"An epic performance: by turns heartfelt, absurd, self-indulgent, self-abasing, silly and genuinely moving. A memoir that manages to encompass riffs about the joys of skateboarding, the woes of high society, the miseries of boarding school and the perils of new money and new age therapies with equal aplomb, a memoir that can make the reader remember—no, re-experience—what it was like to be a wretched child and even more wretched teenager with ridiculous, Proustian ease. It's a book as hip and intermittently tender as Dave Eggers's *A Heartbreaking Work of Staggering Genius*, as gripping and overstuffed as David Foster Wallace's *Infinite Jest* . . . an incredibly powerful performance: a memoir that announces the debut of a remarkably gifted, daring and, yes, very funny writer."
                                        —Michiko Kakutani, *The New York Times*

"Holy moley this is a great read—probably the most compulsively readable book I've picked up in years. At one point I had to burn the second half of it so I didn't distract myself from my own dumb deadlines. Again and again I asked myself, 'Is my obsession with this book due to the fact that I have known Sean Wilsey for a few years?' And the answer is, unequivocally, No. I read plenty of true-life-story sorts of books by people I've met, and this is the No. 1 most intriguing, most hilarious, most jaw-dropping, most reckless and brilliant and insane."
          —Dave Eggers, author of *A Heartbreaking Work of Staggering Genius*

"Sean Wilsey's magnificent memoir spares no one but forgives almost everything; it's a kindly act of retribution that's sure to ring a bell with any adult survivor of parental narcissism. A bell, hell. *Oh the Glory of It All* becomes a veritable carillon of remembered pain, never once losing its wise and worldly sense of humor. I couldn't stop reading the damn thing."
                              —Armistead Maupin, author of *Tales of the City*

"Exuberant, honest, and unforgettable. Wilsey shows that great privilege doesn't guarantee bliss, but also doesn't preclude it. I'm glad he survived this odd/epic youth and emerged from it such a sane, generous, and funny narrator. My only regret is that he's not older than he is, since there would then be more to read."
                      —George Saunders, author of *Civilwarland in Bad Decline*

"His narrative voice reflects a vivid mix of brio, self-awareness and sophistication, and he is able to meld the point of view of the troubled boy he once was with that of the stable and sensible adult that he has, admirably and against all odds, become. What's even more impressive is the way in which he alters pitch and tone as his subject changes from the semicomic misadventures of a hapless kid to the more serious experience of a grown man able to regard his mother with bemused compassion and to view his aging father with an affection and understanding that illuminate several wonderfully tender scenes. . . . Wilsey's portrait of a scheming stepmother is so deliriously searing and so convincing. . . . Among the true glories of it all, as Sean Wilsey so aptly reminds us, is the fact that writing well is indeed the best revenge."

—Francine Prose, *The New York Times Book Review*

"[An] irreverent and remarkably candid memoir about growing up in wealthy eighties San Francisco . . . Evoking both *The Royal Tenenbaums* and Dave Eggers's *A Heartbreaking Work of Staggering Genius*, it's rollicking, ruthless . . . ultimately generous-hearted."                    —Kate Bolick, *Vogue*

"A heartbreaking and hilarious family drama . . . a triumph of tone over tribulation. Wilsey's prose is headlong and rich. . . . *Oh the Glory of It All* . . . is beautiful and funny, and glorious, too."

—John Freeman, *The Atlanta Journal-Constitution*

"Wilsey has written perhaps the best book of 2005 and single-handedly destroyed the comforting Wildean notion that it is only the second-rate writers who lead the interesting lives."                    —Christopher Bollen, *V.*

"Sean Wilsey's *Oh the Glory of It All* is a good four times the length of *Candide*, and I enjoyed it probably four times as much."    —Nick Hornby, *The Believer*

"Recounted with clear-eyed, wry and poignant humor."

—*Time* (one of five "memoirs that you won't forget")

"Fascinating . . . brilliantly written."                    —*New York Daily News*

"A sensitive evocation . . . and a scathing portrait."                    —*People*

"Honest to a fault, richly veined with indelible images: a monumental piece of work."                    —*Kirkus Reviews*

"This memoir busts free from subgenres. It contains socialite gossip, self-help, coming-of-age, drinking and drugs, and no shortage of Stepmommy Dearest. Wilsey chronicles it all with a voice that is simultaneously clever and moving."
—*Booklist*

"Strange, fascinating, complicated . . . the writing is vivid, detailed, deep and filled with fresh metaphors."       —*Publishers Weekly* (starred review)

"An engrossing, entertaining, and often hilarious memoir that is sure to be in high demand."                            —*Library Journal*

"A thoughtful and confident narrative, one that is equally heartbreaking and at times approaches genius with its raw honesty and emotional charge . . . Wilsey has composed an expansive and tragic tour—one that succeeds in being amusing but not smug; sincere but not self-indulgent."       —*Bookforum*

"This delicious memoir . . . soars . . . cool and damning . . . and loving."
—*Entertainment Weekly*

"Wilsey's tour through some of the planet's most interesting reform schools is enough to make you want to call your mother-in-law just to say I love you."
—*Details*

"Dickensian . . . a pungent indictment of the way we (at least some of us) live now, and of the tragedy, for anyone, but especially the young, when cynicism becomes their daily way of meeting the world. That Mr. Wilsey has made this often sad material full of life and humor and yes, even at times, wisdom, is a powerful achievement."                                  —*The Washington Times*

"[A] ridiculously compelling memoir."                  —*The Globe and Mail*

"*Oh the Glory of It All* is being compared, naturally, with . . . *A Heartbreaking Work of Staggering Genius* by Dave Eggers. Both giant books showcase young writers flexing their prodigious talents in creating postmodern memoirs that expand and enliven the popular form in intensely personal and ironic ways. Both have original and enticing strange-but-true tales to tell. Both turn intense navel-gazing into unmistakable literary art."            —*Seattle Post-Intelligencer*

"Think you're burned out on memoirs? Read this book . . . [It] has all the elements of a good memoir. A good memoir is filled with wit, humor, and wisdom . . . is honest—searingly so—and redemptive."           —*Christianity Today*

"Wilsey's engrossing memoir . . . [is] recounted in vivid detail and dialogue, with observations both painful and humorous. . . . [It's] about great wealth, great loss, and personal and creative redemption . . . with a cast of colorful characters, divine locales, and a theme that resonates."           —*Bookpage*

"A fascinating story well told . . . Wilsey wins us over by sheer charismatic writing. . . . He's written a masterpiece of a memoir, ranking with Dave Eggers's *A Heartbreaking Work of Staggering Genius* and Mary Karr's *The Liars' Club* as the pick of the modern crop."           —*Tacoma News Tribune*

"Heartfelt, funny and engaging . . . The author's winning irony . . . will earn him comparisons to Dave Eggers . . . [but] *Glory* has a brittle giddiness that's entirely its own."           —*Time Out New York*

"A truth and reconciliation report sent from the Adolescent Republic."
           —*San Francisco Chronicle Book Review*

"Likely to become the juiciest gossip in years . . . the 475-page memoir has it all, from sex, drugs and marital infidelity to famous names, lavish parties and conspicuous consumption."           —*San Francisco Chronicle*

"The best account of what it is like to grow up in a fractured family."
           —*San Francisco Examiner*

PENGUIN BOOKS

# OH THE GLORY OF IT ALL

Sean Wilsey is the coeditor, with Matt Weiland, of *The Thinking Fan's Guide to the World Cup*. His writing has appeared in *The New Yorker*, *The London Review of Books*, the *Los Angeles Times*, and *McSweeney's* quarterly, where he is the editor at large. Before coming to *McSweeney's*, he worked as an editorial assistant at *The New Yorker*, a fact checker at *Ladies' Home Journal*, a letters correspondent at *Newsweek*, and an apprentice gondolier in Venice, Italy. He was born in San Francisco, in 1970, and now lives in New York with his wife, Daphne Beal, and their son, Owen.

# Oh
# the
# Glory
# of It
# All

·

S E A N
W I L S E Y

PENGUIN BOOKS

*For my mother*

PENGUIN BOOKS

Published by the Penguin Group

Penguin Group (USA) Inc., 375 Hudson Street, New York, New York 10014, U.S.A.
Penguin Group (Canada), 90 Eglinton Avenue East, Suite 700, Toronto,
Ontario, Canada M4P 2Y3 (a division of Pearson Penguin Canada Inc.)
Penguin Books Ltd, 80 Strand, London WC2R 0RL, England
Penguin Ireland, 25 St Stephen's Green, Dublin 2, Ireland (a division of Penguin Books Ltd)
Penguin Group (Australia), 250 Camberwell Road, Camberwell,
Victoria 3124, Australia (a division of Pearson Australia Group Pty Ltd)
Penguin Books India Pvt Ltd, 11 Community Centre, Panchsheel Park, New Delhi – 110 017, India
Penguin Group (NZ), cnr Airborne and Rosedale Roads, Albany,
Auckland 1310, New Zealand (a division of Pearson New Zealand Ltd)
Penguin Books (South Africa) (Pty) Ltd, 24 Sturdee Avenue, Rosebank, Johannesburg 2196, South Africa

Penguin Books Ltd, Registered Offices: 80 Strand, London WC2R 0RL, England

First published in the United States of America by The Penguin Press,
a member of Penguin Group (USA) Inc. 2005
Published in Penguin Books 2006

3  5  7  9  10  8  6  4

A portion of this book first appeared in *The New Yorker*.

Pages 483–484 constitute an extension of this copyright page.

THE LIBRARY OF CONGRESS HAS CATALOGED THE HARDCOVER EDITION AS FOLLOWS:
Wilsey, Sean.
Oh the glory of it all / Sean Wilsey.
p. cm.
ISBN 1-59420-051-3 (hc.)
ISBN 0 14 30.3691 2 (pbk.)
1. Wilsey, Sean—Childhood and youth.  2. Children of divorced parents—California—San Francisco—
Biography.  3. Children of celebrities—California—San Francisco—Biography.  4. Montandon, Pat.
5. Wilsey, Al.  6. San Francisco (Calif.)—Biography.  I. Title.
CT275.W5797A3 2005
979.4'61053'092—dc22
[B]     2004063420

Printed in the United States of America
DESIGNED BY AMANDA DEWEY

*Contents*

Oh

the

Glory

of It

All

.

*Prologue* · **E X C E S S** !

I
N THE BEGINNING we were happy. And we were always excessive. So in
the beginning we were happy to excess.

WE WERE MOM and Dad and I—three palindromes!—and we lived eight
hundred feet in the air above San Francisco; an apartment at the top of a building at the top of a hill: full of light, full of voices, full of windows full of water
and bridges and hills.

Mom was the center. Mom was irresistible. Whatever she was saying or wearing or smelling of was captivating—all our senses were attuned to her. As soon
as I was old enough to walk I tried on her shoes and evening gowns and perfume, admired and wanted to be like her, so much that they had me seeing a
shrink by the time I was three. The shrink said I needed to spend more time with
my dad. But how? Mom was irresistible.

Mom was a writer. Most days she was at her desk, on the phone, with a yellow legal pad in front of her. Mom wrote books, and a column for the San Francisco *Examiner*. I came to see her first thing when I got home from school. *My mom the author!* I thought. When she saw me she smiled, waved, and mouthed the word "Tab." I reversed the maneuver 99.9 percent of my gender performed upon seeing her and went away, back down the long upstairs hall, to the bar off the den. I opened a cabinet, removed a cut crystal goblet, set it down on the Formica counter with both hands—*Bng*—and filled it with ice-maker ice. Then I took a Tab from the bar's minirefrigerator, poured, and carried it back down the long hall. The ice clinked as I walked. The clinks were like music, like happiness; I jostled the Tab for joy, made it sizzle up out of the goblet at me like a miniature stadium full of applause.

Mom had published two books—one about throwing parties, one about battling malevolent ghosts—and was working on a third, about her childhood in Texas and Oklahoma.

As far as I could tell Dad's job was to please Mom. He was solicitous and full of care. He gave Mom everything she wanted. He helped her want things she did not know to want.

Early every morning, Mom, Dad, and I took walks around Russian Hill in matching blue jumpsuits with white piping, *Royal Tenenbaums*-style.

ONE SUNDAY, on a shrink-mandated father-and-son outing, Dad took me across the bay on the ferry, re-creating the commute he made as a boy, before the Golden Gate Bridge was completed, from Catholic school in San Francisco to his home in Marin. Halfway there it started to rain, and we didn't have any umbrellas, so when we arrived we stood in a doorway near the water.

Dad hadn't shaved since Friday morning before work, and he looked rough. Even I could see it. Our matching jumpsuits were sad without Mom. Dad lit a cigarette. We looked out at the water.

A man with a box and an umbrella strode past, glanced at us, stopped fifty feet on, turned, walked back, and handed the box to Dad.

"I can't give you anything else," he said. "But take this."

Dad said, "Thank you," and took the box.

The man looked at me, looked at the ground, walked away.

Dad smoked till the man was out of sight, then he threw his cigarette in the gutter and opened the box.

"He gave us donuts!" I shouted.

Dad looked at me and started chuckling. "That guy thinks we don't have any money." He took a donut, laughed again, and blew powdered sugar out of his mouth.

I ate a glazed, and then a chocolate with sprinkles. Dad ate all the rest, steadily, devouring them with great relish and no preference for jelly over old-fashioned over chocolate or bear claw—only pleasure, and great amusement.

AT HOME I was either left alone, or overwhelmed with attention. Mom and Dad were either oblivious or hyperaware. They disappeared on a trip for seventeen days and left me with the maid. On Mom's return I ignored her when she called my name. She had my ears examined. They were infected. I needed surgery; tubes installed to drain them. I was four. Mom set herself the task of increasing my medical vocabulary, to make the hospital less frightening. (When an orderly rolled me into the operating room I asked him, "Are you the anesthesiologist?") I received books to read during my recovery, and became the kind of kid who spends all his time alone, reading, till Mom noticed my left eye didn't turn all the way to the left; then it was back to the doctor.

I HAD a friend down the hill, in the long shadow of our building, whose mother cooked us meatloaf. When I discovered meatloaf, and that other mothers regularly cooked it for their children, I went home and said, "Other mothers cook. Why don't you cook?"

Without hesitation Mom said, "Other mothers don't write books."

It was the end of that question for me. And thenceforth, as if to compensate for not cooking the food we were eating, she began reading from her books at the dinner table.

Mom was a captivating reader. She'd won the all-state elocution award in Oklahoma, in the forties, and when she told a story, especially a story about her childhood, Mom made me love words.

BUT MOM had lots of other people to captivate. The apartment was head-quarters for a salon-*cum*-luncheon—called the Roundtable—where Mom hosted *conversation*. The guests were notorious strangers. They always came, if for no other reason than to see the view. They were: union leaders; unionized prostitutes; Alex Haley; Native American secessionists; Agnes Moorehead; radical lesbians; Nobel laureates; Joan Baez; Black Panthers; Dear Abby; an astronaut; Eldridge Cleaver; Jessica Mitford; Gloria Steinem; a Catholic priest; a woman who had murdered her husband; Shirley Temple; a lesbian priest; Betty

Friedan; welfare mothers; Werner Erhard; a Soviet ballerina; Daniel Ellsberg. And so on.

Jessica Mitford was an old British woman with huge round glasses who proclaimed, "When I *die* I've given instructions that I want to be buried like *this*," and then pulled one corner of her mouth up and dragged the other one down, and eyed the other guests (the mayor, a plastic surgeon, Agnes Moorehead, Shirley Temple). "I want to make sure you all *check* on it. That's the way I want to look." Eldridge Cleaver brought Dad velvet flower-embroidered shorts that had a codpiece hanging down the front. Once I came home from school and no one was in the kitchen. The cook and the housekeeper—in French maid's uniforms—had joined the table for lunch with Betty Friedan and Gloria Steinem. (Said Mom, "They were the *perfect people* to talk with domestic workers about the difficulty of working in someone else's home.")

Mom presided over the Roundtable with a silver bell that she rang to get everyone's attention. After ringing the bell Mom directed the conversation by asking questions. And as I went about my only-child activities—searching out a wire stripper to connect a camera battery to a nail and make a laser gun; constructing an orange juice dispenser out of Dad's discarded WaterPik dental hygiene machine (so I could have breakfast in my room); synthesizing an alcohol-free imitation wine; using bendable drink straws to siphon and circulate cold water throughout my bathroom during a heat wave—words found their way into my newly drained ears:

MOM: You were once behind walls, weren't you? In a concentration camp?
WOMAN'S VOICE: I was a refugee. My country is Yugoslavia, and we are the
    troublemakers of the world, you know.
DAD: Just you?
WOMAN'S VOICE: In 1941, when the Germans took over, these invaders, the
    Germans and Croats, caught a million Serbs and killed them overnight and
    sent them down to the river. It's not something to talk about at lunchtime.
MOM: We talk about everything at lunchtime here!

The battery heated the nail until it turned bright orange!

MOM: How do you feel you have changed?
MAN'S VOICE: I was a Marxist. I had rejected spiritual values. But then . . . I
    saw the design in nature and I was convinced there was a Creator. . . . It

was a bad time for me. I wanted to go home to the United States. Friends of mine got into power and I thought they would help me but they didn't. The whole bottom of my world fell out. I went into a deep depression. I felt trapped. I had a wife and two children and my children didn't even speak English. They were going to French schools and becoming little Frenchie fried people. One night on my balcony I just caved in. This is down near Cannes on the Mediterranean coast. A lot of people ask me, like, were you drunk, had you been smoking? I was not high on anything. I was looking at the moon, a full moon, and I saw these shadows on it. I saw myself, my own profile on the moon. I had been thinking of killing myself. I had the pistol. And I wondered if what I was seeing was a sign that death was near. And then my image fell away and on the moon I saw a procession of my heroes: Fidel Castro, Mao Tse-tung, Karl Marx, Friedrich Engels. And then the image of Jesus Christ. That was an unwelcome image because I didn't have anything to do with him. It was like the last straw. I started crying. Just gushing out, real violent. I was trembling and I had the sense that my soul was trembling. I was down on my knees hanging onto the rail. And then I ran inside for a Bible. And it was there, this book I never read. I found the Twenty-Third Psalm, which I had learned as a child. But I didn't know where to find the Lord's Prayer. That's what happened. O.K.?

The WaterPik fired orange juice across the room!

MOM: Has winning the Nobel Prize been helpful in your work?
WOMAN'S VOICE: Oh, yes!

I put the synthetic wine in a wine bottle. Dad drank it with dinner and couldn't tell the difference!

WOMAN'S VOICE: What propels you to get rich?
DAD (in a voice that suggested maybe he was putting everyone on, or *maybe* he was completely serious): Greed.

My bathroom got cooler and I ran downstairs shouting, "Mom, Dad—finally one of my inventions works!"

. . .

MOM LOVED her luncheons. Mom loved emotions. "All these strangers, they sobbed like babies," she told me recently. "And they became my dear, dear friends." The apartment was an accelerator for emotions, a controlled environment where they could be witnessed without effect. Neutralized and admired. We were eight hundred feet above it all. Little did I—who had known only happiness or loneliness—know the variety emotion could provide. That pain moved in mysterious ways. That it could fly, swim, tunnel; was amphibious, ambidextrous, aerodynamic; a breeze and a smothering blanket and a storm. That emotions would knock our tower down to the ground, and none of these strangers would help us.

WHEN I WAS five Mom and Dad rented a house in the Napa Valley, and Dad befriended a man called Frenchie Meyers who wore suspenders and owned a junkyard nearby—fifty acres covered in thirty-foot heaps of smashed cars, flat-tired trailers full of old glass doorknobs, two aircraft hangars (one stuffed full of forklifts, tractors, and power tools and guarded by Sam, a glass-blue-eyed wolf dog, the other converted into a machine shop and guarded by an anvil of a bull-dog named Jezebel). Dad let me play in an old school bus parked beneath an ancient willow tree. How old? Centuries old, Dad informed me. I played for hours beneath that green canopy, in that yellow bus, while Dad talked to Frenchie.

Dad made Frenchie an offer to buy it all, said Frenchie could keep on living in his little house on the edge of the junk, rent-free, forever. Frenchie accepted.

Dad built a hill—flood protection—and Mom's dream house on the hill. Mom landscaped the junk into trees and lawns and an hourglass-shaped carp pond. The school bus got towed. I built a tree house in the willow. I tried to construct a car out of Frenchie's leftover junk. On the weekends Dad wore a JC Penney work shirt and led a crew of men planting grass, grapes, and flowers, and shoring up the eroding banks of the Napa River, which ran along the property's edge.

Perfect happiness started flowing. Mom brought Dad cooling beverages while he worked. We had picnics. I made friends with a Mexican kid down the road, and we hammered nails into the tree house. At night Dad showed us World War I movies on an old projector. Mom's best friend, Dede Traina (pronounced Try-een-nah), had a place nearby, and she was over all the time. Hundreds of people came to our housewarming party, where a Catholic priest blessed the premises and Benny Goodman played live. This party blended into another and another. The biggest was a *Gone with the Wind* ball, when Dede upstaged everyone by wearing Scarlett O'Hara's green-and-white hoop dress from the movie, refabricated by the original designer; it was like the willow tree, and I crawled underneath, following her sons, Todd and Trevor. There was a whole world under there!

Mom said, "Sean, get out!"

Dede said, "No, he can stay."

I wanted to spend my whole life there.

MOM'S PREVIOUS best friend had died in a mysterious fire while living in Mom's old apartment, shortly after my parents were married. Dede Traina arrived in Mom's life in the early seventies (around the same time my shrink told Mom to stop spending so much time with me). Dede was new to San Francisco, fifteen years younger than Mom, in her early thirties, unhappily married. Mom liked Dede. Dad liked that Dede came from an old East Coast family. Dede was grateful; every time she visited our house she brought gifts. Once it was a coffee-table book of "history's great beauties."

She climbed up on Mom's bed and they looked at it together. Helen of Troy, Marilyn Monroe, Jackie O.

"You're one of them, Pat," Dede said.

"Oh, Dede, you are making my day," Mom said, beaming.

Before long Dede was the first person Mom would call in the morning, and the last she'd talk to at the end of the day.

One time, when my parents were out, Dede appeared in my doorway.

"Come with me, Sean," she said. "I've got a surprise for you."

I wondered how she had gotten into our house. But it didn't matter. She was Mom's best friend. I went downstairs, got in her car, and we drove to the supermarket. She took me to the candy aisle.

"Let's pretend it's Halloween," Dede said. "And we can have as much candy as we want."

I was tentative. *Yeah? Was this possible?*

Dede started grabbing bags off the shelves, opening them, and handing me Reese's Peanut Butter Cups and mini Hershey bars. She was like a kid with the power of an adult. She told me I could eat them right there in the aisles, demonstrated, and nobody stopped her. It was as though she owned the store. Maybe she did own the store! I started eating. We filled a cart with candy. I was flying on sugar. In the checkout line I chewed a Starburst and drank a Coke. Dede drank a Pepsi Lite and ate hunks of something called almond roca.

"This is my very favorite candy," she whispered. Then she gave me a bite, holding a piece and placing it on my tongue. It was chocolate-covered toffee, studded with little filings of some exotic nut—sophisticated and delicious. *Wow.*

WE MOSTLY SAW Dede and her boys, and sometimes her husband, John, for picnics and bike rides and lunches in the country. Mom had started a bicycling club that took back roads through the valley every weekend. Dede and John and Todd and Trevor always rode elegant European-style bicycles called Univegas, while Mom and Dad and I rode Huffys. Dede's elegant bike was frequently breaking down, but my dad would stop and help her.

IN SAN FRANCISCO Dede and John Traina lived in Pacific Heights, a neighborhood of mansions not far from Russian Hill but stodgy by comparison. During the week she came over to our house by herself. Dede became a member of the family, part my big sister, part Mom's little sister, part something else.

Dede was kooky, like family, too.

One day, after lunch, she told Mom and Dad and me how full she was, and asked, "Do you want to see how I get into my really tight jeans? I have to lie down, like this." She lay down, unzipped—pink underwear stood out against the kelly green of her jeans—"and then wriggle in." She pulled the waist down to demonstrate, and then started yanking it back up as she swiveled her hips side to side on the carpet.

*Very difficult,* I thought.

WHEN I WAS nine I asked Dad about sex. He drove me to the Fairmont Hotel, on nearby Nob Hill, parked across the street in a loading zone, and told me to wait in the car.

Then he crossed the semicircular drive of the hotel, held the door for a woman, exchanged a pleasant word, smiled (lips closed to hide his stained teeth), and disappeared into the building. I looked around Nob Hill: gray Grace Cathedral (where I'd be going to school soon); red-brick Pacific Union Club (an institution Dad reviled—though later joined—because "somebody blackballed me for being married to a Jewish woman," which required a complicated explanation of blackballing and Judaism, forever twinning the two in my mind); shreds of blue bay between old brownstone skyscrapers; green geometric Huntington Park where Thuy, a Vietnamese "governess" (to use Mom's word) whom I'd asked to marry me the year before, stealing a ring from her so I could give it back as a wedding present, once snatched up a pigeon and held it to her breast while she told me her brother had been killed by the Viet Cong.

Dad came out of the Fairmont holding a *Playboy.* He carried it in plain sight. I could make it out from across the street. I watched in awe—a small, beautiful, inadequately clothed woman, arriving with Dad. He got in and handed it to me.

"Here," he said. "We'll look at some women's bodies."

The cover woman looked at me like she *loved* me. *I loved her!*

Dad opened the magazine to the table of contents.

"What should we look at first?" he asked.

"The lady on the cover," I said in a very quiet voice. It seemed faithless to look at anybody else.

Dad laughed, not unkindly, and said, "Well, there's a lot more in here. Let's look at the centerfold."

My vocabulary was getting ever larger.

He unfolded and I stared. The centerfold was the most beautiful picture of the most beautiful woman in the world that month. After a couple of minutes he said, "The centerfold doesn't have to be your favorite. It could be anyone." He handed me the magazine. I leafed through. Breasts. Lace. A completely naked woman in a body stocking—a totally confusing garment. I stopped at a half-page picture of a woman with straight dark hair reclining on a rubber-latticed pool chaise, a gold unicorn pendant on a thin gold chain around her neck, and dangling down between her breasts, which were tanned, dewy, and a bit smaller—*more modest,* I thought—than the other breasts in the magazine. The unicorn stopped me. It was an amulet of power. Like the magic ring in my favorite book, *The Hobbit.* She was beautiful and mysterious and wise and possibly part elvish.

Dad turned back to the centerfold. I had a confusing erection. The centerfold was beautiful. She was tall and blonde and proud, standing completely straight, completely naked, and facing the camera. I had only ever desired toys, and now I desired *her.* She was motivating me. I felt like doing her bidding. I wasn't sure *what* she was bidding me to do. Grab the magazine to my chest? Crinkle the pages as hard as I could. Eat them? Roll around in the backseat with them? Beat someone in wrestling? (I was one of the better wrestlers in my Catholic grade school.) Everything hurt. I had hot magma flowing through my head and arms.

Dad started the car and we drove home, me holding the *Playboy.* In the building's garage he took it back and said, "I'll keep this, but whenever you need it come ask me. We can look at it some more, together. But you can't keep it."

After we'd both looked at the issue a few times, another month came, and the overhill ride to the Fairmont happened again. It became a father-son tradition.

After a few months, Dad told me, "I'm going to keep these in a drawer from now on, and you can come take them any time you want. You don't have to ask me. But you have to put them back when you're done looking at them. I'll be checking on that."

MY PARENTS' third home was a restaurant halfway down Nob Hill, toward the seedy Tenderloin—run-down on the outside, clubby and leathery and lustrous on the inside. I was a nonspilling, silent-when-told-to-be child, so, also when I was nine, my parents convinced the management to make an exception to their unbendable no-children rule, and for nearly a year I almost lived there, too. It was like traveling overseas to a ruleless country. All proscriptions were thrown out. I got to stay up late. I was an adult. The maitre d' told us what a great table he had for us, down the hall, past the cigar lady in her closet—who waved at me as if from a ship—past the bathrooms with their zebra-skin doors, in the dim, glowing hum of the main room, called the Captain's Cabin, which grew louder as we entered, as if we were newspaper thrown on a fire.

A waiter came, took Dad's drink order—"Tanqueray gin on the rocks"—and quickly came back. The air around Dad started to smell like fuel.

Mom ordered. Dad ordered. They ordered for me: an elevated silver platter of spare ribs with a candle underneath, accompanied by a butterfly-shaped dish, one wing full of hot yellow mustard, the other sweet red sauce. Dad looked deeply content. Mom smiled her radiant, irresistible-to-photographers smile. People came to say hello.

Dad drank his flammable Tanqueray gin on the rocks, slowly, and leaned back into the banquette, above which maxims were set into wooden plaques with chiseled Gothic letters. Above him it said:

> *No chord of music has yet been found*
> *To even equal that sweet sound*
> *Which to my mind all else surpasses*
> *The clink of ice in crystal glasses*

I knew about the clink of ice in crystal glasses: It was a sound that meant all was well, everything was in its place, no mistakes were being made, everybody loved each other. I looked at the maxim on the plaque above Mom and Dad and

I knew we were doing everything perfectly, and as long as the crystal and ice kept clinking there was nothing to worry about.

MOM AND DAD got divorced that same year—after ten years without once fighting, and regular reassurances that they would never get divorced—and when they did it was vicious and corrosive and melodramatic and strange, like having all your clothes taken away, being forced to the end of a narrow hallway, and having a flaming car battery hurled at you.

I thought their marriage was perfect until one night in the middle of dinner. This was the second night in a row that Mom had placed her head in her hands and started crying at the table while Dad carried on making conversation as though nothing were out of the ordinary. I said, "Dad, what's the matter with Mom?" He hesitated, and she blurted out miserably, "Something *terrible* has happened." Dad looked unreadable. I realized that this was serious. Dad said, "We're going to tell you about it after dinner." I tried to prepare myself. I tried to think of the worst thing that could ever happen happening.

I said, "Has Dede died?"

Mom and Dad told me that Dad would be moving out. A few days later I went and spent the night with him in the Fairmont Hotel, and for the first time he told me the following, which he would repeat many times over the years: "If your mother had cared as much about being a wife as she did about being a star, we'd still be married."

PART ONE

·

# Useless Emotion

*One* · M O M

WHEN DESCRIBING MY MOTHER it is impossible to overstate her grandeur, her haughtiness, her generosity, her old Hollywood star power, her immaturity, her joy, her entitlement, her suffering.

If you want a sense of what she's like, for grandeur and loneliness and elocution, go see *Sunset Boulevard*. (Like Gloria Swanson, she is a great me-lo*dramatic* ee-nunn-see-ate-oar.) Also see *Gentlemen Prefer Blondes*, for Marilyn Monroe (who looks very much like Mom) doing her bombshell country girl thing. Then there's *Mommie Dearest*, which captures many elements of her postdivorce persona. I had a truly visceral reaction to this film when I was a teenager. Not the meanness, because Mom has never been mean, but the smothering physicality and desperation and melodramatic manic depressiveness: The scene of the self-pityingly bedridden Crawford receiving her Oscar for *Mildred Pierce* took me back to how Mom would lie in bed for days with the drapes drawn, experiencing dismal languors and dispatching me at regular intervals to the store, where I would purchase gallon containers of Dreyer's ice cream (vanilla) and cans of

Hershey's chocolate sauce (this was just before the plastic squeeze bottle came out), which she would consume in their entirety, in bed, in her nightgown, in the dark, me occasionally peeking in to make sure she was still alive. In fact, I saw *Mommie Dearest* with Mom, and I was amazed she was able to sit through it without turning to me, ashamed, and saying, "I'm so sorry." After my two best friends saw it they said, "Jesus, dude, that *is* your mom."

MOM WAS BORN in 1928, and by the time she was sixteen possessed great beauty and charisma. But it was not a soft beauty; it was a chiseled, sculptural, architectural sort of beauty (which has barely faded after seventy-seven years), a rock solid beauty that comes of impeccable bone structure supported by a curvy, zaftig, tense, erectly carried frame and long-fingered hands that are handsome and uncomfortable; her fingers abrupt and strong and nervous and ringless.

Mom's charisma is anchored in her beauty, but it goes deep.

Her parents, Myrtle Caldonia Taylor and Charles Clay Montandon, were both evangelical Nazarene ministers—she gentle in the pulpit and hard out of it, he the opposite—unified in their passion to spread God around the West by constantly uprooting the family, moving from town to town, building churches, and assembling new congregations.

In 1896 my grandfather, twenty-one, had climbed a mountain in Tennessee, looked out west, and received a vision from the Lord commanding him to go and spread the word. He started out in the streets of Chattanooga, and made his way to Texas. Doing roustabout work in ranching country he met, wooed, and married my sixteen-year-old grandmother, purchased a carnival sideshow tent, and took her on the road.

Mom grew up with six siblings. There would've been seven siblings, but one, Betty Ruth, died in infancy, just before Mom was born, and my grandfather, who had a barber's license, and was also a mason and a carpenter, stopped them in Merkel, Texas, the town they were passing through, buried the child, and then carved the headstone himself. They stayed in Merkel until Mom—Patsy Lou Montandon—was born. She was the brazen, silly, gangly, affectionate child who loved being the center of attention, sang loud and tuneless in church, broke her nose on the dash of the car, and had no idea she was pretty, because they never let her know.

The ministering life was equal parts adversity and grace, deprivation and unexpected generosity. Mom and her siblings grew up seeing the best and worst of people, during the *Dee*-pression (as my aunt Faye calls it). Another of my aunts, my aunt Glendora, persuaded my grandmother to write a memoir of these years, which she did, shortly before she died (from gangrene) in 1979—the only one of my grandparents I got to know.

She wrote: "We spent the night out under the stars having a couple of quilts and a pillow for a bed on the ground. We had not eaten dinner or supper the day before. We had about $1.50 and about 75 miles yet to go. My husband stopped at a farm house early that morning to ask if we could get breakfast making clear we would pay for our breakfast. The lady of the house said yes but was curious about us. Later she said she thought we were a couple who had run away from home and married. We were very young. On learning our mission she would not take pay for our breakfast and in addition fed our horse. We became friends for days and years ahead."

Finances were always tight, but they "continued on preaching and working wherever opportunity came, making opportunities when there was none in city jails and on streets under brush arbors too." On one occasion, my grandmother wrote, "I knelt by the chair in the kitchen telling the Lord our needs. A knock was at the front door. I wiped my tears away with my apron to meet a guest and it was a young mother with two children who had recently been saved in our services. She put her arms around me saying, 'Whether you need what I have brought or not, I refuse to feel like I have been feeling the past hour. Here are some groceries.'"

The typical Charlie Clay Montandon sermon, preached at night in lantern light, under a tent or under the stars, emphasized hell, fire, damnation, ashes (heaps of them), and the serpent. He knew how to save souls and inspire repentance. "One night the power of God was so manifest that people saw the light visibly, and hundreds fell before God prostrated. Heaven was so near," wrote my grandmother.

She went on:

The people began to come in droves. . . . One lady started for the altar and her little girl about 11 years of age held on to her saying, "Mama, don't go up there. Them women will beat you on the back." But the mother went right on and was saved. One night here came two brothers carrying their brother. They made a pack saddle to bring him in. They had found him hidden in a wagon trying to get away from them and from God . . . such shouting, such victory. An old drunkard was saved one night and was elected Sunday School Superintendent at the close of the Revival. A Dr. came out from Gouldbusk, Texas one night. It had been noised abroad that Jesus was in our midst. He knew me before my marriage. He said before the service, "Myrtle, I have never seen such." He said, "Many here are paying my old bills. I never expected to collect." He knew them all. He had been their doctor for several years. We were using old-fashioned gasoline lamps. He publicly said, "I will furnish all the gasoline you need to keep this meeting going. I am a shouting Methodist, so more power to all of you for such a work."

•

At Dennis Chapel under a large tabernacle we were laboring faithfully and were having some bitter opposition until one night a goodly number gave their hands requesting prayer. A young man fell at the altar praying mightily confessing all to Jesus who saved him. Others followed and a mighty revival broke . . . we preached, and our labors were rewarded with souls.

•

The Sunday School Supt. rushed to the altar and his hands reached towards heaven. He was calling on God for help. His wife was frightened and thought he was dying. She began to scream and pray within the minutes he had prayed though she was no longer praying for him but for herself. Also, she prayed through so no longer did we need to pray for courage and faith. Faith had turned to sight.

•

I will mention a revival held on what was known as Sunshine Hill about 20 miles from Wichita Falls near Burkburnette. This was an oil field. Many workers lived out there—some in good houses and some in shacks typical of an oil field in those days. As interest increased, some who were known as roughnecks began to come. Their hearts were stirred. Their families were touched. They began to seek God in an old fashioned way. At the close of the three-weeks revival, more than 100 people had found the Lord.

•

An amusing incident happened at Grape Creek in Coleman County at the day service. One morning a small green snake fell down from the branches above in the arbor. Women scrambled for their babies until a man struck it with a stick and killed it. . . . That was the only time we experienced a snake scare in our services. We did have trouble with dogs. They often came into our services. They discovered their masters were going someplace every night. They investigated and would find the way there. Try as the minister might to drive them away, it just couldn't be done.

•

One night a middle-aged man came seeking God for forgiveness. He wept, prayed, then arose to ask Husband to go with him two and one half blocks away to see a man whom he was having trouble with. As they came near, it was a task but he wanted peace. He called to the man to come outside not for trouble but that he wanted forgiveness. He said, "I have a preacher with me." The man reluctantly came out. He put his hand out saying, "Forgive me. I did you wrong." It touched his heart. He said, "I did you wrong, too. Forgive me. I want a better way of life." With the two, Husband knelt in the yard and prayed. The three rejoiced together and went away in peace with God and man.

When they were done saving souls for the day they liked to lie down in the grass together and make one. It was a romantic, wild, daring life. Riding horses. Preaching in prisons. Taking alms (once from the KKK, my aunt Faye recalled, saying, "It was money, it was in the name of the Lord, so he took it."). Cutting hair. Cutting stone. Preaching in oil fields where just before, my grandmother wrote, "an evangelist, not a Nazarene, had his tent and all equipment burned by some disgruntled person or persons. At times it seemed like our fate might be the same." They built and integrated a church, then saw it burned down as a result (KKK again). They lay down to bed in the open air.

. . . Star . . .

. . . Aquilla . . .

. . . Waco . . .

. . . Erath . . .

. . . Grape Creek . . .

. . . Gouldbusk . . .

. . . Hardin . . .

. . . Rule . . .

. . . Bangs . . .

. . . Wichita Falls . . .

. . . Stephenville . . .

. . . Pryor . . .

. . . Knox City . . .

. . . Wellington . . .

... Grassland ...
... O'Donnell ...
... Post City ...
... Tahoka ...
... Olton ...
... Eula ...
... Clovis ...
... Higgins ...
... Waurika ...
... Burkburnette ...
... Dalheart ...
... Tokio ...
... Takoho ...
... Sulpher ...

When they arrived in a new town my grandfather would pitch the tent, borrow a piano, and start preaching. Eventually he'd muster up a congregation, find a suitable plot of land, somehow get it bought or donated, build the church, requisition a full-time minister, and move on. Grandmother wrote: "Always it seemed that each revival was better than the one before. We could have stayed on longer than we did, but my husband felt others could take this work and we would move on ... with no home, no church, and no salary we went. The children used to changing schools would settle down."

Itinerancy was God's will. So Mom's family went along like this for years, all over West Texas, New Mexico, and Oklahoma, first on horseback, then in a horse-drawn carriage, finally in a car. Aunt Faye remembers my grandfather ordering one of her brothers to "take a butcher knife and cut down the high center of the road so we could pass." Grandmother wrote, "Occasionally we stopped and unloaded so my husband could safely go down the hill and up again. Sometimes we had to push with all our might to get through a sand bed." They lived like this till my grandfather's kidneys started to fail, and the family decided to settle in Waurika, Oklahoma, which, of all the towns they'd passed through, had always been Charlie Clay's favorite. My grandmother took over the preaching, but she didn't quite have his spirit. When my grandfather died in 1941, the center went out of the family.

DURING WORLD WAR II, when Mom was a teenager, with only her mother and little brother left at home, the rest raised and gone (my uncle Charles, for example, studying in a seminary and working at a defense plant), Mom realized she was beautiful. A neighbor lady knocked on the door, which Mom opened with a smile. The woman was so struck she exclaimed, "My! You are the most beautiful thing!"

My grandmother actually ran into the room and shouted, "Don't you tell her that! It isn't true." It had never occurred to Mom that she might be beautiful. But in that moment she saw that it was a fact. And that it was powerful. It was an escape. She decided to go to Dallas and become a model.

Enlisted to assist her in this plan was her brother-in-law, my uncle Cecil (pronounced see-sill), who had the concession for all the jukeboxes and peanut machines in Waurika. He went around the town's theaters, cafés, gas stations, and bars, emptied his machines, brought Mom a huge sack of nickels, and said, "Go to Dallas, Patsy Lou." Mom told my grandmother she'd found a job selling hosiery for a respectable women's shop. My grandmother said fine, Mom was welcome to go, provided she bought her own train ticket—impossible—and had enough left over to pay for a week in advance at the YWCA. Mom shook her sack of nickels at her mother and got on the train. She got a modeling job at Neiman Marcus. A week or so later my grandmother, in constant contact with the YWCA, discovered that Patsy Lou was *modeling*, not selling hosiery. She stormed into Neiman's, calling, "Patsy Lou, come out of this wicked place!" found Mom in a dressing room, and yanked her outside by her then still black hair. "We're going to California to live with your aunt Mary," she told her. "If you don't agree to come along I'll call the police on you for being underage and showing your body."

They drove to California. Or, rather, my great-grandfather Taylor, a ninety-year-old part Comanche Indian, who was only licensed to drive during the day, drove them. It was 1945. The trip took weeks. They slept in the car. When they sighted the Rockies, Mom, who had never seen anything in the way of a vertical landscape, thought they were monsters. "I was that ignorant," Mom said, when she told me the story. Then she paused. "Of course, because I was so ignorant, I did a lot of things I didn't know I wasn't supposed to do. Ignorance has served me well!"

In California Aunt Mary and a slew of cousins—all of them fruit pickers—were living in a converted school bus parked in a cherry orchard. Mom took one look and decided to get a job and make enough money to go back to Dallas and model. She started waitressing at a bus station café.

One of her customers was U.S. Air Force Captain Howard Groves, owner of a nearby ranch. He nicknamed her Muggins, admired her figure, left big tips. My grandmother thought Captain Groves was the perfect solution to the problem of Patsy Lou.

Then Mom started having trouble catching her breath, went to see a doctor, and was told that a valve in her heart wasn't closing properly. Without a new form of heart surgery ("closed-heart" or "blind" they were calling it) she would die in her twenties. At that point eleven people had survived the procedure. Thinking she'd probably be dead soon—and that he had money enough to buy her the surgery—she married Groves. It was not a conventional wedding. Mom auditioned and was chosen to be married on a live national radio program called *The Bride and Groom*. "You will be taking with you the good wishes of the entire United States," the announcer said to her and Captain Groves after they'd gone through the on-the-air ceremony. Then she had the surgery, and became the twelfth to survive. Howard got shipped off to an air base in the Azores, and Mom went along. She was an officer's wife for twelve years. Howard crashed and was grounded; Mom put on plays, commandeered planes with her charm, and flew to Lisbon for costumes. She modeled. She was the commanding general's favorite party guest. Her plays were hits. She threw parties every week. She outgrew Howard so thoroughly that he grabbed a woman at a New Year's Eve party and kissed her passionately in front of Mom. Then he hit her—and Mom divorced him. He was, she always says, "boring and sterile—literally, his sperm were incapable of fertilizing an egg—and I never loved him."

Then came San Francisco. It was where she'd had the heart surgery—San Francisco had saved her life—and she felt sentimental about the place. She was thirty-one. It was 1960. She walked into the CEO's office at the Joseph Magnin department store, without an appointment, and asked for a job. He chased her around his desk. She let him catch up, and slapped him. He was so impressed he hired her.

"I like the way you handle yourself, Mrs. Groves."

"*Ms. Montandon.*"

He decided to put her in charge of the high-rolling gentlemen's formal department, called the Wolf's Den—equipped with a fireplace and drinks and salesgirls who dressed up like tarty elves at Christmas. After she racked up the highest seasonal sales in the company's history he put her in charge of managing a new store up in Lake Tahoe, where she met Frank Sinatra, up for the summer, doing a show every night at the Cal Neva Resort.

She got squired around by Sinatra. "He was a perfect gentleman," she said. He always called her "Patty baby," and the word went out that no other man was to address or even approach her. "It was relaxing," Mom told me. "I could eat my lunch without anyone bothering me. And he always took me out for dinner, in big groups, with all his flunkies and friends. I was like the tail of the rat! I had him over to my house for a cocktail party after we first met and he got lost on the way, so he pulled over and knocked on a woman's door to ask if he could use the phone. That lady said 'Sure!' and she never let anyone else touch the phone after that. When Frank got to my place I gave him a drink, and he saw a dog I was taking care of out on the porch. The dog didn't like strangers, but Frank said, 'I'm good with dogs. They like me.' And he went out there and the dog bit him. I bandaged him up and he stayed late talking to everybody. He was so nice. I never saw any of the bad behavior he had a reputation for. He was wonderful to me that summer."

But it was only a summer, and when the season was over Magnin's brought her back to San Francisco. She dyed her hair blond (the only color I've ever seen it). She changed the pronunciation of her last name "back to the French." From "Mawntandun" to "Moan-tan-dawn." She had a date every night. She met and wed her second husband: "It was the only time I ever got married against my heart." (I suppose the first time was literally *for* her heart.) They moved into a beautiful apartment, on the crooked block of Lombard. Six months later the marriage was over. He moved out and Mom kept the lease on the apartment. It was all she wanted for a settlement.

She made it into the society pages for throwing flamboyant parties with the assistance of the window dressers at Magnin's. There was a mod party, an astrology party, a come-as-your-favorite-celebrity costume party, a Mexican fiesta. "Pat is the best thing that ever happened to this blasé city. Now every hostess is on her toes, trying to keep up with her," wrote the society editor of the San Francisco *Chronicle*. "Pat Montandon has no peer when it comes to party-planning," said her counterpart at the *Examiner*.

She met Melvin Belli, the trial lawyer who defended Jack Ruby, and later represented the Rolling Stones. Mom married Belli, her third husband, in a Shinto ceremony in Japan in 1966. It was over three weeks later. "30 Seconds Over Tokyo," wrote Herb Caen, Pulitzer Prize–winning columnist for the *Chronicle*, longtime Mom chronicler, and enemy.

She was invited by a producer to audition for television, and became the host of the *Prize Movie* (rechristened *Pat's Prize Movie*) on Channel 7, with twenty minutes of live on-air talk time. She wore frilly boas and long evening gowns and ad-libbed it. She became a local cult phenomenon. *Pat's Prize Movie* was the highest rated program on the air in the Bay Area. Mom had a fan club. She went to the opening of the opera, stuffy San Francisco's biggest deal, and was greeted by photographers and fan club members holding homemade signs that said "Pat's our Gal." Mom made her smiling entrance, doubled back outside, picked up a cameraman and mic, and covered all the (other) celebrity arrivals live, runway style.

She published a book about giving parties, called *How to Be a Party Girl*.

Meeting Mom is like meeting a celebrity you've never heard of.

Then: Dad. Recently a widower, he read about Mom in the paper and had a friend introduce them. He phoned to ask her out, she said yes, then she canceled. He asked again. She said yes, and canceled again. He asked a third time, and she said no. There was something about his voice she didn't like.

"Please," he said before she hung up. "You could come up to my house for dinner. I live near you. My son and I are here alone for the evening. We've just cooked a chicken."

Somehow this was irresistible. It was kind.

She didn't put on any makeup. He drove down Russian Hill and drove her back up. His apartment was at the top of a new building called The Summit. It occupied the front half of the top two floors—the space generally allotted to six two-bedroom apartments with twin baths, full kitchens, large living rooms. Dad had bought The Summit with his closest childhood friend, a real estate developer who urged Dad and his older brother, Jack, to branch out of the butter-and-egg business they'd taken over when their father had died. He'd already been married in Marin, had four kids, got divorced, raised his two sons Mike and Lad (been given the "mother of the year" award by his local PTA), discovered the woman next door had cancer (they'd been having an affair while he was married to his first wife, who'd moved to Hawaii with his two daughters), married her, watched her die in their bed, taken a shower, called the undertaker, buried her, and a few years short of fifty, moved into this massive, six-apartment-sized penthouse apartment by himself. Dad had left or been left by everyone of significance in his life. He told Mom he was just sitting up there waiting to die, and she'd saved his life by coming for dinner.

She met Lad, who was visiting Dad for the evening. They all talked for an hour, ate the chicken, and then Dad drove Mom home. It was the best evening she'd had since Sinatra. Dad was a gentleman, too. A man who could take care of her. For a second date he cleaned up her kitchen and went home. He discovered how hard it was to reach her on the phone (always busy) and asked if he could install another line so he could get through. She said yes. The telephone was red.

They got married in 1969. It was a civil ceremony, and all the photographs are lost except for the photographer's set, which show Mom smiling hugely in a white eyelet dress, and Dad in a dark suit, looking quietly content, with the word "PROOF" stamped across them. Then her best friend was killed. The coroner was baffled: lower body immolated, but no smoke in the lungs; blood carbon monoxide levels less than what you'd get from a cigarette; all the doors locked from the inside; no reason why she couldn't have woken up when the fire started. The arson inspector suggested she died "from fright." Mom went to bed, mourned, got pregnant with me—and then went into labor when a huge fire started in *our* building. After the fire department left an ambulance came for Mom. She was forty-one.

Around the time *Esquire* magazine declared her "the West Coast's #1 hostess," the *Examiner* hired her to write its society column. This meant reporting on people who didn't *do* anything but had enough money and history to make the present superfluous: people like Whitney Warren, a flamboyant man in his seventies whose father had built Grand Central Terminal. Warren presided over a different sort of salon than the Roundtable. When he threw a wedding party for Jackie O's sister and the guest of honor didn't show, he took Mom by the arm, walked into the street, and handed out drinks to the press, saying, "You never could trust those Bouvier girls." *This* was the kind of thing Dad liked. A lot better than listening to angry/horny Black Panthers and earnest folksingers.

He wasn't alone. Herb Caen had been writing about society, turning bon mots into an art form, for decades. Everybody in San Francisco read his column. (Truly, everyone.) And Dad wanted to be a part of this world, the world Mom and Herb Caen were writing about.

So Dad saw Mom in the paper, did his wooing, did his marrying, joined San Francisco society, had me, built Mom her dream house, gave her everything she asked for, and then left and took it all with him.

# Two · DIVORCE

DAD MOVED OUT to the Fairmont Hotel. Shortly after he'd left (for a room that smelled like his aftershave, Royall Bay Rhum) I found that first *Playboy*, which hadn't gone in Dad's drawer but onto a bookshelf in the library. He'd forgotten it.

In my bedroom, while Mom wept, I opened up the centerfold—blond and proud and gracefully, benevolently smiling. With an X-acto knife I cut a hole where her pubic hair was. Then I turned down the lights—I had a dimmer—took off my clothes, and pressed myself to the 23-by-10-3/4-inch page. I wasn't that much taller than the centerfold in *Playboy*.

Dad had informed me, "The man puts his penis in the woman's vagina and they have intercourse. This is as close as two people can possibly be to each other. It's called 'making love.'" But I did not quite follow. I thought the man tapped his penis against the triangle of the woman's pubic hair, she smiled, and the triangle folded back like a garage door, allowing the man inside, where it was very comfortable and soft and warm, and they would hold each other, hugging and kissing until they could not tell who was who. I had a book that showed cartoons of naked bodies, but it was all very procreative, and when they got to actual penetration the man and the woman disappeared beneath the sheets, and the air above the bed filled with red hearts.

I had no idea that there was *motion* involved in sex.

After cutting out the pubic hair I knew I had made a mistake. It looked wrong. Everything was not O.K. I wondered if the real woman was in terrible pain now. I wondered what to do with the small, triangular patch of hair I'd cut out. Throw it away? Where? Someone would find it. But I still wanted to make love. Maybe everything would be O.K. once we started making love. I put my penis in the hole, scraping my skin against the edges of the paper, knowing my skin cells were getting all over—in science class the teacher had had us scrape our skin with the edge of a glass slide and then look at it under a microscope to see the cells. But I was still excited! I thought she might become real somehow when she felt how much love I had.

I said, "I love you. I want to have babies with you." I pressed myself down and she crinkled. This was not glorious.

"OH THE GLORY OF IT ALL" was something I said when I was alone and things were glorious.

I would only say it when I was alone. It came out spontaneously. It felt like an affirmation of my own identity in the face of my parents' overwhelming identities. I would say it slowly, drawing it out, when the world was more full than I thought possible—when I could not contain myself, when I was alone and I was happy. I said it in the school bus under the willow. I said it when one of my inventions worked. I said it looking out the backseat windows at Chinatown and the Broadway topless joints. The phrase just came out. I remember first saying it alone in the bathroom, when I had finally got a grip on potty training and could shut the door and have the room to myself.

DAD GOT MOM to agree to something called a bifurcated divorce—their marriage was legally over and he was free to remarry just a few months after he moved out. But their disputes over money and property remained unresolved, and they would go to court to settle them.

In court Dad, viciously businesslike, stripped Mom of any claims to his property by producing a signed prenuptial agreement. Mom says she never signed it. She even found thirteen-year-old plane tickets that showed she was in L.A. on the day it was dated. Didn't matter. Dad had several witnesses. One had Mom saying, "I've signed away my right to be rich." Mom naively agreed in court that the signature was hers.

As the trial got under way the *Chronicle* reported, "The intricate accounting of the vast sums in dispute, detailed in arcane accounting and legal language, has left the City Hall courtroom awash in a flood of ledgers, computer printouts and epic-length legal briefs. But the scene has been enlivened by angry outbursts from lawyers and bitter sniping by the estranged couple at each other."

Dad's lawyer was excellent—Mom's wasn't actually a divorce lawyer—but even so, Dad made the unorthodox decision to represent himself. "He strode around the courtroom like a regular Perry Mason," one witness told me. He tag-teamed with his excellent attorney (who told the paper, "It was most enjoyable"). According to the admiring *Chronicle*, "Wilsey whispered to his own lawyer . . . 'This is a subject I know something about. Mind if I ask the questions?' Wilsey then [went] over the hurdles, item by item."

Mom's lawyer was humiliated. He told her to itemize a month's worth of expenses and ask for them as alimony. The list she produced was massive, exorbitant, alienating, embarrassing. She seemed to have taken the largest sums of money she'd ever spent on every single thing in her life and thrown them all onto a list as monthly expenses. Dad told the judge that her expenses were "appropriate for Prince Charles and the deceased Shah of Iran."

The press—society and regular—was on Dad's side all the way. Herb Caen wrote (*underreporting* Mom's alimony request by nearly half):

Ms. Montandon, a female so liberated she refused to use Wilsey's name but daintily accepted his money, wants $33,000 a month from here to eternity, to defray such expenses as doorman (she can't open her own doors?), cook, houseman, secretary and housekeeper; $2,500 a month for clothes, $2,500 for entertainment, and $170 a month for her masseuse. The nameless husband has already given her their $1.5 million Russian Hill penthouse, and is paying temporary "spousal support" of $23,000 a month.

For his part, Mr. Wilsey is willing to pay her $14,000 a month, a sum that any decently liberated woman would find derisory. . . . He also obtained an injunction to restrain her from mentioning his unmentionable name in her thrice-weekly column, a glittering feature that has broken new wind on the afternoon paper. Patsy Lou resisted this on First Amendment grounds, claiming she has to protect herself from "the defamatory innuendoes" of a morning columnist "by fighting back in my column, but with good taste."

I find this all quite moving, don't you?

Mom's list of monthly expenses (all minor for Dad—though this was never mentioned) was reprinted everywhere: $2,500 a month on travel ($4,800 according to one paper); the same on clothes; $50 for firewood; $300 in symphony and opera tickets; another $50 for glasses (she was always losing them); $500 for an allergist; $500 for flowers (casual, everyday flowers—there was a whole separate "entertaining" figure). Every detail was in the paper. One article, called "Millionaire Divorce Trial—Dollar by Dollar," led off like this:

San Francisco Superior Court Judge J. Anthony Kline looked down at Pat Montandon on the witness stand last week and marveled, "Twenty-five hundred dollars a month for clothes? That's $30,000 a year."

"I know, it's a lot," she replied. "It's become a very important part of my lifestyle. . . . I like to make life a special occasion."

Dad's attorney insisted that Mom didn't even need alimony, because "a TV executive might see her . . . and say, 'That's the kind of person I want. Miss Montandon, would you take $100,000 a year?'" Dad claimed Mom had spent all the community property during their marriage, and produced overwhelming quantities of evidence to prove it. (As one article reported, Dad "was so intent on keeping his investments separate from community property . . . that he had accountants keep a running account throughout the marriage on the separate and community funds.") Staring at the "piles of ledger paper" the judge (as reported in the *Chronicle*) said, "You are about pushing me to the limit of my being able to digest these facts." But Mom, ignorant and arrogant, described in one article as "wearing knee-high cherry-red boots, doeskin pants and matching red sweater" on the stand, continued to plead for "vitamin therapy, tennis lessons, and a masseuse." She did everything wrong. And the whole city thrilled to see her lose her mind, her dignity, her husband, and a fortune. For an entire Wednesday a DJ on one of the city's main radio stations simply repeated, "Five hundred dollars a month on flowers," every time he was supposed to do a station ID between songs.

This excerpt from a feature in the *Chronicle* describes the trial:

Montandon and Wilsey have sat shoulder to shoulder every day at the front of the courtroom, occasionally glaring or smirking at each other as their lawyers spar.

After one angry session in which Montandon's lawyer, Charles Morgan, said that Wilsey's attorney was "hoisting himself on his own petard," Wilsey asked Morgan in a friendly tone, "How do you hoist yourself on your own petard?"

"You screw up," Morgan replied pleasantly.

"It's what *you're* doing, Al," Montandon added sweetly.

Wilsey was less friendly when a photographer snapped his picture outside the courtroom. "I'll break that camera in your face," he growled.

Both sides have complained that the drawn-out legal battle is creating other problems in their personal lives.

Montandon insists 10 weeks in court has wreaked havoc with her hair style and manicure. Elegantly dressed in designer clothes, broad-brimmed hats and gloves, the columnist unhappily told a reporter that "I have to wear a hat and gloves, because it's been so long since I was at the beauty salon."

When an observer said that Wilsey probably was missing out on some business, too, she sniffed, "He's got minions to do his work for him."

Wilsey has refused to talk to the press, saying publicity would be harmful for their . . . son. His custody is not an issue, since they have agreed to joint custody.

A photograph showed Mom striding down a courtroom hall in hat and gloves. A smaller one showed Dad, mouth open, caption: "AL WILSEY 'I'll break that camera.'"

Herb Caen came up with a series of nicknames for Mom: "The Blond Dumbshell"; "Ms. Pushy Galore"; "Pat Montrachet (a dry white)." Dad was "the splendid rich chap" and "Mr. Big Bucks Nizeguy."

The writer Armistead Maupin, whose *Tales of the City* was being serialized in the *Chronicle*, brought Mom in as a character:

People said the meanest things about Prue Giroux. . . . They said her looks had gotten her everything. Her social aspirations—they said—were tainted by a kind of girlish desperation which rendered her utterly impotent as a Beautiful Person. . . . Furthermore, her ex-husband . . . had always been "the nice one." She *was* a simple country girl from Grass Valley: a tractor salesman's daughter. One of seven children.

"Prue"/Mom was: "too awful for words," a "hopelessly common woman," a "ridiculous woman," and a "pathetic creature who spends her time bragging about how far she's come."

THE DIVORCE made it all the way to the *National Enquirer*. They ran a full-page photo of Mom under the headline THE WORLD'S MOST EXPENSIVE WIFE (Dad's phrase). It was *Dallas* and *Dynasty* and Danielle Steel come to life. It was like being trapped in a television drama. Having to live and make sense of the world through its rules, scenarios, plotlines, cliff-hangers.

This *was* an eighties prime-time soap opera drama. Except for the pain.

AFTER MY PARENTS separated Mom and I went to Mexico. Dede and John Traina came along with us. Dede came to comfort Mom, but she said she also felt obliged to tell her friend some hard truths. After reading Mom's tarot cards Dede informed her, with heavy resignation, "Forget about Al coming back. He's never coming back. And he won't take care of you. You'll never get any money out of him."

Mom said, "That's not true. I *know* he will behave honorably."

Dede said, "The cards never lie."

Suddenly angry, Mom shouted, "That's *impossible*, Dede!"

Dede said, "Don't kill the *messenger!*"

The next afternoon Dede invited me over to sit with her by the pool of her rented house. In the sun, white and freckled, she told me stories about her child-hood. As Mom was larger than life, Dede was smaller than life—more detailed and intense. She told me about other worlds, about living overseas and visiting her good friends the crowned heads of Europe (mainly the queen of England and the king of Belgium). She described in detail the wonder and happiness that had been her life growing up in Washington, D.C. She and her sister, Bonnie, had their own ponies that they rode around their estate after school. She got a teal Studebaker Avanti on her sixteenth birthday (she still had it, she said, and promised me a ride). Listening to Dede was like reading a book. She was small, strung together seemingly endless narratives, and required no response. I fell in love. Europe, kings, sacks of Starburst fruit chews, Coke, ponies, sugar, *intimacy.* I wanted to have her to myself, take her to school and to bed and to dinner like a book.

By the pool, after hours of Dede's company, drunk on her, a whole new world and identity in my head, I had to go to the bathroom. She said, "Just go on up to my bedroom." It was shuttered and overlooked the pool. I knocked. John said, "Come in," lazily. I opened the door.

John was always tan. He worked in "the shipping business"—though his real occupation was the acquisition of rare objects, like Faberge cigarette cases. A 1999 article in the e-magazine *Fashionlines* described him like this:

John is a consummate collector and connoisseur who focuses on jewelry, fine art, Easter Island sculptures, and antique automobiles and carriages. Sometimes he races his 1954 Jaguar XK120 in Italy or California, and sometimes he hitches up one of his 18 or 19C carriages. Or he might be rebuilding a 50s Alfa Romeo. His carriage collection, recently written up in "Forbes" magazine, began in 1980 when he acquired [his] Napa house.

"It's a Victorian complex, and it just looked as if it should be surrounded by old buggies," he says. Now there are 33, including a surrey with fringe on top, and he says, "With each of my collecting passions, I feel a certain itch after I buy the first item, and I know I'm hooked for life."

He also collects miniature suits of armor and maritime memorabilia.

A year and a half before, when I was eight, and the kind of kid who sang songs to sick flowers and told people that I wanted to be either an inventor or an interior decorator when I grew up, I decided I should put John Traina in the hospital, so Mom and Dad and I could have Dede to ourselves. I thought, *Since Mom and Dad and I love Mrs. Traina, and take care of her, and John never takes care of her, John can't love Mrs. Traina.* My plan was to knock him off his bicycle into a ditch by riding up from behind and grinding his rear wheel with my front one, which, according to a T.V. movie I'd seen, would result in loss of control, a catastrophic wipeout, and months in traction for the front rider. John would go to the hospital with terrible injuries, and I would replace him. I pictured John tumbling with his elegant Univega, its metal bending and splintering, into the gravel and dust at the side of the road, destroying his sweater, his perfect, looped-around-his-neck sweater. The day I tried it I was possessed. I rode up slowly behind him, inching closer, and then closer—*I'm doing this, I'm really doing this!*—till we were just inches apart, our wheels making figure eights, and then—*Do it! Do it! Do it for Mrs. Traina!*—mine touched his, I pumped the pedals hard, leaned forward, and my arms wrenched to the right and sent me over the bars. I flew past John and into a ditch. My bike landed on top of me. John turned, hit the brakes, stopped, jumped into the ditch, and pulled my bike off. I thought he was moving the bike so he could slug me. He knew what I was doing. I said, "No! I'm sorry!"

A look of confusion and concern broke across his tan. He said, "Sean, are you O.K.?"

As I OPENED the door to Dede and John's bedroom in Mexico, John was midway through threading a thin green belt through bright yellow pants.

I said, "Hi, John! . . . *Sorry* . . ." and looked away.

The shutters were slatted to afford a view of the pool. I thought he had probably been watching Dede and me. He was silent. It flashed through my mind that he was going to challenge me to a duel. John was the dueling type. He probably had pistols somewhere. Could you take swords and/or dueling pistols on Aeroméxico? If you were flying first class?

He gave me a slight, almost involuntary eye roll and lifted his profile in the direction of the bathroom. I shut the door. All of John and Dede's toilet articles were on the sink in front of me, intermingled. This was true intimacy. When I came out he had the thin belt looking just right, a matching green cardigan tied around his neck, a red-and-white-checked shirt, open at the throat, and was headed out the door.

"I'll leave you two alone for the afternoon," he said.

*Good,* I thought.

SEVERAL MONTHS into my parents' legal battles Dad pulled me into the living room in Napa, planted himself in front of the fireplace, and, shaking with emotion, told me, "Your mother only thought of me as a credit card."

He looked at me hard. I didn't know what to say.

"She manipulated me," he continued. Then, under his breath, "*She's a barracuda.*"

Even at age ten I knew this was wrong. Mom loved and was utterly devoted to Dad. She'd spent his money because that's what he taught her to do.

Years later I would discover that when Mom and Dad were still married Dad kept a separate apartment around the corner from his office. Dad would have lunch with my half brother Mike, who was then working with him. When he finished eating Dad would say, "I'm going to take a walk," and disappear for an hour. The first time he did this Mike thought, *He wants to take a walk? He never wants to take a walk.* He said, "I'll walk with you if you'd like the company."

Dad said, "No. I want to be by myself." Everybody in the office knew where Dad was going. Dad's employees had a nickname for his apartment: "the nooner."

Mom told me, "I was trusting, I was stupid." Her famous ignorance let her down.

I did not know that "the barracuda" was Dede's out-of-earshot nickname for my mother. It became a San Francisco society pastime to provoke the barracuda.

Mom had been queen of San Francisco for too long. The city was ready for a coup. I imagine it started with a whispering campaign. Then it escalated. At one formal luncheon in the Napa Valley, just before the divorce, Charles Crocker III, one of Dede's friends, pulled Dad out of his seat, saying, "We have a better place for you up here, Al," and moved him to a vacant space at the head table, next to Dede. Mom lost her temper—and when Mom loses her temper she can be counted on to destroy herself. As generous and fun and likable as she is when she is the center of attention, when she feels scorned or belittled she transforms. She will throw a grand, Norma Desmond–style tantrum, featuring slammed doors, hurled objects, generalized damnation, haughty sulking.

It is easy to goad Mom into one of these performances. And with Mom losing her temper, calling Dad names, and damning San Francisco society to hell (like a fiery preacher's daughter), Dad felt all the more justified in his actions. Driving home from the party he said, "Maybe we should split up." It was the first time he'd ever said anything like that.

Halloween, two months before the divorce, Dad wanted us to go trick-or-treating in Pacific Heights instead of on Russian Hill. He did a lot of foot tapping about how we needed to leave *now*, which was fine with me—I was dressed like C-3PO, ready for candy. Mom was annoyed and didn't understand why we couldn't stay in our neighborhood.

"Alfred," she said. "I have *precious* little patience for this. I will *not* leave the house till I'm dressed and made up."

She couldn't really get angry because I was there. I said, "You look great, Mom."

Dad, grumbled, "Call me Al. I'm sick of being called Alfred."

Mom said, "That's your *name*. Al sounds like somebody who works in a gas station."

Dad was silent.

Finally we left, drove down the hill, parked, and Dad hustled us up to the corner of Pacific and Steiner—where we ran right into Dede and her sons, Todd and Trevor: *rendezvous*.

AFTER WE RETURNED from Mexico, Dede's oldest friend, godmother to her son Trevor, called up Mom and asked her to lunch. Mom accepted with surprise. At lunch the woman asked Mom questions.

"Has Al been calling you?"

"No."

"Do you think you'll get back together?"

"*No!*" Tears.

After she got Mom's answers, she never called Mom again.

Within a matter of days one of Herb Caen's best sources, a guy with a "de" in his name, came up to Mom at a party and said, barracuda taunting, "Oh, Pat, Dede says she's having the best sex of her life with Al Wilsey."

*Ka-boom.*

THIS IS what Dede did. She got to know Mom, found her greatest weakness (pride and vanity), stole her greatest asset (family), mocked Mom's presence in a world where she didn't belong (society), lit Mom's fuse, and watched her explode.

Dede's was an extraordinary betrayal. Extraordinary in its boldness, its meanness, and its total unoriginality. The whole thing—not just our whole splashy, public life, but *this woman*—was right out of *Dynasty,* or *Dallas,* or (one of Dede's favorite shows, which she once claimed was partially modeled on us) *Falcon Crest.*

In the end Mom's whole world was taken away from her. A world of wealth and privilege she had never wanted in the first place but now was identified by completely. Dede made Mom ridiculous. Publicly humiliated her. Drove her crazy. Destroyed her. Ditched her. Married her husband. Switched identities with her, taking not only Mom's home and family, but her reputation for grace and honesty and compassion. Instead of looking like a victim, Mom looked scheming, grasping, deceptive. The identity switch was flawless. A year or so

later, when she'd divorced John Traina and married Dad, Mom's ex—best friend
was described as sweet, "Dimpled Dede" in Herb Caen. Society's darling.

When Mom talks about San Francisco society now—Caen and all these
people with their "de" and "von" prefixes and Roman numeral suffixes—it's as
if she's speaking of another century and another country. Though Mom was
part of their world, she doesn't seem to really understand it, or speak its language. She can't pronounce their names. She was never really one of them, and
she never really tried to be. She was just being herself, having fun, and thinking
they liked her for it.

JUST BEFORE DAD left Mom he said he'd been having some financial difficulties and they'd have to change their lifestyle. They would have to let Clifford,
Mom's chauffeur, go. (That's the euphemism for firing both Mom and Dad used:
"let go.")

Dad said, "How would you feel about driving yourself?"

Mom said, "I'm more worried about what will happen to Clifford. Driving
myself will be fine. I did it for years when I had my T.V. show."

*Great. That's a relief. . . .*

But the whole premise was a deception. Dad, meticulous, could cross one
more concern off his checklist—*Find out: will she insist on chauffeur?*—before he
divorced her.

Around the time of the chauffeur conversation Dad took me out of Catholic
school—despite his Catholicism—and enrolled me in Dede's sons' Episcopal
school on Nob Hill. Mom would've fought if he'd tried to change my school after divorcing her, so it was (1) change my school (2) divorce Mom. It was like a
military campaign, the way Dad employed strategy in order to ensure that he accomplished as many objectives as possible before the open declaration of hostil-
ities. Dad was a remover of all foreseeable obstacles.

Everyone in my new, easier-for-Dad-to-commute-to school knew me only
from what their parents read about my parents in the paper.

WHEN THE DIVORCE trial was over, the judge, stating that Mom wasn't entitled "to retain every single vestige of luxury to which she became accustomed
during marriage," gave her twenty thousand dollars a month for six years. He
gave Dad the Napa house (which Mom pined for) and her the penthouse. He
said Mom should get a job. Mom said, "I cannot, on $20,000 a month, support the
lifestyle to which Al Wilsey made me accustomed. I'm talking about equity!"

Dad said Mom could sell the penthouse, buy a less expensive home, invest the difference, and live off the proceeds (all this is per the *Chronicle*). The judge disagreed. He said it was in *my* best interest that Mom keep the penthouse—because I was "comfortable" there. He granted that Mom was in a state of nervous collapse. It was obvious. But this was temporary. He was optimistic: "[T]he fortitude and resilience that characterize her life is such that the court does not believe this present disability should endure much longer than six months to, at the most, one year." She was, he said, "strikingly attractive and vivacious . . . by any measure a remarkable person."

Dad was satisfied. He told the press that the judge was a "paragon of patience for putting up with trial day after trial day of pure nonsense.

"I think it's a disgrace that the courts of San Francisco were tied up for months by the litigious attorney for Miss Montandon on a matter that could have been settled on any afternoon in 1980."

"Your dad *bought the judge,*" Mom declared, then burst into tears and went to bed for several weeks.

I was impressed that Dad was *so powerful.*

I brought Mom her ice cream.

When she finally got out of bed things only got weirder. She hired society divorce lawyer Marvin Mitchelson for the appeal(s) and dragged the whole thing on into the mid eighties, Jarndyce v. Jarndyce–style. Dede divorced John Traina and married Dad. Within a month John Traina was married to Danielle Steel. (Mom had introduced them.) Prior to dating John, Danielle had been having an affair with *Dad* (while pretending to be friends with Mom) but she had lost out to Dede in the battle for his affections, so she picked up John Traina as a consolation prize, had five kids with him, and got a divorce seventeen years later.

Is that all clear?

*Three* · D A D

S AN FRANCISCO looks like a hand. A right one, palm side up, forearm the
peninsula leading down south. And this is true down to the details: the cor-
respondences of palm lines to major streets, whorls to neighborhoods, fingers
to bridges, calluses to hills: the crease of the "lifeline" the smooth arc of highway 80 curving off the Bay Bridge of the pointer; the lower and more diagonal
of the two other main hand lines ("headline" and "heartline" in palmistry) repli-
cates the diagonal of Market Street, while its companion is the kink of the Geary
Expressway arcing into and becoming Van Ness. There's a nameless groove that
doubles for Lombard Street, a perfect crosshatchy area for the alleys of Chinatown, the fat lump anchoring the thumb is Potrero Hill and Hunter's Point, right
where they should be. The Bay Bridge is the pointer, the Golden Gate the ring
finger, the rest of the fingers are gone—unless you count the finger piers.

There are a lot of San Franciscos in this small space. The touristy waterfront
leads to the strip joints of Broadway, which slices through Chinatown, which

separates swank yet bohemian Russian Hill and swanker, non-bohemian Nob Hill, both of which overlook austere, pedestrian-free Pacific Heights.

It's a city that has held and handled and shoved and harbored and stroked and caressed and flipped off and called come-hither to my father's family going back to 1857.

ALFRED SPALDING WILSEY—Dad—was born in San Francisco in 1919, the year the treaty of Versailles was signed. The Spalding came from the doctor who delivered him, though Dad liked to let people think he was part of the family that made the tennis balls.

Wilsey is Americanized Dutch and was originally Wiltsee, which means either "wild side" or "wild sea" depending on context.

Hayes Centennial Wilsey—Dad's dad—was so named because he arrived in 1876, and Rutherford B. Hayes, a family friend, dandled him on his lap, causing my then nameless grandfather to lose control of his bladder (the first in a series of Wilsey incontinences brought on by Republican politicians).

When Dad came along, the youngest of four, Hayes was already a divorcé. It was Hayes who established the matrimonial template that was followed so closely by my father. Hayes married Flora, his first wife, in his early twenties. Dad did the same with Dory, his first wife. Hayes had an affair with his second wife, Ora Carmelita McCarthy, my exotic Spanish-Irish grandmother. Dad had an affair with his exotic—"Lorrie was Jewish!" he always said with pride— second wife, too. After Hayes married my grandmother, he started another affair with his secretary (Gertie), and then married the secretary when my grandmother died of cancer (the same disease that killed Dad's second wife, allowing him to move on to Mom).

Hayes outlived 33.3 percent of his wives.

Dad outlived 50 percent of his.

Hayes:
>       Flora
>       Ora
>       Gertie

Dad:
>       Dory
>       Lorrie

Patsy
Dede

Dad got off two rhyming matrimonial couplets. Hayes only managed one point five.

In 1906, Dad's parents survived the great San Francisco quake and fire. Thirty years later, when Dad was a teenager, they both died within a few months of each other, first his mother and then his hastily remarried father. At seventeen Dad and his older brother, Jack, moved in with family friends and took over the family butter and egg business.

Dad was stunningly and immediately successful in business. His older sister, my aunt Helen, told me how he kept the company afloat: "That young kid would go to the bank and talk them into giving him a million bucks to buy the butter. Borrow a million bucks, buy all this butter, sell it, make half a cent a pound in profit, pay the money back. Your uncle Jack said to me about your dad, 'That kid's good.'"

The company was called Wilsey Bennett (though there had been no Bennett for years). They cut butter into sticks for home use, and devised single-use portions for restaurants and cafeterias. The principal varieties of Wilsey Bennett individually packaged butter were:

Continental Chips: rectangular cubes wrapped in foil
Filpers: filled paper cups with peel-off, wax-paper tops
Readys: thin Continental Chips on little squares of waxed cardboard, with
    wax-paper peel-off tops (nickname: Pats on Mats with Hats on the Pats)

Dad and Jack worked in every aspect of the business. When an employee got his finger sliced off in a butter-packing machine Dad went through all the wrapped sticks until he found the one with the finger, and rushed it and the worker to the hospital, where they were successfully reunited.

They moved into edible oils. They supplied McDonald's with tallow to fry their fries. They bought a drug company, a candy company, and a trucking company. They went into real estate with their childhood friend, Gerson Bakar, forming an investment partnership called Jalson (*Jack Al Gerson*). Dad and Jack got pilots' licenses so they could fly out over the country with their checkbooks, looking for land to buy. They went as far as Oklahoma—Mom country— but made it big with huge parcels north of San Francisco and south of Los Angeles, where they built apartments worth hundreds of millions of dollars today.

Uncle Jack always dominated everything they did. He was the big brother

and the big personality. He took Dad out drinking and fighting and whoring—
Nevada was an easy flight—and Dad always had to get Jack out of trouble. Dad
didn't really come into his own till Uncle Jack died, a few years before I was born.

When I was a kid Wilsey Bennett Continental Chips were on the tables of half
the restaurants in San Francisco. They were even at Denny's, Dad's favorite
restaurant after Trader Vic's. I'd see the cool fifties-modern "WB" logo and think,
*Dad!* At its height the business had fifteen hundred full-time employees. Dad told
me, "More than a thousand people are depending on me for their livelihood."

BUT THAT'S REALLY the extent of my knowledge.

Whatever I can tell you about my father will probably be wrong. I have a collection of theories and incidents and facts concerning Dad, but no comprehen-
sion. I've put him together like an archeologist investigating a lost civilization
while at the same time powerfully longing for it.

HE HAD A Class A, three-axle, commercial truck rating on his license, permitting him to drive buses, coaches, and tractor-trailers with loads in excess of ten
thousand pounds.

He became a helicopter pilot in his midfifties and made his last flight when he
was eighty-one.

He quit smoking every year for Lent, when he took advantage of his U.S. Department of Agriculture butter and cheese inspector's license to feast on epic
quantities of California cheddar under the pretense of inspecting it.

He could name the capital of any state, country, or territory. I'd say, "Zam-
bia?" He'd say, "Lusaka." I'd say, "Tasmania?" He'd say, "Hobart." Then he'd
say, "I am a font of useless information."

He liked to arrive at San Francisco International Airport very early, check in
(first class; British Airways, if possible), and then roam around the airport looking for luggage carts to return for the deposits.

He did business with the Italian Mafia and the Irish Mafia.

Every once in a while, pretty much out of nowhere, he liked to sing out softly,
"Toora Loora Loora, that's an Irish lull-a-by."

DAD, married to his first wife, woke up one night, his skin burning. For several
seconds he didn't know why. Then he realized Dory had a bucket and a sponge
and was rubbing Bab-O Cleanser into his chest.

She said she wanted to get him clean.

. . .

I FOUND THIS clip, marked JUN 25 1954 (shortly after the above incident), and "wilsey, alfred s," in the files of the California Historical Society:

DAIRY OWNER'S WIFE SEEKS DIVORCE

Doris Wilsey, 33, of Kent Woodlands, Kentfield, filed suit for divorce yesterday against her socially prominent husband, Alfred S. Wilsey, 35, owner of a dairy products company.

She said he had struck her June 10, causing bruises and contusions, and had threatened to repeat the act.

She asked $1250 a month support for herself and four children, $1000 in attorneys' fees, and possession of the family home.

The only time Dad ever hit me, he hit me in the head. He and Mom were still married, and we'd been out on a family bike ride in the Napa Valley with Dede and John and their boys. When we came back to our house for dinner Dad told me to do something (I don't remember what), and I told him I'd do it later, because I wanted to show something to Mrs. Traina first. Suddenly the left side of my head felt like it was on fire, and my vision skewed sideways. Dad had stepped up behind and slapped me as hard as he could. I felt a lightning flash of pain, then heard the sound of the slap, and then started crying. It was a head slap like a thunder clap—flash, boom, water.

DAD LOVED FUNERALS. Dad was a funeral enthusiast! When he got older and his friends started dying he loved to call their widows right after the mortuary had removed the body and offer to come along and help them pick out a coffin. He was good at haggling. And coffin salesmen were confused by how much he seemed to be enjoying himself.

He talked in a soft voice that suggested he was putting you on, and managed to be simultaneously flattering and distancing, like maybe this wasn't the *real* Al Wilsey but a special, personalized Al Wilsey, rolled out just for you.

ONE OF DAD'S oldest friends was a guy named Johnny Tremeroli. Dad took me to Johnny's funeral. Johnny's mother had outlived him, and she wailed at his graveside—"Oh Johnny! Oh Johnny! Oh Johnny! Johnny! Johnny! Johnny!"—for the whole service. I had never seen emotion displayed so publicly. I didn't know this was permitted. It was horrible and electrifying, and Dad obviously enjoyed it.

Earlier, in the church, he'd turned to me, cocked his head toward the back, and whispered, with *merriment*, "Here come the pallbearers!"

I looked over my shoulder. Six old men approached, bent under Johnny's coffin.

"I helped pick that one out," Dad continued, almost to himself.

The men passed us solemnly, exchanged some nods with Dad.

"Hope they don't drop it."

I started to laugh.

Then he turned back to me, put-on voice gone, and said, "Someday, that'll be *you* up there, and *me* in the box."

Following World War II—which he sat out because of bad knees—there was a lot of military surplus from the Pacific campaign floating around San Francisco. Dad and Uncle Jack went to an Army auction and bought six jeeps, an amphibious transport with a fold-down gate, of the sort used to storm the beaches at Normandy (called a landing-ship tank), and a truck with rubber wheels in the front and tank treads in the back (a half-track). They cruised around the bay in the landing ship tank on the weekends, shouting challenges to sailboats over the roar of the big diesel engine. *"You wanna race?!"*

When the city installed parking meters on Battery Street, where his butter plant was located, Dad filled the bed of the half-track with cement and parked it there at 4:00 A.M. After it accumulated sufficient tickets a tow truck came, hooked up, and instead of towing, reared on its back wheels, burned rubber, then crashed to the street. A crowd gathered to watch. Another truck was called. The same thing happened again. They called heavier tow trucks. No luck. Photographs of the half-track began appearing in the paper, alongside antiparking-meter editorials. Eventually, the city removed the meters.

THE SIX JEEPS were cannibalized for parts, making one that still runs today. Dad used it to exercise his two largest, wildest, unhappiest dogs: Bo, a yellow Lab, and Yogi, a standard poodle. Yogi and Bo lived full-time in a kennel in the Napa Valley, and were let out for half an hour on the weekends to chase the jeep, in a ritual Dad called "running the dogs."

When it was time to "run the dogs" Dad found me, started up his jeep, and moved the passenger's side to within an inch of the wire door to the kennel, with great precision. This was like a military operation. We got in position, the dogs hurling themselves against the door and falling back to the ground, and then, on a dog rebound, Dad bellowed, *"Now!"*

I sprang the latch and shoved in hard. The dogs exploded through the gap, clambered over each other, and were in my lap. Dad dropped the clutch and we swayed away from the kennel onto a two-lane blacktop, pulling a hard right and barely hesitating to check for oncoming traffic. Then we drove out to a long, straight, deserted stretch of road at the back of the valley, the dogs clambering all over us, licking and drooling, Dad shouting over the wind, "Keep them *off* me—and *off* the *stick shift*." Finally we stopped, and Dad seized the dogs and pushed them out hard. Then he floored it.

Yogi and Bo looked confused as we sped away, then they began to pursue. They gained for the first seven seconds, and for the next half mile or so they stayed about thirty feet back, like water skiers. When Dad shifted into top gear they shrunk rapidly; first Bo, the Lab, who was an awkward, lumbering runner; then drooling, filthy, wired Yogi, who reminded me of myself, his big need driving him forward, chasing *Dad*, wanting *Dad*, tongue hanging out the side of his head like a seat belt. Eventually the dogs became specks, one small and black, the other smaller and yellow, pursuing us desperately. After a couple of miles we pulled onto the dirt at the edge of the road and waited.

When the dogs arrived they got back into the jeep, lay down, pacified, and we stuck them back in the kennel for another week.

IN THE BEDROOM, in a closet, Dad kept safety deposit boxes with guns in them. Also shoe boxes and exotic leather cases containing such objects as a gold tie clip in the shape of a meat cleaver, a combination watch/money clip/pocketknife (that I now have), cuff links, ammunition, badges, lapel pins with strange and beautiful enameled insignias, rings from former marriages—all glinting and clinking together indiscriminately.

He didn't care about these things. They were tokens his thrifty nature wouldn't allow him to discard, so they filled a closet that he almost never opened. After his first marriage ended, Dad's house had burned down (spontaneous combustion) and the contents of this closet were what he'd dug out of the ashes.

Dad hated the past. Dad wanted to reinvent himself. And he did so, so many times. Until he found Dede and made her my stepmother. And then he put Mom and me in his Indifferent Closet of Weapons, Treasure, and Personal History, too. Or, more accurately, he managed to make Mom combust spontaneously, and then

OH THE GLORY OF IT ALL    45

he dug me out of the ashes and stored me away. But before I joined it, Dad's closet was the place that set my imagination on fire. I was in awe of it. *All of his past.* And all the more fascinated that he didn't care about it at all. He didn't even care about the *handguns,* of which there were three. The two bigger ones—a .38 and a .45—had belonged to Dad's brother, my uncle Jack. A friend of Dad's had given him the smallest (a nasty, tinny thing with a vinyl ankle holster) because, Dad told me, "He was afraid of what he might do with it. So he wanted your old man to hold on to it for him."

I said, "What do you mean, 'afraid of what he might do with it'?"

"He was afraid he might get low and kill himself," Dad said. He seemed indifferent. The gun man was part of Dad's *past.* So he may as well have been dead. He never came to see Dad. Dad never pointed him out at Caesar's, the dark old Italian restaurant on the fringe of North Beach, where all the old men looked up from their cards or drinks or racing papers and said, "How ya doin', Al?" Where we went into the kitchen and greeted the owner, who was frying something with Dad's butter (which Dad ate plain, the way other people eat cheese). Where Dad once turned to me and proclaimed, "Sean, look at that—there's nothing better than a clean stainless steel restaurant kitchen."

*What does that mean?* I thought. It was nonsense. But still I admired it—like I admired all things Dad—and took it for wisdom. Everyone in the kitchen looked like they were about to burst into applause when he said it.

Dad was always issuing such declarations.

Since the family Dad lived with after he and Uncle Jack were orphaned was Jewish, like his second wife, any reference to Judaism or Israel or New York City or just a simple "I had a bagel for breakfast" would elicit an "I like Jews!" from Dad, who spoke conversational Yiddish and could recite a Catholic mass in Latin. To Dad Catholicism was the Judaism of Christianity.

When people moved out of earshot he declared, "They like me!"

Upon entering a men's room he'd head for the sink, saying, "You should wash your hands *first,* before you use the urinal. Not after. Your penis isn't dirty. But your *hands* are."

When he saw me eating junk food: "There is no better thing you can be in this world than a lover of fruit."

As a catchall expression of futility: "If your aunt had balls she'd be your uncle." (i.e., Me: "I would have gotten a B-minus instead of a D-minus, but I didn't see the last page on the test." Dad: "If your aunt had balls, she'd be your *uncle.*")

He also had three aphorisms, suitable for any company or occasion:

1. "I didn't choose to be born *bright* and *white,* and because I was, I need to give back for this great opportunity."
2. "There is no such thing as a free lunch."
3. "If I lose everything, I can always drive a truck."

I noticed all Dad's details. And I particularly noticed how he never seemed to notice anything about me. I tried to be funny—my one salvation at school. He refused to laugh at my jokes, though he frequently laughed at things I could not help. Like my walk, which was "too bouncy" and cracked him up, until it made him angry, and then he tried to train me out of it.

I remember walking to the car on one of the rare days he picked me up after school. Coming out of the doors, happy to see Dad, I quickened my pace.

"Stop bouncing!" he hollered. I was the bouncing son of the world's most expensive wife. Busted.

MY TWO BEST friends at my new school were Spencer Perry and Blane Morf.

Spencer Perry arrived at Cathedral School for Boys the same day in 1979 that I did. I was there about half an hour before him. When Spencer walked in with his mother, the only free desk was next to mine, so Mrs. Perry made for it, Spencer in spectacular tow. On the first day of school his new uniform of gray cords, blue button-down, yellow-and-red striped tie, and black shoes already looked ink-stained and threadbare and wrong-sized on this kid who seemed simultaneously skinny and pudgy (pants too big, shirt too small) and had a huge afro of blond hair and a two-inch scar that ran down his right cheek, from a car accident a few years before.

As the class turned around to check him out Mrs. Perry looked at me, looked at him, and exclaimed, "Why Spencer! You remember Sean from *cooking class,* don't you?"

We both feigned ignorance.

"At the Jewish Community Center!" Mrs. Perry continued. We nodded in shame. Mom and Dad had enrolled me in a cooking class at the JCC. I can imagine Dad thinking to himself, *If he's gonna be a queer at least he'll get some smart Jewish friends in the bargain.* Spencer had been there too, because he wanted to be a chef (a fact he was callow enough to admit).

Our new classmates at Cathedral School for Boys laughed so hard at us that it took half the year to recover.

For the next few months common humiliation forced Spencer and me to hate each other. We got into a fight when I smashed a kick ball at him as he was lying on the ground at recess. He'd tried to whip me and Blane Morf—who'd already been at Cathedral for years, and more or less fit in there—with his belt because we were teasing him. He'd been in public school, and this was supposedly what the tough public school kids did when they were truly pissed.

But after a couple of months one thing became clear—we understood each other. And there was no way we couldn't be friends.

Blane Morf was more like a brother than a friend. He was blond and freckled, with a completely guileless face that helped him get away with things. He lived around the corner from me, which enabled us to eat half our meals at one or the other's houses. He also came over and threw things off my deck. For some reason Glad three-ply garbage bags, and their astounding strength, were heavily advertised on T.V. during afternoon cartoons. Walking home from school one afternoon, Blane and I decided to buy a box, fill a pair with water, haul them out on my deck (thirty-three stories up), and toss them off. We could barely hoist them over the deck railings. Before we let go, in a moment of sanity, I told him to put some holes in his so it wouldn't be full when it hit the ground. "It'll lose water, catch air, and not be as heavy."

"O.K.," he said.

I made my holes. Soon mine was dripping all over me. "Ready?" I asked.

"Yes," he said.

"O.K. Go!"

They rolled off the deck railing, spun, and plummeted! Comet trails of water sprayed out of mine. His fell twice as fast and barely dripped at all.

I said, "Blane! Didn't you make any holes?"

"I did!" he said.

"Oh no! Not big enough! Oh God!" I said.

"Oh shit!" he said.

Blane's bag fell straight down thirty stories, like a bowling ball in an elevator shaft, and shattered the rooftop greenhouse of the three-story building next door. Glass imploded, the roof collapsed; we saw wet, swaying trees.

My bag hit harmlessly nearby.

We observed the destruction in silence.

"Those look like palm trees," said Blane at last.

"We have to tell my mom," I said.

Mom immediately sent us down to confess and apologize. Even though it was more my responsibility, I made Blane go first. This was lucky. The woman who owned the greenhouse looked at Blane and simply said, "You boys are so nice to come down and apologize." Then she offered us cookies.

We got off with the best story ever. Our friendship was assured.

Dad was disgusted.

"I can't believe that lady doesn't make you boys work to repair her greenhouse," he said.

I shrugged.

From then on Blane and Spencer (guilty by association) were the wrong kind of friends. But Blane and Spencer were the only friends who didn't judge me for what Mom and Dad were doing.

I WAS ALWAYS struggling, without success, to convince Dad that I was *funny*, not "funny." That I could make people laugh deliberately, and also *not* make people laugh—deliberately. Finally, I just told him. I said, "Dad, you know, I *am* funny. Lots of people laugh at my jokes. I'm considered very humorous in certain circles."

"What circles are those?" he asked, dryly.

"*Over at Mom's house,*" I mumbled.

He turned to me, looked hard, then after a long pause, said, "I know you're funny. But you're not my kind of funny."

HE OFTEN LAUGHED when he saw me. And I also laughed when I saw him. It was how we recognized each other.

I used to find it humiliating that he was laughing at me. But later I liked it. It ran deeper than any other emotion he ever showed me.

Probably it was laughter about the fact that we were father and son. At the ridiculous idea that I had come from him. And the fact that I looked just like him.

FOR THE FIRST decade of my life, when Dad came home at the end of the day he wanted a hug. He was a physical father. He roughhoused. He gave piggyback rides. He said, "Come here. Pull my finger."

His affection went underground after he married Dede. He got awkward. I'd run for a hug when he came home from work and he'd deliver it rapidly, furtively, *one-armed*. I started meeting him in the garage so we could hug and not be seen.

Outside the garage, Dad only showed his affection in church. A Catholic church was an assuredly Dede-free zone. We usually went to Saturday evening mass at a small one near Napa; St. Joan of Arc, full of World War veterans, vestigial farmers, migrant laborers, and a few scrubbed kids. Dad didn't give me much credit for coming—it was a duty in his eyes—though he did repeatedly ask if Mom ever went. No, I told him. Mom did not attend church in anything like a regular pattern—though she was occasionally taken by fits of spirituality and would go to three services at three different denominations of church in a single weekend, catching the Saturday afternoon mass in North Beach, an Episcopal vespers on Nob Hill, and a Sunday morning Baptist service in Oakland, dragging me along.

Dad laughed. *This was funny*. I was *almost* funny for telling him about it.

On the way to St. Joan of Arc he lectured me on my flaws . . . which were mitigated by the hope of youth . . . which I was in danger of squandering . . . unless I learned the value of hard work.

When we got to church everything about him relaxed. We sat in the back, near a statue of St. Joan of Arc. She had long hair, white skin, full red lips, and wore a genuine suit of armor (the metal contoured to accommodate her breasts), and held a helmet in the crook of her arm. She looked sexy, dangerous, compassionate. The priest stepped onto the altar, the service started, and Dad reached over and took my hand. He had dry, comfortable hands. Not rough or soft, just a bit fleshy—hands like a barely sandy gust of wind. They were *pleasant* hands, to use one of his favorite words. I pressed down on the ends of his fingers and they indented, and remained indented for several seconds before returning to normal. I loved doing this over and over, and he never complained.

Dad and I held hands through the various lessons and readings, the part when you pray silently, and were interrupted only by kneeling, hand shaking, and the liturgy, after which I walked down the aisle to take communion, which Dad couldn't take (too many living wives). When I sat back down, the host still in my mouth, I picked up Dad's hand again. He squeezed three times: "I. Love. You." I squeezed back four times, an extra squeeze for "Too."

When the sermon began to drag and he fell asleep and started to snore, I squeezed to wake him up, and then he gave this loopy grin, tipping his head back and letting his tongue loll out of the side of his mouth, like he was absolutely out cold, or dead—and we laughed as quietly as we could.

*Four* · DAD AND DEDE

Aꜰᴛᴇʀ ᴛʜᴇ ᴅɪᴠᴏʀᴄᴇ, with a few months before he could marry Dede, Dad ricocheted across the top of Nob Hill, taking me with him during his custody weeks. He started at the Fairmont, on the far east end; then the Gramercy Towers, a hotel that'd been converted into an apartment building, on the southwest corner (moving into an apartment that had just been vacated by Rock Hudson); then the Brocklebank, a grand, old, post–quake era high-rise on the northeast corner, my favorite of his postdivorce bachelor lodgings.

At school one day I heard that Dede and John Traina were getting divorced. (I had no idea Dad was having an affair with Dede, and would not figure it out till well after they were married. I was the only one more naive than Mom.) When I heard about Dede and John I came up with a plan. And the more I thought about my plan the more an emotion, absent since Mom and Dad's separation, an emotion that I thought I might not see again, began to bubble up in me. It was joy. I felt dizzy with joy. I saw a possibility. I knew *I* could never marry Dede, even with John out of my way—*but what about Dad?* The idea generated a huge amount of warmth in my chest.

*Maybe Dad and Dede could date,* I thought. *Do they know each other? I mean, she's really my friend, but maybe they'd like each other. Could it ever be true?! Do they know what this could mean? Have they thought of this?*

I went crazy during recess. We were playing dodgeball and I thought, *If I cream enough people, I can make this happen.*

After P.E. I walked out of school and saw a black-and-gold Special Edition Trans Am, the one that was in *Smokey and the Bandit,* idling at the curb. I saw it, thought *cool,* and then realized *Dad* was driving. What did this mean?

"Get in," Dad said, all cool.

We shot down Jones and out California. Dad didn't make me fasten my seat belt. The day was classic San Francisco—a cloudy day full of small sunny days—and as we blasted off Nob Hill, skirted Chinatown, took Jackson to Polk, Polk to the Tenderloin, weaved a pattern around California, we moved from yellow to gray to yellow to gray, making a lot of noise. We went back to the Brocklebank for dinner. When we'd eaten Dad said, "Sean, let's drive around some more."

"O.K." *Cool.*

The car had removable, smoked-glass, individual sunroofs—called "T-tops"—over the seats. Dad pulled them off and put them in the trunk.

"We'll put on the heat," he said.

We flew out California—lights blurring, wind coming in from above, me without a jacket, the heat bad, both of us cold, until Dad finally turned into a gas station to reattach the T-tops. I tried to help.

"This is annoying," he said.

*Where did he get this car?* I wondered. He told me he wasn't going to keep it, that he'd "borrowed it from an employee."

The T-tops were stacked awkwardly in the trunk. I came around back and we each took an end of one. When we got above the passenger's side Dad said, "O.K., O.K.," and I dropped my side, making him drop his.

"No! No! You'll break it, Sean!" Dad flexed his fingers, glanced at his watch. "Leave it now!"

I watched. The Bandit never had any trouble with his T-tops. He probably tricked Sheriff Buford T. Justice into dealing with them. Or Sally Field . . . maybe Cledus, his partner, in a pinch. The Bandit was not sixty, thrice married, once widowed, twice divorced, driving around with a ten-year-old, his other four kids in their thirties and married. Dad didn't need to run beer across Texas on a bet with a pair of rich twins, one a giant, the other a homunculus.

Dad had finished with the T-tops. He said, "Let's drive by Dede and John's place in Pacific Heights."

"O.K.," I said.

We drove a few blocks in silence. Dad said, "We're going to check up on Dede."

Silence.

"This is an important night. I need you to sit still with me. We're making sure Dede's O.K."

It was easy getting a parking space on Jackson Street—everyone had a garage. We pulled up across the street from her house, on a downhill slope between Pierce and Steiner. Dad lowered his window six inches and cut the engine.

He said, "Now just be quiet and patient. I'm sorry about the cold, but this is important, and it's important we stay out of sight. Keep an eye out for activity around the windows. That's all you need to do, Sean. If you see anything you think I might not have noticed make sure to tap me and let me know."

It was strange and awesome sitting in the dark with Dad in a freezing, unfamiliar, *way* cool vehicle.

We sat without touching or talking. I thought about . . .
*CHiPs* . . .

Pong . . .

Dede . . .

the Bandit . . .

Dad was patient and attentive.

We were a father-and-son buddy team on a stakeout.

*Bandit and Son. Dede's guardians.*

Dad would always point out wildlife and scenery on drives, and I managed not to see them. "Deer!" Dad'd say, and I'd jerk my head up and say, "Where!," gawk side to side, grab the dash, and then he'd say, "Gone."

I spaced and looked at Dede's house, spaced and looked at Dede's house. What sort of activity was I supposed to keep an eye out for? A tan man in yellow with a knife in his hand? Dede naked? Maybe Dad was checking out her body to see if he liked it enough to want to ask her on a date. I was excited. I felt so close to Dad. He trusted me to spot Dede's body or John's knife or something else significant. Nothing. Nothing. Nothing. Nothing. Nothing. Nothing. Nothing.

Nothing. Nothing. Nothing. Nothing. Nothing. Nothing. Nothing. Nothing. Nothing. Nothing. Nothing. Nothing. Nothing happened. I spaced. *Japanese robots*. Lights went off. *Japanese robot interior decorators.*

*Lights went off?* I jerked up and saw shadows: Dede and John!

I said, "Dad!"

He put his hand on my arm, briefly, coolly.

*The Bandit.*

There was a lot of meaningless activity—lights, shadows, dimming lights, receding shadows, advancing shadows. I said, "Um!" Dad gave a squeeze. A few minutes later, when the lights were gone, he started the car, rolled up his window, and relaxed.

After we'd driven a few blocks Dad said, "Sean, Mr. and Mrs. Traina are getting a divorce. Do you think, if I ask Mrs. Traina to have dinner with me, that she'll say yes?"

*To the Bandit.*

I said, "*I'll* tell her to."

He nodded appreciatively. "I hope things are going to change for the better very soon."

After a moment's silence he added, "I hope she might one day like to marry me." I was in awe. I thought, *Hurry! Go fast! Don't let her slip away.*

I said, "Dad! It's amazing! I was thinking about this! I heard Mr. and Mrs. Traina were getting a divorce and I thought you and Mrs. Traina could get married!"

Dad looked so happy. The Trans Am crossed Van Ness.

When we got home to the Brocklebank, we sat in the living room together and read, the lights warm, him engrossed in some history or submarine book, me in *The Lord of the Rings*. We were closer now than we ever would be again.

DAD AND DEDE. A few nights later Dad came into my room and told me, "I'm going on a date with Mrs. Traina." It felt like a miracle. As the dating went well and Dede spent more and more time over at our bachelor apartment, I began to suspect that I possessed supernatural powers. I had made this happen by dreaming about it. It was briefly another identity. *Superpowered.* I felt fear and excitement at the responsibility. An awestruck sort of self-respect. But it was a brief feeling, an identity quickly swept away by unfolding events, by other, more powerful people's desires, by the reality of Dad and *Mom* and Dede.

. . .

I WAS HAVING dinner with Dad a few weeks later when he asked me, "Sean, how would you feel if Dede and I were to get married? Would that make you happy?" There were fireworks in my brain. I thought, *My dreams have been answered! I made this wonderful thing happen through my efforts and imaginings and prayers!* I had gotten them together through the strength of my love and wishes. I wanted to make a new family, and I had.

I thought, *Oh the glory of it all.*

And I told Dad yes.

Only recently were all these memories skewed by the strange information that Dad had not only been dating Dede Traina and Danielle Steele, but also Dinah Shore, *at the same time*—Dinah Shore who had just broken up with . . . Burt Reynolds . . . "the Bandit" *for real.*

*Five* · DEDE

DEDE IS SMALL, "petite," almost *reduced*, like a sauce or potion—and her smallness seems to grant her an added potency. (Dad loved her smallness. "Look at my slim, little wife," he used to say.) Her eyes are brown and sharp, and she's always fit, though it's a strange, almost inanimate kind of health, sharp, too—like the health of a knife. It's difficult to imagine Dede sick or aged. Inside her I imagine wheels and racks and cogs covered in pink-and-green chintz, with lipstick-stained lapdogs making it all turn. If you want a sense of her values, rent the movies *Gaslight* and *Sweet Smell of Success*. The scheming lead in *Gaslight*, who, bent on the acquisition of jewelry, sweet-talks a wealthy heiress into marrying him and then drives her mad with drugs and doubletalk, *is* her. (Though he actually looks like John Traina.) Dede gaslighted Mom, and later Dad, too. And when I first saw *Sweet Smell of Success*, a movie that depicts a stylized evil so heartless, smooth-talking, and extreme that it seems impossible, I was filled with amazed recognition. *Yes! Yes!* I thought. *This is it. This is how it was. This is the truth. This is her.* Though Dede, at all times, remains pleasant and charming, even as she pierces you with a javelin slicked in shit.

If I seem to be making an abrupt turn here, I do so to mirror the abruptness of her transformation with regard to me. Overnight she went from being my most beloved friend to my most bewildering oppressor.

But how can I explain Dede? She's my evil stepmother. She's an unbelievable cliché.

It seems like the best thing I can do is give the facts. And the fact is, the way Dede was raised—privileged, lonely, bizarre, and surrounded by celebrities—is a lot like the way I was raised.

DEDE WAS BORN in 1943, and grew up in Washington, D.C. Her father was Wiley T. Buchanan, Jr., one of Richard Nixon's close friends, U.S. ambassador to Luxembourg, Eisenhower's secretary of protocol, and U.S. ambassador to Austria. Her mother was Ruth Hale Buchanan, the granddaughter of Herbert Dow—founder of the Dow Chemical Company—and an actual heir to his fortune (which, Dad told me, was placed in a generation-skipping trust, so Dede wasn't a beneficiary, but her sons would be). In his memoir, *Red Carpet at the White House* (E. P. Dutton, 1964), Wiley Buchanan had only this to say about his younger daughter: "Dede . . . has a sharp, incisive mind . . . concerned about politics and practicalities."

In a 1959 profile the *Washington Post* described Dede's father like this:

What kind of a man is Wiley Buchanan? . . . He is of medium height—five feet, eight and a half inches of shrewd determination. . . . Buchanan has the same firm lines around his jaw and the same love of hospitality which characterized his ancestor, the fifteenth President of the United States, James Buchanan [Lincoln's Neville Chamberlain–like predecessor]. . . . His formidable fortune, flowing originally from Texas lumber, cotton, and oil, keeps multiplying through his Washington real estate foresight.

By the time I met him Mr. Buchanan had Alzheimer's. He couldn't dress himself, hardly knew his wife, didn't know Dede, wore a robe all the time, carried a small, red, long-haired dachshund everywhere he went, sat at a desk doodling moustaches on photographs. Midway through dinner he'd depart for some high-speed, reckless Bentley driving. Dede's mother eventually hid his keys. After he got sick enough to be housebound he'd deposit his dachshund on a high shelf, where she couldn't get down, and forget about her. He ate dog food. I thought he was by far the coolest person in the family. Certainly the friendliest. Here's what the *Post* wrote about Ruth Buchanan in 1953:

The lady who will step into Perle Mesta's shoes as chatelaine of the American Legation in Luxembourg is a petite . . . blond with delicate Dresden doll features and blue, blue eyes. Mrs. Wiley T. Buchanan, Jr. will be a striking adornment to the legation, of which her husband has been made Minister. . . . Interior decorating, flower arrangement, photography, children and schools, not necessarily in that order, are her chief enthusiasms.

Dede's family produced a president and performed ceremonial acts of diplomacy on one side; arranged flowers and developed napalm on the other.

DEDE GREW UP ALONE, and in public. She spent summers in Newport, Rhode Island (where her parents owned Beaulieu, a former Astor/Vanderbilt residence of truly stupefying magnificence). When Dede was a girl her parents left her alone with staff, sometimes for months, and put her on a diet till she lost twenty pounds and four dress sizes. She lived in Europe, then came back to the United States. She met a lot of kings and politicians and celebrities. When she was twelve her parents threw a party for the actor Tyrone Power. She was too young to attend, but Power sought her out. The *Post* wrote about the encounter:

"Well, if Dede can't come see me, I'll go see her," said the actor.
Promptly he asked to be shown the way upstairs. On Dede's door was a sign worked out in shining blue sequins which had been put up for Santa Claus on Christmas Eve. It said:
"Be careful of the stockings. No runs, No snags. Thanks, Dede."
That illusion [*sic*] was to the fact that the Buchanan children had hung up nylons for Santa to fill!
With a great laugh at this bit of joking from the witty Dede—at 12, she's no believer in Santa any more—Ty Power went in and carried on an entirely grownup conversation with the little girl who was too young to stay up until the 2 A.M. farewell time of the party.

In 1961 the coverage of her debutante party ran for more than sixty paragraphs in the *New York Times* and *Washington Post* combined. Some highlights:

"Against the background of a shocking pink color scheme, Washington society danced the Twist last night at the Pan American Union . . . [though] certain diplomats began protesting early yesterday afternoon when it was learned that former United States Chief of Protocol Wiley Buchanan had been given permission to turn the premises into a duplicate of New York's famous Peppermint Lounge, where the twist craze was born. But the complaints were largely ignored and some of the best-known names in the Social Register and Who's Who watched with great amusement as the urge to participate in the twist seized VIPs. . . . First Lady Jacqueline Kennedy's mother, Mrs. Hugh D. Auchincloss . . . Time-Life publisher Henry Luce and his famous wife Clare . . . Senate Foreign Relations chairman J. William Fulbright . . . were among the sideliners enjoying the impromptu floorshow when young and old alike began twisting. At 1 A.M. came the second half of the debutante extravaganza. This was the opening of 'Dede's Peppermint Lounge.' . . . The walls of the Peppermint Lounge were hung with red tinfoil fringe. Gigantic peppermint sticks lined up every ten feet. Red and white table cloths covered the tables. . . . Bo Diddleley's [sic] Twist Trio [performed] the music of Dede's favorite dance until dawn. The petite and energetic deb was the most skilled of the performers. The debutante has undergone a strenuous self-imposed slenderizing program this year. Since entering the freshman class at Connecticut College in September, she has lost 18 pounds." This is separate from the twenty pounds.

The debut even featured a theme song—called "Dede"—that went, according to the *Post*, "Dede—Dede—Loves to twirl as she does the twist. . . . Always laughing and always gay; witty, pretty, she's the sweetest gal, she's the swellest pal; she's the tops all the way."

The *New York Times* said: "'Twisting' in the Pan American Union upset Latin-American diplomats tonight. A crisis developed with the discovery that the headquarters of the Organization of American States had been borrowed for a debutante twist party. . . . Apparently many Latins became irritated over the installation of 'Dede's Peppermint Lounge,' with a neon sign, just off the indoor tropical garden. . . . However, a few hours after the neon sign had been installed, it was taken down. It was understood that diplomatic protests had been lodged against it. . . . One ambassador, not taken with the decor, asked rhetorically how the United States Senate would like to discover its chamber redecorated in peppermint for a debutante party. Aside from such complaints, diplomats worried about the timing of the party. Members of the O.A.S. Council will wade through the decorations tomorrow to choose a site for a foreign ministers' conference on Jan. 17. The conference . . . will center on a policy toward Cuba. Diplomats feared that the Buchanan party would create a propaganda opportunity for Fidel Castro's Government to picture the O.A.S. as sponsoring a carnival just before sitting in judgment on Cuba." In the next day's edition the *Times* reported, "Wiley T. Buchanan Jr. . . . dismissed criticism of his daughter's coming-out party last night in the Pan American Union as 'a tempest over nothing.' . . . Creating controversy and agitating about such affairs, he said, were 'typical Communist tactics' used repeatedly to divide this country and its allies."

The national press coverage ended when the *Washington Post* wrote a week later, "Castroites are contrasting the expensive trimmings with the abject poverty of Latin America."

*Town & Country* crowned Dede "Deb of the Year" and put her on their cover. At age twenty-one she met John Traina, Catholic, eleven years older, and decided to marry him, over her parents' objections. "Dede has told us of her intention to get married," her father said, in an official statement quoted by the *New York Times*. "It has come as a shocking surprise." She moved to San Francisco, got a dachshund, got a Victorian, had her sons, Todd and Trevor, moved to a mansion, aired her troubled marriage's several false endings in the *Chronicle* and the *Examiner:* "The . . . marriage of the socially powerful John Trainas would seem to be ending"; "The John Trainas . . . were both lunching at the Villa Taverna on Wednesday, but at separate tables . . . they did wave at each other"; "On the other hand, it's off again: I mean the glamorous but troubled marriage of Dede Traina, dghtr of the socially powerful Wiley Buchanans, and Shipping Exec John Traina"; "Dede filed for dissolution last Tuesday, because, as she said, 'I was in the mood.' . . . She plans to remain in San Francisco and would like to either work or take some college courses."

But no. No college for Dede. My father instead.

DAD AND DEDE were married on the lawn at Underoak, Dede's family estate in Washington, D.C., in mid May of 1981, a week before my eleventh birthday. The same minister who had married Dede and John Traina sixteen years earlier performed the ceremony. There was no prenup. I carried Dede's flowers for her.

At Underoak I slept in "the tower room," a turret on the edge of the house that had been Dede's bedroom growing up. It had been preserved as she'd left it twenty-five years before. I felt like a teenage girl in the 1950s. A window seat overlooked the grounds, and Dede paid me a late visit the night before the wedding.

We sat there together. It was like my imaginings had come to life. This was the place she had told me about by the pool in Mexico, and here I was in the very heart of it. She gave me a present, a small tablet of gold, with my initials and the date engraved in it—as though it were my wedding. It was our last moment of intimacy.

Married to Dad, Dede changed—instantly. Where once I had found smiles and indulgence, I now found indifference or worse. All sugar and kisses and spoiling disappeared.

BACK IN San Francisco Dad and Dede settled into a routine, reported over the years in *W, Town & Country,* the *Chronicle,* the *Examiner,* the *New York Times,* and a number of other publications.

They wrote about Dede's clothing and accessory decisions:

Dede Wilsey turned up in a bright turquoise Scaasi and dripping in diamonds. . . . [S]he said wryly, . . . "I figured gauche is in tonight."

•

Dede was wearing a cute Christian Dior black velvet and red satin number that she had picked up in Paris (with matching ruby earrings).

•

Dede Wilsey would . . . demonstrate that when she is dressed in green she wears emeralds on both hands.

•

Dede Wilsey . . . had on a screamer of a fire-engine red Givenchy . . . but as she stage-whispered to a friend, "Wait till Friday. I'm wearing a Scaasi to kill for."

•

Best jewels of the night award went to Dede Wilsey. . . . "I wore the Shreve stuff for the Town and Country picture at the beginning of the evening but then I said, 'Thank you very much, I'd prefer to wear my own jewels for the rest of the night.' That really got them. I don't think anyone has ever said that to them before."

•

Dede . . . will wear an Oscar de la Renta full, pale pink satin skirt and pale pink satin and silver fitted jacket. . . . "This year, I outsmarted myself. I saw a picture of a dress in *W* and said to Al, 'Isn't that the most beautiful dress you've ever seen?' A couple of months later, I opened up a box, and there it was."

•

Paloma Picasso . . . gave each of her old and new friends a big red box containing a compact, lipstick, eye pencil and mascara. Dede Wilsey applied the lot to her face with gusto.

•

Dede Wilsey slipped on a diamond and gold necklace, and a friend told her, "That would be wonderful with your Adolfos."

•

Dede Wilsey wore a blue Scaasi ballgown with a sock-you-in-the-eye sapphire and diamond necklace.

•

Dede Wilsey [wore] a Galanos of white and black skirt [*sic*] split thigh high, with a bustier of chenille, ribbon and jewels.

•

Leave it to Dede to remark to petite ————, who wore a short Scaasi to the symphony gala, "When are you going to be old enough to wear long skirts?"

•

Dede . . . wore an Oscar de la Renta suit with a jacket in bottle green velvet and a pleated sequined plain skirt in green, white and hot pink. Green and pink are Dede's colors.

•

The couture was haute and the ice was HOT. As Dede Wilsey, one of two women wearing the same coffee chiffon and gold lace concoction (Dede garnished hers with Bulgari from the vault) commented, "Everyone got together and agreed to be fancy."

•

Dede Wilsey, who always outshines everyone else with her dazzling jewels next to a dazzling smile . . . decided on something very un-Dede . . . i.e., something that's not in her signature colors of baby pink and green. . . . Wilsey says she'll get her diamonds and rubies out of the bank and try them on with the gown before deciding which gems to wear.

•

Expensive dresses in the $5,000 and $6,000 range were the order of the night. Particularly gorgeous: . . . Dede Wilsey's ice aqua special-order Oscar de la Renta.

•

One of the big hits of the season is Chanel's new stubby black and gold sling pump. . . . At a recent party . . . Dede Wilsey [was] wearing them. "Al wanted to know how much they cost, and I told him that was between me and the Chanels," said Dede.

•

Dede Wilsey [was] looking quite festive in a bright fuchsia suit and some very large jewelry.

•

In all the right neighborhoods here the click-click of safes can be heard as people bring forth the diamonds . . . like . . . Dede Wilsey's thirty-carat friendship ring that her husband, Al, gave her just for fun.

•

Dede Wilsey . . . has never been afraid of color. "Last year I wore a bright, screaming Schiaparelli pink with a bustle and train. I was stepped on, trod upon and crushed. I thought if my husband steps on my gown one more time, I'm going to have to find a new husband or a new dress."

•

"I have a room upstairs I call the stable, I have so many mules," Wilsey said at a party at her home . . . for the Ferragamos. "I probably have more shoes than Imelda Marcos."

•

Dede graced the room in a soft green taffeta embroidered with pink bouquets of flowers—an Escada couture gown complete with bustle and train. Garlands of roses graced her shoulders and the bustle. Bejeweled with a parure of Harry Winston emeralds and diamonds the Empress Eugenie of France would have envied. . . . ————a discerning judge of such things—remarked to Dede: "I have not seen such beauty since the 17th century," to which Dede replied, "That is my era."

And their lifestyle!:

The Wilseys have just returned from Hong Kong, or, as a friend kidded Dede, who loves to shop, "You mean you returned with Hong Kong."

•

Dede and Mama will make their annual trek to Maine Chance in January with friends like Charlotte Ford and her Mama.

•

The best hors d'ouevres of the week (city competition only) were found at Dede and Al Wilsey's cocktail crush Wednesday.

•

There were . . . close to 200 at the cocktail party Al and Dede Wilsey gave Monday at their new home on Jackson—150 guests and 50 in help (Dede told the caterer to double the number he would usually hire).

•

Dede and Al Wilsey . . . will celebrate their . . . anniversary Saturday night. How? "Opening presents, I hope," said Dede.

•

Throughout her years of worldwide travel and collecting antiques and objets d'art, Dede Wilsey has been successful in finding exactly what she wants.

•

. . . Dede Wilsey's hobby is roses; over 70 varieties are grown at the Wilseys' Napa Valley ranch, where they spend most weekends. "It takes me about two hours every Sunday to cut and strip my roses. Then I transport them to San Francisco in special boxes Al had made. Monday I arrange them for every room in the house."

•

Dede and Al Wilsey entertained the couple [Countess Camilla and Count Frederic Chandon] at dinner; the Count and Al are both helicopter pilots and can talk about whirlybirds in addition to social whirling.

•

Al Wilsey will be honored at the President's Dinner at the Legion of Honor Tuesday, where the Diane (that's "Dede" to her friends) and Alfred Wilsey Court will be dedicated. All major Fine Arts Museums donors have been invited—and those who are really very, very major might be able to have a room named after them sometime, too.

•

With the help of private florist Bob Bell (he no longer has a shop), the Wilseys really did a fantastic job of decorating the house with trees, wreaths, garlands and Dede-pink (her favorite color) tulips with matching bows.

Count and Countess Caramati di Carmate flew in from Los Angeles for the Wilseys' bash.

•

It's Tues. night and we're in the Opera House's mezzanine bar, where Dede (Mrs. Al) Wilsey, the ex-Mrs. John Traina, remarks to ————, "To-

morrow is John's birthday and the next day is Al's." Pause. "What a difference a day makes."

•

[T]he Wilsey order for fish alone at the Grand Central Market came to
$5,000.

•

Even though it's just the tip of the holiday ice-cube, Dede and Al Wilsey's
annual Christmas cocktail party Wednesday was the biggest and the best, so
other hosts can just relax and enjoy themselves. A reindeer led the 325
guests through a forest of Christmas trees into the garland-festooned house,
which was also filled with tulips, roses, wreaths, ribbons and done—in only
five days—by retired florist Bob Bell, who winters in Puerto Vallarta, but
flies in to do the Wilseys. Admiring it all, ———— . . . said, "It's such a
great party. You see everyone you know." But sometimes you won't see
someone you know because the Wilseys make changes in the list yearly.

•

Trader Vic's . . . regulars were accorded the honor of their own tables.
Dede and Al Wilsey . . . Gloria Getty and the Countess Irina Tolstoy all
have their designated dining areas.

•

Dede and Al Wilsey are back from a shooting trip in England, where they
were joined by Dede's mother, Ruth Buchanan, of Newport, R.I., and
Washington, D.C. . . . Mother joined them at Claridge's for a week of shopping before the shooting started. "We didn't take her shooting because we
would have been shot," said Dede. Ruth will fly out for another visit with the
Wilseys next week and for their annual Christmas party December 7.

•

Dede and Al Deck the Wilsey Halls for Hundreds
    It's like Stars on Saturday night; like a First and Last Call Sale at Neiman
Marcus; it's like nothing else: It's Dede and Al Wilsey's annual Christmas
party.
    It's noisy, crowded and exhausting: You have to shout your "You look
fabulous, darlings" to your friends—perhaps even, if you're lucky, to all
375 guests at their party Thursday.
    Al recommends doing the party in a circle: from the foyer to the living
room to the 40-foot-wide garden room (full of marble, Michael Taylor–
designed furniture, and windows that overlook the bay and a garden) to

the dining room and then back to the foyer to dance to music by Walt Tolleson. . . .

"It's beautiful," said Bob Bell, former florist who goes back to the greenhouse for just this party and creates all sort of garlands, flowers and trees. He also helped adorn the slipper Dede's mother, Ruth Buchanan, had to wear on her right foot because of her broken leg: He wrapped it in shimmering ribbons and bows. . . .

Before the party started, Dede and Al and her two sons, Trevor and Todd, posed for their Christmas card photo. Dede wore a gold and green gown with emeralds for that and then dashed upstairs to change into a short, black-and-white bouffant dress and diamonds for the party.

When all the guests finally left at about 10, the Wilseys and family dug into the fabulous hors d'oeuvres and buffet prepared by caterer Viola Yokato. Darlings, we must get her recipe for zucchini rolls; the best. Just like the party.

•

Although Dede Wilsey loves her several gardens in the Napa Valley and takes the lead in their development, she does not masquerade as a "true" gardener who revels in the arts of composting and double-digging.

"My mother had a beautiful three-acre garden at her home in Washington, D.C.," Dede recalls. "One day we were talking and I said I was sad that I'd never inherited the gardening genes that made her want to dig in the earth. And she said, '*Dig?* When have you ever seen me dig?' And it was a sudden revelation: you can have fun gardening without ever getting your hands dirty!"

Laughing at the recollection, Dede says she then bought dozens of garden books and magazines and, on cold winter days, would sit by the fireplace with a huge handmade map she'd drawn of the garden, making crayon drawings and pasting pictures where she wanted the garden to come to life.

And that's how she gardens at the weekend home she shares with her husband, Al. "I really enjoy putting together gardens," she enthuses, "so for the past few years, I've been finding little places that need fixing up, so that I can design the gardens, too."

We set out on a walking tour of her home's spacious grounds and were immediately greeted by the awesome sight of thirty-nine thousand brand-new tulips in long drifts of strong pink and pale, creamy yellow, blooming in all their glory. Ironically, the seasonal demands of her husband's business and her own career as chair of the Fine Arts Museums of San Francisco usually keep them at their San Francisco residence during the peak of tulip time. . . .

Dede confesses, "It's not an elaborate garden or terribly imaginative—I just want to be able to stand anywhere on this property and see flowers that look like they're already arranged in a container." . . .

When we return to the porch, Al is there with their six dogs, waiting for a report on what we've seen and, most importantly, what new plans Dede has in mind.

"Al," Dede smiles, "enjoys the beauty of this place as much as I do."

•

Talk about a dream evening. Dede and Al Wilsey—with the help of Stanlee Gatti, and Dan McCall—created a world of beauty, friendship and, yes, love for their 320 guests Wednesday night in a gigantic tent covering Rodin's "Thinker" courtyard at the Palace of the Legion of Honor. It was Dede and Al's 20th wedding anniversary, and its celebration was unforgettable. Sheer magic.

To be sure, an invitation to this event is coveted like none other. Social, political, community and business leaders were there to honor what this dynamic duo has done for, first of all, one another, and then for their friends, the Fine Arts Museums, Grace Cathedral, St. Ignatius . . . well, the list goes on and on. Just talking about Al Wilsey brought tears to the eyes of my dinner partner, ————.

He couldn't say enough about the strong, wise, giving, caring Al. . . .

The setting for all these tributes was, to say the least, heart-stoppingly gorgeous. Entering at the terrace level, guests felt as if they were floating up a walkway banked with greenery inset with gardenias. The interior Rodin courts were gracefully adorned with large sculptural urns of French tulip umbrellas. Guests were in awe. . . .

———— gushed, "She is just a doll. . . . "

———— . . . exclaimed that Dede "simply radiates with happiness—this is her night." . . .

"Tonight is right out of an Edith Wharton novel," quipped ————. In the same vein, ———— found the evening "reminiscent of Versailles." . . . Of the celebration, ———— said: "I have lived in San Francisco over 30 years and never seen anything so beautiful." . . .

Those already in love had to fall deeper, and those looking for love came a lot closer to it that evening.

This group has grown accustomed to being around the very best of things, yet there was nothing but amazement and appreciation for this extravaganza. This Cinderella is still pinching herself.

Now that she was married to my dad, there was a sudden disdainful cold coming from Dede. It was a though she didn't respect me for how much I loved her. The only thing I could think to do about this was try to be more lovable. I asked Dede, in a rare moment of calm, if I could start calling her "Mom."

*Six* · EVERY OTHER WEEK

---

THE CUSTODY AGREEMENT between my parents had me spending a week with Mom and a week with Dad—like a business traveler— vacations alternating. I packed a bag and switched houses every Monday.

It was the shuttling stage of my life.

AFTER THE WEDDING Dad moved us out of the Brocklebank and into Dede's Jackson Street mansion, former residence of the Episcopal bishop of San Francisco, full of stained glass and secret corridors and staircases. John Traina's old office was my bedroom.

Downstairs, in a corner of the kitchen, Dede's fourteen-year-old miniature dachshund, Sarabelle, slept all day. When she was awake she peered out of her corner with gray blue, cataractous, primeval eyes. Dede'd had Sarabelle since before Todd and Trevor were born, and she used to talk about the dog as her *first* baby. When she was in her twenties (just after leaving Washington and her job as

secretary to Texas senator John Tower) she and John Traina moved into an old
San Francisco Victorian with a furnace that blew heat through cast-iron grates.
Sarabelle would stand on the grates, and when the furnace kicked in her ears flew
up Marilyn Monroe–style.

On June 14, 1981, thirty days after Dad and Dede were married, John Traina
married Danielle Steel, at the hillside home of a famous interior decorator in the
Napa Valley. Todd and Trevor were in the wedding. This being my week with
my father in the world of constantly rotating residences, I was at Dede's weekend house in the nearby Napa Valley town of Oakville, sitting in the driveway
trying to fix a go-cart carburetor, fifty feet outside the back door from which
Dede ran screaming.

"Oh my God—Sarabelle's missing!" she said.

I ran over.

"She's gone!" She whipped her head around, scanning the yard. It was a beautiful day. Very, very hot. Very still. "She's *run off!* She's *disappeared!* My Serr-
eee-belle!"

She was desperate. "We have to look for her. Sean, you go that way!"

"O.K.!" I said.

I would prove myself deserving of Dede's maternal affections by recovering
Sarabelle, even though I was squeamish and afraid to find and be alone with the
dog. Would I have to pick her up? I imagined green teeth biting me. She was
John's dog, too, and she didn't like Dad and me. Still, I looked hard for half
an hour.

I found nothing. I came back, told Dede, and volunteered to scour other areas. Dede said she'd already covered all other areas, *thoroughly.* "Maybe another
set of eyes," I said, using a phrase I'd read somewhere.

"No!" she said.

Dede's eyes filled with tears, and she cried, her intelligent and compact face
becoming more tiny, intelligent, focused with contraction.

"It's no use! She's *lost!*" she despaired.

I said, "But we have to find her! I don't mind. I *really* want to help find her. I'll
look all over the place." My shirt was sticking to my back in the heat.

Alda Polo, Dede's Peruvian housekeeper, stood on the porch, looking concerned.

Dede said, "I'm calling Todd and Trevor. They'll have to come home and
help."

"But Mr. Traina's *wedding!*" Alda said.

Dede said, "*This* is more important! They've known Sarabelle their whole lives. And now she's run away." She went inside to make the call. A few minutes later she drove off, first telling me not to look anywhere else.

Half an hour later Todd and Trevor arrived in three-piece suits. We all got in Dede's Chrysler Le Baron station wagon, with its fake-wood trim and burgundy vinyl interior. Dede drove down a row of vines, and within a minute Trevor spotted the dog, lying in a scrap of shade.

He said, "There!"

Dede stopped the car. Sarabelle looked dead in the dust. But she was still breathing, weakly, through her green teeth. Trevor picked her up.

Dede had driven us right to the spot.

"Hold her up to the air-conditioning," Dede said.

He did.

Sarabelle was fine. She drank some water and recovered. The incident passed. Then, back in the city, a few days later, she died. Alda Polo found her stiff in her dog bed. Dede called John Traina, now on his honeymoon, to give him the news. He demanded Sarabelle be put "on ice" at the vet's. When he got back there was supposed to be an autopsy.

BACK IN the penthouse the next week, Mom told me: "She killed that dog, Sean. Just like she's going to kill your father"—beat—"the bastard."

THEN DEDE SOLD her half of the Jackson Street mansion to John Traina and Danielle Steel, and we moved into a rented mansion on Spruce Street, while a new mansion, *back on Jackson Street*, purchased with the money from John and Danielle's acquisition of the ex-bishop's mansion (and located four doors down!), was expensively renovated.

It was still only the summer, but Dede started dropping hints about the Richter-scale scale of her department-store-shelf-clearing generosity come Christmas—provided I was deserving. Provided I passed certain tests.

In the temporary mansion on Spruce Street I was given the old servants' quarters in the attic. I figured this was because I had a really nice room at Mom's, and I was only there half the time, anyway. Then came the imposition of new rules. No afternoon T.V. No candy or soda without permission. No sugar after 5:00 P.M. No snacks outside the kitchen. (These rules did not apply to my step-brothers. Todd would pop a Coke and go watch *Scooby-Doo*, while I stared after him hungrily. While at Mom's I became a T.V. addict, and an increasingly decadent in-bedroom snacker, filling my dresser drawers with tins of strawberry Quik and tubes of cake icing.)

At Dad's, when I wasn't in the attic, I spent my time trying to find ways to distinguish myself: keeping my elbows off the table; getting up from my chair when Dede arrived; running around to pull out hers; standing if she stood; opening doors; inserting "please" and "thank you" into all possible locations in a conversation; attempting to become an international, Wiley Buchanan–style, Dede-and-Christmas-spoiling-worthy gentleman.

I breathed another atmosphere up in the attic. And it was . . . anticipation. Anticipation. Anticipation of . . . I wasn't sure what. Todd and Trevor were distant. Dad and Dede were always out at society parties, celebrating their union.

When Dede was around, I called her Mom sparingly. I thought that by letting me call her Mom Dede was giving me a great gift. This honor added up to more love than anyone had ever given me before. I savored it the way hobbits savored particularly fine pipeweed or ale. I felt selfish and reverential and insecure about our powerful new mother/son bond. I felt warm and content when I called Dede Mom and nobody challenged me. (Todd and Trevor just gave me dirty looks.) My delusion warmed me up. It was a great, rushing thrill. But the thrill was not love . . . exactly.

No.

It was the thrill of telling a lie that was greater by far than any lie I'd told before. And having nobody question it.

Dad and Dede told me not to let Mom find out I was calling Dede Mom.

"Dad, Mom, don't worry," I told Dad and Dede. "My . . . other mom . . . will never find out."

THE NEXT DAY, when I arrived back at the penthouse for my week with my real mom, she said, "Sean, sit down."

I sat.

After a long, blue stare she told me, "Sean, I have cancer and I'm going to be dead by Christmas."

We were sitting in the "living room." I put living room in quotes not only because Mom was announcing her death there, but because the room used to be our living room before the renovation. I was on a huge white barge of a couch that was built into the wall. Mom faced me in a newly-recovered-in-peach high-back chair. Between us was a six-by-twenty-foot, ten-inch-thick marble coffee table that resembled the cargo area of a flatbed truck. In the last year of their marriage my parents had remodeled, although the place had already been equipped with every imaginable amenity pre-remodel: a Jacuzzi, a chef's kitchen, three fireplaces (the one in the kitchen, fitted with a rotating, chain-driven, rotisserie spit that could do a large pig), VCRs, microwaves (in the seventies!), skylights, two wet bars, a movie screen that dropped out of the ceiling. But they renovated anyway—and what this amounted to was a total obliteration of my father's presence, making it even easier for him to slip out the door. All Dad's warmth was removed and the space was turned into a theater for my mother. I called it "the marble palace."

The good thing about the marble palace was the view. The Summit towered above North Beach and the wharf, facing the bay. If there was fog in the city our apartment was above it. Sometimes, when it rained down at street level, it would snow on the decks. Dad always liked to say (taking great care with the facts) that because of the hill the apartment was the highest point in all of San Francisco. Higher than the Transamerica Pyramid! Higher than the Bank of America building!

Under Dad the floors had been a dark wood parquet and the first story of the space was partitioned into comfortably sized rooms—with a big (useless) glass atrium, like a wind tunnel, in the center—and decorated with a collection of animals he'd hunted: heads from his African safaris; antlers from his years of deer hunting on horseback; horns; a tigerskin rug (with head); a zebraskin rug; bristly gray stools made from elephants' feet; and a huge, sectional, leopard-print sofa. Next to the couch was a worn easy chair Mom nicknamed the American Airlines chair (because it reclined, and was at a high altitude?), where Dad liked to sit and smoke a pack and a half of Marlboro Reds every day, before Mom got him to quit.

The house was warm and weird and safe and masculine.

For the remodeling, all the dividing walls downstairs were taken out and the atrium was covered with a huge glass-paned skylight and incorporated into a five-thousand-square-foot space that contained, all flowing together: a dining area with a circular white marble table that accommodated sixteen; a satellite, intimate dining area, where a small octagonal, solid-marble table was surrounded with elegant armchairs and then blasted off into the cold reaches of space at the other end of the room (this table was where Mom and Dad broke the divorce news); a sitting area where the bargelike couch (seating capacity ten) reigned, along with its companion flatbed-truck-sized stone coffee table; a carved-rock fireplace; a vast arena beneath the skylight where Stonehenge-like white divans with huge, life-raft-sized cushions were strewn among thirty-foot ficus trees of the sort found in the skyscraper lobbies of multinational corporations' head-quarters; a mirrored corner where a black grand piano, polished to be a mirror itself, shimmered in endless copies (and still looked small in context); a crystal chandelier, from the court of Louis XIV, which had been hung from tree branches for royal picnics and was illuminated with candles (Mom lit it with a fifteen-foot brass taper, like something out of the Vatican); and, spiraling down through the trees, at the center of it all, a grand staircase on which Mom liked to linger during parties, greeting her guests from above.

The wood floors were replaced with polished travertine, which was a word Mom loved to say: *"Travertine."* Beneath these cold floors was radiant heating (another word Mom loved to say: *"Radiant"*) that did not work.

All the walls were mirrored. Every vertical surface was mirrored. No architectural detail was insignificant enough to escape mirroring—light switches, doors, *plug covers.* In every direction was the view and yourself and yourself and the Golden Gate and yourself and Coit Tower and yourself and yourself and Alameda and yourself and Alcatraz and you again and Angel Island and ships coming in and helicopter tours and you and DC-10s and a submarine surfacing and a big neon captain's wheel that was the sign of some restaurant on the wharf—and a certain grand loneliness and the clouds and everywhere you, you, you, you, you, you, and Mom.

George Shultz, Reagan's secretary of state, lives there now.

SO THERE WAS space for nine other people next to me on the couch when Mom told me she was going to die. As usual, it was just us. I looked away from her at my reflection. I looked O.K.

Time slowed down. Mom paused, scrutinized me, then continued. "You've been a very bad son, and now there's no time to change. You aren't going to get another chance. You are going to have to live with the bad son you've been after I'm gone"—she choked up—"the way you've *neglected* your mother"—tears began to flow and she coughed out the rest of the sentence: "for"—sob—"the"—sob—"rest"—sob—"of"—sob—"your"—sob—"life."

I had been hoping to read *The Lord of the Rings* and maybe play with the Hot Wheels I was too old for but still embarrassingly into. But here was the new worst thing that had ever happened to me. This was worse than the divorce. *How can all these bad things keep happening?* I wondered. *So fast?*

She was going to be dead. I would be alone with guilt. I imagined living in this cold, echoey apartment.

I didn't understand (or even really *know*) Mom. As a mother, she had been glamorous and wondrous and absent. I had been her admirer. Then she and Dad and the shrink told me I admired her too much. We were separated. Now I was afraid of her. But since Mom had been abandoned by her whole world—Dad and Dede took friends, employees, all the people she used to rely on and see every day, leaving her like one of those nineteenth-century Mississippi river towns, boom to ghost, after an unpredictable change in the river's course—she was turning her full attention to me. I was the only one in the audience remaining. I was the only person who couldn't abandon her. I wanted to be part of the abandonment! I was packed and ready to go! But no. I could only go for a week at a time.

I thought briefly about video games. My brain went white and then started to come back in strange, fragmentary ways. Go-carts, my grandmother Montandon's funeral, Japanese toy robots, Dede, Dad, die-cast Datsun 280-Zs. The more my brain came back the more I started to cry. I felt like my heart had been placed in the precise center of something crushing. Like a car crusher. *A heart juicer.* The on-switch was on. My heart was crushed. The liquid was coming out of my eyes. Simultaneously I felt the strange sensation of knowing this was what Mom wanted. It was performance crying. Both unavoidable and advantageous. Then I hugged Mom. I told her how sorry I was for how neglectful I'd been, for causing her pain, for Dad, for Dede (Dede!—*"Mom"*), for the divorce, for stealing confiscated Hot Wheels out of the music room in first grade, for *everything I could think of.* Her response came in slow motion, dreamy, as if she were already half-dead. Her voice was leaning against a wall to avoid collapse—half in the grave:

*"Oh you're being so sweet. But it can't possibly matter to you. You'll be happier when I'm gone and you can be with Dede and your father. That's where you've made it quite clear you'd rather be."*

I cried hard. She was right. Everything was wrong. I saw that my reflection was all wobbly.

Resharpening her voice, not wishing to comfort me in any way, she said, "There's no undoing that, Sean. Just because I'm *dying.* What you've done you've done, you've made it known how you feel about me, your *mother,* and how you prefer *that woman*—and you're going to have to live with it." Then she said, "You can go to your room now—and think about this."

I went to lie down on my bed. I looked at the bottom of the top bunk. I thought, *I'll be living with Dad soon.*

There was an end in sight.

I waited for her to die.

I imagined a penitent life.

I was solicitous and kind.

"You're so sweet, but I'll be gone soon," Mom said. I got used to the idea that Mom was dying. It was going to be a relief. I would be able to focus on Dede. I needed to devote more time and attention to her.

WHEN DEDE MOVED into Mom's Napa Valley dream house she placed a needlepoint pillow on a couch in the living room, and did almost no other redecorating. The stitching on the pillow read:

> YOU CAN NEVER
> BE TOO THIN
> OR TOO RICH

Mom tried to reach me there, dialing what had for years been her own phone number but was now Dad and Dede's. Dede answered, and this exchange followed:

MOM: "Is this the bitch who stole my husband?"

DEDE (*singsongy*): "Yes iit iss!"

THE ATTIC SERVANTS' QUARTERS at Dad and Dede's didn't have any heat, though heat *rose*, so this was no problem. I wore sweaters and kept my mind focused on Christmas. Mom would be gone, I would emerge victorious from my trials, Dede would embrace me as her son, and I would no longer have to move houses every week.

Calling Dede "Mom" was enough to make me forget the rest of my life. It was rapturous and perfect and obliterating. Knowing that Mom was dying, it was good to have a new mom.

IN NAPA there were things Dad liked to do and Dede hated to do—non–thin/ rich things. So, every other weekend, when I was there, Dad did them with me.

Dad would burst into my room at 6:30 A.M. and say, "Surprise, we're taking the helicopter to the Nut Tree!" I'd dress and he'd fly us halfway to Sacramento, where they had great "hotcakes" (Dad's word) and a dining room aviary filled

with exotic birds. Dad liked to get a hotcake stack ten inches high and stuff butter in between the layers like money in a mattress.

If I had Blane or Spencer over Dad would say, "Sean, if you and your friends
help me pull the helicopter out, I'll take you to the arcade." Then he'd fly us
forty miles over the mountains to an amusement center with tons of video games
and a huge batting cage, set down in the parking lot, keeping his RPMs high to
lift off again quickly, hand us twenty bucks in quarters (he always had rolls of
quarters to make up precise tolls and tips), and say, "I'll be back before dinner.
Listen for the turbine. I don't care if you're not finished with your game. Come
out." He'd disappear into the sky the second we cleared the rotors, heads
bowed, running like marines.

"Your dad's so cool," Blane would say, hefting his roll of quarters.

Spencer would give me his roll of quarters to hold. He'd look up at the departing helicopter and shake his head at what a show-off Dad was.

SHORTLY AFTER Mom told me she'd be dead by Christmas, Dad did his own
version of the same thing. We were up in Napa again. He said, "Let's go out for
a walk, but before we go out, look up the word 'remorse' in the dictionary, and
then come find me."

Dad was big on making me look things up in the dictionary. "Get the dictionary," he'd always say. If I didn't know the meaning of a word he'd never tell me.

I looked up "remorse": "A gnawing distress arising from a sense of guilt for
past wrongs."

On the walk Dad said, "When I die I don't want you to feel any remorse. But
you're going to feel a lot of it."

He was silent for a moment, then he added, "I had you late in life, Sean, so
we're going to have a very limited time together. But Dede will be here long after I'm gone, and you'll have to get along with her. So be good to Dede. Be good
to Dede now. That's how you'll make points and get more out of me." By
"points" he meant affection. By "get more out of me" he meant, What? Time, I
hoped. He went on. "I was fifty when you were born. You missed out on the
father-and-son activities, the hunting and fishing. I'm like a building: a bit run-
down now. And you're a tenant with a short-term lease."

I asked him, "Did you feel remorse when your parents died?"

"No," he said. "I didn't. But you *will* feel it. It's inevitable. But try not to. Try
to avoid it. Remorse is a useless emotion."

After making his remorse speech this first time (it became a bimonthly tradition), Dad said, "Come on," and we walked across the creek that Dad called a "slough" and headed for the helicopter hangar.

On the way we stopped in an orchard he'd planted with Mom. Dad held up a peach with a crater bit out of it, and said, "Birds. They did this." Then he took a bite. "Bird-damaged fruit is still perfectly good. We can't get diseases from birds. But farmers can lose a good percentage of their crops from them pecking and then migrating and other flocks coming through and pecking at other pieces. Birds are a *nuisance*. Two will never peck the same piece of fruit." He lifted a black plastic net that covered the tree. "Netting can stop most of it. Must be a hole in this net." He began to sift it through his hands. "Help me look for it."

What was I looking for? A *hole?* The net was *full of holes*. It was a *net*. But I really wanted to find *the* hole, since I was living in *Testland* and hoped to pass as many undeclared tests as I could.

Dad found the hole and asked me to remind him about it later. I immediately forgot. We continued through the netted trees, Dad picking up more fruit, explaining that the best was the fruit that had fallen. He put an entire peach in his mouth and produced a clean stone. He filled his JC Penney work shirt shirttails with fruit, and had me do the same.

Dad pointed to the big willow tree I'd always loved, and said, "What's the name of that tree?"

What's the Name of That Tree was one of his favorite games.

I said, "It's a willow."

This was the free one.

Then he pointed to a second tree, by the creek, tall, with rough bark.

I said, "Black walnut?"

He grimaced. "That's a *valley oak*."

*Valley oak.*

What's the Name of That Tree was over.

Willows and pines were the only ones I could always get.

*Shit,* I thought.

We walked. Dad accumulated fruit.

His helicopter's wind sock fluttered in the breeze at the bottom of the orchard.

"You want a Coca-Cola," he said with his mouth full. It wasn't really a question.

There was a walk-in fridge in the hangar, full of beer and wine and cases of Coke. I always wanted one of those Cokes.

"It's *sugar* that you like."

I shrugged.

He said, "What if I told you there was sugar in fruit?"

I hated fruit. I was the enemy of fruit.

I said nothing.

"Do you know what fructose is?"

"No."

"Fructose is natural sugar. *Not* the sugar you like, what's in those Cokes. Fructose is *good* sugar." Then he reached into his shirttails, took out a peach, stuffed it in his mouth. Juice ran down his chin, he spat the stone into his hand, stepped back, and hurled it a hundred feet, into the creek, a throw I could never even imagine making. The horrible fruit had granted him superhuman strength.

"It's the kind of sugar you need to *learn* how to like." Then, in his softest, surest voice, he delivered his closing statement: "There is no better thing you can be in this world than a lover of fruit."

WHEN WE WERE done with the orchard Dad strode purposefully toward the hangar and said, "Let's go see what Coppola's up to." Seeing what Coppola was up to meant overflying the patrol boat from *Apocalypse Now* that lay on its side in a grove of trees behind a Victorian mansion. I hesitated.

Dad said, "We'll do Falcon Crest, too."

I said, "Can we fly low?"

He said, *"Maybe."*

When Dad flew low I would strafe the Falcon Crest house with skid-mounted machine guns. We would blow right over the top of the place, me laying down the withering fire. Then Dad would give me a loopy grin and I'd spin my fingers through the air to say, "One more pass?" He'd nod, pull up over the crest of the mountains, stop, hover, make a 180-degree pedal turn, then blast back down and over the house at speed.

The hangar was a big, beige, steel, prefab building with two twenty-foot-tall-by-twenty-foot-wide sliding doors on rails. We rolled open the doors, me racing to beat him, which caused a crash when I slammed into the jamb. Dad gave me an annoyed look. We deposited our fruit in a pile in the shade. He got in the helicopter and started going through a start-up checklist.

My job was to pick up the helicopter and move it outside. I walked across the hangar to Dad's Tug-a-Lug ground handling dolly. This was a squat, long, rolling, motorized, hydraulic lift controlled by a panel at the end of a fifteen-foot stem, which, for some reason (order and aesthetics?), Dad kept flush against the back wall of the hangar. The stem, on a flexible joint, was pushed 90 degrees up and out of reach, so I had to inch the Tug-a-Lug away from the wall manually. This was difficult, since it weighed as much as a car, and Dad kept the small, heavy-duty tires one-quarter flat to give the helicopter a cushiony ride. I pushed hard, crouched low, wedged my feet against the wall, strained. I made faces and squirmed and slowly it moved a half inch forward, then stopped. I thought, shouting inside my own head, *Fuck!* And then I felt remorse for swearing. *Why,* I thought, *is a machine that's supposed to make moving heavy objects easier, actually a heavy object that is impossible to move and that I'm supposed to move?* I looked resentfully at him. Dad was absorbed in his checklist and did not notice. I panted, comically, for his benefit, until he looked up and frowned. "Your young back can take the strain," he said.

Eventually I made enough progress to slide between the Tug-a-Lug and the wall and pull down the control stem so it nestled just below my neck. Then I hit the wrong switch and the whole thing lurched back, pushing me up on my tiptoes, like a bully hanging a smaller kid on a peg. Before Dad noticed, I freed myself and hurried to get the Tug-a-Lug under the helicopter, dodging communication antennae and cop car–like belly lights. When I engaged the Tug-a-Lug's lifting controls the helicopter creaked like old furniture as it went up off its skids. Outside on the tarmac I uncoiled a heavy-duty jumper cord, pulled open the passenger door, and plugged it into a recessed female socket beneath my seat, so Dad could use the Tug-a-Lug's power to start the helicopter. (Maintaining full charge on all his batteries was a priority for Dad.) A click came from deep within the helicopter, followed by a slow, electrical acceleration sound—*whv whv whv whv whv.* Rotors started turning, gradually at first, and then, as they became invisible, the turbine engine kicked on with a *chhfff,* and it was too loud to speak. Everything became noise. Dad gave me a carrier deck–style thumbs-up. I braced a foot on a foot peg and yanked as hard as I could on the jumper cable. Nothing. Hands locked on the red plastic handgrip, rotors siccing the air overhead, all the sound and motion bringing on a feeling that I was about to make a Big Mistake—and when I made the Big Mistake, get *decapitated*—I strained, pulled, failed. Dad watched me, impatient, ready to *go.* Finally I had to cheat it out, working side-to-side, though he'd forbidden this method, saying, "The only way to remove the jumper cable is by pulling it straight out."

*Or what?*

Dad said, *"Air disaster,"* in my head.

I kept at it. It popped loose! I fell back, wheeled my arms to keep balance, coiled the cable (Dad was as exacting on coiling as he was on straight-pulling), put it back on top of the Tug-a-Lug, and, in a crouch, wheeled everything back inside the hangar. Then I shut the doors, latched them with a carabiner, crouch-ran back, hopped in the passenger's seat, donned DJ headphones (with aviation mic), pulled their cord-hanging switch in the "TALK" direction and said, "O.K. All set. Over."

Dad said, "Keep quiet till we're in the air."

The skids lifted off the tarmac; I clicked to "TALK" and said, "We're in the air!"

Dad said, "Quiet!" and I moved into my own head. *You said no talking till we're in the air. We're in the air!*

Sometimes I would actually say out loud, into the noise, what I really wanted to say, and in the next few years it was, "*Fuuuuuccckkk yooooouuuuu! Daaaaaad!*"

Dad ascended ten feet straight up, elevator-style, the Gs pushing me into my seat, executed a perfect ninety-degree right turn, skimmed the adjacent field, and then rose slowly up and over vineyards and reservoirs till we were three or four miles away from our house and higher than the mountains at either side of the valley.

The valley! Valhalla! Ninety square miles of well-drained alluvial soils and viticulturally favorable microclimates. Down below: $120 per person tasting menus; six-month waits for tables at five in the afternoon; "the most exciting place to eat in the United States," according to the *New York Times;* a valley thick with grapes and restaurants offering (per reviewers) "clever creations such as chipotle-rubbed quail with tamales rajas and avocado salsa, and baby back ribs with crispy yams . . . griddled goat cheese polenta with tomato chutney . . . changing, seasonally-fresh menus . . . casual come-as-you-are ambience . . . un-usual wines by the glass—think Blockheadia Ringnosii Zin."

*Yeah.*

But everything above the valley floor was Dad's. It was *his* ninety square miles of airspace. *He was a social climber*—literally. The higher we went, the more Dad could see, the more omnipotent he became.

All the perfect towns and wineries and estates were laid out below so Dad could circle them like they were written on a page, figure out whose cars were in whose yards, who was sleeping with whom, inviting whom, not inviting him, spoil their fun by buzzing low (me strafing), harass from the air, ruin golf games, scout conquests, irritate grape growers with his dust-blowing rotor blast (he was notorious for this), land and charm and surprise people. Flying with Dad was an aerial guide to society! And *that's* why Dad liked to fly. Not for the freedom and joy of it. For the advantage of it. For the way it put everyone else at a disadvantage. Dad wanted his name in the society pages, he wanted to belong to the Pacific Union Club, he wanted to hang out in Newport, Rhode Island—where he began flying the helicopter cross-country every summer—more than he wanted anything else. Because why? It's the mystery of my father's identity.

The higher we went the more afraid I became. I listened for irregularities in the *eyyr* of the turbine engine and the *wrf* of the rotors.

An engine had failed before. Dad was flying back to the city with Mom, just before the divorce, when it banged and went silent and they sailed down into the salt-water marshes at the edge of the bay. Dad's emergency autorotation technique was impeccable and saved their lives. Half an hour later they were rescued by the Coast Guard.

Silent, I thought about Dad's Death, and it got larger and *larger* and *LARGER*. And then, just when I thought it was going to happen for certain, that Dad would die here and take me with him, something in the combination of fear and sky and loud noise resulted in a miracle!

I heard really beautiful music, symphonic pop songs with shouted choruses and backup singers and string sections and harps and smoking guitar solos. I stopped panicking and listened. It was music—no question—but also nothing like any music I'd ever heard before. These songs went for ten minutes and were only getting started—there was a whole album in a flight!—and just when I thought it was getting monotonous, really *was* just the drone of the engine tricking me, and not a miracle, something would change, a gong, or a harpsichord, or seven falsettos would come in. This defied the laws of physics, because we were still flying along at the same altitude, RPMs stable, and *nothing had changed! If I could just get these recorded I'd have a hit on my hands. I'd be set for life! I could live on my own, drop out of school, never again listen to Dad's lectures on remorse and fructose.*

After a few minutes of listening I got the song's structure and the idea of its verses—actual verses always just ahead of my ability to understand them. Then I hummed along, sang along, shouted along. Dad didn't notice. The louder I sang the clearer the words got, till I had: *"JAKESAWAKEOOOOOHJAHYEAH! BRINDLEBRINDLEBRINDLESNNNNOUT!!! ALOOOOOOOOOOOOOSA! BBBBBBBBBOHOHOHUHHUHHUHHUH!HUNKYYEAHYEAHYEAHY UHUH!!"*

In order to understand the lyrics perfectly it was important to scream as loud as I could, though Dad could hear that, I discovered, when I got loud enough to come out with the only two lines I remember. I screamed, as loud as I could: *"TICKTACK HACKENSACK!/I'M TICKED OFF AT HACKENSACK!"* Dad looked over in genuine alarm. From then on I sang quietly.

I looked at Dad. *He can't hear this stuff? He can't hear this stuff.* Dad was holding the main control stick for the helicopter, the cyclic, between his knees, and fiddling with the radio. *Wait. Holding the cyclic between his knees? He's not even flying. He's not paying attention. We're still ascending. Does he know this? We're going too high, the air will be too thin and we'll fall. I should tell him. I'm fucking scared . . . stop swearing . . . just focus on the song!*

Dad had promised me not to go high. Then he tried to *sneak* up there. He always did this. Didn't he know I could read the gauges?

I pressed "TALK" and said, voice trembling, *"Dad, you said we'd stay low."* I pointed to the altimeter.

He replied, "It's safer at a higher altitude. No power lines to get tangled in. And if we lose the engine and I have to autorotate there's more time to act. Now stay off the radio."

*Aahhhhhh.* I despised this logic. At eight thousand feet the helicopter was so high it seemed to be standing still. It was like an ornament hung in the sky, shaped like a bubble, seeming not to move, bright sunlight filling its small cabin, making unbelievable noise.

Dad's father/son quality time.

Now that the song was gone I tried to stare unwaveringly at a fixed point on the horizon. I made resolutions. *I don't blink we don't fall. I stare at the cyclic—* eyes drying out—*Dad does . . . uh . . . not die for at least twenty years. Now breathe in time to the engine. Keep the eyes moving, watch all the gauges: fuel; altimeter; airspeed; oil pressure—keep them out of the red.*

Suddenly a blaring dial tone, followed by the staccato beep sounds of touchtone number punching, jarred me out of my terror-control rituals. Then the sound of a phone ringing. This was why Dad had flown so high. He was making a call on his exotic early-eighties version of a cell phone: a two-way radio connected to a dedicated phone line and a signal booster on the roof above the penthouse, the highest point in San Francisco (so that even after the divorce Dad's conversations got beamed back and were carried on twenty feet above Mom's head). At the right altitude the signal was strong enough that he could use it sixty miles from the city.

Dad was calling whoever's fancy house we were circling to make the quip, "Hello, this is Al Wilsey, and I'm *upstairs.*"

. . .

I KNEW DAD was going to die on one of these flights, and that he took me on walks and told me about remorse so I would be prepared. So I could *act*. So when he died in midflight *I'd land the helicopter*.

And I had a plan.

First I'd shift him out of the pilot's seat. I'd do this while simultaneously holding the helicopter stable with the foot pedals (called duals) that stuck out on my side of the floor. No problem. Once we were stabilized, then I'd stretch over, take hold of Dad, lift him straight up, duck, arc him over my head, spin him 180 degrees like a baton (so his head wouldn't be pointing at the floor), set him briefly on my lap, slide over into his vacated place, leaving him in mine, and take the undisturbed controls. Easy. Mom had told me about a rush of adrenaline that enables mothers to lift automobiles off children, and I was counting on something like that.

This was my most fleshed-out plan. Backup plans were: (1) Stand, face backward, shimmy him over into my seat, take his place; (2) Leave him there and simply reach over to use his hand controls; (3) Sit on his lap and fly with my feet and hands on top of his (maybe the feeling of his hands would help me).

It was like a riddle out of Tolkien: *How to remove the dead king from the pilot's seat of his turbine jet helicopter without losing control and crashing?* I was consumed with finding a solution. And since I revered Dad I missed the only plan with a chance of success, the plan confirmed as feasible by a helicopter pilot to whom I recently put the problem: reach across, feet steady on the pedals, grab the stick, unlatch the pilot's door, and shove him out.

Of course, I was doing this already. Landing the helicopter was living with Mom.

NOW THAT HE was no longer paying for her chauffeur, Dad told Mom she should go pick out a car. Any car. There was no price restriction. But he had one stipulation: It had to be American-made.

Despite the fact that she was going to be dead by Christmas, Mom took me to every American car dealership on Van Ness Avenue.

These were bad years for the American automobile. After looking at several showrooms of shitty Chevys and Fords, and walking past the gleaming windows of Jaguar and Mercedes dealerships from which she was barred, Mom began to despair.

"I want a little red convertible Mercedes," she said.

I knew this was impossible. But I had a flash of inspiration. I said, "What about a DeLorean?"

"I want a Mercedes. A little red convertible," she repeated.

"I know, Mom," I said. "But that's impossible, you *can't have* a Mercedes, Dad won't let you. Mercedes is German. So it's out of the question. But you *can* have a DeLorean."

Silence.

"It's American!"

"I don't want some DeLorean."

"Mom, I don't think you even know what a DeLorean *is*. It's *really nice*." I scrambled to think of a way to make it appeal to her. "It's *luxurious*." *C'mon, what else?* "Uh, it's *stainless steel*. It's *expensive*. And it's *American*. So Dad has to buy it for you!" This seemed like an awesome case. Mom gave me silence.

"You can *resell it*," I added.

"Your mother is not going to become some used-car dealer."

"But Mo-um—I just want you to get something good. You don't even kno—"

*"Don't tell me what I don't know."*

*"You don't know,"* I mumbled. *"You could buy like five Mercedes for a DeLorean."*

Then a salesman approached and said, "Who's buying a car today?"

I got very worried, gave up on the DeLorean, and thought, *What can I do? I should do something. I'm the man here.* The guy told Mom, "I used to watch your T.V. show." Mom was hooked. This was bad. We were in the Oldsmobile showroom. Who'd ever even *heard* of an Oldsmobile? The only one I'd ever seen belonged to the parents of the dorkiest kid in my class, who'd tried to befriend me, until I realized he was only going to make my life worse and mercilessly ditched him. His parents were even older than mine. The Oldsmobile was like the car of the dead. The salesman moved on to remarks about financing and discounted sticker price, prompting Mom to say, "Money is of no importance. My ex-husband is paying. All I know is I want a convertible." He led her to the Oldsmobile in the window. It was not convertible, but it *was* two-tone.

Mom said, "Is it convertible?"

The salesman said, "It sure *looks like* a convertible, doesn't it?"

"It does!" Mom said.

I asked, "How's the gas mileage?" and was ignored.

Mom asked if he thought the car was cute. He thought it was very cute. *Don't ask him,* I thought. *He's selling it.* But ten minutes later Mom had bought herself an Oldsmobile. Its two tones were white (body) and beige (the vulcanized-canvas, nonconvertible top). Its convertible appearance always provoked a brief burst of optimism, followed by an enduring feeling of disappointment. It had a long, blunt, white hood, and a grill and mirrors of chrome-colored plastic.

The next morning Mom saw her new car in the parking garage and despaired. "What was I thinking, Sean?" she asked. Inevitably—as the letter "q" is followed by the letter "u"—her despair was followed by rage at men, at Dad, and at the car salesman.

But it was impossible to return the car, and Dad had got off without having to buy her a DeLorean.

ONE AFTERNOON I invited Blane over to Dad's rented mansion. We were in the kitchen trying to get some snacking done, when Dede appeared and said, "What's this?"

She was holding a glass streaked with chocolate milk residue.

I said, "An . . . empty . . . chocolate . . . milk . . . glass?"

"Right," she said. "I know it's 'an . . . empty . . . chocolate . . . milk . . . glass.' What's it doing outside the kitchen?"

I thought, *Something's up here. It's in the kitchen.* She'd lost me.

"I don't know," I said. I looked at Blane. "Were you drinking chocolate milk?"

"No," he said.

"It's not ours," I said.

"How did it get in your room?" Dede asked.

"I don't know . . . Mom," I said. "I mean, it's impossible—it *wasn't* in my room."

*"I just found it there."*

Silence from me. How could this be? I would never violate the no snacks—especially liquid ones—outside the kitchen rule. I thought back to when she had spirited me away to the store and bought me the whole candy aisle. What was I doing wrong now?

"Don't you know, Sean, that everyone can see through you?"

I thought, *It's a test. It's a test.*

"That is not my chocolate milk glass," I said.

"It is so sad that you're a *liar*, and such a *bad* liar that you don't *know* everyone sees through you."

With great earnestness Blane said, "That is *not* his chocolate milk glass. Sean was *not* drinking chocolate milk in his room."

"Your friend is covering for you," Dede said. "I'm just going to have to make it impossible for you to walk around this house with my glasses. From now on you are only to drink out of plastic cups"—she pointed to a shelf of battered green plastic cups that looked like they had the late Sarabelle's bite marks in them—"and you will do all your eating and drinking over the kitchen sink. Nowhere else!"

Blane was sent home. "Sean, she planted that glass in your room," he said later. Actually, I think Todd probably did it.

When Dad got home Dede took him aside and laid out her case against me. Then we sat down together, and Dad said, "I think you might be better off going to boarding school for sixth grade. You liked the East Coast when you visited for the wedding, and there's a good place out there that might take you."

I felt like I was going to cry. Dad looked weary. He said, "I'm tired, Sean. You think about this. I'm going to go upstairs and take a nap."

When he was gone Dede told me, "Your father is so disappointed in you for lying."

But calling Dede "Mom" was the only lie I was telling. It was a lie I wanted to believe. So it had weight and life. I wanted it to be the truth—so it made me incapable of seeing the truth.

It was a lie in the vacuum of my neediness and loneliness, the useless emotions that were being cold-stored up in the attic with me. I knew I was not loved, but I had decided that love could be represented by permission to call Dede "Mom," permission to act as though I were loved, and if Dad and Dede would grant me that, I would not ask for or require any real love. So calling Dede "Mom" wasn't just a lie, it was an *utter inability to grasp the truth*. And Dad and Dede (and Todd and Trevor) felt embarrassed and ashamed that I just didn't *get it*, that I was sticking around and calling Dede "Mom" instead of getting the hell out of their city and going three thousand miles away to a boarding school for eleven-year-olds. I *sensed* all this. I felt their shame, the temperature changing when I entered the room, as if I were dragging the attic down into the rest of the house with me. I knew I didn't fit in. Everyone's voice and posture changed when I approached. But I kept trying and pretending. And this was embarrassing: that I thought I was one of them; that I was this stupid; that the *patsy* (the *son* of Patsy!) thought he was in on the plot; that I didn't have the decency to disappear without forcing them to get rid of me. I *was Mom* to them, and that fact, combined with the fact that I was calling *Dede* "Mom," was an irony that could not be borne indefinitely.

Dad and Dede were in the strange position of pitying and feeling embarrassed by me even as they eliminated me. And since the rules I was trying to abide by were meaningless (*no snacking anywhere but over the kitchen sink?*), they could only grow more arbitrary. All these actions, reactions, desires, and emotions spun around and around, mixed, and became shame. Shame for everyone! Though nothing stayed pure shame for long. For me shame became revolt. For them it became contempt.

My revolt would not come for another few years. Their contempt came now, blowing out of all the cracks in the rented mansion, just for me. *I* was dead. So they could preserve themselves, I was dead to them. At the same time, I tried to make Mom dead to me, so I could be prepared for her death. Except Mom was the only person I was sure loved me, so I was always emotionally resurrecting her. Nothing made sense. I had no family, while shuttling between two homes, and calling two women "Mom."

This ended one afternoon in Dede's Le Baron. I was in the backseat with Todd; Dede was in the front with Trevor. No Dad. In his absence I always sensed the deep alliance between Todd and Trevor and Dede.

I forced Todd against the right-hand door by leaning needily forward into the front of the car, separating Dede and Trevor.

Dede remarked on the difficulty of parking on Fillmore Street, where we were going to see a movie.

I shouted, "Mom, there's a parking place right there!"

Dede passed it by.

I thought, *What was wrong with that parking place?*

Trevor said, "We're too far away, Sean."

"Oh, O.K., Mom," I said to Dede. Dede was a fast and assured driver. She flew down the hills. Two blocks passed. I said, "Mom, there's one, up ahead."

Silence. She passed it.

"*Mom . . .*" I wanted to be helpful. "In how many blocks should I look? Let me know and I'll start looking then." I checked out Todd, pressed against the door, and Trevor, in his preppy green sweater, and felt a brief burst of confidence. There was nothing to be afraid of here. I was helpful, fun, eager. They were *jealous.* Not *disgusted and embarrassed.* I felt sorry for them. I loved them! Love was spilling out of my skin and running down the hills and taking up parking spaces! Reserving them!

*We're a family,* I thought, with comfort. *And even if they don't like me, we are together now, and it's permanent.*

"We always look for a space right in front of the theater," Todd said.

The theater was on the next block; I looked left and right, said, "Mom, there! Mom, there! There, Mom!" and she swung around the corner, spotted a guy pulling out across the street, hooked a ∪, lined up, and swung back into the space.

Then, without turning around to face me, Dede said, with deadly, precise calm—a tone she inaugurated here and thenceforth used almost exclusively in addressing me—"Sean, don't call me 'Mom' again. You can call me 'Dede.' I'm not your mother. You have a mother. Unfortunately for all of us." She pulled the key out of the ignition. "And I'm not her."

IN AUGUST, Dad, Dede, Trevor, Todd, and I took a trip to New York and Newport, Rhode Island, where we would spend two weeks with Dede's parents in their Astor/Vanderbilt mansion. (I begged Mom to let me go, and she reluctantly agreed.) In New York, Dad left me with Dede and my new stepbrothers while he did some business. Walking up Fifth Avenue, window shopping, somewhere in the Fifties, we passed Van Cleef & Arpels, Jewelers.

"Van Cleef's!" Dede said.

She ran for the window, and we all followed. Behold: a watch face–sized emerald set in platinum surrounded by diamonds, hanging at the bottom of a chain of rubies, surrounded by more diamonds, wrapped round a decapitated velvet torso, under spotlights, behind bulletproof glass.

Minerals formed by pressure and time into light-permeable crystalline structures harvested from the earth by poor men in pits and cut and polished by molish men in bright armored rooms, then sold to a middleman, sold to this company, set in metals that had been similarly harvested, and put on display here on Fifth Avenue!!!

After admiring it Dede said, "Let's see if you can guess the price."

I felt a thrill of hope. Usually I did not register tests till they were over. But this was definitely a test. I was aware of a test, and if I guessed correctly, I would be *passing a test*.

"You go first, Sean," Dede said.

I wanted to go last.

"Can't I go last?" I asked.

"No."

Todd and Trevor both had the same hobby: gem collecting. They had cotton-lined display boxes with glass lids full of precious and semiprecious stones. They served as Dede's jewelry consultants, advising her on what she should purchase, what she should wear out with what gown, and what should stay in her safe. These were things Todd and Trevor had been doing all their lives: appearing in *Town & Country;* gem collecting; jewelry advising; browsing through the Christie's and Sotheby's catalogues. I was a novice in these areas. Standing on Fifth Avenue, I thought hard. Dad had recently told me that his yearly salary was sixty thousand dollars. I assumed it was all the money he made. This thing we were staring at seemed worth that much. But it *couldn't* be *more* than that. Perfect. I felt a feeling I rarely felt—*satisfaction at my deductive intelligence*—and said, "Sixty thousand dollars."

Trevor said, "Two hundred and thirty thousand dollars."

Todd said, "Three hundred thousand."

We walked into the store. The air was manicured. Trevor asked an elegant saleswoman, "Would you please tell us the price of the necklace in the front window?"

The saleswoman said, "Two hundred and thirty-five thousand dollars."

Trevor turned to Dede and said, "Overpriced."

WHEN I GOT back from Newport Mom took me on a rafting trip down the Green and Colorado rivers. She also brought along her niece, Linda, and Linda's son Patrick. It was actually fun to travel with Mom, who was at her best when she was far away from Dad and Dede and San Francisco. In our raft she was too busy worrying about drowning to talk to me about her cancer. We re turned to San Francisco late on a Sunday night. Linda and Patrick, who lived three hours north, in Willits, decided to stay over. Patrick took my top bunk and I got in the lower one with a red Ray-o-vac flashlight and *The Lord of the Rings.* After half an hour I fumbled the flashlight and sent it down the front of the bed, between the mattress and the frame.

Patrick woke up, and I said, *"Sorry."*

Over many years of flashlight reading I'd never done that. I rooted around after the Ray-o-vac and felt something cold, thin, round, with sharp, hard ridges. I found the flashlight and pointed it at the round thing, which lit up, fiercely. The round thing was a ruby-and-diamond bracelet.

I grabbed it, jumped out of bed, booked down the hall, and banged on Mom's locked door. If she didn't open fast I could go back to my room, get my pocket-knife, stick it in the lock, and pop it open. (A building handyman had just shown me this trick.) But this was not necessary. Before I had to jimmy it she pulled the door open.

"Sean!?"

"*Mom*—jewelry!" I held out the bracelet. "I was reading *The Lord*—"

"This is a bracelet from my safe. What are you doing with it?"

"I found it under my bed!"

She followed me back to my room. We woke up Patrick, put on the lights, and pulled back the mattress. Glittering there was an emerald-and-diamond bracelet that matched the ruby one, a big gold-and-diamond pin made to look like a bee, Mom's five-carat emerald engagement ring, and a huge, milky gray, star-sapphire-and-diamond ring Dad had given her shortly before the divorce. (All things she would sell at auction within a year.)

"What *is* this?" she said. None of us knew. Mom woke up Linda and we all went downstairs and sat in the kitchen.

Mom said, "Sean, someone's trying to make it look like you stole my jewelry."

"I didn't take any of this, I swear," I said. "Why would I steal your jewelry? Why would I come tell you about it if I *had?* This is just so strange!"

I was telling the truth, and everyone believed me.

"I know, Sean," Mom said. There was a certain wild light in her eyes.

Mom made tea for herself and Linda, and hot chocolate for Patrick and me. She began to tell us about her personal experiences battling the forces of evil, the subject of her second book (*The Intruders*).

"Strange things like this started happening to me when I lived on the crooked block of Lombard Street," Mom said. We listened. "My doors and windows would come unlocked in the night, when I knew, specifically, that I'd locked them. Strange people with awful *whippet dogs* moved in upstairs. Some dark liquid came dripping through the ceiling. It was blood. And they were making *drugs* up there. Eventually the police came and took them all away."

We were rapt.

"Perfectly normal-seeming men took me out and tried to attack me at the end of the night when they dropped me off at the apartment. They always wanted to come in, and when I said no they went crazy. The police got used to coming over to my place.

"There were weird smells. My dog grew terrified and I had to give him away. I had a man come and perform an exorcism. A psychic told me the house had the worst energy of any place she'd ever visited—she was terrified. And then my best friend, Mary Lou, was killed there."

We were in awe.

But Mom looked brave. She didn't look afraid.

"I found out after I moved that it had been a hanging ground for Russian sailors," Mom said. "Now the largest private collection of voodoo art in the world is housed there."

Hanged Russian sailors had drifted their way up to my room while we were river rafting, wraithed their way through the sliding deck doorjambs that whistled from the wind, plundered Mom's safe, and put the contents under my bed. *My* bed. *Me. Evil knows about me,* I thought.

We sipped our chocolate and looked out at the view. It was clear. San Francisco was all laid out below. We looked down at her old place on the crooked block of Lombard, five blocks away. I felt a great love for Mom. I was always reloving Mom after thinking it was impossible. Here she was being my mom: sympathetic, fun, protective. Dede had barred me from consuming sugar after five in the evening. Mom was giving me hot chocolate at night—*with no deleterious effect.* I imagined living with her full-time, in spite of the malevolent supernatural forces that were maybe pursuing her, and had finally figured out her new location. (*If it took them this long to figure out her new address they can't be that dangerous,* I thought.)

Now Mom was full of calm and excitement. If The Beyond was messing with her, as it had messed with her before, then she must be special. Things were *happening,* and that was good. She was so glad not to be alone. She was engaged and excited and mystified by something outside herself, yet close enough to be interesting.

"It's *imperative*," she said, "that we not say anything about this to anyone else. We'll just wait and see what happens. Someone planted these things under your bed, Sean, and we want to find out who."

THE NEXT DAY Dad called Mom and told her that I was *stealing things,* and lying, and needed discipline. He thought I should be sent to a boarding school called Fessenden for sixth grade. He had already made inquiries and there was a place for me.

Mom came into my room. She said, "Your father and that woman are trying to frame you and send you away to boarding school, Sean. But don't worry, we'll fight them."

She took Dad to court and kept me out of boarding school.

We never figured out how the jewelry got there. *Of course it was Dede,* I ended up thinking. *There was jewelry involved.* Stealing jewelry was the worst possible crime in the world of Dede. She knew I'd stolen my Vietnamese "governess"'s ring when I was eight. And we'd all watched *The Pink Panther* together over at the rented mansion before I left on the raft trip. I'd even said how cool I thought David Niven—*the jewel thief*—was. In my mind Dede planted Sarabelle in the vineyard, and she planted the jewelry under my bed.

A few days after I found the jewelry Mom received a dirty Ragú pasta sauce jar full of dead flowers, dropped off in the lobby of The Summit, and a death threat at the *Examiner,* where she was still writing a column—and had been taking swipes at Dad and Dede and their twenty-four-year age difference. The police said they were taking the death threat seriously, and Mom immediately began to wear a disguise (dark glasses and a black wig). She told me to keep an eye out for her assassins at all times. On the way to a movie we noticed a seedy-looking man in a beat-up car staking out our building. He looked like a killer.

Next, while I was at Dad's, Mom discovered splinters and pry marks around her bedroom door frame, as if someone had been trying to break in. She was terrified, and had an alarm and extra locks installed. I looked at the pry marks and wondered what kind of thief or assassin could get into the house but not get past this crappy door lock that I could pop with a knife.

Mom's new burglar alarm was equipped with undercarpet weight sensors and armed police response. Every door and window was wired, even though we were thirty-three stories up in a doorman building. The first time there was a false alarm the cops drew their guns, pulled out their flashlights, saw ten other guys with guns, and almost blew out all the mirrors downstairs. Mom kept a garage door opener–looking panic button next to her bed. Shrieking air raid sirens sounded whenever it was pressed. Spencer came over after school and picked it up, not knowing what it did.

He said, "Hey, your mom's garage works all the way up here?"

I said, "No! Don't tou—"

Then he pressed it, and we were enveloped in noise.

After Mom called the alarm company and told them it was a mistake, she informed Spencer: "There have been some attempts on my life."

Spencer said, "Wow. I feel really sorry for your mom, Sean."

Dad tried to use all these incidents to bolster his case that I should be sent to Fessenden. He said to me, "Sean, don't you think you'd be so much better off in a boarding school, away from all this drama?"

MEANWHILE, Mom started talking to me about menopause.

"Sean," she said. "I have hot flashes."

She pulled open the neck of her blouse and started fanning her chest, which was flushed and blotchy. "My body is changing. I'm no longer menstruating. It's very difficult for me. And that this is happening just as your father leaves me," volume cranking up here, "for *that woman*." Soft again now. "It makes me feel thrown away, discarded. I'm *suffering*, Sean." I was silent. Mom's voice turned brittle and she said, "I just thought you'd want to know what's going on with your mother."

I began to think of the new Oldsmobile, onomatopoeically, as the Old Mom's Mobile.

"You know what I've been thinking about doing, Sean?" Mom said late one Sunday night, as I was packing to go back to Dad's. Her eyes flashed with desire, swam with confusion, then clouded with fear. All these emotions made me nervous. I was sad and afraid. I was afraid of being sad. Emotions, I knew, were my enemy. They made Mom crazy, they led to divorce, and I needed to resist them. I needed to defeat them in myself. If I was sad then I was lost. I thought, *No. I AM THE ENEMY OF EMOTIONS. Whatever Mom says cannot touch me if I have no emotions.*

Mom's posture changed, became immaculate. She looked like she was on stage as she said, "You know what I think I'll do next weekend while you're in *my* house with your father and *that woman?* I think I'll get in the Oldsmobile and drive up there, turn down the driveway, and just keep on going —right through the front door and kill myself!" She grabbed my arm now. "And kill all of them, too!"

I decided to pay detailed attention to the nuances of her sentences here. She'd said, "You know what I *think* I'll do." It was all speculative.

Now Mom was crying. "They've hurt me so much. They've driven me to it. They've taken everything from me. Even you. Why *not* my life?"

*Technically they have not taken me*, I thought.

"How would you like that, Sean?" Mom asked.

I said, "I don't think that's a very good idea, Mom."

THE RENOVATION of Dad and Dede's new mansion, on Dede's old block, proceeded slowly. With school in session, boarding school evaded, I spent my free time in the attic at their temporary mansion. I watched Dede seal off a room and make it her Christmas workshop. "Under no circumstances are you to enter this area," she said.

A few days later, Dede invited Todd and Trevor and me into the room off the kitchen that she called the "breakfast room." There, on the breakfast table, were three boxes. One was big, the size of a T.V., the other two were half, and half again, the size of the first. They were all gift wrapped.

Dede said, "This is a test to see what kind of person you are."

*Yes!*

"You can pick out any of these packages, and open it *now*. What you pick will mean something about you. We'll find out if you are a generous person or a self-ish person. If you are a smart person or a *stupid* person. It's a test of character and intelligence. What you pick here will affect how I see you, and the presents you get—or *don't* get—on Christmas."

Silence.

"Maybe the big package is the best package. Or maybe the one who picks the small package will be rewarded on Christmas, unlike whoever picks the big package, *regardless* of what's in the small package. Because maybe the small package contains the best present anyone will get *all year.*"

*Whoa.*

More silence. Awed from me. Knowing from the stepbrothers.

"Sean, you can go first."

I hesitated.

Trevor said, "I'd take the small package because good things come in small packages."

Todd stared silently at the big package.

"If you want my advice, *off the record*," Dede said, "I'd pick the middle one."

Dede used to have Easter egg hunts before she and John divorced. She'd filled her garden with a hundred colored eggs and two hollow plastic ones, one silver and one gold, which contained a ten- and a twenty-dollar bill. She'd always point me in the direction of the golden egg. Then, after marrying Dad, she'd told me, "You were so stupid I had to walk you right to it." My mouth had gone dry. The saliva went to my eyes. *Emotion.*

I wanted a good present. And I wanted to prove I was smart.

"You have to pick now," she said.

I picked the medium-sized box. Todd picked the big one. Trevor picked the small one.

They got: exactly what they wanted.

I got: *fruit.*

WHEN CHRISTMAS CAME to the rented mansion it was Christmas like I had never seen even in movies. A fifteen-foot tree was so congested with pink rib-bons and pastel globes, so tightly bound with lights, that not a single branch re-mained visible, and a carpet of presents stretched around it in a circle—thirty perfect feet in diameter. Small boxes contained jewelry for Dede. "I *like* the small boxes," she said tartly, as she went about collecting them—*by the dozens.* (In a few years these small boxes would also be for Todd and Trevor, and contain keys for cars; heavy watches.) Big boxes contained Sharper Image products in rare brushed metal. Stockings contained sterling silver yo-yos from Tiffany. I was caught up in the excitement. But eventually, as unwrapped presents began to outnumber wrapped ones, I noticed my pile consisted primarily of sweaters. (Oh, and a Tiffany key chain.) Hundreds of thousands of dollars worth of jewelry and electronics accumulated in other piles. Finally I got one cool thing: a smoked-glass plaque stating in grand terms that a newly discovered star had been named "Sean Patrick Wilsey." As I got ready to leave for Mom's I asked Dad, "How come Todd and Trevor get . . . everything . . . and I get *sweaters?*"

He said, "Those gifts are from Dede to her boys. It's none of my business."

But I knew I had not passed the tests. And I would never again try to pass them. Dad drove me over to Russian Hill.

At Mom's we listened to carols. Mom cried. I gave her a scarf. She gave me a Japanese robot I'd wanted for months. It was cool of her.

But the weird thing was that Christmas was here and Mom was still alive. I was happy, so happy that I surprised myself. Mom's life was a good present. But then I also felt *stupid.* (Happiness *was* stupidity. And I—it had been proven— was very stupid.) Obviously I just didn't understand something. Then I realized, *She's going to die during the night.*

When it started to get late I said, "It's Christmas. Let's stay up all night, Mom!"

"It's your bedtime, and I'm *exhausted,* Sean."

I said, "Let me run to the store and get you some ice cream."

"Sean, I have to go to bed. And so do you."

*She has to go to her death. This is it. I'll go into her room tomorrow morning and find the body.*

Grim resignation. "O.K., Mom. Good night. *I love you.*"

I could not sleep. Every sound—and there are a lot of sounds at the top of a building in a windy city—was *Death coming for Mom, and maybe also coming for me, not to kill me, but just to like say hello.* I fell asleep around four.

Mom woke me up.

*Mom.*

*Mom!*

*MOM?!*

She was alive. I was amazed to see her alive. She *was* alive? Was *I* alive? *Was* she alive? Here she was. Was this maybe Mom's *ghost?* She did not look menac-ing. I did not want to look stupid. It was a beautiful day. Sun poured in. I stared at her. *Proceed with caution. Play it cool.*

I gave her a neutral look.

And then Mom broke down and said, "You forgot my birthday, Sean."

The day after Christmas, December 26, 1981, was her fifty-third birthday. This was no ghost.

This was Mom.

And I had forgotten her birthday.

I saw pain in her eyes, incomprehension at how I was lying there looking at her blankly, instead of bringing her breakfast in bed on her wicker movie star breakfast-in-bed tray with the built-in newspaper holders on either side (for reading your press), which she loved. Dad used to do this, and it was a tradition I was expected to continue.

*Oh no no no no no no no no no no no no no no no no no no no. Oh God. No!*, I thought, then jolted up, went into euphoric mode, said, "Happy Birthday, Mom!" and threw my arms around her. I had *nothing* for her birthday.

*She's supposed to be dead!* buzzed in the back of my head.

It was too late to go downstairs and make her breakfast.

What I needed was to get Mom *out* of my room. Yes, I had stumbled into a huge new screwup, but my despair hadn't yet caught up with my relief that she was alive. I had to use this euphoria. Make it my dominant emotion. My career as a liar was gaining momentum.

"I must have overslept because I stayed up late last night working on your birthday present!" I said. "I still have to put the finishing touches on it! Can you leave now?!"

Helping me lie was the realization—stunning and liberating—that *she* had not been telling me the truth. It was past Christmas, and it was now impossible for her to be dead by Christmas. I was not a bad son after all. And I no longer had to tell her the truth.

It worked. Mom left. I began ransacking my room for something to wrap and give her as a present.

A gold trophy of Dad's was the obvious choice. I could pry the engraved plate off the front and write "Happy birthday" on it in paint pen. She'd like that. But I liked the trophy too much, so *no way.* I had to be quick. I made a decision, and fifteen minutes later I came downstairs with some strawberry Quik crystals I'd poured into a glass bottle and tied a piece of ribbon around.

Mom was sitting at the breakfast table with some toast crusts and scrambled egg shreds on a bright red plate that said in white around its rim, "You Are Special Today." I felt suddenly terribly sorry for her. Almost as sorry as I felt for myself.

But new Liar Me said, "Happy birthday, Mom! This is birthday powder. Your birthstone is ruby." It wasn't, but she wouldn't know. I mean, she didn't know what a *DeLorean* was.

Mom simply said, "Growing up my family gave me combined presents. They'd always say, 'This is your birthday/Christmas present.'" She started to cry. "All my sisters and brothers got presents on their birthdays and at Christmas, even though we were poor—and we were *dirt poor*—but not me."

"Birthday powder!, Mom," I said, ignoring her sad story. "It's for your birthday."

Mom put her dishes in the sink, left me at the table, and went back to bed for the rest of the day.

I stood over the sink and looked at her plate.

*You are miserable today*, I thought, and this became the phrase I saw when Mom pulled out this plate on all my future teenage birthdays. As for the cancer, I discovered years later that Mom had been exaggerating what ultimately turned out to be a minor, benign growth. She never mentioned it again.

BACK AT DAD'S, in Napa, in the kitchen, leaning over the sink, I made chocolate Quik. My method: five tablespoons of powder, *then* the milk; no stirring allowed. Let the milk seep into the Quik. The liquid would hint at chocolate, while at the bottom loomed undisturbed powder mountains that I'd crush into delectable sludge when there was barely any milk left. In Napa, the sink overlooked the driveway, which was lined with liquidambar trees Mom had planted. I leaned over, drank, looked out the window, thought about Mom. I thought about her kamikaze plans with the Oldsmobile.

Now that she had survived Christmas, I thought, *What are the odds of Mom just killing herself and Dede and leaving me with Dad?*

I took my Quik outside and looked at the front of the house.

*What about this step? Will the car be able to make it over? Will it blow out the tires? Will she survive and embarrass me?*

I'd gone down to the garage at Mom's and checked out the front of the Olds, assessing the clearance. I looked closely at the step. I thought it could clear.

My new policy at Dad's, since I couldn't call Dede "Mom" anymore, was to pretend Mom didn't exist. If I just kept quiet I might appear motherless. But Dede didn't have the decency to play along. Dede talked about Mom. And I was powerless to stop her.

At lunch Dede said, "There's just nothing more awful than a woman who lets herself go," and turned to Dad. "I think we all know someone like that. Didn't we see her picture in the paper the other day? The caption said, 'A woman who's let her rear end get a leetle too large.' That's sad." *This was Mom.* (Even I had noticed that her butt had grown commandingly large.) "I mean, the huge, hideous flabby behind of a failed woman who has just *let herself go.* It's revolting."

I hoped Mom wouldn't underscore her existence, her connection to me, by crashing the Olds through the front door and failing to kill them.

Dede kept talking. She had a machinelike way of going on about a topic, as though she were speaking to imbeciles. She was like a perpetual speech machine. She could generate words in any situation, on any topic, with seemingly no connection to what she was thinking, as though her mouth was moving while her brain was otherwise engaged, as though words were what powered and lubricated her malevolence; and, since they were often trivial, words were what she used to distract her victims. The impossible key was to ignore everything she said and look for the truth elsewhere. But I could never quite tune her out. Her words burned, but I listened. She was an artful and entertaining conversationalist. And I was in her power.

And now that Dede had explained that it was *revolting* to have large buttocks I associated Mom's buttocks with stupidity, with being a sucker, with having a weak brain; and Dede's then tight little knot of an exercised ass with her sharp little mind. Mom's ass was lassitude, what I was trying to get away from, and Dede's ass was power, what I was trying to attain.

Standing over the sink, Quik in hand, I thought of Mom's big buttocks filling the vast, brown front seat of the Olds: dead meat.

Dad and Dede and Todd and Trevor would all gather around the Oldsmobile and laugh at her, slumped over the beige-plastic steering wheel—*Look, her steering wheel isn't leather, like ours!*—all akimbo, blood in her long-dyed, long blond hair, glass everywhere. It would be an embarrassing scene. Then they'd look at me. Dad would take a step back—*nothing to do with me.* Dede and Todd and Trevor would stare.

I stirred and ate the grainy, sweet Quik sludge. It was delicious.

.   .   .

IF MOM and Dad and Dede were all killed in Mom's kamikaze attack I thought I would then be raised by Danielle Steel. And I thought about it a lot. To me Danielle Steel was the logical person, the president pro tempore of the Senate after the president, vice president, and speaker of the house were killed. She was beautiful. She was kind. She was rich. She was maternal. Her ass was not very large, nor was it a sexy, mean little fist. She had a kind ass. She gave me a really cool handheld version of Space Invaders. I couldn't figure out why. I concluded that she just liked me and was generous.

I did not know that she had also been Dad's lover while pretending to be Mom's friend. I did not know that my stepmother was almost Danielle, not Dede. I did not know that around the time of the divorce Danielle had proposed to Dad, and he had turned her down.

He'd said, "I can't marry you. I'm old enough to be your father." Danielle was older than Dede. Had he been hoping for Dinah Shore? I'll never know.

I did not know that I had come that close to paradise—and gone to hell instead.

Danielle would have made a great stepmother! I thought of her every time I went into a bookstore or supermarket. There were Danielle's books, with their dedications to John and Todd and Trevor. It could've been me!

She'd have loved me. I'd have been a big brother to her son. As for her daughter, the beautiful Beatrix Lazard (this really was her name), who was delicate, sophisticated, and, it seemed to me, of refined sensibilities—it would be okay if we fell in love, because we would not be related. In four years I'd get a vintage 1950s Porsche Spyder for my sixteenth birthday and drive it over the bridge with Beattie, wind mixing sea air into her dark hair. We'd take a long walk over the Marin headlands and find a private place to French kiss, while her little brother Nicky (stowed away in the trunk, the rascal) Windexed the Porsche's windshield. Then we'd head back home to Danielle's mansion. This would be great. Mom and Dad had never spoiled me. Dede had first spoiled and then recoiled. I was ready to be spoiled. I would know how to handle and appreciate spoiling. Spoiling wasn't for everyone, but I was qualified for it. *Spoiling* wouldn't *spoil* me. I was adept at being deserving. I could ski the black diamond run of supreme spoiling, pull down my spoilee goggles, fly, spin, parallel, and never stumble. I would know what to do.

AND THEN CAME the culmination of this period, the event that shuttled back and forth between Dad and Mom's with me, the event that is always in the present tense.

I'm eleven, almost twelve. Mom comes out of her bedroom in a long white nightgown and sits down at the top of the steps overlooking the city. She looks defeated, miserable. She's been spending all her time in bed, but not sleeping. She asks me to sit down with her. She has something to tell me. We stare out at the view. "Sean," she says, "I'm going to kill myself tonight and I want you to kill yourself with me."

No "I think," no "maybe," no "may." I try to hear it that way: *Sean [I think] I'm [maybe] going to kill myself tonight and I [may] want you to kill yourself with me.* But I can't. It is a definite.

I am looking forward to the next scene in *The Lord of the Rings.* The scene after the awesome one I just read, when King Theoden awakened to the fact that Wormtongue, his court counselor, had been poisoning his mind, and his "staff fell clattering on the stones," after which he rose "slowly, as a man that is stiff from bending over some dull toil," until, "tall and straight he stood, and his eyes were blue as he looked into the opening sky."

He was going to kick some ass.

Now it's raining. The sky is opening. I have a whole small theological moment as I sit there. I think, *Maybe I'll be able to read the rest of the book in the afterlife.* Then I think, *No, probably not, if I commit suicide I'll go to hell. There are no good books in hell.*

Mom is solemn and determined.

I am convinced that we are going to kill ourselves. Unless I can do something to stop it.

"No, Mom," I hear myself say. "I don't want to die. And I don't want you to die." I realize that I mean it. I feel it. I know it. I have only a few minutes to live, unless I can talk her out of it. This is not some melodrama. And though I threw in the second sentence, "I don't want you to die," as a manipulation, I realize that it's true, too. I don't want Mom to die. I love her. Immediately after I realize this I am overwhelmed with emotion. I am the enemy of emotion. But I can't control it. It's useless. I start to cry. But I *must not.* What is necessary here, what is required of me, what I may or may not possess, and will find out with my life, is skill. I must think fast and talk well or die. I am in another one of those situations, like in the helicopter, and I must act correctly, answer a riddle, or suffer the consequences. In my mind it is: *Either talk her out of it or die with her. That's the choice.*

"Let's talk about it, Sean. Let's talk about how we'll do it," Mom says now. She holds my hand. Her eyes look hard into mine. "How would *you* like to do it?" she asks. Offering me a say; it's as if I'm a grown-up, too. I feel sick.

"I don't want to do it, Mom," I say.

"Would you like to hold hands, so it won't be lonely?"

"No," I say.

"We'll show your dad," she says. (She never calls him "your dad." It scares me. *Call him "that bastard*," I think.) "We'll teach him a lesson together."

We will hold hands, and jump off the deck, and fall. It can be no other way.

I imagine the loneliness I'll experience the moment she hurls herself over if I back out and don't go with her. It will be more horrible than jumping. Being there alone up in the sky, in the dark, with that huge empty apartment behind me, Mom falling down onto Russian Hill, white nightgown trailing behind her, me having to take a long walk through the marble palace's echoey chambers to escape. *God'll kill me before I can make it out. He'll just erase me for letting Mom kill herself.* Death worse than death. Easier to just jump, too. That's how it'll be. I am certain. It is the worst thing in the world.

I will have to make her not go.

I don't imagine anything else. I don't realize that if Mom really wanted to kill herself she would use nembutal, the sleeping pill she'd been taking ever since her heart surgery, thirty-odd years before, and had on hand in plentiful quantities; one bottle for mother and one for son, and then we'd lie down together in her bed.

No. In my mind it is the deck. Mom is attracted to and repelled by the deck. Its drama appeals to her; the beauty and power of falling into and smashing herself on a city that used to love her and now does not, taking with her the boy who used to love her and now does not. I do not realize that the idea of her face and limbs being crushed on the concrete—a closed casket funeral—is something she could never bear.

I say, "No, Mom, I don't want to die. I need you. You're my mom and I need you. I can't live without you, Mom." *I shouldn't have said that.* I want to vomit. *"I don't want to die. I don't want to die. And I don't want you to die,"* I say desperately, through tears now. I have never spoken this way. I am broken. These words are impossible to say, but they are coming out of me easily.

They're true and I wish they weren't.

I say, "I love you more than anybody, Mom."

I say, "I've only been alive for eleven years, and I want to see twelve." I feel a weird vertigo. I'm more calculating and more awfully truthful than I've ever been. I keep going. I state every dream and hope I've ever had for my whole life. "I want to get married, Mom. Like you used to tell me I would. I want to be a writer like you. I want to live in Florida"—this had seemed like a good idea for a while—"and have kids." Each thing I say makes me gasp and cry harder. I throw everything I have at her. I grab her and I cling. I do not want to touch her, or even look at her. And I do not want to let her go. But if it will work I will do it. So I do grab hold of her. I am pure emotion and pure manipulation united. My survival is at stake and I will do anything. I need my mom. I cry into her long white nightgown. I feel her warm, fleshy arm through the soft silk. I say, "I don't want to die!"

Twenty minutes go by like this. I sense that something is changing, that this might be working. We are still alive. *So don't stop now!* I pour it out, pour out my love for her, till I am exhausted, wiped out from guilt and crying and begging and apologizing.

Mom lets me cry and hold her. She remains stiff. I am hyperaware of any signs or responses.

"I love you so much, Mom," I say.

She begins to stroke my back while I am crying. *Good,* I think.

Then, after a long silence, she simply says, resignation in her voice, "O.K., Sean."

I have survived. I am amazed that I have done it.

Still, I do not relax. I must remain vigilant. I am convinced that after this peaceable interlude we will step out into the cold, foggy San Francisco night, there will be condensation on the deck railings, and we will throw ourselves over them.

I remain convinced of this for the next seven years.


WE GO INTO her bedroom and watch T.V. I sleep in her bed that night, making sure she doesn't change her mind. Somehow, I realize the next morning, over the course of the night the responsibility for her life has been given to me. From now on I must save her from killing herself; and I must save myself by saving her with my love, but also by never getting too close, and saving/being myself with sarcasm. And this paradox rules my life, every other week.

*Seven* · P E A C E

I T ' S   T R U E   T H A T   M O M  was born "dirt poor." That's why she felt entitled to be filthy rich. It explains and excuses a lot. She didn't want money because money was *power;* she wanted it because she'd been poor, and money cures poverty. (When she was married to Dad she was profligate in her generosity, regularly making outrageous gestures of kindness, such as adopting an entire Appalachian school.) But beauty is like money from God. And Mom has always been beautiful. Suddenly she saw her beauty's true purpose: She would save the world's children from nuclear annihilation with her beauty.

I N   T H E   F A L L  of 1982 Mom, taking after her father, received a vision that altered the course of her life. She, too, considered it a message from God. And, as with her father, this vision required of her a great deal of itinerancy, with a great number of children.

She was in a "guided meditation" with Sheila Krystal, her Berkeley psychologist. This, in the still unpublished book she wrote about these years (*Whispers from God*), is how she describes what she saw:

It was as if I was viewing a movie, or an event in the distance. But it was as real as anything I had ever witnessed. Fascinated I observed [an] inky blackness form into a circle.

"It's the earth, Sheila, I'm seeing the earth. It's as if I'm looking at it from the moon." And then, as the picture in my mind continued to unfold, I saw the perimeter of the circle explode in huge bursts of orange and red flames like those we see in photographs of the sun.

My heart raced, sweat beaded my forehead. "Oh no!" I cried.

"Oh my God, my God, Sheila," I moaned, "I'm seeing the circle of the earth. Not our beautiful blue planet but an inferno."

"Take a deep breath Pat. What you're seeing isn't real it's symbolic. You can open your eyes anytime."

"The earth has been destroyed!" The illusion held me in its grip. "My God, oh my God, there's been a nuclear explosion!" I gasped. "I'm seeing the annihilation of the earth . . . the seas are lava, boiling oceans, all the buildings are rubble . . . there's nothing left, people, animals, plants, trees, have all evaporated. Oh my God, my God," I wailed. "Why am I seeing this?"

"Open your eyes, Pat. It's okay."

"No, it isn't okay." I sobbed as the horrific vision continued to unfold.

"Oh," I persevered. "There are children standing in the debris, in gray ashes amid broken buildings, they're terrified, wailing. They're crying out that no one cared enough to stop this holocaust. They've lost everything, everyone. They are the only survivors. They . . . they . . . they're shouting, 'Why didn't you help us?'" My grief was piercing. What I had seen was authentic.

"Breathe deeply," Sheila instructed. "You can open your eyes anytime, you know."

"No. There's more. Now I see a white-winged horse. It's Pegasus, Pegasus," I repeated, "flying out of the ash-filled sky, gliding inside a bright light. The horse has a rider." I paused, watching the projector and screen in my brain. "The rider is reaching down with rays of light, lifting the children onto the horse, carrying them to safety; away from our destroyed planet."

And so, with Pegasus, the strange postdivorce limbo period ended.

Mom had begun seeing Sheila Krystal—who was originally based in Oakland, but would soon relocate to Berkeley, in a move I always linked to the large sums of money Mom's epic-length, daily visits pumped into her practice—after the first miserable postdivorce year seeing the same shrink as Dad. This man had told her, "There isn't even any point in talking to you. Your husband has made up his mind and that's that," and then continued to talk to her and bill her. Before that she'd seen a marriage counselor with Dad. (Dad had agreed to this on the advice of his lawyers.) The marriage counselor was attractive, young, agreed with Dad on all counts, flirted with him during their sessions, and—rumor has it—let him seduce her. Wow, Dad.

MOM SEIZED UPON her vision with all her energy. She became consumed. She returned from Sheila's and started talking about nuclear weapons and "the children." She also mentioned something called "the black void," and used the word "annihilation." Mom had never brought up the cold war before.

From *Whispers from God:*

"Sean . . . do you ever think about nuclear war?" He looked at me as if I had just emerged from the Ice Age.

"Get serious, Mom."

"What do you mean?"

"Well, you know, get serious. Yeah, I'm scared of nuclear war." He was busy making a peanut butter sandwich. "I wonder why I even go to school or anything. When the Russians push the button, we'll all be blown away. Or even if we push the button—wham-oh! All my friends are scared too."

This was unacceptable. The cold war had to end.

Then, the next day, a man called Gerry Jampolsky, whom Mom described as working with kids "suffering from catastrophic illnesses like cancer," came to see her, and brought a book he had put together called, *Children as Teachers of Peace.* The book compiled kids' drawings and sayings about peace. Mom took this as another sign. Jampolsky asked if she could help him promote it. Mom threw herself into the task. With great speed she put together a series of children's peace rallies in San Francisco, all culminating in the arrival of Jehan Sadat, the widow of Anwar Sadat, who was also involved with the book, and who Mom always re-

ferred to, grandly, as "Madam Sadat of Egypt." They held a press conference together.

At the press conference Mom watched Mrs. Sadat closely. She was a handsome woman: regal, poised, full of dignity.

Mom could do regal, she could do poised and dignified. After watching for a
few days she transformed herself from sexy society divorcée into widowed
stateswoman. And then she no longer needed Madam Sadat.

Armistead Maupin, through one of his male characters in *Tales of the City*,
had this to say about it: "That stupid twat thinks she's Eleanor Roosevelt now."

Mom did not care. She was impervious, bigger than all that. She had a mission now.


MOM ORGANIZED a huge Saturday morning concert, downtown, in Union
Square, at which she expected hundreds of kids to show up with "messages of
peace for world leaders." Mom had advertised and promoted the event, had been
in touch with schools all over the Bay Area, and a big turnout was assured.
When the day arrived there was a torrential downpour. There were mud slides,
cars washed off roads. The rain showed no signs of abating.

"There won't be a concert today, Sean," Mom said. "Maybe we should just go
see a movie."

I imagined us coming home after the movie, Mom depressed, obliging me
to crawl up on the bed with her and watch the raindrops streak down the
windows.

With conviction I said, "Mom, if even one kid shows up we have to be there."

Mom locked eyes with me. I held her gaze. She said, "You're *right*, Sean. We
must go." She donned a designer raincoat, got her keys, got in the elevator, and
prepared to roll down Russian Hill, up and over Nob Hill, to Union Square.

From *Whispers from God:*

Turning my windshield wipers on full, I eased into the street. The wind had
quieted, but the rain was like Niagara Falls.

"We're late, Mom, but no one will be there anyway, I guess, so can we go
to a toy store?"

Pulling up to the curb near the plaza, I answered. "Maybe, but for now
go on up there, while I park the car."

Hurrying up the steps to join my son in Union Square, I arrived just as a
flash of lightning illuminated the scene. I stopped short, taken aback, dis-

mayed by the number of wet bedraggled children waiting there. There were hundreds. Umbrellas of every color sheltered them as they, along with adult chaperones, attempted to keep dry in the deluge. Another lightning flash, thunder rumbled, and then, above it all, a song. We Shall Overcome. The words had been changed but the meaning was the same; We Shall Live in Peace Someday. The children's voices were high and sweet, rising and falling on the rain soaked wind blowing across Union Square. Huddled under umbrellas, clutching their plastic wrapped mail, I was reminded of a scene from the film Our Town in which the community gathers in a downpour to bury Emily. . . .

Youngsters crowded around, eager to find out what we were going to do with their offerings.

"Where have you been?" a kid asked, recognizing me. "I saw you on T.V. and you said you'd be here at ten."

"I'm sorry, I didn't think anyone would come out in this weather."

"This is real, real, important." The boy's red jacket was wet and bunched around his ears.

"We were afraid you wouldn't come." Sprinkles dripped from the girl's eyelashes, her nose was running. "We've been waiting a long, long, long time."

"We're scared," the boy was about nine and smelled like bubble gum. "We want our letters to get to those guys who can blow us up, you know the guys in Russia. Are you going to get our letters to Russia?"

They were determined.

"We're really, really, really scared. Will you help us?" The petition came from a chorus of Asian, black, Caucasian, and Hispanic children.

With startling clarity, I realized these were the children in my vision.

"Yes," I answered, barely able to speak. "I'll mail them, even to Russia."

Sean pulled at my slicker, "Mom, they'll end up in a shredder! We've got to go there. We've got to take them ourselves!"

"Are you going to go there?" The children were incredulous. "To Russia?"

My fate was sealed. "Yes, we'll go there."

Sean's arms went around me as others pushed forward in youthful exuberance, wrapping themselves around my legs, pulling on my raincoat.

Thank you, I whispered, looking up at the blustering sky, thank you. I didn't know, that day, that above the rolling peals of thunder a far greater sound was directed toward me. It was a mighty whisper from God.

As I remember it I was holding open a bright green canvas bag with a large red "P" on it, the first in a set of five bags that spelled out the word "PEACE." (Mom called them, "the PEACE bags," and always kept at least one letter in the trunk of the car, along with an original Rodin sculpture she was trying to sell, "to fund my work.") Kids came up to me and put bundles of plastic-wrapped mail to Reagan and Andropov in the bag.

A blonde girl asked, "What are you going to do with all the mail?"

Mom said, "We will send it on to the world leaders. I have their addresses."

"They'll just throw it away if you send it to them!" said another kid.

I saw confusion on Mom's face—*she hadn't thought of this.*

I said, "It's *true,* Mom. They'll just throw them away." She stared at me, other kids had gathered around, and I realized I was fucking up royally. Mom would blame this on *me.* Not on herself. Not on these other kids. *I* was betraying her, showing my allegiance to Dad—and, as I'd learned to do within the confines of single sentences, sometimes single syllables, I needed to make a necessary, life-saving about-face, switch away from Dad and back to her, make her angry at Dad, at the world leaders who would throw these messages so callously in the trash, and with the word "away" still in my mouth I made the switch, saying, "*We* have to *take* them!"

There was a moment of silence. All the kids were amazed. And then Mom declared, with the children gathered around her, "*We will take them. We will carry your messages of peace to the world leaders.*"

And from that statement our lives changed again, forever.

"You're really going to take them to Russia?" a kid asked.

Mom's eyes teared up. She nodded, solemnly. She took my hand and the hand of another child and said again, "*Yes. We will take them. We will carry your messages of peace to the Soviet Union.*" And then she began to sing. Mom sang, "We shall overcome," changing "overcome" to "live in peace."

*We shall live in peace*
*We shall live in peace*
*We shall live in peace*
*Some day-ay-ay-ay-ay*
*Oh, deep in my heart*
*I do believe.*
*We shall live in peace some day.*

I sang, too. Everyone joined her. She smiled down at me. It was a taste of what was coming.

MOM HAS ALWAYS had a weird thing about pronunciation—changing the modest, plainspoken Oklahoman Montandon ("Mawntandun") to the French "Moantan-dawn"—but when the peace work began I noticed how Mom had a second voice. It appeared suddenly, taking over her regular speaking voice, so she could say things she felt very deeply, or things she wanted very much to be true, that were maybe not true. With this new (evangelical) way of speaking she hoped to convert others to what she felt. But my favorite thing about language, written language at least, is its stability, its faithful adherence to rules and principles—contrasted with an infinite potential for expansion and recombination. Words had long been my friends (thanks to Mom) and I respected them. But now Mom was trying to cheat. Words were stable like elements—Mom was trying to split them. This felt dangerous.

Her voice changed completely. She slowed down. As if she were talking for cameras, or posterity, even when she was only talking to me.

She began to invest—irradiate—her words with emotion. She needed obedience from words, and she didn't know how else to get it.

Mom's gift for elocution had mutated into a highly specialized method of delivery, in which even a true statement was overstated to such a degree that it became untrue. She'd take a word's literal meaning, and then threaten, emote, and force it into meaning what she needed it to mean. It was like watching Mom become Dede. A hurt, unfocused, hesitantly ruthless Dede. Briefly manipulative (Dede's cardinal quality) but with no idea what she *really* wanted. (Beyond her own redemption—being seen as something other than "the world's most expensive wife." Also: world peace.) And so Mom would briefly become Dede and then she'd return to herself. And during these transformations she was doing to words what Dede'd done to me. (Of course Dede also played with words. But she did it with the opposite of Mom's drama. With her it was cool and calm and professional. Chemist's great-granddaughter that she was, Dede donned a white smock and performed lab experiments on her vocabulary. She spliced the genes of the truth to create a horrible form of lie that could not be disproved. And Dede is so very modern and powerful and American in this way.) When Mom spoke in her new voice I could hear that it was need and desire—not calculation—fueling the manipulation, drowning or burning the truth out of her sometimes-even-true statements. She was desperate, and if you knew much of anything you were not convinced. It was a pathetic kind of dishonesty and manipulation. It was like she was betraying me and words and herself all at the same time. And really fooling no one but herself. "Betrayal," by the way, was a favorite Mom word of this period. She used it to describe what Dad and Dede had done to her. And sometimes she used it to describe what I was doing, too. What I was doing was survival, not betrayal. And calling *me* the betrayer: THAT WAS THE ULTIMATE BETRAYAL! I MEAN, HOLY FUCKING SHIT!

Anyway.

This was a statement Mom loved to make: "We must protect the children of the world from the threat of nuclear annihilation." Her favorite parts of the phrase were the words *children* and *annihilation*, which she loved to enunciate with maximum syllabic elongation, wanting to take as much meaning as she could from these words, pump them up beyond recommended levels of inflation, pump them up so full of pathos that I looked around desperately for a heavy table under which to crawl, because they were gonna blow. *No good can come of it!* I thought (in a Sean Connery voice). *"Children" and "annihilation" will send us all to kingdom come!*

*Of course* there was something scary and dangerous and unqualified about Mom's new use of words—to use a *Lord of the Rings* analogy: Mom was the corrupted wizard Saruman, tainted by too many dealings with Sauron/Dede. Mom was playing in Dede's laboratory and who knew what the fuck she might mix together. She might kill herself, and kill me, too. Though she wanted to save the world.

Sometimes words didn't cooperate with her. They balked at this treatment. Annihilation never seemed to want to be overemphasized—being itself was enough—so there was tension within the word, between its letters, like it really might break apart and explode. I'd been trying to figure out what this would look like on the page when I realized that it was like her half in the grave, I'm dying of cancer voice: When she talked this way half her letters went italic and the other half stayed roman. "We must protect the *chi*ld*re*n of the world from the threat of nuclear *a*nni*hi*l*a*tion."

I thought of it as The Mom Voice, and as soon as she started to use it I stopped listening. I closed my ears in order to protect myself. Because, especially as I got older, I would have to mock her when she spoke this way—somehow I could not not mock her, especially if there was an audience. My accustomed Mom-mocking audience was Blane and Spencer, both of whom found Mom-mockery extremely funny. Whenever Mom started talking about *peace* and *chi*ld*re*n Blane would whisper, "Sean, your mom's doing her special voice," I'd impersonate it, and he'd collapse with laughter. Spencer was more respectful. "Your mom's really theatrical," he'd say. But he'd laugh, too, and then she'd become enraged, and then I was boned for being stupid enough to make fun of her to her face. But still, the mocking was necessary. I had to keep my distance in order to keep my integrity. (Also, I could not resist a laugh—getting laughs was one of my few talents.) After making fun of her I'd immediately kiss her ass, or keep talking, de-emphasize my punchlines by delivering them inside innocent sentences, jokes audible only to Blane and Spencer, and once they'd caught them I'd switch immediately into long discourses on world peace and how Mom and I were going to bring it about, while my friends struggled to control themselves.

ON MY SHELF is a videotape Mom sent me when I turned twenty-five. After her watershed moment, deciding to take the messages of peace to the world leaders, she hired a series of documentary film crews. This tape was shot shortly after the events described above. It's a typical Mom gift, in the same sentimental vein as the eighty-page epic poem she wrote about our mother-son relationship and had leatherbound for my eighteenth birthday. (Now, unfortunately, lost.) The video is titled *A Message of Love. . . . To My Son. . . .* (ellipses hers). In it we're sitting next to each other, Indian style, in a group, singing and performing the synchronized hand gestures that went with the song.

"From *thee* I *receive*," we sing, and fold our hands up to our chests. "To *thee* I *give*," and our hands unfold out in front. "*Together* we *share*," hands open wide, then settle on the knees. "And from *this* we *live*," hands stretch way out to the sides.

The camera zooms in and out on Mom and me. I'm participating and not participating, detached but not disparaging. I look baffled and good-natured. Next to me, Mom is spilling her banks. Tears are streaming down her face. This song is penetrating the innermost chambers of her heart!

I'm reaching over, patting (*not stroking*—too much unbroken contact in stroking), and comforting her, but also trying to keep her away, keeping some strength and tension in my patting arm—calibrating the distance I can maintain, the fractions of space and the required pressure/duration of hand on back) without provoking dejection at my resistance, envelopment at my yielding (wondering to myself where the real and where the fake begin and end in Mom's totally real/fake tears). I'm comforting and recoiling (it's like all my hair is standing up and leaning away while I put my arms around her). I *had* to keep my distance in order to keep my integrity. I had to come close in order to keep my life. And so my identity was compressed, crushed into the smallest of interstices between these two things; between these two powerful forces; between Mom and Dad, really. And in the same way that the letters of her emphatic words did battle with each other, some pulling to italic, some staying straight, the sides of my brain, and the auricles and ventricles that made up my heart (a heart half Dad and half Mom!) were at war with each other.

And I thought this was what *emotion* was. I thought emotion was a public thing, performed in front of cameras to a song. I hated it. So I strove to resist emotions, to be sarcastic. Which is hard to do when you are filled with emotion.

Emotions were my enemy. They made Mom crazy and I could not succumb to them. *No.* Emotions were what had fucked up my life. They weren't the result of life being fucked up, they were *why* life was fucked up. I felt stained and polluted by them. I was terrified and I needed to avoid them. Every emotion felt and shared with Mom brought me closer to an unwanted hug, to an inextricable bond—and an inextricable bond meant that the next time she made her evil proposal I really would have to kill myself with her. Emotions lead to death. *Fuck death. Fuck emotions! I declare war. I AM THE ENEMY OF EMOTIONS.*

As the enemy of emotions I refused to capitulate to them, but was, of course, not strong enough to refuse them, so I felt the one acceptable stifled emotions byproduct: anger. (Also rage, hate.)

And I was working for peace.

AND THIS WAS how it was. Mom trying to end the cold war; me trying to end the war in my head; watching her go from proclaiming the importance of "giving children a voice in their future" to telling me that she was going to go to bed, take nembutal, and not wake up. And I thought, *What do I do? It's my problem.*

Meanwhile, the San Francisco of "From thee I receive," a San Francisco that I'd never encountered, spilled into the penthouse. A man who played "music of the spheres" on special glass bowls came to give a concert—and offered to sell his spheres to Mom. Mom put a wandering minstrel on retainer. The minstrel was also a psychologist, and she'd met him at the mental health clinic she occasionally checked herself into, telling me, "Sean, while you're with your father and *that woman*, I'm going to Langley Porter Psychiatric Hospital for the care I so *desperately* need." She acquired a massive, horse-sized, white satin Pegasus. Children's choirs sang on the staircase. A troupe of young ballerinas (one of whom was a thirteen-year-old Puerto Rican who took the rubber bands off her braces and gave me my first French kiss) performed for her. Crystals! Crystals were

everywhere! The penthouse was filling up with so many crystals—for meditation and decoration and transubstantiation—that, coupled with the mirrors, it
was as if Superman's arctic Fortress of Solitude was levitating hundreds of feet
in the air.

When I described the scene to Dad he said, "All these people are in your
mom's court so they can take her money. Which is *my* money."

I HADN'T SUGGESTED taking the mail because I believed it would work.
Without giving it much thought, standing there in the rain, it seemed to me that
the mission of delivering children's messages of peace to the political leaders of
the world was a vast one that would distract Mom for some time, and almost certainly for the rest of the day. I could see only one day ahead anyway.

I have always, always underestimated my mom.

In twelve days Mom arranged to deliver the mail to Washington, Rome,
Moscow, and Cairo. She was effectively combining the professions of her father
(minister) and Dede's father (ambassador).

She gathered children. Children of all races. Naturally, I was one of them.
She called us, "*Ambassadors Without Portfolio.*" What did that mean? It probably didn't mean anything, but it contained two words Mom liked to say: "*ambassadors*" and "*portfolio.*" And so she said it a lot.

She had buttons printed up that said "CHILDREN AS TEACHERS OF PEACE" in
big green all caps on a white field. Mom made me wear mine everywhere (I took
it off when I got to school). It was as big as my head. She ordered unwearably
dorky T-shirts that matched the buttons. She designed a purple banner embla-
zoned with "Children as Teachers of Peace" and hands with flags on them,
reaching for a heart, in the center of which was printed, in cramped-looking letters that Mom had had appended after helping an old man across the street and
being struck by the realization that the elderly were important, and sort of like
children, too: "Generations Together." She gave the wandering minstrel/
psychologist a stage name by taking two parallel streets on the slopes of Nob
Hill and running them into each other: Mason Taylor. Then she put him in the
studio (with a children's choir) to record two songs he'd written, the "We Are
the World"–like "Children as Teachers of Peace":

*Peace is a rain-bow above the storm,*
*Peace is a migh-ty tree,*
*Peace is a bluebird's song of joy,*

*Peace is being free.*
*Peace is grand-ma's homemade bread,*
*A hug when the day is through,*
*Peace is a touch from Dad-dy's hand,*
*And say-ing "I love you."*
*Peace is a chi-ld that can't see why*
*Na-tions dis-agree,*
*Peace is lov-ing somebody smaller,*
*Some-one just like me.* [Only the children sang this line.]
*Peace is an ea-gle fly-ing high,*
*The bear and the lamb laying side-by-side,*
*Peace is the spir-it of trusting each other,*
*Something deep inside.*
*Peace is our fu-ture!*
*Our best chance of a sunrise!*
*Peace is the prayer we pray,*
*Peace is beauty,*
*The sweet sound of laughter,*
*Peace is a child at play.*
*The rul-ers of nations!*
*And wise men on mountains,*
*Are trying their best to lead*
*But the quiet within us*
*Says follow the child-ren*
*Children as teachers of peace.*
*Peace is our future!*
*The best chance of a sunrise!*
*Peace is a dream we seek,*
*So come walk beside me,*
*And we'll make the journey,*
*For children as teachers of peace,*
*As child-ren as tea-chers of peace.*

And the groovier, folksier, "Room for You and Me":

*Can you hear my heart beat?*
*Yes, I hear your heart beat.*

*Do you like the sound?*

*And I like the sound.*

*Would you like somebody?*

*I would like somebody.*

*To wrap your arms around?*

*To wrap my arms around.* [Mom, standing behind me, would wrap her arms around me and breathe the words "wrap my arms around" directly into my ear here.]

*Look into the future and tell me what you see.*

*Is there room for love there?*

*Is there room for me?*

*Shout it from the mountains,*

*Across the great divide.*

*Tell it to the nations.*

*Let it come inside.*

*We have found an answer.*

*We know just what we need.*

*Peace is what we're after.*

*Love will be the seed.*

Both were pressed onto a 45.

She hired a publicist and began issuing press releases. She hired her first documentary film crew to follow us around and chronicle these historic events.

She meditated with Sheila and visualized the world's leaders meeting with us. In one of these visualizations Sheila asked her to visualize a home that would forever be hers, a home for a peacemaker. Mom closed her eyes, and felt the light from the center of the earth move along her spine and up through the top of her head. Then she saw an Indian tepee.

"What do you see?" asked Sheila.

"I see a tepee—I don't want to see a tepee," said Mom. "I want to see a castle."

"Just go with it," said Sheila. "This is *your* tepee. No one can take it from you."

"I don't want a tepee," said Mom. "*Let* someone take it!"

But then she agreed, focused, and experienced a past life as an Indian maiden.

"I saw the deerskin straps that held my tepee together. The furs on the floor. Things I didn't even know about," she told me. "It was a *past life experience,* Sean."

"Wow, Mom," I said.

Then she told Mason Taylor about it. He looked at her, put down his guitar, took her by the shoulders, and said, "*Pat,* do you *realize* the acronym for this movement, for Children as Teachers of Peace, is See A *Te Pee?!*"

"Sean—it's a miracle. Your mom's a visionary!" Mom said.

*What about the "of"?* I thought. *Shouldn't it be C.A.T.O.P.?*

I looked at the horse-sized Pegasus that dominated the living room.

At school Blane and Spencer would always ask me, "Hey Sean, how's *Pegasus?*"

THERE WAS GROUP meditating, too. We meditated on our mission and we did crayon drawings to supplement the mail we'd collected from kids. We came up with slogans. I became adept at portraying the earth with a stick of dynamite through it. I also drew the Peace Frog: fat, laconic, heavy-lidded, the style ripped off from *Garfield*, a bubble coming out of his mouth saying, "PEACE IS THE TASTE OF FLIES IN THE MORNING." It was the perfect way to mock Mom and love her at the same time.

WE LEFT ON the first peace trip on Christmas Day 1982. The plan was to go first to Washington, D.C. and present a bag of mail to Reagan. Then we'd go on to Rome and meet the pope. Then Russia and Andropov. And finally Egypt, where we would be welcomed by Mrs. Sadat.

Mom assembled a random and multiethnic group of kids by placing ads in the paper and calling on friends. We were: Rachel Skiffer, eight and black and precocious; Raquel Bennett, twelve and Jewish and more precocious; my cousin Patrick, who had discovered he was a Republican and acted like Michael J. Fox in *Family Ties;* Matt Nolan, a freckly, blond, Dennis the Menace–resembling kid; Jonathan Dearman, black, fifteen, a varsity football player, idolized by Matt, hilarious and sarcastic and sincere; me. Mom and a handful of other mothers acted as chaperones.

WITH OUR CONFUSING banner and our recordings of "Children as Teachers of Peace" and "Room for You and Me," which Mom put on a boom box and had us sing along to whenever there was a break in the peacemaking action, we boarded a large Pan Am jet to Washington, via Houston. Mom felt the Christmas departure was appropriately symbolic, and said so to the reporters who came to see us off. When we arrived in Houston Mom's sister, my aunt Glendora, met us at the airport with a choir, a Santa Claus, and more reporters. The lights flashed on atop T.V. cameras and Mom was radiant for the rest of the way to D.C.

Thanks to Karna Small, a White House publicist (later Reagan's appointee to the National Security Council), and a longtime acquaintance of Mom's, Reagan was supposed to meet with us. But when we arrived there was no meeting. Mom had also been in touch with Caspar Weinberger, the secretary of defense, who'd promised to put in the good word with Reagan, but no luck there, either.

Mrs. Sadat hooked us up with a man she knew in Egyptian affairs at the State Department, named Wingate Lloyd. In a side alcove of a large State Department office building's lobby we sang "Room for You and Me" (Mom holding Lloyd's hand and showing him the lyrics so he could sing along) and dumped mail on an exhausted-looking couch. Lloyd seemed like a man experiencing the low point of a career.

Afterward Mom insisted that we go to the White House. We stood outside the gates and unfurled the banner. Mom told me and Rachel Skiffer to form a biracial delegation and beg the security guard to let us in.

"Tell him you want to see Reagan and give him your mail," she said.

We did, reluctantly, unsuccessfully.

"Sorry kids, president's busy, and I can't take anything for him," he said.

Then Raquel Bennett went up and begged the guy to at least take some of the mail "from American children who really care about the future." He shook his head.

"Don't you care about the future?" Raquel asked.

He looked like he cared about the future of the Washington Redskins.

Mom jumped in and said, "You should be ashamed of yourself! We're going to tell the press that President Reagan doesn't care about children! It's *shameful!* Don't you think that's shameful? That the president doesn't want to see the children of his country? The press will think so."

He said, "I'm sorry."

Mom gave him a piercing shot of her blinkless blues and said, "You *should* be sorry. Don't you have children?" She was wearing a huge fur-trimmed hat with a burgundy felt top. It looked like a sea urchin.

He said, "I'm not gonna talk about my kids with you, lady."

Mom said, in a voice of great empathy, "What are their names?" her head angled to the side in its sea urchin hat, his face only a foot away.

He slid closed a Plexiglas door and locked himself inside his closet-sized guard booth. We left. Then we went over to ABC News and occupied their lobby in an attempt to get upstairs and see Peter Jennings. When we were kicked out, we went to the Vietnam Memorial. Mom made us stand behind a group of three stoic vets in camo, bearing huge American and black POW/MIA flags.

Then we sang "Children as Teachers of Peace" while a couple hundred confused tourists filed by and watched. Mom stood proudly, like some peace warrior
version of the vets. The POW/MIA flag blew in my face. Then she made us
sing "Room for You and Me" in front of Lincoln, at the Lincoln Memorial, until
a guard shut us down, saying, "Guys, out!"

I thought, *Oh, fuck. Mom's going to get suicidal now for sure.*

BUT SHE DIDN'T. Mom decided that at the end of every day we would have a
"rap session" where we'd all get together in her hotel room (always the only
suite), discuss what had happened that day, and be videotaped. "These will be
historical documents," Mom said.

Rap sessions started with a general discussion of the day's events. Mom would
often cry, or try to get us to cry. The tone of this first rap session was discouraged and anti-American, though Mom did say about the cop at the White House,
"I really got to him with that question about whether or not he had kids. That
made him think."

Then the session segued into a meditation.

Meditations involved visualizing ourselves in a circle of light. My circle of
light existed in a dark world of shadows and smoke and neon that resembled a
music video. I'd always see myself standing there awkwardly, shuffling, thinking, *Okay, here I am in the circle of light.* Then Mom—who directed these meditations—would tell us to place another circle of light in front of and just
touching our own, "forming a figure eight," and bring into it whatever world
leader we were after. She always used their full titles, and placed emphasis on the
more exotic countries and names: "His *Holiness* Pope John Paul II"; "Prime
Minister of *Israel* Menachem Begin"; "*Union of Soviet Socialist Republics* Com-
*munist Party* General *Secretary Mikhail Gorbachev*"; "President of the United
States of *America* Ronald Reagan"; "Premier of the People's Republic of *China*
Zhao Ziyang"; "*Chancellor* of West Germany Helmut Kohl"; "Prime Minister
of *India* Indira *Gandhi*"; "Prime Minister of *India* Rajiv *Gandhi*" (all of whom
we would, in fact, eventually meet).

After our defeat with Ronald Reagan we put the pope in the second circle.

"See him in your circle of light blessing our mission," Mom said. "Visualize
front-row seats." She had arranged, with the help of a Catholic priest friend,
who also used to have a hit Bay Area television show, for us to attend a medium-
sized public audience with the pope.

We flew to Rome the next day. Mom went to pick up our pope tickets at a convent near the Vatican. It turned out that we had a block of front-row seats and a block midway back, but on the main aisle.

Our audience, the next morning, was in a modern building adjacent to St. Peter's. Outside, we waited behind barricades for an hour staring at the Swiss Guards. They looked like clowns with swords.

"What the hell could they do?" I said to Jonathan Dearman, who I was trying to impress. At fifteen Jonathan was the oldest. And he was one of the only black students at the same Catholic high school my dad had gone to.

He said, "They're like ninjas. They can stop bullets with their swords. You could unload a whole Uzi at one of those guys and they'd be fine. And if you even got *near* the pope." He assumed a karate stance and uttered a drawn out, badass, "Hoooooooooo-aaaaaaaaaahhh . . ."

Around us everyone was singing. There was a joyous throng of people who had been waiting all their lives for this. Africans. South Americans. Italians. Irish. Eastern Europeans. Then they let us into a Quonset-roofed building with a stained-glass, elliptical, rose window taking up the entirety of one end.

Dad had told me that if I got to meet the pope—which he seriously doubted (though he knew enough about Mom's abilities not to discount it completely)— "you should kiss his ring and ask him to bless your old man."

I said I'd do it because I didn't think it would happen. It was the weirdest thing I could imagine, kissing a strange man's ring. How did you kiss a ring without kissing the hand, too? This seemed totally unacceptable. And it was a dilemma I thought I would not have to face. But now Mom had given one of the front-row seats to me. I walked down, down, down toward a huge golden throne, till I arrived at the front row. I sat there thinking about The Ring. Rachel Skiffer ignored everything and read *Are You There God? It's Me, Margaret*. There was so much crowd noise that it filled my ears and felt like it was creeping down my throat.

The nuns were ubiquitous. People sang "Ave Marias" with French, Slavic, Italian, and Irish accents. Flowers, Virgins, and cameras waved around in the incense.

Our row filled up and steel barriers were locked into place at either end. Three-foot-tall wooden platforms were set up at regular intervals along the center aisle. People pressed against the barriers and leaned out looking for the pope. The scene was oceanic. The people along the aisle had their feet rooted and their arms waving as if they were sea anemones. Mom, ten rows back, wore a white dress—to match the pope—and a tightly wrapped coral-colored turban. It made her look like a piece of reef. Schools of nuns in light blue outfits darted through.

And then came the pope! All in white, with an entourage of men in black: black suits and thin black ties, long-tailed black tuxedos, white ties, and silver watch chains, priests in their flat, black shirts. When they made their entrance at the top of the main aisle, the pope in the center like a boxer surrounded by train- ers, the ocean started *boiling*. People kneeled, stood on their toes on kneelers, cried out. It came together into a huge adulatory crash.

The pope walked down the aisle toward the throne. In his long white gar- ments, with his red face, he looked like a butcher. He climbed the platforms, a man holding each of his hands, then turned to either side of the hall so that the entire congregation could witness him. The men in black suits collected gifts, passed them back, and received new ones, like a bucket brigade in reverse.

At home on the nightstand next to my bed I had a framed picture of the pope. Dad had given it to me. I thought the pope was cool. No other religion had a man who dressed exclusively in white and ruled his own city-state. As he drew closer I thought about how impressed Dad would be if I actually got to meet him, if we had a conversation, if he laid his hands on me, if we became friends and he decided to be my advocate, if I was tying up the phone one evening and Dad asked who I was talking to, annoyed, and I said, "Karol," and he furrowed his brow into the Al Wilsey accordion and I handed him the phone, and he said, "Carol?" and the pope's Polish Darth Vader voice said, "Yays. Karol Wojtyla. Bayter known to you, my soan, es Johannes Paulus Secundus, speaking."

I'd grab another extension and say, "The pope."

"*Tak*," the pope would say in Polish, fondness in his voice.

"Vicar of Christ. Bishop of Rome. The Holy Father, Dad," I'd say.

"*Tak, tak*. Eet ees very spaycial young men thayt you hev there," the pope would say. "Eet ees a very great sadness for me, aynd for God, that you do note understand the value oav him."

The pope would come to San Francisco and stay in the top bunk of my bunk bed for a few months and help me wrestle with some of my difficulties. Dad and the pope and I would start hanging out. They'd both appear at the door of my classroom, the teacher would let me leave early, as I did when I went to the psy- chiatrist's, and I wouldn't have to lie and say I was going to the allergist's. We'd all three hold hands at the back of St. Joan of Arc on Saturday nights, then get some pizza, maybe go to the arcade. The pope would have tons of quarters.

He'd give me the ring when he went back to Rome. In a gesture of solidarity, to help me get through troubled times.

At the airport, on the tarmac, he'd put his hand on the back of my neck, press the ring into my palm, look fondly into my eyes, and say, "You will tayke thees, Sean. I cain geet enoather. I know good jeweler een Rome. I will say I loast eet een the shoawer."

Then he'd board the papal jet.

"Cool," I'd say, drawn out and soft.

I WOULD WEAR IT, and every once in a while Dad would fall to his knees and kiss it.

"*Dad*, come on, *Dad*, that's not necessary," I'd say.

The pope was the only man my father would listen to.

WHAT REALLY HAPPENED was the pope ascended the altar and sat on his throne and a man read a roster of delegations present at the audience. When the name "Children as Teachers of Peace" was announced he raised his arm and shook it approvingly. Then, after the service, when I thought the whole thing was over and Dad would never be impressed, the pope suddenly came down, slapped a young priest on his shoulder like they were on the same team and the young priest would get in the game soon, took Rachel's chin in his hand while *Are You There God? It's Me, Margaret* sat on the pew behind her, gave her a kiss on the head, looked at all of us, looked at Matt, and said, "Irish?"

A woman with a brogue shouted, "Everybody from Galway sends you their love, Holy Father!"

I was leaning out so far I almost lost my balance. I said, *"No."*

He looked like this information was disappointing to him. I had disappointed the pope.

Matt said, "Um. American."

The pope said, "American!"

The pope grasped one of our head-sized pins, with Mom's big green all-caps on it, and read out, very slowly, "C-H-E-E-L-D-R-E-N T-E-A-C-H-E-R-R-S."

"Galway, Holy Father!" the woman shouted.

"P-E-E-Z," said the pope.

Then he came and stood in front of me, everyone's eyes following. I handed him my pile of mail. He looked me in the eye and said, "Thenk you. I em very grate-ful to you and all your *fraynds*." He looked at me hard. "Uhh, so meny," he said.

*"Yeah,"* I said.

It was good having him there in front of me.

"God blays avery wone of you, your femilies, aynd your *fraynds*."

He looked at me hard again on friends. I thought, *Like we're friends!*

"Thank you," I said, and gave him a smile that said, *Dude!*

"Thank you, Your Highness," my cousin said.

"Veery, veery welcome," he said to me.

Then he put his hand on my shoulder, and just stood there. I could feel the starch in his clothes. They were very clean, and luminous.

I said, "We really want peace."

He said, "Peace ees a beautiful thing."

He turned so a Vatican photographer could snap a picture of us—which I have—and then he stood, leaning forward, enveloping me in the starch, talking to the Irish lady from Galway. His robes were all around me. It was a white-out. I soaked in the starch against my face. I looked at the ring on his finger. It looked heavy. He smelled Dad-like. I thought I could hide in those robes and go with him. And then he was gone, the steel barriers were removed, and we filed outside.

Outside, when I told her what had happened, Mom said *she'd* sent the pope to me.

He'd been coming down the aisle, getting up on the observation platforms, stopping at every tenth row or so, and then Mom, who'd been meditating so hard on this moment, was rewarded. "I knew he would come to me," she said. "I just knew it. He singled me out like a laser.

"He told me, 'You are doing God's work.' And when he tried to walk away I tugged his sleeve and said, 'Please go to the children, they're on the front row.'" And he did.

So we were blessed.


FOR RUSSIA Mom had obtained visas with great and unusual speed. She had walked into the Russian consulate without an appointment and asked for the consul, who happened to be walking by the reception area at that very moment. Struck by her beauty, he invited her to tea under a large portrait of Lenin. She pleaded her case until he agreed to call Moscow.

"Can you call immediately?" she asked.

He looked at his watch, said, "I will call immediately," and disappeared. After a long absence he returned and told her that her request would be granted.

This aroused the interest of the FBI, which began keeping a file on Mom right then.

And Rome was the first of many places and occasions that she said, "Sean, I know that we're being followed."

A hushed postpapal dinner in a small restaurant featured much conversation about how we were being tailed by the KGB, FBI, CIA. Various members of the group spoke up, saying they'd seen men ducking into doorways.

We'd met the pope and were being followed by spies.

We were going to Russia, where we would be bugged and tailed by even more! I could almost forget my real life.

OUR AEROFLOT FLIGHT landed in Moscow the next afternoon, with the light already gone. An Intourist guide named Val met and obviously disliked us. We stayed in a vast hotel called the Cosmos, which curved like a sickle and had been built for the 1980 Moscow Olympics. In a park across the street a golden statue, on the scale of the Washington Monument, depicted a tiny rocket atop a massive, fiery exhaust trail, commemorating the accomplishments of the Soviet space program.

It was December 31, 1982, and we had arrived just in time for the New Year's Eve ball at the Hotel Cosmos. After putting our bags in our rooms and giving our keys to a woman stationed at a desk near the elevators (our belongings were combed through, we would discover later), we went down to the basement ballroom, where several round tables had been set aside for us, and found it filled with hundreds of drunk Russians.

All I knew about Russia was that all the women were unattractive and all the men were unhappy, and bent on making the rest of the world unhappy by taking away our material comforts. But this was nothing like that. There was loud music and dancing, sexy women in costumes, couples in sixties-looking clothing, obliging waiters. The adults—Mom, her documentary film crew, and her retinue of other mothers—took a table for themselves and left us on our own.

Heaping piles of blinis and black caviar and sour cream arrived. There were balloons tethered to the tables, and at each setting was a large, lacquered, brightly painted wooden spoon. Pepsi had cornered the Soviet cola market, and the waiter brought it to us. Then my cousin, Patrick, discovered an unmarked bottle of clear liquid. Vodka! Someone had the cool idea of mixing vodka with Pepsi, which had arrived in abundance—little bottles of Pepsi were all over the table, as well as a bucket of ice, tongs, and tons of glasses. Mom was happy, distracted by spies and bugs and miracles. Patrick mixed our drinks. A feeling of independence and plenty and freedom washed over me. The Soviet Union was the perfect distance from Mom's unhappiness and Dad and Dede's power. There were no rich friends and social connections here.

Patrick handed drinks to me and Jonathan and Matt. Raquel and Rachel split one reluctantly. It was the first time I'd had more alcohol than the sip of crème de menthe Dad let me drink during chess games when we were living like bachelors together.

We bashed balloons around with our long-handled wooden spoons and shouted, "Comrade!" Our waiter helpfully told us that the spoons were used for mixing vodka and sugar—he pointed to a sugar bowl—and slurping it back after toasts. We filled our spoons with vodka and sugar. Jonathan started toasting the various branches of the American armed forces: "To the army! The navy! The air force! The marines!"

Rachel said, "I don't think we should be toasting the U.S. military when we're in the Soviet Union on a peace mission."

I laughed so hard it felt as if I might pass out. I was elated.

We went back to bashing balloons. Vodka and sugar flew around and stuck to us. Then the Soviet champagne arrived!

We popped it. Pop!

Sugar and vodka came out my nose. I had not felt so good in my entire fucking life. I was *euphoric*. I *loved*, *LOVED*, *LOVED* everything! I was carefree! I threw my arms around Jonathan and Patrick. Thanks, alcohol!

"Let's cruise the elevators," I said, pulling everyone out of the ballroom, telling the oblivious adult table we were going to go to bed.

"Did you drink some of that Soviet champagne?" Mom said.

We all laughed. She let us go.

Growing up on the thirty-third floor of an apartment building, I knew elevators and the fun that could be had in them. I also knew hotels. I'd spent every other week with Dad at the Fairmont Hotel after the divorce, sneaking into its kitchens and riding its elevators. We called one, held it, called another, split into two groups, and raced to the top of the Cosmos—higher than the rocket sculpture.

Soviet elevators tended to shudder violently, drop, lurch, halt between floors for strange extended periods of time with their lights flickering, and then fall down and open on sinister, ill-lit, sickle-shaped floors, where a bunch of drunk, racially diverse American kids could briefly jump out, get a dirty look from the walruslike women who sat there guarding room keys, realize we were lost, and then get back in again, all the while laughing and frightened and thrilled.

The more the elevators fell and shuddered the more I felt euphoric and safe. I was far away from my own insignificance. I had just met the pope and he had laid his hands on me in benediction. I had Mom beat, nailed, wrapped around my fucking finger—*snappwooh!*—and I had got some laughs off Jonathan Dearman!—*who was so cool*—when I'd toasted the CIA. ("Yo! Don't be toasting *them!* Not *here!*" he shouted and laughed.) I felt a new personality opening up. Maybe this was my new life. Papally blessed, vodka-swilling, peace-sowing provocateur behind the Iron Curtain, yeah! Yeah! Yeah! Yeah! *Stumble* . . . Woooooooweeeeeee! Because—and I really felt this—I was returning to some lost and rediscovered real version of myself. I could do no wrong in the Cosmos! I was in a faulty elevator and I could finally relax! *Oh the glory of it all* . . .

I got the sense that I could be cool. In one brief, drunken, twelve-year-old adrenaline rush. Todd and Trevor were cool—they had a whole world in which they were cool. Now I had found one, here in Russia, here in drunkenness, mixing vodka and Pepsi and making people laugh and smiling and not being ignored, overlooked, harassed, or smothered, but here in Russia, shining, shining!

If only it would translate to back home, put me back on track in the competition with Todd and Trevor for Dad's love, if I could use the pope's blessing and Soviet technology to beat the Americans—unholy, imperialist Todd and Trevor—to reach past them and grab my dad back.


WE WERE IN Moscow for five days. The next morning, happy and unhungover as only twelve-year-olds can be, we met Val, the Intourist guide, for a tour of Red Square followed by a meeting at the headquarters of the Soviet Peace Committee, an entity for which Val had a cynical smile.

The Peace Committee building, on Prospekt Mira, was large, impressive, and set on a corner, with the word for peace (*mir*) written on its facade in many different languages. We entered, checked our coats in a beautiful marble entrance hall downstairs and then went up a grand staircase to a second-floor lobby filled with velvet Art Deco furniture. High windows looked out over the huge, mysteriously trafficless boulevard.

The Soviet Peace Committee existed to better the image of the Soviet Union abroad, a job at which it was failing. Still, it seemed to be a very well funded institution, with many white-curtained Lada and Volga staff cars, and it was impressive in a way that made us all think, though we'd never heard of it before, *The Soviet Peace Committee . . . WOW—I am in a very important place.*

A pair of double doors swung open and we entered a large wood-paneled room. Screens for overhead projectors hung from twenty-foot ceilings. A gleaming, polished, U-shaped meeting table was set with glasses, bottles of water, and U.N. General Assembly–style headphones for simultaneous translation. It reminded me of Mom: a great show, but considering we'd never heard of it before, probably important only to itself—powerless.

And in the waning years of the Soviet Union it would turn out that Mom and the Soviet Peace Committee were meant for each other. They loved each other immediately. They wound up together for years. They made each other happy.

We sat down along the bottom of the U. A quartet of Peace Committee representatives, a woman and three men, attempting to look cheery but looking mostly boiled, deprived of essential vitamins, and underrested, occupied the arm to our left, while on the right were four attractive Soviet children and a stern woman with a huge fur hat and unfashionable glasses. All the Russian adults seemed to want sleep and cigarettes simultaneously. We put on our headsets. Words of welcome were translated, in an inflectionless newsman's voice, by a man in an elevated glass booth at one end of the room.

The man in charge spoke English, and when he addressed us the booth man got a break.

Mom, wearing her sea urchin hat, brandished the "Children as Teachers of Peace" book and said, "Peace is different things to different *people*. For some peace is, as they say, 'Grandma's homemade bread.' But *never* is peace *war. Never.*"

Then she had us sing. We sang badly. When we were done Mom declared, "Love is the motive, peace is the message, compassion is the emotion, and hope is the outcome."

There was a silence.

The Peace Committee representative said, "Uh . . . Peace is not a bureaucratic thing." Then he gave a long preprogrammed–sounding speech. I spaced out. After a long time he concluded by saying he hoped his grandchildren would live to see "a thousand sunrises." I thought, *Does he mean literally wake up early and see them? Rather than live through them? Because a thousand sunrises is . . . like, less than three years!*

Mom now had us tell the Peace Committee what peace meant to us. Jonathan said, "No ego trips. Just listen. It's an easy goal." Patrick said friendship. I said, junior diplomat–style, "I think that we're all on this mission to make the Soviet Union and the United States realize that their people are really the same, so that they can get along better and bring the two nations closer together." Raquel said, "We're a few of the many billions who want peace." Matt said, "Talking things over." And Rachel blew us all away with, "I think peace is something that everybody should have. Not just people but animals. It's just—peaceful."

Everyone laughed. There was some chatter. We had some back-and-forth with the Soviet kids. Then Mom said, "I feel quite ignorant being in your country and only knowing *spiceeba* and *parjalsta* and *da* and *nyet*. I was trying to learn 'hello' and I can't even learn 'hello.'"

The man said, *"Strasvoitya."*

Jonathan whispered, *"Strasvoitya."*

Mom looked at Jonathan, then repeated, *"Strasvootiay."*

The man said, "Almost."

Mom said, "Almost!"

The man said, "Are they also from all over the country here that you've brought or are they from the, eh . . . Bay Area?"

"They are from the Bay Area and Houston, Texas, we had a stop in Houston, and also New York City."

He said, "Excellent."

"There were many, many more than this, but it was impossible to bring them. And we do hope to send them. In fact, not only do we hope, we will send them."

"Do you mean that, eh . . . there are such, eh . . . well, since you're not an organization but movement as children as teachers of peace but, eh . . . they have them in New York, in Houston, as well as San Francisco?"

"It's beginning to move that way. We're finding that as we go across the country that more and more people want to be involved in this. It's a pro movement, it's not anti. It's *pro* peace. We are *for* peace."

*That's not true*, I thought. *What is she talking about?* At this point C.A.T.[o.]P. had given some concerts in San Francisco, solicited kids' mail, received the endorsement of Mrs. Sadat, and put together a book of children's drawings—and Gerry Jampolsky had done the last two!

The night before, while I was drunkenly asleep, Mom had entertained a mysterious Russian visitor. I vaguely remembered someone coming to the door. Here's how Mom describes this visit, in *Whispers from God:*

Pulling the door open, I was startled to see a stranger standing there, a very large stranger.

"My name is Joseph Golden," he whispered in a husky deep accent. "I must talk to you Pat. Special human rights agents told me you were here."

Joseph Golden fit the description, "a bear of a man." Overweight, medium height, with a round, rough-hewn face, thick dark eyebrows, wearing a black coat and fur hat, I would have known he was Russian anywhere.

"Is important we talk," he repeated, his voice low. "Your trip to USSR is break for all Russians. So, you have meeting with Soviet Peace Committee; is very important I speak with you. Yuri Zhukov, President of Peace Committee, hard liner, has power, can get you in Kremlin."

Joseph propelled himself into my room and sat down. Without bothering to take off his coat he proceeded with his monologue. "So, Russians respect force, Pat. So, must be forceful. Is very important." Fascinated by the man's intensity and conviction, I was staring at him.

"Who are you? How do you know my name? Who are these special human rights agents?" If I was a smoker, this would be the time to light up.

The small sitting room was scarcely large enough for the two of us. It was to be the gathering place for our group, but I hadn't thought I would be entertaining a visitor, certainly not a huge Russian man in the dark of night. The room was dim, sinister. Green horsehair furniture stacked with suitcases, packets of soap, pens, and samples of perfume, brought as gifts, cast long shadows against the gray walls. I should have been afraid, but I wasn't.

"Pat," Joseph was lighting up a gross smelling cigarette, "is no problem who am I. Problem is tomorrow. Tell Soviet Peace Committee that our own Mr. Andropov has said is time to stop slogans and get to work. Insist going to Kremlin. Get foreign newspapers to cover visit. Is very important Soviet people and world know you are here, that you allowed to be in country that refuses to let citizens travel." Joseph appeared to be pacing while sitting.

"Must go now, might be arrested. Put in mental hospital. So, Pat, is necessary you act as I have said." Departing, trailed by cigarette smoke, he walked in the opposite direction from our floor lady guard. Was he a crazy person, I wondered. Instinctively, I felt he could be trusted.

Golden had given Mom code words to use with the Peace Committee, pass phrases to get into the Kremlin. He also told her about a giant television screen that would allow Russians and Americans to look at each other and forget their differences. Mom told me the next morning that Soviets respected strength. That you were to *demand* what you wanted, strongly. They were to be treated like shopkeepers!

Here's a transcription (from video) of what happened next:

The camera wobbles across the meeting room to Mom. She gestures with her hands.

MOM: And there is nothing that people can really find fault with. Uh . . . Nonprofit, nonpolitical. And we're finding that people anyplace and everyplace we talk to about this want to be part of it. And when we get back to the United States, it will be our mission as the core group, and certainly *my* mission, to see that this is expanded all over the world. I would like to see it be everywhere. And how this is going to come about I don't know yet. But it will be done. And that's why I keep going back to television. There's a man named Joseph Golden, a Russian gentleman—Soviet gentleman, I'm learning the difference between Russian and Soviet.

She laughs.

MOM (*cont'd*): And he was telling us about how this giant screen can work. And about how a script has already been written so that we can get Children as Teachers of Peace united literally all over the world. Within *a month*. As I said before, we're working under a time stress. I don't feel that we have time to just sit back and say, "Let someone else do it." No, we've got to do it. Each of us. We've got to do it. Or it won't be done. And I think that there will be a war. And we'll all be killed. And I feel that, uh, if we really care about the future, then we've got a great job ahead of us. And while it may seem easy, I think . . . it's so simple, it's so easy that it seems complicated. Because we allow it to be complicated. And it doesn't have to be.

We close in on her face.

MOM (*cont'd*): It can be straightforward and simple. And I know there're games of politics and all this, but I feel that we can cut through all of that. We've been doing it so far. We leave here, we will go on to Egypt, where we will be received by the president of Egypt. And that, unfortunately will be out last stop—unfortunate only in that we would like to go on all over the world, but the children do have to go back to school.

She smiles.

MOM (*cont'd*): But this is our first trip of this type, not our last. And I would like to know from you how we can present our letters.

RUSSIAN MAN (offscreen): This is what I was thinking and trying to talk with eh . . . eh . . . the boys here in the committee. As I said, eh, Mister Andropov has left for Prague and they have the, uh, political committee meeting starting, I believe tomorrow.

We pan around to show the Russian man, who has strong eyebrows and holds a pencil.

MOM (offscreen): Can we go to Prague?
RUSSIAN MAN: Well . . . uh.

He laughs.

MOM (offscreen): We'll go.
RUSSIAN MAN: Well, who can stop you from, eh . . . It's just a question—

He laughs some more.

MOM (offscreen): A lot of people can stop us.
RUSSIAN MAN: No, I can not stop you from going to Prague, to Czechoslovakia, it's just a question of getting a visa and a ticket. That's it.
MOM (offscreen): But can we see Mr. Andropov?
RUSSIAN MAN: Well, that will depend on the Czechoslovakian authorities already. Uh, but anyway, I ask to find, eh, the ways and means of, eh, trying to arrange something, eh, to give you a chance to meet somebody from higher up. Because it's all unexpected, you know, had it been known couple of weeks ago, or a few days ago, uh, but with, eh, holidays and—
MOM (offscreen): I did get in touch with your Soviet Consulate General in San Francisco, who's been most helpful. And I sent a cable. So they did know.
RUSSIAN MAN: Probably they sent, uh . . . the word since you came through the help of Intourist. And probably they sent, eh, advice to Intourist to look after you and so on, but, uh . . .
MOM (offscreen): They didn't know we were so determined.

Both of them laugh.

RUSSIAN MAN: They didn't know you were so determined! That's right.

MOM (offscreen): We can only be determined with your help.

(The Russian man stammers out a few more words, totally off-guard.)

We pan to an older Russian woman, who sits next to the Russian man. She listens stoically.

MOM (offscreen): We feel—and I've often made this description—and walking through the snow today and watching those snowflakes fall — we don't see that in California.

RUSSIAN MAN (offscreen): Yeah.

MOM (offscreen): Unless we're in the mountains. I said we are but snowflakes. We—all of us—are the snowflakes that go to make up the snowball that will create the avalanche for peace.

We pan back to the Russian man, who suppresses a smile.

MOM (offscreen): And we have to start with the snowflakes.

RUSSIAN MAN: And it's important that we shouldn't be melted!

We pan back to Mom, who smiles and nods.

MOM: That's right!

The whole room laughs. Mom claps.

MOM: And that's why we're so determined. So if you would give us an answer when you get it about where we can deliver this mail, the children and I and all of the adults who are with us will be more than happy to lug it to any place we have to carry it.

We pan back to the Russian man.

RUSSIAN MAN: What, eh, what are your plans for today, eh, I mean this afternoon and tomorrow?

MOM (offscreen): Our plans are to deliver the mail.

RUSSIAN MAN: No, I mean today.

We pan back to Mom.

MOM: Anything we have planned to do, we can cancel.

RUSSIAN MAN (offscreen): Where will you *be?*

MOM: Well, we'll have to ask our guide, who knows more about where we
  will be than we know where we will be. But I think we were to go shopping
  this afternoon, which is not important to us. The mail is important. In the
  United States, we have a saying: "The mail must go through. Through
  rain and snow and sleet and dark of night."

The Soviets conferred. I was two seats away, so I heard Mom say softly to another adult on the trip, while the Soviets were occupied, *"Where's Prague?"*

The meeting was wrapping up. We would not be leaving our mail here, as
they wanted us to. Mom said, "Thank you very much. Thank you for your work
on behalf of peace. We love you for it. We appreciate you for it. And we hope
that what we have done today will help further the cause of peace, because that's
all important to all of us and that is why we are here. So we give you our hearts
and we hope to give someone our mail."

Then I lit a candle, and the meeting was done.

BACK ON the bus, Mom called an impromptu meditation.

She said, "Picture us being received in the Kremlin. Picture Mr. Andropov ac-
cepting the mail. *Reading* the mail." We all closed our eyes and breathed in the
bus fumes. When we opened them Val said, "Eet weel note heppen." He scoffed.
"You will not be invited to Kremlin. No one is invited to Kremlin."

"I see it happening. It will happen. I believe in miracles," Mom said. "Why are
you so negative, Val?"

WHEN WE got back to the hotel (after shopping at the hard currency store,
where Mom purchased caviar and lacquer boxes) an envoy was waiting in the
huge marble lobby. He pulled Mom aside and told her that he needed all our
passport numbers and names. He was sweaty and breathless with excitement.
There would be a meeting in the Kremlin first thing the next morning. We
would be received by Vitaly Petrovich Ruben, head of the chamber of national-

ities, one of the two chambers of the Supreme Soviet. I can only imagine what they thought of Mom. She was something they'd never seen before. She was a shining advertisement for every new product the West had to offer. She had come to them talking of peace, telling them, "Shopping isn't important to us." She wanted them. And they wanted her.

THE NEXT MORNING we drove through a guarded gate to the Kremlin.

"I promised you a miracle, Val," Mom said as we passed through clean and beautifully cobbled streets in the private part of the fortress. "Here it is. Ta-da."

Val was silent, better dressed than usual, not smoking.

We pulled up to a large, yellow, stone building, entered through a side door, checked coats, and then, four at a time, ascended to an upper floor in a private elevator, which was quiet, wood-paneled, and red-carpeted. There was an elevator operator dressed in livery. Everything felt different here than in the rest of Russia—the product of a different country than the one that had made the rooms and elevators at the Cosmos. This was not the Soviet Peace Committee. Henry Kissinger had ridden in this elevator.

When everyone had arrived a man led us down a wide, silent corridor that had begun at the elevator. He hurried. Red carpet ran up stairs and around corners. A few hundred feet of hallway later we stepped through a door into a room full of black-suited men. Several poles of television lights lit up—*whoomp!*—and the details of the room became unnaturally, flamingly distinct. The red room was on fire. Shutters were released and flashes popped.

Mom lit her own smile like a torch for the cameras. She smiled and smiled and smiled. This was what she'd come for. She was home. When those lights came on she was back on T.V., putting on a show. Then, still smiling, she turned to Val and without breaking the smile said, "Val, are you the same person who told us we were crazy? That we would never be received in the Kremlin?"

More shutters. Val, also barely moving his mouth, said, "Eye doan't beleeve eet."

"Believe it, Val," Mom said. "It's happening."

I wondered if there was going to be vodka at this meeting.

A valet in a gray suit led us into a paneled room of cool magnificence, with a connecting door to the chambers of the Supreme Soviet (which they showed us later). Mom went first. I followed. The room was Chairman Vitaly Petrovich Ruben's "office study." Floor-to-ceiling windows with thick, white drapes looked out over wooded Kremlin grounds. There was a large desk and a grandfather clock. Glass-fronted bookcases were built into the wood panel and filled with leatherbound Marx in Cyrillic. There were strange buttons and switches in the wall. In front of us was a long, clean, polished conference table. Plush armchairs surrounded it. At six places (for ambassadors without portfolio) were red, intimately detailed, Kremlin-shaped boxes containing Soviet chocolates (chalky, unmeltable). Silver trays of refreshments were laid out—an amber liquid called kvass, no Pepsi here, other multicolored liquids in bottles, fruit. Elsewhere on the table were napkins, glasses, knives for slicing apples. The wood paneling ran ten feet up the walls and stopped five feet before the ceiling, where portraits of Lenin and Brezhnev hung. There was an oriental carpet on the floor. I was awestruck.

The muzzled press followed us in and set up their television and radio equipment on the far side of the room, near the windows.

Mom said, "Oh, how pretty! How nice! How nice to see everybody. Where should we go?"

The valet in gray said, "Please," and indicated a solid, very red man, with lank, fluorescent white hair, wearing a black, pin-striped suit, a subtly striped tie, and silver sunglasses with yellow lenses: Chairman Vitaly Petrovich Ruben.

Ruben bellowed in Russian: "Welcome, American children, to Mordor—also known as the *Kremlin!* Recent home of *Stalin!* Lord of the dread Nazgûl. Also, Sauron, who will awaken again to glory some black day—presently he sleeps below, in Red Square, in his dread mausoleum! Have you seen it?"

A young translator with acne and a nasal voice translated, simply, "We would like to welcome you here in Kremlin."

Mom stared at the translator for a second before she realized he was finished. She said, "Thank you."

Ruben spoke more Russian. Mom smiled. "And I'd also like to meet my young friends! Please."

Mom said, "Yes, yes, let me get out of the way!"

Ruben went to Rachel, bent over, and said, "I would be glad to shake your hand!" Then he shook all of our hands, looked at the banner, and said, "The poster is very expressive!" Cameras flashed. The translator continued madly translating. "I understand it as expressing the desire of all the peoples on earth to live in *peace*." More cameras clicked and flashed. "Now I may invite you, my dear friends, to be seated at the table."

Reporters, aides, Ruben, underlings, us—we all sat around the table. Ruben had perfect posture when sitting.

Mom said, "I can see that you're very good with children!"

Ruben shrugged and removed his sunglasses. The grandfather clock chimed.

Mom looked up in wonder and said, "Oh, how beautif—" But Ruben cut her off. He began speaking without pause—at unbelievable length—blinking frequently.

"Dear Mrs. Montandon, distinguished ladies, and my dear young guests, my friends, the children of the United States of America. I am glad to welcome you here in my office. As you can see, this is an office which is not very large . . . but we the Soviet people have a saying which has it that even if there is not very much space around, everybody can be comfortable. The more so the closer are the ranks of the partisans of peace, the more assurance we can have that peace on earth will be eternal!"

I looked around. The place was gigantic. Ruben was at the head of the table. In front of him were two phones, one a rotary, the other some sort of special push button in case he needed to order up some MiGs, or a missile strike. In the middle of the rotary phone was the Soviet sickle and oak-leaf cluster. In front of the phones, facing us, was an ornate pen holder, with two pens, and an even more ornate, wood-and-gold Faberge-style clock. The translator, on Ruben's left, scribbled on a pad of paper, trying to keep up.

"I'm very glad to have both the privilege and the chance to meet with the future of America, the American children. In this study as well as in the Kremlin Palace, I have had meetings with American senators. In particular it was in 1975 when Yuri Aleksandrovich Zhukov [head of the Peace Committee] present here today with us and myself met with a delegation of American senators led by the late Senator Humphrey and Senator Hugh Scott, who is now retired from active political life, and during those meetings we have talked about peace since the atmosphere was undoubtedly favorable at that time for such kind of conversation between us. And I must be frank to say that at that time, the atmosphere for a talk was more favorable than it is now, when I'm having the privilege to meet the future of America, American children. In the first place, I'd like to tell my dear guests very shortly about what the Soviet Union, about what the Union of Soviet Socialist Republics is. About one hundred and thirty nations and nationalities live in the Soviet Union, in the Union of Soviet Socialist Republics. And all our peoples, regardless of race, color, or religious faith are absolutely equal."

I looked out the window. There was a big cathedral out there. *Where is Mount Doom?* I wondered. *I must sneak away from this meeting and find it. I will throw the ring into its fiery depths. I will ask to use the bathroom . . .*

Ruben looked at Mom, said something in Russian, and she laughed insanely.

I spaced out again. Ruben was talking about the Soviet Union's many allies, its various Autonomous Oblasts and Autonomous Okrugs, the men of Far Harad who would come if Gondor chose to make war. He said, "I'd like to reemphasize that all of those people regardless of their faith or race or color or nationality are absolutely equal in their rights. And I am not merely talking of an article in the constitution of the USSR, which provides for the equality of peoples in the Soviet Union. For it is a genuine and true equality in everything and every sphere of life. It is an economic equality between all of our nations and nationalities. Peoples of all nations in the Soviet Union have jobs. We have no unemployment. All our peoples have equal access to the achievements of our multinational culture."

"Can *we* say that in this country?" I would say to Dad, parroting Ruben upon my return home. "No!" I was liking this guy. The Kremlin wasn't Mordor at all!

The translator kept translating: "And education is free of charge for all. It is free of charge starting from the elementary school and up to the highest grades of education. The common language of communication between all of the nationalities in the Soviet Union is the Russian language. But in every republic children are taught in schools both in their native language and in Russian. They also can study various foreign languages according to their options. It is sometimes claimed about that in the Soviet Union a sort of a Russification is underway with regard to all of the population. I will try to show you whether it's true or not on the example of my own family. I am a Latvian. My wife is Russian. My junior grandson, Vitaly Petrovich Ruben, Jr., is studying at a secondary school in Riga, and from the first grade he's been studying English. All teaching in that school is in English, but children also study Russian and the Latvian languages. As of today my grandson already has a perfect knowledge of Russian, Latvian, and English."

Ruben gestured "no" with a wagging index finger, then held up three fingers.

"But he is not content with command of only three languages! For a year already he has been studying Italian in an optional course. . . . Dear young American friends—we Latvians have a saying. A saying which has it that you are as many times a man as many languages you know."

Mom, in a Southern belle voice, said, *"My."*

I spaced back out. Were these phones for calling in missile strikes? The clock would be a good place to keep the launch codes. And if Ruben and Zhukov were to spin the two fancy pens in the pen holder, in synchronicity, then maybe the clock would open and . . .

Waitresses in matching red dresses began to serve us tea in glass cups.

Ruben was back on American senators. "Myself, I have talked about it with senators Humphrey and Scott. At this very table I have told this to Senator Cranston and Mr. Mondale. And I can also remember other responsible and well-known Americans who are in charge of ensuring the well-being of the American people, the security of the American people and other peoples on earth who are responsible for the destiny of all mankind. To my profound regret, I must admit that so far those talks that we've had with them all and the dialogue that we've had and my attempts to convince them of our sincere desire for peace have been *fruitless.*"

His voice grew grave and entreating. "My dear young friends, American children, I can assure you, I'd like to assure you in all sincerity that the Soviet Union will never start a war against anybody who does not attack it."

I was completely convinced.

"I know that you have brought here with you a message to Yuri Vladimirovich Andropov. I have seen the sacks that you have brought here to my study. I believe that with all the sincerity, with all the purest sincerity of children you have expressed your dearest wish to live long on our old mother Earth. And this is also the desire of my junior grandson that I've talked about to you of, Vitaly Petrovich Ruben, Jr., who has already studied many languages in order to make friends with many children and many people round the globe, and so that in future there be no kind of iron curtains dividing us and also no language barriers, which are also sometimes difficult to cross too."

Mom gazed at Ruben with rapt, devouring attention.

Ruben smiled, gestured wildly. "So please believe I'll be very glad to accept your letters to Comrade Yuri Vladimirovich Andropov, and I shall hand them over to him and we shall consider those letters as the most serious and most sincere expression of your desire to live in peace and to cooperate peacefully with us!"

This seemed to conclude one phase of his remarks. Now he talked of U.S. aggression and of the unrequited efforts of the Soviet Union to reduce its nuclear arsenal, made baffling references to SALT ratifications that the U.S. had delayed, and told us in detail about all our ordnance, its overwhelming quantity and wide dispersal.

And there was something charming about this. I liked him a lot. He would be a fun grandfather. It would be cool to come and stay with him for the summer, maybe learn Latvian, meet some attractive Soviet girls. They were *totally* attractive! All those rumors about Russian females being ugly were wrong. There were a lot of lies going around in America, and I'd have to straighten them out when I got home. What Ruben was saying made a lot of sense. He ordered an aide to distribute a stack of books and pamphlets on the subject of disarmament.

The grandfather clock chimed.

I wondered, *Why do we have all these missiles pointed at this country of chocolate Kremlins?* I felt sure that Dad would have a hard time explaining. I would nail him on this point.

Ruben had not touched his tea. Mine was gone. He said, "I would like to conclude my statement. I'm not quite sure, though, if I have managed to make my message clear to you that the Soviet people seeks friendship, peace, and cooperation with all the peoples on Earth and, in particular among them, with the people— or it would be even more precise to say the peoples—of the United States?!"

I thought, *It's totally clear! And this is good news!*

"Did I make it quite clear to you?"

We all hollered, *"Yes!"*

He added, "And let me stress that in my eyes you are not less important, responsible, and serious as representatives of your country than are the adults, the official representatives like senators, vice presidents, congressmen, and others who come here to have talks with us. And I believe in your sincere and strong desire to live in peace and to preserve peace on Earth forever. I would like you to excuse me for abusing your attention, for as far as I know in American schools lessons are sort of shorter than the conversation we have just had. Thank you for your attention once again, and please dear Mrs. Montandon, if you have something to say, Mr. Zhukov and myself would be happy to listen to you."

Mom said, "Thank you, thank you very much, Mr. Zhukov, Chairman Ruben. We come to you with love, pure innocence, and caring about all the children of the world."

The translator translated.

"I think it was *appropriate* that when we walked in, the clock was chiming." A pause. Mom looked at the translator. He let her go on. "Because we feel we're working under the stress of time for peace and there isn't that much time left for any of us unless we *actively* achieve peace and work at it. Perhaps the most simple way of expressing ourselves is sometimes the most effective. And the children, *Children As Teachers of Peace*, have a clarity of vision without *ego*, without the *facade* we all build in order to get through life."

The translator translated. Ruben nodded, frowned, pointed to Mom, said, "I very much agree with you."

"Ah. I'm so glad!" Mom said.

Smiles were exchanged. Mom continued, slowly, pausing for translation every tenth word.

"It seems to me that you were talking about communication. And communication is the essential thing that will bring peace." Courteous Translation Pause. "Nineteen eighty-three, this brand new year we have just entered [C.T.P.] has been declared by the United Nations to be the year of communication. [C.T.P.] The children have communicated, all of the children, your children as well as ours, through their drawings. [C.T.P.] Their drawings are all alike. Whatever children we're dealing with, their drawings say the same things. [C.T.P.] They want to live in peace. They don't want bombs. This is a child from the Pioneer Palace."

She handed Ruben a drawing.

"There's always sunshine, there are rainbows, and they invariably say 'no bombs.' [C.T.P., during which Mom stared into Ruben's eyes, then gestured across the table.] Our children say the same thing. [C.T.P.] June first has been declared 'Child Protection Day.' [C.T.P. The clock chimed again. Mom looked at it lovingly, then continued with great intensity.] And it seems *appropriate* that on that day we should have a *giant, satellite hook-up* with a *giant television* screen which has been available to us in many nations throughout the world where we connect and where we communicate with directness and honesty and we really see each other as we are. [C.T.P.] We have with us a camera crew, Eli and Rob, who are doing a *documentary* of our trip. [C.T.P.] So what we're saying, and what you were saying and what has been said by the *pope*, what has been said in the *United States*, what will be said to us in *Egypt*, will not only reach our small group, but millions of people we represent, children all over the world. [C.T.P.] I think it's best now if I let each child present you with a token letter, then give you the bag of mail, if you can tell us where the mail can be placed, and they will read to you a token letter because we want the children to speak. They speak much better than I do. [C.T.P.] Rachel Skiffer, who is eight years old, will you present Chairman Ruben with your—"

Before Mom could finish, Rachel, brandishing a big piece of construction paper, said, "Kiss and make up. To Mr. Andropov and Mr. Reagan." Then she mumbled, "Read by Rachel," and showed the drawing to Ruben.

Mom said solemnly, "'*Kiss and make up.*'"

Ruben, pointing at Rachel, said, "Mr. Andropov is ready to do that and Mr. Reagan should also get ready!"

Rachel dumped out her sack on a table. Mom said, "Now I must tell you something very funny. [C.T.P.] We've been traveling since December twenty-fifth at seven-fifteen in the morning. [C.T.P.] And in taking mail for President Reagan, for Pope Paul, for the president of Egypt, as well as Mr. Andropov, some of it has gotten mixed up. [C.T.P.] So you may get a letter or two for President Reagan and he may get a letter or two for Mr. Andropov."

More laughter from the press. Ruben laughed and said, "I'll send them over to him."

Mom said, "And that may be a very good thing, to read each other's mail!" (This inspired line, ad-libbed here, was something Mom would wind up saying to half the world's leaders.)

I stood up and presented Chairman Ruben with a drawing (not the Peace Frog—Mom had nixed that) and told him, "Peace is helping each other."

Chopping the air with his hand, while angling his body at me, he shouted back something grandiose. I tried to get away, but he wouldn't let me. The translator said, "That's quite true. A *perfect* truth and an *eternal* truth."

I asked Ruben if they'd send Russian kids to America.

Ruben said, "Please know we shall always welcome and support such initiatives as yours, and will give your proposal the most serious consideration."

I thought this was kind of a dodge. But that was O.K. He probably had to talk to Andropov.

Mom said, "If we may, Chairman Ruben, we would like to light a candle for peace. We carry them with us for this purpose."

Ruben said, "I will be grateful to you. It is noble to cast light into the world."

Jonathan Dearman lit a votive candle in an ashtray on Ruben's desk and said, "I'm lighting this candle to unite the leaders and adults of our countries, hoping they can see with our eyes. The children are already united."

Ruben said, "Thank you for coming. Your visit gives us hope," and the meeting broke up.

In *Whispers from God* Mom describes what happened next:

Just across the threshold of the building, still on Kremlin territory, Sean yelled, "We did it!" Raquel, Matthew, Jonathan, Rachel, Patrick, the camera crew, we all responded, "We Did It!" The words echoed and re-echoed across the tundra [there wasn't really any tundra], circling the golden onion domes, attracting the attention of four guards. They stood watching us, young men, not knowing what to do as we began throwing snowballs at each other, and at Val. We were acting like crazy people.

And then half laughing, half crying, we came together and, right there, within the walls of the Kremlin, under the Soviet flag, and near an enormous mural of Lenin, we howled with joy.

We had lit a candle for peace in the Supreme Soviet, talked about the similarities between our children and theirs, and we had asked for an end to the cold war, and an exchange of children. All the things we had set out to do only a few days before.

As we stood there, under the perplexed gaze of Russian solders, not feeling the cold, for a brief moment even Val allowed a flicker of emotion to cross his face, as we, with American exuberance, included him in our warm embrace.

After this we were greeted by banks of press wherever we went. Everything we did was a news story, broadcast throughout the Soviet Union.

We were taken to a winter carnival, given horse-drawn sleigh rides, and more vodka. The next day, at a huge communist youth activity center called the Pioneer Palace, thousands of kids, a whole stadium worth, wearing red rayon kerchiefs and white shirts, danced for us, and then with us, pulling us out onto the floor, and gave us Lenin pins while clattering newsreel cameras and sixties-looking television equipment filmed everything: Mom striding valiantly through the snow, in sumptuous designer boots trimmed with fur and leather, her own film crew racing ahead of her, banner unfurled behind, looking like a revolutionary icon come to life in a fashion shoot.

There was brief confusion when Mom stepped off the path and grabbed two small children, bundled in huge, down coats. She snatched them away from their mother, and continued walking proudly with them holding each of her hands, the mother chasing after, increasingly frightened (but out of the frame), the children unable to resist the thrill of it all, the lights and cameras and this blond American movie star who was now saying to all the Russian children, to the T.V. and radio people, to the reporters from TASS and *Pravda*, to her own documentary film crew, "I love you! I love you! I love you!" shouting it, getting Soviet kids to take up the call, making all of us do it, too, throwing the words like flowers into the crowd, "I love you! I love you! I love you!" She asked Val how to say "I love you" in Russian.

"*Ya lyublyu vas,*" he said. Then Mom cried out, as loud as she could, full of joy, "Yellow blue bus! Yellow blue bus! Yellow blue bus!" to the left, to the right, right at the cameras. "I loav you! I loav you! I loav you!" Delighted like a child, like a star, she took a bouquet of flowers, and in a huge chorus of "I love you"s ascended into the bus, hugging, kissing, kissing, kissing, throwing kisses everywhere, letting go of the children, whose mother ran to retrieve them. Then back to the Cosmos, where she prepared some chocolate flavored Alba 77, the diet shake powder she consumed in lieu of food and made in a blender that she carried with her and which, along with the necessary plug and voltage adapters, took up half a Louis Vuitton bag.

This scene, on Soviet television that night, became a refrain. It was like coming home for Mom. Coming home to the sixties. Coming home to fame. It was coming home to her childhood of church, and siblings, too. All these children combined with all this singing and public adulation. She wanted it over and over again. And I saw her repeat it many times, in Moscow, in Cairo a few days later, pinning C.A.T.[o.]P. buttons onto the rags of street kids, walking with a throng of more button-wanting kids, begging and screaming behind her, saying, "I love you," in Arabic, and it always filled me with anxious amazement to see my mother plunging into crowds of children drinking up their love and vowing to represent their needs as "the most powerless group in society."

At the end of that first trip, when we got to Egypt, we saw Madame Sadat, on whom Mom had modeled herself so successfully, and it was strange to see them together. *Now there are two of them.* We were greeted with much fanfare in the former presidential residence. I have a cool photograph of myself with Mrs. Sadat. I'm wearing a Bedouin headdress and we're standing together in front of a huge oil painting of Anwar Sadat in full military regalia. A few months later Mrs. Sadat invited me to spend the summer with her, but Mom refused to let me go. Though she did take me on two more trips. I had a good time writing "stud" on numerous customs forms, in the blank for "profession," showing it to Mom, watching her freak out—"You've ruined this! Now they won't let you into the country!"—then adding "ent." The joke never got old.

I met Helmut Kohl, Indira Gandhi, and Menachem Begin. Kohl slapped me on the back and told me I reminded him of himself. I said, sincerely, "Peace to me is something you really have to work for and get out and really . . . try your best." He grabbed my face, in an affectionate, Germanic, statesmanlike way. Mom grabbed his hand and held it while we sang. Indira Gandhi told me, with great sincerity, "Try and convince people and see that the movement for peace is not a political movement but a real people's movement." Menachem Begin had really bad teeth and looked baffled by everything we were doing, especially Mom holding his hand. He pulled away and patted hers. In Hiroshima a man recounted his experiences on the day of the atomic bomb. A woman told us about having to strip naked before a panel of radiation experts. I realized that what we were doing mattered.

I also began to realize that nothing could be too grand or surreal for Mom: a processional through the Arc de Triomphe with children singing "Peace, peace, peace! Pat, Pat, Pat!"; a crowd of admirers bowing before her as she stepped from behind a silk curtain in the Forbidden City, *Last Emperor*-style; standing atop the Great Pyramid of Giza in a flowing white dress with doves wheeling about her head and the desert sands below covered with cheering, weeping crowds of children. Imagination was the only limit.

MOM WOULD GO on to create many moments of profound grandeur and sur-reality. She airlifted a twenty-foot replica of the Statue of Liberty to Moscow and asked permission to erect it in Red Square. She learned the Russian word *"Chaika!"*—limousine—and repeated it over and over again, shouting, "I love you!" and "Limousine!" to the crowds and T.V. cameras. She gave a Dior night-gown to a starving child in an Ethiopian famine camp. She gave "the key to our hearts and the key to my apartment in San Francisco!" (gold plated, on a Tiffany key chain) to numerous Eastern European leaders as a gesture of goodwill. She auctioned her clothes and jewelry in the ballroom of the Fairmont hotel, raising over two hundred thousand dollars to fund the International Children's Peace Prize. She got West Germany, China, the Soviet Union, and India to send chil-dren to the Peace Prize ceremonies, taking money from their defense budgets to pay for the travel. She dressed exclusively in white robes and a dove-of-peace choker one year (after selling her wardrobe). She dressed exclusively in Indian saris the next year. She got Indira Gandhi and Zhao Ziyang, the premier of China, to sign a document called the "Declaration of *Dependence*." She tried to get Rajiv Gandhi to sign another that read, "I do hereby pledge to the children of the world that as proof of my country's most sincere desire to be peaceful we will dismantle one of our most powerful weapons of war in a public ceremony within one month of signing this document." (Rajiv said, "It has to start with the big powers.") Mom, hair flowing, stood in a white, ruffled, floor-length gown, with décolleté galore, and a huge black bow on her shoulder, while Gorbachev told her, "Your activity is a sign of the times in which we live. Times character-ized by the real direct involvement of the peoples of the world in international affairs." She was an honored guest at the opening ceremonies of the World Congress of Women, in Moscow, seated on the dais with Gorbachev, and next to Fidel Castro's sister. When she got up to speak, with her hair flowing, all in white, a C.A.T.[o.]P. pin at her shoulder, her latest project, "The Banner of Hope," was unfurled by children who came marching down the aisles. A boy declared, "On the banner we have brought into this hall are written the names of *children* killed by the violence of war! We want to live! We want to grow! We want to see! We want to know! We want to share! What we can give! We want to live!" A crescendo of music rose and a small Japanese girl came racing up to Gorbachev with a crystal globe from Mom. He picked up the girl, gave Mom a meaningful look, teared up, pulled a handkerchief from his right jacket pocket, then held the globe up while he and Mom smiled to a cheering standing ovation from the crowd. It was the highlight of Mom's life.

When I asked Mom for help getting the facts straight about her peace work and the various world leaders she'd met on her thirty-three trips with children, she sent me the following e-mail back:

Subject: World figures/& Leaders

I gave up and typed the list into my e-mail.
President Mikhail Gorbachev - many times
Raisa Maximovna Gorbachev - many times - very kind
Prime Minister Indria Gandhi - New Delhi
Prime Minister Rajiv Gandhi - New Delhi
The Peoples Republic of China, Premier Zhao Ziyang
Chancellor Helmut Kohl
Pope John Paul II - 2 times
Mother Teresa - in Calcutta
PM Menachem Begin - Israel
Prime Minister of Iraq - Mouidin - I think. His name was the same as the
    PM of Egypt
Madame Jehan Sadat
Prime Minister Gro Harlem Bruntland - Norway
King Olaf - Norway
Prime Minister of Egypt - Mouidin
President Oscar Arias - Costa Rica
Soviet Ambassador Yuri Dubinin (very well known and important)
President Shevardnadze, of Georgia - formerly Soviet Georgia
President Ronald Reagan (actually I didn't meet him but [the kids] were
    whisked away for the "accidental" meeting, purportedly in the hall of
    the white house, I was ignored)
President Bill Clinton - at a social, read: fundraising, event in SF I pressed
    my advantage but alas to no avail—too old I suppose.
Vice President Ulanhu, PRC
His Holiness the Dalai Lama
Queen Noor of Jordan - her husband, the late King Hussein, interceded
    for us to get our visas to go to Baghdad

Many different ministers of the Supreme Soviet - Substantive meetings.

Valentina Tereshkova, the first woman in space, a cosmonaut, was quite
  helpful to me during the Gorbachev reign

Sean do you remember when we were in Turkey and went to a museum.
  People holding flags were lining the road, and while you went to get us
  tickets, the President of Hungary arrived. I was standing at the
  entrance to the museum and the man got out of his limo, walked up to
  me, bowed slightly and then shook my hand as if I were the official
  greeter. Funny.

And on our African Trip the Prince of Swaziland joined us. A TV crew
  and still photographer arrived at our camp to film the Prince. My photo
  ended up on the front page of the Beira, Mozambique paper with the
  caption Papsie Lou Wilsey, bla, bla, bla. you were hiding in my belly at
  the time. But I'll bet you remember it!

I do seem to attract these incidents from the old world members of this and
  that. Remember the letter I got from Yeltsin regarding his gratitude for
  the humanitarian aid? Did me a lot of good with the Mafia!

But for all the good intentions and gratifying spectacle, Mom was no less mercurial and unhappy. She could still turn in an instant. In India some kids had a
pillow fight, got too loud, were told by migrainous Mom to be quiet, and then
half an hour later, I was jumping in the hall with my friend Kei Grant, who was
like a black Blanc Morf (ironic and kind), laughing and shouting, when Mom
threw open her door, hair full of rollers and beauty chemicals, and said she'd
had it with us. She called a trip meeting to tell us what *disgraces* we were and that
she was sending us all home—Indira Gandhi be damned. An inexorable, solemn
guilting ensued that felt totally arbitrary (*she said no pillow fighting, not no jumping and laughing*) and left us with no option but to abase ourselves completely
and apologize with such slavishness that we were like sinners recanting heresies
against Mom, patron saint of Peace and Glamour. We apologized. And then,
with a frown and a raised nose, Mom said, "O.K." We could stay.

In 1985 I played her the Sting song "Russians." It was a peace song, and I
thought she'd like it. It seemed perfect for her: "Believe me when I say to you/I
hope the Russians love their children, too."

Mom said, "That's ridiculous! Of course they love their children! Turn
that off!"

She could be warm and embracing and outgoing to an extreme, and to that same extreme she could be cold and haughty and imperious. In 1986, the year Elie Wiesel won the Nobel Peace Prize, she was nominated by a member of the Nobel committee she'd met in Scandinavia, and she worked hard to get the nomination seconded by a number of politicians in the U.S. She was convinced she'd win. "Somebody has to win, why not me? I *will* win the Nobel Peace Prize, Sean," she said (over and over). "It will be a wonderful affirmation for our work." A friend even gave her an executive desk bauble, a glass pyramid with the words "Pat Montandon Oslo 1986" suspended in its crystal depths. When it was announced that Wiesel had won, Mom, crushed, threw the pyramid into a mirror. It bounced off and hit my leg. I picked it up. Cracked at its heart. Mom locked herself in her room, pulled all the drapes, and ate ice cream. It was the introverted opposite of her one-woman "I love you!" parades. I got her a silver cup at a trophy store and wrote the words "A. Nobel Mom Prize" on it in paint pen.

I imagined calling the Nobel committee and saying, "Please give your award to Mom and save my ass."

I imagined telling Mom, "Maybe you could get the Nobel *Tantrum* Prize," and her saying, "There is no Nobel Tantrum Prize! Don't be ridiculous, Sean!"

But what she was doing was also so sincere and moving, and when she was doing it she gave me the best experiences of my childhood. We'd go around the world, to fame, accolades, and adventure, then back to San Francisco, the penthouse, her bedroom, loneliness, the curtains drawn. No friends but the people who occasionally recognized her from mornings home sick in their sixties childhoods, spent in front of the T.V. No one to talk to but employees. Not a single intimate but me. With all her extreme behavior Mom became the source of all my humor. And half my despair.

Upon our triumphant returns from these trips Mom, whose primary experience with children had been with me, became the great friend and advocate of children. Where once she had been photographed with celebrities at her famous parties, now she was photographed with children. To promote her Children's Peace Prize, Mom posed under the dramatic rotunda of city hall, surrounded by kids with olive branch crowns on their heads. She posed in black in front of a black backdrop surrounded by a group of eighteen multiethnic kids, all of them wearing black and holding up their hands making peace signs. In the printed photo all you see is darkness with lots of smiling, rainbow-complected faces and peace signs and Mom's radiant smile, halo of hair, her lightning-strike zigzag of a commanding, broken nose, and her resolute jaw, shining out at you.

## *Eight* · DAD'S HOUSE

AFTER RETURNING FROM that first trip in 1983, my head full of Chairman Ruben and the pope, it was time to go back to Dad's. I had almost forgotten what life was like over there. Dad picked me up downstairs at Mom's, and in the car he asked me, "So, now that you've been all over the world, do you think your mother has accomplished anything with this peace business?"

I thought so. I loved Mom. I admired her. I had seen her do unbelievable things.

"No."

This was the correct answer. And it pleased Dad. My end of the deal, implicit in him asking me this question, was to say no. The dismissive psychoanalysis of Mom was one of the only things Dad and I could collaborate on. Dad seemed to love me when we were dismissing her together.

He said, "Your mother is awfully good at playing the star."

I said, "She's great at that."

"But she's self-destructive. She shoots herself in the foot."

"Yep."

"She just wants press, Sean. I know that from experience. Your mom's happy if she's in the newspapers. That's all that's important to her. What she's doing now is not really for peace. Your mother doesn't care about peace. She cares about herself. She cares about publicity. And if the press isn't paying attention to her, she's miserable. If your mother had worked half as hard at being a wife as she did at being a star we'd still be married."

I started to turn on him. *Not this shit about how you'd still be married,* I thought. *Maybe you'd still be married if you hadn't slept with her best friend.* It would take me years to say this out loud.

Dad went on. "She may get a lot of press in Russia. But it's not a free press. And those Russians don't care about peace. They're just using your mother to make us look bad."

Chairman Ruben had given me a book on the arms race called *Whence the Threat to Peace*. The first part of the title appeared at the top of the cover— *Whence the Threat*—and the second part—*to Peace*—at the bottom. In between flew an American ICBM, fire pouring out of its tail, the words U.S. Air Force written in big black caps on the side. The meaning being, as I understood it, *"This Is Whence."*

The threat to peace was coming from the U.S. of Fucking A.! The book detailed, in page after page, our purchasing and deploying of nuclear missiles, and our outstrippage of the Russians on both fronts. Maps showed our missile emplacements in Germany and Turkey, pointed at nearby Moscow, while their missiles huddled in sad little clusters thousands of miles away from America, waiting for bread or something. Blue missile icons outnumbered red ones all over the globe. American tanks massed on the borders of Eastern Europe. American subs prowled the Pacific. American medium-range mobile nuclear missile launchers crawled all over Europe. Our bases were spread across Japan. It was outrageous!

At home Dad's taxes were low. His portfolio was rising. With his marriage to Dede he'd finally joined the social aristocracy he so admired. He'd established permanent residence in a lavishly renovated mansion, in the best neighborhood in San Francisco. ("Specific Whites," as Spencer called Pacific Heights.) He owned his own jet. Dede's parents and their Newport, Rhode Island, old-money society had embraced him. He flew to London and dined at "Harry's Club"—members only—right next to Fergie. He was having the best days of his life. In his office was a framed caricature of Ronald Reagan, thumbing his nose at the world.

I said, "Yeah, well, it's pretty *easy* to make this country look bad and attack its commitment to peace and diplomacy using the actual facts—I mean, did you know that the United States has enough missiles and . . . bombs . . ." *Was that right? Did we still even have bombs?* . . . "in its nuclear arsenal to destroy the entire planet more than one hundred times?" The words came out quickly. I wondered if I was exaggerating, and Dad would use this against me, pointing out dismissively that we could only destroy the world, like, a dozen times. What did "destroy the world" mean, anyway? All life extinguished, but the rock and core still around? Or the whole thing blown up like Alderaan—Princess Leia's home planet in *Star Wars*—after the Death Star fired its beam? Obi-Wan would say, "I felt a great disturbance in the force, as if millions of voices suddenly cried out in terror and were suddenly silenced"? If that was the deal, then the United States was one hundred times *more powerful* than the Galactic Empire!

"Unlike in the USSR," I said, "the U.S. education budget is just a fraction of the defense budget. I mean, we're not even at war!"

Dad had a *Where (Whence?) do I even begin?* look on his face. He said, "I would be happy to explain the doctrine of deterrence and mutually assured destruction to you at some point."

I said, "Yeah, yeah—I know about that. It's completely crazy!"

He snapped, "Taking a bunch of kids around the world, in my opinion, is crazy! Thanks to that defense budget, and the stimulation it's giving to the economy, which trickles down to all parts of the population, you won't have to work and struggle like I did when you get out of college, if you even *get* to college, which, with your poor grades, I doubt. You're going to have to do a *heck* of a lot better. I wanted to go to college but I had to drop out. I had to work because my parents died and left me an orphan when I was seventeen. My brother and I ran the family business. I didn't choose to be born bright and white and in this country of opportunities, but because I was, I was able to do things I wouldn't have been able to do if I were a *communist*. I didn't ask for help. I worked. If I'd had all the opportunities you'd had I certainly wouldn't be a communist."

We were always having some variation on this conversation.

With the Napa Valley getting more and more fashionable, Dad had started describing himself as a "grape grower." It was as if he were no longer in the butter business. As if he were tending his vines all day. On the peace trip I'd heard from Jonathan Dearman—the cool older kid I admired—that alcohol was a bacterial waste product.

Now I said, "So Dad, I recently learned that wine is grape juice mixed with bacteria excrement."

He said, "What?"

I said, "Bacteria excrement. That's what alcohol is. And so bacteria excrement is a big part of wine."

He said, "You don't know anything about wine making."

I said, "Fermentation occurs when the grapes are crushed and bacteria excrete alcohol."

"No."

"*Yes!*"

"No."

"You deny that bacteria excrete alcohol? That that's where it comes from?"

"It comes from bacteria, yes."

"And they're excreting it!"

"It's a by-product."

"It's a *waste* product."

"*By-product.*"

"Like *sweat* then?"

His jaw clenched. He said nothing.

*Ha!*

This ridiculous exchange marked the only time I ever pierced Dad's logic with an observation. I constantly got to him with my actions. But he found my observations and remarks—my brain—easy to ignore, dismiss, defeat.

It was Trevor Dad took seriously, and he was so fond of Todd he'd listen to anything he had to say. We'd arrived at the new mansion now. Todd, Trevor, Dad, and Dede–land, far from Russia and safety. Dad opened the garage door and we drove in.

I ADMIRED my stepbrothers, and I changed in every way I could in order to be like them, and I failed. Todd and Trevor were cool. They *actually were* cool.

It was now January 1983. I was in seventh grade, Todd was in eighth, and Trevor was a freshman at University High, the most exclusive school in the city. Suddenly we were old enough to be into music. They liked the Police. I had not heard of the Police. My favorite song was the theme song from the Royal Viking Star cruise liner. This was a ship that Mom and Dad had taken me on when I was seven. The theme song, played over the public address system whenever we left port, was sung by a falsetto-voiced chorus, and exulted:

*Here she sails away!*
*Like a French chalet!*

*All the lords and ladies smiling!*
*We have left the world on the shore!*
*That's what paradise once was for!*
*We are all aboard . . .*
*Going for-ward!*
*On the Royal Viking Star!*
*On the Royal Viking Star!*

Upon disembarkation the Royal Viking line gave everyone 45s of it. I'd played mine over and over again. It made me cry and my heart soar. It was so totally inspiring!

Todd and Trevor could never know this. Quickly I realized I needed to make the Police my "favorite group," too. And in a way that made it seem like they'd *always* been my favorite group. I also needed to pick a favorite member of the group: Sting, Stewart, or Andy.

Stewart was Todd's. Trevor had Sting. I made Stewart mine, too. I told Todd we were stepbrothers and Stewart brothers! Todd, testing me, asked what phrase Stewart had taped onto the skins of his drum kit. I did not know. Stewart had a different word of the phrase "Fuck Off You Cunt" taped onto each of his drums. Todd pointed this out in some concert footage. "Fuck" "Off" "You" "Cunt" said Stewart's drums, running left to right. Then Todd said, "Fuck off, you cunt, you can't have Stewart, too."

*Oh, O.K.*

I didn't want to piss off Todd, the only member of the family who—in private—was tolerant of my company. I'd take Andy. Absolutely. Of course. *Yeah.* *Andy*'d been my favorite all along. Andy was like me. He was a foot shorter than the others. He'd joined the band late. His name began with a different letter. They bossed him around. As Sting said in an interview about one of their live recordings, "There's a very good Andy solo in there, though it's very short because we only ever let him have eight bars." I spent my allowance on Andy's side project, *I Advance Masked*, which sucked (and was confusingly titled. Was "I" supposed to be first person singular or roman numeral one? I didn't know. I called it *"One Advance Masked"* sometimes and *"I Advance Masked"* other times). Where were all the cool songs? The "Roxanne"s and "De Do Do Do, De Da Da Da"s and "Don't Stand So Close to Me"s? They did not exist! I listened to it anyway. Though I didn't like it, I wanted to be true to Andy.

My new room in the renovated mansion was on the top floor again (though it wasn't an unheated attic). Todd and Trevor's rooms were on the second floor with Dad and Dede. Their rooms were hotel suite–like, with big walk-in closets, deep carpet, immaculate fixtures, cable television, spacious bathrooms, dressing *parlors.* Mine had a walk-in closet, too. But then, since this closet had a second, exterior door, Dede sealed it off and redesignated the space a storage room for the gifts she stockpiled. (It was a very Dede concept—buying presents and not giving them to people.) There was a whole huge basement she could have used, but she chose my closet. The second door connected to a landing where the house's manual, open cab, 1910 elevator stopped. She never went to her gift room via the stairs, which led past my door, but always took the elevator, entering my ex-closet undetected. I'd hear rustling while I was reading and think, *Dede's in my closet.*

I was not supposed to use the elevator. It was for Dad and Dede. Every other week, for the rest of seventh grade, as I tried to be cool, I'd come back to Dad's, run upstairs, put on a Police record, air guitar with Andy, watch MTV, put on red pants that I thought were New Wave cool, put a lot of hair gel in my hair, towel it like mad, get it going in a rock star sort of direction, check myself out in the mirror, air guitar more furiously, avoid homework, and do some cowardly patting down of my hair for dinner, where Todd and Trevor (who had great, naturally thick, wavy, cool-guy tennis-player hair) would dominate the conversation.

WHEN DAD was in his late fifties and still married to Mom, I'd sometimes see him naked, like kids always see their dads naked—and I would stare at what seemed like the ideal body, though it was already a body on the wane: strong, but with loose and lazy skin, muscles hanging a bit, not so firm on the bone, the whole physical impression almost indolent, lounging, careless, like a teenager leaning back in a chair.

And old man/teenager is perfect Dad. He was full of the sureness and weakness of each.

The bathroom was the nude zone for Dad. If we were in there together, neither of us were at all self conscious. I'd be completely impressed by Dad's body, and Dad would enjoy how impressed I was. He would run the razor across his face with a flourish and fart theatrically, while singing songs like "Hinky Dinky Parlay Voo?" or, as a duet with me, "Do Your Ears Hang Low?" If he wasn't naked he'd be wearing only dress socks, and sock garters. A lot of the time he was sitting on the can. He'd let me come in and use his shower. Like most kids, I'd only ever taken baths. He showed me how to shower, grabbing hold and inspecting some part of me in the process—sunken chest, fallen arches—shaking his head in disappointment, and then quickly reassuring me that I still had a "fine, healthy body," and there was lots of time for me to change—and be more like him. These moments were always gentle, if humbling.

Shortly after I returned from the peace trip, Dad sent Clifford Mooney, his retired Marine Corps sergeant major/factotum/revoked Mom-chauffeur, to purchase two metal-handled gas station–style squeegees, tax free, at the Presidio PX. Clifford bought them and put them in the trunk of Dad's car. I met Dad in the garage, we did our furtive hug, he popped the trunk, and handed me a bag.

"This is for you."

I looked in the bag, saw the squeegees, and said, "What are these?"

He said, "They're for you to clean your shower. If you wipe the glass down every day after you shower it'll stay clean."

I took out a squeegee.

"Why are there two? Do I have to do it double-handed?"

"The other one's mine. I'll be doing it, too. Use it after every shower. I'll be coming up to check."

"It'll be like working in a gas station naked, Dad."

Dad gave me a sour look. "Let's go upstairs and I'll show you how to do it." We took the house's elevator. He shut the outer door and safety gate, then pressed the top button. The elevator moved slowly. We watched the concrete shaft go by. Then the concrete stopped and a pair of bare, female legs and a long, chromed, precision-forged helicopter part came into view. This was the bottom of a life-sized, autographed poster—showing a woman in a skimpy blue helicopter mechanic's uniform—that Dad had hung in the elevator shaft. Clifford had brought it back from a convention. Dad chuckled. We kept moving. After a painfully long wait, a saucily outthrust hip appeared. Then a hand high on the hip, a flat stomach, boobs, cleavage, and vertical words:

Sean,
love to you!
Kathy
"Miss Tall
International"
80–81
P.S. You're a
cutie—
Admit it!

Then a big smile, huge blond hair, and the bottom of the door to the next floor.

I always felt humiliated by this poster, which Todd and Trevor and Dad and Dede thought was hilarious. Todd was always talking about sex, quoting the end of *Caddyshack*, when Rodney Dangerfield shouts, "Hey everybody, we're all going to get laid!" Cuties did not get laid. I did not want to think of myself as a cutie. It was Dad's one decorative touch in the new mansion, his version of the needlepoint throw pillow Dede'd brought to Mom's abducted dream house.

Dad pulled the elevator gate aside, pushed open the door to the third floor, brandished his squeegee, and said, "Come on." I followed him to my bathroom, where we stood before my glass-walled shower.

Dad called Alda and Paca, Dede's housekeepers, "the girls." "It's difficult for the girls to clean the glass once the water's dried on it," he said. "We have hard water."—*hard water?*—"It comes out of the Hetch Hetchy Reservoir and leaves mineral deposits—here." He pointed. "Those grayish streaks. Right after a shower there's an opportunity to avoid this."

Dad adjusted his grip on the squeegee's handle. "Put some water on the shower walls."

I turned on the shower and spray bounced off the floor and pebbled the walls. "*Wetter.*"

I slapped a few handfuls onto the glass.

"Fine. Now if you pull in a straight line, with constant, even pressure, the water will come off and leave nothing behind."

Dad leaned in, placed the blade of his squeegee at the top of the glass, and pulled to the floor in one motion—as if he were removing a tall woman's floor-length dress. What remained was a perfect band of transparency.

He did it twice, then handed the squeegee to me.

"It takes less than two minutes to do this properly after you shower. And your body will dry in the process, so the girls won't have to change so many towels. You try."

I reached in, planted my rubber blade as high as possible, pulled, and it stuttered and ricocheted down the glass, leaving wet-and-dry stripes behind.

"Get in there, it'll be easier," he said.

"Are Trevor and Todd going to have to do this?" I asked.

Dad gave me a what-does-that-have-to-do-with-anything look and said, "Trevor and Todd are Dede's kids. I don't make any decisions concerning them. But you and I are doing this."

I stepped in.

"Not in your *shoes!*" he yelled.

I pulled off my loafers and socks, holding his arm for balance. Then I got in and tried again.

"Straight. You're *curving*. Are you listening? Even pressure. *Better.* Don't let it bounce. O.K. O.K. *Decent,*" he said. "Now once you've got it all off the walls you should also get down and pull all the water into the drain so it doesn't pool and mildew." He took his squeegee and demonstrated. When he was done it looked as if the water had been shut off for years. Like the shower was a closet.

"Now get down to breakfast," he said.

THAT SUMMER I was sent away to camp in Arizona. Before leaving, I went up to Napa for a weekend. Blane came, too. We took the brown-and-white van Dad had bought to carry Dede and her retinue. On the road, Todd said to Dad, "Al, I heard this joke I think you'll really like."

Dad said, warmly, "Let's hear it."

Dede rode shotgun. Todd and Trevor were in the first bench seat. Blane and I were in the second. Alda and Paca (the girls) were in the third with the family lapdogs, which were growling at Blane.

Todd looked around and said, "A big, bare-chested black sailor walks into a bar carrying a magnificent, three-foot-tall parrot on his shoulder. This parrot is *incredible.*"

"Sounds like a macaw," Dad said.

"Really stunning plumage," said Trevor.

(Around this time Dad took away one of the few compliments he used to bestow on me—"you have an excellent vocabulary"—and gave it to Trevor: "but Trevor has a better one.")

Todd said, "Shut up, Trevorus."

I thought, *Here comes another great Todd joke.*

Todd continued, "The bartender looks up and says, 'Wow! Where'd you *get* that?'"

Dad smiled.

"And the *parrot* says, 'Oh, Africa. There are millions of them!'"

Laughter rolled through the van, skipping me and Blane.

From the third row I heard Alda translating the joke into whispered Spanish.

*"Negro . . . papagayo . . ."*

.   .   .

THAT SAME WEEKEND, eating lunch by the pool, Dede said, "Sean," and Todd, Trevor, Dad, and Blane all paused their spoons for a moment.

"You've managed to disgust Kaisa de Tristan," she continued, glancing at Dad. "*That's* not easy to do."

I had been studying French with Kaisa de Tristan, a European woman in her thirties, who was some sort of displaced aristocrat. She'd tutored me for two years before I started taking French in school, so everyone expected me to excel. Instead I got Bs for the first two years of review, and in my last seventh-grade report card, I'd reverted to my usual C. (*C—satisfactory,* I always thought. *Satisfactory!*) Dad—who had an obvious crush on Kaisa—was humiliated that I didn't get As after studying the language for two extra years.

"*Two years* more French than anyone else and you're still only getting *Cs?*" Dede added.

"*B-minuses,*" I mumbled.

"Your accent is *horrible*. I've never heard anything like it. You shouldn't even speak, you should just listen—as a favor to French speakers. Can you even say the most rudimentary phrases in a passable accent? I mean, *can* you? Can you say, 'Where's the train station?' Something *anyone* can say. 'Where's the train station?'" She looked upset. Kind of sexily so.

*Wow,* I thought.

"*Can you?*"

Silence.

"*Can you?*"

*I've met the pope,* I thought.

Dede turned to the rest of the table—all absorbed in eating a between course palate cleanser of homemade fruit sorbet from the orchard (which Dad had planted with Mom)—and sneered.

"You can forget the *accent,* Sean. Just *say* the *sentence.*"

"Dede, enough," Dad said quietly.

"No. He has to try to say it," she said. "I want to hear you say it."

I said, "*Whale lager?*"

Dede laughed. "Do you have *any idea* how much of your father's *money* you're *wasting?* Tutors and private school—*God* what a waste. It almost sounds like you're joking. I know you're *not* joking with that accent."

Silence.

"Are you stupid, Sean? Is that what it is? Are you just stupid?"

I was smiling now. The smiling happened suddenly.

"*Ooh-alellgrrr?*" I said again with more phlegm. Everyone was quiet for a second, and I thought I might have got it right.

Dede said, "We should send you to public school and save your father the money." Her voice got tart. "Though then he wouldn't be able to see Kaisa."

Silence.

"West lager?"

Dede nodded at Trevor, and Trevor said, "*Où est la gare?*"

"And that's without any private lessons with Kaisa."

There was a humiliating silence, and it seemed as if maybe the conversation was over. Then Dede said, "I feel sorry for you. But you know who I really feel sorry for? Your *poor father.*"

To my amazement, Dad said, "Stop it, Dede."

She ignored him. "Poor Kaisa. I feel sorry for her, too. She needs the money, so she'll keep teaching you. But you're hurting her business."

Dad *shouted*—it was the only time he ever did this—"*Now!* Dede! *Stop it now!*"

Everyone was silent.

My painful smile turned into a real smile. Blane grinned at me. Dede was silent for the rest of the meal.

Then, after lunch, I saw Dad kissing Dede tenderly and whispering into her ear.

IT WAS as if they were speaking French all the time at Dad's. It was like the court of Louis XIV—cruelty and cleverness, repartee and appearance prized above all. They were all downstairs wearing powdered wigs and delivering bon mots.

Every accent and wry word from Todd and Trevor was met with appreciative laughter. Todd was the most effortless conversationalist I had ever encountered. He could smooth his way gracefully through anything. When he started high school he stank of booze and pot and cigarettes, got Cs, and got my piece of dessert (revoked over nothing). And the more time I spent with him and Trevor and Dede the more awkward and inarticulate I became. But I tried to be funny. I had to try.

The fall of eighth grade, back in the city (at camp in Arizona I'd played a lot of Dungeons & Dragons and generally failed to fit in), I tried practical jokes. I hung an animal head from one of Dad's sixties safaris in Todd's closet. When he opened the door there it was, glass eyes shining, horns curling outward. He screamed and jumped back.

Hey!

Todd short-sheeted my bed.

I turned off the water in his room.

He turned off the power in my room.

I was preparing my response when Dede took me aside and said the practical joking was to end right there. Immediately.

How else could I be funny? Someone had given Dad a 45 of the early rap/ R & B hit "Double Dutch Bus," by Frankie Smith, because it contained a non-sense lyric that sounded like, "Wilsey is a piss-ant/the double du-dutch." (Wilsey *was* a Dutch name!)

He gave the record to me. I took it up to the country one weekend and played it continuously (on my child's record player):

*Wilsey is a piss-ant*
*the double du-dutch*
*the double du-dutch*
*the double du-dutch*
*Wilsey is a piss-ant*
*the double du-dutch*
*the double du-dutch*
*the double du-dutch*
*Wilsey is a piss-ant*
*the double du-dutch*
*the double du-dutch*
*the double du-dutch*

At lunch, on the patio, "Double Dutch Bus" under discussion, Trevor said, "I mean, what is a piss-ant? *Ooh*—a piss ant. Step on it!"

Trevor was the smart one, Todd was the funny one. Here was Trevor being funny. That demanded respect.

Everybody chuckled.

Then, inspired, I shouted, "A *step* aunt—*piss* on it!" Everybody roared but Dede, who stared at me coldly. It was the only intentional laugh I ever got over there.

THAT YEAR Dad decided to have a go-cart race in our field in Napa. He called it the Wilsey Grand Prix, and told Todd and Trevor and me that he'd had special prizes made for everybody.

Trevor said, "If I know Al it'll be something suited to everyone's personality."

I thought, *What would that be for me?* I had no idea. Just a vague sense that it would be bad.

Now that fall had come, the topic of boarding school, absent for the last two years, was reintroduced. A recruiter from St. Mark's School, in Southborough, Massachusetts, visited Cathedral School for Boys. St. Mark's was prestigious enough for the recruiter to tell us about students going on to Harvard and Yale, and show us some pictures of turning leaves and Tudor buildings. Dad asked me if I'd like to visit St. Mark's, and said he'd take me. I said sure. It seemed like a good way to spend time alone with him, outside of the helicopter or the garage or St. Joan of Arc.

Dad took me to visit eleven boarding schools in eleven days. The trip comprised the most time we'd spent together in years. When I got back I told Mom I thought I wanted to go "back east for school" (quoting Dad). Mom was distraught, but she said it was up to me. I was confused: I wanted to make Dad happy, and I wanted to stay home—but there was no way I could do both. The best thing about being "back east" was having Dad there with me.

IN THE NEW mansion in San Francisco Dede monitored a row of plastic buttons on the multiline phone at her bedside. They corresponded to different lines, and lit up whenever another extension was in use. She always knew when anyone had been on the phone and for how long. The illumination of one button was sufficient to attract her attention, or awaken her from her slumbers. I'd discovered the phone-light phenomenon when Todd started receiving compliments on the length of his phone calls with girls. He was a freshman at University High, where I was secretly hoping to go, too. (Stewart and Sting were there, so why not Andy?)

One evening, at dinner, Dede said to Todd, "Last night's phone call was really something else. I saw the phone light was on for two hours. How do you keep them entertained for so long?"

I thought, *He's not even supposed to be on the phone that late at night.*

"Oh, I just let *her* talk."

"And you fall asleep," Dad chimed in affectionately.

Todd mimed being asleep and holding up a phone: "'Mmm-hmm. . . . Yes, how fascinating, Sweetie.'" Then he said, "Sometimes I let them talk to Tilly." Tilly was his toy fox terrier.

Dede then turned to me and said, "Sean, you should spend less time on the phone."

Dad said, "Crack the books instead. That's how you'll get into St. Mark's."

I said, "I never talk on the phone for a long time."

Dede said, crisply, "I know how long you talk. Though, of course, you're only talking to Blane. I watch the phone light by my bed. When a light goes on I watch it and I look at the clock and I know exactly how many minutes you've been on the phone."

The mansion's elevator had a rotary dial telephone that did not light up the cubes on Dede's extension. From then on I brought the elevator up to the third floor, so Blane and I could make our plans. We called the elevator phone "the secure line," and it was where all important business was conducted. "I'm on the secure line," I'd tell Blane, and then he knew we could talk about important matters. (That year we started sneaking out and going to North Beach strip clubs at night. Actually, we stood in front of them and looked through the curtains at the girls, and then ran away when the barkers hassled us, but there was still an element of adventure to it.) I only had to make sure to have the elevator back downstairs the next morning so Dad could take it from breakfast to the garage. Discovering the secure line was one of the few verifiable signs of my intelligence, and one of the only ways I outmaneuvered Dede. It was such rare evidence that it was hard for me not to confess it—I wanted Dad and Dede to know about it almost as much as I wanted to get away with it.

IN JANUARY of eighth grade, following another Christmas peace trip with Mom (Japan, China, India, Russia, France), Dad, Dede, Todd, Trevor, and I went skiing in Sun Valley, Idaho. At dinner in a dim restaurant, looking for a good conversation starter (nobody asked me about the trip), I remarked on the colors of a sweater Dede'd given me for Christmas. They were always talking about the color and pattern of draperies, or the rare hues and qualities of rugs— I thought I'd give it a shot. The sweater was dark green with three horizontal bars across the chest. Putting it on that evening I'd noticed that the center stripe was white and the other two were pale yellow: This seemed like *conversation.*

I said, "Hey, one of these stripes on my sweater is actually *white,* not *pale yellow,* like the other two are. They all *look* the same, but the center stripe's white!"

Dede said, "They're all yellow, Sean."

This was exciting. Dede considered herself an authority on color. Here I'd noticed something she hadn't noticed.

I said, "I think it's an optical illusion. Because it's *between* the other two it looks yellow, too."

Dede said, "No. They're all the same, Sean."

I said, "It's hard to distinguish between white and pale yellow in here. But I looked in the sunlight. That's how I noticed the difference. And you've probably only ever seen it in store light, when you bought it, and now, in candlelight." I was getting nervous.

Dede paused for a moment, then replied, "I bought that sweater for Trevor four years ago. All three stripes are identical. You're color-blind, Sean."

I said, "My left eye won't turn all the way to the left—but I'm not color-blind!"

"Sean—enough!" Dad said.

I thought, *Am I color-blind?*

The waiter came. He took all their drink orders. When he got to me I said, "Can you tell me what color the stripes on this sweater are?"

He said, "White?"

I said, "Look closely."

"Oh, is one different?"

Dede said, "Do not look at his sweater! Do not talk to him about his sweater! He will have *water* to drink."

I said, "No Coke?"

Dede said, "You will not talk about this anymore with anyone. Not with the waiter. Not with Trevor. Not with Todd. Not with your father. And you will not have any dessert. You are hyper on sugar."

I was still convinced that the truth mattered. That the truth was the truth and it would come out eventually. But that was just one of my many mistakes.

Back in San Francisco I tried to get Dad to look at the sweater when we were alone in the garage. He growled, "Enough about the sweater, Sean."

COLOR MEANT MORE to Dede than it did to other people. For Dede, having a favorite color was as crucial as having a name. After she and Dad bought their new mansion she was picking out paint and asked what my favorite color was.

I said, "Red."

Dede said, "Red can't be your favorite color. Pick another one."

I said, "Green."

She said, "You don't have any imagination, Sean. Green's your *father's* color." So my new room ended up being painted gray.

Dede also changed the color of my eyes. I was demoted from hazel, the eye color Mom always said I had, "just like your father" (Dad nodding in assent), to brown, which was Dede's corrected assessment. The rest of the family, she and

Todd and Trevor—brown-eyed the lot of them—had dark eyes she compared with jewelry. They were "deep jade green" or "chalcedony."

Dede got a brown Mercedes convertible (the same model Mom wanted). Dad bought it for her. When I asked Dad why he made Mom get an Olds and Dede got a Mercedes, he said, "I bought the Mercedes used, so the money stayed over here." When I called the Mercedes brown Dede said, "Brown is the color of your eyes. My *Mercedes* is *chocolate*."

Eventually, though, she had her Mercedes repainted teal to match the Studebaker Avanti that she'd had since she turned sixteen.

IN DAD'S new mansion I couldn't help noticing my absence from the dozens of photographs that crowded the marble-topped surfaces of ormolu-legged secretaries and "Louis XVI wood and gold-filigree trumeau"s (to quote an article about the place in *House & Garden*). These showed Dad and Dede in tuxedo and gown, on their way out for an evening; Dad giving a thumbs-up in the helicopter as he prepared to launch off into an afternoon of Napa Valley social-air-dominance; Dad and Todd and Trevor, smiling, in matching blazers; Dad dancing with Dede's mom at a ball in Newport; Dad on a Harley, in a biker jacket, wearing a knotty, long-haired wig and grimacing; variations on all of the above, but with the addition of small dogs held in the arms. I did not exist.

On the back stairs leading to the second floor from the kitchen, there was a photo of Dede in a long, tight, hot-red dress, the fabric pooled around her legs, a smoldering expression on her face, modeling for a perfume ad. If I stopped to look at it I'd get a boner. To get rid of it I could go round to the front stairs where there was an oil painting of Dede in a voluminous pink dress, puffy-sleeved and full-skirted, with gems painted around her neck. The eyes followed you in this one.

Todd had a picture of Dede in her debutante days up on the wall in his nongray room. She was beautiful in this photo; but, more importantly, she looked doable. This was a whack-off pic if there ever was one! She was showing a lot of cleavage, and she looked like she *wanted it*. I always thought, *Dude, why do you have a whack-off pic of your mom up on the wall above your bed?* And then I'd get turned on from standing there looking at it and run upstairs to whack off.

In the new mansion, Dad's death and its imminence was always being hinted at—hanging in the air like an odor that neutralized any sweetness (I think of this when I hear the phrase "the scent of death," and the fact that it smells expensive is unmistakable: Death: It's the one extravagance *everyone* can afford!). This was part of the newly vigorous argument for sending me to boarding school: My presence was making life hard for Dad, hastening his death. Dad's death was the foregone conclusion to our life as a group—like the handover of Hong Kong to the Chinese. How would we all fare after that? What would happen to us? We were meant to wonder. But none of us wondered as much as *Dad*. He began stressing the following aspect of his remorse lecture: "When I die I want you to be good to Dede." This was the condition the London of Dad was constantly trying to impose on the Hong Kong of me. And the Beijing of Dede said, "You'd better get used to dealing with me now, because when your father dies you'll be dealing with me all the time." This also made boarding school more attractive. When it came time for me to apply to high schools, I didn't apply to a single one in San Francisco, though I still hoped for a last-minute boarding school reprieve. I thought maybe I could go to St. Ignatius, where Dad had gone. I figured if things started going better with Dede, he'd get me in, no problem.

DEDE GAVE EVERYBODY an assigned place at the table during meals. You could not sit anywhere besides the assigned place. She'd acquired a plate-glass, octagonal dining room table, and according to her design, she and Dad and Todd and Trevor sat in an arc of four, then there was an empty space, and then came my place, with two more empty places on the other side.

I asked, "Why can't I sit with the rest of you, you know, where this space is?"

She said, "That's impossible. It would throw off the symmetry."

At meals we each were given pastel napkins in pastel napkin rings. Great significance was always attached to the different shades of pastel. I typically got pale yellow, which was the color Todd and Trevor didn't want. Occasionally I would get mint. I never got any of the esteemed napkin shades, like lavender or mauve. We always ate off a different set of dishware. One of Dede's subsidiary interests—always subordinate to jewelry—was the acquisition of dishware. She had *thousands* of different dishes, though, strangely, these dishes (which now fill an entire wing of the abducted country house—the dish wing—where they are arrayed in brightly lit display cabinets) all looked the same: like the unholy offspring of a kiln and a chintz sofa.

At breakfast, before he married Dede, Dad used to make me perfect poached eggs on toast with the crust cut off. "That's too much work for Alda," Dede said when we moved in together. Now Dad bantered with Trevor and Todd while I sat alone on the other side of the table and Alda made breakfast, to Todd and Trevor's specifications, and served it on pastel breakfast plates—always the *same* plates at breakfast, the ones I remember most clearly being turquoise, a color against which breakfast rarely looked appetizing. Dede was not a regular at breakfast. She was a late sleeper. Passion for pastel notwithstanding, the proximity of the dawn hurt her.

Most breakfast conversation was between Trevor and Dad. They were always the first at the table. Trevor read the *Wall Street Journal,* and Dad read the *New York Times* and the *Chronicle.* Sometimes I would race downstairs early, in an attempt to beat Trevor and get to spend some time with Dad. If I timed it right (25 percent of the time) we'd get ten minutes alone, and read the funnies, then do the word jumble together. Half the time Trevor would already be there with Dad, or be there by himself. The other 25 percent of the time *nobody* would be there, not even Alda.

Trevor followed the stock market and made wise forecasts about it. His conversations with Dad concerned Wang and IBM and Dad's favorite defense contractor, EG & G (Edgerton, Germeshausen and Grier: former NYSE call sign, EGG, later to buy a competitor, take its name, find itself briefly, spectacularly, overvalued, and subsequently destroyed). Trevor also followed foreign stocks.

He drank coffee. I drank milk. ("We are *never* giving you coffee, Sean," Dede said.) Since no one was interested in including me in a conversation, I had to blurt things out.

Here's a typical breakfast:

I'd arrive late and say: "Can I have the funnies?"

Being late I'd have to wait till Dad was finished with them. He'd fold them up and hand them to me. I'd unfold them and read from bottom to top: bad ones first, good ones last. *Steve Roper* was my least favorite, but sometimes I'd get caught up in the serial plots.

Trevor would be reading about a foreign stock.

Dad would say: "You should go American, Trevor."

Trevor, deferential but firm: "A good company is a good company, Al."

Dad: *smirk*.

Trevor: *smirk*.

Me: *Why does he love him so much?*

Trevor, continued: "The markets are global. So I follow stocks regardless of their nationality."

Dad: "Pretty smart."

Then Todd would arrive at the table, Alda popping out of the kitchen to give him an adoring "Hi Todd!" in her Peruvian accent.

Todd: "Hello, Sweet." Then he'd tell her what he wanted to eat.

Dad would flatten his mouth in mock censure, and say: "Todd, you were tying up the second line on the phone for over two hours last night." Dad's morning voice was full of gravel from thirty years at a pack a day.

thoroughly and found not a flea on her. Can you explain this?

—M.O.

Any airway obstruction, even a partial one, should be considered an emergency situation.

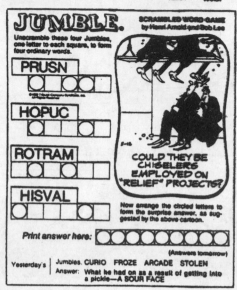

"I was on with Derby," Todd would say, "discussing the events of Saturday night. We had to offer some assistance to a female who had partaken too amply of the refreshments. A female"—putting on a sour face—"who then did a substantial amount of vomiting." Dad smirked. *Todd, what a rascal,* he seemed to be thinking.

"*You* never would get involved in such things," Dad would say. There would be a hint of *flirtation* in his voice. The flirtation that occurs between adults and other people's children.

He seemed to think all this—the long phone call, the party, the fact that Todd was friends with girls named Sidney, Serena, Victoria—was *cool*.

Todd would continue: "Of course not, Al. We just came to her assistance."

"Todd and Derby to the rescue," Dad concluded.

I turned to my favorite funnies:

San Francisco Chronicle

And then it'd be time to go to school. Trevor would drive Todd. Dad would drive me.

Whenever Todd talked about girls at breakfast, Trevor tried to change the subject back to business. Half the time during my eighth-grade year Todd looked angry and tired and hungover. He'd say things to Dad that would have gotten me the remorse lecture.

On one occasion Todd said, "Derby and I smelled repugnantly of beer and cigarettes last night. That's what these parties are like, Al."

I looked up from the funnies. He was saying this because he was afraid Dad might have noticed.

Out of the corner of his mouth, to Trevor, Todd continued—in the same voice he used to say "Fuckoffyoucunt"—saying, "andanodorthati'mtoldismarijuana *Trevor*."

*Wall Street Journal* rustling covered a reply.

I wanted to jump in and shout, "Dad! I'm sitting here with milk and the funnies and they're talking about stocks and *pot!* That's what they're discussing over there behind the *Wall Street Journal, pot!* Todd calls it 'greenie' or 'Mary Jane' or 'buds,' but he means *pot.*" I shifted in my seat, thoughts flying.

Then I stopped on the following thought: *Dad knows about the pot and thinks it's cool. And this is where I'm failing. I'm not cool enough for Dad.*

By now Trevor had moved the conversation on to business.

"Al, hybrid corn—"

"——500 percent more resistant to disease,

with yields—"

"—soft drink

companies!"

"—high fructose corn

syrup!"

"—removes trade barriers—"

"—middlemen—"

"—*and* exchange rates."

I read the funnies, thinking about how uncool I was, and half listened.
I was done.

"A lot of cane's grown in *Hawaii*," Dad said. "You don't want to put Hawaiian farmers out of work."

I needed to become Todd and Trevor. Todd could charm his way into and out of anything. Trevor had great grades, shrewd investment strategies, and made savvy drug deals. I thought, *This is what I must do.*

When there was a break in the sugarcane conversation I said, "I found out I can run fast on carpet!"

Cathedral School for Boys' biggest athletic event of the year, called Field Day, was coming up in a few weeks. I usually came in last or second to last in all events.

"You know how I haven't done so well on Field Day," I said.

"Yes," Dad said. This was a continuation of a conversation Dad and I had been having my whole life about my lack of coordination and his deep desire—yet total lack of faith—that this might change.

"It's because all those events take place *outside*, on *dirt*, instead of *inside*, on *carpet*."

Silence.

"But yesterday Tersh Barber and I raced down the hall from the fifth-grade room to the eighth-grade room, which is like three hundred feet, and I beat him."

This was true. Flying down the hall in my school uniform, gray corduroys, leather-soled shoes touching carpet, then going up in the air behind my back, sky-blue Oxford untucked, school tie, navy blue with little red and white crests of a bird, and a book streaming over my shoulder, I saw Tersh's face and he looked stunned. I really *had* beaten him. And he was the fastest runner in my class.

"I beat him. I won the race." Dad looked skeptical. "I think maybe he stopped trying at the end, but that was because I was already way ahead, so he wanted to make it look like he wasn't trying. But he was trying."

Silence.

"I'm really fast on carpet."

Pause.

"I think I'd be the fastest kid in school if we ran on carpet."

Dad said, "It's too bad Field Day won't be on carpet."

DEDE WAS ALWAYS at dinner, so dinner conversation was different. These were the approved topics for dinnertime conversation: precious stones; miniature dachshunds; toy fox terriers; the endearing unintelligence of small dogs; debutante parties; escorting debutantes; debutantes "coming out" (a topic that left me completely confused); Todd and Trevor's amazing popularity; Todd and Trevor's amazing social exploits; Trevor's amazing grades; Todd's amazing ability to chat up girls; a Chinese/Greek girl in Todd's grade named Wei Ming Dariotis, who Todd was not interested in chatting up, but whose name he could pronounce in a tart, bemused voice and reduce Dad and Dede and Trevor to helpless, tearful, convulsive laughter; people in Dad's employ with humorous shortcomings (particular favorite: deafness); *Dallas* and *Falcon Crest;* strangers to whom I had never been introduced, but who Todd, Trevor, Dad, and Dede talked about like old family friends. I remember Dad saying, with great boyish amusement, "Harry de Wildt has always been a real anal aperture," and Todd and Trevor and Dede laughing at his wit, while I said, "Who's Harry de Wildt?" which made them laugh harder, so I laughed too—my rule being: *Whenever they are laughing, I'd better laugh.*

In my room, instead of doing my homework, I tried to come up with good one-liners for use at dinner. I was the only *M\*A\*S\*H* fan in the house. I wanted to be Hawkeye Pierce. Maybe I could use Hawkeye's wisecracks, the ones they never heard, to get ahead at dinner. I labored to retool them. I didn't realize how difficult it would be to make them sound right coming from a thirteen-year-old living in wealthy eighties San Francisco, instead of a weary, disenchanted Yankee surgeon in fifties Korea.

I wrote down:

"I will not carry a gun (napkin), Frank (Dede). When I got thrown into this war (house) I had a clear understanding with the Pentagon (Dad): no guns (napkins). I'll carry your books, I'll carry a torch, I'll carry a tune, I'll carry on, carry over, carry forward, Cary Grant, cash and carry, carry me back to Old Virginia, I'll even 'hari-kari' if you show me how, but I will not carry a gun (napkin)."

This seemed funny. I'd have to work on it a bit.

The next two were good as they were. Sort of. They were definitely funny when Hawkeye said them:

"I've eaten a river of liver and an ocean of fish. I've eaten so much fish, I'm ready to grow gills. I've eaten so much liver, I can only make love if I'm smothered in bacon and onions."

And:

"I can take umbrage, I can take the cake, I can take the A train. I can take two and call me in the morning, but I cannot take this sitting down."

I scrawled these lines in shorthand on my hand, for covert use at the dinner table. I wrote in tight, dense handwriting, each phrase hard up against another phrase, all of them completely covering my palm, and, in the case of the longer phrases, extending out the length of my fingers. The pen tickled on the fingers.

At dinner that first night there were no silences and no chances. The biggest laugh of the evening came when Trevor, carrying on that morning's conversation, said something to Dad about a foreign stock, and Todd said, "Perhaps Trevor should consider investing in a foreign corporation I've been following called Wei Ming Dariotis."

Everybody roared.

Todd looked pleased with himself. Trevor rolled his eyes.

MY *M\*A\*S\*H* NOTES faded in the next twenty-four hours. I tried to do a touch-up. I had to use them! The following night there was a silence. My chance! I looked at my cheat notes and saw nonsense. My brain couldn't reassemble them into their joke form! *Don't miss the chance! They'll fade!* I started to speak. "Hey guys,      I've eaten      river      "—then I went silent and stared at my hand.

One, two seconds. No idea. *Abort,* I thought. I hoped they wouldn't notice.

"What? What is it you are saying, Sean?" Dede asked, fully alert, derisive, and focused on me. "And why are you looking *down* like that?" She was homing in fast. "What's all over your hand? Take it out of your lap. Have you written something there?"

I said, "Oh, you mean this stuff?" and pointed to the black scrawls covering my hand like a tribal tattoo. "Just some things I wanted to remember."

"What things?"

"Um." I looked at Dad. He nodded severely.

In a very small voice, "Just some things Hawkeye said to Frank Burns on *M\*A\*S\*H.*"

"What?"

"Just some things Hawkeye said to Frank Burns on *M\*A\*S\*H?* I wanted to remember them because they're funny?"

Dede was amazed. I thought she was going to ask me to recite them, the ultimate humiliation, but instead she made a sour face and said, "It's getting all over my good napkin."

Dad said, "Wash your hands, Sean. Don't come back till you've got all that stuff off." He was angry. I had embarrassed him in front of Todd and Trevor and Dede. I walked back to the kitchen and started scrubbing.

IN THE SPRING of eighth grade, on the night of my school's second annual dance with its two affiliated girls' schools, I came home at eleven, right after the dance ended—having danced with no one. I called Blane on the emergency phone in the elevator.

A year before, in seventh grade, I'd gone to the same dance. This was the first time anyone in my class had ever attended a dance with girls. I'd had no expectations, so things had gone well: I danced with Jody Steiner, who wore a dark green sweater (*not pastel*). She had bright eyes, lush, curly, brown hair, and she said "Yes" with such frankness when I asked if she'd like to dance with me. It was an evening of amazing luck, and it added crucially to the small store of hope and evidence that there might just possibly be another destiny for me besides the obvious one of loneliness and failure and unfunniness (all these were stored in abundance—but then there was this small quantity of something else, to which Jody Steiner added immeasurably).

I didn't kiss her, but I got her number. We talked on the phone. She told me about her family vacation to Machu Picchu, and the beauty of the sunrise there. I struggled to equal Todd's record two-hour-conversation-with-a-girl-mark. I did it. This was like making it into space. What was I supposed to do next? I had no idea. I knew Dede was watching, and that was what was important to me. After our two-hour conversation I never again called Jody with any real purpose. Our talks fizzled into nothing. I never asked her out. It always seemed inevitable that if we met in person again she'd be disappointed. Soon she stopped wanting to talk with me. I gave up calling. It was the last time I would talk to a girl for a long time.

In eighth grade I was a failure at the dance. I stayed close to the wall, talked to no one. Jody had another boyfriend (had I even been one?). Blane didn't go, but we agreed to sneak out and meet up later. We would go to the Palladium. This was where all the cool people with fake IDs—and *girls,* who didn't need fake IDs—supposedly went. Blane had been talking for weeks about how we'd get in and then . . . the plan was vague . . . stand around flicking overfilled Zippo lighters and offering the towering flames to girls! Something like that. More important, and I hadn't told Blane this, I was going to *tell Dad* about it the next morning, just like Todd told Dad about his exploits. That was my prime motivation. Dad was going to ask about the dance, and I needed to have something cool to tell him. He *wanted* me to do stuff like this.

On the secure line, Blane told me he couldn't sneak out.

"I'm gonna go *alone* then," I said. I thought this would shame him. But instead he said, "My mom's up and I can't. Sean, I'm sorry. Good luck."

We hung up. I sat on the floor of the elevator. The house was silent. Here was another failure. One more reason for Dad to love the amazing stepbrothers and try to get rid of me. Then I had an idea. I crept over to the regular phone and pulled the receiver off the hook. The line lit up. I felt a burst of daring. I kept the receiver in my hand for a hundred count.

I didn't have to go out; I just had to make them think I'd gone out.

THE NEXT MORNING Dede was at breakfast.

"I *saw* the light. Don't try lying about it," she said, and turned to Dad.

Dad said, "Who were you talking to last night past your bedtime?"

It was working. This was ironic. The only way to convince them I wasn't lying was to lie. Now I *had* to go for the whole thing.

"Ah, *Dad,*" I said, trying for the right Todd and Trevor tone. "There was a lot of drinking and smoking going on last night at the dance. A bunch of us were talking about going home and then sneaking out. I wasn't going to, but I decided I'd better—just to keep everyone in line." I put a little sarcasm on this last part, Todd style.

"Who were these youngsters?" Dad said.

"Uh . . ." Why hadn't I thought of this? They needed to be cool people. "I really shouldn't say?"

"You'd better say, or you're going to regret it."

"Billy Getty and . . ." Dad nodded.

Billy Getty was part of the Getty Oil family. I'd known him in *preschool*.

Did Dad know so little about my personal life that he would believe I was friends with Billy Getty?

He was waiting for more names.

"Like some other people . . ."

"Such as?"

*Who are Billy Getty's friends?* I wondered.

"B.J." I said.

I had never met "B.J.," who was a famous cool kid. I had no idea who he was or what his initials stood for. I just knew he was cool. (For all I knew "Getty" was spelled with a J—"Jetty"—and pronounced "Getty" and Billy Getty *was* B.J.) B.J. was notorious because he had taken acid and screamed, "I'm on fire! I'm on fire!" in the middle of his seventh-grade homeroom at Town School, Cathedral School's much cooler, secular rival. They took him away in an ambulance, packed in ice, though still looking cool. He was a legend after this. I'd never met him.

Dad seemed to buy B.J., too.

"I came to make sure nobody got carried away and, like, *took acid,*" I said.

"You were a *chaperone?*" Dad said.

"Yeah."

"And how did this all come to pass?"

I could not stop. "I got home and made that call—that must have been the light Dede saw—then I snuck out of the house and met Billy and B.J. and some girls. I'm really sorry, of course I shouldn't have done it, but I didn't want those guys to go out alone. I was just doing the right thing . . ." I trailed off.

Dad's face was surprising me. Where was the conspiratorial smirk?

It was only then that I realized I couldn't possibly have done anything worse than tell him this story. He was *scowling*. I was screwed. But still, it was too late not to add the final detail, "And we went dancing at the Palladium."

"What's the Palladium?" Dad asked.

Dad doesn't know and care about the Palladium and think it's cool?!

I said, "It's a club."

"Means 'the safeguard,'" he said.

"A dance club," I added.

"And where is this place?"

"On Broadway?" I wasn't quite sure.

"You were out at a dance hall with Billy Getty, B.J., and probably Blane Morf, last night?"

"Yeah . . . *not Blane*," I mumbled.

"Do their parents know this?"

"Uh. Yeah! Of course. They definitely do."

Dede had been regarding me with disgust, like something unpleasant impaled on the end of one of her high heels. "I'm going to call them right now," she said. I said, "What?!"

She stood up. She was going to call the parents of the coolest kids in San Francisco and tell them their sons had been out at a dance club with me, and I would be exposed, humiliated, doomed. Boarding school was better than that.

"Wait!" I said. "I'm just *kidding* with you guys! I didn't do any of that!"

Now the truth sounded like a lie.

I had to stop her. There was only one way to make the truth believable, which was to tell them *everything* and sell myself out.

In a rush I said, "When I want to talk on the phone and not let you know I always talk on the elevator phone it doesn't make the phone lights light up I just picked up the other phone last night so you'd see the light and I could tell you this story I wanted you to think I'd been out last night . . . doing cool stuff." I looked at Dad. "Like Todd and Trevor."

Todd and Trevor looked shocked. Dede looked surprised. Dad looked embarrassed. I was a goner.


DAD AND I took the elevator down to the garage. I pointed to the phone and reiterated that it didn't light up the other extensions.

"I don't know what to believe," he said. "I'm troubled by this, Sean."

Long pause.

"You should have gone to Fessenden a couple years ago."

I never told on anyone, but I was desperate, so I said, "Todd and Trevor go out and drink and smoke *all the time!*"

Completely unsurprised, Dad said, "That's Dede's business. You're mine."

. . .

THAT NIGHT a rare thing happened. Dede came up to my room. She entered without knocking and did not sit down, but kept herself stationed by the door, leaning against the frame, her left shoulder blade against the light switch, which was from the fifties and required a thumb to pull it up with a resounding *clopk*.

My gray room was perfectly square. On the eastern wall was the door and Dede. Next to this was a dresser from a cheap set Dad had Clifford buy at the Presidio PX. On the adjacent south wall was a matching dresser. To allow for the opening of drawers in both dressers, they just touched at the edges, leaving a square gap in the southeast corner of the room, occupied by a trash can and a rolled poster Dad had gotten for free from the power company. The poster encouraged frugality and conservation. "Make It Last!" was printed beneath a shining cartoon lightbulb. He'd put it up in my room at the Brocklebank one week while I was at Mom's. I was forgetful about turning off the lights, and he hated paying the power bill. But he hadn't bothered to make sure I put it back up in the new mansion.

Next to this dresser, which also held my Montgomery Ward stereo, was a sliding glass door to a roof deck, which was located above Dede's dressing room. Dede could hear me walking on it, so I usually just slipped across the sill, slid shut the door behind me, and stood there (smoking, soon enough). The fog came across Alta Plaza Park and in over the deck where it would thicken under the overhanging roof.

I did all my homework on my bed while watching T.V. I was watching T.V. now. My T.V. was old, and didn't have a remote like Todd's and Trevor's, but I had hooked it up to a Clapper-style sound-sensitive box. This one was activated by a shrill whistle, made by a piece of soft, hollow plastic, molded to look like a remote—you squeezed, it whistled, and the T.V. would go on or off. I had learned to imitate its whistle by taking a deep breath and forcing air between my tongue and upper teeth.

I looked up at Dede, took a breath, and blew hard, *"Sssssseeeet!"*

Dede winced. The T.V. died.

"This whole time has been a test, Sean," she said, looking at me as if I were an idiot and gesturing behind her, back into what I took to mean the past. "And you've failed. I've been watching you. Your table manners. Your consideration for others. You've missed the whole point. You've been blowing it. And now this." With the news that I had blown it I felt a smarting sensation and wanted to slap my own head—*blown it, idiot!*

Dede was Dad's oracle. She was always interpreting him. She inserted herself into every relationship he had, with everyone in his life. With me she liked to convey the sense—absolutely definitive—that it was *too late* to make right the many un-undoable wrongs I had already committed. That something I had done, and had done thoughtlessly, had secured permanent banishment from his love. That doom had already been secured. As she put it one time, "Once you irritate him, once you cross him, he is unrelenting. He is the *coldest* person in the world—and you can't come back into his good graces. Once the door is shut, it's *shut.*" This view of the world utterly pervaded my subconscious. For years, when I dreamed, I almost exclusively had nightmares about: a) inadvertently destroying what was most valuable to me, usually a woman, a child, or an ancient artifact; b) failing to prevent a nuclear holocaust through cowardice, laziness, or haven't studied enough–style incompetence; c) killing someone by accident; d) impregnating a woman and discovering that she wanted the child, yet I lacked the resources, emotional and financial, to provide support; e) losing my job and all my money; f) becoming an invalid and therefore; g) incapable of working to support myself (often at the same time as "e"); h) crippling someone else through carelessness, and in my inexorable guilt taking responsibility for their life. These nightmares were Dede's legacy. She was a master at engendering hopelessness.

Now she said, "With this you have really *blown it.* And I'll tell you why. Because your father will never trust or respect you again. And I'll tell you something about your father—he doesn't give second chances. Once he's made up his mind that you've crossed him, he is not interested in you anymore. I've said to him, 'But *Sean* is your *son.*' And his response was, 'No, not anymore. He blew it.'" This sunk in, deep. *I'm not his son.* I'd blown it. It was over between me and Dad. "That's just the way your father is," Dede continued. "When he makes a decision he sticks with it.

"I'd hate to be in your shoes. I hope I don't ever wind up on that side of your father. I hope I never see it directed at me.

"Your father wouldn't come up and talk to you. And he didn't want me to. The only way he will ever forgive you for how you've embarrassed him is if you go to St. Mark's and make him proud. He can get you in there with a donation, but then it's up to you. If you want to get back into his good graces you'd better get serious, fast." She turned to go. Then she turned back and added, "I know about the way you sneak down to the garage to see him when he gets home. He hates it, but he couldn't tell you himself. That better stop, too."

· · ·

I KEPT the T.V. off.

I had discovered something.

The useless emotion in my life was love. My love for Dad.

It was useless to care without reciprocation.

But we were father and son. So we were stuck together. My nonhazel eyes aside, we were identical in appearance. Much to Dede's annoyance, I looked like his shadow, trailing fifty years behind.

Anyway: The useless emotion was love.

There was no use for my love.


WHEN I WAS accepted at St. Mark's I was elated. I would go there and make Dad proud.

Two things happened before I left:

First, in the van again, with Dad, Dede, Todd, Trevor, Alda, Paca, and Blane, just past Napa, several dozen black bicyclists were slowing traffic. A snarky, smug, mean silence descended. I sensed the formation of a cutting remark.

Before it could be made, putting on a Dede-style WASP jaw lock, I shouted, with more sarcasm than I'd ever employed, "Oh, *God,* no, Al. *Niggers* in *our valley!*"

The silence changed—from smug to shamed—and nobody said anything. It lasted for miles. It was like a burst of light through the clouds. I sat there and re-alized, *I know who I am. It is not one of them. And it is a good thing.*

*Oh the glory of it all,* I thought.

It was the only truly courageous thing I ever did—resulting in the only true joy I ever felt—in their company.


SECOND: IN THE country, a patio was carved into the willow-lined banks of the creek that bisected the property, and we sat there and ate light lunches—Bibb lettuce salads, poached salmon or chicken with dill, chardonnay for Dad and Dede, and that fresh fruit sorbet. (Blane told me years later: "The sorbet was good.")

I'd been accepted to boarding school. Dede looked at me and said, "You and I are going to be very close one day. When you're a grown man you'll come to me for advice. You'll seek me out and we'll be confidants. I'm only going to tell you this once, because your father is *very jealous.* But it's true. We'll have a special relationship."

This was enough for me. Everything shifted into a new light: *I am not yet strong and able enough to be her partner. I don't yet deserve her love and respect. Dad is still alive. But one day he will die. And one day I will be ready. I must never forget this.*

*I'll take over from Dad.*

*When he is gone.*

*And she is telling me this in front of Dad. So he knows that it is inevitable.*

*That is why they are always punishing me—to be worthy of her.*

Everything made sense!

*Dede did love me before she married Dad. But Dad is very jealous. So she's been cold. But Dede and I shall love again. I must be patient, and our time will come. She is testing me, to see if I am worthy. She conceals her deep passion for me because it is so very deep.*

After that, when she berated me, I would sometimes get an erection. On one occasion I had to conceal it beneath my yellow pastel napkin.

·

# PART TWO

# Useless Education

*Nine* · S T.   M A R K ' S

I F   S T.   M A R K ' S, the one-hundred-and-nineteen-year-old Massachusetts boarding school where I arrived for freshman year, were to change its crest, which depicts a stern, sphinxlike winged lion clutching a book in its paws, I'd suggest the following triptych: a small asphyxiated pig, its skin blue, lying on a bathroom floor with a $CO_2$ cartridge at its side; a multipanel tableau showing two bears urinating in a trash can over the course of several weeks, and then dumping this can all over the clothes and possessions of a third bear with bad posture and a sensitive muzzle; and, finally, a group of seven donkeys, some dressed in sport jackets and ties, some in lacrosse gear—all coltishly braying! daring each other to participate in a *Clockwork Orange*–style gang rape of an inebriated, long-lashed doe, dressed in an unbuttoned Oxford shirt.

When I got to St. Mark's, the first scene in the above triptych was said to have occurred the year before, when a boy's allergic reaction to some inhalants seemingly caused him to drop dead. The piss-in-the-trash-can scene happened during my sophomore year, to the freshman boy who had inherited my old room. The rape, which was initiated by a fellow sophomore, happened just before I was kicked out, also in my second year.

I arrived in 1984. The school had only recently and awkwardly become coed: The senior class contained forty-seven boys and twenty-one girls; my class contained thirty-two boys and twenty-two girls. Drugs were rampant but unaddressed. Hazing and senior privilege were sacred. The school operated on the English "form system," which wasn't a system but a relabeling, in which the terms "freshman," "sophomore," "junior," and "senior" were replaced with "third form," "fourth form," "fifth form," and "sixth form"—for no reason. It was a perfect example of snobbery: imposing distinctions where there need not be any. Sixth formers had near-faculty status. They sat above the rest of the students during the weekly chapel services in the school's old Episcopal church, in elaborately carved wooden armchairs (called "the thrones") that were built into the paneled walls of the building. They were the only students allowed to walk on the school's central courtyard, called "the quad," a rectangular acre of manicured grass at the heart of the oldest section of campus surrounded by imposing Tudor-style buildings on three sides and a brick-and-brownstone colonnade at the front (its gate, the main entrance to the school, surmounted by a grave-looking stone lion). Should any underformer tread on the quad, even accidentally, they would at that moment forfeit all their freedoms and become a prisoner of the sixth form. The quad gave off an almost electric energy of privilege and risk. It was hard to walk by without considering a dash across. And the sixth formers would patiently wait for some dumb stray kid to touch it so that they could nab him.

Since the quad was overlooked by half the school's dorms it was the most visible place on campus. Sixth formers would play Frisbee or Hacky Sack or pickup football on it, or just lounge around, waiting. If a trespasser was spotted he was run down and then yanked into the quadside sixth-form lair—a suite of dark wood rooms decorated with wall sconces, paintings, a fireplace, and a billiard table, where the coolest of the seniors hung around perpetually watching *Scarface* and *Red Dawn* on their newly acquired VCR. Slavery would begin with someone forcing you to lick the floor, or fetch their snacks, or admit you were "a fag." An indentured period as a bed maker or personal waiter or room cleaner would follow. A couple of years before I got there a kid had been tied up with piano wire and left naked in the crypt beneath the school chapel, where he was instructed to sing hymns. Or so the rumor went.

No one ever seemed responsible for these flashes of violence. They happened.

They turned into legends. And then everyone acted as if it were all in the past. Instant history.

For years, when I encountered people who went to prep school, they'd ask me, "What did *you* get kicked out for?" "Drugs" was considered a pretty acceptable answer. The expected answer. *Cool. Drugs.* But I just failed. I couldn't concentrate or think or stop to see the page in front of me.

Recently I looked at the 1985 St. Mark's yearbook. I looked at the sixth-form section, where each member of the graduating class was given a page to decorate and memorialize his or her four years at St. Mark's. Pictures with friends and family. Song lyrics. Thank-yous to various teachers and coaches. I scrutinized them as closely as I had when I was a freshman, desperately, friendlessly, trying to figure the place out.

In small dark photos, jammed in the gutter, and in some bright, obvious, explicit full-page photos, I counted the following items:

Beers: 32
  Brands:
    Heineken: 4
    Miller: 1
    Stroh's: 1
    Henry Weinhard's: 9
    Tuborg: 2
    Huge draft beers (being consumed on vacations in Europe, or Asia): 2
    Budweiser: 13
      Bottles: 7
      Tallboys: 5
      Small cans: 1

Liquor bottles: 63
  Brands:
    Beefeater: 7
    Bacardi: 7
    José Cuervo: 7
    Seagram's VO: 7
    Smirnoff: 8
    Gilbey's: 7

    Jack Daniel's: 6
    Unidentifiable: 14

Other bottles: 14
    Wine, champagne, wine coolers: 8
    Sake: 6

Miscellaneous:
    Peyote: 1
    Bong hits: 1
    Handguns and rifles: 24
    Garments bearing the name of St. Mark's or an Ivy League university
        (worn casually): 75

Two guys combined their pages into one tableau—which runs across a
spread—showing them passed out on the floor of their dorm room with a bottle
of Jack Daniel's. Another spread shows two grinning boys sitting on a couch in
their room; on the coffee table before them is a two-liter soda bottle full of
milk—beside a bottle of Smirnoff. A series of photos on several senior pages
show a group of the football players standing on a wooden porch holding rifles,
shotguns, pistols, and liquor bottles, while on the porch railing are arrayed a
dozen more bottles—the contents of an entire liquor cabinet. In some shots they
point the guns at the camera. In one a kid crouches on the ground while the others point their guns at him. There are more wine coolers and bottles of sake in
the yearbook than there are black people.

"THE CHAFF" IS what the people who didn't make it were called, listing us
every year on a page that immediately preceded the sixth form section. For some
reason the school allowed me to remain enrolled for two years. Then, just before
I was expelled, before my little piece of chaff sailed away, I was told that I had the
lowest G.P.A., maintained over the longest period of time, in St. Mark's history.
    I had all this energy that was used to panic situations, fast, reactive energy de-
veloped for the appeasement of glamorous, mercurial, suicidal, self-enamored
older women; not, though I tried retrofitting it, for the members of the I.S.L.
Eberhardt Division title-winning boys varsity hockey team. The situation at St.
Mark's was impossible. There was not sufficient time. The attacks were too fre-
quent. The animosity came in on too many fronts. There were so many people

to be wary of that it was like being in a video game. Mom trying to kill herself. Jocks trying to kill me. Dede loving/hating me. It all blurred into one overwhelming panic.

COE HOUSE, where the third-form boys lived, was the most antiquated (least heated) of St. Mark's dorms, where the school's nineteenth-century origins were most in evidence.

It consisted of three hundred-foot-long halls with about ten rooms on each side. The rooms were tight and narrow, about seven feet wide by fifteen feet deep, but they had very high ceilings, thirty feet at least, extending past the dormers of the building's slanted roof. We slept in jungle gyms of bolted-together wood beams, like something built by the wood elves from *The Lord of the Rings,* climbing long ladders to our sleeping platforms. (Stealing bolts from other jungle gyms was common practice, and a good way to fuck with your enemies.) Every room was accessed through a tunnel beneath the jungle gym. At floor level were twin built-in desks and closets, full of sport coats and hockey sticks. If a desk chair was pulled out there was no room to pass. At the back of the room was the ladder to our beds and a small open area that my roommate— a devious, Dickensian-named scoundrel called Matthias Plum—and I filled with big foam-stuffed cubes of brown and orange plastic, provided by the school as furniture. We sat on them and looked out the window onto the quad.

Up the ladder was a platform where it wasn't quite possible to stand straight. This was adjacent to Plum's bed, and provided just enough room for a bedside table and someplace to crouch. Above this, another six rungs up, was my bed and a second platform, a large space where I could stand up easily beneath the sloping roof, with room for a chair and table. I slept there, safe from hazing, until Plum and I were declared bad influences on one another and I got moved down the hall to a single.

ALEXANDRA "TOOKIE" FOLGER was a girl I'd known when I was a little kid in San Francisco. Tookie went to Convent of the Sacred Heart Elementary School, where they wore white, rounded collars over sky-blue dresses. She had short hair and smiling lips. When we were five or six we planned on getting married. She was my girlfriend and best friend until around age nine. I'd lost touch with her after that, when I switched schools and my parents divorced. Since then we'd seen each other only at a dance class for seventh- and eighth-grade private school kids, where she would touchingly leap across the room to pick me when it was "girls' choice" night, and I would then ineptly discuss Atari. She also went to St. Mark's. And at St. Mark's she was immediately popular. Everyone had a crush on her. Everyone wanted information about her. It was my one social in. A brief hope in a brief period that preceded the securing of my position as a total loser.

One night after lights out, before we were separated, Matt Plum and I were talking and I was trying to convince him Tookie and I had been going out just before we came to St. Mark's, but I had dumped her to "keep my options open out east." I hoped to sound cool without giving Plum any specifics. But Plum was no fool.

"Bullshit, Wilsey. Tookie never even *liked* you."

"She liked me. She liked me a lot," I said.

Plum snorted.

I didn't really need to impress Plum. He'd been decent enough to me. But I was pissed, because Tookie really had liked me when I was six.

"I mean," I said, "we always kissed and made out. I don't think you do that if you don't like somebody."

He was silent.

"One time we virtually had sex."

"Oh. *Yeah*," said Plum, who suddenly became fully alert.

"Really," I said. "Not *quite* sex, but absolutely everything else but."

"Shut the fuck up."

"It's true."

"You're lying!"

"You're just jealous, Plum."

"So, what—a dry hump, Wilsey? Or a *hand job?*"

I was drawing on a memory from when I was six, of going over to Tookie's house and playing house in a big box. She was the mom and I was the dad. We had breakfast. I went to work. We had dinner. Before long it was time for us to go to bed. So Tookie lay down in the box, which was dark and private and on the landing of her staircase, and said I should lie down next to her. We took our shirts off. We pretended to put on pajama tops. Then she said I could say good night and kiss her. I said, "Good night." I kissed her. She said, "I love you."

I said, "I love you, too."

We held each other. Then I said, "We should do that over," and kissed her again.

This was a perfect moment. (In fact, I think I went for years trying to repeat this moment.) Then another kiss. I just remember being intoxicated with kissing and saying "I love you." Then we had to get up and deal with our baby, who was Tookie's sister.

"Yeah," I said to Plum. "It was a dry hump."

"And where were you for this *dry hump?*" he asked.

"Her house," I said. "On the floor. We started kissing. And then we took our shirts off."

"You were just 'on the floor'?"

"Well, we were on a rug."

"On a *rug?* Like a bearskin rug? In front of a fireplace, sort of?" He was laughing.

"No fireplace," I said.

"What time of year was it?" he asked.

"Oh a year or so ago."

"So this time of year."

"Yeah, I guess it was . . ."

"Weren't you cold without a fireplace?" he asked.

"We were in front of a radiator," I said. It was the stupidest thing I'd said yet. A fucking *radiator?*

Plum laughed. "Ah, so you were making out in front of a *radiator,* instead of a fire or something . . . Didn't want to start a fire, Wilsey?"

"It was a radiator," I said again. "She didn't have a fireplace, or we would've used that."

"Oh shit," said Plum, laughing. "That's pretty fucking studly, Wilsey."

"Don't tell people," I said.

By the next day topless dry humping on a rug in front of a radiator was all over the school. The radiator became key to the story, the one detail that everybody seemed to know. People passed me in the halls and said "radiator." Tookie (so kind) never spoke to me about it. She hardly spoke to me at all.

THEN I WAS sitting at my desk during study hall (before I was banished to supervised study hall in the library) when Derek Steward, the kid across the hall, shouted, "How goes the beating off, Wilsey?!"

Derek was from Columbus, Ohio, and was one of the few—seven—black kids in the school. He was popular. And the reason he was saying this, I realized in terror, was because of his sidekick Charles Anderson, the other San Francisco kid at St. Mark's (we'd gone to grade school together), whose trademark activity was to climb a wall overlooking the bathroom stalls and pour cups of water on people. I had been in one of the stalls that afternoon masturbating, during a free period—closing my eyes and picturing my fantasy fifth former, who was the queen of the basement butt room (the smoking clique)—when I heard a clunk, like a body dropping from a height, and then the door shutting. Charles had been watching me. The fact that Charles and I were spending the same free period masturbating (me) and spying (him) encapsulates the reasons we failed at St. Mark's. We were simultaneously placed on academic probation (the letter my parents received informing them of this mistakenly refers to me as Charles) and were kicked out within a couple months of each other the next year—him for stealing a television set from his dorm's common room, me for the grades.

"I don't beat off, Derek. You've got me confused with someone else."

"You were beating off today, Wilsey."

"Yeah, Derek."

"That's right, 'yeah'—I *know* you were beatin' off."

"Yeah, on the quad, Derek." This got some laughs.

But me getting laughs pissed Derek off. After that he was not fucking around.

"Yeah, you can try to make it a joke. But it's true. You. Were. Beatin'. Off."

Angry.

Then, every five minutes or so—just when I'd begun to think it was over—for the rest of the evening, Derek would break the silence of study hall by saying, "Beatin'. Off." Until everyone was laughing.

IN FRENCH CLASS I flirted with the teacher. At first I barely knew I was flirting. It just started happening. And then it was funny. And then I tried to make it so that everything I said to her contained some innuendo or double entendre. Everybody laughed, particularly when I asked, in a suggestive voice, if I could be excused to go to the bathroom—the implication being that I was going off to masturbate.

As long as everybody thought I was a masturbator . . .

PLUM AND I were separated (in the hope that solitude would increase my studiousness). Now my only friend was Alex Rodberg (born Oleg), who had emigrated to the United States from Russia a few years before, and was at St. Mark's on a scholarship. Alex was kind and funny and smart and liked me without reservation. He thought the radiator story was stupid, and I was an idiot, but he didn't hate me. Nor, miraculously, did he assume I was gay because I was from San Francisco, as everyone else did. He didn't even care about the beating off (which, anyway, I continued to deny).

Dad came to visit for parents' weekend.

I don't remember much about the visit, but he wrote the following when he got back to San Francisco, sending it to me much later:

This will be an account of a trip ASW [Alfred Spalding Wilsey] took to Boston to see Sean at Saint Mark's School for the first parents weekend of the school year.

I left San Francisco on Friday morning October 26 on a UAL flight on a new Boeing 767. This plane is designated as a "heavy" aircraft of the wide bodied type such as a DC 10 or 747. The flight left San Francisco at 8:00 AM direct to Logan Field Boston with an in transit time of about four and a half hours. This segment is rapid because of the heavy easterly winds in the fall of the year. Logan Field Boston is only reached from the main part of the city by a two lane tunnel each way. Traffic because of this is stop and go and it can require as much as an hour each way during heavy traffic periods. After picking up a car at Avis, which is reached by a bus from outside the baggage area of the terminal. In the cold weather this can be slow and difficult. After getting my little car I headed out of the airport in the midst of the end of the day Friday evening traffic. It took me over two hours from the Avis terminal to the Sheraton Tara Hotel in Framingham, Mass. I checked into the hotel, listened to the programmed pitch of the bellman, dropped my baggage, set out to go to Saint Mark's which is about six miles from the hotel. Eastern roads are somewhat different than those at home because turn offs are not as clearly marked as they are at home and the signs are not as clearly identified as I would like. [Strangely—typically—a large percentage of our conversation during Dad's visit concerned these Dad-subjects: winds and signage.] After arrival, I parked and started looking for Sean all over the place. First all around the entrance, then the reception area alumni office, faculty area, dining room, Coe Hall (where he lives) and then finally found him in the computer room with a friend. It was good to see him. He has continued to grow, although not around as he is quite thin but looks healthy and well taken care of, except for his hair in the back of his neck which is quite long.

I suggested that we go out for a milkshake and Sean asked if we could take along the friend who had been with him in the computer room. I said "of course" and Sean introduced me to Alex Rodberg; we took the car and drove through Framingham passed all of the favorite stores, which from the conversation between the kids was familiar territory to them. Sean asked to stop at Pier One where he conned me out of a fabric wall hanging, a wastebasket and something else. I can't remember what. We then went to one of Framingham's finest restaurants . . . Wendy's. While we ate and talked, I realized that Alex was the Russian boy that Sean had spoken about several times. Not only Russian, but Jewish. The family had lived in Kiev and had received an exit quota in 1978 and left for the West with just what they could carry with them. His father is an electrical engineer; his mother a medical doctor and his older brother now a student at Exeter. Some family. Alex is obviously bright and gets along well with Sean and other kids as well. After our visit I took both boys back to school and left for some sleep. I was scheduled to start in the morning at 8:30 with a session of fifteen minutes in each of Sean's classes with his teacher and what parents were there. His classes are: A music understanding course; Algebra I; Introduction to computers; English and French II. I was impressed with all of the classes and the teachers. After the five classes we went to the auditorium where the headmaster talked and heard a discussion of school rules and regulations by a panel of students and administration people. I would guess that there were about 400 parents present. . . . During all of this we talked to a number of parents and students including the Folgers from San Francisco. At one o'clock I had a fifteen minute appointment with Sean's faculty advisor, Mr. Berryman (also his music teacher). I feel that this man has the ability to assess a child very well. He described the problems that both Sean and his roomate, Matt Plum, had at the beginning of the term with homesickness and difficulty in adjusting. . . . The result was very poor study habits for both of the boys and subsequent bad grades. The two were separated and put in single rooms on October 23. The effects have not been determined. Sean has now been put in a controlled evening study group in the library. . . . Sean is to be encouraged not to be the first one out of class and to try to pay attention and appear to be interested in the subject. He is required to visit each teacher every Monday to see if he has completed all assignments given the previous week. Mr. Berryman indicated that Sean is liked by teachers and students and that there is no question that he can make it at Saint Mark's if he wishes to. He asked me to strongly encourage Sean to seek advice and encouragement from him at any time and told me that he had all of his students to his house and that Mrs. Berryman had been well impressed by Sean's manners and personality. . . . He talked to me twice the allotted time and I was very pleased with his obvious desire to have Sean do well. He likes him. As I left the area I ran into Mr. Barlow, the headmaster, and asked him if he thought Sean could make it and his answer was a strong "heck, yes".

I then ran into Sean who had suited up for soccer. That day the girls teams played Brooks and the boys teams played Milton Academy. Sean did not play but helped out with things on the field etc. He has broken one of his shoe inserts and they don't want him to play until it is replaced. When the games were over . . . Sean had permission to spend the night with me. We slept quite late the next morning, had breakfast and went to Mass in Southborough. After that we went to Grungies, the local pizza parlor for lunch and back to school. . . .

I helped him organize his room until three o'clock when I had to leave for the airport. He still had a lot to do when I left but we made a lot of progress.

It took me just forty minutes to get to the tunnel in Boston and then another hour to get to the plane check in area.

I think Sean and I identified most of the areas where he needs to work. He needs to organize his daily schedules; program his class, study, athletic and recreation times; set up his clothes, laundry and so forth and I will give some thought to this when I write next.

At Christmas I went home to Dad's, where more problems could be identified. Mom was off on a peace trip, traveling by rail through the eastern bloc countries, with a camera crew from a local network affiliate. My role as a peacemaker had been usurped by another boy my age, Michael White, who was, Mom said, "equally articulate, and very good on camera." The trip started in Rome. White got wired with a remote mic, walked up on the high altar, knelt, and had a conversation with the pope, asking him, "Will you bless our mission?"

The pope said, "Yays," and gave White a huge papal candle with big golden keys on it.

I sat around Dad's, jealous and bored.

During a tedious rotation on MTV I went down to Dad and Dede's room to find out if I could have a Coke. I stood at the threshold, knocked, and called, "Hello!" No answer. I did it again. Still no answer, so I stepped inside onto the thick, new, pastel carpet—a cabinet full of Faberge knickknacks to my left. I heard the sound of swishing fabric from the open door to Dede's dressing room. I said, "Dede?"

Silence.

"Dede? Hello? It's Sean."

I stepped around the cabinet, turned into the doorway, and there was Dede, in nothing but a bra and panties—and *garter belts*. She looked at me and smiled.

The only woman I'd ever walked in on naked was Mom, who always screamed and rushed to cover herself, and shouted, "Get out, Sean! Get out! I'm *nude!*"

I stood and stared at Dede. I looked at her panties, which were black lace, with a little decorative flair at the edges; her matching garters; her breasts, which I could see plainly through the black lace bra; her nipples; her face. She held our eye contact, turned away, and continued to smile at me through the mirror. Now was this Dede—since I was looking at her *through* the mirror—or Dede's opposite? Benevolent Dede! No. The lingerie would've been white. *White lace,* I thought, *Ohoh.* I tried to smile back. My mouth moved, but not quite right. It made not-under-my-control spasms. Then I thought, *This must be the way she snared Dad. Garters. Black lace. Black magic.* I took a step back, then another, lost my balance on the carpeting and stumbled, severing our eye contact for a second, which seemed to break the spell. I ran. I pounded up the stairs, thinking: *Dede wants me! Dede married Dad so she could be with me. She loves me. But she couldn't marry me, so she had to marry him. And I look like Dad! Everyone says so. And I'm younger. I have youth on my side. Yes.* I pounded, leaped three, a second of levitation. *She totally wants me! She totally wants some young meat!*

I called Blane.

"Dude!" I hissed in a manic whisper. "Listen, you won't believe what just happened. I go down to ask Dede a question and I knock and walk in because the door's *wide open* and there she is in her like, totally *sexy fuckwear, a bra and black lace panties and garter belts.*"

"*Garter belts?*" Blane asked. This was proof that she was obviously a sex master.

"Garter. Belts," I said. "I *swear* to it. She was wearing garter belts. She was just standing there in her *bra* and *panties,* wearing fucking *garter belts.* And when she saw me she *smiled. Dude,* she *smiled.* Like she *totally wanted me!* And that smile meant, 'We can't do it here and now, but look what you're gonna get when the time comes!' Like when my dad dies!?"

Blane and I were both silent for a second.

Then I made a resolution. "*Dude,*" I said, "*I'm gonna fuck her!*"

A few days after the garter incident I was on the regular phone with Blane, a little after ten o'clock. Dede picked up in the middle of our conversation and said, "I see when the phone light is on. I *notice.*"

"Dude!" we said to each other.

"She *wants* you," Blane said before we hung up.

Thenceforth, when I talked to Blane on the phone, he'd ask if it had happened yet, if I'd fucked Dede, and I'd abandon phone caution and say, "I haven't got her alone yet, but I'm *gonna* fuck her, Dude!" *Half-hoping she was listening in.*

I suspected Dede heard all my phone conversations. I assumed she was always there. But I kept talking about her. I liked that she was listening. I wanted her to know exactly how I felt. I was convinced she could pick up her extension black magic, voodoo style, without making any clicks. And this added to my fantasy. I said to Blane, "How can someone who notices the light on the phone stand in her garter belts and leave the door wide open, with nobody in the house but me?" Silence. *Dede?* "That was no accident, Dude. That's all I'm saying."

"Good point."

"*Dude,* she knows, she *totally knows* what she's doing! That little smile she gave me. I could've had her right there. I've just gotta wait and get her alone."

"Yeah."

"Yeah."

"Oh, yeah!"

MASTURBATING MY CHRISTMAS vacation away, I pictured Dede in the garters, then I bent her over or pushed her down or sat her on the sink top and we did it in front of her mirror. I did it with evil Dede and benevolent mirror Dede. It was a *threesome!* I said, "I've wanted you since that moment I walked in and you were in your garters and panties. You gave me that smile, and I knew."

Or sometimes my fantasy went all wrong, and instead of slipping her panties down her legs, she said, disgusted, "Get out of here, Sean. Get out of here now! You're not half the man your father is." I could not force the fantasy to cooperate.

But it *had* happened. *It happened,* I reminded myself. It was one of the only good things I had to hold on to. Dede in garters, and the pope.

It meant everything to me. It restored my faith.

Then I went back to St. Mark's.

MY NEW SINGLE was tiny, with a bed about six feet off the floor, in hazing range. My first night some sixth formers busted in and blasted me in the face with a fire extinguisher. In the morning, walking to the shower, I encountered a stocky, pretty guy named Rob Leggat, whose friends called him "Legs."

I wore a T-shirt and boxers under a towel, in case someone tried to pull the towel off and start snapping a rattail at me. There was a cult of the rattail at St. Mark's, where gym towels were tenderly rolled and moistened and remoistened, and then deployed with sufficient force to pop open a locked bathroom stall, or knock a dent in a hollow-core door. *Slam!* The halls were full of the sound of whipping rattails. They made it difficult to study, or listen to synth pop. Rattails were thunderous when they impacted on a surface like a wall or a door, sending a report and sowing fear down the halls of the dorm. When a rattail hit skin it raised a welt.

Leggat came out of his room, bare chested in a towel, and lazily stretched his arm out to block my way.

He smiled, and in a low, breathy, drawn-out, mock amorous voice said, without opening his mouth, just exhaling through his teeth, "*Hiii* Sh*aaa*wn." He kept smiling, widely and sarcastically, and batting his long lashes.

"Hiii Raaahb," I said back in a similar, smaller voice.

"Hiiyyyy Sh*aaa*wwwn," he said again, drawing it out even more, and maybe leaning forward a bit.

I was about to do the same thing back when he disengaged his hand from the wall, dropped the wide smile, and started advancing at me.

"You're really such a little *fag*," he said, clipping off the last word and saying it really fast and mean and vicious.

"Little *fucken* fag."

I said, "You've been whacking off to my picture again, Legs?" in the mock-amorous voice, but I was scared, and he knew it, and he ignored this, and just kept advancing and insulting, first in a kind of baby-talk whisper, then in a sharp hiss, until we arrived back at my room, which was at the end of the hall. Other kids were watching at this point. That made it better, and worse. He pushed and stared me fifty feet down the hall, intently saying "fag" and "Wilsey" and "Shaaawn" over and over with increasing not fucking around–ness, until I had to stop just past my room, at the wall where the hall dead-ended, and then he slugged me in the arm contemptuously, and I pretended it didn't hurt, and hit him back as hard as I could, which obviously *didn't* hurt, and some tears sprang out of tear storage and wobbled there in my eyes, just barely not running down my face, and I got the last sarcastic face-saving word: "I looove yooou toooo, Raaahb." My throat hurt from not crying. I still had to make it to the shower. Rob's friend T.D. Thompson started laughing. T.D. was a big, lanky Swamp Yankee with a loud, nasal, insinuating voice. He hated me because he was patriotic, and I was from San Francisco, which was not really America, and my best and only real friend was Russian. T.D. called us "brothers" and "comrades" and gave me the nickname "Chernyenko." He said it really drawn out, nasal and whiney, "Hey Chair-knee-*yenk*-ohhh," every time I walked past him. Now that Rob had pushed me down the hall calling me a fag in my towel and T-shirt, T.D. laughed and said, in his twangy, angry, sarcastic voice, "Take a shower Chair-knee-*yenk*-ohhh, you stink."

I took a shower. It was a sad, nervous, hurried shower. I hoped my weakness hadn't inspired somebody to trash my room. Room trashing was a popular pastime that involved entering a room—there were no locks—and ruining everything in it: ripping buttons off shirts; throwing sheets off the bed; shattering the lightbulbs; ripping the posters from the wall and tearing them in half (if you had a poster of Heather Locklear exiting a hot tub, as I did, her crotch would be torn out and tacked to your door); hocking up phlegm on the doorknob; throwing paint on the desk; knifing boom box speakers; tossing shoes out the window; and then gathering a little group of ten or so others to come and watch the victim's reaction (all the while remaining completely anonymous). On more than a few mornings that was my fate, and I wouldn't know who'd done it, though a crowd would be there awaiting my return. I'd walk down the hall and accumulate a wake of people as I neared my door, and everybody would start looking at me as if I were famous, as if I were about to meet with a world leader. My first instinct would be to smile, but just then I'd realize I was heading home to a trashed room. Sometimes someone would go into the bathroom and talk with me in order to keep me occupied until the trashers had finished a particularly ambitious trashing. I'd think, *Why the fuck is this guy who usually hates me in here talking with me and smiling, unless . . . fuck fuck fuck!,* but it was always too late to catch them in the act.

LEGGAT AND T.D. Thompson were usually backed up by inviolable, shit-kicking Tucker Hall, who looked like a little Aryan tank, and whose dad, Brinley Hall, was the head of admissions.

Tucker lived right next door to me after I got separated from Matt Plum and viewed my room as a convenient place to get free things. He stole whatever he liked of mine. I would then sneak into his room, find whatever he'd stolen, take it back, and then neither one of us would speak of it. Tucker also had the weird habit of occasionally skipping an opportunity to be cruel, maybe just by not making a disparaging remark when I passed him in the hall—something Leggat and T.D. Thompson could never resist.

I frequently encountered T.D., who liked to run through the dorms with a fake Mohawk glued to a bald wig, which, since he was already large and unpredictable, made him terrifying. He was in the fifth form, but he had been spurned by his age group, and he chose to hang out with the third-form jocks. He was bitingly sarcastic—the most impregnably sarcastic person I'd ever encountered. It was dazzling how sarcastic he was. He never called me anything other than "Chernyenko." Rodberg was sometimes "Andropov" and sometimes "Brezhnev." It varied. But T.D. loved to say "Chernyenko." He had a real genius for saying it and drawing it out and making it very funny. It was the perfect airtight put-down. What do you say back to a guy who is hulking, two years older, wearing a bald wig with a Mohawk glued to it, and calling you by the name of the ailing Soviet leader? Eventually he came up with alternate nicknames for Rodberg and me. "The Schnoz" for Rodberg and "The Forehead" for me.

Rodberg was generous, kind, morose, fond of chess (though not especially good), dingily attired, caustic, an avoider of showers, about the only Jewish kid in the school. He didn't quite have a grip on America *or* Russia. He was sweet, oblivious, and in the sentimental habit of wearing a tracksuit from the boycotted 1980 Summer Olympic Games in Moscow.

He would learn the hard way.

I STOPPED AT Alex's spartan room every morning after my shower to wake him up for breakfast. (The third form was required to attend breakfast.) He slept half-dressed, in a button-down, opaque black socks, and institutional, Soviet-looking, brief underwear. The light in his room was gray. He'd pull on a pair of ash-colored slacks and we'd walk down to the dining hall. Hockey players would be zestily wolfing down bowls of cereal. Someone would look up and shout, "Hey Chair-knee-*yenk*-ohhh!" Beautiful girls with sexily mussed hair sat with the jocks.

We'd shuffle to the center of the huge, churchlike, wood-paneled dining hall and write our names in a ledger, proving we were there, then leave. We'd go back to Alex's room. He'd get back in bed. We'd split a package of Pop-Tarts and a Coke. This was the best part of the day, a brief half hour when we could talk. Alex was fine, sardonic company—though no one else saw this in him. Then he'd get up, put on the ash slacks, put on a tie, pour some cologne in his palm and spread it through his hair, don an exhausted hand-me-down sport coat, and head off to class. Already dressed, I'd do the same.

. . .

THEN I REALIZED Rodberg was the source of my alienation. I had to dump him.

This was easy. I shoveled snow into his bed when he was brushing his teeth, before lights out, alerted some cool kids, and hung around with them to watch the discovery.

He smiled wryly until he realized what had happened, and then he looked so deeply dismayed that I thought he might cry. "Why did you do this, Sean?" he said, simply.

I said, "I thought it would remind you of mother Russia, *Schnoz*. A little taste of home."

Everybody laughed.

*Dad will be pleased*, I thought.

Dad only ever called Rodberg "the Russian," and didn't seem to think he was the right kind of person to become friends with. The next time we talked on the phone he said, "How's the Russian?"

"We're not friends anymore," I said.

He said, "Oh," and we didn't talk for a long time after that. I called, but he was always out.

IN MY SINGLE I realized I could take advantage of another unusual architectural feature of Coe House.

Each room could be opened up and connected to its neighbor by way of a sliding door. These had all been nailed firmly shut. My single was second to last on the hall, with a vacant room next door, locked and used for storage. Only faculty and a few sixth formers had access. I figured I'd open the party door and use this room as a lounge. The main appeal of having a lounge in the storage room was that nobody would ever look for me there. I would be able to hide out.

At night and during free periods, for a week, I pried the nails out of the sliding door, carefully, slowly, so as not to make noise or leave evidence. At the end of the week I was done. It was early afternoon, toward the end of one of my free periods. I slid open the door, walked triumphantly into the room, which was hot and mostly empty, and found something completely unexpected sitting in the middle of the floor: a huge sack of crushed Budweiser cans.

It was a clear plastic sixty-gallon sack. The cans were densely packed and smelled yeasty in the closeness of the room.

It was like finding a dead body! These beer cans had been massacred. Drained and crushed. *Hundreds* of cans. One hundred? Two hundred? More. Financially, the ability to purchase such a vast quantity of beer was totally beyond me, let alone the finesse required to negotiate the acquisition of fake IDs, transportation, friends. All this flashed through my mind. I was looking for a place to hide. And here was a reminder of what I was trying to hide from. I could not hang out with this. I couldn't even believe it had been lurking on the other side of the wall from me for months. I felt sick. It was part envy. I'd come home to Mom's for spring break that year so filled with the St. Mark's notion of glamorous drunkenness that I swiped and drank a full bottle of Myers's rum, posed in the mirror drinking it and singing and making suave faces and getting happy, passed out, and woke up the next morning covered in a film of vomit. I never did it again. I thought I'd been lucky not to drown.

I looked at the sack. It was disgusting, excessive, like some kind of contaminated egg sac—all the lips of the people I hated had been all over all those cans. I had to get the thing out. Out of my redoubt. My hideaway.

I thought, as I opened the window, *This belongs to the seniors, so they can fucking have it,* got ten feet back, where no one could see me, surrounded by beams and trusses for the room's jungle gym, and hucked the sack. Somehow it sailed straight through, silently, without snagging or even *grazing* the sill, then continued its trajectory, way out, and smashed down on the quad. It was a perfect throw. I experienced an unexpected moment of grace. The sack blew apart, releasing its hundreds of beer cans. I went back, resealed the party door, grabbed my binder and books, and went to class.

THE SACK SAILED as if it had been catapulted over the walls of a medieval city. Smashed cans rolled across the grass. Stale beer scent filled the air. The sack sacked the quad! In a moment everything was laid bare. Paradoxes were united. The whole drink'n'haze-our-way-to-Yale bullshit of St. Mark's, the faculty looking the other way while everybody posed with their vodka and shotgun in the yearbook. This pretty quadrangle masking this zoo of evil.

Beer on the quad! It was an allegorical tableau!

I don't know why I was so lucky. Probably because I did it without thinking. If the thing had snagged just a little bit on the sill it would have fallen straight down from the window, along the outside wall of the building, and onto the path that ran next to the quad. Somebody would have seen it falling. Spotted the window. Or it would have made noise nicking the sill and somebody would have looked up. And these scenarios would have made the whole thing just the act of some thwarted kid looking for a hiding place. It was the apparitional quality that attached itself to the incident that made it so perfect. Plum, full of newfound respect for me, likened it to a supernatural visitation. Like the thing had just been beamed there, *Star Trek*–style.

I never got caught. And whoever put the beer there in the first place never came after me. But there was a clampdown on the whole sixth form. Their party was over! First they had to clean it up (since it was their quad, they were the only ones who *could* clean it up). Then a probationary period descended. Privileges were revoked. All the swaggerers walked around cowed for the rest of the term. The class of '85 went out with a whimper.

Right after it happened, as I walked to algebra, one of the cool, stoned-out seniors, a burner who never so much as made an extra gesture, came running up the stairs and down the hall of Coe House screaming, "There's a *baad* scene on the quad!"

BLANE MORF had gotten a skateboard while I was away at St. Mark's. When I came home for summer vacation—on probation for my straight D-minus average—I discovered that he was a skater. Skating had been in a dormant phase since its heyday in the seventies. But San Francisco was one of the places where it was beginning to come back. S.F. was the city where *Thrasher* magazine was published and half the photos in it were taken. But Blane didn't know any other skaters. The kind of personality that's drawn to skateboarding isn't the kind of personality that's given to sociability.

Skateboarders are lonely. Skateboarders are not well loved.

I was lonely and not well loved!

I tried his board. He taught me a few things. It was no fun watching while the other skated. He begged me to get my own. I got some money out of Mom, went down to the skate shop, and bought myself a skateboard. Then I climbed to the top of Russian Hill.

At the crest of Green, where it meets Leavenworth, is the lower of the two summits of Russian Hill. Green then slopes down again, leveling off midblock on its way to Jones and my house, behind which is the higher summit, at the top of Vallejo. By San Francisco standards, this half block of slope isn't a hill, because it kinks back to horizontal after about 150 feet.

I set down my board, stepped on, pushed off. My plan was to roll the whole slope and use the flat to slow down gradually before the intersection. I had no backup plan.

The acceleration was instant. In a matter of seconds I was moving faster than my legs had ever taken me. After thirty feet I was moving faster than I'd ever moved outside of a car. Faster. Without thinking I locked my legs at the knees and stood as if I were trying to look over a fence, the instinct—a terrible instinct—being to get as far away as possible from the rushing tarmac. My knees should have been bent, body low, arms out to the sides. The board started rocking side to side, trucks (the metal suspension/steering system) slamming back-and-forth, fast, hard left, and then fast, hard right. It felt like the board was possessed and wanted to throw me off. I had what's known among skaters as the (dreaded) speed wobbles. And once they start there's no way to stay on.

I bailed just before the bottom of the slope and tried to run it out, knees aching when I hit the ground, going so fast it was like a wind was pushing me from behind. I kept my feet for ten feet and watched my new board rocketing down the block toward the intersection. Then the speed shoved me over. I pitched forward, screamed "Fuck!" with more anger than I'd ever expressed in public (skateboarding, like learning a foreign language, offers a whole new personality), and as I heard my voice echo off the buildings I slammed onto the street, hands first, torso second, thighs third, calves and feet up in the air behind me—and began to slide.

This was like bobsledding! I had all the speed of a bobsledder. But without the sled, or snow. There was just me and some fabric and the concrete.

I was no longer going down the center of the street, but, since my last step had been off my right foot, I was plowing into the oncoming left lane, toward the parallel-parked cars on the far side of the street, my destination the front tire of a dark-blue, two-door Honda. I braced for impact, closed my eyes, missed the tire, and instead went under the driver's-side door—a deeper dark filled my head—and kept going, calves banging against the car's plastic frame and flopping back down, head dinging off something in the undercarriage and then down to the street, until I was wedged under the trunk, between gas tank and pavement, my cheek jammed up on the curb.

The curb is the piece of the city that skaters are most often concerned with. Mine was cold, and I could smell it: oil and salt. I also could taste it in the back of my throat. I'd never looked properly at curbs until I learned to skate. Steel-edged ones make for long, fast grinds (slides on your trucks). Regular ones make for loud, sloppy grinds. This one was plain and clean and angular, no rounded steel edge (coping, as skaters and masons call it). I was feeling a strange mixture of sensations: pain, embarrassment, isolation, and a pleasurable sort of intimacy with the hidden parts of the city. I felt like I had just survived a rare experience. I was glad to be still. I thought that beneath a Honda might be a good place to lie low for a while and nurse my wounds. I had never crawled under a car on the street before. There was something good about it. It was like a cramped and filthy fortress.

Then—*shit!*—I remembered my board. I scrambled back out.

I stood, but I couldn't move. The slide beneath the car had ripped my pants off. I stood on top of Russian Hill in my underwear, ankles cuffed together. I pulled my pants back up. They were full of holes. My shirt looked like someone had thrown acid at me. My chin was sore. The skin was grated off the palms of my hands. I started to run.

A man and two women, all middle-aged, came running towards me. The women hollered, "Oh, my God!" The man bellowed, "Are you O.K.? Are you O.K.?"

"Yeah, yeah—I'm fine! *Fine!*" I said, angry, and then I ran faster, chasing my board, which had made it across the intersection, my hamburger hands throbbing, holding up my pants, feeling slow. I got on and pushed the last twenty feet to my house.

From then on being from San Francisco meant being from the world capital of skateboarding. After sliding beneath the car I came out in another city. I'd never understood skateboarding before that fall. Skating is a feeling— if you really want to get it, you have to do it. And being from San Francisco was something to be proud of.

THAT SUMMER, the more I thought about it the more I was convinced: I was gonna *get it on* with Dede! It was only a matter of time! She wanted it. I wanted it. She knew it. I knew it. We were just waiting for the opportunity. I expected her to pull up next to me in the teal Mercedes while I was skateboarding on Market Street. She'd be wearing a Burberry raincoat, high heels, nothing else.

"Get in," she'd say, and drive me down to one of the motor lodges on Lombard.

I started looking at her slyly, as though we shared *a secret*. When Dede told me to do something I said, "Ummm-*hmmm*. Oohhh-*kay*. Dee*dee*," like I was *in on it*. I moved slowly—*sexily*—to comply, keeping my eyes on her all the time.

*Obviously she wants me.*

*She gave me that smile.*

*She has to have it.*

*She's in her thirties—that's a woman's **sexual** prime.* (Actually, she was in her forties.)

*She's been trying to resist me. But now I am becoming a man. She cannot resist for long.*

MOM HAD JUST heard something scandalous from Danielle Steel, who'd heard it from John Traina, who'd heard it from Alda Polo, Dede's housekeeper.

At some dinner in Dede's formal dining room, back when everyone was still with their original spouses, Dede had disappeared into the basement in search of another bottle of wine, taking Dad with her since, Dede had said, "he knows so much about wine." They were gone for what seemed far too long. Alda went down to see what was keeping them, and there, supposedly, was Dede on her knees, giving Dad a blow job. After recounting this story Mom confided in me, with sweet, strange innocence, "I wondered what they were doing down there for so long in the basement."

I thought, *This is an inappropriate thing to be hearing from my mother. I wonder if it's true.* And, *I wonder if I could get a blow job from Dede.*

DEDE REMAINED the main focus of my libido until José, a doorman I was friendly with at Mom's building, alerted me to a girl who'd moved in on the twenty-third floor.

"Jessica on twenty-three—she's fine," José said.

I alerted Blane, and Blane ended up riding in the elevator with her one day. He confirmed it: "She's totally hot, Sean."

This was huge. The main impediment, as I saw it, to meeting girls in San Francisco was that I never was in proximity to any. But now. The Summit was *my* turf. Fine/hot Jessica would be mine, too.

I began cruising the elevators at times I judged likely for Jessica to be on the move: early evening, when she might be going to a movie, or out to dinner with her family; Saturday afternoons. I would call an elevator to the penthouse, jam my skateboard in the door to keep it from shutting, and then call and ride the remaining one—if she was going anywhere she'd have to get in with me. I would dress as cool as possible (a *Ghostbusters* hooded sweatshirt and khaki cargo pants), sit on the floor, read *Thrasher* magazine, and wait for someone else to get in—holding my breath and scrambling to my feet every time the car entered the lower twenties and slowed, then leaning into the corner and nonchalantly tapping a black Converse All Star. I smiled at women in their sixties complaining about how long it had taken for the elevator to arrive, impatient husbands heading for the garage, all people who knew me and my parents. I said, "Hello

Mrs. . . . ," over and over again. Then, when I was most bored and least expecting it, Jessica got on. The elevator stopped on twenty-three. I looked up—*Oh
shit*—and then she was standing there, like some kind of apparition (hot *indeed*),
and I was still on the floor and couldn't think of anything to say, and then she
was gone. I went back up to our floor and Mom was standing there, on her way
out, having just discovered the other elevator, its emergency buzzer sounding,
skateboard stuck in its door—"What *is* this, Sean?"

After that I decided to be bold, write Jessica a note, in collaboration with
Blane, and leave it on her door.

> *Howdy.*
> *We were wondering if you and a friend want to go see a movie? Preferably*
> *Ghostbusters definitely not The Karate Kid.*
> *Call us.*
> *Sean and Blane 775-2813*

There was no response. When I ran into Jessica in the elevator a second time,
a month or so later, I was with Mom and wearing my hooded *Ghostbusters* sweatshirt, which made it obvious that I was the one who'd written the note. It had occurred to me by then that holding up *Ghostbusters* as wholly superior to *The
Karate Kid* might just be alienating rather than a bold assertion of taste, and that
girls enjoyed and even loved *The Karate Kid*. Jessica looked at me, looked bored,
looked at the floor, got out.

HALFWAY THROUGH the summer, up in the country, after months of boast-
ing and fantasizing and masturbating, I found myself alone with Dede. Todd
and Trevor were with their father, and Dad was flying. The house's longtime
caretakers had just been fired, and Dede was interviewing replacements, so we
were completely alone. Dad had tried to get me to come with him, but I'd looked
over at Dede, smiled (*sexily?*), and said, "No thanks, *Dad*. I'd really like to stay
here with *Dede*." When I heard him take off I thought, O.K. . . .

Dede was at the pool, in a green and white one-piece bathing suit. I was in
plaid Gotcha shorts. I took off my shirt. I tried to catch her eye.

I said, "Can I get you something to drink?"

"You want a Coke, don't you, Sean?"

"No! I mean, *sure*, Coke would be nice. But I want to bring *you* something."

"A Pepsi Lite," she said without looking up.

PepsiCo had discontinued Pepsi Lite a few years before. The local gourmet store had a standing order to hold it for Dede if they found any. It was her favorite drink, and she had stockpiled large quantities of it in tall glass bottles ("the way it tastes best," she said). I sprinted up to the house, took a side door, went down a hall, then into a pantry. On the floor were dozens of six packs of Diet Pepsi, her replacement beverage, in identical bottles. The Pepsi Lites, in their light blue and lemon-yellow cardboards, were at the back, behind the Diet Pepsis. I turned on the light, went to the back, and found that every Pepsi Lite carton was now filled with Diet Pepsis. I checked each slot to be sure. Finally, I grabbed a Diet Pepsi, took it to the kitchen, found one of the tall, green, beveled-plastic glasses she favored, filled it with ice, poured, and brought it out to the pool.

Dede was on her back now. I scoped out her ass. It was beautiful, doughy white. I thought I should say something suave, like, "I figured a Diet Pepsi would go down better on a day like today," but instead I said, "Dede, I'm sorry, I couldn't *find* a Pepsi Lite, I looked all over, but all the Pepsi Lite cartons were full of Diet Pepsi so I'm really sorry, but, seriously, you're out . . . I brought you a *Diet Pepsi!*"

Dede sat up, annoyed. I looked at her breasts. They looked great. "I should never have sent *you* to find one. I'm not out. I know exactly how many I've drank, and no one else is allowed to touch them." She spun, planted her feet in a pair of sandals, and started up to the house. I followed, still carrying the Diet Pepsi. It fizzed at me. I watched her ass. *What am I supposed to do with this Diet Pepsi?* I thought. *I'm not going to drink it.* Then I realized, *We're going inside.*

I padded after her into the pantry, where she bent over in her bathing suit and inspected the cartons.

I thought, *This is it! This is it, Dude! She's led you back here to a dark room and now she's bending over for a reason! She knows there's no Pepsi Lite! She didn't want to fuck you outside in case Dad flew over in the helicopter! She wanted to get you back here where it's safe. And dark and sexy. The Pepsi Lite was a ruse. It's the perfect seduction! She's waiting. She wants you! She's bending over and offering it to you! Make your move! Go! Go! Grab! Grab it! Grab her ass! Pull down her suit! She wants it! This is it! Come on! Come on come on come on come on come on on on on on on! . . . Whip it out! Put down the Diet Pepsi.*

The Diet Pepsi continued to mist my hand and I looked for someplace to rest it. I couldn't pull out my penis and grab her ass with a Diet Pepsi in my hand. There was a shelf full of blackberry preserves, canned by the couple Dede had fired. I thought of them. They had taken me catfishing. I leaned against the shelf, rattled the jars, and Dede looked up. Her face was angry.

"Where are my Pepsi Lites?" she said. "Someone's been drinking my Pepsi Lites."

"I don't like Pepsi Lite," I said weakly.

Dede straightened, put her hands on her hips, said, "Someone's in big trouble," and exited the pantry.

THAT SUMMER the panty raids began. In the country Blane and I snuck into Dede's huge closet—formerly Mom's huge closet—when Todd and Trevor were at their dad's, Dad and Dede were at a party, and the new couple Dad and Dede had hired, Knute and Eileen Flynt, were both in bed. (Knute was a ruined millionaire turned butler, also formerly pilot of his own helicopter, and quite deaf. Eileen was deaf, too, as well as dowdy. And they were each the subject of great amusement to Dad and Dede and the stepbrothers.)

Blane and I headed right to Dede's panty drawer, to her soft, dark, sexy, lacy panties, like moths (us and them), and sniffed. We pressed them to our faces and inhaled, reverently. They were "sweet" and "musty." We smelled some more.

"Juiced," we said to each other.

"Smell these ones, Dude."

"Ahh."

Again, Dede, who knew all about the length of my phone calls, didn't know about this. We decided we were safe if we didn't steal a pair.

HAVING MADE IT through the first year at St. Mark's, with an unsounded abyss of a G.P.A., I was allowed to come back the next year with the understanding that I had spent the summer reviewing math and French and English. I had skateboarded and sniffed panties. But sophomore year I was cleverer *and* stupider. In order to get another single I convinced my roommate, James Souvlis, a newly arrived student who I christened "Biker Dude" because of his interest in cycling, that I had a cocaine problem. I crushed up aspirin and snorted it during study hall. I smoked it in a corncob pipe I'd bought at the sundries shop in town. He moved out. But snorting aspirin was too beer-on-the-quad fun to give up. It became a performance. I got a razor and mirror and a rolled-up dollar and went around snorting it in public. I walked up to a group of students talking in the hall, looked around with exaggerated nervousness, sniffing, rubbing my nose, then pulled out my mirror, set it down on a windowsill, cut a couple lines of smashed aspirin, inhaled, looked around, as if it had just occurred to me that this might not be the most private drug-snorting location, pressed one nostril closed and inhaled deeply through the other, switched sides, threw my head back, snorted hard, then ran.

I went to French class with a little white powder arranged around my nose. I sniffed loudly. I got bloody noses and had to ask to be excused. (When certain cool girls got bloody noses in class a reverent hush would fall—it was a profoundly glamorous event.) Eventually I snorted so much aspirin and ended up with so many bloody noses Dad had to take me to get my nostrils cauterized on Christmas break.

I stopped when two sixth formers took me aside, nervously, and told me they were coke users, and it was serious to them: "It's not some joke, man," they said. They were reputed to be dealers, too, and I must have been fucking with their business by fucking with their glamour, making it all a joke. But it was a ridiculous warning. They didn't really know what to say. I stopped not so much because I was afraid, but because I couldn't imagine it getting any better than that.

ONE BENEFIT of ditching Rodberg the year before was that Matt Plum had decided to be my friend. Plum and I were walking by Rodberg's room one day when Plum turned and barged straight in on Alex and his new roommate from the United Arab Emirates and challenged the former to a fight.

I followed somewhat apologetically behind. Rodberg looked up. Plum shouted:

"Fight me, Rodberg!"

"No."

"Then fight Wilsey."

Beat of silence.

"*O.K.*"

And it was decided. Plum signed me up, arranged a time, and then we left. I was fighting Rodberg in three days. It would be at night, in his room, after study hall. There would be a small crowd, but not too many people. Seven or eight, tops.

Plum was all confidence. "We'll kick his ass."

"We?"

"I'm your trainer. I'll get you in shape. Give you some tips. You can't back out of this."

It was to be a "punch fight." A punch fight, Plum explained knowledgably, was different from a fistfight in that the opponents took turns throwing punches one after the other. It was like a slowed-down, structured fistfight. You couldn't hit in the face, and you couldn't hit below the belt. A punch fight went on until someone fell on the ground or failed to return a punch. Endurance was key. It was to your advantage to be meaty, which Plum was, and Rodberg wasn't, and I *really* wasn't.

Three days later we arrived playing what Plum called my training song, "Born in the U.S.A.," on a boom box. The lyrics were embarrassing and had nothing to do with me, except for maybe the part about "covering up." There were about ten spectators, including a couple of seniors, one of whom stood leaning against the door to prevent anyone from walking in on us. The fight began half an hour before bed. We flipped for first punch, and Rodberg won. I'd never been hit full force in the gut before. Plum told me to tighten my stomach muscles during our training. I did. Rodberg gave me a thick-browed stare. I held my stomach muscles tight. He was wearing a gray T-shirt instead of his usual untucked, semitransparent dress shirt. I looked at his wispy mustache. *Can't do this forever,* I thought. Then he hit me. It hurt, but not that bad! I was still standing. I had not instantly crumpled! I had survived! I felt cocky.

Now it was my turn. "C'mon, Schnoz," I said, "is that the best you've got?" I taunted him a bit more. "You ready to go down, Schnoz?"

"Don't waste time, Wilsey," he said.

I hit him, twisting my fist as I connected, like Plum told me to. Alex didn't flinch. I saw a thought flicker behind his eyes. It was: *I'm stronger.* Then he hit me again, fast, and I took a step back with the impact. I returned with a weak shot that glanced away between his stomach and arm. I fell forward into him.

"Sorry," I said, and straightened. He hit me again.

I hit him back. He hit me again, instantly, center of the solar plexus, knocking me back, sending a sour pain through my stomach.

"Jesus," I said. "Give me a chance to get ready . . . Schnoz."

He laughed and said simply, "Hit me, Wilsey." I could hardly believe how tough he looked.

I righted my stance, pulled back, looked him in the eye, hit him as hard and straight as I could. I felt the connection. Better. He gave a little grunt. Then he hit me high, in the bones of the chest, which surprised and hurt me in a different way. I hit him back in the same place, but the angle was wrong and it was a weak shot. He got me in the chest again. I tried it again, hurt my hand.

Plum yelled, "C'mon Wilsey, straight arm!"

I stood back. Rodberg nailed me in the stomach again. The pain was cumulative, one blow adding to the next. I pictured my torso infrared. He looked fine.

My punches were harmless. I might as well have been crumpling up balls of note-book paper and throwing them at him. Fritos. The only light was Rodberg's desk lamp. We were so close to each other. I couldn't help remembering how much I had liked him. I *still* liked him. He was the only one who had stuck by me after that bullshit radiator story. He wasn't the reason everybody had hated me; he was the only one good enough not to hate me. Though now he hated me for real.

Rodberg was the Iron Curtain. I realized he was never going to give in. He could take more of this than I could. I was taking more and more time with my punches. Everybody was yelling at me. I joked feebly. "Schnoz . . ." and everybody shouted at me to hit him. I thought, *The second I hit him he's going to hit me.* Then I made a decision. I hit him. Rodberg hit me. I cried out, buckled over, and hissed, "That was below the belt! You *motherfucking cheater,* that was . . . Below. The. Belt! You *fucking slime,* Schnoz!" Then I ran, stumbled, pushed the guard-standing senior away from in front of the door, and fled down the hall.

Such gleaming cowardice!

The next day I woke up with cuts and bruises all over my chest, which was throbbing—so tender I could barely touch it.

"Jesus! You look awful, Wilsey," Plum said when I ran into him in the shower. He touched me. I winced. He frowned. "I'll go see how Rodberg looks." A cou-ple minutes later he came back and reported, "He's fine. Not a *single mark.*" He touched me again. He seemed worried about me. "Maybe you should go to the infirmary? No . . ." Confused. "It's like he didn't even get hit."

THE ONE THING I liked about St. Mark's was the oldness of the place. I loved wandering through all the untouched dust and solitude and peace of the base-ment, where students weren't supposed to go. I would sneak down there late at night or between classes and find things: a quarter-mile concrete passageway—full of pipes and conduits and offshoot crawl spaces, like something out of a sub-marine movie—that led all the way across campus to a generator building full of huge, loud machinery; a firing range, complete with targets and pulleys, covered in so much dust it looked like the wreck of the *Titanic.*

Plum and I discovered a filthy crawl space that dropped us through a ceiling into a room where they stored all the Cokes for the soda vending machines. We stole case after case and hauled them to our rooms in our laundry bags.

We stole a ring of keys to every door in the school out of the night watch-man's booth. Using them we entered a locked wing of the basement and discovered the school's main circuit breakers. They were ancient, primitive, brass things with wooden handles. Plum and I loved hardware stores, and it was amazing the things we were able to buy in them (including a plumber's blowtorch we used to incinerate our stolen Coke cans). After discovering the breakers Plum bought a huge pair of insulated rubber gloves. He donned them, said, "Here goes," and shut down the entire school.

A lot of students had arrived for fourth form. And some of the new kids thought this was pretty cool. I found people who wanted to be my friends. There were two other skaters, and we formed a little fellowship.

BACK IN THE FIFTIES James Thurber came to do a reading, got drunk, and graffitied pornographic cartoons all over one of the bathrooms. The school immediately removed all the tiles, boxed them up, and placed them somewhere in the vast basement. So on my sorties I was sometimes looking for the Thurber tiles, sometimes looking for a fabled secret passage that led to the gym (or "Field House," as St. Mark's called it), and pretty much always looking for something off-limits or illegal, such as the key to the fridge where they kept the wine for visiting alumni and trustees. That one hadn't been on the night watchman's ring.

There was a whole sexual undercurrent to the basement, like an emanation from the Thurber tiles. The basement was where the butt room was and, consequently, where my worldly-seeming fantasy girls hung out. A passageway in the basement was where the spy hole into the girls' showers turned out to be.

I roamed around down there with a small complement of fellow fuckups. We were probably the most marginal group of people in the school—not even the tolerated "artsy" butt-room crowd, but nearly invisible little particles flying through a foreign atmosphere. Trying desperately to form ourselves into a legitimized, cohesive group, we were the perfect insignificant people, dingy, unaccounted for, half of us Chaff, attracted to all that dust, while up above the school of real people engaged in real activities. We were the brotherhood of the basement.

A boy who I'll call Damon March looked like the blond Duke boy from *The Dukes of Hazzard*, only short, conniving, with a mouth full of braces, and from Massachusetts. Together we discovered the shower spy hole. We had been sneaking around at night, and one of us thought to follow a water pipe into the locker room where the day school girls changed and showered, and pry off the molding where it passed through the wall, so that if you stood on a chair and pressed the side of your face to the pipe, you could see into the shower stalls.

Unfortunately, it was a hot water pipe, so when a few showers got going the heat was unbearable. March and I had red, pipe-shaped imprints on our right temples till we figured out to wrap a towel around it.

To March it was, without misgiving or embarrassment, the coolest thing that had ever happened. He started venturing down there on his own, without proper lookouts. Eventually, in his overzealousness, he got spotted, and the hole was sealed up, which was almost a relief. Seeing these girls that we knew and some-times even talked to—the day students were the most accessible girls in the school—completely shifted the planet. It seemed like an impossible violation of the laws of physics, beautiful at first, but then frightening and wrong. Like split-ting the atom.

THEN MATT PLUM brought a video camera back from Thanksgiving vaca-tion, and everything changed. A bunch of us decided to make a movie. We were a band of superheroes, called G-string, out to save the planet from an evil crea-ture called The Baad Thing, in honor of the senior who came running through Coe House shouting about the "baad scene on the quad." We made *The Baad Thing* and *Baad Thing II—Baad Thing Rising* and showed them to the school one Friday night. Suddenly we were celebrities. Two girls came up to me and said, "That was really funny. We didn't know you were *cool*." I didn't know what to say. A girl named Jen let me take her to the practice rooms in the music building and touch her breasts. She shoved my hand back as I attempted to move her shirt up enough to see a nipple. I just barely glimpsed it before she said, "No!" I could touch, but not look. She didn't let me take her back to the practice rooms, but she was nice to me.

Another new kid and I managed to get hold of a bottle of vodka, got drunk, and went to see Allen Ginsberg give a poetry reading to the school. He played a bongo, read "The Tyger," and then read his own stuff. When he read the line "Come in my ear!" we exploded with laughter and had to leave. I was starting to have fun at St. Mark's.

WHEN THE RAPE happened, and the school was descended upon by reporters and concerned parents, an issue of almost equal concern on campus was the fate of one of the most popular seniors, who had walked into the dorm room where the drunk girl had been laid out naked (or, according to the *New York Times* ar-ticle about the incident, "dressed only in an unbuttoned shirt"), seen a host of guys around her, taken a look, and decided it seemed consensual. The school had to discipline him, and everyone was worried that this might affect his early admission to Yale. In the end they decided to suspend him and allow him to finish the term at home, and Yale let him come the next year. One more St. Marker on to the Ivy League.

The feeling of having it made—rapist or not—certainly pervaded St. Mark's. My father, who was of this you're-at-St.-Mark's-you've-got-it-made-for-life opinion, bragged about my presence there (the only thing he'd ever bragged about in connection with me) until I made it clear that I didn't have it made, by failing, failing, failing, for which he then resented me.

Here's how the headmaster described the rape in his letter to St. Mark's parents:

On Wednesday evening, December 11, two fourth formers, a boy and a girl, drank a large quantity of vodka in the woods. They returned to the main building and checked into their respective dormitories. Later, the boy went to the girl's room and they engaged in sexual intercourse. They were intoxicated. The girl became ill and went to sleep. The boy returned to his dormitory. After some conversation with his roommate, the boy went back to the girl's dormitory and brought her back to his room. She was clothed in a buttoned shirt. The girl remembers nothing of these events. The boy's roommate alerted some students of her presence and the word spread in the dormitory. Several students, many of them seniors, entered the room at various times. Some awakened others to bring them to the scene, some offered insulting and demeaning suggestions and comments. However, at no time did any of this larger group actually touch the girl. Some who came upon the scene were revolted and walked away. Some were stunned and shocked and tried to influence other members of the group to bring the scene to a halt. Later a group of students did return the girl to her dormitory.

Elsewhere in this angry and searching letter, he says, "We must ask ourselves what kind of attitudes toward the opposite sex St. Mark's fosters." How hard would it have been to look at the yearbook? Flip past the picture of third-former bras strung up in the dining hall with sixth-form jocks raising their hands in victory beneath them ("'85 members commenced their reign of power by decorating the dining hall with thirty-seven newbie bras!") and check out the following few examples. Picture: A teacher leering and walking behind a group of girls in plaid field-hockey skirts. Caption: "I'd follow these girls anywhere." Picture: Two girls talking earnestly. Caption: "Meg, have you thought about an abortion?"

Picture: A guy and a girl by the school store. He's taking out his money. Caption: "Five now and five after."

OF COURSE, the fourth-form boy at the heart of the incident was Damon March.

I wouldn't say that I felt responsible. Because I didn't. But I felt affiliated. I felt like I should have known. It felt inevitable.

What March was doing was fitting in. He'd hit on something that would give him status, and he had no remorse. He'd taken home the same yearbook. He'd studied it like me. He was providing proof of his conquest, since the girl would never have admitted to sleeping with him. He was doing what St. Mark's had taught him to do. That's what was so sinister about it.

I can just see Damon smiling and feeling so cool that all these sixth formers were with him there, watching him with this beautiful naked girl.

No one would ever have believed him otherwise.

A photograph on the back page of a recent *St. Mark's Magazine,* which goes out to alumni, shows W. H. Auden, who was a guest teacher for one month in 1939, posing on the quad and having a cigarette. He's wearing a three-piece suit with a handkerchief in the breast pocket, and behind him, on the other side of the grass, a couple of sixth formers are lounging against a window frame. It all looks just the way it did forty-five years later. Right above Auden's head is the school's clock tower, and to the left are the windows of Sawyer House, the boys' dorm where the rape occurred. Two windows beyond the picture's frame is the room where it happened. Just over Auden's right shoulder is the room where I fought Rodberg. It's 2:10 in the afternoon.

WHEN I GOT kicked out for poor academic achievement I had to fly back with my dad to get my stuff. I was two months shy of sixteen. We packed up my room together, and then I told him I wanted a moment alone. While he waited outside I graffitied the fuck out of Sawyer House.

## Ten · WOODHALL

A FTER DAD AND I flew home, on his private jet, he took me to an educational consultant—a sort of real estate broker for schools—who recommended a place called Woodhall, in a town called Bethlehem (Connecticut), run by an ex-nun and largely supervised by a man who had preternaturally elongated appendages and the face of Jesus.

The Woodhall School's pamphletlike catalogue from 1986, which provided my first glimpse of the place, showed boys in straight-backed New England chairs beside mantels and ticking clocks, wearing knit ties, striding down wooded paths. It described the school's teaching approach as "individually designed to build basic skills and to make up educational lacunae." These goals were accomplished using "the time-honored pedagogy of the one-on-one Socratic method." The pamphlet promised a "solid restructuring of a student's scholastic patterns."

The reality was five hours of study hall during the day, and then a couple more hours of study hall in the evening. Classes lasted twenty minutes and were one-on-one with an instructor. When not in study hall we engaged in organized sports and "newspaper reading." To quote the pamphlet: "Because Bethlehem is host to the longest continuous annual hunt in America's history, there are many opportunities in town for equestrians."

This was not exactly the case. In fact, if any of us had read the pamphlet, instead of just looking at the pictures, we could have told you it was all a bunch of bullshit. That in reality the place was a trailer park mixed with a funeral parlor located in the muddiest boglands of western Connecticut and inhabited by Jesus, Mary, and twenty-five stoners.

There were no equestrians.

I would soon find out that all the students called the place "Woodhell."

But what was Jesus doing in hell? If Jesus had been taken down from the cross after five or six hours and transported to New England to live a sedentary life as a mathematics teacher he would've been indistinguishable from Mr. Chant, who taught algebra, supervised us in our limited evening and weekend free time, and lived above the dorms—in a tower directly above the T.V. room, at the top of the only significant flight of stairs on campus.

Mr. Chant had the lean, sensitive, intelligent face of Christ as depicted in every Renaissance painting and illustrated Bible, complete with wispy blond beard and deep-set, thoughtful, milky-blue eyes. The blueness of his eyes was emphasized by the fact that their whites were tinged blue, too. He was tall, slender, and loose-limbed, with disproportionately long arms and legs, toes, and fingers—these last being so long as to be spidery (the actual medical term for this is "arachnodactyly")—and a strangely shaped chest: truncated and pushed out, like the front of a locomotive.

He looked as though he had been stretched almost to the point of breaking.

He smoked, even though he had weak lungs. His legs were too long and fragile to hold him up on their own, so he walked with old-fashioned wooden crutches. These made a creaky sound to which we all became attuned, though he was extremely adept at masking the noise when he needed to.

On the rare occasions he failed to achieve perfect stealth, you'd think you were hearing creaking outside your door, late at night, as you were talking or smoking or sniffing something, and fall silent. Then, after a couple minutes, you'd hear it for sure: Mr. Chant heading away, like a boat rowed with oars deep in the water—not splashing, only creaking faintly.

But I didn't notice any of this. I didn't realize Mr. Chant had a rare condition called Marfan's syndrome that was transforming his resemblance to Jesus into a living tableau of the Crucifixion. I simply thought he was a tall, unusual-looking man, who'd maybe injured his legs skiing or something and now lived in a tower in Bethlehem, Connecticut.

Dad had lost hope and interest in me, and I could feel it. When the educational consultant recommended Woodhall he enrolled me hastily, dreading the idea that I might have to stay home, the most important factors in his decision being that the school was three thousand miles away and willing to admit me immediately. With St. Mark's he'd finally gotten me to boarding school. But in getting expelled from St. Mark's I had thwarted the perfect arrangement of being far away, out of his life, yet also somewhere that he could discuss without embarrassment at the society functions where he "literally dropped in, piloting his money-green jet helicopter" (to quote the *New York Times*).

Mom was too busy with her peace work to interfere. So Dad flew me out to be interviewed by the headmistress, an ex-nun called Sally Campbell Woodhall, who agreed to take me, after I wrote the following letter.

*March 20, 1986*

*Dear Mrs. Woodhall:*

*I would like very much to attend Woodhall and I am writing this letter to tell you why. It is obvious that I need a different approach to edgucation than the one I was getting at Saint Marks, and I think Woodhall has the right approach. The System of one teacher to one student is perfect for me to learn by, Also I am glad that the main focus is on academics so that my my mind will not wander as at Saint Marks. Under the supervision and care given at Woodhall I can do my best schoolasticaly. I really want to succede and I think I can get back on my feet at Woodhall. If you will accept me I promise to work my hardest.*

*Sincerely*

*Sean Wilsey*

Mrs. Woodhall told Dad I was exactly the kind of boy she could help.

WHEN I TRY to remember where the things that happened to me while I was a student at Woodhall actually happened—the location of the mall where we most often bought pot; or of the other mall where we smoked "dust," uprooted landscaping plants, and then threw them down into a central atrium, while I claimed I could see "tracers" flying from the soil that spun off their roots (I could not); or of the movie theater where I got really, really high and made people laugh on purpose and felt glamorous—*I can't*. Looking back, geographical ignorance and dislocation seems like an integral part of my experience: *Having no idea where I was*. Woodhall was in western Connecticut, but I had no clue about the geography of New England. I once took the bus to Boston instead of New York because I thought it was closer. I did not know that Connecticut, at least the portion surrounding Woodhall, was essentially an extended suburb of New York City. I did not even know that Connecticut had a coast. All I knew was that it had mud and snow and lots of towns with grim names—Killingworth, Killingly—linked together by strip malls. Perhaps this was my way of pretending I was not there.

Though I *was* there. And it was as if the sadness and failure that I could not shake had followed me and attached itself to the names and landscape that surrounded me.

At least that's what I thought while getting buzzed from beers ripped off from the local market, which, on Sundays, covered its alcohol in a black shroud and extinguished the lighting in that aisle—making the shoplifting easier.

INSIDE WOODHALL, all was wood.

A gray-brown wood paneling covered all the walls in the dorms and was so easily mutilated—fingernails tore right into it—that it seemed like balsa.

On the battered walls were sad, small, mounted posters from the MoMA (like Edward Hopper's twilight gas station), placed at irregular intervals, usually where there was no light, their corners soft and blurry from being rubbed by the winter coats of students, streaked brown by airborne arcs of Coke flying from cans not quite finished before getting hucked in the trash.

Everything felt wrong—doors that should have opened out opened inward; windows at the wrong height faced onto walls—and this feeling bled into everything:

. . . dim light . . .

. . . low ceilings . . .

. . . dingy carpet . . .

. . . low-watt bulbs . . .

. . . hasty construction . . .

. . . sweet, worn-out smell . . .

. . . easily disconnected smoke alarms . . .

. . . white sky . . .

. . . pasty people . . .

It made you want to stop trying.

Coming back from excursions to the mall we passed a junkyard right after passing the Bethlehem town line, and we knew we were home.

It would be hard to find a place where there would more obviously be less of a chance of something good happening.

BUT THERE WAS absolutely nothing malign or evil about Woodhall. St. Mark's *was* evil, whereas Woodhall was Mrs. Woodhall, and Mrs. Woodhall, the force behind all the contradictions, the Woodhallishness of Woodhall, was a small woman who lisped and taught French and wore tweed skirts and vests and white blouses with tuxedo ruffled fronts, a cameo nestled in their folds. Her hair was short and curly and boyish and brown and her eyes were twinkly. She had freckles. She looked like a real nun. She was just shy of plump. The staff referred to her as either "Mrs. Woodhall" or "the head" (her official title), with the exception of Mr. Chant, who called her Sally. Behind her back, all the students called her "Sally," too—out of affection, not disrespect. She was so good, so well intentioned, that we all wanted to protect her from how awful we were, and from *how terrible her school was.* Having thought about it for years, I can only conclude that she was unable to see bad in others, because there were *so, so, so many* bad kids there, and we were only getting worse. We all loved her. She was one of the very few people who gave a shit about us.

I visited Woodhall recently, walked into my old room, and found this written in big sloppy lettering that switched in and out of cursive, on the underside of my overturned former desk:

"I was normal
Didn't do Drugs. Didn't
Want to do Drugs.
I came to Woodhall.
I did drugs.
I got caught
I got expeled
Why did I come to
Woodhall?
I never should
have!!"

This was perfect. My experience exactly.

I was bent over marveling at it when Mrs. Woodhall walked in and caught me. She read it, too. When she was done she shook her head and said with beautiful, nunlike compassion, "Ah, yes, this was David. He just couldn't make things work for himself here."

I thought to myself, *Jesus Christ, you still have no idea.*

WOODHALL WAS so small. I can describe every student who was there while I was there.

The entire student body, nineteen boys, was about the size of a small clique at St. Mark's. So in the eyes of the outside world there was nothing to separate me from the Japanese ESL student who got bullied into getting a Mohawk, allowing everyone to ogle the scars from his brain surgery; or from the little, wasted carapace of a kid with a broken arm who would shoot up under his cast.

I was a Woodhaller.

I was describable in equally reductive terms.

I had found my clique.

As a group the one thing we all had in common was the fact that we were fuckups, which was the one thing we wanted to hide from the world, so we were all constant, painful reminders—and consequently brutal and cruel—to each other.

Any Woodhall assembly or outing always included four or five bearded twenty-year-olds who wore boots and smoked constantly and seemed mildly ashamed and mostly resigned about being there. These guys had bombed out of Connecticut public schools years ago and had made some last-ditch deals with their parents—usually involving offers to take care of children, pay off debts, purchase cars—that had got them to Woodhall, where they would hopefully "make up educational lacunae" and get their high school diplomas. These guys trudged to class alongside the sad foreign kids sent to learn English as a second language and the wiry boys like me, whom they would soon help to become stoners, doomed to fuck up, linger on, never go somewhere better, eventually go somewhere worse.

When I asked Mrs. Woodhall about one of those older boys she said, "He's drinking and working in a mill now, I'm afraid."

MY FIRST-YEAR ROOMMATE was Peter Taft, who was uncool, big-nosed, freckle-spattered, marshmallowy. Across the hall from me and Taft was Tim

Steiner, a blond, strong, two-towns-over townie kid who my dad—in the midst of delivering me to the school—took the time to glance at and then declare, "That one looks like a hood. You might get some trouble there, so I'd try making friends with him." It was a perfect (and prescient) thing for Dad to say as he was about to get on his private jet and fly away. He said it with a certain relish. Dad was pissed that I'd done this. That I'd wound up at this school of losers. As if I'd done it *to spite him*. So he took whatever pleasure he could in the fact that I'd be having a harder time being there than he'd be having explaining where I was. His observations about Steiner were all the send-off I was getting from Dad. He was chilly and abrupt and then gone. Back to the airport, into the sky, and home to Todd and Trevor and Dede and "the Wilsey home in San Francisco . . . a spirited collaboration between the owners and interior designer Michael Taylor," as it was described in *House & Garden*.

Once Dad was gone I looked around and saw that he had a point. What he said about Steiner was good advice. Tim would be the first test I had to get through at Woodhall. And the way I handled it would determine how the spring would go.

This became clear on my second day at Woodhall, when Peter Taft walked into the T.V. room and said, "Hey guys!" in a friendly voice, and Steiner erupted from a couch and started mincing around, saying, "Hey guys! Hey! Guys! Hey!" getting right up in people's faces, grimacing, and spitting, "Hey!" almost breaking into a laugh, but then remembering how angry he was and stifling it, before spreading his arms wide to the room, "Guys! I'm Peter Cottontail. I'm a happy faggot rabbit!" After which he went all dead-faced and mumbled in this acid voice, "With a big fucking schnoz." He then stared at Taft for an uncomfortable several seconds, turned away, and told the T.V.  as if Taft weren't even worth addressing—"Shut the fuck up, you little fag."

This completely terrified me.

He came up to me in the hall an hour later and said, "Taft is such a fucking *dick*. And you're living with him. So *you* must be a dick." He stared at me for a long moment, until I looked away, and then he declared that he was going to start making my life miserable for being Taft's roommate: "I'll give you a real Woodhall welcome."

This activated something ruthless in me. I was not going to be lumped in with Taft. I was not under any circumstances going to make the same mistakes I'd made at St. Mark's. I was not going to befriend someone vulnerable or different. Not even briefly. I was going to become invulnerable and/or invisible, and I would menace and harm and keep Taft off balance. I had to make it *clear* that I was different. I immediately saw the advantages to making Taft's life miserable and putting myself unequivocally above him. I knew what I needed to do. The solution also lay with Dad. Dad had told me stories about how he and his brother menaced another neighborhood boy called Jack Arms. They pulled pranks on him and made him a laughingstock. Taft was going to be my Jack Arms. Everything I would do to him I would do to try to be like Dad. And I would fuck with Taft worse than Steiner had even dreamed of fucking with Taft.

The next night I removed the slats that held Taft's top bunk in place and skewed the mattress so that it was wedged into the frame and barely resting up there, held from the sides. I did all this while Taft was in the bathroom brushing his teeth. I'd observed that he went to bed promptly, about half an hour before lights out, to read. I invited Steiner to come over and hang out, telling him I had something for him to see. Ten minutes later Peter returned—wearing a robe and boxers and carrying a cup of water. It was such a Victorian image that memory has added a candle and a nightcap. He said, "Hey, guys," frightened at the presence of Steiner, who smiled friendlily. Then, probably thinking to avoid confrontation, he climbed up his ladder, hopped onto the bed, and the entire thing, *mattress, bathrobe, book, pillow, cup of water, blankets* plummeted like an elevator with a cut cable—wham!—*bounced*, and then threw Taft onto the floor. It happened, so perfectly—as if it had been choreographed—and Taft himself had such a genius for awkwardness, that Steiner and I hit the floor, too. I laughed harder than I had laughed since getting kicked out of St. Mark's.

Taft was so frightened and confused that he couldn't even stand for a good fifteen seconds, which made us laugh even more. We were *crying*. We were on the floor. *And, wait . . . he was crying,* and *he was on the floor,* too! *We were all lying on the floor with tears coming out of our eyes for opposite reasons.* Steiner and I were shouting. Howling. Other kids started walking in, looking at the scene, cracking up, and drawing more people in to crack up, until within a few minutes the entire school was laughing. I felt a flicker of sadness, though I was still weak and convulsing and barely able to speak from all the laughter. I knew I was doing the wrong thing. But when the laughing finally died down, and it took a while, I got a firm slap on the back from Tim Steiner. "You're cool, Willzey. Sorry you have to live with *this* fag." Only when everybody had cleared out did I help Peter fix his bed.

That night, lying in my bottom bunk, beneath his now properly secured mattress, I thought:

*I am cool.*

*I am mean.*

*I am saved.*

I knew I had done the right thing.

Taft was my Jack Arms.

I was fitting in.

DAN GRIFFITH was the prototypical Woodhall student. He was weird and thwarted and compelling and repellent and smart and idiotic all at once. He was a smoker, like everyone at Woodhall, though Dan was a sixteen-year-old *chain-smoker*—nervous, fidgety, cigarette always in hand, ashes fluttering around and up from his constant jangly motion, settling like frozen dew in his frizzy hair. He flicked his cigarettes continually, even when there was no ash, sending lit cherries meteoring across rooms to smolder pits in carpeting. When he wasn't smoking he would talk fast and bang out drumbeats on chair arms.

Study halls, where smoking wasn't allowed, were impossible for Dan, and were made tolerable only by the fact that about a third of the teachers smoked, and they allowed him to smoke in class, so if he could make it through a forty-minute segment of study hall, twenty minutes of a nonsmoking class, and then another forty minutes of study hall, that would be the longest he'd ever have to go, since odds were his next class would be taught by a smoker. We all smoked in sports. And Dan smoked in bed.

I first spoke to Griffith during one of his sixty-minute cigaretteless sessions in morning study hall. He got out of his chair, crept across the room to where I was sitting, smiled, and said, "Hey. Hold out your hand." I did. "No. Palm down." I turned my hand over. Then he reached out, dug his fingernails in, wrenched them back, tore out a rip of flesh, and ran back to his desk, where he folded his hands and sat up straight.

I sat there stunned. It hurt. Blood welled up.

Looking at my hand I realized that Griffith sharpened his nails. I thought that there seemed to be some mysterious correlation between this and how several of the older Woodhall students kept one fingernail long, *"for cocaine,"* as the whispering went.

But Griffith was no cokehead. What he was was crazy, and a guitarist who didn't use picks, and likable and sweet and girlish. He was a little like me, in the ways I most wanted to disguise. (He crossed his legs at the top. He was effeminate. He had limp wrists. He would've been called a "fag" at St. Mark's.) *Why has he done this to me?*

In each of the next two periods of study hall I ran to Dan's desk and tried to scratch him back. Each of these times he got me again, worse. Finally I was so furious that I agreed to his challenge of official combat, the rules for which were: "No hiding hands. Scratch as much as possible. The first one to pull away loses." Within twenty seconds he'd torn out enough skin to fill the space under his nails and left me with such deep bloody lines on my left hand that one of them is still there today. Mr. Chant broke us up. Blood was bubbling out of my hand, but I pretended it was no big deal. Chant let it go. The pain came on about thirty seconds later, a septic aching, as if my hands had been grated and plunged in sewage. As in the punch fight with Rodberg, I had done practically no damage.

Back at my desk, left hand bleeding on a binder, with a smarting headache from holding back tears, I thought to myself, *I will have to do something to Taft again.*

Dan appreciated my silence with Chant, and he was just too weird and charming to start a feud with. Walking to the T.V. room that night he looked at my hand and said, "Shit, dude, I used to get it that bad all the time before I got *skilled.*"

Dan was from Georgia. He loved Lynyrd Skynyrd and a band called Nazareth, whose best known song was "Hair of the Dog," aka "(Now You're Messing With a) Son of a Bitch." He formed a Woodhall garage band. It consisted of him singing and on guitar; Vinnie Pizzarelli (who had a mustache and referred to himself, in the third person, as "The Italian Stallion") on bass; and a stoner blond kid whose name I can't remember on drums. They did not know what to call themselves. First they were "Dan Griffith Band." But there were complaints of narcissism from the secondary and tertiary members. So, since Griffith and the drummer were Southerners, he suggested that they call themselves Three Parts Southern, even though there were only three people in the band, and the Stallion was from Connecticut. Griffith said God was Southern. But this was lame. So they continued to hunt around, coming up with names that would last a night and then going back to 3/4ths Southern—2/3rds Southern just sounded wrong—and eventually going full circle back to Dan Griffith Band, which was what everyone called them anyway.

The one thing that wasn't ever in a state of flux with Dan Griffith Band was the repertoire, which was a single song called "The Peppercorn Tree."

It went like this:

Ooh, *I love*
*my peppercorn tree.*

*You don't know what it does*
*to me!*

*It's got magic in its roots*
*and love in its leaves.*

*Come sit with me*
*under my little tree.*

*And nobody's gonna* take *it!*
[*Rah-nah!* The guitar came in here and they began rocking out.]
*Away from me!*

[*Rah-nah! Na-na!*]
*Oooooooh, the peppercorn tree!*

Then some unguided guitar. Then they'd fizzle. Maybe a pause for cigarette lighting. Some desultory drumming. *Hmm, bum-dum-da-rum-ba, ba-dum?* Bit more fidgeting. Flicking of Zippos.

Silence. Then they would decide to start up "The Peppercorn Tree" again.

The song carried all the way through campus, to the most distant dorm rooms. It pulsed through the balsa-wood Woodhall walls. *Nuh, nuh-huh, na nuh nuh nuh knee,* over and over, eight, nine, ten times a night, more, interspersed with constant cigarette breaks and free-form drumming sessions, when the Stallion would grab the sticks as the blond kid smoked. Strangely, I liked the song. In fact, we all did. It was catchy. We all got behind it—making it a Woodhall anthem on trips to the mall to watch movies and buy drugs, or on outings to Wykeham Rise, the nearest all-girls school, the slogan for these trips being: "Dick-em at Wykeham!"—which probably would've made a better name for the band.

. . .

SHORTLY AFTER MY introduction to Griffith I opened the dorm fridge, in a grubby kitchenette off the T.V. room, and found several catatonic house flies on top of a pizza box. I said something like, "*Fucking* nasty. There are flies in the fridge," and a commotion came from the T.V. area as Griffith hurled himself from a couch and hollered, "Don't kill them. Don't fucking kill them! Those're mine!"

Dan captured and refrigerated flies. He did this so he could keep them as pets. And fly-snatching was the best example of his guitar-playing, hand-maiming, ultrafast reflexes. He could sit in the T.V. room smoking and talking, and then suddenly steal a fly out of the air in midsentence, without harming it at all. Then he would throw it in the fridge, where the sudden drop in temperature put flies into suspended animation. (I don't know how he figured this out.) When they were immobile he tied thread or dental floss to their legs, attached these filaments to his long, sharp-nailed fingers, and waited for them to revive, at which point he would *wield them:* Dan walked the halls, hands held high, tethered flies trying to fly off, buzzing in frustration. Sometimes he'd just sit and watch MTV with them.

SO, if Griffith, in all his weirdness, was the prototypical Woodhall student, the rest of us were his constituent parts, his Dan Griffith Band.

Covering the unpredictable side was Tim Steiner and another guy we called the weight lifter—I can't remember his name—who was even scarier than Steiner. He was huge and sweaty—like a thermal spring stanched with clothing—and humorless and insecure and constantly lifting weights and eating steroids, but he was also safer than Steiner because he kept to himself and didn't come nosing into your room. (Occasionally, though, he would get really pumped up and come marauding through the dorms, pointing to people who would have to follow him to the weight room so that he could bench them.)

As Griffith was sweet and unselfconscious, so was Mike Brown, a nineteen-year-old former Eagle Scout who was still involved in scouting, and sometimes would don his full Scout's regalia—brown shorts, little cap, and a crisp shirt covered with a broad chest of merit badges.

Also sweet was Peter Taft, my unfortunate roommate, and Jean Wagniere, the waifish, bespectacled, thirteen-year-old Swiss ESL student, who everyone called "Wags."

Singing the same song over and over again, living in the same worn groove, is what all the older students had been doing for years. In addition to beards these guys had condoms and b.o. and entrenched habits, like drinking coffee and then having a cigarette first thing in the morning, prior to which they were absolutely unapproachable.

In this group was:

A gentle, funny, defeated alcoholic from Maine, with long greasy hair and a roughneck beard, who looked like Bono and whose name I feel obliged to omit.

A corn-belt intellectual from Kansas, with long hair and John Lennon specs, called Rich DeVore. Rich had an interest in literature, and a pained, world-weary attitude.

Another student who will remain nameless, and who might have received zero respect in another setting, as he weighed about three hundred pounds and was always heaved over on a couch, from which he would talk about his father's butcher business and express his evil political views while snacking.

A guy whose name I've forgotten, who drank Jägermeister, had children, and was Kiefer Sutherland's doppelgänger. He would hang out in the weight/pool room while Griffith was practicing "The Peppercorn Tree"—the smell of steroid-tinged weight-lifter sweat mingling with cigarettes and hot amplifiers—and lead a bunch of twenty-year-olds and teenage acolytes in shooting eight ball and spitting chew.

Robin Montgomerie, who once invited half the school down for the weekend to stay in his huge Upper East Side apartment, with the promise to Mrs. Woodhall that we would be well supervised by his mother. His mother was sloshed when we arrived, and made us blender drinks all weekend. Robin was suave and good at tennis. He seemed like the kind of guy Dad wanted me to befriend, and I wanted Dad to know I'd hung out at his house, which was fancy in the Dede vein—lots of gilt and heavy drapery and ormolu bathroom fixtures—but when I told him I'd been there Dad didn't give a rat's ass.

Also from Manhattan was a sly, dark-haired kid who was like the Artful Dodger without the sweetness. (I've forgotten his name, too.) He was a skilled pickpocket, a serious pothead, and a total performer, who, in the middle of shoplifting beers from the market, would turn to me and say, "Is this on sale? I think *it is*."

"Maybe so," I'd say gamely.

"Oh, no. No maybes. Definitely." Looking more closely at the bottle in his hand, and then holding it up to me, "See, it says right here. It's on the"—he'd wave his fingers through the air like he was playing a flute—"five finger discount." And into the lining of his overcoat it would go. He taught me how to pick pockets, which I put to use at a St. Patrick's Day parade.

On the periphery were:

A kid from New York called Rosenkrantz (fittingly enough for a peripheral character) who did "blow," had nostril edges like hot barbecue coals, and constant sniffles.

A guy with advanced male-pattern baldness.

A handful of fellow teenagers, some in the bully mold, some in the cagey mold, some in the bland mold, and some just plain damaged, like the guy who'd been dropped on his head as a baby and could barely speak.

And finally there was Chris Scalley, who behaved normally in all other respects, but shared, in name at least, Griffith's most eccentric habit: He sat at his desk throughout evening study hall, not studying, but bent over a vise he'd bolted to his desk, twisting catgut around feathers, tying flies, which he would use to go fishing on weekends. He was the gentleman sportsman.

Varied as we were, we nearly all embraced a common interest: seeing the entire school simultaneously stoned. This goal was put forward by the unbelievably cool twenty-year-olds, and it was accomplished when the only holdouts (Eagle Scout Brown and ESL Wagniere) were cornered in their rooms and hit after hit of smoke was blown in their faces. All of Woodhall was stoned!

THERE WERE NO cliques at Woodhall. There were no jocks or sufficient numbers of any other type to coalesce into a group. The only time some kind of social status came into play was during a popular T.V. show. There were social hierarchies in place for the distribution of couch space.

The dynamics of moving from a couch or relinquishing part of a couch when you were stretched out on it were negotiated with care. The ideal move—and the status-enhancing one—was to hold an entire couch while other people sat on the floor. Certain people you could tell to fuck off (Taft, Wags), other people you would welcome with just a little resentment (Rosenkrantz, the shoplifter, Griffith), and certain people you had to both bow and assert your status to. If Tim Steiner wanted the couch I'd say, sarcastically, "Ooh. I would *love* to share this couch with *you*, Tim," and talk to him for a while about how much pleasure it would give me, what a great addition he'd be to the couch, while at the same time not moving, just bluffing him on, asserting autonomy and disinterest in pleasing him immediately, so he would not think, *Weak*. This would have to be timed just right so as not to escalate into a confrontation, but merely an affirmation of the boundaries. After which I'd sit up and move over.

If Tim did think you were weak he would be all over you and in your room and eating your food and joking at your expense and borrowing your money and your little patch of Woodhall would be overrun. Taft never saw this. He just didn't understand how important it was to stand one's ground to the necessary degree, even if you were afraid—especially if you were afraid—something I only understood because I was more afraid of what would happen to me if I didn't.

Status at Woodhall was all about conning, lying, keeping people off guard, the employment of guarded sarcasm, and confrontation—but never direct confrontation. (Nor could you succumb directly.) Everything had to be sidelong and casual—noncommittal, but serious; obstructive, but friendly.

Of course, certain people were exempt from all this. I moved my legs promptly and unquestioningly for the twenty-year-olds. The three-hundred-pound butcher's boy got a whole couch because he was frightening and could not have been younger than twenty-three and would actually threaten to *sit on you.*

The T.V. lounge is where I met Todd Rhame, the only real—and extremely fleeting—friend I had my first year at Woodhall. I had just done the bunk-bed thing. So I was watching T.V. and I wasn't feeling at bay, defensive, wary, just alert, since I knew that the purchase I had on cool was probationary and easily eroded by vulnerable or even inattentive behavior. I definitely didn't want my real self to come out in a moment of absent-mindedness. I wanted to avoid the long oxygenless climb from loserhood I had been forced into at St. Mark's.

Todd, who looked like Paul Simonon from The Clash, though everybody thought he looked like Billy Idol, and told him this, had on an earring and was effortlessly holding a couch by himself. He had no friends and wanted it that way. And he did not fit into any of the above listed Woodhall categories.

Todd was a year older than me and lived at the end of one of the dorms, in a room a hallway's width bigger than any of the others, and furnished with twin beds instead of the standard bunk beds. It was the coolest and largest room in the school (measuring ten by sixteen instead of the usual ten by ten) and was actually ripped out the next year—when they put in a doorway at that end of the hall—as though no one but Todd was worthy of it.

Todd was a skater and rode a no-bullshit blank board with black wheels.

During a commercial I was inspired to go on a sarcastic riff about the power company. I was the chief executive calling the control room at the nuke plant to demand more power so that I could watch the Playboy channel with maximum clarity on my giant, wall-sized T.V. (the wall-sized T.V. being an idea with its origins in that first peace trip). It made Rhame laugh.

Then he said, "Hey. I'll pierce your ear."

I was stunned. *Whoa.* Everybody stared at me.

I knew that there were great opportunities for coolness here. But also great opportunities for shame. There was instantly a discussion among everyone in the T.V. room about how painful piercing was if you didn't do it with a machine at the mall. Todd said that was bullshit, he'd done it himself, it didn't hurt much, he had an extra stud, you just iced the lobe till it was numb, soaked the stud in hydrogen peroxide, shoved it right through.

The decision was shame or pain. I could become Wilsey the Bold, *Invulnerable to Pain*—with scarred hands and pierced ear. Or I could remain Wilsey the Timid, who was always a good boy and never got credit for it anyway. (Dad had a habit of delivering sidelong jibes about the fact that everyone said I was a nice kid, as if there were at least something to be proud of in being "a hood" like Steiner, and I was doubly contemptible because I was both nice *and* a fuckup—it was one of his most confusing tropes.)

"Yeah. O.K. Let's do it," I said.

Rhame went back to his room to find his stud, and I began icing. Everyone was psyched. Others began to arrive and wait in anticipation. Rhame came back with a gold bar, fat and rounded at one end, pointed at the other, and too dull and thick looking for this to go well.

We went into the bathroom and the T.V. room followed. Tim Steiner got out a pen and marked an insertion spot. I checked it in the mirror and said it looked good. Then Todd pressed the stud to my lobe and started pushing. He got through the first wall of skin easily—*crrrp*—but then he got stuck in the carti-lage, and the stud began slipping around inside, like it was greased, at all sorts of strange angles.

I said, "Dude, what's going on?"

He said, "It's slippery."

I said, "Sensitivity is returning to the ear."

He continued to push. It continued to slip. He continued to push. It burned. I was about ten seconds away from letting tears seep spontaneously from my eyes. Todd may have sensed this, and didn't want it to happen. "Ice it some more and then I'll pour hydrogen peroxide on and we'll finish up," he said.

I sat down with the earring sticking out of my ear like an arrow. I thought about Dad. He would loathe this, which thrilled and mostly scared me. What was I thinking? He noticed everything about my body—every new blackhead. Even if I took out the earring, there was no way he was going to miss the hole.

He looked me over every time I came home, held me by the shoulders, put on his half-frame reading glasses, started with my hair—"needs cutting in back"—then the face—"these blackheads, hmm, these blackheads," and then he'd run his finger over my blackhead-studded nose and forehead, maybe halfheartedly try to extract one, and usher me into the bathroom, where he could train some really bright lights on the situation, get out some witch hazel, make me hold still—a situation very similar to the one I was in now—and do his "level best" to get them out. He was patient and focused, and these sessions could last for an hour, Dad all the time putting steaming hot water on a washcloth and pressing it to my face to "loosen things up," then going in with his big short fingers. I loved this. Intimacy with my father, his reassuring touch—it was so different than with Mom, who had her own terrible version of this ritual, which involved me laying down on her bed, night-table lamp on, shade skewed to throw light, long sharp nails biting into my face. At the end of a welcome-home blackhead session with Dad he'd give me the bottle of witch hazel and some cotton, which always made me feel special, tell me to take off my shoes and shirt and pants and get on the scale: "Too skinny." Then walk across the room: "Too bouncy." And tell me we were going to the barber's at 8:00 A.M. the next day.

I was defacing Dad's property.

I went back into the bathroom.

Todd resumed pushing, the thing kept slipping and scrambling around. Finally, I braced my head against the mirror, Todd grabbed the lobe with his left hand, and I said, "Push as hard as you can, man!" Tears seeped, and then I heard a huge "*crrssp!*" and the stud was through. Done! Success! Tears retreated unnoticed. "Yeah," Todd said. He put the cap back on the stud, and I looked in the mirror. My earlobe was big and red and swollen, with a gold dot almost hidden in the center.

Before lights out Rhame took me back to his room and gave me a shot of whiskey from a flask. I remember feeling warm and about five years older. I was drinking whiskey for a reason. I'd been accepted into the fraternity of men by piercing my ear. This was so great. We brushed our teeth at adjacent sinks in the same bathroom where he'd done the piercing. *There, that's my blood on the mirror!* I thought.

I said good night, and went to bed almost crying with happiness, dreaming of my new life with an earring and Todd as my friend.

And this dream came true. Rhame and I plummeted into friendship. The next night we watched T.V. and made fun of the power company while both wearing earrings. All were impressed. No one this cool had ever been my cohort before, not without making a few jokes at my expense, just to make sure everyone knew how the hierarchy worked.

On Sunday Rhame invited me down to his large room. He wanted to play me a band called the Violent Femmes that I'd never heard of. He put a cassette in his boom box, pressed play on side one, track one, and then did a perfect lip-synch to "Blister in the Sun," smiling and jamming and strumming and drumming on his skateboard and nailing every last word and nuance. It should have been stupid, but instead it was majestic.

He made it seem like *his* song.

I sat across the well between beds from him as he fake strummed and looked not so much intelligent as crafty. When someone tried to come in Rhame tossed off a southern "Fuck yooooooou," kicked the door, and they went away.

Then we went skateboarding at the post office in town.

By the end of week one of this friendship I began to confide in him. Be vulnerable. Tell the truth.

On the second weekend of our friendship we went into the woods to play "commando." Todd loved playing commando, which entailed getting dressed up in camo, smearing mud all over his face, and crawling around through the leaves and mud on his stomach pretending to be after the VC. We did this for hours. He was hard core about it. I remember returning to my room covered in mud, Taft being intimidated, and then showering, checking out the earring, having a cigarette, and thinking I had it made. *Made.*

THEN GIRLS were reintroduced into my world. A very proud Mrs. Woodhall announced that we would be hosting a dance in the dining hall for the girls (*sluts!*) of Wykeham Rise, the nearby, comparably run-down girls boarding school that was willing to engage in coed activities with Woodhall.

This was huge. Everyone reacted accordingly.

The twenty-year-olds (who all had girlfriends, or wives, or ex-wives) made a lot of knowledgeable remarks about statutory rape and the probability of prosecution in Connecticut. They quoted laws, presented their opinions, and discussed the legality of hand jobs and finger fucks with an air of longing. Everyone's pulse was racing. *They are coming! They are coming!* We were the crew of a vessel long at sea. *They. Are. Coming!* Coming through the air lock—into our atmosphere. For me this information was *inflammatory.* I had been making a lot of progress in the direction of coolness. And now here was a shot at getting somewhere in the seemingly impossible quest to lose my virginity. If I could get a girlfriend out of this situation. . . . If I played it right. . . . Would my coolness translate? I had to think of some more funny things to say about the power company.

The night of the dance we converged on the dining hall and stared out the windows as a van containing nine girls arrived.

Woodhall's cook, a perennially unshaven Vietnam vet, was our DJ. A few slobs had unearthed Izods either too small or too new and were doing their best to look preppy. Scalley and Griffith were wearing Duckhead pants and pressed shirts. Steiner had on a jean tuxedo. I was wearing pegged and faded jeans with artfully ripped holes and a plaid shirt that I thought had a sort of ska vibe. We all had on cologne. It surrounded and protected us like the Mutara Nebula in *Star Trek II: The Wrath of Khan.*

The girls came in—all freshmen and sophomores—and we evaluated the situation.

There was one girl our eyes turned to. She was as tall as me, thin but curvy, blue-eyed, blond, with clear skin, a delicate oval face, long legs in blue jeans, and a single, three-foot, beaded braid. All the other girls studied her, studied us, gathered around her. She seemed composed and indifferent. I stood there in my jeans with their artful holes and was motionless, hungry, scared.

For half an hour she danced with no one, just moved to the music with her friends, that long braid swaying in front of her face, and I assumed it *meant* something, that the braid was subtle and significant. I was staring, watching, trying to decode, while my hormones were shouting, *"Help us! My! God! Do! Something!"*

Then my self-restraint snapped, I thought, *Fuck it,* and walked across the dance floor, running out of air as I went. Better a total blow off than just knowing what a coward I was. When I got to her, in my terror and desire to appear suave, I actually said, "May I have this dance?"

"Sure," she said.

She took off her jean jacket, volcanoes erupted covering the dining hall in lava and hot ash—Frodo had destroyed the ring—and we danced. She had small breasts in a small white T-shirt, and I thought, *Maybe this is why she's nice, because she has small breasts,* which I found attractive, anyway. When the song ended we just stayed on the floor and automatically danced again, though vicious, self-promulgating tornadoes were battering the dining hall. "One more time?" I said after that, smiling, not knowing what I would do after all this dancing, but loving that everyone was watching us. We danced again. And again. And again. Till finally I was more tired than nervous and I asked her if she wanted to take a break. Then I asked her if she wanted to take a walk.

*Was this really happening?* I walked her past the dorms and made disparaging remarks about their architecture, and she did not laugh, and when we arrived in the field where we did sports between cigarettes I offered her a cigarette, and she said no, and so I refrained, and we looked at the stars, and eventually her jean jacket seemed inadequate over such delicate lightbulbs of shoulders, and I performed a manly, weather's-chilly-let-me-warm-you, arm-around-her move, which was awkward, because she was my height, and I was numb with fear, but being commanded to do this by hormones that had never run the show before—*this girl likes you: we're taking over,* they said. She didn't mind.

I asked, "What bands do you like?"

The question, "What bands do you like?" was the slightly cooler version, I'd just discovered, of "What rock groups do you like?" Suddenly rock groups could be called "bands," even though "bands" conjured up epaulets and tubas. This was irony! It was my first intentional use of irony.

She said, " *'Bands'?* What do you mean?"

Then I felt better about myself, a little superior, gained a little confidence, loosened up, and instead of answering let my hormones shove me forward and kiss her.

She kissed me back. So I carefully put my hand up her shirt. Her skin was so soft. She shivered and there was much adjusting of the jean jacket, making for cramped space in which to work and weird hand/wrist angles. But I persevered. We kept at it for a few minutes: hand questing—*Is that a nipple? Or just some concentration of lace work on her bra?*—tongues curling, faces wet, wind blowing, moisture evaporating, lips chapping.

Then we took a break and she said she would smoke after all, though she never usually did. We talked in softer, deeper voices, with that new intimacy that always comes with someone you've just kissed. We were standing and holding each other.

"Are you going to tell me about bands?" she said.

"I just meant rock groups," I said.

She told me she was fifteen, though she was actually fourteen, for another month, before which our relationship would be over. Likewise, I was almost sixteen, though she would never see me at sixteen. I made some jokes and she was very quiet and did not laugh. She spoke in a staccato rush of words. I tried to kiss her again and she kissed me back for a second, strong and almost *childishly*, the way kids move too fast toward things, and then she said, "I should go!" As if she'd forgotten where she was. We walked back to the parking lot and saw that we were just in time. We were holding hands but she let go when we got close. Everyone was outside the dining hall and the other girls were getting in their van. She got in, too, without kissing me good-bye in front of the boys—thus weakening my story—and then she was gone.

Tim Steiner started off the postdance shit-dispensing session with, "Did you fuck her?"

Griffith said, "Did she blow you?"

The weight lifter asked, "You eat her out?"

I was evasive. I just shrugged and smiled, which I hoped would lead people to conclude that maybe I had, but which, for some reason, led them to conclude that I had not.

"He didn't do *shit*," said Steiner.

Still, everybody thought I was pretty cool. Griffith was enthusiastic. I'd shown some hidden talents. Everybody respected this. But not Todd Rhame. Todd was silent and pissed. I thought he was disappointed because I had not fucked her, or been sucked off, or eaten her out—I had let him down. I was not worthy of him and his friendship.

THE DAY AFTER the dance Mrs. Woodhall came into the T.V. room and said there was something for me from Wykeham Rise and that I should come and get it. There was a lot of excitement, and *"Dude,"* and backslapping, and laughter. Steiner literally *capered* behind me. I followed Mrs. Woodhall to the dining hall and was presented with a vase containing a red rose and a note with the blond braid girl's dorm pay phone number, telling me to call that night. I was speechless. Touched. No girls ever gave guys flowers. It was unheard-of.

This meant that I must have fucked her or got sucked off or eaten her out!

I was a stud. This was the only conceivable reason for the rose. From then on no one would doubt me again. My "maybe so"s would now be seen as modesty about my great prowess, which resulted in deep female gratitude. I was too cool to brag. This was the only possible explanation. Girls did not send guys roses.

In the halls that week everybody said, "Wilsey must've found her G-spot!"

Knowing what had really happened, no one was more surprised than me.

In their places I would've thought the same thing.

Suddenly, within the confines of Woodhall, my cool status was irrevocable, no matter what I did. I could have even acted like myself! If I'd still known how. I had vast and admirable bedroom talents. *The most beautiful girl at Wykeham sent him a rose.*

Thenceforth I was respected. Nobody fucked with me. To the contrary, *I* shamelessly used *it* to *fuck with people.* Griffith bragged about how much his girl-friend back in Georgia loved him, and I said, "I don't see her sending you any roses." Steiner came looking for couch space and I said, "Steiner, take the couch. I pity you. For you will never satisfy a woman." It was invincibility for the re-maining five weeks of the term.

My romance with the rose girl, whom I called that night, consisted of one visit to Wykeham Rise, during which she told me she was sorry she could only afford one rose, and we made out in the choir loft of the school chapel. She took off her bra up there, and we cuddled. I felt honored, and wanted to feel a connection with her. I wanted to be in love. Then I visited her house for the weekend, and we made out on a chilly beach, I have no idea where (though it was news to me that the east coast *had* beaches). We had nothing to say to each other, and broke up. This further elevated my status at Woodhall. Everybody thought I'd got bored of fucking her.

But Todd Rhame did not buy any of this. He was hurt and insulted and maybe even a little bit humiliated by it.

Recently, when I started to think back on our friendship, I thought maybe Todd wasn't just some cool guy. Maybe he wanted a real friend and had been waiting until he thought he could find one, and then picked me.

Our friendship started foundering, though neither of us wanted to be lonely, so we hung out, him trying to slap me down to secondary status, me trying to lord my bullshit over him, until finally he just stopped talking to me. He refused to even look up when I said his name. He would stare at me and shake his head and look serious and reptile-eyed and stay silent a long, long time, and then sud-denly break his silence by shouting and startling me and then laughing hollowly. Finally, he fell 100 percent silent, and never initiated a conversation again. Then the end of the year came and he was gone. Ours was a classic fast friendship: briefly inseparable, never to see each other again.

But first we made a trip to Emma Willard, a tarnished but venerable girl's school in Troy, New York, that was hosting a spring carnival and dance. Amaz-ingly, Woodhall had been invited.

Lots of other boys came, from prestigious places like Deerfield Academy, but we Woodhall boys—with our drug stashes and earrings and bandannas and beards and flasks (necessary for any Woodhall outing); our Zippo tricks and roll-your-own cigarettes; our psychotic weight lifter—were intimidating and mysterious and caught everyone off guard. No one had ever heard of Woodhall before. *Who are these guys?* they seemed to be thinking. And they were scared. We ruled the building where they had everyone bunking, a huge Victorian-Gothic ex-infirmary full of horny boys, median age sixteen. Our contingent was brazen, loud, adrenalized, median age nineteen. I felt proud to be a Woodhaller.

In the shower, some preppy Leggat–like jock from Deerfield started giving me shit and the weight lifter stepped in, got right in his face, told him to "say that shit again *to me* or fuck off and apologize." Apology accepted. It was so cool I wanted to hug him right there in the shower. And when some smart-ass little shit started making anti–weight lifter remarks, Steiner and I fucking castrated him with sarcasm. High-five between me and Steiner!

Using our unique talents we romanced more Emma Willard girls than any other school. We were freaks and mutants. We were the X-Men. But compared to all the little prepsters, we were studs. The *XXX*-Men. (Steiner: *Heh.*) Usually we were stoned or otherwise neutralized, but on this occasion we were able to use our mutations in concert.

We cleaned up. We applied cologne. We menaced the prepster competition. Then we came cruising into the big Saturday night dance, cologne wafting ahead, and deployed our unconventional tactics. We saw that there were balloons, so we began popping balloons, making noise, creating little explosions around ourselves, attracting attention, and then gathering up the colorful deflated skins and giving them to suave Robin—the icebreaker—Montgomerie. We'd been noticed, people were staring at us and wondering, *Who are these bearded kids destroying the decorations?* He turned all this to our advantage, by *charming the ladies.* We all followed behind as Robin cruised the periphery of the dance floor, country-club preppy, cleft-chinned, dressed in an immaculate seersucker, posture impeccable, bearing his handful of deflated balloons with great dignity, beaming a totally sweet, affectless, well-bred smile, and proffering them to clusters of girls with the words: "May I offer you a prophylactic?"

*"May I offer you a prophylactic?"* We were dying.

And the girls loved it. They gathered round. They liked us. Rich DeVore, the intellectual from Kansas, with his mysterious and compelling long hair and John Lennon specs; brooding Rhame; the twenty-year-olds; even Steiner—we were something new to these girls, with their huge gabled stone campus, their sprawling lawns and rooms high up under lead roofs. They were *interested.* (Which was a revelation to us. We felt like we were made of the same cheap shit Woodhall was made of.) And as they gathered, the weight lifter scared off any competition; Kiefer Sutherland pulled out the alcohol; we passed the flask; I stood around trying to look like suave rose guy; DeVore supplied the intellect; Steiner the comedy; Rhame the handsome silent mystery stuff. My usual feeling of standing on the outside of a group and longingly making fun of people was actually absent. *I was on the inside.* We had broken in. This was working. And the moment was expanding, rather than contracting. My loneliness and longing, which would normally increase as a song I loved came on—the distance between the fantasy the song conjured and my present reality crashing down— were *shrinking;* and as I walked across the dance floor (over to the water fountain) and "If You Leave" by OMD came on, I felt giant, as though it had come on for me, in my honor; the moment was for me, about me and the song, and everybody was looking at me, at my pegged pants and Chuck Taylors that looked luminous, splendid, and my hair, Studio-gelled up, all but one area, where it dangled down over my left eye. *I was on the inside. This was working. I was glamorous. Happening. Accepted. Using Woodhall and shrugging off Woodhall.* And suddenly I was talking to the most beautiful girl I'd ever talked to.

We started talking at the side of the dance floor after I'd done my glide over to the water fountain. Her name was Whitney Ann Weber and she was Southern and wanted to know who the hell we were. I told her, and then I told her about my mom's family and our roots in the South. She seemed to want to keep talking, so I told her about San Francisco, which I was discovering girls thought was a cool place. She was blond. Her eyes were cool and blue and clear. There was something a little bit hard about her, like she knew things. She was sophisticated! She was experienced. I darted a couple of glances at her breasts. *Oh. Gorgeous.* She looked like the governor's daughter in *Benson.* Was she only talking to me as some sort of experiment? The rose girl had just been a freak occurrence. She'd been too immature to see how immature I was. But *this.* This was a full-fledged girl, too much to hope for, yet she seemed to be interested, and she was not looking around for her friends. She was looking at me. She was slightly caustic. But she seemed genuine.

She asked me to come outside and smoke a cigarette with her. This was when I knew that I loved her. I started feeling geothermal activity in my stomach. I felt warm and giddy and full of hope. And then everything that she did, every way she turned and said hello to a passing friend and flicked her ash, started burning beautifully into my memory.

After we'd been out smoking for about three minutes Todd Rhame joined us. My happiness was complete. *This is great,* I thought. *We're hanging out together again.* Then I thought, *Oh. But. Wait.* Whitney and Todd were talking about the South. They were having a great time. *I haven't said anything for several minutes and . . .*

Todd and Whitney paired up and went off. Everyone was pairing up! Even if Todd had cut me out, it was inspiring to see.

By the end of the night the weight lifter (who was kicked out three days later for some act of violence against Griffith in between performances of "The Peppercorn Tree"), in a moment of pure joy, picked me and Todd up (I gave Todd a smile; he looked away) and carried us up the huge flight of stairs to the second floor of the infirmary, on his shoulders, grunting, us whooping, others falling in behind. We then paraded down the main hallway, smelling like booze and smoke and steamy make-out sessions, everyone holding up a phone number, repeating a girl's name, shaming all the Deerfield boys in rugby shirts sitting on their bunks. We were the mutants and we were strong.

Though, in my case, also depressed. I saw Whitney the next day and she was friendly and did not mock me, but she kissed Todd. And for the three remaining weeks of the term they talked on the phone. Todd never talked to me again. As far as he was concerned our friendship was dead. He went back to Georgia, where he was supposed to finish high school. I went back to San Francisco.

*Eleven* · S K A T E B O A R D I N G

Whil e I was at Woodhall, my friend Spencer Perry had twisted all the deodorant out of a Speed Stick—like one big log, right into the trash—and inserted in its place a blackboard eraser, folded in half lengthwise, into which he then poured a bottle of ink and started writing all over the walls of his bedroom.

Unlike Blane, Spencer didn't skate. He'd become a mod. So he wrote things like "Piaggio" and "69." But he let Scott, his thirteen-year-old skater brother, get in on it with a can of spray paint, adding silver, screaming dreadlocked kids, and phrases like "Skate and Destroy" or just "SK8."

The room looked out over an unkempt backyard that was full of random pieces of scavenged lumber and debris. It was hard to see beyond the backyard—Spencer lived in one of San Francisco's microclimatic fog belts, and looking out his window was like looking into a washing machine where hills, cars, Muni buses, and bare trees made brief appearances between sudslike clouds.

Mr. Perry was forbearing and rarely seen. Mrs. Perry was sick with cancer, bedridden, and sweetly crazy. Spencer's little brother, Scott, had fought off his own bout of cancer with chemo and gone bald when he was eight. It had made him the type of self-possessed kid you just did not worry about ever. Probably because it hurt too much to worry about him.

Scott was the lord of the T.V. room, which was the only room with any life in it; the rest of the house was all dead furniture and lamps with dusty lightbulbs. There was graffiti in there, and a couch that had given up trying to stay a few inches off the floor and just *settled,* at the perfect angle for viewing the T.V. There was a deck off the T.V. room, carpeted in matches, where we smoked clove cigarettes (they stank too much to smoke inside), did Zippo tricks, and tried to spy on some girls Spencer said he'd once seen *sunbathing.* Scott would always be on the collapsed couch, sometimes holding a rifle (he collected guns).

Spencer's place was like San Francisco's grungy/benevolent answer to Woodhall. If it was raining and I couldn't skate, that's where I'd go. Even though we went for months without seeing each other, we'd always be able to pick up where we left off. I'd light up a cigarette, give Mrs. Perry a kiss or a wave if she was awake, get a little box on the shoulder from Mr. Perry if he was around, a grin from Scott, and sit down to watch T.V. and recount, during the commercials, the latest drama from my strange life. They found it entertaining. I was a refreshing presence, with my larger-than-life obstacles and adventures and advantages. Whenever I walked into the T.V. room Scott would shout, "Yo! Ferris Bueller's here!" I told them about everything: Mom's suicide proposal; Dad's remorse briefings; Dede's panties. They pitied me. This was great! In spite of the cancer and the sadness and the empty refrigerator, the dusty lightbulbs and the fog, they felt sorry for *me.* They thought my life sucked, and I was grateful.

But Spencer's house was way across town, so it was hard to get there very often. Blane was just a few blocks from Mom's, on Russian Hill. My two best friends didn't see much of each other anymore. Freshman year they'd both gone to St. Ignatius, the Jesuit school my dad had attended, but by the summer of sophomore year they'd both dropped out and gone to public schools in their own neighborhoods. Spencer was a mod and Blane was a skater, and mods and skaters didn't associate unless they were related, or Spencer and me.

For me skating had become a devotional lifestyle, complete with language, values, strict dress (all culled from *Thrasher* magazine), and rigorous practice. That summer, when Blane wasn't working, we met up at a Chinese elementary school, scaled their fence, and skated their multilevel concrete playground. After a few hours I'd smoke some cigarettes (Blane didn't smoke) and we'd head back to his place. If his mom was home we'd shut ourselves up in Blane's minuscule room.

After subtracting what was taken up by his bunk bed and closet Blane had about six by four feet of floor space, and no light, just windows that looked onto a back hallway into which fog-filtered sun filtered through opaque plastic skylights.

Economically, the Morfs had suddenly blown it four years earlier, back in 1982 (sixth grade), and within a few months they'd been unable to fix the BMW. Then they'd sold the sailboat, dashed Blane's hopes for a boom box with a graphic equalizer, divorced. Mr. Morf had run off somewhere and was never to be seen. But Mrs. Morf managed to hang on to the building they lived in, which contained three other apartments she rented out. She had Blane working as the superintendent/handyman, which was the subject of much complaining and many lost Saturdays, and resulted in lengthy, unprofessional repairs (I would assist). When we wanted to go skate, we'd spend the morning fixing the washing machine. After detaching its water-supply hose, removing whatever was obstructing the flow, then reattaching it with a vise grip, Blane would tell his mom, "It's essentially fixed."

" 'Essentially,' Blane?"

"Yeah, essentially, it is."

"I concur," I'd say. "Its essential state is now fixed."

"Well then you can go put some nails in the front staircase." The Morfs' front staircase, which rose three stories like a scaffold, was always about to collapse. This was not an exciting job. (We only got excited when the thirty-year-old woman on the ground floor had a leaky faucet.)

Like Spencer, Blane also had a little brother. Joseph Morf was nine years younger than Blane, and idolized him. Blane was always kind and patient with him. And Mrs. Morf was unfailingly generous to me. She fed me half my meals, and I spent the night over there as often as I spent it at Mom's. Blane's was just a short skate down the hill.

What Blane and Spencer had in common was that their families were sad, and they made me happy.

DAD HAD ALWAYS wanted to get me away from both of these friends, and that summer he was going to do it.

He told me that I would be spending the summer in Wyoming, hiking through the Wind River mountain range, learning survival techniques, with something called the National Outdoor Leadership School (NOLS).

I looked at the pictures in the pamphlet Dad gave me from the National Outdoor Leadership School, scrutinized them as I always did, picking out every small detail that would indicate what kind of people I would be dealing with this time. I saw huge expanses of nature being marveled at by kids in Patagonia fleeces and mirrored Vuarnet sunglasses, carrying massive backpacks. I could already imagine the first night around the campfire when some kid, upon learning I was from San Francisco, would say, "the gay bay," and I'd chuckle and jest and distance myself and pretend I was from Napa. "Ho, ho. Fags," I'd say.

I wanted to stay in San Francisco. I wanted to get a summer job and skate and be with Blane and Spencer and steal Mom's car and possibly meet girls, if Todd Traina would take me along on one of his famed nights out in his new Audi GT coupe. I had learned things I wanted to show Dad. I had started to figure out how to be cool, and I wanted him to see this. I told Dad I wanted to work on my relationship with Dede. I also pointed out that Todd and Trevor were spending half the summer with him and Dede in Newport, staying at Dede's mom's mansion, Beaulieu, and the other half in Sardinia jet skiing with their dad and Danielle Steel and their friend the Aga Khan. I'd come back from past summers' banishments to camp and heard about all the parties and the friends of Todd and Trevor who had been at the country house and how Dad had flown them in his helicopter and what a familial time everyone had minus me. I pleaded with him to let me be part of the family.

Over all my protestations and promises he booked me into six weeks of NOLS. We flew out to Wyoming in his jet. Dad had his pilots wait at the airport, rented a car, and drove me out to the remote town of Lander, where NOLS was headquartered.

As we drove we talked. I was cheerful and cooperative. Dad was happy about this. We passed a historical marker and Dad pulled over to take my picture beside it. For years Dad told me that he would pull this picture out of his desk drawer and try to see the traitor in me. Then he'd become infuriated and disappointed and depressed, and put the picture away.

Lander, Wyoming, had several gas stations, one of which featured a big, snarling, brightly painted, fiberglass wild boar impaled on the end of a pole like a standard. We exited the highway, made a right, and pulled up outside NOLS— a surprisingly tall brick building next to the boar station. There was no one on the streets, and no sign of life in the NOLS building. Lander was like a ghost town, which was perfect. I was adrenalized, my pulse flying, my voice shaking. I turned to Dad and said, "Dad, I want to go in and face the guys myself. I don't want to walk in with my dad holding my hand. I need to do this on my own. So let's say good-bye here."

I had rehearsed these lines, and as I said them they seemed completely phony. If I'd actually intended to go to NOLS for six weeks, I'd have wanted Dad to come in and meet "the guys." Dad was cool, everyone always thought so, and he sometimes made me look cool, too. (Even Tim Steiner—who could have seen him only for the same thirty seconds it took Dad to declare him "a hood"— said, "Your dad's cool.") But Dad did not even know me well enough to know this.

I had never outsmarted Dad, face-to-face. I'd only ever conned him out of a few toys and some Saturday mornings sleeping in. We made direct eye contact, and I did not look away.

Then he said, "Sean, I respect that."

We got out of the car.

We seemed to be the only two people in Lander, Wyoming. It was one of those rare moments in which, had a single thing gone differently, my whole life would have turned out some other way. All that needed to happen was for someone to see us. We were there for three minutes. Dad got out and opened the trunk. I grabbed my stuff. We exchanged a hug, which, as always, felt good, said we loved each other, and he got back into his car and drove off.

Then he was gone, more or less for the rest of my life.

I HAD CAPITALIZED on one of Dad's weaknesses. He hated to spend the money to make his pilots wait. He wanted to get back to San Francisco. He had taken me there. Why should he have to waste any more of his time?

My plan—which I couldn't believe was already working—was to run; hitch back to the airport; arrange to use my prebought return ticket six weeks early; call NOLS pretending to be Dad's secretary and tell them that Sean Wilsey would not be able to attend because he'd been injured skateboarding; have them send a refund to Blane's; fly home; lay low; find employment; skateboard religiously; and show up at the airport six weeks later, where Dad would pick me up, and I would pretend I'd had a great experience at NOLS.

When I'd outlined this plan to Spencer and Blane they were incredulous that I would even consider it.

Blane said, "With *your* dad, dude. *Jesus.* He will be pissed. He will fucking blow a gasket."

I said, "Dude, he will never know."

Spencer said, "Good luck."

.  .  .

*Grandfather Wilsey*

*Grandmother Wilsey*

*Half a page from my baby book. Captions by Mom.*

*Mom, front right, with cousins and my aunt Glendora (curly hair) in Gouldbusk, Texas, c. 1934.*

*Myrtle and Charlie Clay Montandon with my infant uncle Carlos, 1911. She's seventeen.*

My brother Mike sent me this old trade magazine cover with a note that said, "Look familiar?" Dad, left, 1965, looking a bit like I do now.

Mom with third husband Melvin Belli (p. 23), at the opening of the San Francisco opera, 1966.

Mom with her fan club, 1967.

Mom and Dad. The back of this photo reads "Venice 1972." Dad always used to say, "Venice is the most romantic city in the world—for three days. Then it's time to leave." Eighteen years later I apprenticed with Gino Macropodio, the gondolier who's rowing them.

*Mom, Dad, Ping-Pong the dog, me, the view, 1974.*

*Only existing picture of Mom (a), Dede (b), Todd (c), Trevor (d), and me (e), taken in front of Dede's now rebuilt house in Oakville (f) (pgs. 431–434), Easter (p. 94), 1979. Photographer: Dad?*

*Dad's Magnum PI chopper cut off by Dede's (teal) Studebaker Avanti.*

CHRISTINA KOCI HERNANDEZ / SAN FRANCISCO CHRONICLE

*Dede, 2002.\**

JOHN O'HARA / SAN FRANCISCO CHRONICLE

*Dede and Dad, 1994.*

*\*Knowing almost nothing about jewelry, I took this picture up to the Diamond District in New York, where an appraiser at Lader and Weisberg Diamonds, on the corner of Sixth Avenue and Forty-seventh Street, told me, "She's probably wearing a million dollars right there—wholesale."*

*Clockwise from below: the marble palace
(apparently un-redecorated by current resident,
former Secretary of State George Shultz);
Pegasus, unknown child, Mom, and Star
(l. to r.); me, Raquel, Pope John Paul II;
the pope and Mom.*

*Jehan Sadat, me, Jonathan Dearman, in Cairo (last stop on trip 1).*

*Mom and me (back row) with Indira Gandhi, New Delhi, 1984 (trip 3)—confusing banner behind us.*

*Menachem Begin and me, trip 2.*

*Ruben and Rachel, trip 1.*

*Mom addressing the 1987 World Congress of Women (and CPSU General Secretary Mikhail Gorbachev).*

*Dad had me pose for this picture during his visit to St. Mark's, November, 1984. The "quad" is in the background.*

*A month later, post NOLS.*

*Typical Blane and Sean, Blane's sixteenth birthday, June, 1986. I left for NOLS a few days later.*

*Science at Woodhall, 1987.*

Spencer sent me this photo of himself at age seventeen, writing, "Hey Sean . . . I can find some younger, but the LAST thing I want immortalized in your book is any image of me from, say 10–17 . . . baaad years." He was working here, at Marcello's Pizza, when he delivered the heroic speech on page 351.

Grief can take care of itself, but to get the full value of joy you must have somebody to divide it with.    (Mark Twain)

*Merry Christmas, Sean    with love, Michael*

Ron (pgs. 373–385), Amity Christmas.

The entire Amity School —me, Charles, Benjamin, Leandro, Donald, Jason    on a field trip. This picture, framed, was a Christmas present from one of the counselors.

Dad and I took this picture together when he visited Amity. The next year I sketched the school as a gift for him. He kept it above his desk till 2002.

Daphne.

Pages 478–479.

AS SOON AS Dad's car was out of sight I ditched around the side of the NOLS building, crossed the concrete apron of the boar service station, and hid behind a Dumpster until I was sure he was a mile or two down the highway. There was still no sign of any NOLS personnel. I never thought the plan would go this well. I knew I'd better move fast. I ran up to the road, stuck out a thumb, and was picked up immediately by a young guy in a Subaru station wagon who said he'd take me as far as someplace that was about halfway. He let me bum a cigarette off him.

After he dropped me off I stood on the road for about twenty minutes failing to flag down anyone else. I was still fifty miles away, and I began to worry that I might miss the next flight out and not be able to make it to San Francisco. But eventually a car stopped: a couple in their seventies. I endeavored to be my most charming, and after about twenty minutes the wife told the skeptical husband that she thought they should drive me straight to the airport. I told them that I was going to my sister's wedding in Napa, California, and she was all the family I had besides my sick aunt with no car out here in Wyoming. At the airport the woman gave me their number and told me to call them collect when I made it, so they'd know I was safe.

"Have fun at the wedding," her husband said.

"What?!" I said. "Oh! Yeah. Thanks! I will."

I leaped out of the car and went to the ticket counter, where I was told that there was availability on the next flight to Denver, with a connection to San Francisco, and that I'd be able to use my ticket, with no extra charge. It was arranged with ease. Then I got several dollars worth of quarters, found a pay phone, got the number for NOLS from information, and called it, and when someone said, "Hello?" delivered the following speech, in a long uninterrupted rush (while pumping quarters into the phone to stay ahead of the charges):

"Hello yes I'm calling in regard to Sean Wilsey who *was* to be arriving today for your six-week Wind River Range survival course—I'm his father, Mr. Wilsey's, secretary—and I say 'was'—'*was to be arriving*'—because I'm afraid there's been an unfortunate mishap: he's broken his leg in *three places* skateboarding [it made me cringe to say the word "skateboarding," since, like *Thrasher* magazine, I always called skateboarding "skating"], and so, obviously, he will be unable to attend the program, which he was so looking forward to, and is terribly disappointed about, but there's really no choice, since this is a major break and will require a lengthy convalescence . . . recuperation . . . and obviously he can't participate in the program [it was right about here that I realized winging it was not exactly the best move, and that I should have rehearsed this—I just never believed that the plan would get this far], but, and we know that this is late notice, and that even a partial refund may be impossible, but if it is possible to recover some of the payment for the program even at this late date we would be grateful if you could send a check to Mr. Wilsey's *summer address*, which is 25 Culebra Terrace; San Francisco, California 94133." This was Blane's house.

I paused for a moment. They asked again about the leg being broken in three places, *such a major break*. I said it was "tragic," confirmed the address again, and realized that this story was stupid—overkill. A sprain would have done. *Fuck*, I thought. *Too late now*. They put me on hold for a second and then told me that it would be possible to refund most of the money, four thousand dollars, and that it would take a week or so to process. *Whoa*. I said, "Well, hopefully next year!" and hung up. I thought, *What the hell?*, made a face at myself in the reflective chrome part of the phone, ran to the gate, and got on the plane.

While changing planes in Denver I called Blane, who said he would borrow his Mom's car and meet me at the airport.

In San Francisco Blane *and his mom* met me. They were smiling and shaking their heads. "What are you going to do now, Sean?" asked Mrs. Morf, in a worried and amused voice. I started talking fast about plans for the summer, about where I'd work and how I'd lay low, and laughing giddily with Blane about various permutations of Mom, Dad, and Dede spotting me skating down a hill as they drove up it, doing a double take, thinking, *Was that Sean?*, then maybe looking at one of their ubiquitous bottles of prescription medication, the fucking addicts, and shaking their heads, *Nyah, couldn't be*.

Blane and I laughed. I felt good. I was grateful to Mrs. Morf. As she drove, Blane and I acted out these spotting-me scenes, with me as Dede, trying on a huge rock at Shreve's, and Blane as Dad, handing over a credit card, and then seeing a flash on a skateboard. "Is that *Sean?!*" I waved; Dede dropped the jewelry, cracking the display counter.

Blane was Mom. She'd just bought a little red Mercedes convertible, the one she'd been wanting for years. (Though she kept the cursed Oldsmobile for the housekeeper's use.) He imitated her with the top down, acting like a movie star, then seeing me, and flipping, *Dukes of Hazzard*–style. I did Dad in *his* new car, a Cadillac Eldorado, jumping the curb. *Was that . . . was that, Sean!?*

The next day we went skating and job searching. I asked about sales jobs at my favorite skate shops, but mostly just rolled around and experienced a feeling of joyous liberation. That night I swore to Mrs. Morf that I'd find work and help Blane with his superintendent/handyman duties. I'd be no trouble at all. But

Mrs. Morf said to me, "Sean, I really think you need to tell your parents what's going on here. I don't want to have to do it."

SOMETIMES Mom's building would punch its way through the clouds. The next day was one of those days. It was gray, and the cement of Russian Hill rose up from the bay and turned into sky. I walked slowly, carrying my skateboard, not wanting to get there too quickly. I slouched up the hill, into the lobby of our building—mild surprise from the doorman—into the elevator, up. When David, the cook, pulled open the door, it was sunny up there.

"I'm back," I said, dramatically.

I went upstairs and walked down the hall, into Mom's room. She was sitting at her marble desk, looking out through the floor-to-ceiling windows, across the sunlit cloud tops, talking on the phone. I sat down in an armchair next to her desk. She did not notice me and continued talking. After twenty seconds she looked to her left, fumbled the phone in surprise, and hung up immediately.

She said, "Sean!? What?"

"I'm back, Mom," I said.

We were silent for a moment.

I said, "I couldn't go to that place. But Dad wouldn't listen to me. So I came home. I *had* to."

Her phone rang, instinctively she picked up, and it was Dad.

He *knew*.

Mom said, "*Al?* Yes. He's sitting here right beside me."

A sense of doom settled in.

Clifford Mooney was sitting in Dad's office when he got the news. "I'd known Alfred Spalding Wilsey for nearly twenty years," he told me recently, "and I never saw such a look on his face. You got him, and he didn't know what to do. I'm glad he didn't ask me what I thought, because I might have suffered a bout of honesty and told him I thought it was great."

*Yeah.*

Mom said, "He just came walking into my office. I didn't know anything till a few minutes ago."

Dad shouted, so loud I could hear it, "Better get his ass on a plane and back to NOLS!" He was furious.

"I had nothing to do with this, *Al,*" Mom said tersely. "And I think you should listen to what your *son* has to say."

There were a few more harsh exchanges. I was terrified of being put on the phone with Dad. But it was decided we would all meet and discuss this further with Mom's vision-guiding Berkeley psychologist, Dr. Sheila Krystal, acting as a mediating party.

THAT AFTERNOON, for the first time in seven years, I found myself in the same room with my parents. It was a very Berkeley room. Sheila held her sessions in a pillow-strewn nook with the sun shining in through high windows and cats pacing and purring and crystals blazing and Shivas waving and sandalwood scent molecules offering massages to molecules of oxygen. Predictably, Dad was there early, and I was afraid that he was going to hit me on sight—just slug my ass. But he didn't. He looked up and said nothing. Mom and Dad and I waited for Dr. Krystal with the sound of tinkling bells and waves crashing around us.

Sheila Krystal looked like a young Nastassja Kinski crossed with a middle-aged Yoko Ono. She wore a jumpsuit made of rust-colored crushed velvet, which was roomy and very low cut, and provided views of cleavage and dangly jewelry. She moved around her office bending and fluffing pillows, scooping up cats. She was sinewy; her cheekbones and jaw were sharp. She was sexy, prosperous (she drove an Aston Martin), braless, with auburn hair and deep red highlights. Sheila was feline and limber. She was full of wisdom and wonder. Sometimes she would stretch languorously and cock her head to the side in mid-sentence and fall silent. My dad called her "the airy fairy."

Sheila was straightforward and willing to give advice. Often extraordinarily kooky advice. Of which I would get a great deal in the subsequent two years.

We sat three abreast on a row of pillows opposite her. I was in the corner, then Mom, in the middle, then Dad nearest the exit.

Dad started the session by saying, "This is a waste of time. He needs to get on a plane and go back to NOLS."

I said, "I want to get a job and stay home."

Dad said, "What job?"

I said, "Something. I don't know. I'm away all year."

Mom agreed. Dad crossed his arms. I begged.

Dad said, "Are you going back to NOLS or not?"

I replied, in a high, nervous voice, "Dad, I left that place for a good reason. I told you I didn't want to go there and you just ignored me."

I told him NOLS offered a refund. I said I'd work for Wilsey Butter, on the docks or something. I'd do anything, just for another option, to see that he could listen to me.

Dad said, "You don't tell the truth. You *lied* to me. You're a liar. That place will be good for you. Give you a sense of independence and self-worth. You'd better get your ass back there."

I said, "If you really cared about what's good for me you'd listen to what I *thought* sometimes."

"You haven't earned the right to be listened to. I *listen* and you *lie*."

"*I* lie? What about you? What about the lies *you've* told me? About Mom, about Dede, about your marriage."

Dad went silent for a moment. Then he said, "I've said all I have to say. Either you go back to NOLS or I will have nothing to do with you anymore."

I said, "Well, I'm not going back to NOLS."

And that was it. Suddenly everything switched into a different tense.

Dad relaxed his shoulders. He said, with such deliberateness that it must have been on his mind for quite some time, "I will support you financially. I'll pay for your school until you're eighteen. But I'll have nothing to do with you otherwise. I will not see you or talk to you. You are not to come into our house ever again. I will have the contents of your room packed up and sent to you."

Mom and Sheila both jumped in at this point and said that, whatever happened, I would need to be seeing a psychoanalyst.

Dad said, "He can do what he wants, but I'm not going to pay for it." He looked at Sheila. "You should be telling him to go back to NOLS."

Mom said, "*I'll* pay for it, then," expecting Dad to do it.

Dad said, "O.K."

Then he got up and left. I tried to give him a hug, which he refused.

DAD WAS GONE.

There wasn't anything left for Mom and Sheila and me to say. The meeting broke up.

But I was free, too. I had won. He had won. It was a win-win.

TWO DAYS LATER boxes arrived from Dad's. Clifford Mooney had packed them up. He told me, "I was packing everything carefully when Dede came into your room and said, 'Clifford, this isn't how you pack boxes! You pack them like this!' and swept everything off the shelf."

. . .

THE LAST TIME I'd been home long enough for a summer job I was twelve and had worked as a messenger for a magazine called *Scene,* edited by Mom's then boyfriend. *Scene* had folded. I'd already tried skate shops.

*Now what?*

Mom said I had to get a job, because I would not be getting any allowance— after Sheila Krystal's bill she couldn't afford it. I managed to negotiate ten dollars a day (a fortune!) for lunch money while job hunting. Mom reduced it to five dollars when I had no luck after a week. "You are not pounding the pavement hard enough, Sean," she told me. So I tried Burger King and McDonald's. The manager at Burger King just shuffled out from the back, looked at me, and said, "No way." My second favorite McDonald's in the city, on Van Ness and Golden Gate, took my application and then called me in for an interview. I was excited. The night before the interview I went to bed thinking, *Free McDonald's!* The next day I looked around at all the other interviewees and thought I had it made. My English was much better. But the manager, a slim South Asian, said, "I'd like to hire you, but I know you won't stay." I went home and told Mom that even McDonald's had rejected me. "With inflation and unemployment what they are, my prospects are not good," I said.

Mom was unusually concerned about her finances that summer because I was not the only minor in her care. There was also a girl called Starling Rowe, who Mom called Star. Star was a nine-year-old ballet dancer. Her mom was a street vendor who had a stand on Ghirardelli Square and sold jewelry she made from feathers, silver, and turquoise. Star was sweet, wry, bold—she'd met Mom by coming up to her on the street and saying, "I know you. You're Pat Montandon. You can give me a ride." Star charmed Mom, told her the street vending business was not good, that she and her mom were moving around a lot, and then asked if she could come live in the penthouse. Mom said yes. So Star lived with us for the summer.

I liked Star and thought she was a good mascot.

Blane liked to call her "the star child."

Mom liked to do Star's hair, though she was terrible at it, and the result always looked painful, severe, Texas-Nazarene.

I asked Star, "Does she, like, plant her foot on the back of your head and yank as hard as she can?"

"*No.*"

"That's what it looks like."

But I was kind to Star. I respected her. She saw through all my bullshit in a way Mom never could.

(Later that year Mom would arrange for a Soviet girl, a child actress called Katya Lycheva, to come to the United States on a "peace tour" and meet with President Reagan—echoing what an American girl called Samantha Smith had done a few years before in Russia. Star was Katya's companion on the "peace tour," which received a lot of national press, and which Dad called, "Your mom's best stunt.")

When I told Mom I'd bombed at McDonald's she said, "I've noticed how well you and Star get along. Why don't you volunteer with the Big Brothers of America?"

This was a random suggestion. Maybe she'd seen something about them on T.V.? I didn't think they were looking for sixteen-year-old big brothers as much as looking for big brothers for sixteen-year-olds. But I was in no position to argue. I called the Big Brothers and talked to a woman who told me that as a minor I couldn't *be* one, but I could come in and stuff envelopes. They needed all the help they could get. When I told Mom she said, "Fine. Since you can't find a paying job you are to volunteer five days a week with the Big Brothers." I agreed, abandoned the job search, showed up at Big Brothers, and stuffed envelopes for a week. After Mom called me there for the third time I pretended they were angry about volunteers receiving personal calls and told her not to call again, lest I lose my job. Then I stopped going and started skating full time. I successfully negotiated for ten dollars in daily lunch money, now that I was working, and though this would prove difficult to extract, sometimes resulting in a Mom-made lunch—Campbell's Cream of Mushroom in a Thermos—I could usually get lunch for around three or four dollars, supplement it with some snacks at Blane's, and keep the rest.

I left the house at eight-thirty and couldn't go home until five. The days got filled with whatever adventure we could come up with. Sitting on a bus making fun of some graffiti that read "Fulton Street Mob," I said, "Fulton Street Mob? What's a *mob?* Is this like the nineteen-twenties?" Blane laughed. A kid in a hood, seated in the very back, said, quiet and menacing, "They'll blow up your house." We all got off at the next stop. I laughed, thought *Good luck blowing up Mom's house*, but carried my skateboard like a club for a few blocks.

I got good at jumping over the hoods of parked cars. One time I stopped in the middle of a quiet street where a Porsche was parked and said, "Dude, do you think I can jump *over* this car?"

Blane said, "I don't know."

"Do you dare me to jump over this car?" I asked.

"Sure, I dare you."

Then I got back as far as I could, ran, leaped, landed a foot hard on the far edge of the Porsche's hood, denting it and setting off the alarm. We yelped, "Oh shit!" and skated away fast.

We ripped the receivers off pay phones till we had a whole collection of them.

We did nitrous oxide in the back of the bus and let the spent canisters roll down the aisle.

We climbed up the sides of buildings and sat on their roofs.

We jumped into parked convertibles and pretended they were ours.

When I knew that Dad had left California for Newport Blane borrowed his Mom's car and we drove up to Napa, to Dad's house. We walked in and introduced ourselves to his nervous new caretakers (Knute, the deaf former millionaire, and Eileen, his deaf wife, had been fired). They said they were going to call the police. I calmly went to my old room and took the only thing that I could absolutely and undeniably claim as my own: a plastic Roman centurion's helmet. Then we drove back to the city.

While Blane was babysitting his seven-year-old brother, we took the car to a mall where MTV VJ "Downtown" Julie Brown was making an appearance. We planned to shout, "Hey Julie, wanna see us piss blood?" Instead we stood in the back of the crowd, I mumbled the question, and we laughed nervously while Blane's little brother looked confused.

We rented porno movies at Choi's Home Video, on Lombard and Van Ness. The first one we rented was called *The Fine Art of Cunnilingus*. We assumed it would be about a smooth operator named Gus who tricked a lot of women into sleeping with him by being very cunning: "The Fine Art of Cunning Gus." We were surprised, and then, when we figured out the truth, we thought we were Renaissance men.

Most days I woke up, smacked a bunch of gel in my hair, toweled hard, so it stood up and *out*, in every direction, shiny and crunchy (soon to be full of sweat), begged my ten dollars, grabbed a Coke and my skateboard, flew out the door in my black Chuck Taylors, stuck my earring in in the elevator, and skated out into the sunshine, over to Blane's, via a circuitous route—since Mom was watching from above to make sure I really was going to Big Brothers. I had to go ten blocks out of the way to be safe. I would fly down hills, turn the board sideways and slide the wheels to decelerate, then pull the slide all the way round into

a 180, ride backward, then kick-turn forward again, then do another slide, plant
one leg and boost ("boneless") off a notch cut in the hill for someone's garage,
fly, replace my foot on the board, land, roll, pop off the curb into the intersection
at the bottom of the hill, keep going. The skateboard is the most versatile urban
conveyance. In a crowded city, no one on foot or bike or in a car could ever hope
to keep up with you. Up and down stairs. On buses and trains in an instant.
Holding onto the backs of delivery trucks. The city a body of water. I was a fish.

I'd pick up Blane, and then it was off into the city together.

ON ONE of these amazing days of freedom Blane and I were cruising down
Market Street toward the bay. I wore pegged black Jimmy'Z pants with a Velcro
fly and built-in Velcro belt and holes in the knees from past falls; a *Thrasher*
skateboard magazine T-shirt with a recipe for "shark tacos" across the front; and
an old, stained, beige dress shirt from some thrift store, unbuttoned and fluttering behind. About ten feet ahead of me Blane looked like a lacrosse player who
just happened to be standing on a skateboard: short hair, cargo pants, clean white
T-shirt.

Market Street is like a river for skateboards. It slopes slightly, heads toward the
bay, and requires almost no effort to ride to the end. It takes you past run-down
buildings and drunks in the Tenderloin, canyons of buildings and businessmen
in the financial district, and then both mixed in with tourists at the end, as it
empties out like a waterfall into the basin of the Embarcadero Plaza, where
all the city's skaters used to gather. Market's sidewalks are made of polished
brick and laid so beautifully as to be almost seamless (only a mason or a skater
would notice). The seams are just wide enough to make a lot of noise without
slowing you down. When you click over them they send a wall of sound ahead:
the unmistakable skateboard rumble of rolling urethane interrupted by wood
tails hitting cement and occasional squeals of wheels going sideways
into slides. *C lop pssh . . . RRRaaaaooooowwwwwwwrrrrrrrrrrrrr—reeeeeeeeeeeeeeeep
ppp—rrraaaaooooowwwwwwrrrrrrrppp. . . .* The noise put us in a trance. We'd
push off for more speed, the decibels would spike, heads would whip around up
ahead of us, conversation would go back and forth.

After a few minutes we passed a dirty brick building. A punk kid—skinny,
bitter expression, tight, pale face broken out with zits, black pants pulled close to
his legs with glimmering silver safety pins—stepped out of its doorway, looked
at Blane, sneered, cocked his head at me, and said: "Skaters *suck*."

Then he kicked back and smirked.

I looked him in the eye and said, "*You* suck." This was something I would never have said as a pedestrian.

His face fell in surprise. "*What?*" he said, jerking straight. "What did you say?" "*You* suck," I said.

He faded into the doorway. I thought, for some reason, that he was hiding in shame—then I heard a voice shout "fuckers" in a San Francisco accent (an accent that makes "San Francisco" sound like "Sam Rocisco"): "*Fawkers!*"

I drew level with the doorway. He reemerged. And four skinheads in flight jackets and Doc Martens popped out behind him. The punk pointed at me and shouted, "Get *him!*" All four leaped and missed.

"Holy shit!" Blane and I shouted together and started flailing our legs— kicking way out in front of our chests and all the way back behind us—and propellering our arms, crouching down low, doing all we could to move our boards as fast as possible. They started running awkwardly in their heavy, many-eyed boots. We pushed hard, going for all the speed we could get, our skateboard sounds amplifying and people in front of us turning and scattering—which, through my own terror, I was just able to register as totally cool.

Their boots weren't stopping. They weren't just trying to scare us. They kept shouting, "Come back here!" explaining how they were going to kill us—first pummeling us down to the sidewalk with our skateboards, then kicking and stomping. We skated harder. We were going to get away unless we hit a big crack.

From the point of view of two sixteen-year-olds, skinheads were the most terrible force in America. There were fabled skinhead murders, and whole San Francisco neighborhoods—the Haight—under their dominion. We had aroused sufficient anger in them to provoke pursuit: This was an honor, like being in a movie, or the pages of *Thrasher*. *We were skating for our very lives.* A single skinhead possessed the might of an entire high school. *But four of them?* If we won, it would be truly awesome. Like having skate-granted superpowers. Our skateboards made us better than them. And skateboards were what had provoked them. *They were envious.*

After a couple of blocks I dove down a stairwell for the monoline subway that runs the length of Market Street—useful as a sort of skateboard chairlift to get you back up so you could flow down Market again—kicking my board up into my hand without stopping, almost falling down the stairs, then leaping the turnstile while Blane ducked into a dusty sports memorabilia shop. On the platform there was silence, no sound of pursuing boots, and then a train. In the sports memorabilia shop Blane feigned interest in an autographed San Francisco 49ers

Super Bowl game ball (there was nothing skateboard related). After fifteen minutes of browsing he got the owner to see if it was safe to leave (this always
amazed me, a store proprietor helping a skater, but Blane brought out such qualities), and then skated away to the Embarcadero.

We arrived at the same time, told our story to the twenty or so assembled
skaters in an adrenalized rush. And then a semihomeless skate-rat kid who I was
friendly with stepped out of the pack and said: "You shouldn't go fucking with
skins. You're gonna get our asses kicked."

Everyone was silent until he smiled, a chip-toothed skater's grin (one that I
would copy after slamming directly onto my upper incisors a couple of weeks
later), and shouted: "*You* suck!"

Skating was a community, and now I felt I was part of it.

THIS WAS BETTER than a survival program!

FOR ONCE something I'd told Mom and Dad was true. I had goals for the summer. I was determined to become a better skater. I was determined to learn how
to buy pot. I was determined to lose my virginity. Though two out of three
would be fine.

If we didn't go to the Embarcadero we rolled around the seedy, drug-dealer-
filled Haight risking the wrath of skinheads, ate McNuggets at our favorite Mc-
Donald's, on Stanyan, lurked outside Fogtown Skates, on Waller, the coolest
shop in the city, and then went over to the panhandle of Golden Gate Park,
where we attempted to purchase pot and got ripped off. We laid down twenty-
five dollars and came home with a bag of throat-mucous-stripping dried brown
leaves mixed with mean little sticks that made us sick and dizzy. But we were determined to be stoners. We went back to the Haight and bought some more, and
this time it was good.

As for the virginity: Dede'd gotten rid of me, and would not be pulling alongside in her Mercedes. I was a loser in San Francisco, and had been for years. The
rose girl at Woodhall was an East Coast anomaly, and not a trace of that rose
confidence had made the trip back home with me.

To mollify my libido I plotted to fondle the breasts of random women on the
street—I'd grab them and fly away, skating as fast as I could, like with the skinheads. I was afraid I might hit a crack and fall and the fondled woman would come
and berate me and some man would have seen and beat me up and I would be arrested as a pervert and get sodomized in jail. Still, I wanted to do it. I was even

more afraid that I would never again touch a breast than I was afraid I'd get beaten up or imprisoned for touching one without permission. And I *needed* to touch one.

I was like some kind of primitive man who had seen fire and was trying to make it out of incorrect, resolutely incombustible, materials, like lettuce. *I have seen that girls like boys and I'm a boy so I must make a girl like me.* My observations of girls in movies, prep school, and San Francisco society led me to believe that they were smarter than I was, liked drugs, and liked guys with drugs, cars, courage, and athletic prowess.

All beautiful girls were also geniuses until proven otherwise, and as geniuses they understood all cool and subtle and audacious gestures of defiance—if I could make such gestures in front of them, then they would see how unique and special and cool I was! I'd been learning about pot mostly because I thought it would help me find favor with girls. I had never heard of a girl who didn't want to get stoned. It was something that they were drawn to, much as they were drawn to good looks and Audis and athleticism. Girls were corrupt.

OUR FAVORITE ACTIVITY became something called the "Hit and Run."

We came up with the Hit and Run one weekend when Mom—who often did such things—said, "I need to be pampered: I need a spa treatment," and announced that we were going to a fancy hotel/spa called the Sonoma Mission Inn, north of the city, in the wine country. I worried that Mom would soon go bankrupt. She was always saying that Dad had screwed her "out of his millions." She was supporting me and Star and sending kids around the world and buying cars she couldn't afford and paying her credit card bills with other credit cards. Soon, she said, the cook and the maid would have to be "let go." She'd already let them go once, only to rehire them. Then she hired a couple more people. She hired these people so she wouldn't have to be lonely. I asked if she could pay for Blane to come along to the Sonoma Mission Inn and, unfailingly generous, she said yes. So Blane came, too. And, of course, Star was coming. We all piled into the new red Mercedes convertible that Mom could not afford and that Blane and I couldn't wait to steal, and crossed the bridge. When we got there Blane and I got our own room, located a good distance from Mom and Star's. Immediately we cracked the minibar, drained the vodka bottles, replaced their contents with water, smoked a bowl of pot, and headed out to the swimming pool. At the pool a preppy girl in a plaid bikini immediately became the object of impossible fantasy and speculation, along with two women in their thirties—their sexual prime!

We swam and gazed at the preppy girl, thought she just maybe looked at us, weren't sure. When she left we returned to our room, watched T.V., and began drinking the minibar gin, which was the only remaining clear liquid. We had room service for dinner, and ordered beers. Star came by, knocked on the door, heard us racing to hide everything, and rolled her eyes when we let her in.

"Don't worry, I won't tell Pat what you're doing," she said.

"The star child is cool," said Blane.

"Don't call me 'the star child,'" Star said, "or I will tell."

Blane looked mock scared.

"Plus, your name's Morf," Star said. "That's a weirder name."

"The star child speaks wisely," I said.

"Shut up!" they both said.

When Star left we smoked some more pot. It was very festive. We were getting away with lots of bad behavior.

The next morning Mom said she'd pay for a *massage* for each of us. We went to the spa part of the hotel and were told by an attractive woman in her thirties to take off our clothes and get under some towels. We consulted.

"Dude, that can't mean boxers, too, can it?" asked Blane. (We had only recently switched to boxers—the underwear of cool people who smoked pot.)

"Well, *Dude*, she *said* 'take off your clothes.' Boxers *are* clothes. So I'm definitely taking off my boxers."

A few minutes later we slid under our towels, shoulders shawled in acne, wearing our boxers. Two women in their thirties started oiling us up. We felt like dogs eating human food. We made conversation. We tried to seem cool and older and "from the city."

When the massage was over, our hormones were roaring through our heads. We went back to our rooms and sat on our beds. *QUIET, HORMONES! FUCKING QUIET! PLEASE.* They would not be quiet. They were *loud,* scary, insistent. Being a teenager was like living in a haunted house, or being possessed—our hormones screamed and clanked their chains, made us do things against our will. There was whistling wind. *Woooaahhahhahwhh!* It was impossible to think. We both wanted to masturbate, but we were in the habit of pretending that we did not masturbate. Our thoughts turned to the preppy bikini girl.

The only way to get through this was to smoke pot, lots of pot, and we only had a little left. Then I had a strange and wonderful inspiration: the Hit and Run.

I said to Blane: "Since everyone at this place is some rich old person, and that girl, she must be bored—she'll be impressed if we do something to just flip it all off, to just show it all up for the bullshit that it is. So let's . . ." I outlined a plan, and we acted.

In our room we packed a big bowl-load, the last of our pot, then walked over to the main entrance to the pool area. I waited with pipe in hand while Blane strolled through to the pool itself, past the girl—he gave me a nod to indicate that she was there (she was there!)—and then continued on to a gate that led off into the parking lot, where he stationed himself, looked around, gave me an all-clear sign. I took a deep breath, summoned all my adrenaline, then ran at top speed to the middle of the pool area, held out the pipe, smiled broadly, flicked my lighter, and took a huge hit, right in front of the girl, some swimming kids, and their parents. I held my hit and gazed around—making sure my presence was registering. Everyone stared at me in alarm, *awe,* girl included. Then I exhaled a huge cloud of smoke and ran away, with a whoop and a leap over a deck chair, off into the parking lot.

When I got there I turned around. I thought this would impress her to such an unstoppable degree that she would whip off her top and pursue, shouting, "Wait!" like the skinheads, but then adding, "My hero!" But she wasn't following. I started laughing—all lust obliterated by the insanity of the whole thing. We left a few hours later, still laughing—and the Hit and Run was with us to stay. I started doing it for its own sake. I picked places that reminded me of my father. Later that week, when I was supposed to be at Big Brothers, I ran into the marble and pile-carpeted lobby of the Fairmont Hotel, hit, held, released a big pot cloud, and ran. Summer was passing, and I was distracted.

Then Mom received an invitation to go to Russia, gave me a week's worth of lunch money, fifty dollars!, and got on a plane—taking Star with her (for an audition with the Bolshoi Ballet). I was left unsupervised.

I knew Dad was still away from the city, in Newport. I'd skated by and seen that workers were renovating his house, enclosing a two-thousand-square-foot porch that offered sweeping views of the bay. When completed this room would be identical in materials and appearance to Mom's marble palace: travertine floors; floor-to-ceiling windows; overstuffed white couches; bay and sky; and a huge metal-and-glass skylight, just like the penthouse's, except that this one slid open, splitting into two halves that rolled apart at the push of a button to reveal the open sky. Reagan's MX missile project was always in the news at the time, so Dad and Dede were building themselves a silo.

The French consulate was next door, and the *Examiner* had called for a quote about the construction. An item in the society notes read: "Asked about the scaffolding all over his neighbor's pad on Jackson Street, the consul general explained: 'Dede Wilsey is building a new closet.'"

The scaffolding for Dede's closet made it easy to climb around the side of the building, adjacent to the consulate, and scramble onto the soon-to-be-enclosed back porch, with its sweeping views of the bay. Blane and I did this on a sunny weekend afternoon. The house was empty, and nobody saw.

I walked across the porch and opened a heavy iron-and-glass door that was always unlocked. Immediately, the alarm went off, and a security chain stopped the door from opening more than six inches. *Fuck*. There were also two sets of French doors leading onto the porch. One of these had external hinges, so I took a screwdriver, banged out the pins, and all at once the left-hand door fell on top of me, a pane smashing down squarely on my head. I don't know what kept me from going right through, glass shattering, face slicing, but I was lucky, the glass just vibrated, and I fell onto my back with the door on top of me and the alarm ringing even louder now that we weren't hearing it through closed doors. Blane helped me lift off the door, and we stepped into the house, where the alarm was blazing even louder still. We began tracking Converse All Star footprints (as recognizable as a phone light to Dede) in the deep and perfectly vacuumed cream carpets. I am sure that it is one of Dede's deepest regrets that the police did not come and catch us in the act. But I knew it always took them forever when Mom set off her alarm.

We went directly to the master bathroom, opened up a cigar box–size malachite box Dad kept on his sink top, and took thirty dollars—that's all (though Dede claimed I took several hundred dollars from the maid's room). Thirty dollars was enough for a *Thrasher* T-shirt at Fogtown and two movies. Then we went back downstairs, out onto the soon-to-be-enclosed marble MX-silo porch, slotted the door into its dead bolt, rehung it on its hinges, jumped onto the scaffold, flashed past the consulate, leaped onto the street, and away.

I thought I did this because I needed a T-shirt—*to clothe myself!* Not to say, *"Fuck you if you think you can keep me out! Fuck fuck yooouuu! Daaaaaaaaad."*

*Twelve* · S E X

B Y  SEPTEMBER I'd accumulated a small pot stash by hoarding some of my Big Brothers lunch money. I'd also swiped a huge jug of Jack Daniel's from Mom's (she never touched it, so she'd never notice) and packed it into my suit-case. I was ready for Woodhall.

Woodhall seemed like it might be something of a relief from San Francisco, where my sneakiness was starting to backfire. When Mom returned from Russia she heard from Dad. He called to accuse me of having broken into his house and stolen money from Alda, Dede's housekeeper. I denied this with conviction. But Mom didn't quite believe me. And Dad didn't even bother listening. He just kept insisting that I return the money immediately. To Dad my reputation as a liar and a thief was insoluble. This filled me with shame. I abandoned my hopes for a reconciliation. I hated him and I hated myself, and Woodhall seemed like a good place to go and be very angry.

My new Woodhall roommate was Chris Johnson. Johnson was infatuated with *The Breakfast Club* and had long, dark, straight bangs and big nostrils that made him look like Judd Nelson—an association he encouraged by wearing fingerless black-leather-and-mesh gloves, a trench coat, and constantly quoting Nelson's lines from the movie. Johnson acted as if he *were* Judd Nelson, or as if Nelson's character, John Bender, had been *based on him*.

In study hall, when Mr. Chant left the room, he shouted, "It'll be anarchy!"

He mumbled, returning from French class with Mrs. Woodhall, "Molière really pumps my nads."

He did a perfect facsimile of Nelson/Bender's monologue about his home life:

In a drunken father voice: "Stupid, worthless, no good, goddamned, freeloading son of a bitch, retarded, big mouth, know-it-all, asshole, jerk."

In a whiny, weary mother voice: "You forgot ugly, lazy, and *dis*-re-spectful."

Whipping his arm back to slap the second voice he delivered the line he loved best, back in the dad voice: "Shut up bitch! Go fix me turkey pot pie!"

Then, as himself/John Bender/Judd Nelson: "What about *you*, Dad?"

"Fuck you."

"No, Dad, *what about you?*"

"Fuck you."

Now screaming, *"No, Dad, what about you!?"*

*"Fuck you!"*

Then he reached out, started drilling punches into the air, and fell down on the floor.

Which was pretty cool.

His second favorite speech was delivered in a rageful, spitting frenzy:

"YOU KNOW WHAT *I* GOT FOR CHRISTMAS THIS YEAR? IT WAS A BANNER FUCKIN' YEAR AT THE OLD BENDER FAMILY! I GOT A CARTON OF CIGARETTES. THE OLD MAN GRABBED ME [he thrust out an arm] AND SAID, 'HEY! SMOKE UP, JOHNNY!'"

Often, without warning, he'd just shout, *"SMOKE UP, JOHNNY!"*

Then he'd light a cigarette.

Johnson also excelled at nodding yes and saying "No" (difficult if you are stoned); lighting one of his boots on fire and then lighting a cigarette with it; hocking a loogie, knocking his head back, spitting it straight up in the air, catching it in his mouth again, and swallowing. Generally this would happen in the T.V. room. It took him a while to master, and early on it was not uncommon for the spit to arc off to the side. Johnson would lunge over, violently, crack heads with whoever was sitting next to him, and the spit would land on his cheek or their shoulder, which would be followed by shoving and slapping and cussing. If the neighbor was Tim Steiner, Johnson would wind up in a headlock, and they'd roll around on the filthy carpet together.

But once he'd mastered it he could unleash one with perfect accuracy, in study hall or in the middle of dinner, and reduce us all to tears.

Chris and I got stoned in our room, and then he played the song "Medicine Show" by Big Audio Dynamite over and over, because it contained, after a sample of some outlaw saying, "Duck, you suckers," a full thirty seconds of Gatling-gun fire, combined with the sound of panicked, neighing horses. Johnson donned a green trench coat with a West German Army patch on the sleeve, dangled a cigarette from the corner of his mouth, cradled an imaginary machine gun, and opened fire on me and our room. I either ignored him or decided to join him, in which case he rewound, cranked the volume, and we walked out into the T.V. lounge, cigarettes dangling from both our mouths, and took out the whole school—everybody giving us the finger and shouting, "Fuck off," while we just kept on shooting.

I was a Woodhall veteran now. I endeavored to be stoned *at all times.* Johnson was a capable ally in this endeavor. We woke up and smoked pot, smoked some more after breakfast and lunch, smoked more after dinner, and watched T.V. all evening.

When I wasn't stoned I threw myself against a wall outside.

The entire Woodhall campus was unpaved (mud) with the exception of a small slab of concrete next to a big windowless, wood wall, the end of one of the dorms.

I tried to ride this wall—skating toward it, kicking my board perpendicular to the ground, sailing up onto the vertical, and then popping back off onto the slab—though I never managed to do it very well. Usually I just popped the board onto the wall, lost my footing and then bounced off and skidded along the rough wood, getting splinters in my hands and face. I had more success with wall walks: skating to the wall at ninety degrees, popping the board on while leaning down and planting a hand on the ground, then shooting the board up, planting my other hand, popping off into a handstand, board balanced on my feet, back arching, shirt falling over my face, then grabbing the board and landing back on the ground again just before the arm gave out. This was a cool trick, and doable, except when my arm unexpectedly buckled. At the end of a night on the slab I'd skate down the hall and do double "bonelesses"—planting a foot, jumping with the other foot still on the board, then returning the planted foot, sailing through the air, and landing—bang!—down the two flights of stairs that led to my room.

I managed to regularly replenish my pot stores by making drug deals with the new kids next door or at the local mall on our occasional Saturday night trips to the movies. In San Francisco I had acquired cool pot paraphernalia. Paraphernalia—all the James Bond accessories—and the idea that it would get me girls were the main attractions of pot. After my skateboard my most prized possession was a little piece of brass machinery called the Proto Pipe. It was an architectural-looking thing designed to be the ultimate in efficient, waste-reducing pot-smoking technology. A notched cylindrical storage canister twisted elegantly into an opening behind the bowl, the notch mating with a peg—no threads, since the edges had to be smooth for scraping resin from the detachable resin trap. A hardened-steel poker slid in beside the storage canister, interlocked with a flange coming off it, and then mated with a tunnel in the back of the bowl, so the poker could hold the whole thing together. The Proto Pipe had a swiveling "sneak-a-toke" lid that prevented the escape of any excess smoke, doused cherries, and allowed you to keep the bowl loaded and ready for a quick hit at all times.

*Ah, pot.* I loved the sight of green buds packed closely beneath the Proto Pipe's swiveling brass lid, with its twin embossed "P"s. I scraped for resin in times of great need, when supplies were low, once coaxing a huge black resin booger out of the stem and greeting it with joy and awe. When I was desperate I stole other students' pipes and smoked their screens, screens that had originally come from the sinks in the dorm bathroom—the water always shot out of the Woodhall sinks in a messy, unaerated flow. A great sense of security came from walking around with the Proto Pipe fully charged, its storage pod at capacity, its bowl full and well resinated, a baggie tucked away in my room. I felt like a prosperous German burgher, ready for winter. Pot was the one thing we Woodhallers *knew about,* our area of expertise, our extracurricular activity—everything I can tell you about drug culture, all the stupid terminologies and dumb-ass double entendres, I learned that second year at Woodhall. We must have been the school with the highest ratio of stoners to nonstoners in all of America—especially considering the stoner teachers like Mr. Chard, a new arrival who taught biology, looked like John Belushi, and wheedled away at me for weeks, saying, "C'mon, Wilsey, show me your stash. I know you smoke. I just want to see it," and then, when I relented, confirmed that it was "good shit," and asked if he could have "just one nice big bud," for which he repaid me with an inflated grade for the term.

Woodhall's literature talked about covering "two years of high-school in a year and a summer." But the school's real specialty was turning out accomplished stoners in half the time it took other boarding schools to do it.

Around Thanksgiving a new student arrived at the school. He said he'd come from a "psych ward" in Cleveland, and been a drug dealer before going crazy. This was Jason (the first of three Jasons I'd get to know in the next two years), and he would very slowly become my best friend at Woodhall. Jason was not cool, but he was fiercely intelligent. He was big, soft, smooth, and he wore baggy, fashionable, silly, designer clothing. He was a completely different kind of kid for Woodhall, full of sarcastic humor, yet kind and friendly and eager to please. I noticed him immediately, and wanted to befriend him in the same way I imagine Todd Rhame had wanted to befriend me the year before—because he was so different from everyone else at Woodhall. Because there was some hope in him.

He noticed me, too. I was walking through the T.V. room, on my way to go skate, wearing a shirt from a Cure concert I'd attended that summer, otherwise in *Thrasher* gear, Proto Pipe in my pocket, and Jason glanced up from a couch and gave me a look of *admiration*. This froze the moment permanently for me. It was the first time I'd been *admired*. I'd been liked, looked at fondly, scorned, disliked, envied—but never admired. In that moment I realized that everything had changed at Woodhall. There were fewer twenty-year-olds, Steiner was neutralized, Griffith a friend. I had my footing. I didn't have to be guarded. I could be . . . *myself* (whoever that was). There was nothing to be afraid of.

Suddenly I was Rhame, and Jason was me.

I made overtures of friendship while simultaneously exploiting a willingness in Jason to do me favors. If Johnson and I needed some pot, Jason, who was rooming with the single biggest freak in the school, a guy with unfailingly high quality drugs, would take care of all the arrangements, and even help pay for it. He said he'd overdosed back home, so he no longer did drugs, but he was willing to help us. He bought pizza and a pitcher of Coke on Sunday afternoons, since I was deigning to hang out with him. He was like my patron. Nothing like this had ever happened to me before. All he seemed to want in return was talk.

We talked at my desk. He sat across from me in Johnson's chair. I drank, socially. My desk was really more of a bar than a desk. I had pulled it out from the wall, turned it around to face the door, and kept my jug of Jack Daniel's only marginally concealed underneath, along with a few shot glasses (film canisters) stashed in a cubby intended for books. Behind me, in the corner, I'd taped full-page photographs torn out of *Thrasher* all the way up to the ceiling, papering the walls.

Jason came in and sat in Johnson's chair and Johnson performed and tried to seem mysterious, and somewhat dangerous, and I hauled out the jug of Jack Daniel's and presided.

We liked to read the ads in *Gent* magazine, which specialized in women with extraordinarily large breasts ("Home of the D-Cups"). Our favorite was for something called the "Hands-free Masturbator." Employing a voice of earnest wonder Jason read the ad and gave a testimonial about all the time this device could save you. "The hands-free feature allows me to simultaneously pursue my many other professional objectives!" he said.

He read from the Woodhall pamphlet, too, the stuff about "educational lacunae" and "equestrians." His voice filled with glee and he shouted, "It says that shit, man!" I loved the way his voice changed—from his usual anesthetized deep monotone—when he was really amused, and got higher, livelier, like a kid's.

He read something. I read something. We tried to impress each other. The more we impressed each other the more purposeful I felt. It was better than doing drugs. Johnson was left behind. He would shout, *"SMOKE UP, JOHNNY!"* and we would look at each other like, *This guy just is so fucking wasted.* Johnson *was* wasted. And with our eyes we would say to each other:

S: You're a genius!

J: You're a genius!

We were geniuses!

Genius was a consolation prize for the inability to be a person. *I am a genius, Dad.*

Being a genius was the new thing that was going to save me and get me laid and earn me the respect of my dad.

On a Sunday, when everyone else was getting stoned, dropping acid, watching T.V., Jason was often engaged in artistic pursuits, like the construction of a shrine to the number nine. "It's the largest single digit number. It deserves to be honored," he once told me. And I thought, *Is that genius or what? The nine shrine!*

But Jason and I, in our new fast friendship, were also into the low, not just the high. Our genius minds were capable of appreciating a *Gent* magazine spread showing two women having sex in an automobile shop, using a torque wrench as a dildo, and then taking things to the next level—coming up with the most debased and sickening ideas. Saying things like: "What if you took a big, long, solid shit, and then froze it, so it was really, really solid and hard, and then used it as a *dildo—fucked somebody with it*." Laughter. "Fucked Dede. *Fucked her with shit*. Now that would be revenge."

"Dude," I'd be the one to say. "Fecal dildo. That is genius. Do you think anyone's ever thought of that before?"

And in moments like this Jason would put himself in the superior genius role, saying, "I think there's a fetish for everything and nothing is new. Everything's been thought of before. We've probably even existed before. There is no originality. Only remembering and forgetting."

"Dude."

But then, as I got more vulnerable and open and confided in Jason, was it my imagination, or was Jason's "You're a genius!" actually getting a little more contingent? It seemed that he was really saying:

J: I am a bigger genius.

So I could only respond:

S: I am attractive to women.

Trying to keep him down, hoping he wouldn't see how insecure I was.

I WAS NOW a regular guest on the campus of Wykeham Rise, on a mad dash to lose my virginity. There was a certain kind of girl over there who actually seemed to find me attractive.

Over the summer Wykeham Rise had occupied a large place in my imagination. I thought it was my best chance in the quest to lose my virginity, virginity being the main obstacle to my happiness and success. Once I had lost my virginity, everything else would be gained. I would rise up like Aragorn from *The Lord of the Rings* and take the mantle of my power. I would ride the high winds to California with a crown upon my head and suddenly Dad would see who I was—great, fun, not a virgin, funny, like him—and that people liked me. Everything good about me would be revealed. I would be resplendent. I had no idea about the emotions of sex. *Emotions?* I did not want to feel emotions. I wanted to be a stud.

I knew two Wykeham Rise girls, because they'd answered the dorm phone when I called the rose girl the year before. Their names were Kit and Cecily, and they were the punk rebel girls of Wykeham Rise. Matt Broussard, also new at Woodhall that year, a blond, sweet, blissed-out fellow skater kid with whom I liked to get stoned and try wall rides, was obsessed with Cecily, and said reverently, in his skater accent, "Suss-lee, she looks like Siouxsie from Siouxsie and the Banshees." And she did, with her round white face and all-black wardrobe, her long skirts, confusing, shredded, black, semidiaphanous tops wrapped around her, intermeshing with her ripped black T-shirts, so you could never quite tell where the outer fabric ended and the inner began.

Kit was a skinny girl with a little childish pudge left in her face and white-blond curly hair cut short, tufting up, and dyed green and pink in streaks. She was cute, and wore torn, black, cutoff cargo pants, or camos, or shredded fishnets and a miniskirt with a Cramps or Sex Pistols or Minor Threat T-shirt. Kit's many safety pins clinked and sparkled.

Somehow I started going out with Cecily. She kissed me at the end of a dance, and we talked on the phone for a week—me incredulous and confused and enjoying Broussard's envy. But the next stoned Sunday at Wykeham, out by a *swingset,* Cecily was annoyed with me, and Kit was not, and Cecily went inside, and Kit did not. Kit was suddenly very friendly, flirtatious, then *nuzzly,* then she was pressing herself up against me. We were alone. Broussard was off with Jason and some other guys who'd come over on this trip, meeting Wykeham's two celebrity children: Tony Bennett's daughter, who was wearing a big purple rabbit fur coat, and George Lazenby's daughter, to whom Jason said, getting a huge laugh, "Your father was a shitty James Bond." Everybody was still laughing about this on the van ride home. Though I barely noticed. Because . . .

I was alone with Kit, and then we were kissing. Her kisses were slow and deep and aggressive and very thorough. And . . . *So. Fucking. Wonderful.*

It was extremely flattering that Kit would fuck over her best friend, for what— *for me?* To kiss and touch *me?* Kit was such a good kisser. She was the best kisser I'd ever kissed. She tasted like gum and smoke. And she took my hand and said, "I think you should come in here," pulling me into a basement classroom with windows at the ceiling letting in gray light. We shut the door and paced around a bit, talking in that murmury way you do when you've already decided that you are going somewhere and are waiting just a little bit longer. It didn't matter what we said; talking was just a way of anticipating what was to come. And then, suddenly, we were kissing again. I was sitting on a desk and she came and pressed herself into me and twinned her legs and thighs with mine. Then she was between my legs and pressing hard against me and that felt so good that I wrapped my legs around her and I couldn't remember if, for us to have sex, I was supposed to be between her legs or she was supposed to be between my legs. Things were moving so fast, faster than I could think to figure this leg question out. And there were seemingly no limits. *Hands* were then *in* pants. Our mouths were all over each other. I was breaking all sorts of records and barriers I'd never crossed before. I slid my hand into her underwear and she made a *moan* (of pleasure?), and she was wet and she felt so soft, like the music of The Cure when it got all melodious and *doot doot doot do,* and I wanted to protect and investigate her thoroughly. O.K. Things were not stopping. She was giving every indication that this could keep on going. She shoved her tongue deeper into my mouth as my finger went inside her. She moved her thighs in small quick hiccups and shuddered and laughed and we really seemed to like each other and have great chemistry and there was nowhere else for it to go but for us to take all our clothes off. But could it possibly get any better than this? I had never felt this much. And there was supposed to be *more?* That seemed impossible. I thought, *Will you?* We stopped kissing for a moment and her eyes said yes. I unbuttoned her black cutoff cargo pants and moved to slide them past her hips when there was a noise in the hall and she startled and said, "Oh, no. Not here—come on!" and ran for the door pulling me after her, and I was drunk with hope and would follow her anywhere and do anything: My brain was only interested in her, stuck on the words "Come on."

Out in the daylight her pink and green and white hair was glowing and her white skin was rubbed red around the mouth. Her Doc Martens led off through beaten leaves and bark. She brought me to a place beside a path where the ground sloped up a bit and was not too muddy. We stood there kissing again, hands all over each other. Then she sat down awkwardly in the wet leaves, and I kneeled between her legs—my head had cleared enough to remember where I was supposed to be, *between them*—and looked side to side to make sure we were alone.

When I looked back her pants were down. I missed this moment. A woman had never taken her clothes off for me. *We're about to see her naked,* my hormones said. But what I saw instead was white cotton underwear, patterned with delicate little strawberries, and I was stunned by the sight—her little strawberry-covered butt on the wet ground.

Then she said, in a scared, apologetic voice, *"I've never done this before."*

And in that moment, her in the leaves, this phrase in the air, me kneeling with the breeze blowing cold, Kit no longer a bad girl in a dark classroom but a virgin like me, wearing underwear her mom had bought her, I felt only tenderness for her, and smiled, and felt so much better and clearer about myself and my loser virginity. I relaxed, though I still wanted her incredibly—my hormones receded, courteously, and I wanted to talk to her, talk to her tenderly, allow us to take our time so we could both lose our virginity together.

*Oh the glor . . .*

Suddenly we heard shouts. They were coming from Mr. Chant and Broussard and Jason and Steiner, all in high spirits. They were all shouting:

"Wilzey!"

"Wilzey!"

"Willlzeey!"

"Get down here! We're going! Get in the van or your ass is never coming back here!"

They were getting closer. The tenderness disappeared. My hormones roared, *FUCK THIS GIRL NOW. YOU WILL NOT GET ANOTHER CHANCE. FUCK HER NOW.* I looked at the strawberry underwear and reached to pull them down. Then we looked at each other in the bright winter light. She undid my belt, reached into my boxers, and touched me gently, regretfully, like something expensive in a shop that she had decided not to buy, after much consideration; longingly, but mind definitely made up against it. And I held still and hoped that she would pull down the strawberry panties herself and then pull me down and then inside her, and with that it would finally be over, my accursed, fucking virginity. She looked sadder and sweeter than anyone had ever looked. It was not going to happen. And I understood that. And then I *had* to act. The voices were loud and close by. So I pulled up my own half-down pants and took one last look at her, and thought she was beautiful, and the moment was sort of delicious anyway—and—*Oh, man!*—I kissed her fully for five seconds, pressing my feelings into her mouth, and she kissed me back just as much, and all the hormones surged back to life then, but too bad, because she said, "Call me," and I was running with an erection and leaving her there on the ground (I don't know how long she stayed there) and not looking back again.

I spent the whole van ride stunned, silent, while everybody gasped with laughter repeating Jason's conversation with George Lazenby's daughter. *Your father was a shitty James Bond.*

Kit was expelled that week, before I could go back and we could lose our virginity together. She just disappeared. I got a call from her a month later. She'd run away from home or wherever they'd sent her next and told me that she was living in a house somewhere off in the confusing geography of New England, hours away, with a bunch of other kids; a punk squat.

She said proudly, "I've gotten over that little problem."

Her virginity.

"You should come see me," she added.

.   .   .

THERE WAS NO one to talk to about such things. Nobody who loved me and wasn't crazy and whom I could trust. I tried, disastrously, confiding in my half-brother Lad while home for Christmas. He invited me over to his house for the weekend. I loved Lad. He was twenty-five years older, and I wanted him to think I was cool. He asked, "So is my little brother still a virgin?"

Hoping to please him, thinking of Kit, I said, "Nyah. Lost it a while ago. In fact, I just got a blow job from this girl in the woods who didn't want to have sex because *she* was a virgin. So she gave me a B.J. instead."

Lad was driving, and pulled over the car. He was suddenly furious. "That poor girl!" he said. "Why did you do that? It's not right to take advantage of a girl like that." The rest of our weekend together was strained and miserable.

I was ashamed and confused. *Isn't this what he wanted?*, I thought. *I mean, this is how guys talk to each other, right? Fuck.* I wanted to tell him it was all a lie.


WHEN I GOT back to Woodhall after Christmas I managed to lose my virginity for real. I had sex on the floor of the Wykeham Rise photo lab with a bossy, racy, preppy girl named Heather, who told me, as though I should be flattered, that she was "so sore" afterward, and then never wanted to see me again. It was brief and fumbling and done.

And then Woodhall was invited back to Emma Willard for a long weekend. I spent most of it trying to dodge Whitney Weber, the girl I'd met at the dance the year before and then lost to Todd Rhame. I assumed Rhame had told her what a fraud I was. I lurked in the back of a basement smoking lounge, trying to make conversation with a girl named Noelle, who toyed with me by letting her bra straps show, and wearing boys' boxer shorts in public, and having a dime-sized mole beneath her left clavicle. I followed her into some bushes to smoke cloves (which you couldn't smoke in the basement) and confessed that my favorite actor was Alan Alda. Then she and her beautiful subclavicular mole laughed at me, at length. This was not a cool thing to say to a girl smoking cloves in the bushes in boxer shorts.

After being laughed at I walked dejectedly across the Oxfordlike campus, heading for the building where everyone from Woodhall was staying. Then Whitney came up, fell into step, said, "Remember me?" and looked at me with genuine interest and animation. Was this a joke? Was I being manipulated or made fun of? That *was* what women did. But no. Whitney was sincere, vulnerable, real. She still looked exactly like the governor's daughter in *Benson*, but with a serious smoking habit. We walked and talked and smoked for the last hour before the Woodhall van left. I'd thought all was lost with my Alan Alda confession, and then this. In the parking lot, as we were walking to the van, in front of all her friends and all the Woodhall boys, she said, "Aren't you going to kiss me?" After she said it she was suddenly shy and pale. I kissed her and she kissed me back. There were some "Hurray!"s from both sides. And I felt redeemed.

Back at Woodhall I talked to Whitney for an hour every night and billed the call to Jason's parents' calling card. She was easy to talk to. And with Whitney I was sure that everything was going to be fine. I had found my perfect match. I would never let her go. Not for any rule or person. This was love. And love would kick everybody's asses. If we looked and did not blink the world would understand and have to capitulate. Anyone who stood in the way would be standing in the way of something true and beautiful and be struck down and destroyed. Within a week I needed to tell her I loved her. I was full and aching with the need to express my love. And so I told her, and she told me that she loved me, too! And I was so elated that I even called Dad, who I hadn't talked to in months, and said, "Dad, I'm in love! A girl from . . . a prestigious place."

He was silent for a moment, then he asked me, "When are you planning on admitting that you broke into my house and stole money from Alda? And can you explain to me why your grades are getting worse again?"

The answer to both those questions was: *I'm in love!* And that trumped everything. "I'm in *love,* Dad!" I said again. Thinking that if I kept drilling it into him he'd become overjoyed and forgiving. Instead he told me that he had just about convinced Mom to sign off on sending me to a "year-round school" first thing come summer. I felt a sense of doom, shouted again, angrily now, "I'm in *love,* Dad!" and slammed down the phone.

But Whitney and I kept getting closer. Now we knew we didn't have much time.

A couple of weeks later a few of us were invited for a return visit to Emma Willard. Jason had been corresponding with a girl who he said was a genius, and with whom he was also in love. I spent a day walking around Troy, hours away from Woodhall and Connecticut and my real life, with Whitney, Jason, Jason's genius girl, and Chris Johnson, who carried a boom box, playing the Psychedelic Furs. Jason bought us all pizza. Then we went sunbathing on the banks of the Hudson, laying in a row on a grassy slope atop a retaining wall. The girls briefly took off their shirts and lay in their bras in the sun.

Wonderful.

Except that suddenly, now that we weren't on the phone, Whitney and I didn't have as much to say to each other, and it all felt too momentous, as though our love needed to *save us from too much*.

And "Heartbreak Beat," which Johnson insisted on playing over and over again, was a depressing song, with lyrics like, "And the beat don't stop/And we talk so tough/And there's a perfect kiss/Somewhere out in the dark/But a kiss ain't enough."

And I had crab lice. I suppose I got them from the preppy girl I'd lost my virginity to. She claimed she'd gotten them from me, in a postcard from "the crab pits" in San Francisco that said, "Hey Asshole. Thanks for the crabs."

At the time I didn't understand what she was talking about. I was convinced I was itching so much because I had jock itch.

The following week, back at Woodhall, trying to distract each other from Whitney and the genius girl, Jason and I plotted to break into the school office and read everyone's private files. The idea came when I was in the office for some routine purpose, reached over, and unlatched one of the windows. That night we snuck out of the dorms, through the ubiquitous mud, and then through the window. We pulled down the blinds, switched on a lamp, located the file cabinets, and started yanking out folders and laying our fellow students' most private information out on a desk.

We expected to find that everyone was some kind of dunce or psychotic, and that we were geniuses.

I found my own file, and after going through the familiar St. Mark's transcripts (embossed with winged lion and magnificent Latin) of my Ds and Fs, I found a nine-page, typed, single-spaced document titled, "PSYCHOEDUCATIONAL EVALUATION," and stamped "CONFIDENTIAL."

Jason said, "Oh, yeah. I had one of those. It's an intelligence test. I blew the curve."

I started reading, expecting it to confirm my genius.

It said:

PERTINENT BACKGROUND INFORMATION
AND REASON FOR REFERRAL:
Although Sean has been attending the Saint Mark's Preparatory School, he was recently asked to leave. This was not due to any behavioral problem on the youngster's part, but rather apparently caused by poor academic performance. Thus, Sean was on academic probation during this year, and fin-

ished last semester with three F's and two D's. Prior to attending Saint Mark's, Sean was a student at a local school (Cathedral for Boys) and, according to his father, maintained a "B" average. However, in an immediate prior interview with the father, Mr. Wilsey also suggests that Sean "has never worked very hard." The father also states that Sean, when questioned about his poor performance, says he just "doesn't know" as to why he has earned such low grades. However, upon further questioning, it is clear that both Sean and his father feel that the youngster's "oversocializing" with peers has taken time and energy away from his studies.

It should also be noted that Sean comes from a divorced family; his father has since remarried. (Sean's custody is shared by his mother and father.) Mr. Wilsey also mentioned that Sean has been in psychotherapy (apparently for being rather withdrawn as a child). Basically, the boy does not participate in team sports. Sean's father feels that the youngster is "insecure" due to the divorce between his father and mother. . . .

BEHAVIORAL OBSERVATIONS:
Sean is a very presentable dark-haired young man who, in responding to his low grades at Saint Mark's, said he was "not surprised" that he was asked to leave, although the boy was rather upset at the way it was handled by the school. Basically, Sean felt that he should have been warned and had his extra-curricular (i.e., social life) activities restricted, rather than merely asked to immediately depart from the school. However, the youngster was quite happy at Saint Mark's and would (hopefully) like to return if his grades were to improve.

Sean does readily admit to oversocializing with peers, stating that he has derived great satisfaction from these activities. However, Sean also feels that he can concentrate on his studies to a greater degree and will do better in the future; the youngster did state, for example, that he had "no problem" with his grades while he was at Cathedral School for Boys in San Francisco. Sean is also currently visiting a psychologist in Berkeley, ostensibly to help improve his grade standing. Within the classroom, Sean states that his best subject is English, whereas math is least favored by him. Sean wishes to attend college (preferably Dartmouth, if possible). When asked about future vocational plans, the boy said that he felt that his father would wish him to become affiliated in his business, although almost in the same breath, Sean also mentioned that he would enjoy becoming an actor. In his spare time, the youngster likes to skateboard, as well as "hang out" with peers; his three wishes were to (1) return to Saint Mark's [I thought this would solve all my problems.]; (2) get into a good college; and (3) make my parents happy.

At this point I started skimming, looking for the genius numbers, occasionally getting stopped by interesting paragraphs.

Personality testing suggests a quite anxious and insecure youngster who sees the environment as being a very difficult place in which to function and who often tends to mask or otherwise "smokescreen" his true feelings from the world at large (and significant others in particular). At surface levels, Sean appears to be practically a model of decorum and lightness (which the examiner feels has been aquired through the teaching of important social functioning skills to him, both inside as well as outside of the home environment). However, and also at surface levels, Sean's considerable need to overstructure himself as a means of containing his anxiety yet remains a factor with which he and others must contend.

At deeper levels (and in spite of the fact that Sean has quite good social awareness and participation skills), there is evidence to support the considerable problem the youngster manifests in relating to father figures and to his masculinity in general. To the degree that one's masculinity is expressed through more obvious or "macho" endeavors (e.g., team sports), Sean would find it difficult to proceed. At the same time, maternal figures are also related to with anxiety and insecurity. This may well be due to his sources of anxiety possibly bearing upon aspects of Sean's being an only child and coping with his parents' divorce when he was still a rather young boy. At core levels, Sean does manifest some difficulty in terms of his self image; although ego boundaries are intact, this youngster does invest energy in containing his anger, which is certainly present. Indeed, it may well "fuel" larger aspects of avoidance and distancing that the boy may well manifest under stress. It must also be recognized that a significant amount of internalized anger within him may emerge at times, break through his controls, and be seen in acting out sequences of an episodic variety. In fact, Sean sees himself as having difficulty in "fitting in," and dealing with others' expectations; moreover, he appears to be bothered and upset about what this may portend, in terms of his future. However the fact remains that he has not yet "worked through" feelings of loss of family and/or rejection (however passive it may be) that currently affect his lifespace.

I turned the page and there they were:

Verbal IQ = 118 (88th Percentile)
Performance IQ = 90 (25th Percentile)
Full Scale IQ = 105 (63rd Percentile)

105. I was floored. That number was indestructible. It was a fact. I was 105. I looked over at Jason, who was absorbed in somebody else's file. He was so so so smart, while the temperature could rise above my IQ all over the country during the summer.

The first thing I felt was that I had let Jason down. I shoved my file back in the cabinet and felt ashamed. My IQ was supposed to prove that I was Jason's equal, that I was superior to my various oppressors, a vindication of the fact that I was a *misunderstood genius*, not an understood mediocrity, that I was O.K. after all, that there was hope for me yet, that I would be somebody someday, in the future—with some high number there like a fact to prove it. Jason told me how his parents and various educators had reacted to him with awe and respect after his IQ had been measured. I was behind Dan Griffith. (His IQ was well over 105.) My supposed identity was blown.

Jason was absorbed in somebody else's file. He said, "Oh, my God, he only has one testicle." He held his stomach and started crying to hold back the laughter.

Even though we never got caught, and breaking into the school's files was a boast-worthy episode, I wished it had never happened.

But Jason, now that he had all this privileged information, started making prank calls, posing as the school shrink. Everyone in the T.V. room gathered round to listen. He didn't have to change his deep voice to do it. He started out conservatively, established credibility, then told Woodhall parents things like: "Your son is dangerous, potentially psychotic. I think, probably, one of the most frightening youngsters I have ever encountered. Please let me explain. . . . Yes. Of course you're surprised. For many years he has had a highly controlled persona. But now, outside the home, in the real world, his ego boundaries are fracturing. You may recall the incident when he urinated in the flower beds, because he was frightened of the public toilet. That was a very mild symptom of a syndrome that has become exacerbated, and that we must combat, but not with psychotherapy alone. I think brain surgery, a partial lobotomy. . . . Yes. I know it's a shock. No, no, impossible. . . . I'm afraid it's gone well beyond that point. And returning home is out of the question. It would not be safe for him to travel. . . . We can do it here at the school. Mrs. Woodhall will assist—" We were all laughing too hard to hear the rest of what he said. But he never broke character, and he was completely convincing.

He went through this routine with three or four kids, called a suicide hotline posing as Peter Taft, my roommate from the year before, and was more entertaining than anything on MTV. Finally the office started getting calls from alarmed parents, and Jason was pulled in for a conversation with Mrs. Woodhall. He was charming and emerged unscathed. I don't know how he managed it. "I know how to talk to Sally," he said. And she never did find out we'd been in the files.

I was shaken. I knew I was a liar, not a genius. Soon Jason would realize. I started smoking a lot of pot again. My grades collapsed.

The next report card Dad received solidified his determination to place me in a year-round school and gave him lines he would quote for years: "Sean's behavior has taken a turn for the worse this term. He has attempted, unsuccessfully, to play the charming con artist. . . . He consistently resisted waking up in the morning. He was given to episodes of immature behavior with his roommate, and at times was responsible for dormitory vandalism. Furthermore, Sean often engaged in nocturnal meanderings. . . . As the adage goes: 'When he is good, he is very, very good, but when he is bad, he courts disaster.'"

My clearest academic memories are of Mr. Chant, who was a kind and patient teacher, and allowed me to double-check my homework in class before he graded it. I redid assignments I'd had hours to complete, while he watched and suggested and smoked. Then he taught me, and I learned things from him.

Mr. Chant smoked throughout class, but he wouldn't let me smoke because I didn't have permission. In the Woodhall registration form there was a line that read "The above student (has/does not have) my permission to smoke." Dad had underlined "does not have," and double crossed out "has." So I was not allowed to smoke *in class*. There was never any effort to prevent me from smoking in any other location on campus. Only when I was sitting across from Mr. Chant in his office/classroom was there any enforcement of the smoking policy. At the start of every math class I pulled out a pack, asked him for a light, was refused, and then reluctantly got down to redoing my homework.

THAT YEAR a new teacher arrived. He taught Shakespeare to us in Woodhall's one group class, at least until he got fired for teaching in a bathrobe and, in a confrontation that took place in front of all his Shakespeare students, refusing to change.

Genius!

We idolized him. He was witty and irreverent and young and cool and, alas, he just wasn't into me, didn't seem to find me smart or interesting, tended to cut me out of conversations by looking at and responding only to Jason, whom he was always inviting over to play long chess games, which I would sometimes come and watch. One night he told Jason he kept all his money under his mattress. Jason told me. It seemed like such an ill-advised thing to tell a Woodhall student that it must have actually been: Genius! So now there were three geniuses at Woodhall, though the other two, being legitimate geniuses, probably realized that the third was an imposter.

Grades slipping, pot smoking on the rise, I scrounged to keep up my quota of genius remarks, jokes, perceptions. I was desperate, terrified that I'd be found out. I tried to memorize some Shakespeare. It was like being back in San Francisco, having dinner at Dad and Dede's.

During this grim period I accepted Jason's roommate's invitation to come over to his and Jason's room and smoke some high-quality New York City marijuana. I turned up with my Proto Pipe at the appointed hour, well after lights out, leaving an envious and uninvited Johnson behind and bringing along Matt Broussard, Woodhall's other skater. We sat down in desk chairs beside the bunk bed and handed my well-scraped PP up to our skinny benefactor, who was wrapped in blankets and enthroned on the top bunk. There was the sound of a plastic bag, bedding rustling, and our anticipatory chatter. Jason lay on the lower bunk and watched.

Our host lit up and took one, two, three big hits. He handed the pipe down to me, and I took one, then handed it over to Broussard, who hit once and passed it back to the top bunk, where Jason's roommate did four hits in a row, so that by the third I was crazy, distracted, thinking the damn bowl would surely be ashed by my second turn. But then he stopped and kindly packed in a little more, passed it down, and as I flicked my lighter and pressed the stem to my lips in relief an eruption of sound came from the direction of the door as someone forced it in six inches, pulled it back, and then forced it all the way, defeating the crude chair-under-knob lock we'd placed there. The lights came blazing on—Jesus Christ, Mr. Chant!—and I was captured in a perfect tableau of bust-ableness, frozen, with pipe poised and lighter at the ready, before I dropped them both and the pipe went rolling under the bed, spilling glowing pot across the carpet, which began to smolder.

Mr. Chant crutched in with amazing speed, swept up the pipe, stamped out the pot, and sent us back to our rooms. Twenty minutes later Broussard snuck in and we decided to take the blame for the whole thing, which worked. Everybody knew and believed that Jason didn't smoke, which he didn't, so he was off. I don't know how Jason's roommate got off, but we claimed that it was our pot and our pipe and we'd just come into their room to smoke it in their company, and that was good enough for Mrs. Woodhall and Mr. Chant.

Broussard and I were suspended. But our parents didn't want us home, so we were suspended "on campus," which meant "manual labor from 7:45 A.M. to 4:30 P.M. each day," as the letter that informed my parents explained. We laid a neat brick path from the dining hall to the admissions office. Then we helped in the kitchen, where the Vietnam vet cook, who was supposed to be making us *scrub* pots, stood lookout while we sat on lawn chairs in the basement smoking cigarettes and more pot from Jason's grateful roommate.

Winter thawed and Jason invited me to come to Cleveland, and then on to Naples, Florida, with him and his parents for spring break. I said O.K. as long as Johnson, who would be bringing a lot of pot, could join us. There was room in the Florida condo, and it was fine with Jason's parents, so all was arranged. Jason and I went to Cleveland, where we got along great, our genius/subgenius, cool/subcool dynamic inoperative in the real world. Then we went to Florida and met Johnson, and I started trying to act cool. Johnson and I ditched Jason one night and found ourselves supplying pot to a group of girls in a hot tub, which was an unbelievable spring break dream—girls; hot tub; us?; everybody high thanks to us?—but then somebody called the cops because of all the noise we were making, and they arrived just as Johnson was taking a hit, which reordered the universe along more Woodhallian lines. Johnson got caught by the cops, just like I'd gotten caught by Mr. Chant. I ran down the beach and back to the condo and was in bed by the time the cops woke up Jason's parents, banging on the door and presenting Johnson. The next morning Jason's dad put him on a plane home. I was allowed to stay. Over the next two weeks Jason and I solidified our friendship. Our dynamic of balanced jealousies disappeared. I was myself and he was himself, and by the time we got back to Woodhall we were best friends. I resolved to stop hanging out with Johnson—and stop smoking pot.

And with my abandonment of him for Jason, Johnson exited his *Breakfast Club* phase and entered his *Apocalypse Now* phase.

He removed the ceiling bulbs in our room so that the illumination was always dim and inadequate, and began wearing his dad's green jacket from Vietnam, with "JOHNSON" stitched across a patch on the chest. He wore it with fatigues and jungle boots; black, with green mesh and numerous drainage holes, muddy all the time. He talked about being in the jungle "lookin' for Charlie." (He breathed this phrase out low and soft, between his teeth.) He crouched in the darkest corner of the room in his boots and a camo shirt and his dad's jacket, sharpening his dad's bayonet, quoting lines from the movie: "Every minute I stay in this room I get weaker. And every minute Charlie squats in the bush he gets stronger. . . . Charlie was dug in too deep, or moving too fast. His idea of great R and R was cold rice and a little rat meat. . . . I love the smell of napalm in the morning. . . . The horror. The horror."

Otherwise he would just lie on his bed smoking and musing on the severity of "crotch rot" in the jungle. "Crotch rot," he repeated over and over. "*Crotch rot,* Wilsey."

And this was too much to bear: Because it was right after getting back from Florida that the crab lice I thought was jock itch hatched their young and started to make walking, thinking, laughing—anything other than scratching— absolutely impossible.

Sunday night, before the weekly sit-down dinner, I ran out of Tinactin jock itch spray. My crotch was frosted white with the stuff, it was Christmas in my crotch, but it was making no difference—all I felt was a stabbing, rasping, pinching itch. So I counted out the exact change for a new can—I knew the price by heart—ran through the woods into town, speed making me forget my misery, hoping the store would be open. I got there, bought it, and ran back into the woods, dropping my pants and spraying as soon as I was out of sight of the road, yanking them down in midstride and delivering a concerted blast, spraying so much Tinactin into the air that it enveloped my abdomen and began fogging up the fen where I'd crouched, as if some kind of germ warfare test were being performed. The spray was cooling, and my head cleared for a second. Then I hauled my pants back up and ran. It took only two strides to realize that the in- dustrious activity, the smelting mill in my pants, was *still going full blast,* was possibly even more motivated by my offensive against it! I'd just made it *angry*. It was *roiling*. I ran harder, the motion keeping me from going crazy. I could run all night until I collapsed. Maybe that would help. But I had to have sit-down dinner. I was late. The whole school would be waiting. And now I had to change my pants, since they were streaked white. I made it to my room, ripped down the pants, and, brain reeling, eyes bulging, wild, miserable, spotted Johnson's hot-shit Braun electric razor and seized it in desperation. *Shave your pubic hair!* This was the only thing I could think to do. I flipped on Johnson's razor, sprayed more Tinactin as lubrication, and started shaving: *RRRROOWRRRRRRRRRPPP!*

As I did—*Wha?*—someone started *banging* on my door. I hollered, in my agony and confusion, "Just a fucking second!"

Mr. Chant said, "Don't say 'fucking' to me! You are late and you are coming to dinner now!"

*Mr. Chant? Jesus Christ!—Mr. Chant!*

He turned the knob and I jumped, pants down, razor in hand, pubic hair white, and wedged my foot against the door.

The door jiggled. "What's this? Open up, Sean!"

Now he thought he had me cornered smoking pot. I'd come running out of the woods. I was telling him not to come in. There was the steady sound of an aerosol being sprayed.

"I'm shaving, just a second!" I said. But my foot against the door made everything worse—all this suspicious activity was going on in a room from which a faculty member was being barred.

"Come! Out! Now!" he shouted.

All I could do was surrender. I wasn't going to shave my pubic hair with my foot against the door and Mr. Chant shouting to get in. I pulled up my pants, opened the door, came out, and went to dinner. Mr. Chant looked at me sternly, sniffed the air, and came with me. I didn't know what to say. I felt too insane to be ashamed. I felt truly mad, unruled, wild—I'd lost my grip on everything.

And that night the crab lice migrated to my armpits. Suddenly I was itching wildly, there, too. By morning my shirt was wet and stained yellow in the armpits. I felt like I had a tropical disease.

Mrs. Woodhall wanted to see me.

She said, "Sean, what is happening with you?"

I could not say a word.

"I'm not going to be able to keep you here. . . ." She trailed off.

I'd hoped that if I worked really hard and impressed Mrs. Woodhall she would recommend against following Dad's plans. But the crab lice I thought was jock itch were making that impossible. Maybe Dad and Dede had planted them in my bed like Mom's jewelry? I could pay attention to nothing but my crotch. They were a physical manifestation of my state of mind. With summer just a couple of months off, it was looking like year-round school for me. The crab lice would remain unidentified, and come along with me.

IT WAS MAY, term was almost over, soon I would be going to my next school. But there was still time for me to add three more fuckups to my roster.

Fuckup number one came on a Saturday, when a tough New England Italian girl with feathered hair, acid-washed jeans, and crazy-baggy sweaters regularly visited the school. She used to date Dan Griffith, but dumped him for Vinnie Pizzarelli, Dan's bassist, effectively breaking up the Dan Griffith Band and ending the reign of "The Peppercorn Tree." I can't remember her name, but she had breasts, and a car, and so was treated reverently. She came over on weekends to pick up Vinnie or sometimes just to hang out with him in the Woodhall T.V. room.

Dan pretended that she was still his girlfriend and he was loaning her to Vinnie. Jason's parents had arranged for Jason to stay at Woodhall for the summer. This gave Dan an idea: Jason should take his/Vinnie's girlfriend. He would *loan her to Jason* for the summer.

"Give her a try for the summer, Juice,"—Griffith's name for Jason was "Juice Ball." "C'mon Juice," he said. "How can you pass her up? Her dad's got a pontoon airplane. [Weird but true.] And she's got a car."

Jason started asking her sarcastic questions, playing up the joke, acting as though he wanted to find out if they were right for each other. She mostly ignored him, but one afternoon, when we were all in the T.V. room, Jason started really talking with her, asking normal, friendly things, drawing her out, getting her to open up. He kept at it until she had turned all the way around in her chair and was looking at him instead of the T.V., listening and responding to his questions. And then, in a conversational tone, he asked her, "Do you have vaginal warts on your pussy?"

In the silence that followed I lurched up, turned to Jason and sputtered out, "It doesn't bother me if she does. I haven't had any in *weeks!*"

She ran out of the room in tears.

Before following her Vinnie said, with remarkable dignity, that Jason was "a scumbag with no respect for a lady," which made us laugh even harder. Then we had the T.V. to ourselves, which was what we wanted.

But then we were called into Mrs. Woodhall's office and seated across the desk from her. My crab lice itched. She replayed the entire incident. "Baiting this poor girl," she said, appalled. "I have never in all my years as an educator . . ." The usually tolerant and genial Mrs. Woodhall lectured us until she'd worked herself into an indignant rage, getting redder and redder in contrast to her high-collared white lace blouse. Finally she stood up and shouted, her lisp coming through clearly, "'*Vaginal whawts on yowr poosy?*' '*Vaginal whawts on yowr poosy?*' How dawe you?!" in disgusted, enraged bafflement.

I forgot about my crab lice.

I never thought I'd get to see an ex-nun driven to do anything like this. Jason and I stared at her. (Later all we would have to do was look at each other and we would erupt with laughter.) Hearing Mrs. Woodhall recite the words "vaginal warts on your pussy" was like experiencing a miracle.

After the lecture, we were sent to apologize to the girl. "I'm sorry I asked you if you had vaginal warts on your pussy," Jason said. "I'm sorry I said it didn't matter if you did because I hadn't had any in weeks," I said.


THE NEXT DAY, Sunday, fuckup number two: I was sitting in my room with the increasingly eccentric Johnson, who had recently acquired a perfect replica of an Uzi submachine gun—solid steel, with heavy metal shells that ejected when fired.

After letting him blow me away, showering our little ten-by-ten room with shells, I got an idea, a great idea. I donned a long, dark, wool overcoat that I'd bought the year before in New York, hid the Uzi in its folds, and walked up the driveway, out along a lane, and finally onto the main road that ran through town. I crouched in the bushes until a car was almost on top of me, leaped out, tore open my coat, yanked out the Uzi, and started firing. The car swerved into the oncoming lane and sped away. *It fucking swerved! Ha!*

I reloaded. Hid again. Attacked again. Reloaded. Hid. Attacked. Yelled, "Stay out of Bethlehem, fuckers!" I chased a guy as though I were Han Solo chasing stormtroopers on the Death Star, Uzi over my head, shells spilling onto my shoulders: "Yaaaaaaaaaaaaaaaaaaaaaaaaaaaaaaaaaaaaaaaaaaaah!" Screaming. Laughing. Smoking. Laughing so hard I was crying. It was cold. I was by myself. I lost a couple of expensive shells in the wet brown leaves at the side of the road.

Fifteen minutes later, back in the T.V. room, Mr. Chant came in and announced that Connecticut state troopers were outside and wanted to speak with me.

· · ·

FUCKUP NUMBER THREE came six days later, when Mr. Chant volunteered to drive everyone to the Naugatuck Valley Mall for a movie. Jason and I decided not to go, and for three or four hours we were unsupervised.

"This is a perfect opportunity to investigate Jean Wagniere," Jason said. "He's got no personality. And he's got the Swiss flag up on his wall. Like he's 'neutral.' And then there's the fact that the Swiss flag is *square*. Have you noticed that? *What the fuck?* He *is* the most frightening kid in the school."

I went to Wagniere's room with Jason and we riffled through his stuff.

When the school got back from the movies Jean Wagniere went to his room, and then went to Mr. Chant, who went to Mrs. Woodhall, who came to us. That was it: I was restricted to campus for the remainder of the school year. The letter my parents received explained that I had been "bullying . . . a young and vulnerable foreign student."

Being restricted to campus meant someone would have to buy my Tinactin for me. It meant I could never see Whitney again. Mrs. Woodhall said there was now no way she could convince my parents to let me stay at the school.

Soon thereafter came word from my parents, official, *unified* word: My new school would be the Cascade School, located in the logging country of Northern California. I was scheduled to arrive on June 15 and go nowhere for at least a year.

I FELT NO continuity between any of these events. The last three years were meaningless and fragmentary. Beer on the quad! Crucified Christ! Flies on strings! NOLS escape! Pot! Genius! Crab lice masquerading as jock itch! I felt as if I was reinventing myself with every new place and every abandoned and replaced friendship. Reinventing myself, almost invariably, as a worse and worse person.

PRIOR TO MY departure for Cascade, Whitney and I spoke on the phone twice a day. We were sure we loved each other, and now that I would be disappearing for a year we decided we were ready to make love. But we would not be able to. If I couldn't leave campus, it was impossible. *I had to see her.* So I went to talk to Mrs. Woodhall. I told her that I loved Whitney and begged to see her one more time before being sent away.

Mrs. Woodhall, whose kindness was more than I deserved, asked her daughter Abby (who also went to Emma Willard) about Whitney, and Abby vouched for her good character. Mrs. Woodhall offered me a special dispensation. Whitney could come and visit. I would be allowed to walk around Bethlehem with her during the day.

The weekend came. It was gorgeous, warm May weather. We took a blanket and Johnson's boom box and sat in a meadow under a tree and smoked and kissed and talked and listened to Yaz, a band she liked that I'd never heard of before, and drew out our anticipation of making love.

We spent the whole weekend anticipating, extending our anticipation as much as we could. After sitting on the blanket in the secluded field and talking for a few hours we walked through town with our boom box and checked out a little league game.

I felt so cool. I'd never walked around with a boom box and a girlfriend. Whitney said, teasingly, "You've got your girl on your arm. Everybody's looking at you. You're the coolest boy in Bethlehem." (It was redemption. Having Whitney. Anticipating making love. It was all I'd ever dreamed of.)

And it was true! I was wearing my lucky Cure shirt. I was getting admiring looks from some other teenagers. The crab lice were keeping quiet. Back at Woodhall everybody was impressed that a girl would travel several hours to come to a place we considered to be hell, and that she had done this because she loved me, and I loved her, and we intended to make love together, that weekend, in hell. It gave everybody hope. Johnson cleaned our room. Everyone was kind. The weather was good. Woodhall was at its best for Whitney. The school wanted to help. Goodwill was with us. I felt proud of the place.

We discussed having children, seeing different parts of the world, airports, naming all our children after airports: Orly, LAX, SFO . . .

Sunday was like Saturday until we realized we only had an hour before someone was supposed to drive Whitney to the bus station. The pleasure had been in knowing we had time. But now our time was gone. We panicked. Then Whitney took charge. She led me off into the woods, spread out the blanket as if she were laying a picnic, put Yaz on the boom box, and then lay down beside me. We started making out, and then she took off her clothes. I took off my clothes while she kissed me. I held her, and felt her skin blend and bleed into mine. Yaz was in the air. Branches and blue sky were behind her head. Underwear was off. This was the first time I'd ever seen a naked girl who could also see me. I wanted to look and look, take her and the moment in slowly. But there was no time.

*Hurry,* I thought. *You need to make love, have a simultaneous orgasm, get dressed, pack up all this stuff, get Whitney to the parking lot, and say good-bye for a year (at least) in the next five minutes.*

I tried to get inside her. She took me gently in her hand to help. I shoved, she pulled. We couldn't make it happen. It got more and more awkward, and then I was too soft. She let go of me. I looked down, knowing we had to go, and then I came. I felt an overwhelming feeling of dismay. She sat up on top of me.

"I'm sorry," she said.

*I'm sorry,* I thought.

There was no way to talk about this.

Yaz played. We gave each other looks of fear and need and helplessness. She needed reassurance. I needed reassurance. I wanted her to do something and she wanted me to do something.

We touched in silence until we knew there was no time. And then we gathered up our blanket, put on our clothes, grabbed the boom box, came running out of the woods.

She called the first time her bus made a rest stop.

When I picked up she said, "Sean? I love you."

Then she started having trouble getting the phone to accept more change, and the operator came on the line and threatened to cut us off. She tried to explain that the phone kept returning her coins, while simultaneously apologizing for what had happened in the woods.

*Why is she apologizing?* I thought.

Then she said, "Some guy kept coming on to me on the bus until I told him, 'Leave me alone, I have a boyfriend.'"

I was confused and sad and slightly hopeful: *She still considers me her boyfriend? Who the fuck is this guy? Is he a stud? Can he fuck her? But she loves me. And she's apologizing. Maybe this is her fault and not mine.*

She said, "I went into the bathroom just now and I look crazy. How can you like me?"

"I love you!" I said.

"I love you, too," she said.

"Is that guy still on the bus?"

"Yeah," she said distractedly. "It's fine now."

"Don't let him bother you. I'm your boyfriend," I said.

Then the operator said she was terminating the call.


I SAW WHITNEY one more time, the day before I flew back to the West Coast and Cascade. You weren't supposed to be able to rent a hotel room when you were seventeen and looked fourteen, but Whitney managed it. The hotel was big and empty and near the Albany airport. Our room had an interior courtyard view and two queen beds. We sat down, one on each bed, close to the night-stands, both leaned forward, our hands at our sides, and kissed, our mouths the only parts of our bodies that were touching. It was around 6:00 P.M. We stopped kissing and nervously walked around the hotel, letting time pass. Then we came back, slowly took off our clothes, and got into bed. I kept my boxers on and she kept her dark blue girls' Jockeys on. We caressed and kissed each other everywhere. She briefly touched her lips and tongue to my penis, through the boxers. I kissed her through the fabric and felt how soft she was underneath. Neither one of us could take the next step. After hours of mournful, frustrating sexual noviceness we started to get drowsy.

In a small voice she said, "You know a lot more about sex than I do."

I thought, *What does she mean?* Then, *Maybe I really do know a lot about sex? Oh the Glory . . .*

No. I knew a lot about fear.

She said my penis reminded her of a banana. I laughed. I'd never talked to anyone about penises who didn't have a penis. She fell asleep. I was angry at her for not taking charge, for expecting me to be in charge, for failure slipping into inevitability. I felt like I was stuck being myself. Then I fell asleep with the T.V. on and woke up with a start in the morning.

We took a shower together, which was more hygienic than sexy. The fluorescent lights shone brightly. We were both exhausted. There were planes to catch. I soaped her breasts, and they were slippery. Here I was getting something true to brag about, and knew I wouldn't.

We went to the airport, and I felt empty and relieved when I kissed her and she disappeared down the jetway. I told myself I was disgusted with her, she had been a burden, that now I was clean and free. These lies made me want to cry immediately, with such force that slipping on my Walkman was all I could think to do. It felt like warming half my body while the other half was dangerously cold.

But at least I was never going back to Woodhall.

*Thirteen* · C A S C A D E

M Y HALF-BROTHER Mike told me recently, "None of us understood why you were sent away to school. You'd always been a good kid, despite your eccentricities. So I asked Dede, and Dede said you'd pulled a knife on Dad and that's why they had to send you off. She said you'd threatened him."

So I was supposed to have threatened Dad with a knife. Threatened what? To kill him? "I'm gonna stick you!" Is that knife talk?

I have no idea what exactly I was supposed to have done. But Dede said Dad was so frightened that I had to be sent away.

*Dad*, afraid of *me?*

MOM WOULD BE taking me to Cascade. It was now June of 1987. The night before I left Blane came over for dinner and to say good-bye. I'd spent the last ten days in San Francisco skateboarding around with him and an 8mm Olympus video camera that Mom had bought to further document her peace work—Mom was always throwing away money on things she didn't use. I'd begun working on short films. I was going to be a filmmaker!

Waiting for dinner, I packed, and Blane fooled around with the camera, then got bored and pulled out a gun I'd taken from Dad's closet in the country the summer before, just before the NOLS incident. I'd kept it well hidden since then. The gun was a long-barrel .38-caliber police special that had originally belonged to Dad's brother, my uncle Jack. I'd taken it because it reminded me of Dad, and had fired it twice: once at a pond, and once at a dirt pile. Suddenly Mom knocked on the door, I whispered, *"Dude, hide the gun,"* and he shoved it between some clothes in my suitcase.

After dinner Blane left and Mom came up to check on my packing. She reached into my suitcase and screamed.

I turned to see her holding up the gun.

"Sean, what is this?!"

Recovering as quickly as I could, I said, a bit too smoothly, "Oh, that's a .38 replica that Blane got from the Sharper Image. He must have left it here by accident."

But she didn't believe me.

Now Mom was afraid of me.


THE CASCADE SCHOOL grew out of another school called CEDU— phonetic for "See" yourself as you are and "Do" something about it. CEDU, which still exists and was reportedly sold for seventy-two million dollars in the 1990s, to a corporation that operates private schools, grew out of a tangle of cults and communes in sixties Southern California. Originally the school was an alternative to juvenile detention. The state sent kids to CEDU and saved the money it would have spent incarcerating them. The counselors at Cascade had all been students at CEDU in the sixties and seventies. But by 1987 Cascade was decidedly affluent and white. Cascade had gone where the money was.

The first phase of their philosophy was to strip away all indicators of where a student stood in the outside world—your "image," as they called it. Natural adolescent hierarchies didn't exist at Cascade. Jock, stoner, artsy, nerd—these weren't *identities,* they were *images,* and the school intended to remove them.

I arrived wearing my coolest stuff, carefully selected for maximum, unambiguous, I AM COOL impression-making on whoever the cool people were. I was going for an intellectual skater look: pegged black pants, black Chuck Taylors, a white dress shirt over a T-shirt, and a bomber jacket with cat paws I'd painted on the back in homage to The Cure's best song, "The Love Cats." My bangs were stretched down over my eyes. But before another student could see me a counselor whisked me and my stuff directly from the parking lot into an empty communal dorm room, where I was strip-searched, my baggage was examined, and all items deemed "unacceptable" were taken away.

The following were unacceptable:

Black clothing
Anything with a hole in it
Bandannas
Band shirts
Anything related to skateboarding
Dr. Martens
Anything tight
Anything baggy
All leather (except for belts and shoes)
Jewelry
Stickers
Anything trendy, or with a conspicuous designer label
Anything altered with bleach, ink, safety pins, or thread
Makeup
Perfume
Short skirts
Music
Walkmans

Like most of the other boys I was left with the khakis and button-downs my mom had packed. I looked like everybody I'd hated at St. Mark's.

The girls were left with blouses, Easter dresses, polo shirts, sweats, and maybe some too-big jeans.

Suddenly we were all wearing these unfamiliar clothes and forced to squint at each other's earlobes and nostrils to see if they had been pierced, or stare hungrily at tattoos during the brief moments when they were permitted to be *unbandaged* (literally: If you had a tattoo, no matter how large or small or where it was located, you had to keep it covered with a bandage at all times) in preparation for a shower.

Then the staff explained the rules, which were not called rules, but "agreements." I could not use the phone. I could not write letters. All conversations with my parents were to be monitored. Mom and Dad had told me nothing, just that the school was year round. And that's what the school wanted. If I'd known the rules I would not have come willingly. Those who did find out and refused to go were regularly brought to Cascade against their will by ex-cops working as "escorts." They'd bust into your room while you were asleep, handcuff you if you were uncooperative, and escort you to Cascade. It was a cowboy time in the "special education" field.

The most intricate and difficult Cascade agreement concerned music. Certain music was "unacceptable." Unacceptable music was any music that did not have a positive, uncomplicated, life-affirming message—all "cool" music. Any mention, hint, reference to, or innuendo of such music would be cause for disciplinary action. That music no longer existed. I greeted this with resistance and disbelief. But it was true. No one dared discuss unacceptable music. At dinner a week later another new student, who wanted the Tabasco sauce, asked, "Could somebody pass the Red Hot Chili Pepper sauce?," thinking he was just going to get a laugh, or perhaps that he was being so clever and subtle that he would get a few underground nods of approval, since it was actually kind of an obscure musical reference in 1987. Instead he was turned in by the table, taken out of classes for the day, and put on a work detail.

The following music was unacceptable:

Most rock
All heavy metal
All punk rock
All rap
Anything with a specific fashion attached to it

Unacceptable music was carefully codified into a whole series of lists. As you progressed through the school you were rewarded with a new selection of bands that you were allowed to discuss, listen to, and think about. The first list included all the Police and the later Beatle albums. (The early albums were already acceptable, so everyone could walk around humming "Love Me Do," but new students got work detail for "Eleanor Rigby.")

As a new student, the only music besides early Beatles that you could comfortably hum or sing out loud was fifties music; oldies.

Mentioning an unacceptable band was called "popping off," and if someone heard you pop-off they'd "pull you up" (a "pull-up" occurred when one student confronted—elevated?—another on breaking the rules). Pull-up protocol required the person who'd popped off to then go and confess to a counselor. This was called "copping out." If it was an unacceptable music violation you'd tell the counselor, "I said, 'the Red Hot Chili Peppers,' which is unacceptable." Then they would punish you. The counselor was usually twenty years older than you, and had no idea who the Red Hot Chili Peppers were. But a crowd of spectators, having noticed the pull-up, would gather to hear the pop-off a second time when you copped out, and so these bands accrued sort of talismanic power. If you managed to say "The Velvet Underground" in front of a few people you might get in pretty serious trouble, but you would also be associated with them forever (without the pressure of having to prove any sort of extensive knowledge of their oeuvre). You were an honorary exiled member of the band in everyone's eyes.

The other major rule, among a host of minor ones, was that you could not have any romantic contact: no kissing, no fondling, no *flirting*, no sex. No smoking, either.

Oddly enough, swearing was O.K., and so everybody swore—but words like "dude" or "rad," words that were very specifically youthful—were forbidden. You could say "fuck" but you could not say "cool."

Cascade's campus was made up of several communal boys' dormitories and several communal girls' dormitories, kept at a great distance from each other, on either side of a large main building, called "the house" or "the lodge," that had a central L-shaped meeting room. Outside was a beautiful and abused California landscape: red dirt and overlogged vistas, young scrub forests, the distant, snow-capped Cascade mountain range, and a campus peopled with the most extreme 5 percent of the adolescent population. Cascade was a high school made up of the rejected students of many other high schools, the opposite of the cream, the most marginal characters to lurk in the corners of a normal high school. We were angry, self-confident, rebellious kids; mean, shit-kicking jocks (who'd maybe come to Cascade after doing something violent on steroids); hackers; D & D-playing pyromaniacs; nerds; airheaded southern princesses; silent, smart, hesitant, alienated girls; outrageous sluts; serious baked-all-day stoners; cokeheads; and a wide swathe of uncategorizable kids who were just freaks, the outcasts who had never managed to form themselves into a marginal group, because they hadn't been able to convincingly wear their pants low and baggy, or put soap in their hair, or skateboard, or whatever was required of them to obtain the tenuous refuge of a subgroup—*the truly rarest and strangest of the strange.* Now our behavior made no sense: A guy in my dorm invited me to *lift weights* with him, took me down to the weight room in the basement (which was as sweaty and close and frightening as any weight room), and instead of beating me up or making fun of my weakness gave me an encouraging talk, saying, "Bulking up is good for a body like yours. It'll help your self-esteem. We'll start lifting together. I know you can do it." Cascade was a place of such unsettling frankness. I was a skinny kid, but I'd never had anyone besides Dad tell me something like this so directly, without being insulting—like he *cared*. I did not know what to do. Maybe we *would* start lifting together.

All these strange kids congregated in the main room of the house/lodge, from seven-thirty to nine-thirty in the evening. At Woodhall we would have watched T.V. At Cascade there was no T.V. This T.V.-less time was called "floor time." There was only one counselor in charge of supervising the entire school during floor time, but, in fact, supervision was coming from everywhere. As the *New York Times* reported in 2003, writing about a group of off-shore behavior-modification schools, in language that applied equally to my experience at Cascade, "Children were divided into . . . levels, the lower ones forbidden to speak freely . . . the higher ones free to discipline and punish inferiors." The levels at Cascade were called "families" and I was in the lowest one.

Floor time was not to be confused with free time. During floor time, we were expected to have edifying conversations with the students in other families. Floor time was Orwellian. Floor time might have been the single most unsettling thing about Cascade. Everyone was dressed in semi-formal clothing, nice pants, collared shirts, and blouses, and engaged in intense, sometimes tearful conversation. Everyone glanced over the shoulders of their interlocutors—alert to pop-offs the way the sixth formers at St. Mark's had been alert to trespassers on their quad. I had arrived in early summer, and a whole wall of the main room of the house/lodge was made up of French doors, which were opened to the night air. A two-step staircase led into the short arm of the house/lodge. I walked back and forth through these two rooms, pacing them off, because I did not know what else to do. Had this been Woodhall I would have started making sarcastic jokes, and then spoken with anyone who'd laughed. This was how friendship worked. At Cascade, sarcasm was unacceptable, and even when you liked someone and wanted to become friends, if they weren't in your family, but were at some other level in the hierarchy, they often had certain curricular obligations, and could not hang around and talk to you, unless a counselor had told them to talk to you. Then they'd bound up eagerly. If a student was in your peer group you'd be told, as I once was, "You two have nothing to talk to each other about yet." During floor time the only person you could talk to as a new student was the person who had been assigned to you as a "big brother"—meaning that he was a member of something called the "Friends Committee," which selected various older-in-school-time students and parceled them out to supervise new kids. (My big brother was three years younger than me.) Of course, there weren't enough older-in-school-time students to go around, so new students were invariably left with free time, in which we'd pop-off, or wind up talking with each other, and consequently get in trouble. The kids on the Friends Committee would have one or two other appointments to keep—they referred to all conversations as "appointments"—during floor time, and would be feeling the pressure. So what socializing I did took on a harried, interstitial quality, punctuated by pacing, which, that first night, brought me into contact with something that shocked me. A heavy man in his late fifties who was squeezed into tight jeans, a button-down shirt unbuttoned over a T-shirt, no shoes, was lying on the floor, his arms spread out wide, and around him, with their heads resting on his chest and legs and shoulders and on satellite pillows placed as close to him as possible, their limbs also draped over one another's, was a pile of about thirty students, boys and girls. The man was Neil Westin, my family head.

I walked off as quickly as possible. I must have looked stricken, because an older student came up to me almost immediately. After descending the pair of steps that led back to the long arm of the L, I felt a hand on my shoulder—my fourteen-year-old "big brother."

He said to me, "That's a smoosh pile."

This was a Cascade tradition, the "smoosh pile."

I said, "Who's the old lecher?"

"Uh . . . he's family head of Fountainhead," he said.

"Fountainhead?" I said.

"After a book you should read."

I would soon notice many people reading it.

"Let's spend some time," he said.

What to talk about? Current events were out. (Too shallow.) Pop culture was out. Sports were O.K., as long as they were more or less mainstream sports . . . but the best thing that you could talk about was yourself and your *feelings*.

In this first conversation with an older student—in typical Cascade style—a blazing earnestness overwhelmed the fact that we did not really know each other, and were not allowed to get to know each other in the normal way, by seeing if we had anything in common (Cascade just bashed down the front door to intimacy, never went round the back). After forty minutes of awkwardness that must have been just as exhausting for him as it was for me, the boy (having fulfilled his obligation) pulled me into an embrace, and told me that he loved me. Then he hurried off to another appointment.

Now what to do? I had a John Irving book to read, but non—Ayn Rand reading was discouraged. Only people who didn't want to read were encouraged to read. If you liked reading you were avoiding edifying conversations and called a "bookworm." (Disjunctive 1950s-ish terminology was classic Cascade, and woe to you if you mocked it.) A girl in my family named Jane—who, incidentally, loved to read, and so was forbidden to ("book bans," was the official term for it)—was called "Plain Jane," for being so quiet and unobtrusive. I liked Plain Jane, and tried to talk with her, but we were quickly separated. The counselors initiated juvenile name calling—"Plain Jane is a bookworm!"—and then older students took it up. I never got put on book bans. But reading was conspicuous, since all the other Cascaders were having conversations, and an older student would quickly pull you out of a book and suggest that you and he—they would never be of the opposite sex—have a deep/hasty conversation right then and there. I rarely got through more than a page without this happening.

So there I was, not allowed to smoke, no way to set myself apart, wandering the house, effectively banned from books, though I clutched one anyway, faced with an obese man in his late fifties draped in fourteen- through eighteen-year-olds, wearing clothes I hated, cut off from home and friends and wondering if they were going to start calling me something infuriating like "Plain Jane," too. Fortunately, no; I didn't get a nickname. But when Neil wanted to address me he wouldn't say my name, he'd just imitate the habit I had of pushing my hair back out of my eyes.

If they weren't collaring you on the spot the eager young older students would usually approach during the day and ask if you'd like to make an appointment to talk that night. *I'm pretty much wide open, engagementwise,* I'd think. Anyway, you had no option but to agree.

That first night on the floor, after seeing Neil and the smoosh pile, and after the hastily convened appointment with my big brother, who, for some reason, I saw very little of thereafter, curious students from my family briefly crowded around; they now felt free to talk with me because I'd had my appointment. They were all eager to know one thing: "What was your image?" They asked this in hungry, eager, direct, almost anthropological tones.

I was baffled. So they looked at me and made pronouncements based on what shards of clothing or vocabulary had remained intact. One girl told me my image was "artsy fartsy," but that I was a poseur because I probably couldn't paint (this was established as definite in an art class the next week).

But they were mostly eager to give their own answers:

"Metalhead"
"Punk"
"Jock"
"Stoner"
"Skinhead"
"Skinbitch"

I'd never heard other kids speak of themselves this way.

A few, like Plain Jane, even said "nerd" or "studier," in that sort of 1950s, lollipop, ba dum-dum-dum, Cascadey way. These were our *images*. But we were all friends now.

MY FIRST PRIVATE MEETING with Neil served to strengthen my resolve to get the fuck out at any cost. He sat me down in the advising office, a glass-walled room at one end of the house/lodge, and supervised the one call I would be allowed to make to Whitney. I wouldn't be able to talk to her (or any friend) again until I left the school. I told Whitney that I loved her. Neil sat there and took notes. He was wearing his big, tight blue jeans and sitting in a low chair that thrust his knees level with his shoulders. With Neil canted back like that, my attention was drawn to his belt buckle: silver, about the size of a lightswitch cover, inlaid with big chunks of turquoise that spelled out N-E-I-L.

After a few minutes he said, "Say good-bye."

I started to cry. Whitney did, too. Then I hung up. I sat there looking at the floor. Neil, from deep in his reclined position, came out with, "You don't have any true friends. But you might find some real friendships here at Cascade. And you might get to know what friendship means."

This infuriated me. Blane and Spencer were true friends. Even the *pope* knew I had good friends. He'd told me he was *grateful for me and my friends*. I knew what friendship was!

I was always a polite kid, even as I failed and lied my way through most situations, but here I lost it.

"Oh yeah," I spat. "Why should I listen to *'Neil?'*—*'Neil'* with the *belt buckle*."

Neil sat up in his chair, taken aback, and said, "You don't have to be insulting."

ONE OF MY favorite lines of Neil's (in response to the accusation that they were brainwashing us at Cascade) was: "Your brains could use some washing."

But it didn't make as much of an impression as his other frequently uttered line: "If you don't make it here, then you're going to Provo. And at Provo they'll bend you over a bunk bed and shove a dick up your ass."

Provo was the Provo Canyon School, a more extreme version of Cascade, reputed to employ straitjackets, violence, and Mormons, located outside of Provo, Utah, and considered to be a last stop before Juvenile Hall. A lot of kids went there from Cascade.

He made this threat to anyone of either gender in Fountainhead who gave him any resistance. He'd say it loud and drawn out. And I believed him. If Mom and Dad had been willing to send me to Cascade, then why not Provo?

NEIL WANTED US all to open up and share our feelings.

In our group therapy sessions he devoted himself to extracting the saddening and shameful stories we had long been concealing. With Neil's urging, one guy told us about how he used to smear ice cream all over his penis and then make his dog lick it off. He said he later learned to contort himself so that he no longer needed the dog. "Who of you hasn't tried to do the same thing?" Neil asked. "You *all* have. *Yes.* Even the girls." The girls laughed embarrassedly.

*I haven't,* I thought. Though I still had crab lice.

Most of our triweekly sessions were spent seeking out this kind of tearful confession. Raps, as they were called, were held Monday, Wednesday, and Friday. They started at three in the afternoon and ended around six-thirty in the evening, just before dinner. I remember a few "mixed" raps, where older students from other Cascade families—one was called Camelot—would be thrown in with midlevel students and new kids like myself, but usually it was just Neil and the fucked-up young Fountainhead family.

Raps began with the whole school gathering in the house where students' names would be read off a list that corresponded to whatever rap they would be attending. The atmosphere during rap assignments was giddy. Obviously, some of us were about fifteen minutes away from having our shameful stories extracted, while those of us who'd refrained from unacceptable acts and been sincere and cooperative (although mere cooperation would inevitably get you in trouble for passivity), knew that we were in for some incomparable entertainment. Raps were always intense and exciting, and if you had been "working" (avoiding pop-offs, engaging in edifying conversation) you could enjoy the spectacle. But this was rare. Only the older students ever seemed to feel confident about their rap prospects, and only on mixed rap days, when they were "hatchet men"—this was actually the term employed—deputized to go after us Fountainhead fuckups.

So if you were rebellious, or docile, or sullen the most you could hope for was to pull a rap through which you could cringe in fear while they focused on people who had been worse than you.

But *everyone's* adrenaline was up. Everybody was chatty and scared.

Once we got our rap assignments we left the main building and trekked off to whatever dorm or other outlying structure it was being held in. Since raps were loud, they were always held at maximum possible removes from each other.

During the walk to the rap the atmosphere changed. Now we knew what we would be getting. Everyone was in a state of heightened awareness. The outdoor light and shadow seemed distinct and significant. We'd listen to the scrape of our shoes against the crushed gravel of the school paths and watch the little clouds of red clay dust our feet were throwing up.

When we arrived in our rap room we unstacked a bunch of chairs lined up along the wall and placed them in a circle. There would usually be ten to fifteen of us, plus Neil (who got a more comfortable chair). Placed dramatically in the middle of the circle was always a box of Kleenex. It would get kicked over to the first person to begin crying. (Usually the first of many.) Raps were all about carefully structured, almost operatic crescendos of emotion.

There was a little gentle chatter during the unstacking, and then a communal silence set in—no clowning, no whispering, just dead quiet. When Neil arrived he might launch into a monologue—this was a man who loved the sound of his own voice—but then he'd join the silence for a long, awful minute before saying, "Let's begin."

The catalytic emotion was anger, so raps began with an airing of grievances. Usually there were two or three people who were obviously "dirty." "Dirt" was the Cascade term for an unconfessed violation of the Cascade "agreements." Anything counterproductive got you dirty. Dirt could mean sarcasm, lies, shirking, talking about unacceptable music, reading, or thinking too much. A direct confrontation in a rap was called an "indictment." And we the dirty would be indicted. An indictment might come from Neil, but it was highly preferable for it to come from within the group. There was a great deal of prestige attached to an indictment, if it wasn't a phony or opportunistic one, but a pure, truthful, and thus courageous one. This did not happen so often in Fountainhead raps. But in mixed raps there were always older students and aspiring midlevel students who would leap at the chance to bring forward an indictment.

When Neil said "Let's begin" our silent, frightened moment elongated. We were poised and waiting, either to hear our own names, or to call out someone else's. There were only about fifteen seconds in which someone had to do this before Neil would start laying into the whole group, and then—scornfully—go after whomever he thought needed it most.

Logistically, this is how raps worked. If you chose to indict someone you had to be seated at least two chairs away from them, to prevent things from getting physical. If your target was within this buffer you had to change seats before you could indict. Ideally, you would move across the room. To get there you would stand up, bisect the circle, and stand in front of the person whose chair you wanted. They would have to get up and go to your old chair, and you would sit down and face the person you wished to address. As this little mechanical adjustment took place the four people on either side of your just evacuated position would try to guess which one of them you were planning to talk to, or, I should say, *shout at,* since the preferred volume of indictment was loud, to show conviction. You had to prove that you meant it. If it sounded fake you were ruined. It would backfire. The rap would almost always turn against you. The kids who excelled at a crisp, loud, righteous, to-the-point delivery were always the staff's hatchet men, rotating into raps where there was a lot of dirt, in order to do the cleaning.

Once you were reseated you would begin your indictment with the person's name. That was always the very first thing to break the silence. A name. It would be pronounced in a clipped staccato, snapping off all the speculation. As soon as this happened one of two things could happen next. Less good for whoever was delivering the indictment (the term they used was "running"—"running an indictment," like it was a heavy piece of machinery): a brief, alert silence before the indicter had to continue past the person's name and launch into whatever they had to say; best for them: a sudden scrambling activity as one, two, or even three or four other people leaped out of their chairs to cross the room and join in. With this kind of support the indictment was certain to go the distance, be taken up by Neil, and wind up in tears, snot, some kind of revelation for the indicted, glory for indicter, and a kicked box of Kleenex.

For someone who was dirty the smartest and most courageous thing to do in a rap was say, "I want to talk," and head people off before the indictments came.

Because if you didn't, they would surely come, until even the quietest, most seemingly apathetic and disinterested kids were leaping out of their seats to join in. An indictment might start with two or three righteous main figures, but sometimes such an overwhelming consensus would form that it could arrive at a point where everyone in the rap was screaming at one person, all our frustrated, pent-up, adolescent energy coming out on this one unfortunate target—would-be indicters leaping up to change seats and being refused because their desired seats' occupants would be on deck just waiting to get a chance to yell too, and then the chance would come, and as soon as they'd finished their yelling they'd be instantly replaced, and this would continue until the indicted was completely pliant and tearful and routed.

Then Neil would step in.

Once you broke, depending on how you broke, you'd get either mockery or real sympathy. If you were in any way faking contrition by being slightly petulant or resentful of your recent group obliteration, even then, *after you were beaten*, Neil would jump in, and he would be *scathing*. He would almost surgically ply you with details about your life and history that had been supplied by your parents, guardians, and all the private or state psychiatric records that had been made available to him (and the complete availability of such records was mandatory at Cascade). Raps were designed to make you more and more vulnerable—to remove any vestiges of privacy or secrecy you might be guarding. The rap would get to know everything. And then it would be sympathetic.

Though it could about-face at any moment. A rap was a fluid, slippery thing and one's position in it was never too secure. Indictments were incredibly liberating, because you got to tell people exactly what you thought of them, and as long as you were honest you could not go too far. But a rap was always a dangerous place. There were no limits to what was acceptable in a rap, in direct inverse proportion to the severity of the limits on behavior outside of one.

Thinking to ingratiate myself with Neil, I once pitched in on a campaign to make a sarcastic boy cry about how his dad never talked to him about anything other than sports. But that didn't save me from Neil turning—as this boy finished crying—and saying, "Well, Sean, isn't it interesting that you're indicting someone for being sarcastic," in a voice dripping with sarcasm. And the best I could do was say, weakly, "I've been trying not to be sarcastic."

"You hurt people," Neil replied.

A couple of other boys from my dorm shifted seats. I'd been joking around with one of them, a boy named Jason, whom I'd started to become friends with (Jason #2). We'd been running fake indictments on one another before the rap. A former heavy-metal kid named Seth, from L.A., started speaking to me. He was the assistant dorm head and in charge of making sure I did my morning chores.

"Why do I have to tell you two or three times how to make a bed or clean a shower, and why are you always rolling your eyes at me about it?"

Neil's baritone kicked in: "He's always had a maid. Why should things be any different now?"

"That's not true, man!" I said, though of course it was.

"I'm not your fucking maid!" Seth shouted.

Jason, whom I'd been joking with before the rap, had only been there a few weeks longer than I had, and our tentative friendship was mainly based upon exchanging subtle signs that we were not part of the whole brainwash operation. He spoke up, saying, "You know, it's impossible to have a serious conversation with you. Everything's just some kind of joke with you."

He was a fellow skateboarder. During floor time we'd read the apartment listings in the San Francisco *Chronicle* together. When a listing had said "gd trans" we'd pretended we were on the telephone with the landlord, saying, "Tell me about these transitions." In skateboarding a transition meant the change from horizontal to vertical on a ramp, so the ideal skater apartment was a big cylinder in which you could skate constantly! We'd both thought this was funny:

"Yeah, uh, six hundred dollars a month . . . how're the transitions? . . . Uh-huh." He put his hand over the pretend receiver and said, "Says they're good." Then he took his hand away and said, "So that's, essentially, a gradual transition to vert?"

I said, "Rad"—unacceptable—gave him a thumbs-up, and we agreed to take the apartment. We were dirty.

When he began indicting me in the rap I felt betrayed. Neil had probably taken him aside and told him to help me and himself by copping out to his dirt—and taking me down.

THE FIRST TIME I called Mom Neil sat in the room listening and taking notes. As soon as I reached her, before he could react, I said, "Mom, you've got to get me out of this place. They're crazy. My counselor, who is sitting right here, listening to my call, and he'd be a liar to deny it, tells me that if I don't make it here

I'll get sent to someplace in Utah where they'll—quote—bend me over a bunk bed and shove a dick up my ass!"

Neil snatched the phone out of my hand and kicked me out of the office. Standing outside I heard him tell Mom that I was a manipulative liar.

There would be no more calls home.

AT CASCADE the bathroom stalls didn't have doors. The only place I could be alone was the shower. So the shower was where I did my planning. At all other times it was essential to remain guarded and alert. But each morning (it was a Cascade rule that you had to take a shower every day, and wash your hair every other day) I would turn on the shower and promise myself that I would escape. Then I would solemnly recite a lyric by The Cure, reaffirming the existence of the outside world, which had become increasingly remote and unreal.

The school was generally considered escape-proof.

It was important not to seem as though escape was in my thoughts. That would make them watch me harder and press me further in raps. So I was able to learn very little about how others had escaped, and what I did learn was imparted in the form of antiescape ("splitting" was their word for escaping) propaganda I could not seem too interested in without arousing suspicion. The fact that the driveway was seven miles long was the essential piece of discouraging (though false) information. Other carefully gleaned facts about the driveway were that it was connected to many small logging roads, making it easy to lose your way; wolves prowled it; and at the end was the unsympathetic town of Whitmore, where a lot of the faculty lived, and where the police, and the other fifty inhabitants, most in some way connected to the school, would send you back.

You couldn't talk yourself out, which would have been my preferred method, because they never allowed you to talk to anyone outside the school except in the most controlled circumstances. I heard a couple of stories about kids whose pre–Cascade friends had managed to track them down, then driven up and tried to bust them out. But these stories all ended in glamorous failure. One guy had just stood there amazed and couldn't bring himself to go. One girl got in and headed off, but the school got on the phone to the police and by the time she'd made it down the driveway there was a roadblock. Another girl walked the driveway by night and then hitchhiked her way to San Francisco, giving blow jobs to truckers, only to be caught and sent back when she got home.

As soon as students went missing the police were always called in. Even if you made it out of Cascade, past the roomful of other sleeping boys (and the night watchman who patrolled the campus) and down the driveway, there were thirty miles of two-lane blacktop before the first strip mall where you'd have much chance of catching a ride or laying low. The blow job trucker girl had gotten lucky. Each morning in the shower I would turn the possibilities over in my mind. I ruled out running away by night. The chances of failure were high, and if I were caught I knew they'd watch me so hard I'd never get another chance. I didn't want to just rebel or make a statement. I wanted to leave. I wanted to make it. I was waiting for an opportunity. But I had to do something quickly.

"CELEBRATIONS" WERE all-day, all-night, top secret, thematic raps that the school put each peer group through every two months.

I arrived at Cascade just after Fountainhead had gone through its first, the "Truth Celebration." Just before the second, the "Children's Celebration," Fountainhead was broken into two families, and I was made the senior student in Fountainhead #2. But new kids kept coming. I knew it might only be a matter of a few weeks before Fountainhead #2 was large enough to go through its own "Truth," and I didn't like the way the people in Fountainhead #1 seemed altered by the experience. Whenever Neil brought up Fountainhead #1's experiences in the "Truth" everyone grew pale and silent.

In preparation for the Children's Celebration the staff gathered the entire school together for what they called a warm-up. It was around seven in the evening. Fountainhead #1 was dressed in loose-fitting, comfortable clothes, looking nervous and alert. All of Cascade sat and listened to "Children of the Universe," by John Denver, Joan Baez's version of "Forever Young," and "Shower the People," by James Taylor, on auto repeat. Hugs were exchanged, good-byes were said, and Fountainhead #1 disappeared to a remote building at the edge of campus.

At around six the next evening there was another gathering in the house/ lodge to welcome them back. We waited (all the older and midlevel students and me), watching the far shore of the school lake, beyond which the Celebration was taking place, squinting against the low, summer evening sun. My crab lice itched. Everyone kept saying that they'd be *transformed*. It got dark as we waited, and a tape played through several times. I noticed that certain songs on this tape would send identical ripples of emotion through the older students. People would burst into tears, and cry in groups. Then there would be a lull. Then a wave of laughter or chatter would run through the room.

When Fountainhead #1 arrived, fuzzy-eyed, raw, and full of love and gratitude for older students, walking up the porch steps into the house, I looked for Jason, my skateboarder friend. I walked up to him and saw that his eyes were bloodshot and *twinkling*—then they misted in *panic* when he saw me. Sensing his panic some older students took him aside and hugged him while he started crying. George Benson's version of "The Greatest Love of All" was playing, and most of Fountainhead was crying now, too. A group of older students closed in to hold and comfort them.

I was afraid.

Jason's personality had been wiped away by some overwhelming force.

In the following days Fountainhead #1 began to cry much more often in raps, and speak in a deeper, impenetrable jargon. I knew that I had to get out before I started going through these things, too.

A FEW DAYS LATER there was a meeting of the whole school for a special announcement. The Cascade Summer Olympics—a much anticipated, all-school sports extravaganza—was being canceled for something they were calling "Bust Ass Work Ethic Week."

This was not to be some superficial week of straightening up. This was going to be the Cascade Summer Olympics of competitive labor. We would be evaluated on our attitude, supportiveness, speed, and diligence in fulfilling minute and painstaking tasks, like cleaning the grout between kitchen tiles back beneath the dish-washing sinks, where no one could see, with a toothbrush; and major endeavors, like completely clearing a four-acre, steeply graded tract of wilderness (where the school would build a dining hall), using scythes and saws, and carrying all the wood down from the hill, past the house/lodge, around the school pond, to another crew that would saw up the trunks with two-man handsaws and chainsaws, and stack them up in a woodshed or under a tarp. The seven people who worked hardest would be rewarded at week's end by a trip into Redding, the largest nearby town, thirty-five miles away, for pizza and a movie.

This was my way out!

The wood carting was the most highly visible task of Bust Ass Work Ethic Week. It brought you by a couple of crews cleaning the house/lodge, another one working alongside the lake, and a steady stream of people headed across campus. It was the best opportunity to demonstrate my work ethic.

I was assigned to the first rotation of this crew, two days of hefting logs, and I was going to make the most of it. I would get out of the program by getting with the program. This was the best chance I'd seen.

In the shower I imagined the scenario—what I'd do when we got to the theater—every BAWEW morning, psyching myself up. We'd all be seated in a
row, the ass-busting work ethicists, and I'd try to get the aisle. I'd watch an hour
of the movie, and then say I had to use the bathroom. They'd either let me go
and I'd just walk off into the night, or they'd send someone to keep an eye on
me: Seth, the ex-metalhead, now dorm head, I imagined. The idea of hearing
some last idiot command or prohibition, like "wash your hands" or "take two
minutes, no more" and not giving a hint of anything but obedience, appearing
absolutely sincere and with the program, and then fucking *deceiving them* and
running free out onto the street—this filled me with *impossible bliss.* I imagined
how far I'd have to run before I could dive into a Dumpster and stay there,
silent, for hours—days if necessary, hiding. I imagined it in great detail. I
dreamed about it at night. How crowded the streets of Redding would be. The
odds of hopping a bus. What the movie would be. I imagined that if they didn't
give me a chance at the bathroom, some opportunity to run would have to present itself on the way out of the theater. I'd have to just dash and hope they didn't
have a fast-running older student there to chase me down. (Neil would be easy
to outrun.) I thought that if I didn't pull it off just right they'd grab me and
force me into the school van and keep me in a headlock until we were back out
on the logging roads. I imagined stealing a skateboard and using it for my getaway. That's what I'd do—wait till I saw a skater, tell him I needed to borrow
his board because I was a brother skater in terrible jeopardy, and then away! I'd
be uncatchable (and *unacceptable*).

THERE WAS a lot of noise and excitement at the next school meeting, to kick
off Bust Ass Work Ethic Week. The school gathered in the house/lodge. The
headmaster and eight or nine counselors stood up front (instead of the usual one
or two that led more routine gatherings) and more were sitting down among us.
Each of them took a turn to explain what aspect of the week he or she would
run, and to talk about goals. One guy, an American Indian with thick hair, light
skin, and an amazing build, did a whole boisterous number about the wood crew
and how the toughest of the tough would be tested for all they were worth with
him. His muscles stuck out impressively, like ornaments on Victorian furniture.
There was a cult of the muscle at Cascade. "I used to look like you," he told me
later that evening, the implication being, *If you work hard during Bust Ass Work
Ethic Week, you can look like me.*

We were formed into a tree-felling crew, a brush-clearing crew, a log-hauling crew, a ground-leveling crew, and a log-sawing crew. Other crews were dedicated to the obliteration of dirt and decay from all areas—from the most remote crevice to the highest beam. Cascade—whose name I always associated with the dish-washing detergent—believed that intense cleaning led to emotional and intellec-tual order. Bust Ass Work Ethic Week wasn't extraordinary in this respect. They made us clean everything, all the time. Sometimes we'd just be between activities and a counselor would gather a few of us into an impromptu cleaning brigade.

The guy in charge of the kitchen said, in a sort of mock oratorical style, "You know those greasy grout lines way back behind the stoves? The gray ones? The time has come to make them white."

Everybody cheered.

Michael Allgood, Cascade's boyish and charismatic headmaster who kept a perfect distance from the students, making only rare (and fun!) appearances (he would occasionally have lunch with me in his office, and I would want to tell him about Neil, but never could bring myself to do it), gave us a pep talk. Michael was the last speaker, and was self-deprecating in a way that all the others hadn't been, and for a moment he made it seem as if there was something honorable about Bust Ass Work Ethic Week. He spoke calmly. He was warm and convinc-ing. Michael was able to articulate the benefits of hard work in a sincere yet slightly ironic and therefore all the more convincing way. He was humorous and mellow—the antithesis of Neil with his turquoise-studded belt buckle. He was the kind of man you hoped you could be like. So when Michael talked about Bust Ass Work Ethic Week we listened, because we wanted to believe him.

It was almost impossible to believe that this place was his doing. "Some of you don't know what work is," he said. "You really don't. But we're going to teach you. And you're going to thank us for it."

Later that evening, in my dorm, before the first day of log hauling, Michael came around to boost morale. He was like a celebrity visiting the troops. (It oc-curs to me now that Michael was probably so concerned about Bust Ass Work Ethic Week's success because if it lived up to expectations it would clear the way for some major construction projects and the expansion of the school.) He spoke with a lot of charm and humor. He bantered and attracted everyone's attention. Most of the faculty, Allgood included, had begun at CEDU—and Michael was particularly good at telling grisly, weird, depraved CEDU stories, which everyone relished and retold. There was one oft-repeated story about a guy who'd confessed to a shotgun murder in a rap, and another about a guy who'd been caught early one morning on the school's farm trying to have sex with a chicken.

As Michael was about to leave someone called out, "Michael! Can we give each other massages?"

He turned around and smiled. "Yeah, O.K." Then he gave a stern look and added, "As long as there are no flailing penises."

WHEN BUST ASS Work Ethic Week started I tried to never pick up a piece of wood that weighed less that the most I could carry. I took a whole trunk, rested it on my neck, wrapped my arms around it—Christ-style—and trudged along the lakeside to the spot where the sawmill had been set up. After a few hours, bark had rubbed half the skin off my neck. I didn't care. There was an older student standing on the porch watching—shaking his head at girls who tried to get away with carrying single sticks—and he approached me, as I walked rapidly back from the mill to get another trunk, and said, "You're working really hard. People are noticing. Keep it up." I did. And I was helpful and encouraging to others. They rotated me to other tasks, and I cleaned, scrubbed, polished with focus and determination. At the end of the week I was the only winner from the Fountainhead family. I was the last winner they announced. Neil said, "Can it be?" and did his pushing back my hair impersonation (though I'd been forced to get it cut the week before).

Then it was announced that pizza and a movie in town was actually going to be pizza and a video on campus. No explanation given. I was in despair.

The next Sunday, swimming in the middle of the Cascade pond, someone dared me to swim to the bottom and bring back proof that I'd made it. I held my hands up to show that they were empty, took a deep breath, and started heading down. About twenty feet under I heard a sharp bang, like a firecracker going off in my left ear, which was followed by the sensation of rushing bubbles—air exiting my head through my ear. I kept going for four or five more kicks until I touched mud and weeds, grabbed a handful, and turned back towards the surface. When I broke through and opened my eyes the whole world was ninety degrees off kilter, and my balance was so off that I thought I was falling while swimming. I could shut my mouth, hold my nose, and exhale through my ear.

In fact, blowing air out my ear is what I had to do to convince Neil that something was wrong. He pressed the side of his huge, gray head to mine, I blew, and when he heard the gurgly sound of air escaping ear he agreed that the situation was serious enough to merit a trip to the doctor. Since it was an emergency, and no counselor could be spared from duty on the floor, they put me in a car with one of the women who worked in the front office. She was a secretary, someone who would not run a rap, probably didn't really know what raps were, and wouldn't really watch me closely. So—in spite of the altitude change on the way down to town, which hurt like hell—it was one of those rare moments, as in the shower, when I could relax my guard. The doctor told me I'd blown a hole in my eardrum. I'd be all right, but he wanted to see me again after I took a week's course of antibiotics, and again a week after that, at which point he would declare me sound.

Walking out of his office two weeks later I ran into Knute Flynt, failed millionaire, ex–helicopter pilot—Dad's one-time butler.

Stunned, I said, "Knute!"

He said, "Sean!"

"What are you doing here?"

"I'm picking up a prescription."

I remembered that he and Eileen's hearing had always been bad. (Dad and Dede and Todd and Trevor used to love to make fun of this. They called Knute and Eileen "the knuts," and Knute and Eileen never heard.)

"We're living in a trailer up here now," Knute said.

"Wow," I said, dizzy with the coincidence of seeing him. And then the secretary from Cascade said we had to go.

I stepped out of the office and followed her to an Express Mail drop-off. We'd been to the doctor's twice now, and she trusted me. After mailing a package she took me to the supermarket. I couldn't speak. It was a serious breach of the rules to let me in there. I was being exposed to band magazines, beer, checkout girls, and unprescreened music, which drifted through the conditioned air. I was thrilled even as I knew I was going to make a run back to the world where this was the everyday. I just couldn't decide when to run. Here in the store? After we walked in the automatic doors she got confused trying to spot the aisle she needed—there were two candidates—and I considered offering to split up and look down one while she checked the other, then double back and run while she thought I was still in the store, buy some time that way. This would've been smart. But I was strangely unable to do anything but follow her. I was afraid for a moment that Cascade had seeped in and neutralized me somehow; that I would not be able to break free. Who was I? I was frozen with the fear that I couldn't act—that Cascade had cast its spell on me. I realized I was ready to break down and capitulate completely if I went back to the school.

I walked through the store, through the checkout, and as we headed for the secretary's car I turned to her—she seemed to turn to me as well—and said what I suppose I needed to say directly, rather than indirectly, by sneaking away, in order to break the Cascade spell: "Good-bye! I'm leaving!"

She screamed, "No! No! No! Don't go!"

And then I ran for it.

AS SOON AS I was across the parking lot and out of sight, around the side of a building, the woman called Cascade, and Cascade called the police. I ducked into a bait-and-tackle shop, glanced around, and asked them, "Do you have a backdoor?"

They pointed to the back door, which, since I'd run around the building to get in the front door, led to where I'd come from. I reexited the front door, turned left, and made for a Swensen's Ice Cream parlor, where I locked myself in a bathroom and did my best to alter my appearance. I pegged my pants. I put water in my hair. I'd worn two shirts that day, so I took off the top one and tied it around my waist. Then I ran onto the highway and hitched a ride. *Knute* drove right by me, in an old four-door Oldsmobile, waving happily. I waved back. Then an old man who looked like he'd been around since the gold rush pulled over.

He said, "Where ya going?"

I asked him to leave me at "the mall."

"The *big* one?" he asked.

"Yes, please," I said. A large mall would be a good place to blend in, find a phone, start making some calls.

We puttered down the highway, half in the right lane, half on the shoulder, and he showed me a sentimental arts-and-crafts project, stowed in the passengerside leg well: old license plates, reproduced at home with a hand-crank metal press.

"See that glossy red on the numbers," he said.

"Yes," I said.

"I did that with *nail polish*," he said proudly.

"Cool," I said.

I could say the word "cool" . . .

He dropped me at a large suburban mall, a big white slab of wall with a door in it. Walking into a wide, air-conditioned, fluorescent-lit space was like climbing out of a well and seeing the Statue of Liberty. I remember the feeling of letting my guard down for the first time; eagerly, defenselessly, soaking up everything around me, knowing that I was not being watched and evaluated. Walking through the place I began to think back to the kids in Fountainhead, their pants unpegged, their thoughts censored, surrounded by trees and brainwashing and caffeine-free drinks. I was thirsty and I found a water fountain. I had no money. I stood in the A/C with my pant cuffs snug to my leg, checking out the advertising and humming "Boys Don't Cry," by The Cure. I would never forget how lucky I was.

I went to a record store and started going through their bins. I wanted to reassure myself that unacceptable music still existed, that it was still real. I didn't have any money and there was no practical reason to do this, but I just needed to know. First I looked for the bands I loved—The Cure, The Dead Milkmen. Then I started laughing with gratitude and looking up every stupid unacceptable band I could think of: Mötley Crüe . . . Dokken . . . the *Sex* Pistols!

I couldn't find a pay phone in the mall. Someone told me to cross a bridge over the freeway. There would be several phones in the first strip mall on my left. Worried about the cops, I set off. A cruising squad car passed me, but it didn't stop, and I reached the relative safety of the strip mall's wraparound porch, now nervous, feeling exposed, and looking over my shoulder. I called up Spencer Perry.

He was home. "Spencer!" I said.

"Sean!"

I told him I'd escaped and that I needed him to try to get a hundred dollars and Western Union it to me right away.

"You have no idea how many *freedoms we enjoy*, man," I said.

"I think I can sell Scott's Fender Mustang at one of the pawnshops on Sixth Street," he said.

"Don't worry. I'll figure out a way to pay you back somehow," I promised.

I called Mom. She was terrified and hysterical.

"Sean, where are you? What's happening? The police are looking for you. They told me you'd run away!"

I told her, "Mom, I am never going back to that place. I'll call you back," and hung up.

I called Spencer and he said he didn't think he could get his hands on the money before tomorrow, but that he and Scott were doing their best. I told him to try for this afternoon, and then called Western Union and asked when they closed. They said six. I called Spencer and told him that. Then I called my mom back and she said that Michael Allgood would call the cops off if I agreed to talk with him. I took his number and called him. I was nervous. I didn't know what kind of Cascade voodoo he might use on me. He said I should come back to the school and talk to him in person. I told him that there was no way I would *ever* do that. I must have convinced him, because his voice took on a strange disengaged tone for the remainder of the call. I realized I'd won; but I also felt sad about it. I had liked the way this man was interested in me. His new tone seemed to mean that I was beyond hope. *Our way is the only way, and if you do not follow it you may as well be lost.* I was furious about this for months. I had dialogues with Michael and Neil in my head, telling them, *But what if you're wrong?*

Spencer ended up keeping the Fender guitar. Mom agreed to let me come home. She wired ten dollars and a bus ticket to the Greyhound station in Redding. I walked there in an hour, joyfully.

At the bus station they handed me the money and I bought a pack of Vantage cigarettes. When the bus came I sat next to a diabetic girl in her twenties. She was sexy, seedy. She showed me her case of needles and insulin and bought a six-pack of beer for us to share once it got dark.

In Carquinez, crossing the Sacramento River, an hour or so outside the city, we passed the C & H Pure Cane Sugar sign. The "C & H" bubbled, its lights winking on and off at random, making the letters look carbonated. Then the words "Pure Cane Sugar" were illuminated, one at a time:

"Pure"                              "Cane"                              "Sugar"

And then I was home.

# PART THREE

·

# Repetition

# Fourteen · DESTRUCTION

O PEN YOUR PALM. Imagine it surrounded by water. Look at the center. Build a building on a hill there, eight hundred feet above the water. I'm there. I'm back. I'm in San Francisco again.

When Mom let me come home I went straight to bed. The next morning I locked myself in my room, slid open the glass door to the deck, sat outside, smoked a Vantage from the pack I'd bought in Redding, and saw water surrounded by mountains, a bridge with fog rolling up and over its road, threading vapor through the open bottoms of its support towers as sun ricocheted off their tops, and hundreds of sails filled the bay, like triangular shards frozen then snapped away from the fog and scattered. Sun hit Mount Tam in the distance. Cranes gleamed in the naval yards of Alameda. The hills and houses leading up to our building shone white, as if S.F. were some Greek island town full of unrusted sixties European sports cars—BMW 2002s and VW Karmann Ghias and Volvo P1800s and Alfa GTVs.

I'd never really noticed any of this. I'd always taken the city for granted.

Mom was depressed and humiliated and suicidal. Mom experienced brief spasms of superhuman energy to save the planet, to shop, to be pampered, to escape, to combine all of these desires. Dad was hardworking, ambitious, a striver, a social success at last. He and Dede ruled from their fortress of wealth. I had escaped from St. Mark's, Woodhall, Cascade. I was home.

I was about to become more like my parents—and grandparents.

WHEN MY GRANDFATHER, Hayes Wilsey, was a boy his mother didn't want a boy so she let his hair grow long and called him "Sadie Girl." His father, Amassey Wilsey, trained horses to pull pumpers for the fire department, to tolerate fire and noise, till an arsonist—"jealous and mentally ill," as Hayes would explain it to his children—torched the barns in the middle of the night, fire-tolerant horses trapped inside, knocking out his whole life savings and killing him with a heart attack from the shock. Hayes was still a boy. He started boxing. He was a good boxer—small, fast on his feet, a welterweight. A promoter came to see the widow Wilsey and asked if he could turn Sadie Girl into a prizefighter. Out of the question. Then she died. My grandfather was on his own. By age fifteen he'd lost both of his parents and got hit in the face for money.

He dropped out of school in ninth grade, boxed, and worked as a messenger on a riverboat up and down the Sacramento River until he got a job as an animal handler on a Hawaii-bound sailing ship that had a hold full of horses. The sea was lonely, the sailors gave him the same lamb stew day after day, but he was good with the horses, and that got him through.

In Hawaii Hayes established a generation-skipping Wilsey male migratory pattern of western expansion followed by eastward recoil that has continued to this day. (The family started in New York—part of the original Dutch colony—where I've returned, as Hayes would return to San Francisco from Hawaii.) First he climbed the Koolau Pali, high above the windward portion of Oahu, stared out at the Pacific, hoping for a glimpse of California, and cried. (Much as Charlie Clay Montandon, Mom's dad, similarly deluded, would try to spot Texas from a mountain in Tennessee.) Then Hayes went home.

San Francisco was even more beautiful one hundred years ago than it is today. Looking at nineteenth-century black-and-white photos and imagining them full of color and dimension and smell and music and temperature is almost unbearable, like having your heart broken by someone you'll never know. The whole Embarcadero was lined with sailing ships, masts rocking. The surrounding hills rolled away, pristine. Saloons drew fresh steam beer. Ornate fireplaces and cut-glass fixtures cast starlight in rooms full of speculators, Indians, sailors, trappers, actors, prostitutes, Davy Crockett hats, black suits and bolo ties, high-collared dresses slit high up the leg. At a $1.50 boardinghouse you could wake up in the morning with the light shining through lace curtains while the foghorns bemoaned: different weather for every neighborhood in San Francisco. Men wore their hair in long braids. Women hobbled up hills in rocker-soled shoes while children in blazing saffron silk robes ran ahead of them. It was the first great Chinatown, next to the Latin Quarter, up against the Barbary Coast. *The Barbary Fucking Coast!* San Francisco was the capital of the frontier, the end of the trail, the most beautiful city in the country—where skyscrapers and grand hotels were built on gold (to be shaken and reshaken and burned to the ground).

Hayes got married, had his daughter Meryle, the aunt I never met or even heard about until after she was dead, and worked candling eggs in the wholesale district. He was industrious, bought butter from creameries, packed it, shipped it, cut some up for local merchants on the side, and turned into a butter-and-egg man, eventually starting the company that would outlive him. Then he noticed long-black-haired, Castilian-Irish Ora Carmelita McCarthy, my grandmother. The earth shook, buildings fell, and fires rose up.

WHEN MY GRANDMOTHER Ora woke up on Wednesday, April 18, 1906, at 5:12 in the morning, her room was shaking and the shaking was complicated: "horizontal, vertical, wavelike, and rotary," in the words of one witness—all at once. Her bed began to slide to the center of the room and turn in a half circle. Downstairs, in the parlor of the rooming house where she lived, theatrical portraits were hanging on the walls from long wires. They swung out, hovered in the air, spun, and smashed back to the plaster face first, as if their subjects simultaneously refused to watch. Glass shattered. The shaking stopped. Church bells were ringing. It was dark. Ora tried to get out of her bedroom but the house was leaning so hard off center that all of its doors were wedged tight in their frames.

The great majority of life had been tragic for my grandmother. Her father, Daniel McCarthy, had been a civil engineer for Southern Pacific. He was spending the night in a caboose, shunted off on a siding, when somebody switched the tracks and a locomotive sped through and killed him. She was nine.

"He was just absolutely all broken up," Dad's sister, my aunt Helen, told me. Ora's mother was pregnant. Southern Pacific paid the widow a pittance and suddenly they were poor. Ora took secretarial and bookkeeping classes. In 1900 her mother died and left my grandmother with a baby brother and no way to support him. She put her brother in a Catholic orphanage, moved to San Francisco from Oakland, where she'd grown up, and took a job as a fruit seller in the wholesale produce market. Occasionally she'd moonlight as a secretary-bookkeeper with Hayes's butter-and-egg firm.

In 1900 Market Street was known as "the Slot," and everything on the wrong side of Market, where my grandmother moved, was South of the Slot. It was the most flammable part of town, a disposable wooden neighborhood of drunks, artists, foreigners, bachelors, musicians, itinerants, "working girls." Spinster sisters ran the boardinghouse where Ora lived, and principally took in actors, the most respectable and regularly paid demographic in a neighborhood of disrespectables. Ora was a grieving, sedentary, raven-haired, white-skinned, teenage, Castilian-Irish exception in a new world of grease paint, melodrama, blackface, Shakespeare, chorus girls, bearded women, Ibsen, seduction, alcoholism, vaudeville, trained seals, promiscuity. It was a world my grandmother at first feared, and later came to feel a part of. She was moody ("a great crier," per Aunt Helen), artistic and musical—like the neighborhood. Aunt Helen told me she started to "run around with a bunch of musicians." She had a beautiful mezzo-soprano voice, and when she was melancholy she sang. She joined a choir to stay respectable. My grandfather noticed her in the wholesale district. She noticed him noticing her, but he was married and lived in Oakland, and she preferred the society South of the Slot. She lived there, single and unattached, all through her twenties.

South of the Slot used to be the Mission Swamp. When the swamp was filled it was filled with dirt and debris and pavement and cheap buildings. The quake hit hardest there, heaving landfill like water in a tub, with houses floating on top. Buildings fell into the street, imploded, or leaned hard, then went down in the first aftershock. "[H]ysterical women with painted cheeks vomited forth from brothels and dance halls," wrote *McClure's* magazine.

But the quake was just the prologue. The filled swamp briefly became liquid—then became incendiary. In ten minutes there were ten major fires in fifty square blocks, and dozens more small ones.

The fires opened like mouths, like a choir, singing. Ora got out of her room, found her brother, Dan, now a teenager, sprung from the orphanage, and found the building was barely standing, timbers vibrating from the earthquake, actors running over the tilting floors. They grabbed their trunks and got out. On the street there was pandemonium. Stampeding cattle had gored a man and were running free through the smoke and dust, until the first aftershock knocked a leaning warehouse on top of them.

Ora and Dan headed for Golden Gate Park, thirty blocks away, uphill, dragging their trunks. It was a beautiful day. Thousands of other trunks rumbled against the cobblestones—a sound that carried through the city and bounced off its hills. Men and women rolled pianos, sewing machines, vendor's carts, hitched themselves between the poles of wagons. Jack London galloped to town on horseback and described it like this for *Collier's:*

The hills of San Francisco are steep, and up these hills, mile after mile, were the trunks dragged. Everywhere were trunks with across them lying their exhausted owners, men and women. Before the march of the flames were flung picket lines of soldiers. And a block at a time, as the flames advanced, these pickets retreated. One of their tasks was to keep the trunk-pullers moving. The exhausted creatures, stirred on by the menace of bayonets, would arise and struggle up the steep pavements, pausing from weakness every five or ten feet.

Often, after surmounting a heart-breaking hill, they would find another wall of flame advancing upon them at right angles and be compelled to change anew the line of their retreat. In the end, completely played out, after toiling for a dozen hours like giants, thousands of them were compelled to abandon their trunks. Here the shopkeepers and soft members of the middle class were at a disadvantage. But the working-men dug holes in vacant lots and backyards and buried their trunks.

In Nob Hill and Pacific Heights—neighborhoods that weren't burning—everyone ate breakfast. The soft members of the middle class woke up like Ora, beds shaken to the centers of their rooms, bric-a-brac smashed on the floor, but there wasn't a huge amount of damage, and there was no panic. Spectators gathered on the hilltops to watch South of the Slot burn. Then they were hungry. The Palace Hotel, where the opera star Enrico Caruso was staying, was filled with people eating breakfast and the smell of coffee brewing in great urns.

In Hayes Valley, the neighborhood between my grandmother's boarding-house and Golden Gate Park, a housewife lit her stove for breakfast and set her kitchen on fire. The new fire—christened "The Ham and Eggs Fire"—spread quickly, meeting no resistance. People cut around it, trying to get their things to safety, as it doubled and redoubled in size, emptying out more and more buildings and blocks, and headed east toward City Hall. The whole fire department was twenty blocks away, trying to keep the South of the Slot fire south of the Slot. The first fire had started in my grandmother's neighborhood. It drove her into Hayes Valley, a neighborhood with the same name as my grandfather, where the second fire started. These fires would destroy San Francisco. Soon my grandparents would marry and destroy each other.

The two postquake conflagrations were big enough to generate their own wind, drawing air into the city like Caruso drawing breath into his lungs. Sailors out on the bay reported a great funneling sound as air rushed into the city. When they raised their sails they were pulled to San Francisco without steering.

Just beating Ham and Eggs, Ora and Dan hauled their trunks up some of the best skateboarding hills in the city, throwing themselves down exhausted when they reached the head of Haight Street. Ora then told her brother to guard her trunk, and she ran back the way they'd come. She'd escaped her building, she'd escaped the fires—where was she going? Her whereabouts for the rest of the day are unknown. She came back hours later to find Dan dispossessed. "Thieves whipped the trunk out from under him," Aunt Helen told me. It had contained everything she owned.

I can say only what I do know about Ora's trip back into the city: She headed toward the destruction.

The many mouths of the South of the Slot fire unified into one screaming around Mission and Third, then the conflagration split in two directions. Half went down to the Embarcadero, failed to burn the piers (covered with seawater by fireboats), then turned north on East Street (now "Herb Caen Way"), gutting the saloons, flophouses, and brothels of the Barbary Coast, crossing the Slot, where it dead-ended by the water, sparing the Ferry Building but demolishing the wholesale and retail districts and laying siege to the Latin Quarter at the foot of Telegraph Hill, where flames were held off for two days with wine. The other half of the fire traveled up Mission and the south side of Market Street simultaneously, blasting right through office buildings, department stores, the opera house, and the now deserted Palace Hotel—dishes not yet done from breakfast—heading toward Ham and Eggs.

Ham and Eggs crossed Van Ness, gutted City Hall, then jumped Market (something no one thought was possible) and met South of the Slot at midnight.

United, there was no stopping them. San Francisco was theirs. Nob Hill, Russian Hill, the valley between them, Chinatown, half the Mission—all were eventually destroyed. Every main in the city was broken. The hydrants were useless to firemen. The only water came from sewers and cisterns—both soon pumped dry—and the bay, which was too far away. Mobilized soldiers moved ahead of the blaze, making fire breaks with dynamite. They might as well have been spreading rose petals. They tried backfiring, torching whole blocks with kerosene and knocking down whatever still stood with field artillery, but this was done so badly it *helped* the fire. Citizens were evacuated to safe ground, set up camps, started cooking meals, singing around rescued pianos, and watched the unstoppable fire approach until everything around them was as bright as daylight and they were fleeing midsong. The commanding officer at the Presidio described the dynamiting as "so continuous as to resemble a bombardment." That was Wednesday. On Thursday and Friday the fires finished the north slope of Russian Hill and North Beach. Friday's Oakland *Tribune* headline (complete with hasty typo) was: "An Awful Furnace of SeethinP Flame." Finally, the army destroyed every building along the west side of Van Ness, to save Pacific Heights. By Saturday the fire was out. There was almost nothing left to burn.

Three days of burning obliterated 3,000 acres, 500 blocks, 30 schools, 80 churches, 250,000 homes (three-fifths of the city's residences), 3,000 people.

In the aftermath, Pauline Jacobson, a staff writer for the San Francisco *Bulletin*, wrote:

Have you noticed with your merest acquaintance of ten days back how you wring his hand when you encounter him these days, how you hang onto it like grim death as if he were some dearly beloved relative you were afraid the bowels of the earth will swallow up again? . . . Some take it that we are such "brave, brave women," such "strong, strong men. . . ." Bah! That's spreadeagle, yellow journalist rot! . . . To talk of bravery is previous. Wait till this novelty has worn off, this novelty of having been spilled out on the world like so many rats caught in a hole, like so many insignificant ants on the faces of the earth, petted objects of charity and of kindness, the focal point of all the world. Wait till we have settled back into the old trying grooves of traditional civilisation with the added trying struggles inherited. . . . It is then time to bring out one's adjectives of bravery and courage.

The city was closed, but people came from all over the country to volunteer, sneaking or talking their way past military checkpoints. My grandfather came on the ferry from Oakland every day, leaving his wife and baby girl (a chimney had fallen through the roof next to her crib) and sometimes not coming back. There was ash everywhere. Flyers like this one covered the city:

MISSING Mrs. Bessie O. Steele Age 33, dark hair, brown eyes, 5 ft. 5 in., weight 135; slender; Helen Steele 6 years old, brown eyes; Donald Steele 2 years old, blue eyes; Mrs. H.O. Wheeler Age 55, iron grey hair, eyes grey, 5 ft. 2 in, heavy set, weight 150 lbs. Were supposed to be stopping at Rex Hotel, 242 Turk St. Report to Masonic Temple, Oakland, or to 857 19th St., Oakland, Phone Oakland 4096. W.E. STEELE-WHEELER

For months Ora lived in an army tent near the park police station. The mayor banned all cooking indoors. Everyone cooked on the sidewalks. Men who'd been arrested for looting cleared the streets of rubble. Female looters washed the dishes and soiled linens of the police. The photographs of the devastation resemble Dresden or Hiroshima, except when you look past the destruction. San Francisco's survivors look like they're having a good time. It was spring. The whole displaced population was living in the open air, no walls, let alone neighborhoods, separating Chinese, Japanese, Irish, Italians; everywhere underclothes, casks of rescued wine, "flirtation and love making" (according to one eyewitness). Men and women sat side by side, leg against leg, at open air messes. There were no social divisions—class and race were temporarily suspended. If you've already lost everything, why not your identity, too? My grandmother was homeless and poor, with a beautiful voice. She started singing in bars with her musician friends. It was the happiest time of her life. But she was also aware of the precariousness of her circumstances. She saw more and more of the still married Hayes Wilsey. Aunt Helen didn't know the specifics of their courtship, only that my grandmother resisted his advances until the quake and fire pushed her over the edge, at which point she gave him stiff terms she never thought he'd meet. She told Hayes she'd marry him if he left his wife, moved to San Francisco, converted to Catholicism, and took in her kid brother. It took some time, but he hired lawyers, studied for communion and confirmation, and did all these things, even helping with my grandmother's support in the meantime. Hayes was smitten, and only when he'd finally attained Ora did he lose interest. For Ora it was a pragmatic union that slowly went sour. She would come to regret her decision. At first they lived together out beyond Pacific Heights, close to the ocean, in the Richmond district. There was some happiness. They had a daughter, Helen, and a son, Jack. Then Ora's brother went off to war in Europe and came back deranged from the gas. After Dad was born, in 1919, Hayes convinced my grandmother to move to Marin. They had a big house and the whole family, parents and children, slept together on a screened porch above the kitchen. Hayes slowly disappeared back to San Francisco. He was having an affair with his secretary at the butter plant. He'd moved the family to Marin so he'd have an excuse not to come home at night. Aunt Helen told me about a small earthquake that woke up the family in the middle of the night: They all gathered together, but Hayes wasn't there.

Ora hated the suburbs, and she began to hate her husband. He'd bribed her into marriage and tricked her into living far away from all the actors and singers who'd been her friends and sustained her spirit in the city. She was miserable. Aunt Helen told me, "I think she must have had a clinical depression. And they didn't know what to do with that in those days. I can remember her just standing there, crying—and nobody could do a thing about it. She was just like a block of cement."

The only thing that seemed to bring her any joy was Dad's company. "She was crazy about Al," Aunt Helen told me. When Dad was old enough to understand why his father was never around, and that it was hurting his mother, he hung a bell over his bed on the porch and ran a cable from the bell to the backdoor. It would ring and wake up the family whenever my grandfather came home. My grandfather, who preferred his older son, resented Dad's accusing bell and started making the two boys box. Uncle Jack beat up Dad and Dad cried and ran to Ora.

Ora was sick now. She never left the house. She had migraines. She stayed in bed. She was harsh to everyone. "We were always sitting on the edge of our seats, wondering what she was going to criticize us for next," Aunt Helen said. When Dad was fourteen Ora was diagnosed with advanced breast cancer, had a mastectomy far too late, and lived another year before the cancer metastasized and killed her. She died at home in bed, on the porch, during the night. In the morning, everyone thought she was asleep and tiptoed around trying not to wake her. She was buried on a hillside, in the rain. Hayes married his secretary within a few weeks. At fifteen Dad decided to become a priest. Then Hayes died of a massive heart attack. The secretary got a lawyer and tried to get half the butter-and-egg company, which Uncle Jack was running. At seventeen Dad abandoned his plans for the priesthood (he'd been touring seminaries) and went to work in order to help his brother pay her off. Instead of wearing black and hearing confessions, he became a butter-and-egg man, driving a truck and wearing a white apron on the factory floor (things he was always a little ashamed of). The priesthood was how he'd imagined getting away from his family. Now social prominence, bettering his place in society, became his ambition—the social prominence to which I owe my existence. The first step was to make money, and Dad found out he was good at that.

HERE'S A FACT that captures something essential about San Francisco: Only a few weeks after the quake and the fires, "social notes" (society gossip) replaced the lists of changed addresses and appeals for information on missing friends and family in the paper. These social notes would continue uninterrupted for the next fifty-five years, when they would be dominated first by Mom, and then, when she'd burned out, by Dad and Dede.

# Fifteen · CORRUPTION

A s a welcome home Mom took me to the opening of the opera, San Francisco society's main event.

Mom's greatest triumph, which helped solidify her San Francisco fame, had happened at the opening of the opera in the sixties. The city opera had decided to replace the ancient gold brocade curtain that had hung there for decades at the end of the previous season. This was big news in San Francisco society. There was much editorial lamenting of the old curtain: The opera would never be the same; the curtain was irreplaceable, the inaugural, postquake, post–Enrico Caruso curtain first raised in the rebuilt opera house in the reborn San Francisco. It was a storied piece of fabric.

This all gave Mom an idea. She got in touch with the opera and obtained a piece of the old curtain, got in touch with a designer from her department store days, had a cape made out of it, lined the cape in blue silk, and arrived at the opening *wearing* the old curtain, complete with dangling gold tassels and a hood! She walked the red carpet for the television cameras and newspaper reporters, flashes going off everywhere to shouts of "Pat! Pat! What are you wearing, Pat?" The old curtain got to stay at the opera after all! It was exuberant. Triumphant. Fun. Brilliant. Irreverent and respectful simultaneously. Inspired. Mom could do no wrong. She sat in the best box. In the orchestra Dede must've looked up and seen her. Off in Marin, living in his little house that would burn down, rejected by the Pacific Union club for having dirt under his nails and a Jewish wife, Dad did see her. According to one of his oldest friends, Dad was watching T.V., Mom came on, and he said, "I want to meet *her*."

It was that history that made Mom want to keep coming back to the opera.

We arrived in a vintage Bentley Mom had rented. I wore a white bow tie and a long, black tailcoat. We were photographed.

We sat in the orchestra. Dad and Dede sat up above us in their box. In the lobby at intermission I saw Dad cutting through the crowd in a hurry. When he was two feet away I smiled, said, "Hey, Dad!" and he brushed by without a flicker of hesitation, giving me a half second of eye contact.

I ran after him, grabbed his shoulder, and said, "*Hey. Dad*. It's *me*."

He nodded absently and looked off over my shoulder.

Then I put my hand on his stomach—we had that easy physical rapport—and said, "*Sean, Dad*."

He said, "Hello, Sean—I know it's you," with a hint of a smile, and then walked off. A few minutes later, when Mom insisted we go to the bar, I saw him sitting at a marble table with a reserved sign, sipping champagne, Dede on his right and Herb Caen on his left. I came up and introduced myself. I was scrutinized by Herb Caen. He was a small man with a soft voice and sharp eyes. He said nothing to me. Soon I ran out of things to say. I walked back over to the bar and rejoined Mom, who was doing a complicated facial-expression juggling act—glaring at them and smiling an electric smile at everyone else. She held a flute of champagne.

She said, "Sean, we should pour champagne all over Dede and your father, to wipe those looks off their faces. They wouldn't look so smug drenched in champagne." Shifting a bit from foot to foot. "I might just do it. What do you think of that, Sean?"

I said, "I don't think you should do that, Mom."

After intermission, back sitting with her in the orchestra, Dad up in his box, I felt myself—my identity—disappear, and then reappear as shit: a huge pimply ass shat out my legs, and another my torso; a pair of dogs came by, squatted, and shat my feet and shoes, more asses, more parts of me—my tuxedo, bow tie. People sang opera. A woman pulled up her dress and shat my head, my brown eyes, my brain. Some birds flew down from the gilt ceiling and did my hair and the details of my features. Then I was complete. Shitboy at the opera.

THE DAY AFTER the opera our photos appeared in the paper. Mom looked at the society page, held us close to her face, and said she wanted me to see a dermatologist—my acne was too noticeable. The dermatologist prescribed Accutane, which shut down my oil glands. He then asked me in passing if I'd been having any other skin problems. I told him about my jock itch. He looked at my crotch and said, "This isn't jock itch. You have crab lice. My God, I've never seen such an infestation."

Then Mom wanted me to see Dr. Sheila Krystal, her psychologist. I took BART under the bay to Sheila's Berkeley home. Sheila performed Reiki work, which was indistinguishable from massage, but involved "channeling healing energy" from practitioner to recipient. I thought we might get it on. I tried my best to look down her shirt. Then I got on my skateboard and bombed the hills from her house back down to BART.

Full of healing energy, free from Cascade and from itching, I started sneaking out at night to meet Blane. Mom had taken the precaution of setting the burglar alarm to keep me in, rather than keep her burglars and assassins out. I could not crack the code, so I had to figure out how to circumvent it.

My room and Mom's room were located on the far end of a hallway that ran perpendicular to the top of the stairs on the second floor. It was an open hallway until Mom received her death threats and blocked it off with a dead-bolted, solid-core security door, behind which we were both now barricaded each night. To escape I had to unlock and open the solid-core door, leap over the alarm's undercarpet pressure sensors, which began at the jamb, and land on a narrow concrete strip that ran down the edge of the curving staircase, anchoring the banister—the only inch of space where they couldn't imbed any sensors. Then I leaned back, closed the door, and slid down the banister, landing on marble, sliding on socks. (I carried my shoes.) At the end of the slide I took a single hop and smiled at the mirror. *Yeah.* Then I crept through the marble palace to a mirrored swinging door into a room Mom called the "butler's pantry" where a nearly vacant cabinet contained hooks for twenty keys, and labels listing all Dad's long absent vehicles: Jeep; Rover; Speedboat; Firetruck; Motorcycle. I grabbed the lonely spare set for Mom's Oldsmobile. The onomatopoeic Oldsmobile. Her over-the-hill Oldsmobile that I was about to fly over hills.

To get out the alarmed back entrance I unscrewed the wireless alarm box on the door, removed the small cylindrical magnet, and placed it *on top* of the wired companion box on the door frame (it nestled there neatly and almost invisibly: *click*). Now the door could be opened without bells ringing and the police being called.

Outside the backdoor I put on my shoes and ran down the fire escape, which smelled of urine—because I was always pissing down it, to watch the streams slowly disintegrate into rain as they fell past the twentieth floor. I ran at top speed—a plunge that put me into a trance as I went farther and farther, the same motions repeated again and again, running, leaping, cornering, leaping, running, hand brushing railings covered in my dried urine. Down ten floors this way, then I grabbed the elevator at twenty-three so that the doorman watching the monitors from the lobby wouldn't see one coming up to the penthouse. I went to P4, the fourth floor of the parking garage. I backed out of Mom's space, drove down four stories of ramp, tripped the opener for a big, solid-metal roll gate, grabbed one of Mom's many blonde wigs from the passenger seat, kept there in case of a glamour emergency, put it on, and gunned it past the doorman, looking the other way. It was my favorite moment of all. The wig! The escape! The city!

As I rolled the Olds on to Russian Hill I cranked The Cure, the music like a wave breaking and rolling me inside itself. Taking Jones down toward the bay and Blane's house was like getting in a barrel and plunging over Niagara Falls. The hills were like waterfalls for cars. I'd been skateboarding down S.F.'s hills every summer and vacation, and my grandmother had dragged her trunk over them eighty-one years before.

Many of the steepest hills in San Francisco lead up to and around Russian Hill, which isn't a hill, but a series of hills.

From North Beach, at the bottom, you can see Russian Hill's hills rolling, planed into paved geometry, but rolling underneath. The steepest of these crests is in the middle of Filbert Street between Hyde and Leavenworth. The pavement midblock seems to disappear into a sudden sheer drop, like an incomplete section of elevated freeway. It looks as if the street is dangling nine hundred feet in the air. When you drive a car up to the lip it drops too steeply to even see over your hood. The drop is demarcated by two yellow-and-black signs that say "STEEP GRADE AHEAD BUSES AND LARGE TRUCKS NOT ADVISABLE" and "SHARP CREST 10 MILES PER HOUR."

Less than a week after returning from Cascade, I met Blane on the corner of Filbert and Hyde. He got in and we eased up to the lip of the hill, everything still, the streets just a little slick with night fog. He got out, checked to make sure the slope was clear, then got back in, and we reversed to the beginning of the block and buckled our seat belts.

"We're like six seconds from the lip," Blane said. We checked our watches, put a new cassette into the tape deck, played, "What You Need" by INXS, and checked how many seconds elapsed till it "kicked in." Then we subtracted six seconds from the kick-in point to get our ignition moment. We rewound to the beginning, sat still for the opening few seconds, and then Blane declared that a particular upcoming guitar twang meant preignition—"That one!"—then, "It's the next guitar—coming up," and then, "Now! Now!" And I floored the Olds, getting it up to forty as the song exploded with drums and guitar and shouting and we launched off the hill's lip and hung in the misty air, nothing but sky, second-story windows, street lights and darkness around us, the music filling the interior of the car as if we'd plunged into an ocean of it, at which point we finally screamed, and immediately slammed hard onto the hill, huge, gas-guzzling engine hauling the front down with such force you could hear the slam echo off Telegraph Hill a mile across North Beach, suspension scraping the whole way down to Leavenworth while I stood on the brake.

After we got this right—it took several tries—we drove over to the crooked block of Lombard and saw how fast we could slalom its eight tight curves. We played "Bitchin' Camaro" by The Dead Milkmen. Then I put on Mom's wig and headbanged on the steering wheel to a stretched Def Leppard tape of Blane's. As a finale, we drove up—*up!*—the crooked one-way block of Lombard, the music as loud as it would go, choking on our adrenaline.

At the end of the night, dawn coming, a few delivery trucks on the streets, I dropped Blane off, put on Mom's wig, waved to the doorman, and went to bed.

The next day José, the daytime doorman, said to Mom, "You were out *late* last night, Ms. Montandon."

Mom said, "Yes, that's right—on a big date, *José*." Then to me, "What's he *talking* about?"

"Dunno."

When Mom's housekeeper drove the Olds to Safeway that week it died on her. I'd killed it. I would have to turn my attention to the Mercedes.

WHILE THEIR MOTHER was dying Dad and Uncle Jack found a blank key to the family Studebaker, and Dad filed it down so it fit the ignition. Aunt Helen told me, "When everybody was in bed, those two would take the car out. My father was sure it was a lemon. But it was because those kids beat the heck out of that car."

Dad's half-sister Meryle, the aunt he never told me about, snuck out of her bedroom window to a bar down the hill where she played jazz piano. Sometimes she disappeared for days. "She was a little like you," Aunt Helen said. "She would get upset about things and take off."

THE PRIVATE high schools of San Francisco were impossible to get into. But the Urban School of San Francisco prided itself on being exceptional—by being unconventional. "Narrative evaluations" were given in lieu of letter grades. Students called the multiracial faculty by their first names. There was no dress code. Students were openly gay. It was right in the Haight, which still felt dangerous and countercultural—or at least dirty and hostile. Urban had a reputation for getting kids into good colleges. I thought I had a chance of being accepted. I managed to get an interview with the head of admissions. Sitting in her office, making excellent eye contact, I told her I'd been hazed and misunderstood in my three previous schools, that I knew my transcript didn't look good, but I was ready to change, I was ready to learn, my father didn't understand me, that all I wanted was to be in San Francisco, my hometown, where I knew I'd "live up to my academic potential," succeed, if I was given the chance to express myself. I meant all this. They accepted me.

Almost immediately I started to fail.

I did my homework in bed or on the bus in the morning. I made friends with the smoking, disaffected segment of the school. I was arrested for graffitiing hammers and sickles on Haight Street, and released when my accomplice took the rap. I got a ticket for drinking a beer on the sidewalk after class, and Mom had to pay it. Soon I was receiving comments like:

I would like an active student, not a ghost.

Sean basically did no work in this class, and, at the start, was rather aggressively disruptive. . . . Sean needs to bring his attitude and behavior under control; he has to abandon his superficial, glib persona and resolve to be honest with himself and the people in his life. It is time for him to take responsibility for his actions.

Sean . . . was the source of agony to me and the rest of the class. . . . I hope he will stop digging his own grave and learn to give what he can without fighting.

Sean failed this course. . . . I do not think he understands what it means to be a student—he is incapable of serious work. He is unprepared to continue and succeed in any educational environment. He needs to become a responsible <u>person</u>.

Following my first evaluation, which coincided with the public drinking, I was grounded indefinitely.

Walking around the Haight during lunch at Urban I found an Anglican priest's shirt on the rack at a thrift store. It was plain black with a smooth front and buttons at the back. It had a detachable white collar. I knew Dad had wanted to be a priest, so I bought it. I wore it to class: priest's shirt, black pants, black Converse All Stars.

When I walked out of school that day I saw Dad. He was sitting behind the wheel of his new, baby blue Cadillac Eldorado. He frowned when he recognized me. We hadn't been alone together in more than a year—since the drive through Wyoming to NOLS.

He rolled down the window and said, "I'm giving you a ride home, kid."

I got in and we hugged across the huge front seat. He said, "You're wearing all black."

I said, "Priests wear all black."

He said, "You look terrible," and started driving.

Several blocks of silence. He drove through the Presidio. When we came out on Lombard he said, "Your mom tells me you got a ticket for drinking in public."

"Yeah."

"You know your uncle Jack had a drinking problem. That's what killed him. You may have one, too."

"I don't have a drinking problem."

Dad shook his head. He seemed to have decided on the spot that I was the second coming of Uncle Jack, who died in the sixties, a few years before I was born. When I was a kid Dad told me stories about Uncle Jack. These stories were meant to be cautionary, but Dad only managed to make my lost uncle glamorous. He first told me about him when I was three. We were looking at Dad's closet of guns and cuff links when he said, "My brother, your uncle Jack, had a lot of guns, and he got into a lot of trouble with them."

We were at a traffic light on Van Ness. He said, "Lean over here. Let me smell you." I leaned over. He said, "Cigarettes. Terrible."

I said, "You used to smoke. For like forty years."

He ignored this and said, "You want ice cream?"

"Yeah, sure."

"*Yes.*"

"Yes."

He turned up Union and pulled into the bus zone on the corner of Hyde, in front of Swensen's. We both got thin mint.

"Get some napkins," he said. I got them. We got back in the car.

Silence.

"Good ice cream," he said eventually.

"*Really* good," I agreed. "Though I don't know why they call it thin mint. It should be mint chip."

"Nothing thin about it," said Dad.

I laughed.

"So your mom's got a new car," he said.

"She's had it for a while," I said

"Do you know what she paid?"

"No."

"A lot, I bet."

"Yeah," I said.

"Why did your mother waste all that money on that car?"

"Don't know."

Silence.

"You should go back to Cascade."

"I'll never go back there."

"That place would've straightened you out."

"That place was *evil,* Dad," I said. "You wouldn't believe the things they did to us there."

"You think things are going to work out for you at the druggie school?"

"The druggie school" was his name for Urban.

"Urban's a good school."

"It's a druggie school," Dad said. "That's why they took you."

There was a slight, barely detectable tinge of amusement in his voice. Maybe Dad knew this was ridiculous. Then I wondered if I was ridiculous. It was much more likely that he was laughing at me.

"You're never going to cure yourself of booze and cigarettes at the druggie school," he said.

I said, in my peace-speech voice, "*Dad—Urban* is a *great* school. Competitive with any school in the Bay Area. College placement is as good as University and better than St. Ignatius, seriously."

His ice cream was done so he started the car. We drove back to the penthouse in silence.

"*Hello*, Mr. Wilsey!" said José, when he saw my dad.

Dad said hello.

He turned back to me and said, "You should go back to Cascade."

"That's like saying, 'You should go back to *Hell*,'" I said.

Dad looked closely at my shirt. "What's that shirt?" I had the collar in my bag.

"This is a Catholic priest's shirt," I mumbled.

"You're not a priest." He looked closer, touching the fabric. "It's an *Anglican* priest's shirt," he said. "And I don't know why you're wearing it."

I said, "I know it's Anglican, but I'm a Catholic. Like you. So it's Catholic."

"You're not a priest," Dad repeated. "You shouldn't be wearing that."

Silence.

"The white part of the collar only shows in the very front on a Catholic priest's shirt," he clarified, a shadow of the amused look on his face again, but quickly replaced with an irritated look. "Some priest probably needs that shirt."

I laughed.

"You're just a troublemaker," Dad said.

"I'm not a troublemaker," I said. "I'm a . . . provocation." *Shit*, I thought. I knew there was a word for what I was trying to be, but it would never come to me.

"I'd really like to see more of you, Dad," I said.

"You just want a ride home."

THAT NIGHT I managed to get hold of a spare set of Mercedes keys, which had been closely guarded. I did the usual escape and met Blane at 2:00 A.M. on the corner of Lombard and Larkin. The Mercedes was too nice to fly off hills. We decided to drive out into the country and see how fast it could go.

On Highway 101, the first long straightaway in Marin, we hit 109 mph, pedal to the floor, and the car started vibrating as if it had the skateboard speed wobbles.

"So that's it?" Blane said.

"Yeah. Disappointing," I said.

Then we decided to test its cornering. We pressed on for Napa. Halfway, at the Stornetta Dairy, I took a curve marked "45" at 70, went onto the gravel shoulder, spun a perfect 180, gravel flying, and kept going, *backward*. We screamed, *"Fuuu-uuuck!"* till the car came to a stop in the center of the road. It was 3:00 A.M. We headed back to the city. The Mercedes smelled like gas, and from then on it always did. Mom was never able to figure out why, or get it repaired.

A few days later, when I tried to steal the Mercedes again, I set off the burglar alarm as I was going out the back door. It was the middle of the night, and I was dressed completely in black. When the bells started ringing I ran into the kitchen and grabbed a jar of peanut butter. I ran into Mom as I came back up the stairs.

I said, "Hey, Mom, I was just getting a snack."

Bells continued to sound around us.

She said, "You've set off the alarm trying to sneak out of the house."

I said, "What?! I'm just getting a *snack*."

She said, "Why are you dressed completely in black?"

Then I must have said something snide, because she went to slap me, hard. It was something she had never done before. I caught her wrist. We stared at each other. Then I went to my room.

ONE WEEKEND Uncle Jack paid an unexpected call on a married friend who had a farm in Marin. Jack wanted to show off his brand-new '55 Cadillac convertible, white with white interior. He pulled up with the top down, shouted hello, and asked his friend's two sons, twelve and thirteen (the younger of whom told me this story), "Who wants to hunt some rabbit?" It was fall and the fields were mowed but not turned, full of stubble that was full of resinous black pitch. The boys jumped in. They expected Jack to drive farther out into the country and take them hunting on foot. Instead, he handed the boys two rifles and told them they'd be hunting from the car. They tore off into the fields. Jackrabbits flushed. Jack steered with his knees and produced two pistols, which he shot out either side of the front seat. The boys bounced around so much they could hardly aim. Jack floored it. Black sap slowly crept over the car's hood, up its sides, inside, and along the leather upholstery, until Jack, the boys, and the white Caddy were completely black. When they got back to the house the only white left was the spot where Jack had been sitting. They were all laughing. They hadn't shot a single rabbit.

The next morning Jack drove the car back to the dealer and said, "I don't want this anymore. You take it back." He bought an identical new one, and drove it away.

.  .  .

BLANE AND SPENCER both came over one Friday night when Mom was out. None of us could think of anything to do. No movies. No money. No other friends. Since we had the house to ourselves we played with my small arsenal: a crossbow that fired graphite-tipped arrows capable of piercing the phone book up to the mid Ps (the phone book was full of deep, perfectly symmetrical, inexplicable-looking punctures that Mom never noticed, because whenever she needed a number she dialed 411); a weighted throwing knife Dad had given me; and a small, mean, eye-extinguishing, pistol grip slingshot (formerly Uncle Jack's) that fired handfuls of BBs with the velocity of an air gun and the spread of a shotgun. The arsenal was severely crippled without Uncle Jack's .38.

Blane loaded the crossbow and shot all of San Francisco's businesses and citizens. Spencer looked nervous fooling with the knife. Blane said, "Christian's got so weird. He's got long hair past his shoulders and he always wears a black cowboy hat with bones and teeth around it."

Christian and Trevor Ristow were brothers we'd been in grade school with, who used to be like us but had now become cool. Christian went to University High and Trevor went to Urban.

"He's like a death rocker?" I asked.

"He's like Crocodile Dundee or something. And he carries this *hatchet* on his belt all the time. So last Saturday this kid ———" Blane looked at me when he said the name, which I've now forgotten, and I shook my head. "Sean, you know who he is." He was one of the kids who took acid in seventh grade and got kicked out of private school.

"Oh, *yeah*," I said.

"Anyway, he threw this party last week while his parents were out of town. He lives in this big mansion in Pacific Heights. Christian came dressed all Crocodile Dundee, with the hatchet, and ——— called him a freak, and Christian just said 'Fuck you!' so ——— kicked him out of the party. Christian went outside and found this big, like, fifteen-foot really nice landscaping tree in ———'s yard, and *chopped it down with his hatchet,* and the guy ran out and tried to stop him, and Christian threatened him with the hatchet and finished chopping the tree down. ——— called the cops and the cops came and Christian didn't even run, and when ———'s parents got home he was in huge trouble because he couldn't pretend he hadn't had a party, because Christian basically, like, tricked him into calling the cops on his own party."

This sounded like something I would've done—except it was really brave, and Christian also had straight As at University High School and early admission to Columbia University. His younger brother, Trevor, was the smartest and most popular kid at Urban.

How was I ever going to become that cool? And *courageous?* And very quickly. I fiddled with the slingshot.

"But Sean," Blane said. "The craziest thing is their dad just got them their *own apartment.* They're living on their own in Pacific Heights. They have a maid who comes in and makes the beds and cleans and everything. And their dad pays the rent."

I spun, screamed, *"Fuuuuck!"* and hurled the pistol-grip slingshot out the window. It cut a black half arc across my room, glinting in the track light, and then disappeared into the night. A beat of silence. Then we all said, "Oh, *fuck!"* ran out on the deck and looked down. Nothing.

UNCLE JACK became an increasingly dangerous alcohol and firearms enthusiast. He carried a handgun everywhere he went. He liked to sneak into employees' offices at the butter plant and startle them by firing it into the ceiling. He was always pulling out his gun on the street. He shot out the traffic signal on his block, because the light kept him awake. Dad often had to come down to the local bar and take Jack's guns off him.

MOM DECIDED that even if she had to set the burglar alarm to keep me in, I would be O.K. left alone and unsupervised while she went on a two-week trip. I wasn't very interested at the time, but recently I asked her where she'd gone. She told me Moscow, to join, according to a telegram from the Soviet government, the "intelligentsia of the world for a Forum on Human Survival." Mom attended many forums, symposia, eminent gatherings of the crumbling left in this period. In the documents she sent me about this one, her bio is next to Norman Mailer's on the impressive list of attendees.

An Aeroflot Ilyushin 86 flew to New York to pick up Mom and the other American participants. Mom was an Aeroflot expert and knew well the enemy of luxury that was the Il-86. After boarding she walked to the back of the plane, where the seats folded forward and you could put up your feet. The ones at the front were fixed. A crowd of intelligentsia headed forward, where they were accustomed to finding first class. *Ha, ha—no,* Mom thought, settling in. Soon, spotting her comfort, Yoko Ono, Gregory Peck, and Jann Wenner, the editor of

*Rolling Stone* joined her. For the next twelve hours Mom held court, tutoring them on Russia, regaling them with tales of her celebrity behind the Iron Curtain.

COMPLETELY UNSUPERVISED, I methodically searched the house for Uncle Jack's confiscated .38 revolver. I failed to find it. But in the small safe in Mom's bedroom I found a dozen Polaroids of her naked, striking poses. Most of them were straightforward and almost medical, but a few showed her with her hand behind her head or a hip stuck out, pinup style. They were sweet and innocent and embarrassing. They were recent, I could tell, because I recognized the room she was posing in from a weekend house she'd rented a year or two before. I took them all.

I did it because I thought I might have to one day blackmail her. Brandishing the pictures, I might say, "If you kill yourself I'll send these pictures to *Hustler!*" and that might make her decide to stop. I wanted to have some serious leverage. And, actually, rather than *Hustler*, my plan was to threaten to sell them to one of San Francisco's many hometown pornographic newspapers—vending hardcore porn from coin-operated street-corner machines. She was a celebrity in San Francisco, and I figured someplace sleazy would do it.

I was unaware of the symmetry of this plan. At sixteen Mom had run away to Dallas to "show her body," using the proceeds of vending machines to get there. I would blackmail her if I had to, and if she didn't give in her body would end up being shown in a vending machine.

When I couldn't find the .38 I took Mom's video camera and started work on a short film called *The Spanish Inquisition of '87* (*TSI-'87*). I'd been planning it for a long time, but required Mom's absence, and funds to purchase a prop for the undertaking. Blane discovered a store called the Light Opera in Ghirardelli Square that sold various Russian art objects and antiquities, among them lacquer boxes. *Lacquer boxes!*—Blane thought—*Sean has lacquer boxes.* (Mom always returned from Moscow loaded with them.) I rummaged through her walk-in storage closet, found five or six, went down to Ghirardelli Square, talked with a thin man in a white shirt and gold-rimmed spectacles who knew they were stolen, and offered me two hundred dollars, no questions asked. Done. This was a fortune.

The prop, which cost thirty dollars, was an eighteen-inch "double dong" dildo. It was a thick foot-and-a-half of pliable, firm yet bendable flesh-toned plastic with a molded penis head at either end. I bought it at a porn shop on Broadway off Columbus, a couple of doors away from the famous Condor, where a bunch of strippers had come to meet Mom's plane when she and Mel

Belli (who represented Carol Doda, the grande dame of S.F. strippers) had come back from Japan a married couple in 1966. Blane and I went there directly from the Light Opera.

*TSI- '87* opened with a steady shot of the facade of the main Catholic church of downtown San Francisco, as seen from across Washington Square Park. The soundtrack was Gregorian chant. Then it cut to Blane walking into the church. He sat down and listened to the sermon. The camera moved between him and the priest. The priest said, "The Lord is our shepherd." A laugh track cut in. Blane pointed at the priest and slapped his knee. Then he picked a hot dog up off the pew and ate it with gusto. The scene ended when an Italian grandmother, all in black, her voice quavery with fury, grabbed Blane and hissed "Did the *priest . . . tell you . . . to do that!?*"

With the prop we filmed the next scene:

Back from church, Blane cooked two packs of hot dogs on a huge flat grill we had in the center of the stove at the penthouse. The song "Tequila" played in the background. There was a lot of smoke and sputtering noise. Blane wore a dirty baseball cap and an untucked oxford. A cigarette dangled off his lower lip. He drank a beer and pressed the dogs with a spatula so they hissed. He nodded to the music.

The camera pulled back and a girl called Ariana—a pack-a-day smoker from Urban who Mom disapproved of—entered the frame, looked at the grill, and said, "Hey, what's cookin'?"

Blane raised his eyebrows, smirked knowingly, puffed on the cigarette. Ariana (who'd laughed at enough of my jokes in first-period history class for me to convince her that she should "be in my movie") made a painstakingly choreographed expression I'd instructed her to make because I thought it was sexy (she thought it was ridiculous). She tipped her head back, closed her eyelids, rolled her eyes back behind them, and ran her tongue slowly around the outside of her mouth. Then she opened her eyes, nodded her head back down, inclined her chin at the grill, full of hot dogs, smiled, and bit her lower lip. The camera tracked over to the grill. The dogs sizzled. I cut. Everybody held their place. The dildo went on the grill. The camera started again. The dildo, spanning the whole grill, seemed to appear out of nowhere. (*From the female subconscious.*) Blane raised his eyebrows.

UNCLE JACK and Dad threw a party together. Before the guests came Dad changed his whole appearance, everything about his body, his carriage, his face, his voice—so nobody would recognize him. He lay low for several weeks, allowed his beard to grow out, dyed it gray, didn't shower. Before the party Uncle Jack said Dad was sick.

When the guests arrived Jack opened the door and whispered, *"I've got this old man staying with me. He can be strange, but he doesn't mean anything by it. Please be kind to him. He was a friend of our dad's from way back, and now Al and I are all he's got in the world. We have to look after him."*

"Of course," they all said.

Jack put something on the hi-fi, started mixing cocktails. Dad shuffled around bringing people their martinis, his dirty-nailed fingers sticking conspicuously down into them. Everybody had a drink. Dad lit a cigar and stared fixedly at a young woman's breasts. When he'd smoked the cigar down a good inch Dad reached over and tapped its ash into the woman's cleavage.

"What are you *doing?*" she said.

Then Dad reached down her shirt in an attempt to retrieve the ash. The woman screamed, dropped her glass, which shattered, and her husband cursed at the old man, who ran from the room with surprising speed.

"Where's he gone? Where is that goddamn dirty old man?"

"Now just settle down," Jack said. "He didn't mean anything."

Dad reappeared with a broom, which he started flailing around, knocking another drink off the coffee table, ice and glass skittering all over the place. Everyone jumped back. Confusion. The guests looked at Jack. Jack smiled indulgently. Dad took advantage of their distraction to get a good back swing and spank the cleavage woman with the broom. Her husband lunged at Dad, who loped down the hall into the bathroom. The man locked him in, then stormed back to the living room. "I locked the fucking old man in the can." Everyone started laughing. Dad was standing behind him, now half out of costume. The man, who was a business partner, never spoke to Dad again.

AT THE FORUM Mom was seated next to William Styron. She talked about *children* and *innocence* and *annihilation*.

In the crowd of cosmonauts, ranking party officials, ballerinas, official artists, Mom got jostled and spilled red wine all over herself and Valentina Tereshkova, the first woman in space. Mikhail Gorbachev turned to her and said, "You know Patricia—better red than dead!"

Mom gave a speech about the children's clarity of vision, and how they would lead the world to peace (with her help). Afterward, Graham Greene lurched up, drunk, and told her, "Your sentiments have nothing to do with reality. All children are violent. They're mean and savage. There's nothing peaceful about children."

"That may be true," Mom said, in maximum Nobel nominee mode, "but like most of us they have both *qualities*. They have to struggle to decide which part to honor. As adults, we can endorse the good or focus on the negative, Mr. Greene."

I WANTED TO have a party, but I was afraid people would break things and judge me.

I decided to invite Christian and Trevor Ristow over for a screening of *TSI-'87*. They were curious about the famous penthouse, featured in so many magazine spreads and newspaper articles, so they came. I showed them the burglar alarm and my circumvention strategies. I gave them beers. I showed them how to piss down the fire escape. I brought them out on the deck. They marveled at the view.

"Come up to the edge and look down," I said. This was one of my few fearless areas. I would even stand on the railing. They were impressed.

Trevor, the enthusiast of the pair, grinned and said, "Dude, this is fucking awesome."

I noticed a cab was coming up Jones toward our building. I ducked back into the kitchen and grabbed an orange, and when it crossed Vallejo, still a block away, I threw it, with just a murmur of outward thrust.

The orange—bright orange—and the cab—a blue Luxor—drew two lines together into a right angle. We watched breathlessly till it hit. An explosive impact, dead center on the roof. Mist and peel fanned off. The cab did a fishtail stop and remained motionless for a second count. Then the driver burst out, whirled around, looked up. We ducked back, elated. Mom kept a lot of fruit in the house, as decoration. Trevor and Christian spent the next ten minutes throwing Mom's oranges, lemons, limes, and finally, desperately, *grapefruits,* and hitting parked cars, the parking levels that flared out at the bottom of the building, the roofs of buildings across the street, but never the intended targets. I watched. All that remained were leather-skinned pomegranates, which Mom always liked for their exotic appearance.

Jones Street was all exploded fruit and dented cars. We might as well have been firing weapons into the street. José the doorman, who liked me and usually claimed ignorance of who might be responsible whenever something like this happened, was going to have a hard time. The sound of a car alarm drifted up to us. It was a beautiful day. The air smelled like clean hair. Christian and Trevor begged me to do one more. It would be a tough throw. Pomegranates are hard-skinned and aspherical, tapering at one end into a little aerodynamism-affecting crown. I waited for the right kind of car. Even Christian, usually unflappable, was animated with anticipation. After a couple of minutes a blue Ford from the sixties, beat up and rusty, with a flat bed where the backseat and trunk should have been, was clearly heading into the target area.

"Oh, *perfect*," Trevor said.

I released the pomegranate, with slightly less confidence than before. The pomegranate and the Ford headed for each other. All eyes flicked between the fast-racing fruit and the slow-cruising Ford, and then the pomegranate hit the right front fender, just above the headlight. Not a bull's-eye, but still a hit. We all yelled, and the car did a repeat of before. But this time the guy leaped out and immediately looked straight up. We saw him shake his fist before we ducked out of sight.

I don't know what kind of damage a pomegranate thrown from that height will do to a car, but it could probably kill a person.

I asked Christian and Trevor if they wanted to see some of my movies. They said sure. I showed them the following:

*How to Identify Cute Fuzzy Animals Outside the Bathroom Without Mastur-bating.* This was a short film in which I'd superimposed cartoon animals over spliced footage of hard-core porn and Soviet military parades. The soundtrack came from a children's record, over which I shouted animal names in a demented voice: "The duck! The duck!"

*The Search for the Perfect Girl:* This longer project starred Blane and Spencer and me as porn stars on a quest for something more meaningful than constant sex. For most of its twenty-five minutes we got in strangers' faces and asked them what constituted the "perfect girl." In one scene a fat man sitting on the back of a truck said, "I don't know, but she'll probably have a bow in her hair."

*Mr. Perfection.* The title character, played by Spencer, strolled around in a suit and a little porkpie hat, scolding jaywalkers, picking up trash, and placing it in "the proper receptacle." He read the obituaries and crossed the names out in the phone book.

*Rita's Phone Sex:* Spencer, playing a businessman, seated at a desk and wearing a suit, pulled a porno mag out of his In box, looked at the back cover, and said, "Rita's Phone Sex! Gorgeous live girls! Better give it a call!"

Cut to a darkened room where I was seated in an armchair, feet on a table, smoking a cigarette, wearing an angora sweater and lipstick. The phone next to me rang. I picked it up and said, in a deep voice, "Rita's Phone Sex, Rita speakin'."

Spencer said, "Oh, *yeah*, Rita *baby*, what're you *wearin'?*"

I said, "I can't tell you what I'm wearing till you give me your credit card number. You got a credit card?"

"Yeah! Yeah! It's—" He read off some numbers excitedly.

I slid two balloons under my sweater, picked up one of Mom's blonde wigs, put it on, looked at the camera, batted my eyelashes, and said, in a high voice, "I'm wearing nothing but panties and looking for a long lean bone job from someone just like you, baby."

Etc.

Christian and Trevor were impressed. We decided to collaborate on making a movie. Since I couldn't show them the .38 to seal my cool before they left, I showed them the naked photographs of Mom. I made jokes.

"Dude," I said to Christian, "in this one she's about to do a karate kick and smegma's going to go flying everywhere."

UNCLE JACK had a cocktail party that ran later than he wanted. Guests were sitting around the fire, having a great time, ice tinkling, logs crackling. Then Jack said, "Everybody go home." They said, "Forget it, Jack—we're all having a good time. Nobody's going anywhere. Go to bed if you want." Jack took his drink and disappeared. A few minutes later he came back carrying a 1920s tommy gun, with a round ammo clip and a wood pistol grip, fully loaded. The guests laughed. Uncle Jack fired the entire magazine into the fireplace. Sparks, smoke, ricochets, drinks falling to the floor, stone chips from the big mantel sailing all over the living room, guests dropping to the floor and fleeing through the smoke. Jack went to bed.

MOM RETURNED from the Forum where she had hung out with Peter Ustinov, Paul Newman, Milos Forman, Klaus Maria Brandauer, and Kenzaburo Oe. (All the men but Graham Greene had loved her.) A cover story in the Sunday *Chronicle/Examiner Magazine* was titled, "Peacenik Pat." Subhead: "In San Francisco, Pat Montandon can't get any respect. In the USSR, she's the Soviets' favorite socialite celebrity."

Looking around the kitchen Mom said, "Sean, I'm so pleased to see that you're eating all this fruit."

Then she discovered that her liquor bottles were empty and her lacquer boxes gone. José the doorman told her about the fruit. Mom stormed into my room and slapped me in the face, successfully this time.

The next morning she knocked on my door and said, "Your dad's going to come give you a ride to school."

I ate breakfast and started on my first-period homework. There would be time for second-period homework during the five-minute break between periods. At 8:00 Mom said, "Time to go. Your dad's waiting." I went downstairs.

Dad was waiting. I got in his Cadillac, then Mom got in beside me. I didn't know where she'd come from. I was wedged between Mom and Dad.

The three of us hadn't been together in a car since I was nine. It reminded me of driving up to Napa. I thought, *They're getting back together.*

Mom said, "You've betrayed our love and trust. You've stolen from me. And I know you were rummaging around trying to find that gun you took from your father."

"That was your Uncle Jack's gun," Dad said.

Mom continued, "I'm convinced Cascade is the only place that can help you."

I wondered where Dede was. She should've been there to complete the trio. I also wondered how they were planning to get there. I figured we were driving. I could jump out at the first gas stop. Dad's Caddy could never make it to Cascade without filling up. But first I thought it would be good to spend a few hours in the car with them, to see what it was like.

"Your father is going to drive you to the airport," Mom said.

"We're flying up in the jet," Dad said. "The pilots are waiting. The school is expecting you." He gave Mom a look that meant he wanted her out of his car.

Mom said, *"Goodbye, Sean,"* held me tight, kissed me, and got out. I watched her go back into the building. I could have jumped out right then. But I decided not to.

Dad started downtown toward the freeway on-ramp. I had a few almost opportunities to hop out at stop signs, but he went through them faster than usual. *Just be patient,* I thought. I did not want to miss what he had to say.

He said, "I finally got your mother to agree to send you back to Cascade. It wasn't easy. She sees that I'm right now."

"How'd you manage that?" I asked.

"You were lousing up even at that druggie school. Your grades were terrible.

Your mom can't handle you"—slight smirk here—"and she and the airy fairy are out of ideas."

I laughed. "Yeah, I've been kind of beyond their abilities."

Then Dad remembered I wasn't his friend but his failure—the only failure he couldn't divorce or get away from.

"Your grades have been awful," Dad said.

"My grades aren't bad."

"Your grades stink."

"They don't give grades."

"They send reports to me."

I had no idea that Dad received reports. "*What* reports? My reports have been *good.*"

"I *pay* for that place, so they send me reports, and they have been *god-awful.*"

"I thought Mom paid," I said.

"Your mother doesn't have any money that isn't my money." I was in awe of this statement, its obvious truth to Dad, the rage it would've provoked in Mom.

"Dan, my U.S. history teacher, says I have a strong grip on U.S. history." (Dan had actually said I was "beginning to relinquish the strong grip on U.S. history" he knew I had.)

"'*Dan?*'" Dad said. "You call these people by their first names?" He'd called the Jesuit priests in high school "Father."

"They're good teachers," I said, though they hated me for being a rich, white, punk fuckup.

"They don't think you're such a good *student,*" Dad said.

"Oh, *Cascade*'s got a really stellar academic program, Dad," I said, with an angrier edge than I ever showed him. "Do you mean the fat man who told me, 'Make it here or you're gonna get a dick shoved up your ass!'? That was really educational. And you're sending me back there? I was, like, better educated than the *faculty* there!"

Dad said, "They'll shape you up. That's what you need."

I said, *"Ha!"*

"Cascade's the best chance you've got, kid," he said.

"'*Kid*'?! *You're the kid!*" I shouted. We were at a red light. I hit the button, popped my seat belt.

Dad said, "What are you doing?"

I opened the door. Dad grabbed my arm. I pulled, got one foot on the sidewalk, felt him losing his grip, he felt it, too, I looked him straight in the eye, he

said, "Sean, come back, come back to me!" and I said, *"Fuck you,* Dad!" as I
yanked my arm away from him, savagely, with contempt that he thought he could
keep me and make me do anything he wanted. He looked like a weak old man.

He said, "Sean, come back to me!" plaintively this time, but I was already
gone, and there was no him to come back to anyway.

A last moment of blistering eye contact, water in my eyes, not really sure what
emotion was producing this water, hanging there in midstride on the sidewalk,
the Cadillac door open, car creeping forward into the intersection. Dad's foot
was coming off the brake as he leaned over the empty passenger seat. Then I ran.

I CALLED URBAN and told them I was sick. Then I headed back to Mom's,
approaching the building with caution and suspicion, finally deciding it was safe,
taking the elevator up from the plaza, heart pounding. Mom said, "Pack your
bags. You can't stay here. Either go back to Cascade or you're out on your own.
Your father's waiting for your call."

I said, "All right, I'm leaving, but you've gotta give me some seed money."

She said, "I will give you three hundred dollars."

I said something wheedling, hoping to get more. She said, "Nothing more.
Pack your bags. And pack carefully. You're not coming back for anything else.
You'll take what you can carry now."

"What about my stuff? My stereo. I'll need that."

"Too bad," said Mom. "Your stuff's *mine* now."

I packed Converse All Stars, boxer shorts, mismatched socks, priest's shirt,
video camera into a big, old, black-and-gray leather suitcase of Dad's. I started
thinking of all the things I could buy with three hundred dollars.

I threw the suitcase into the trunk of Mom's gas-smelling Mercedes convertible
and we drove to the bank on Columbus, just a couple of blocks off Washington
Square Park, to extract my three hundred dollars. She parked in a bus stop—
"Parking in bus stops is my specialty," Mom always used to say—and told me, "I
can give you two hundred dollars in cash, and a check for the rest."

I said, "Can't you make the check for a little more? Like one fifty?"

"I *cannot.* I'm flat out, Sean. Your father is withholding *my* money."

She went to the bank.

I waited. *Should I steal this car?* I thought.

Mom had left the keys, a gesture of unthinking trust.

I didn't.

Mom returned with two hundred-dollar bills and a postdated check.

She said, grandly, "*Here's your three-hundred dollars. I never want to see you again.*"

I said, "Good luck with your life, Mom," and opened the thick little red car door. I slammed it, popped the trunk, grabbed Dad's beat-up suitcase, banged the trunk closed, and strode off.

I WAS ON my own, with my trunk, in San Francisco.

All these patterns being repeated by generation after generation, playing out the same dramas on the same streets; it was like an intergenerational musical starring Hayes, Ora, Dad, Uncle Jack, Dede, Mom, me, and the extremely attractive city we lived in:

*Hayes and Ora:*
*Earth is shakin'*
*Eggs 'n' bacon*
*Fires blazin'*
*Hey!*
*We lit a match*
*And covered San Francisco with ashes*

*Dad (circling above in the helicopter) and Dede (waving below):*
*We're a match made in hell*
*Look at us if you need to know where the cash is*

*Mom (from the balcony):*
*I call servants "help."*
*I'll fall furthest—heeeeeeeeelp!*

*Me:*
*I'm a spoiled, rotten, sacrilegious little shit.*
[whining now]
*All I want is Dad*
*to point to his lap*
*And say, "sit."*

*Dad:*
*Made my first million*
*From the Continental chip.*

*Got into pats*
*On mats*
*With hats*
*On the pats*
*(That's*
*no Freudian slip.)*

*Mom:*
*I'm gonna jump, I'm gonna jump*
*Call the press, call the pope*
*St. Patricia, Pat, Patsy*
*Has run out of hope!*

I took Dad's suitcase over to the bus stop and waited. When the 41 Union came I took it over Russian Hill and got off just west of Van Ness. Christian and Trevor had been talking about a particular pair of hard-to-find sunglasses that were for sale in a shop on this block. Wearing coveted sunglasses and carrying a suitcase would be an impressive way to show up on their doorstep.

I went into the shop, set down my suitcase, and asked to see the sunglasses. A label in the display case said they were one hundred and ninety dollars. It was more money than I had ever spent on anything. The saleswoman handed them over, and I slid them on. They were black, steel, well made, with thick, reddish-black, bruise-tinted lenses. Everything looked dark and bloody through them. They felt *valuable.* I looked in the mirror. How did I look? I had no idea.

"I'll take them," I said.

Then she said how much they cost.

"Oh! Wait! I thought. It says. They're. Um . . . It says a hundred and ninety on the label."

"Tax."

"All I have is two hundred."

There was a moment of silence—an opportunity to not do this. Then, for some reason, the saleswoman said, as if I were a child and not a Red-Eyed Death Rocking Robot God, "Fine, since you're paying cash, I'll take the tax off."

I gave her the two hundreds.

She polished the glasses, slipped them into a little case (promptly lost), handed them to me with a ten.

I said, "Thanks."

She said nothing.

I stepped back out onto the street.

It was afternoon now, just before school would be letting out, and everything was quiet. Winter was almost over. A line of evergreen trees did some rustling. I slid the glasses out of the case and onto my face. Everything dimmed and turned a beautiful, taillights-at-night red. The trees and the sun on the sidewalk shifted tone and became more particular in detail. Everything unflattened, opened up—and in that moment the purchase seemed wise.

I thought, *I'm going to need these to start my new life.* I hefted my suitcase and set out down the block. I resolved, meaning it, that I would never take them off. Why should I? I could build a home behind the lenses of these glasses.

Then the sun went behind a cloud. I sensed something huge and unavoidable out there.

I SPENT the ten dollars taking a cab to Christian and Trevor's. I knocked on the door wearing the sunglasses.

"Where'd you get those?" Trevor asked.

I explained.

"Sean, you spent all your money on sunglasses!"

I nodded.

"Can I borrow them?"

Trevor borrowed them.

I moved into their living room. The sunglasses were the only rent I could pay. I ended up giving them to him. For the next two months I split my time between Christian and Trevor's—which we dubbed "the Ristow Hotel"—and Blane's top bunk.

Christian, Trevor, and I started working on a movie called *S\*C\*U\*M*.

*S\*C\*U\*M* was the story of a pornography-obsessed superhero trio who possessed a magic candle that granted them great powers. The candle was stolen. To recover it they had to battle an evil nemesis who took pride in having extremely swollen legs. Along the way they consumed a lot of alcohol and cocaine; paid homage to the pope; murdered hippies; consulted an oracular, talking pear; assassinated Ronald Reagan; and campaigned against cigarettes (by wresting them away from smokers and smoking them themselves, with great relish).

Here's a scene:

EXT. PARK—DAY
Rex [Sean] and Joe-Bob [Christian] walk through a park in search of Luigi [Trevor], the missing member of their group. Joe-Bob carries an Uzi. They look in a garbage can. Rex sticks his head in it.

REX
Luigi? Luigi!

JOE-BOB
Na, not in there, man.

REX
No, he's not in there.

CUT TO:
A park bench with Someone [Trevor] asleep on it.

JOE-BOB
(offscreen)
Luigi!

REX
Pope John Paul?

JOE-BOB
Hey, maybe this guy's Luigi.

REX
Nah, Luigi would never degenerate to this state.

They tap the Sleeping Man on the shoulder and roll him over.

JOE-BOB
Hey.

REX
Hey you—

SLEEPING MAN
Hm?

REX
Vagrant scum.

JOE-BOB
Hey you, you seen anybody named Luigi around here?

REX
Yeah!

SLEEPING MAN
Luigi?

JOE-BOB
Maybe he *is* Luigi.

He puts the Uzi to the man's head.

JOE-BOB
Check the birthmark! Check the birthmark!

Rex pulls down the collar of the Sleeping Man's shirt to reveal a birthmark.

REX
It is! Luigi!

Now that I had someplace to stay and a promising career in film, it was time to retrieve my stuff from Mom's. This stuff consisted of: a rectangular wooden box, encircled by blue neon and divided into two squares, one a clock and the other a rotating marquee of old ads; an Olympia beer sign that said "The best of the Rockies" above an illuminated photograph of a waterfall (with a spinning pinwheel behind it to simulate motion); a silkscreen on stretched canvas of a 1970s skateboarder tucked into a downhill slalom run; a stereo; and a backlit plastic Heineken beer sign. It was the accumulated treasure of my life.

After much discussion with Spencer and Blane it was decided that an out in the open, bold-like-Christian Ristow–style frontal assault was the only way to go.

We picked a night when Blane's mom was going out on a date so we could use her car, a huge, brown, dented, early seventies Oldsmobile. It had serious trunk space. We picked up Spencer and headed over to Mom's. We didn't drive to the front, but up Vallejo and down an alley to the "plaza," an open, windswept, gray-concrete level located seven stories above the street at the front of the building but flush with the hillside behind. It was swept by a pair of rotating security cameras. Though Mom had taken my house keys I had made sure to retain a plaza/elevator key. Blane backed the car up the alley so it was pointing out, ready for the getaway. We vaulted the low, locked gate, wet with condensation, sprinted past the cameras, unlocked the door to the elevators, called a car, got in, and pressed "PH"—penthouse.

Silence.

This was cinematic. The moment before the big job. We were calm, adrenalized, ready for anything.

I said, "We ring the doorbell and when they open it—at this hour it'll be David the cook—no matter what they say we walk in—there's no way they're going to stop us. Head right upstairs to my room and start grabbing my stuff, don't let anything slow us down. If my mom's not here it'll be easier, but even if she is here and she starts screaming we'll just stay focused, get the stereo unhooked, form a chain, and move out of the room and down the stairs to the elevator. Then one of us stays and gets an elevator and holds it while the other two keep bringing stuff down. It'll buzz loud, but don't worry, nothing'll happen, I've tested it."

Blane said, "I'll deal with the elevator when we've got enough downstairs."

I said, "O.K. Spencer and I'll finish getting the last stuff. Then on the plaza we'll chain it again into the car. If there's anything to deal with because of my mom I'll deal with it and you guys just keep going. I can handle her."

The elevator arrived at the penthouse.

David, the cook, opened the door, smiled, clouded. Behind him was Cecilia, the housekeeper. She was not usually there at this hour. "Who is it?" I heard Mom say from the top of the stairs.

"I'm sorry, David, but I am coming in to get my stuff," I said, walking past him and taking the stairs.

Blane and Spencer said "sorry"s and followed. Mom recognized my voice and began *screaming* before she even saw me. She charged down the stairs as I came up and we met in the middle, Blane and Spencer right behind me.

"Get out! You're breaking into my house! Get out! *Get out!* I'm calling the police!"

I strode past and said, "What? To tell them I'm here taking back my stuff? That's not stealing. I'm only here for my stuff."

Spencer and Blane said polite "Hello, Ms. Montandon"s and slipped past into my room. They began ripping out everything valuable.

Mom said, "I bought you that stuff and I've taken it back. It's mine now."

I said, "Ha! This is such *bullshit.*" I had planned to distract her with an argument, or even attempt diplomacy, but this was now impossible. I couldn't control myself.

Mom was offended. "How dare you talk this way to your mother?! *What have you* become, Sean? You're stealing. You're a *criminal.*"

"'Become?' 'Stealing?' What the fuck? *You're* stealing, Mom! At least Dad sent me all my stuff when *he* kicked me out. *You're worse than Dad!* You know what? *Fuck you, Mom!*" I said. Now I'd said it to both of them.

Mom was stunned for a moment. I walked toward my room. She recovered and said, "*Don't take one further step.*" I walked through my door. She shouted, "You're going to be in *a* lot of trouble because of this!"

Mom ran to her bedroom shouting, "I'm *calling* the police!"

"Fuck," I said. Blane had got one speaker. I pointed out the other one, said, "I gotta go deal with Mom," and ran out of my room.

David and Cecilia were standing at the top of the stairs, watching. I picked up an extension. They watched me. Mom was on with 911 saying, "My son is here robbing me!"

The operator asked, "Ma'am, what is your address?"

In a slick, condescending voice I interrupted and said, "*Grand-ma,* are you bothering the police again?"

"*That's* him!" she snapped. "My son: the robber!"

"*Grandma,*" I said. "I'm *so* sorry. She does this *all the time*. Always making up stories. Come on, Grandma, it's time for your *medicine.*"

I gave David and Cecilia a little conspiratorial smile that they did not return.

Mom said, "How dare you? How *dare* you?"

Blane came by laden with speakers.

The operator said, "Do you need assistance, ma'am?"

I said, in a too-sweet voice, "No. Everything's *fine*. I'm so sorry that we bothered you."

Mom shouted, "Of course I do. I'm being robbed!"

The operator repeated, "Ma'am, do you need assistance?"

"I told you! Yes! Absolutely I do! My address is—"

"Grandma!"

"999—"

"Grandma!"

"Go ahead, Ma'am," said the operator.

"999 Green Street."

"Do you believe her?" I asked the operator. I could tell she did.

"Ma'am, we're sending a squad car."

"This is really thoughtless," I said.

"*Penthouse* number one!"

"Officers are on the way, Ma'am."

I dove back into my room and told Spencer. "Cops are coming! We gotta move!" He said, "We're just about ready."

"I got that beer sign," I said.

Blane came back and grabbed a full rack of components, stacking them from his belt to his chin.

"I got the elevator," he said.

I made for a corner bookshelf where a second speaker sat, pulled it down, yanked up the speaker wire, scanned the room. Spencer walked out with the skateboarder silkscreen. We had almost everything.

On the landing I could hear the elevator buzzing its warning buzz below. Spencer, ahead of me, had run into Mom.

Mom said to him, "The police are coming! You're all going to jail!"

Spencer stopped, looked her full in the face, and said, "This is all your fault. Sean's a good person and you don't even know it because you're caught up with yourself and all your children for peace. What about him?" He pointed at me. What was this? Nobody'd ever said anything like this. "You'll send him to jail for taking back his stuff? You are fucked up. You are a bad mother. I have *no* fucking respect for you."

*Holy Fucking Shit, Spence,* I thought.

Mom tried to summon up the Mom Voice. But it failed.

For years afterward Mom said, with an odd respect, "Spencer really let me have it."

"You should be ashamed," she said now.

"No. You should be ashamed," he said calmly.

I said, "*Spence,* let's go!" Then I said, "Bye, Mom. Sorry."

We ran down the stairs and out the front door, which Blane had wedged open, and shoveled the last of my stuff into the elevator. Cords were everywhere, looking like seaweed, as though all this stuff had washed up on some beach. We began to descend.

At the plaza, another perfectly coordinated evacuation—we were all *on,* attuned to each other, like Spencer had been attuned to some inner righteous eloquent thing when he took on Mom. I'd never seen anybody do what he'd done. Not Dad. Nobody. We moved in a chain out of the elevator, through the vestibule door, across the eerie, cold breezeway of the plaza, over the fence, into the trunk, each of us thinking ahead and anticipating obstacles. The lobby security monitors showed images of us in gray tones unloading all this stuff and racing across the plaza. We were like the 4077th M*A*S*H when they had to pack up camp and you saw what a crack team they were behind all the wisecracking. We got into the car and pulled down the brick-paved alley, unchanged since the nineteenth century—the very center of the only portion of Russian Hill that wasn't burned in the 1906 fire. We heard the approaching sirens. They were coming! Blane chirped the tires and we blew out the alley. He swung a tight turn, then another, triple curved a perfect chicane down the ramp that led to this oldest, highest section of Russian Hill, the car swaying on its springs, stereo components held steady on our laps, down empty Vallejo, and away!

The police went to the front of the building and never saw us.

We shouted. Blane snapped on the radio.

Of course, all this stuff I'd worked so hard to rescue would wind up lost, neglected, and eventually stolen.

DAD AND UNCLE JACK did a lot of traveling together, mostly going to business conventions and the occasional Nevada brothel, where "everybody was in everybody else's bed," as Dad's longtime secretary put it to me. Jack liked to fly his own plane on these trips. That way he could bring his guns and drink as much as he wanted. One time he almost killed himself and Dad when he mistook a pier in New Orleans for the airport runway. Dad was a bit more cautious.

AFTER A WEEK at the Ristow Hotel, working on *S*C*U*M,* I spent a couple of nights at Blane's. Blane thought the Ristows were cool, and was impressed that I was hanging out with them. Trevor and Christian didn't think Blane was cool. I was suddenly a little embarrassed by my best friend. I decided to start shit-talking Blane when I was with them.

Trevor had a scooter that he rode to school, so Blane and I decided to steal a scooter. I convinced Blane he wouldn't have to take the bus or borrow his mom's car if he stole one. Meanwhile, he had discovered that if you stuck a flat-headed screwdriver in a scooter's ignition, clamped a vise grip to the handle of the screwdriver, and turned, the headstock would unlock and you could press START and drive away.

We snuck out. Fifteen blocks off Russian Hill, in the trough of the landfill that's the Marina, we found an unchained Yamaha Riva 180. The situation was ideal. A dim, empty street. 3:00 A.M. All windows dark. No traffic lights, just stop signs. The Riva was red; 180 meant that it was 180ccs, almost a motorcycle. It was parked way out on the edge of the sidewalk, as if it had been abandoned, as if someone wanted us to steal it. Had some other petty thieves left it here? Would the screwdriver and vise-grip trick work? We walked up.

Blane said, "It's been plugged!" The lock on the ignition had been completely removed. He stuck his screwdriver in the hole where the ignition should have been, twisted right, the dash lit up. Blane hit START, the motor caught, and he shot off up Russian Hill, jacket billowing behind him. My friend was gone. The burst of speed was unbelievable. He'd blasted away, out of dumb-ass take-the-bus adolescence. I saw him make a hard right and figured he was going to wait for me. When I reached him he smiled and said, "Sean, this thing is *so fast!*"

I said, "Dude, you were *flying* up the hill."

We inspected the vehicle. The whole ignition had been cleanly and professionally extracted. You could even stick a house key in the hole and turn it on.

"Way less conspicuous than the vise grip and the screwdriver," he said.

We decided it had been stolen and abandoned. We weren't stealing it first. We were second stealers.

It became our joint possession. We decorated it with stickers. Blane put the Grateful Dead on one side, and I put The Sisters of Mercy, Trevor Ristow's favorite band, on the other. I stole a new license plate, with an up-to-date registration sticker, from a motorcycle. A dollar fifty filled up the tank. It was cheaper than riding the bus.

Blane taught me how to ride. Then I took the scooter away from him. I peeled off the Grateful Dead sticker and replaced it with The Cure. It was mine now. I felt cocky. I cruised the city. I got drunk. At a red on Masonic I pulled up to a two-door car with a pretty girl driving. Her window was down. I smiled and said, "Wanna race?"

She smiled back. Then her car started to shake. A skinhead yanked himself out of the passenger window and glared at me over the top of the car. Three more were in the backseat, making angry noises. The glaring one shouted, "Wanna fight?"

I yelped, terrified, pulled a ∪, then a left, and shot down to the bottom of a dead-end street. "Shit!" But they weren't following.

I had no idea the front brake was supposed to do most of my stopping. I just ignored the front brake and stomped down on the rear one. Soon the rear brake was shot.

In 1957, after Dad's first divorce, he went to London and shared a suite at Claridge's Hotel with Gerson Bakar, the friend he'd moved in with after his parents died, and who was now his and Jack's business partner. Jack and Dad enjoyed harassing Gerson. Saturday night, Gerson went out to a music hall. Dad stayed in and went to bed early.

At the music hall Gerson met a chorus girl, spent the night trying to get her back to the hotel, and finally succeeded, just before dawn. Entering the suite they woke up Dad, who listened for a bit, then dressed and came out to join them in the sitting room. They were having drinks. Gerson got up to use the bathroom. When he returned Dad and the girl had both donned coats and were walking out the door. Gerson said, "What are you doing?"

Dad said, in that maybe I'm serious or maybe I'm putting you on voice, "It's Sunday morning. I'm taking her to church."

One Tuesday, after I'd had the scooter long enough to think of it as my own, Christian and I went out to look for another one, him on the back and me driving. With the bad brakes and the extra weight we drifted midway through crosswalks before I could stop us. We found a silver Honda Elite, unchained on a quiet block in the Sunset district. It was on the sidewalk, midblock, below the low-overhanging, T.V.-lit windows of a white house. Christian shoved a screwdriver an inch into the ignition, clamped it tight with the vise grip, twisted to "On," and then pressed the "START" button.

It started.

*Pppppppp.*

He jumped on and took off fast, me following, through the park and into the Richmond district, where we switched plates with another scooter, *to throw off the cops.* We did this with Christian's beautiful set of German tools, moved on and did it again, near the ocean, then felt safe.

Christian said, "Let's get on the Marina Green and spin some donuts on the grass."

"O.K.," I said.

I had gained much status by demonstrating the vise-grip trick (giving no credit to Blane) and for suggesting the clever, cop-thwarting multiple plate switch. I was relying on Christian for my lodgings. This evening had the potential to be legendary, an incentive for prolonged hospitality. Even though my brakes were gone, I could not refuse.

If my ultimate goal was to impress cool people like Christian, my secret ultimate goal was not *just* to impress cool people like Christian, but to impress them so thoroughly that they would love and want to become close to me. I wanted to impress Christian into intimacy. And then I wanted to show this closeness to Dad, say, "Look, Dad, look at the people who have chosen to become close to me—the coolest people in San Francisco." Society people were the only people Dad seemed to care about. Christian and Trevor lived in Pacific Heights, and their father was a well-known plastic surgeon (with a *von* in his name). This was what Dad valued. Closeness to *Dad* was always my real goal. So crime done out of the desire for closeness with Christian leading to closeness with Dad, who socialized with Christian's father, who had taken a sort of benevolent and bemused stance toward my presence in his kids' apartment, where he paid the rent (and had refused Dad's request that he evict me), led me to spin donuts on the Marina Green. (That and the fact that I thought it would be cool.)

We drove east on Geary ("heartline" on the palm of San Francisco), then up and down the big hills of Pacific Heights, Christian leading the way, my brakes so shot I was drifting into the actual intersections now. The Marina Green is a big lawn that follows the bay from the Golden Gate Bridge on-ramp to Fort Mason (army headquarters during the battle with the '06 fire). It's not so much a park as a treeless green doormat. We drove through the parking lot and right up on the grass, which was as well lit as a stage. Christian planted his right leg and gunned his scooter around it like a pivot. The scooter kept getting away from him and laying down on its side. I gunned mine for fifty feet, then slammed on the brake and slid another thirty across the wet grass. Christian saw and did it, too. We did it together, side by side. This was fun! We were growing closer!

After ten minutes of "power slides," Christian laying his bike down once, but getting up unharmed from the grass, we went back to donuts. I took a shot, half-heartedly, unsuccessfully. Christian nailed it. I laughed at the perfect circular trench Christian was carving out of the grass with his rear tire. Then I saw three bright white lights, approaching fast. Two were down low, at headlight level, and the third was higher up, pointed directly at us, as if it was being *aimed*. It did not seem menacing, just strange. I thought, *Some dudes have brought a motorcycle in the back of a pickup truck,* Mad Max–*style. They're here to party with us.* Christian noticed, too. He stopped middonut and stared.

I straddled my scooter. Christian stood in his donut. Car doors were opened and left open. I heard two men and the sound of a voice on a radio. When the man on the left moved closer I realized he was a cop. They were both visible now, one white, one Latino.

The white cop, the driver, said, "We got a noise complaint. What're you doing on the grass with these scooters? Shut off your motors and let me see your licenses and registrations." We shut off the scooters. Christian handed over his license and said he had no registration. I said I had neither. My ID was my passport, full of stamps from peace trips.

"We *found* these scooters, Officers," Christian said.

"You *found* them," said the white cop. He walked around us, saw we had no keys in our ignitions, looked closely at mine, and said, "This one's been plugged."

He got out a pad and wrote down our plate numbers, then got back in the car to run them. I thought about bailing, but they had Christian's license and I had no brakes. The courage to push the START button was unsummonable. Christian whispered through his teeth, with urgency, *"We'll-tell-them-we-were-joyriding-and-we-found-these-behind-the-Presidio-Wall."* I thought, *The Presidio Wall? What's the Presidio Wall?*

The white cop came back and told the other cop, "Stolen."

The Latino cop said, "We have to take these guys in."

"Tow truck's on the way," the white cop said. "We just gotta wait for it." Then, to us, "Step away from the vehicles, place your hands on the squad car, and spread your legs apart."

*Were we on T.V. or something?*

They patted us down, pulled our arms behind our backs, closed cuffs around our wrists, tight, and put us in the back of the squad car. We sat in the dark backseat while the two cops stood outside, waiting for the tow truck.

Christian, like a lawyer, whispered, *"Joyriding. Joyriding is just a misdemeanor. We've got to say we were just joyriding. We found them behind the Presidio Wall. They were abandoned. We stumbled on them. We were just driving them around. That's what we say. O.K.?"*

"*Uh, where's the Presidio Wall?*" I asked.

"*The Presidio Wall,*" he hissed, louder, jerking his head back towards the Presidio.

"I don't know the wall," I said.

"Right where we all used to play softball."

I never used to play softball. Christian was moving away. I knew we would never again be friends.

"Oh, O.K. Yeah," I said.

We were silent. The cops leaned on the hood of the cruiser. A tow truck arrived. The driver talked with the cops, wheeled our scooters into position on either side of his rear winch, mine nearest, wrapped two heavy belts around their frames, and lifted them into the air. As mine rose the Cure sticker on its right side was illuminated in the cruiser's headlights. I knew I was fucked.

The scooters dangled and spun like red-and-silver ornaments. They were secured with some guy wires. The cops stood, the tow truck washed us with lights and pulled past—cop asses *cushed* into cruiser vinyl, and doors thunked home. Christian said, "It was just joyriding. We found those scooters behind the Presidio Wall. We were just joyriding."

The white cop said, "Tell it down at the station," and turned up the radio. "*I* believe you, but we have to take you in."

"We understand you were just having fun," the Latino cop said. Then, sounding a little less like our friend, "Hey, we get a fucking complaint, we get a fucking complaint."

The white cop said, "Then we check it out and find these two ruining a public park."

"On stolen vehicles."

"We were joyriding, Officers."

"One of them," said the white cop, "almost *eighteen.*"

This was me.

The Latino cop said, "We'd hate it if you had to go to jail instead of juvie."

I thought about this as we pulled out of the parking lot. Then the radio squawked and the Latino cop answered. After some conversation, he switched on the siren, and the car sped up. We drove east on Bay Street, cut over to Broadway, got on the Embarcadero Freeway (condemned following the '89 quake, a few months later), and the white cop floored it, getting all the way to 110 mph. Christian and I looked at each other and shouted, "No way, 110!" Our seat belts were unbuckled. They were showing off. We were kissing their asses. Two minutes later we got off downtown and cut up Market into the Tenderloin, went right onto Mason, the wrong way, then left onto Eddy, also the wrong way. We fishtailed into a diagonal, blocking the street in front of five or six men. The cops jumped out. It was like they were our big brothers, driving us around and trying to impress us.

For the next five minutes our cops established their dominion over the winos of Eddy Street. The winos looked at the pavement. Then our cops got back in the car, hit the freeway again, and drove to city jail, where we pulled into a fluorescent-lit breezeway. They walked us into a big, beat-to-shit elevator. Upstairs we were uncuffed and booked. It was 3:30 A.M. and I was starting to feel sleepy. A new cop put a placard around my neck and took my picture three times—left, straight, right. Then he inked my left and right index fingers and rolled them over two empty slots in a ledger full of other fingers, pressing down hard, which woke me up. Another cop poured detergent on a paper towel, grasped my inked fingers with it, and pulled. He threw the paper towel into a trash can overflowing with inky paper towels.

After we were booked we were recuffed. The Latino cop pointed at me and said to his partner, "Maybe we should leave this one here, split these guys up so they can't make up a story, take him downstairs to city jail, save ourselves some work."

I said, *"No. Please."*

His partner said, "Well, we gotta drive the younger one out to juvie. Might as well take them both."

I said, "Please, please, take me to juvie."

We got in the elevator. "You sure?" the Latino cop said. He hit the button for city jail. "Jail's right here." The car dropped and opened on the jail floor. Dark. Bad smell. I was about to piss my pants.

I said, "Please, please, not jail. Please, juvie."

They paused. Finally the Latino cop said, "The kid wants to go to juvie; guess we better take him to juvie." The doors shut.

"You got a break," the white cop said.

We drove out and up Market, to the foggiest part of San Francisco. The cops parked in another breezeway and brought us into a narrow corridor, where a man sat behind a high counter. The floor was black linoleum worn white. They uncuffed and checked us in. It was like arriving at the night desk of a motel. The cops signed a book and walked out the door.

I shouted, "Bye!" after them.

The juvenile corrections officer behind the counter instructed us, "Remove all your clothes, watches, and jewelry. That includes earrings. You can keep your socks and underwear." He put two sets of juvie-issue sweats on the counter. They were covered in tags and gang names. Mine said, "Fulton Street Mob."

A lot of what I was wearing belonged to Christian. He watched me put his black cardigan on the counter, looked at what I had on under it, and said, "That's my shirt."

The shirt was purple-black with a Nehru collar. I said, "You loaned it to me."

He said, "I want it back."

I said, "But I'm wearing it."

He said, "You have to take it off now, anyway. And since it's mine it should go in my envelope, with my stuff."

Christian and I both knew he'd get out first. He didn't want this shirt stuck in juvie as long as I was going to be stuck there. I'd been dragging him down. He was going to blame me for being a bad influence when he talked to his father.

I said, "You've got my clock." My cool neon clock was in his room back in Pacific Heights, at the Ristow Hotel.

He said, "It's *my* shirt, Sean." I gave him the shirt. I reached down and pegged my sweatpants. Christian, watching, noticed that my shoes were also his—thick-soled, round-toed, black-leather creepers, with suede tongues and heavy, silver, western-tooled buckles. They were cooler than the thin-soled, pointy-toed, all-suede, delicate silver-buckled pair of shoes that he was wearing. Mine were semi-tough. His belonged on a Christmas elf. Christian said, "Let me take those, too."

A juvenile corrections officer took us through a steel door, across a large, half-dark room, and down a hall of metal cell doors with small, wired-glass windows high in their centers. He unlocked a door on the left and put Christian behind it. Then he took me another twenty feet, opened a door on the right, and left me there. A bed was cantilevered from the wall and covered with a half-inch foam pad. The rest of the room was empty. Another small, thick, wired-glass window looked out on a cement exercise yard, with a couple of netless basketball hoops.

Two hours later a guard banged on my door and called me out into a lineup. Fifteen of us came out of our cells and stood in a well-lit room at the end of the hall. I fell into the far end of the line, nearest our cells, beside Christian, who was beside a tall, gangster-looking black kid with long, wet-looking Jheri curls and a pissed expression.

We were counted. Christian and I were given towels and told to shower. Everyone else went to breakfast. In the shower Christian, whose mind had been turning in legalistic circles, hissed over the water, *"We tell them the Presidio Wall, right? Right?"*

"Right," I said.

I was uncharacteristically planless. I hadn't even thought about a story.

AFTER THE SHOWER, and contrary to expectations, they told us we were allowed to make as many phone calls as we wanted. To do so we simply had to ask a guard, stationed at a curved nurse's station–style desk, to dial whatever number we wrote in pencil on a slip of white paper. He would then put it through to a white phone mounted on a wall about ten feet away. Christian called his dad. I called Urban, affected a scratchy throat, and told them I was sick and would be out for the next day or two. Maybe the whole week. Then I called Mom.

Mom answered in the Mom voice: "*Hello!*"

I said, "Mom, it's Sean."

"Sean?"

"Yes."

"What do you want? Why are you calling?"

"There's been a mistake and I'm calling you from juvenile hall."

"*Juvenile hall?*"

"Yeah."

"What are you doing there?"

"I was joyriding a stolen scooter."

"You can *rot* there!"

*Click.*

"Mom?"

She'd hung up.

*Now what?*

I couldn't call Dad.

*What about Mrs. Morf?*

Then the tall, Jheri-curled kid walked up and said, "You're playing Monopoly." He pointed to a bunch of foam furniture where two twelve-year-old versions of himself and a Mexican boy my age were sitting around a Monopoly board. Christian had disappeared. A skinny skinhead was watching soaps.

"Yeah, O.K., cool," I said.

Then he looked down at my sweatpants, laughed, and said, "You in the 'Fulton Street Mob'?"

A lot of the pieces were missing. The tall kid took the race car. His sidekicks got stuck with a piece of broken pencil and a Bic pen cap. The Mexican kid got the wheelbarrow (*la carreta*). I got the thimble.

The Mexican kid was the banker and we all got our money. The tall Jheri-curled kid said he was a Crip, "Up from L.A." S.F. juvie was the airport bar on a tedious business trip. He was making the best of things while his travel agent sorted out the trouble.

In a calm, serious voice, he said, *"Nobody lands on Boardwalk."*

Silence.

"Or Park Place—less they want their *ass* beat."

He reemphasized this whenever one of us got close. Then, when he was in the zone, he said, "Boardwalk! C'mon!" rolled, missed. After missing a bunch of times he landed on and bought Park Place. Next turn he cheated and put his piece on Boardwalk. After that he told everyone, "C'mon, c'mon—*Boardwalk!* Land on *Boardwalk!*"

In between turns the Mexican kid, in perfect English, told me, "This is the receiving unit. The R.U." He flicked his eyes to where a cheery banner said, "Welcome to R.U." "Everybody comes here first."

"Then what happens?" I asked.

"You'll meet your P.O. And he'll talk to you about sentencing. Unless you've got a guardian who can get you out."

"P.O.?"

"Probation Officer."

When Christian reappeared I had Marvin Gardens, but it was still an empty lot. I bailed on the game and said, "Dude! What's going on?"

"I'm leaving," Christian said, and a guard took him out the way we'd come in the night before. After the guard had relocked the door he told me to come with him to meet my P.O. The Mexican kid, watching, somehow interested in befriending me, came up and said he'd play my piece while I was away. My P.O.'s office was halfway down a hallway of small offices not much different than our cells. The guard waited outside while I went in and sat across from a skinny man with a close-cropped red beard and hard, tired eyes. He asked me what had happened with the scooters.

I told the Presidio Wall story.

He listened, then asked, "Where is the Presidio Wall?"

"You know, it's that wall . . . at the edge of the Presidio."

"And where were the vehicles?"

"They were on the other side of the wall."

I imagined the scooters bedded down sideways on leaves and roots and dirt, like sleeping animals, beside a rustic stone wall, inside the Presidio. It made no sense.

"We just found them."

"How'd you get them out?"

"Just started them right up!" Or was I supposed to say we'd found them *running?* Had I just fucked up? I added, "The engines were warm."

He said, "The plates were switched? Did you do that?"

"The people who stole them must have."

Silence.

"My friend just left. Am I going to be able to go now?"

"His father and a lawyer came and took custody of him. Can someone do that for you?"

Being in a small room with a disappointed white man was a familiar situation, and it restored some of my equilibrium.

I said, "I have no parents."

He looked skeptical. "So who's responsible for you?"

"*Me*. I'm responsible for me."

He said, "Your friend told me the truth. You should think about that. He wasn't so worried about what would happen to you."

I was silent.

"We'll talk more tomorrow," he said.

The guard took me back to the R.U.

The Crip was building hotels. My thimble kept hanging on, but not for long. Soon the Crip had all the money, and the game was over.

The Mexican kid said, "You play chess?"

I said, "Oh, *yeah*," cockily. I thought I was good.

Dad had taught me to play chess. We were on vacation—in Mexico, actually—just before the divorce. I was nine and convinced I was talented because I beat him once, and he had not let me. I felt this massive, egotistic burst of self-respect, which was obnoxious, but also good, something you want kids to feel. I felt the brief potential of my adult maturity, of growing up, and the desire for it. I felt the urge to do chores and do them well. I remember also catching the biggest fish of the vacation. I was so proud. And this was the last time I would feel this way. Soon Dad married Dede and she beat me back into childhood, a bad kind of childhood, an entitled, spoiled then gypped, and sniveling and injuredly thieving childhood that at age seventeen and eleven-twelfths, I still hadn't left behind but was wallowing in.

Chess held this sentimental feeling for me. I assumed I would defeat the Mexican kid and he would become my admiring bodyguard. I'd need this if I was going to be stuck in juvie.

The first game, my best game, I lost in fifteen minutes. The Mexican played confidently, made his moves quickly, and did not make mistakes.

We played another, in silence, until he said, "Checkmate."

Spectators arrived: the skinhead and one of the Crip's sidekicks from Monopoly. Five minutes into the next game I made a bad move and the skinhead *tsk*ed. My performance was weakening his case for white supremacy.

The Crip sidekick said, "You should've jumped over his man and killed him. You gotta kill that thing that looks like a dick! *Aww*, you *suck*."

The Mexican kid quietly said, "You're not very good, are you?"

The skinhead answered for me, the only word I remember him saying, "No."

Then a guard came and said, "Time for school." He ushered us over to a rectangular, Formica, art class–looking table where a kind, tired, fiftyish woman was shuffling some papers. I sat immediately to her left and tried to charm her and make a good impression.

The Crip slumped at the far end of the table and stretched his legs out underneath. The Mexican kid sat across from me, on the teacher's right. The others were in-between. School was two hours. It started with a math test—basic addition, subtraction, and multiplication. The Mexican and I finished in a couple of minutes while the rest of the class took the full forty. The teacher read out the answers and did some explaining. The Mexican and I both aced it. I thought, *Mexican: 1. Sean: 1*. Next was English. I prepared to dust the Mexican. *English is my language, Chess master*. The teacher gave us a photocopy from *Huck Finn*. I thought of clever things to say. When discussion time arrived I regurgitated what I'd learned at St. Mark's in third-form English. I used terms like "religious symbolism" and "foreshadowing." The teacher nodded. It was the first time I'd ever felt the pleasure of being the kid who speaks up. I was the smartest kid in my class!

After school we had dinner and they put us back in our cells.

AS SOON AS I lay down I began crying. I could not stop. The crying was quiet and wet. It was impossible to sniff it back or swallow it down my throat. It just came and kept coming, like a steady leak. It seemed that something was broken inside me. It was not normal to cry this way.

Whatever toughness and resilience I thought I had was gone. I'd been fighting emotions for years, since the earthquake of my parents' divorce. Now emotions had me surrounded, and I had to let them do whatever (destructive, terrifying thing) it was that emotions did.

I hadn't been in a place from which I could not escape, in some form or other, in years. I had been trying to avoid this. But it was the only thing I should have been doing.

The emotions kept leaking. Then I hit upon a fact.

*Mom and Dad don't love me.*

And I burst into phlegm. My crying became loud and violent. This was true. This wasn't self-pity. This was fact. Mom and Dad loved, and always had loved, themselves—far, far more than they ever had, would, or could love me. I'd been able to play one against the other. Dad would love me when I dismissed Mom with him. Mom would love me when I was dazzled by her glamour and charisma, or persecuted by Dad. They loved me when I agreed to be their accomplice, or fan. But they did not know or love me for me. (Only Blane and Spencer did that.) Finally, they were unified in not loving me.

I had been so angry at them, for so long, that I did not realize how much I loved them.

Then, against my will, I started to remember things. I remembered, with great clarity, all the moments from the past when I'd thought we loved each other. Dad and I holding hands in church; Mom teaching me medical words; Dad reading with me in his bachelor apartment after we'd spied on Dede in the Trans Am; Mom saying she'd started the peace trips because of me; Dad showing me the school bus under the willow tree; all three of us together at Trader Vic's.

I fell asleep and woke up still crying.

It felt like a miracle. An evil miracle. But still, one that needed to happen.

Now I knew what had been motivating me.

The next morning I felt leveled. I was next to the Crip in the morning lineup. Tears continued to slide out of my eyes. I tried to stand very straight to compensate. The Crip, one leg bent, one straight, looked at me hard, leaned in, and shouted in my face, *"What the fuck's the matter with this guy!?"*

I did not react. He laughed, and turned away. But I caught a flicker of something in his eyes. He didn't want what I had.

After lineup and breakfast I got a call from Mrs. Morf.

*"Sean!"* she said. "I've been trying to get you out. But they won't release you to anyone but your parents or a legal guardian."

"Can I make you my legal guardian?"

"Do you *want* me to become your legal guardian?"

"Yes. Please, Mrs. Morf."

"Yes. O.K. I'll talk to a lawyer and see what I can do. But it's not going to be very quick. It may take a month or so. I'll call you later this afternoon."

When she called back later it was to tell me her lawyer didn't think it was possible for her to assume my guardianship in less than two months, maybe a month and a half, by which time I'd be eighteen anyway. Then I went to see my P.O. In the hallway, on the way to his office, after passing through the locked doors from the R.U. and longer term cells, I ran into two girls I knew from Urban, and Mom. They all shouted, "Sean!" Then Mom looked at the girls, realized they were there to see me, too, and banished them with a few violent words.

MOM AND I sat across from my P.O. She said, "I can take you home right now if you agree to attend, for at least a year, a school your father and I have found for you." I looked at my P.O.—thin, intense, bearded. He nodded.

"You can go if you agree," he said.

"*It's not Cascade?*" I asked. "*I won't* go if it's Cascade."

"It's a school like Cascade—but it's in Italy," Mom said. "You'll be one of the first students. The school is called Amity."

*Italy.* That's where I'd met the pope.

I said, "If it's not Cascade—or someplace like Provo—I'll go. But you have to swear to me, Mom."

"*I do swear, Sean,*" she said.

"O.K.," I said. "I'll go."

"*Swear to me,*" she said.

"I swear, too," I said.

I was ready to stop running.

I WALKED OUT of juvie in Christian's rejected clothes, an oath sworn to go to Italy. We drove down the curvy part of Market, then into the Slot, back into the heart of the city, mostly silent, except for Mom, saying in woeful tones, "Oh, Sean. You looked like a whipped dog back there. Oh, what has happened to us?"

*Italy,* I thought. *What's the language? Spanish?*

*Italy.*

Italy . . .

THE NIGHT BEFORE I left, for what would end up being four years, Blane skated over to say good-bye. We met out on Russian Hill. I gave him my skateboard to look after, then we hugged, and I said, "I love you, man."

**Sixteen · REDEMPTION**

U<small>P TO HERE</small> my life had been like one long chase scene—eighteen years of *Smokey and the Bandit*. But suddenly everything changed. Or chaser and chasee changed. I was no longer being chased and running. I stopped. And then I started chasing after something.

What happened was simple: People took a benevolent interest in me. And when they did I saw I had some value, and I began to *slow down*.

I was no longer in a state of furious escape, a euphoria of running.

I felt safe.

I<small>N ONE OF</small> my favorite books, *Norwegian Wood*, by Haruki Murakami, the nineteen-year-old narrator receives a letter from his girlfriend inviting him to visit her in a very strange mental hospital called the Ami Hostel.

Beyond the woods I came to a white stone wall. It was no higher than my own height and, lacking additional barriers on top, would have been easy for me to scale. The black iron gate looked sturdy enough, but it was wide open, and there was no one manning the guardhouse. [A] sign . . . stood by the gate: "Ami Hostel. Private. No Trespassing." . . .

I came to an interesting old building that had obviously been someone's country house once upon a time. It had a manicured garden with well-shaped rocks and a stone lantern. This property must once have been a country estate. Turning right through the trees, I saw a three-story concrete building. It stood in a hollowed-out area, and so there was nothing overpowering about its three stories. It was simple in design and gave a strong impression of cleanliness. . . .

I heard the soft padding of rubber soles, and a mature, bristly haired woman appeared. She swept across the lobby, sat down next to me, crossed her legs, and took my hand. Instead of just shaking it, she turned my hand over, examining it front and back.

"You haven't played a musical instrument, at least not for some years now, have you?" were the first words out of her mouth.

"No," I said, taken aback. "You're right."

"I can tell from your hands," she said with a smile.

There was something almost mysterious about this woman. Her face had lots of wrinkles. These were the first thing to catch your eye, but they didn't make her look old. Instead, they emphasized a certain youthfulness in her that transcended age. The wrinkles *belonged* where they were, as if they had been part of her face since birth. When she smiled, the wrinkles smiled with her; when she frowned, the wrinkles frowned, too. And when she was neither smiling nor frowning, the wrinkles lay scattered over her face in a strangely warm, ironic way. Here was a woman in her late thirties who seemed not merely a nice person but whose niceness drew you to her. I liked her from the moment I saw her. . . .

She took a pack of Seven Stars from her breast pocket, put one between her lips, lit it with a cigarette lighter, and began puffing away with obvious pleasure.

"It crossed my mind that I should tell you about this place, Mr.— Watanabe, wasn't it?—before you see Naoko. So I arranged for the two of us to have this little talk. Ami Hostel is kind of unusual—enough so that you might find it a little confusing without any background knowledge. I'm right, aren't I, in supposing that you don't know anything about this place?"

"Almost nothing."

"Well, then, first of all—" she began, then snapped her fingers. "Come to think of it, have you had lunch? I'll bet you're hungry."

"You're right, I am."

"Come with me, then. We can talk over food in the dining hall. Lunchtime is over, but if we go now they can still make us something."

She took the lead, hurrying down a corridor and a flight of stairs to the first-floor dining hall. It was a large room, with enough space for perhaps two hundred people, but only half was in use, the other half closed off with partitions, like a resort hotel in the off-season. The day's menu listed a potato stew with noodles, salad, orange juice, and bread. The vegetables turned out to be as startlingly delicious as Naoko had said in her letter, and I finished everything on my plate. . . .

"Are you Naoko's doctor?" I asked.

"Me? Naoko's doctor?!" She squinched up her face. "What makes you think I'm a doctor? . . . I teach music here. It's a kind of therapy for some patients, so for fun they call me the 'Music Doctor.' . . . But I'm just another patient. I've been here seven years. I work as a music teacher and help out in the office, so it's hard to tell anymore whether I'm a patient or staff. Didn't Naoko tell you about me?"

I shook my head.

"That's strange. . . . I'm Naoko's roommate. I like living with her. We talk about all kinds of things. Including you."

"What about me?"

"Well, first I have to tell you about this place. . . . The first thing you ought to know is that this is no ordinary 'hospital.' It's not so much for treatment as for convalescence. We do have a few doctors, of course, and they give hourly sessions, but they're just checking people's conditions, taking their temperature and things like that, not administering 'treatments' like in a regular hospital. There are no bars on the windows here, and the gate is always wide open. People enter voluntarily and leave the same way. You have to be suited to that kind of convalescence to be admitted here in the first place. In some cases people who need specialized therapy end up going to a specialized hospital. O.K. so far?"

"I think so," I said. "But what does this 'convalescence' consist of? Can you give me a concrete example?" . . .

"Just living here is the convalescence," she said. "A regular routine, exercise, isolation from the outside world, clean air, quiet. Our farmland makes us practically self-sufficient; there's no TV or radio. We're like one of those commune places you hear so much about. Of course, one thing different from a commune is that it costs a bundle to get in here."

"A bundle?"

"Well, it's not ridiculously expensive, but it's not cheap. Just look at these facilities. We've got a lot of land here, a few patients, a big staff, and in my case I've been here a long time. True, I'm almost staff myself, so I get a substantial break, but still. . . . You know . . . this sanatorium is not a profit-making enterprise, so it can keep going without charging as much as it might have to otherwise. The land was a donation. They created a corporation for the purpose. The whole place used to be the donor's summer home, until some twenty years ago. You saw the old house, I'm sure?"

I had, I said.

"That used to be the only building on the property. It's where they did group therapy. That's how it all got started. The donor's son had a tendency toward mental illness and a specialist recommended group therapy for him. The . . . theory was that if you could have a group of patients living out in the country, helping each other with physical labor, and have a doctor for advice and checkups, you could cure certain kinds of sickness. They tried it, and the operation grew and was incorporated, and they put more land under cultivation, and put up the main building five years ago."

"Meaning, the therapy worked."

"Well, not for everything. Lots of people don't get better. But also a lot of people who couldn't be helped anywhere else managed a complete recovery here. The best thing about this place is the way everybody helps everybody else. Everybody knows they're flawed in some way, and so they try to help each other. Other places don't work that way, unfortunately. Doctors are doctors and patients are patients: the patient looks for help to the doctor and the doctor gives his help to the patient. Here, though, we all help each other. We're all each others' mirrors, and the doctors are part of us. They watch us from the sidelines and they slip in to help us if they see we need something, but it sometimes happens that we help them. Sometimes we're better at something than they are. . . . Patients with problems like ours are often blessed with special abilities. . . . You're one of us while you're in here, so I help you and you help me. . . ."

"What should I do then? Give me a concrete example."

"First you decide that you want to help and that you need to be helped by the other person. Then you decide to be totally honest. You will not lie, you will not gloss over anything, you will not cover up anything that might prove embarrassing for you. That's all there is to it."

Everything said about the Ami Hostel could be said about the Amity School. The gate to Amity was the same gate, with the same wall. The mood was the mood of Amity. (Or the good mood of Amity, the calm side of the school.) The place gave a strong impression of cleanliness. Most people smoked. We grew our own vegetables. (I was in charge of squash.) We were quiet (when we were not encouraged to scream). People were direct, disarming, and physical. The school was beautiful. It was on an old country estate. The food was delicious. There was no T.V. or radio. We couldn't go to town. We did physical labor. The building was underfilled for most of the time I was there, which is why the place was so successful for me: lots of attention. People would stay and stay and stay (seven years would not be unusual). There were people in their twenties and thirties who were half staff and half student, moving back and forth between the two states. Students were teachers and teachers were students. The place was expensive (except in the many cases when it was free). Total honesty was practiced by all.

And of course there's the name. Amity was half Murakami's Ami Hostel and half Cascade School. But Amity got all the details right where Cascade got them wrong. And I was lucky to be there at the right time.

THE SCHOOL WAS in Tuscany, on the outskirts of a town called Arezzo, mid-calf on the boot of Italy, in a sixteenth-century villa: stubbly-textured, yellow, rectangular. The entrance was through a ballroom, which had a vaulted ceiling painted like a grove of birch trees, with philosophical slogans written in their branches. Entering the building was like stepping into a block of butter (Dad's) and finding a forest. I reached the villa after passing through a stone gate topped with disintegrating terra-cotta lions, paws resting on shields. Then came the vertical darkness of cypresses, lining the drive like tall doorways, through which I at first imagined escape. Olive trees shone silver gray in the hills behind. The school was in Italy because most students couldn't speak the language, and this made it impossible for us to escape.

I had finally found someplace where I could belong.

The students were tuition-paying Americans, Irish scholarship kids from a Dublin halfway house, and a handful of English-speaking Italians. The youngest of us was eleven (the hyperactive, uneducable son of an Italian T.V. star) and the oldest was nineteen (a Southerner who'd freaked out when his appointment to West Point hadn't been confirmed, gone to New York, tried to enlist at the army recruiting center in Times Square, and been declared mentally unfit to serve). For most of my time at Amity the students were outnumbered by the counselors.

These counselors were charismatic, unprofessional, utterly devoted people who had been us twenty years before. They'd attended Cascade's predecessor, CEDU (*see* yourself as you are, and *do* something about it), swore it had saved their lives, and that now they were going to save our lives. Some of the staff had also been involved with Findhorn, an organic gardening commune in Scotland immortalized in the film *My Dinner with Andre*. This resulted in delicious, Ami Hostel–worthy vegetables.

The school belonged to John Padgett, the headmaster. It was his singular vision. He had been the headmaster at Cascade just before I got there, but broke away to start Amity. John was the son of an evangelical Baptist minister, and he'd always dreamed of being a missionary. His mission with Amity was to take "American state-of-the-art special education," as an article quoting him in the *International Herald Tribune* put it, to a place "where it didn't exist." A renegade Guggenheim heiress supplied the money, and he'd opened the school with a single student just a few months before I arrived. He chose Italy because it was the site of the Renaissance and, as he liked to say, "We believe every child should have his own Renaissance."

Were he not bawdy, crass, fat, hilarious, John might have been my grandfather, the revivalist. John knew no shame, and would say anything that was on his mind, usually at top volume—his conviction being that all his thoughts were either wise or profoundly funny (or, more often, both). He did devastating impressions of people. He swore with inappropriate frequency. But he was no Falstaff. He was one of the smartest men I have ever known. And kind at heart. And very strange. Silence in his presence would be filled by weird, offensive non sequiturs (often *sung*) like "I wanna be a toilet!" that put everyone on edge and were intended to sum up some hidden truth about you that he had identified and was determined to out. The very first words he said to me were "What the *fuck* are you wearing? Is that a skirt?" I was wearing Bermuda shorts. He went on, "You *would* wear a skirt if you thought it would get you some *goddamn* attention!" Then he stared at me—and I remember the sensation, which was flattering and frightening, of being *really looked at*.

John seemed invincible. He was the Great God Padgett, destroyer of worlds, wielder of the might of the ages, tender of the flames of truth. Also, thankfully, tender. He was warm and loving. He became a father figure for me, eventually asking me to call him "Pop." I both wanted to and didn't want to.

It was because of John that Amity came to be, but it was because of John that the place was doomed. If the school had existed in somewhat lesser circumstances, it might have survived. But restraint was not John Padgett's style. John's style was to live in a magnificent villa and drive a 5 series BMW. And when the Guggenheim heiress died, just after I finished the program, the money went away. The school lasted for seven years, 1987–94, and I was lucky enough to be there at the right time, when John had the money and was running the place out of love and altruism and just the right amount of egotism.

John terrified and seemed to see right through everyone. His office was in the villa's former chapel, and he liked to talk to us about sex. He wanted to know when was the last time we'd masturbated. "The last time I masturbated," he'd say, "was this morning."

In group therapy sessions, called raps, as at Cascade, John's voice was so deep it seemed like it could only be coming down from the sky, or up out of the earth. It was warm and suggestive of massive power held in reserve, no matter how quiet it might get. He liked to whisper one sentence and then bellow the next. John's father, the evangelical Baptist minister, had paraded through the streets of the small town where John grew up, carrying a man-size cross on his back, and calling for repentance.

Afternoon raps took place beneath a frescoed ceiling in the library, a beautiful, old, leather and age–smelling room. People generally cried after the shouting. Sadness, we were told, was "the emotion beneath the anger." But it was important to get angry first. Shouts bounced off the walls. Wet Kleenex piled up on the terra-cotta floor.

After shouting, resonantly, and getting the details on our masturbatory habits for three hours, John would call it a day, and take his wife, and perhaps a lucky student or two, to a sublime restaurant in the woods, or the hot springs of Bagno Vignoni, an ancient Roman spa, to take the water. At Bagno Vignoni the water, which was scalding hot, came shooting out of a sluice and hit John in the shoulders like his own voice. He'd stand there for half an hour, his great bulk wreathed in steam: a Roman emperor, driving a silver BMW, with Rome plates. When he was hungry he used to drive the car at top speed around a stone cistern honking the horn for his wife to come out. His wife, Marci, was gentle and kind and maternal and had the softest, most delicate skin—it would bruise in a breeze—and everyone loved her. The woman in Murakami's novel reminded me of her exactly. If she wanted someone to rub her feet she said, "My feet are crying out," and we all rushed to get there first. She was the mother I'd never had. I loved to touch Marci, and I loved to be touched by her. Her physical presence was a perfect antidote to the two women I'd called "Mom." But she could also be terrifying—especially to the girls. The most memorable thing I ever heard her say, to a five-feet-one-inch seventeen-year-old, was "You've got a *cast-iron cunt!*"

And the weird thing was we all knew what she meant, the girl included.

LIKE CASCADE, Amity began with a strip search. They were looking for drugs (pot, mainly) and adolescent paraphernalia (concert shirts, tinted contact lenses, miniskirts). But they were less concerned with adolescent paraphernalia than Cascade, and it was O.K. to wear the color black. The sartorial philosophy was that a coat had to be just a coat, a shirt a shirt, etc.—not a symbol of anything else, or a stand-in for your identity. But they weren't too dogmatic. A little *style* was O.K. with them. This was Italy, after all.

All the unacceptable items went up in the attic (it was too complicated to send them home). This was a huge, spooky, beautiful space full of dust motes that hung beneath a gently sloping dormer roof with little sixteenth-century flowers painted between its joists. There was a hallway up there that ran the entire length of the building, on either side of which was huge room after huge room, some empty, some filled with antique Italian furniture that the school had removed from the lower floors because they didn't want us damaging it, others increasingly taken up with our contraband.

It was a place of suspension. We lugged our suitcases up there—five flights, each step worn to a little hollow in the center—and effectively abandoned everything we'd used to set ourselves apart back in America. The attic took on a sort of mythical status, as if our former selves were living up there. For me it was the psychic companion, the inevitable conclusion, to the St. Mark's basement.

After my clothes were taken away, and John had told me I'd wear a skirt for attention, a counselor named Ron took me to Standa—the Italian JC Penney—and filled the gaps in my wardrobe.

The trip was made in silence. I did not talk because there was a vague sense of menace—the possibility that Ron might explode. He'd read my file. He knew everything about me. I had attended, and escaped from, Cascade, where a lot of the faculty at Amity had once worked. I thought he might try to exact his vengeance while we were alone at the Italian JC Penney. I knew the way Cascade counselors worked. I knew they screamed and berated and threatened. Ron bought me a thirty-dollar bottle of Armani cologne. Welcome to Amity. Welcome to Italy.

I SAW A LOT of Ron in my first few months at Amity. He bought me Dunhill cigarettes, shouted at me in raps, forced me to remove dirt from hard-to-access locations, and told stories. When Ron talked about his life it was impossible to tell if he was joking or telling the truth. He was militarily clean-cut, extremely fit, with a mustache trimmed to a precise millimeter. His skin was dark and he claimed to be Pakistani sometimes, Afghani other times. He was a Navajo Indian.

"I used to root for the cowboys in Westerns on T.V.," he said. In the seventies he'd arrived as a student at CEDU, in the mountains of southern California, with hair down to his ass, his only possession a suede fringe jacket. After entering the CEDU program, which was significantly more aggressive and humiliating, they made him wear a sheet and walk around with a broom all the time.

"I don't know why," he said. Then he raised his voice: "But it did me *good!*"

I wondered what he would do to me.

He taught me how to work.

He loved the villa, and he was in charge of making us take care of it. He showed me a cannonball lodged in one of the empty fountains in the garden. He told me he'd heard a ghost in high heels *tic-tac* through the entry hall late at night, leaving behind the scent of her "strong, floral perfume." His voice was soft, just on the cusp of being inaudible, unless you asked him to repeat something—then he'd holler, laugh, and show his perfect teeth. He smoked one cigarette a year, on his birthday. He liked country music, especially its subgenre, *truck driver music,* a compilation of which he played in the evenings, when we students were supposed to be having edifying conversations about the errors of the past that had brought us here to Italy, beneath a vaulted ceiling painted with trees and slogans, like *"Per Aspera Ad Astra"*—"Through Rough Paths to the Stars."

Ron parroted the trucker songs in a slow, ironic deadpan:

*The highways that wind and wander*
*Across this lonesome land*

*Sure can get weary sometimes*
*'Specially when you get a flat on the old diesel*
*I was barreling down old 77 one day*
*And I just passed a hobo who'd given me the thumb*
*And I gave him the thumb back and kept goin'*
*And wouldn't you know it?*
*About a quarter of a mile further*
*I pulled up on the shoulder with a flat on the right rear*
*And as I stood there looking at it*
*Shaking my head*
*Utterin' some profane syllables*
*The hobo walked up and said to me, "Have a flat?"*
*"No thanks I got one."*
*"It ain't too bad, it's only a flat on the bottom."*
*Oh brother, you could tell this guy'd been out of circulation for a long time.*

Ron liked to make fun of people who faked their emotions in raps by quoting another song off the trucker compilation. If you were fake crying he'd say, "My eyes watered like I had a bad old cold."

Evening time, like at Cascade, was called "floor time." It was our only free time (the rest was raps and work crews), though we were still obliged to be in the main entertaining rooms of the villa while we had our edifying conversations.

Occasionally something cool and untrucker would come on the stereo during floor time. A breath from an ironic world. Like Talking Heads! Later we'd sing whatever it was, and someone who hadn't been there might say, "That's not acceptable." We'd say, "Ron played it on the floor!" Debate would ensue. When something that had been unacceptable became acceptable, whoever decided to "acceptablize" it was asserting the school's general enlightened superiority over its predecessors. As one of the first students I felt as if I was witnessing the dawn of a radical new age. The school was like the Paris Commune! We debated the obsolescence or permissibility of certain things from past, decadent cultures. Whether they could be part of the revolution or not. Whether the revolution was so feeble that it could not withstand them. We thought we were the most significant thing to happen in Arezzo since Piero della Francesca painted the *Legend of the True Cross*.

Murakami says this about the Ami Hostel's equivalent of floor time: "[It] had all the atmosphere of a specialized-machine-tool trade fair. People with a strong

interest in a limited field came together in a limited spot and exchanged information understood only by themselves."

MOST OF the other counselors and staff happened to have "M" names: Marci,
John's lovely, straight out of Ami Hostel wife; Michael (thirty-six, second-in-
command, former Hollywood playboy, the man all the male students wanted to
be when we grew up); Mona (soft, loving, good to hug, also a good shouter);
Merv (the only one with a license to practice psychotherapy, and the only one
who wasn't a shouter); and Matthew (late twenties, ex-navy, tattooed, John's
pick to take over the school after he retired, and the ultimate ruiner of
everything). Meryl was the English teacher, and Martin, a forty-year-old Englishman whose puttylike broken nose lay flat to his face, was my favorite teacher.
There was something both brutal and sweet about Martin. John felt we needed
exposure to the Renaissance, so he found Martin to teach us art. Martin chain-
smoked filterless Gauloise cigarettes and told us about Piero della Francesca.
He'd been in Italy since a Venice biennial sometime in the sixties, when he (supposedly) ran the British Pavilion. The best story about Martin concerned his
visit to the Sistine Chapel while it was being restored. A friend took him up on
the scaffolding. Martin wandered away, looked around, stood up on his toes,
pressed that fascinating nose flat to the roof, and *licked*.

There were also Italians. My favorite was Giulio, the villa's caretaker. He'd
been there since World War II, smelled like wood smoke, and told stories about
bedding down ten girls in a hayrick while simultaneously hiding from Nazis.
(They'd used the villa as a command center.) He spoke about the Nazis as the
tenants before the tenants before the tenants before the school.

THERE WERE SIX fellow students when I arrived, and others trickled in slowly.

Jason (my third and last) came over on the same TWA plane as me. We both
sat in the smoking section—smoking—and though I didn't notice him he spotted me walking around trying to look cool for some smoking girl or other. He'd
thought I was a typical Italian. This was because of my clothes: When we met
officially, at the Rome airport, I was sitting on top of a trash can wearing ab-
surdly pegged jeans, basically skintight from the ankle to the knee, which took
twenty safety pins, creepers like the kind Christian had taken away from me in
juvie, a biker jacket, and a dark purple shirt with the collar torn off. He was
wearing brand-new jeans, a pressed button-down, and cowboy boots. He was
sixteen and had been going to Alcoholics Anonymous meetings for several

months. Italians and their supposed machismo were a vague menace to Jason. He was always getting brushed by men passing him on staircases or narrow streets and taking it as a challenge to his manhood. He came from Columbia, South Carolina, where his dad had a medical practice, but in some ways he could have been from anywhere. His mom was married to the colonel who commanded all U.S. forces in the Sinai. The one time she visited him she came in a heavily armored Mercedes sedan. Jason always called his stepdad "the colonel."

Charles, Amity's first student, never quite stopped being cool. We bonded over vocabulary, thumbing through the dictionary looking for words that amused us, had practical applications, a vague pornographic ring, or obscure unacceptable associations that were unknown to the rest of the school. Prolixity, valetudinarian, plethora, intransigent, groin (used architecturally), apotheosis, bohemian, halitosis, hypotrophy, nosegay, and bilavian fricative skin bridge (which I claimed was the more technical term for the perineum)—these were our favorite words, and we used them in conversation as often as possible, particularly when we discussed the contemporary art scene, as described in *The Painted Word*, by Tom Wolfe. Soon we were discouraged from hanging out together.

Leandro was the boy who became my best friend. He was fifteen years old, and Charles's opposite. A couple of days after my arrival he sat me down and told me, without apology or adornment, a private and painful story. He spoke with such courage and plain dignity I forgot that he was a ridiculous dresser and liked the wrong kind of music, was unaware of the Bauhaus movement, and was someone I never would have befriended in the "real world." We've been like brothers ever since.

Patrick, on "Guggenheim scholarship" from Dublin, avoided Italian food and lived off banana sandwiches, unless forced to eat Italian, in which case he went monochromatic: pasta, no sauce. He spoke in an incomprehensible Dublin street accent and smoked a constant stream of Rothmans. After I'd been at Amity for a year John Padgett decided Pat and I were both too underdeveloped and needed regular exercise, so we started biking to the municipal pool together in the evenings. Pat smoked while he pedaled. Following in his smoke felt like biking through Dublin.

James was a very sleepy former Woodhall kid.

"James, *come stai?*" I'd ask him.

"*Sono stanco,*" he'd reply. "I'm tired." It was the only Italian he ever learned, and the only reply he ever gave.

Heidi was a sharply beautiful seventeen-year-old Southern girl with a shell no amount of shouting could crack. Marci Padgett got through to her eventually, as she could with almost any girl, and Heidi wept for an entire three-hour rap. Afterward they let her ring the bell atop John's church in celebration.

Sarah had lost an arm, a breast, and half a leg in a fire. The burned skin, which covered her right side, was shiny and inelastic and hard like plastic to the touch. She had to put a cream on to keep it pliable. We treated her with great care. She had terrible migraines and the whole school would go silent for her.

Alexis was a British/Italian girl who always wore matching primary-colored outfits. Whenever she wore her all-yellow one (barrette, turtleneck, skirt, tights—all identical) I'd walk up to her and say "Banana" and she'd laugh and repeat it back to me in her sweet, singsongy little-girl British voice, "Bah-nah-nah."

I asked Alexis about her stuffed animal, Kitty: "How's Kitty today? Did Kitty sleep well last night?"

"Kitty slept quite nicely, thank you," she replied, very precisely.

(The safety of Amity made all the dorkiness seem insignificant. It was a dream to be able to behave this way at age eighteen. I let all my inhibitions go. I was in the habit of singing Gilbert and Sullivan songs on work detail: "He re-maaiiiiaaaiiins an Englishman!")

Alexis looked like Strawberry Shortcake crossed with Sophia Loren. The matching primary-colored outfits clashed excitingly with a Mediterranean complexion, curvy body, and plentiful piles of brown hair. John thought Alexis and I would make a perfect couple, which I found insulting—and extremely compelling.

Nicole was a pixieish, small-breasted, big-hearted, angry girl (with a white-leather bustier in the attic). She loved English, and claimed she was at Amity for failing math. I fell in love with her despite the public outing of her cast-iron cunt.

Benjamin was a very quiet Italian boy with a narrow face, slight frame, clear, shimmering blue eyes, and ridiculous bouffant hair. He was dorky in the way that most young Europeans seem to most young Americans: tighty whiteys instead of boxer shorts; a slingshot bathing suit instead of trunks. He tried to be funny, but could not tell a joke. Attempts featured lots of arm-waving and European sound effects (*"Boum!"* for *"Bam!"*). But he was also athletic and self-confident and 100 percent sincere. No sordid background. No monumental fuckups. Benjamin had just pulled a few too many schoolboy pranks and his dad (Italy's foremost wine authority) decided to send him somewhere where they'd straighten him out and improve his English, too. (John also seemed to get some choice wine out of the deal.) We always thought of Benjamin as a one-person control group for what would happen to a normal person at Amity.

. . .

WHILE AMITY OCCUPIED Villa la Striscia—the Striped Villa—it was probably the most historically faithful building in Italy.

The villa was built in the 1500s by the Occhini family, which still owns it. When the school signed the lease for fifteen million lira a month (about ten thousand dollars then) they got a beautifully proportioned yellow structure that contained, on six floors: three family-sized apartments; a large painting studio; a dining room with a Tuscan cooking fireplace and seating for seventy; ample administrative office space; a library the size of a 7-Eleven; a grand entry hall/ballroom; four more only slightly less grand social and entertaining rooms; two carriage houses, symmetrically placed on either side of the main building; two large servants' quarters above the carriage houses; a cool, cavernous room where they used to drag the potted lemon trees during a frost (called the *limonaia*); the desanctified church that became John Padgett's office; and at least half a dozen rooms whose original purposes were a mystery. There were eleven bathrooms, one hidden behind a fake bookcase. Beyond the main building there was a derelict bathhouse, a porcelain warehouse, a swimming pool, a tennis court, vegetable gardens, and a pond.

Two staircases came down from either side of the front porch and joined in the middle to form a landing from which a single flight proceeded down and level with the driveway. Mirroring these double stairways were two mounds of grass adorned with star-shaped flower beds and delicate flowering trees. The grass mounds were part of some semiformal gardens at the front that ended in a high hedge punctured by a straight, gradually sloping driveway about a kilometer long and flanked by vineyards. On the front of the villa hung the Occhini crest. Occhini means "little eyes," and the crest, which looked like a large elliptical platter pulled into twin points at each end, consisted of a pair of narrowed eyes centered above a big organic-looking heart beneath an array of cookie-cutter stars. Adjacent to the villa was a small wood full of bugs, grottoes, rustic stone benches, pathways, and a Roman-style pool—surrounded by more decayed sculpture—that bred mosquitoes and frogs. In the gardens were large cisterns that fed several fountains through a mysterious subterranean network of iron pipes. Only one fountain still worked, sporadically. The others held standing water and bred more mosquitoes. In the middle of one stood a whimsical cast bronze statue of Pan.

Villa la Striscia was the most beautiful living, breathing building I'd ever seen. A place that by all rights should have been a museum but was a school and a commune and an experiment.

Amity, because of John's feudal nature, re-created a unique sort of vitality that used to be inherent to such places, which were built to house extended families, servants, dependents, animals, guests: a description the school fit with a perverse, totally unwitting accuracy. John (Pop) was the lord and master, an inviolable and intimidating man with total authority to order our lives, who made every major decision for us. There were always at least three dogs on campus. There were chickens. There were geese. We, along with other tertiary staff, were John's servants and guests and extended family. A servant pays the lord a tithe to work the land. We paid tuition to work for the school. We were serfs with a benevolent duke. John was perpetuating the historical use of the place. It felt Shakespearean. It was romantic. (And repressive, which made it *more* romantic!) Like an old way of life resurrected—though what the school was doing was just a short retroactive interval before modern Italian society would recapture the place. Amity's existence was like a seven-year back skip of some historical needle into a two-hundred-year-old groove.

A series of hills rolled away behind the villa, away from Arezzo, and at the very top of them all was a gnarled tree we called the "lone cypress." There was a lot hidden in those hills—wild boar hunters, grappa stills, private chapels, Tuscany folding massive amounts of information and history into itself. The landscape was like the subconscious. And it seemed to represent the mysteries they expected to unfold for us.

Italy is stealthily large. It looks like a small country—smaller than, say, Libya—but if you could open it, flatten out all those hills and furrows and mountain ranges, Italy could fill the Mediterranean. Tuscany was the brain where nobody was going to find us.


AT FIRST I thought I would resist Amity. But then I saw it would be incredibly shortsighted and unimaginative not to take the counselors up on their offer of help. I knew I was a fuckup. And there was good, unfuckedup stuff here. There was stuff that anyone with an imagination could use. It wasn't some *program* or *brainwashing* operation. It was a bunch of crazy zealots who'd got ahold of an Italian villa and were trying to change the world.

Unlike Cascade, it was the most homegrown, least corporatized place imaginable. And as one of the first students there, I was getting the school in its purest, most idealistic form.

*Sign me up, sign me up for the circus!* I thought.

. . .

THE OPERATIVE therapeutic principle of Amity was to prime you, open you up, make you understand something, and then heal you. It was extraordinarily dangerous and effective. The school's strategy for reforming us resembled a bone-marrow transplant: making us vulnerable, wiping out resistance, and then replacing everything they determined to be defective. (In my case, the most obvious thing in need of destruction and replacement was my deceitfulness. This was the first thing they went after.) And there were side effects. In the same way a common cold can kill after a bone-marrow transplant, after three months at the school I was so vulnerable and sincere, so truthful, direct, and open to my emotions that any Elton John song could produce in me ecstatic joy or deep woe— just about simultaneously.

The locus of all this change was a physical place. It was "the gut." The gut was a crucial Amity location. "Where do you feel your feelings?" John or Marci asked when they were trying to open me up in a rap. I pointed at different parts of my body—"My chest? It's a tight feeling." Head shake. "My stomach." "Closer," they said. And they kept guiding, until I got it right. "I feel it in my gut." And then, by God, fuck all, I really did. I cried like I had in juvie. And I wasn't alone.

I have never experienced emotions so powerfully, mysteriously, unwillingly, and eventually, gratefully. Skepticism and sarcasm, the former forward scouts of my identity, went into deep remission. They were laid low. They were almost killed! My personality was completely wiped out. Amity gave me a new one. Whereas before I had been a wounded sarcastic wiseass, a self-serving liar, and a sneak, I became A Beautiful Man of Honesty and Integrity (in the parlance of the school's grandest extravaganza, a *five day*, virtually sleepless thematic ritual called "The Summit"). Italy was the perfect place for such a transformation. It is an emotive country. And it is a country in which I had no points of reference— about which I knew nothing. I could start over. It was the strange yet welcome experience of *acquired innocence*.

It was like *A Clockwork Orange*. (Which was unacceptable.)

The school was a foreign culture within a foreign culture. I cried, cleaned toilets, sang, and occasionally stumbled on Italy. For forty hours a week I inhaled the smell of European Mr. Clean (*Maestro Lindo*) as I mopped marble floors and washed dishes. I learned that the Italian word for emotions is *sentimenti*. I screamed and cried during raps, or *"chaos,"* as Giulio the caretaker called them. I got to know fifties bubblegum music and horrible bands like Jay and the Americans. ("The morning sun is shining/Like a red rubber ball!") I adopted a policy of total transparency about the astounding frequency of my masturbation. I walked into the bathroom and said, my Italian improving, *"Vado a fare la sega!"*—"I'm off to jack off!" Literally, "do the saw." (*"É una segheria qui."*— "This place is a sawmill," Benjamin used to say.) I smoked. Since smoking was the one vice they allowed us, we all smoked. Then Marci encouraged me to quit, and I did: cold turkey. I abided meticulously by all the rules, right down to the one that sanctioned no more than two glass-dispenser shakes of olive oil on a piece of bread. It was fun to be a zealot.

Ron and John and Marci told us about our legendary predecessors at Cascade and CEDU: the guy who tried to have sex with a chicken (I'd heard about him at Cascade); the girl who'd escaped in the back of a laundry truck; the guy who had to walk around for weeks with a sandwich board that said "I Want To Take A Shit On You"; the guy (also famed at Cascade) who confessed to a shotgun murder in a rap, got turned in, and went to prison.

I spent my time in Italy crying and comforting and getting snot on Jason and Leandro's shirts. I became so raw and sensitive that the slightest sarcasm or insensitivity (which came only from Charles and the new students) burned like acid (and was avenged accordingly in raps). Emotions (my former sworn enemies)—joy, pain, fear, sadness—were cherished and immediately expressed. I could outemote the most outgoing citizens of my adopted country. I had the strange experience of feeling jealous when someone else was crying and I was not. Within three months I treated everyone at Amity with a total unironic tenderness. Or, when angry, with unapologetic, top-volume, affronted rage. One new student, Serge, the busted drug dealer son of a player on the Zairean national soccer team, stood up and threw a chair at me in a rap because I was screaming at him with such abandon, such unchecked rage, about the fact that he'd agreed to meet and have an edifying conversation at a certain time, and then did not show up. "I was *waiting* for you, *Serge!* Does my time mean *nothing?!* Are you that *selfish?!*" The veins in my forehead pulsed. Something in him snapped. "What the fuck, man?" he said in his French/African accent, hands clenched after throwing the chair (which missed me). Ron stood, too—neck muscles bulging, looking like a badass. Serge backed down. He was expelled. Nothing like that ever happened again.

On another occasion, much later, when we were allowed to leave the campus, a group of us went to see *Dances with Wolves*. After the movie Jason, Leandro, Nicole, Alexis, and I huddled together, wracked with sobs, holding each other and wailing in sorrow and guilt over what our ancestors had done to the Native Americans, while baffled and genuinely frightened moviegoers fled up the aisles toward the exits to either side of us. Here was a spectacle. A *spettacolo.*

AFTER BEING at Amity for a few months I finally faced what had frightened me most at Cascade: the dreaded all day–all night "Celebrations." They were called "propheets" at Amity.

I skipped the first two, the Truth (where Ron would wake you up at two in the morning and for the next sixteen hours make you confess everything you'd ever done wrong); and the Children's (where he'd do the same thing, but also play music from the *Velveteen Rabbit,* throw a bubble-blowing contest, feed you PB & Js, and generally remind you that you were once a child). The first propheet I went through was called the Brother's Keeper. It lasted twenty-four hours, and was on the theme of friendship.

It started with confession, which was performed in small groups, seated in a circle on the floor (called a "cop-out circle"), with a counselor overseeing us. Momentum would develop as we went around the circle. Ron played a Kenny Rogers song, at top volume, to put us in the mood.

> *Tell it all, brother*
> *Before we fall*
> *Tell it all brothers and sisters*
> *Teh-eh-ell it ah-ah-aal*

Leandro confessed in a matter-of-fact voice. Jason in a *sinner* voice. Charles in a courtroom voice. Truly shameful things were revealed, side by side with pathetic nonsense. Some of us had nothing but pathetic nonsense to offer (pulling hair, stealing candy). Others confessed dark things scarcely believable coming from a teenager (incest, prostitution).

> *How much you're holding back on me*
> *When you say you're giving it all*
> *And in the dungeons of your mind*
> *Who you got chained to the wall?*

I couldn't wait to say everything—though it was hard finding the right tone of voice. How was I supposed to inflect the information that I'd ripped off nudie pics of my mother for blackmail purposes? Contrite? Yes. But not too phony-solemn. I had to just say it as uninflectedly as possible and let the shame come and do its thing to my voice. Also, it was a memory challenge, struggling to come up with everything so that I could really come clean. And if I ran out of good cop-outs I'd just start scraping around and confessing some of the stupid-est, most trivial and ridiculous things—blowing my nose and sticking my hand in the silverware holder while there was still some vestigial snot on it; not doing my dorm cleanup job properly.

> *Tell it all, brother*
> *Before we fall*
> *Tell it all, brothers and sisters*
> *Teh-eh-ell it ah-ah-ha-ahaal*

> *Did you plant your feet on higher ground*
> *To avoid life's mud and stone?*
> *Did you ever kick a good man*
> *When he was down*
> *Just to make yourself feel strong?*

I had kicked a good man named Alex Rodberg at St. Mark's. I had shit-talked Blane to look cool.

> *Tell it all, brother*
> *Before we fall*
> *Tell it all, brothers and sisters*
> *Teh-eh-ell it ah-ah-ha-ahaal*

> *Tomorrow just might be too late*
> *Now is the time*
> *To get your jumbled mind straight*
> *And seek a new dee-sign*

> *Have you ever walked before a crippled man*
> *Pretending you were lame?*
> *And what made ya think one feeble hymn to God*
> *Was gonna make him call your name?*

The first three propheets were run by Ron and Marci and Michael. They laid the foundation for what Amity called "emotional work." John took over for the remainder, in which deeper emotions were to be experienced and more complicated lessons were to be learned. Propheets were held in the basement. The villa's basement was usually Giulio the caretaker's domain. It was vast, with high vaulted ceilings, and filled with barrels and bottles and stoves and fermentation vats that sat beneath the dorms and carriage house and ballrooms. (Amity, in many ways a recovery program—several students were alcoholics—was operating on top of a winery. I remember standing outside the back door one day smoking, fresh from some rap in which I'd been screamed at for my sarcasm, when Aleghero, a blasted-looking old white-haired drunk who helped Giulio out with the grape pressing and took naps all over the property, appeared at an iron-barred ground-level window and thrust forward a brimming glass of red wine.)

For the propheets we went into the cellar. The school sealed off a room down there, carpeted it so we could sit on the floor, put inspirational slogans on the wall, and installed a stereo. When John took over he didn't bother to put us through confession. He only had to look at us and we felt guilt and shame and sadness. Magically, a snotty boulderscape of Kleenex appeared on the floor. A big, moist sacred offering pile appeared before each of us. Hecatombs of Kleenex—offerings to John, the propheet god. In my piety I did not want to waste too much Kleenex or overdramatize. I'd reach back into a used pile to blow my nose, or just let the tears run down my face, or in my grief, reach into someone else's wet discard pile and not care; my snot, my brother or sister's snot, it was all a sacrament.

John sat in a regal, carved wood chair decorated with grapevines and directed our emotions. Beside him, on an elegant table, was a lamp, papers, a vase of flowers, and the stereo—his choir. When we were sufficiently open, he would teach us.

My grandparents would have recognized what was going on here. It was a revival meeting, but with Truth, Friendship, Dreams, Values, and Innocence (the themes of the first five propheets) subbing in for God. And the same emotions that had moved my grandmother and grandfather would move me.

My grandfather preached in a voice Mom described as "thunderous, only to stop and resume as quiet as angels on tiptoe: '*THIS MAY BE YOUR FINAL HOUR ON EARTH! BROTHERS AND SISTERS, YOU HAD BETTER MARCH UP HERE AND GIVE YOUR HEARTS AND SOULS TO GOD!* This could be your last opportunity to make things right with your maker.'"

John bellowed (his geothermal voice resonating in my sternum): "*WHAT YOU HAVE IS SHIT AND YOU KEEP STRUGGLING TO MAKE IT WORK! YOU WILL NEVER MAKE SHIT WORK! YOU CANNOT LIVE ON SHIT. YOU CANNOT EAT SHIT AND SHARE IT WITH YOUR FRIENDS!* So stop trying, *Sean.*" Pause. Then softly, "Didn't you have a dream once?"

My grandfather read from the Bible.

John read from *The Prophet,* by Khalil Gibran (hence the name propheet—"giving *The Prophet* feet"), and he read from it in a true ministerial voice, calm and majestic, his throat muscles relaxed. (I could imagine him in the bathroom next door, limbering up his throat.) He would sermonize for a bit, discuss the meaning of the passages he was reading, or the enlightening slogans on the wall ("THE TRUTH SHALL SET YOU FREE"; "NO MAN IS AN ISLAND"; "TO THE DEGREE THAT YOU FEEL—TO THAT SAME DEGREE YOU ARE ALIVE"; "WORK IS LOVE MADE VISIBLE"; "IMAGINE"), and then employ more music and provocation. John picked songs that were in tune with his lessons, guaranteed to make us cry, and thereby, through the alchemy-of-tears/crucible-of-emotion cause us to internalize his words as gospel. John put his songs on repeat, playing them until they had the desired effect.

That standard cartoon image of a baby crying, like Swee'pea in *Popeye*—with the tears flying out of the eyes, head thrown back: that was us when John preached his revivals.

Unexpected things were deeply moving. A particular frankly struck piano key. The harps in the song "Abraham, Martin, and John." The tuba in "What the World Needs Now Is Love." Neil Diamond's tear-jerk trifecta: "Captain Sunshine," "He Ain't Heavy, He's My Brother," and "I Am . . . I Said." In the Brother's Keeper I wrung a spongeful of tears out of my eyes to "You've Got a Friend" by James Taylor. In every one of the propheets tears plummeted into the carpet, and I saw Jason and Leandro seized with such profoundly deep emotion—bawling over lost childhood wisdom or regretted misdeeds—that they leaned back, spread their arms, and cried out into the open air. It was stunning—ripped my ego and my heart right out—to see a fifteen-year-old boy crying like that, full face to the room. No matter how uncool I thought Leandro was. No matter how alien Jason was. Because here was their nobility. I looked at these boys crying out their deepest pain and saw that I was in no way better than or different from them. And this was a humbling, beautiful realization. They were my friends. I remember thinking, when I first arrived, that I'd never be close with anyone, and then it came as a revelation that I would and could be. That the boundaries of friendship were not delineated by coolness and common musical interest. That I was happy to be among the freaks.

My first propheet was an epiphany. Something was restored to me. Emotion was *not* the enemy! (Then I became addicted to emotions.)

Each new song and lesson seemed to exhume a truth long but unquietly buried. I knew what friendship meant. I'd had dreams as a child. I cared about truth and integrity. Lyrics like, "Did I ever tell you you're my hero?" from Bette Midler's "The Wind Beneath My Wings," or "A working-class hero is something to be," from John Lennon's "Working-Class Hero," or "May you build a ladder to the stars and climb on every rung," from Joan Baez's "Forever Young," and "Wish I could find a good book to live in," from some song I'd never heard before hit me, and the tears plummeted and the snot flowed and I began building another warm mountain of Kleenex. (I knew it was ridiculous, but I did not care.) I was overcome by Joan Baez, her full, fearless voice. How had I grown up in San Francisco and missed all this sixties shit? She'd even been a guest at Mom's Roundtables.

Marci would come over, stroke my back, and tell me to breathe. I'd hear gentle piano notes, and I was off—crying on the first play of whatever John's choir was singing. I'd cry through play three, and then dry up on play four, only to find a whole new way into the sadness of the song, a whole new interpretation—seeing it from another's point of view, thinking of Mom and Dad and some unexpected memory from when they were still married—on play five, and cry anew, until my brain started to fuck with me on play seven (a "mindfuck" was John's term for any intellectual interference with emotions), and I'd cry less naturally, a bit hiccupy, stop 'n' go, stuttery, until John had me hold Jason—the colonel's stepson—and all mindfuckery was washed away as the crying grew more fierce and unfettered than it had been before on any of the seven plays.

I thought, *Wow, emotions, I love emotions*, and held this angry Southern kid.

Between songs propheets were full of wails, gasps, animallike moans, genuinely pained and sad and pitying, drawn out and sweet "oh"s, sounds like laughter but from a completely different source, keening almost, but bigger, lungier, more full and open. Deep, very personal noises came out of everybody. We were boys and girls in a landscape of strewn Kleenex, bawling altruistically, in Italy.

And when we were open like this John planted the lessons of the propheet in us. He taught us about values, about integrity, about friendship, about dreams. We took it all in. We thought about his teachings. We let John brainwash the mindfucks away.

When John gave me Jason, we were an island together. Around us everybody was crying, too. I started to cry harder, out of gratitude, and I saw John benevolently watching us. Then the other counselors brought other kids to us who were in need of comfort. There was always a point, in every propheet, when we would hold each other in coeducational groups of three or four. I held the girls gently, going out of my way to avoid my deeply desired illicit contact with their breasts. I was a man of integrity. I wanted to right the world's wrongs. I was a child again. I can remember the way each of the girls' bodies felt when they were crying: Alexis hot and heavy and very damp, like a small child; Heidi, lithe and tense, with long hair that got in my mouth. It was such an uncomfortable honor to hold her, though inevitably I'd cry less because I was distracted by her sexiness. Nicole was heavier, denser, softer than she looked. Sarah was smaller, more fragile, smelled good, her head wrapped in a scarf to hide the burns on her scalp, her freckles glistening with sweat. We listened to "One Tin Soldier." The line about cheating a friend made me think about what I'd done to Rodberg, and what Dede had done to Mom for Dad's love and company, his butter treasure and jewelry-purchasing power. I cried and shook my head back and forth full of wonder and astonishment about the repetition of history, and the fact that I had wound up here, saved.

AND THEN MAYBE a break. The night would be over. The sun would be rising.

In the bathroom I'd look in the mirror and see a puffy, red, bloodshot, dazed face—a boy who looked like he'd lost his family and lost a punch fight.

We'd take a silent nature walk as the sun rose. I'd feel so pure and

s                              l                         o                         w.

Everything had clarity and meaning. Insects on the walk—*they're our friends, too.* Plumbing in the bathroom, *a miracle.*

At the end of my first propheet Jason said to me, "I love you." And, "You're such a beautiful man." And, "Your friendship means so much to me." And I said, "I love you." And, "You're such a beautiful man." And, "Your friendship means so much to me." I found myself saying things that were real and unexpected and true and came out of some unrehearsed place in me, like, "It feels so good to be held by you." And there was some face touching. Then a loooong hug with everybody.

COMING OUT into the world felt like being reborn!

The whole school would have a dance. We would dance with abandon, and dance beautifully, euphorically—to horrible songs like "Nothing's Gonna Stop Us Now," by Starship.

I loved it all.

*This freak show!*
*This stationary circus!*
*This halfway house!*
*Those eighty cypress trees!*
*Sancho, my armor!*

My voice would drop several registers. For days I'd blow my nose very gently because it was so sore. Initially I was bothered by this. Then proud.

THERE WERE MASS purges of clothes after a propheet. Shirts that we didn't feel represented us were discarded. An attempt to dress from the soul and the heart would follow—an attempt to look good and pure and clean and radiant at all times. There was something Latter Day Saint–ish about it. We were disciples of Amity. Spreading the holy word.

The book Mom had been writing when Dad left her—the one she'd read to us at the dinner table—was about her childhood. It contained this description of one of her father's services:

Mother banged away at the piano as the choir, wearing the mournful expression of career saints, sang:
*Softly and tenderly, Jesus is calling,*
*Calling for you and for me.*
*Come Home, Come Home. O-o-o-h sinner,*
*Come H-O-O-me*
. . .
"O-O-O-H," I wailed as the tears coursed down my face. "I don't want to die a sinner."

At the first O-O-O-H, several of the devout enveloped me as if they had found a genuine diamond on a kid's treasure hunt. They propelled me to the mourner's bench where I fell on my knees sobbing. "Here's little Patsy Lou, Lord Jesus, a sinner," intoned the supplicants. "Only you know what dark deeds she has done, what evil thoughts she has had. Oh God, we pray for her deliverance. . . ."

In the background I could hear others shouting, "I've got religion!" My mind wandered from my own sins long enough to peek and see if Brother Cantrell was going to throw a songbook like he sometimes did when spiritual enthusiasm overwhelmed him. Sure enough he was winding up. Father ducked as the book sailed through the air, its pages fluttering in the breeze.

After my first propheet I felt what my grandmother felt after her first weekend-long revival:

There were shouts of praise going up to God. Much prayer was heard throughout the grounds as well as praise. God seemed so near. . . . One night the power of God was so manifest that people saw the light visibly, and hundreds fell before God prostrated. Heaven was so near.

As we returned [home], some of these joys were much in our thoughts, but a burden was on my heart to work for the Lord. Though only six years of age, the hand of the Lord was upon me.

There were eight of these experiences. They came every two months. The first six were all day and all night. The seventh was three days. And the last, The Summit, was five days.

The three-day one was less about crying, and more about *exercises*. The exercises got stranger and scarier. I was instructed to lie on my back in a dark room, clamp a tightly rolled towel in my teeth, grasp either end of it, and "fight the fight of your life!" by trying as hard as I could to pull the towel out of my mouth, while straining as hard as I could to keep the towel in my mouth. I clamped my teeth and bit and gagged till I dry-heaved, arms pulling and shaking while counselors ran round the blacked-out room—where other kids were doing this, too—cheering and shining flashlights in our eyes. People vomited and cried and the atmosphere got strange and overwhelming and debauched. When the fight was over a bunch of counselors and students picked me up and rocked me like a baby, to a song that had been specially selected for me—"Somewhere Out There," from the Disney movie *An American Tail,* about European immigrant mice who come to the United States and lose each other in the vastness of the new world. This was my theme song. My *identity* song. And it sucked. It was all wrong. Incomprehensible. Not moving. Though its big hammy duet chorus had a certain emotive power, enabling me to put out a respectable amount of snot, until an overproduced electric guitar solo—the world's *worst,* seriously, I challenge anyone to find a worse one—came along and stopped me back up. This was fucked. Some of the other songs were so good. I mean, "You Are So Beautiful." It's Joe Cocker. It's a piano. Strings at the crescendo. That's it. Superb. *I* wanted the classic old stuff. "Captain Sunshine" went to chain-smoking Pat from Dublin. I thought *I* was Captain Sunshine.

Then came a guided visualization exercise right out of Mom's peace trips. I closed my eyes and Marci Padgett took me on something called "The Fantastic Voyage." In the journal I kept at Amity I wrote the following:

I saw a golden light . . . and I stepped out into it.

I found myself on a path, my path. It went through a valley with trees (pine) on the left and hills on the right. My tour guide [Marci] asked me if I heard or smelled anything. The air smelled sweet and I could hear water running nearby. The water was a flowing brook. As I walked I saw a big sign on my right. The sign said The World. My path is The World. I continued on my path. It was cut into the hills on my left and the pines were still off to my left. On the path I saw an envelope. It had Sean written on it in script. I opened it and took out a beautifull but plain card. On it was written in black

You are my special son.

love

Mom

I had lost this letter. I had dropped it. I folded it up and put it deep in my left pocket. I kept on walking and my path rose into the mountains. I could see the whole world around me white and beautiful. My path was on the mountain sides and I saw ahead of me something gleaming. There were three golden keys lieing on the path, linked together with a ring. I picked them up and looked at the first one. My tour guide asked me what was written on the first key. I looked at the key and I saw the word home. My tour guide asked me to look at the second key. I looked at the key and I saw the word love. My tour guide then asked me to look at the third key. I looked at the key and I saw many words, but none of them felt right to me. After a long time I told my tour guide that the word was friendship. She asked me if that was really the one and I said no. She asked me if the key was realy dirty and I saw that it was. I wiped the dirt away and I saw the word people. I continued on my path and it climbed up to the peaks of the mountains and continued going from peak to peak. My path was on top of the world. All around me I could see beauty. Below me white mist covered parts of the world and the sun shone bright and beautiful through the clouds. The mountains were both white and rocky and my path glowed white like a ribbon going from peak to peak. Before me at the peak of a high mountain was a white marble staircase that led up into the clouds. I walked slowly to the staircase and I began to climb. When I got to the top my tour guide asked me if I was alone. I said yes and she asked me if that was ok. It was I was alone but not lonely. I was with me.

The staircase led to my right big toe and Michael pulled me out and back onto the mattress.

Thanks to Amity, I had now been to Middle Earth.

The final Amity event, The Summit, was based on *Love Is Letting Go of Fear*, a book by Gerry Jampolsky—the same man who'd brought Mom a collection of kids' drawings and sayings about peace, getting her going on her peace trips eight years earlier.

With all the group holding we'd been doing in propheets, Leandro and Jason and I were convinced The Summit would involve an orgy. It did not. In The Summit we decided which of our friends would live and die, based on how much good we really thought they'd do out in the world. We performed funerals for ourselves. (Another Amity/*My Dinner with Andre* connection—this exact thing is described in the movie.)

The next day we were warned "there is to be no physical violence in this experience unless instructed by a counselor." Then Jason and I were positioned facing each other and he was told to hold up his hand and be prepared to strike me. He kept his arm up until we were both shaking.

After that the stereo blasted almost exclusively John Lennon's Plastic Ono Band, the songs he wrote when he was in primal-scream therapy. We were jangly and sleep deprived, and the tears came hard. I looked up and saw a slogan from Gerry Jampolsky's book that said: "THE PAST IS OVER IT CAN TOUCH ME NOT." It made sense. Past: Over. No can touch. A moment of incandescent clarity.

For The Summit's finale we struggled to honestly and accurately reveal everything bad and flawed and callow and cowardly about ourselves, and then create a character that embodied all these things. We constructed costumes that brought our characters to life. Then there was a party where we all ran around *being* these characters, our most hated selves. (Except for Nicole, of the cast-iron cunt, who got to be her best self.) After we had been ourselves in the full bloom of our worst qualities, we had to stand up in front of everyone and formulate a statement that expressed our inner best that was an antidote to this character, a statement that we could ritualistically enunciate, and then follow with our names—which some of us had changed (people routinely changed their names in The Summit)—like the statement was a *contract* and we were signing it. The name at the end was the signature. "Sign it! You've got to sign it!" everyone shouted. If your voice was right, deep and resonant enough, everybody would "tsss." As if to say, *"Hot shit."*

After The Summit, armed with our contracts, which would slay all doubt and fear, we were told to go out into the world and befriend strangers. There were legendary stories about former post-Summit friendships. One CEDU girl had met an elderly man at a mall, and when the man died a decade later he supposedly left her millions of dollars. I took the train to Florence and met a stonemason named Marcello, who was restoring the Florence Duomo.

"The entire church—it all dates back to the sixties now," he told me confidentially. "We've rebuilt the whole thing."

After we'd talked for a while he offered to give me one of Brunelleschi's original obelisks, which he had removed and just finished refabricating, as part of his slow and secret process. But there was no way I could carry it.

AT AMITY I received regular calls and letters from Dad. He was frank and open and loving and supportive. He said he knew what I was going through was difficult and painful. He wished he could be there to help. He was praying for me. He was firmly behind me, no matter how long it took. At the end of every letter and phone call he said, "I love you," often adding, "and now I *like* you, too."

When Dad came to the school to visit me we sat across from each other in the choir of the old church that was John's office, a rose window behind Dad's head, and I confessed, easy stuff first: stealing Uncle Jack's handgun from his closet; stealing his cars; drinking; drugs; lies—I told him everything. He nodded with understanding.

Then came the following moment, which the school insisted on.

I said, "Dad, when you and Dede were out and I was at home I would sneak into Dede's closet, open her drawers, and sniff her underwear." Silence. Maybe I hadn't been clear. I added, "I'd, like, bury my face in them and inhale."

I mimed bending my head down, breathing in deeply.

He nodded, seemed to understand, didn't seem surprised.

The school let us go out for dinner in town. We sat under a staircase in a stone-walled medieval basement, and Dad drank a bottle of wine.

He laughed and said, exuberantly, "This place is so good for you!"

I devoured two plates of pasta.

When dinner was over we walked back to the school. On a steep hill Dad said, "Sean, you've gotta slow down and wait for me."

"Sure," I said.

"I've got emphysema. I have to walk slow and take breaks."

I thought about how we used to walk everywhere in S.F. in our matching blue jogging suits.

We stood and looked at the old buildings lining the street. We walked a little more, stopped again. There was wood smoke in the air.

*Emphysema, shit,* I thought.

"It's not so bad," he said. "I just get short of breath. From all those years of smoking. I'm lucky I don't have it worse."

"You'll be all right?"

"I'm getting old, Sean." He paused, a little melodramatically. "I'm gonna die." This was familiar.

He was breathing hard standing there.

Then, alarmed, he announced, "Now I've really got to speed up! I'm having trouble with my bowels!"

He started up the hill.

"Do you know where there's a bathroom around here?"

"Maybe the bar on the other side of the hill."

"It'll be a hole toilet," he said grimly.

We did a fast, tense three hundred feet, then he stopped, breathing hard, held my arm, looked at his shiny leather shoes, and said, "It doesn't matter," in a tone of utter, self-loathing defeat.

"What?" I said. I didn't understand.

"I've just lost control," he said.

We turned and walked back to his hotel in silence. He told me, "Sean, stand close behind when I walk to the elevator so the people at the desk won't see." I did. He had on khaki pants. Looking down I saw a small stain and thought, *No big deal. He shouldn't be embarrassed about that.*

We got into a wooden closet of a European elevator, me covering his back, and silently watched the shaft slip by. Dad opened his door and calmly went into the bathroom. I sat on the bed talking to him as he stood at the sink, took off his pants and white Jockey underwear, and carefully, domestically, hand-washed them. It was a small room, a departure from his usual grand hotel suites. I looked carefully at Dad's body, smaller than it used to be, reduced. I loved him terribly. After he'd washed the pants and hung them on the radiator to dry, he changed and walked me back to school. He stopped at the end of the long driveway, gave me a hug, said he wasn't going any farther, and said good night. Then he walked back to his hotel and failed to get any sleep.

He told me, "I forgot my pajamas, the room had no heat, and I caught a terrible cold."

The cold persisted. Dad stayed sick for months. Then, just as he was recovering, he aspirated a peanut and developed necrotizing anaerobic pneumonia, which put him in the hospital and almost killed him. It was the start of a decade of visits to the hospital. But I would not know any of this for a long time. After the visit he called and said, "I can't tell you how pleased I was to see how well you looked, and how proud I was of your attitude when I visited you."

I said, "I really love the school. And I loved seeing you."

He said, "You're coming along so well. You'll have some ups and downs, certainly. But I feel confident that you have your act together."

I said, "Thanks, Dad."

He said, "I think about you so often. I love you."

Now that I was six thousand miles away, we'd never been closer.

MOM, ironically, didn't understand Amity. She wrote to John Padgett: "My concern is that in an effort to ingratiate your school with Al Wilsey, in order to receive money, you have turned my son against me. . . . [S]omething very negative has taken place between Sean and me and I am very upset about it."

I've only retained one piece of her correspondence from this period, a telegram she sent when I graduated (in June of 1990, at age twenty):

MY DEAREST AND ONLY SON SEAN, ON THIS SPECIAL DAY MARKING YOUR GRADUATION FROM HIGH SCHOOL I WANT TO THANK YOU FOR BEING MY SON AND FOR YOUR HONESTY IN ASKING ME NOT TO BE AT YOUR GRADUATION. IT MUST HAVE BEEN DIFFICULT FOR YOU TO TELL ME THAT. MY THOUGHTS, LOVE, AND PRAYERS ARE WITH YOU ALONG

WITH CONGRATULATIONS FOR COMPLETION OF THIS MILE-
STONE IN YOUR LIFE IN SUCH AN EXCELLENT AND BRIL-
LIANT DISPLAY OF YOUR TALENTS AND GOOD GRADES.
SEIZE THE MOMENT MY SON AND ENJOY EVERY SECOND OF
YOUR LIFE. LOVE YOUR MOM

It had taken me six years to graduate high school—and I still didn't have an accredited degree.

Crazy and silly as it all was, thank God there was a place, briefly, where tenderness was possible, in exchange for money. That was the missing element of
Cascade. Its program was institutional. Tenderness—the key element of my
success at Amity—had been stamped out. Amity's was *inappropriate* tenderness,
to be sure—but it was essential. Tenderness can't be institutionalized. My success at Amity was so fortunate and particular. Cascade was a commercial enterprise, full of corporate despotism, fearmongering, and corporate cheer. That's
why I hated it. I wouldn't call Cascade a success, even though it carried on, aca-
demically accredited, after Amity was long gone.

John's heir apparent slept with a student (reinterpreting John's feudal pre-
cepts to allow for the exercise of droit du seigneur). The school exploded. John
couldn't handle it, the money dried up, and then the kids stopped coming. Amity
self-destructed, and soon John Padgett did as well. He died of cancer in 2000,
heroically, after a failed bone-marrow transplant, which he described in harrow-
ing detail via e-mail. I was lucky to have known him.

Once Amity opened us, much of our time was spent lamenting. Now, with the
*school* closed, we former students lament—I do—the fact that there's no more
school in which our successors can open up and do their lamenting. Complete
transference of lamentation. First I lamented being there. Then I realized I was
there to lament. Now I lament the school's destruction. It's like a bygone political regime that will affect my life forever. A tiny island of lost and lamented to-
talitarianism. Oppressive, unjust, but still worthy of sentimentalizing.

To quote my dad, "That school was a salvation for you. It saved you."

It was the noblest of failures for itself.

WHEN I FINISHED the program I remained so intensely obedient of the rules
that Mom thought I was "afraid of the world." I just wanted to be true to my religion. Now I knew what it meant to respect a group of people and principles,

trust in them, and live by them. I hadn't had faith in anyone in a long time. Here came a shift in the narrative of my life. Because now I felt a weird kind of belonging.

My grandmother wrote about Gouldbusk, Texas, the small town where she grew up, "The community was made up of Baptist, Methodist, and some irreligious people. My parents were the only sanctified people in the community. I was awakened to the fact even in school that Holiness was not very popular, and they had rather not have us. But somehow the desire for God and Holiness was burning in my young heart."

After Amity I knew what she meant. I was ready to go forth into the world and spread the word. The Amity School was burning in my heart.

Here's an old journal entry that does a good job of capturing, post-Amity, the way the place got into my head—and stayed there:

Very Amity moment. The idea that you can save people. Passed on Broadway and 93 a slender attractive woman in her late 20s/early 30s with long black hair wearing shorts and a white T-shirt with no bra and drinking a Budweiser tall boy out of a brown paper bag. At first, when I saw her nipples, I thought, *sexy*. Then, when I saw the beer, I thought, *Oh, woah*. Then I saw the expression on her face, which was a mixture of willing self-abasement, disgust, derision, hopelessness, and vague lust. The lines of anger around the mouth. The wildness. The intoxication. She passed. I turned around and watched her. She was weaving just a little from the beer. She seemed to be heading towards a cop car, as if to taunt it, as if she belonged in it, and then she kept on down Broadway. I immediately had two fantasies about her. One was wild sex. And the other was me saving her life, helping her find herself, and with a proud modesty watching her become an important intellectual or concert violinist (after her first book/Lincoln center gig going out to celebrate and reminiscing about all the hard times but how I stood by her). *She needs saving,* I thought.

Of course, a religious person probably could have written this, too. (Albeit a horny religious person.)

NOW AMITY *is* a hospital. The villa sat empty for a few years, until the owners leased it to Casa di Riposo Residenza Sanitaria Assistenziale <<Villa

Fiorita>>. Old Italians with no family have filled it. Ambulances come and go. I visited in the summer of 2001. A nurse showed me around. They'd installed *elevators.*

From the room where we used to have raps a voice screamed, "*Oh Dio! Oh Dio!* What are they doing to us?!"

The nurse said, wearily, "It was better when there was a school here."

I replied, "It was different."

*But not that different.* Here was anger, helplessness, shameless emotion. It was as if the patients at Casa di Riposo Residenza Sanitaria Assistenziale <<Villa Fiorita>> were the students, freeze-dried and rehydrated seventy years later— or freeze-dried and not adequately rehydrated. All of us a bit desiccated and shriveled. Only the joy was gone. The joy had hit the fucking road.

And where once there was country, the city was encroaching. The vineyards had been torn out next door and replaced with a concrete park—some municipal plum handed out to the contractor with the most connections—covered with a wondrously banal collection of graffiti.

Fuck the pigs! Go away.
Nail Bomb
1.000.000% hate

Follow              we have [anarchy sign]
Me (in Hell)       no rules

I walked over to see Giulio, the old caretaker, who was still there. The nurse said there might be some "mementos of the school" in the old *mensa*—the mess hall. Giulio had the key. We looked. There was only a single, beaten, gray plastic, institutional silverware holder, which he offered me. I *wanted* it. I'd confessed to misdeeds with that silverware holder. But I said, "*No, grazie.*" It wouldn't fit in my luggage.

We stood in silence for a long time.

Then Giulio asked if I wanted to hear about his daily routine.

I said yes.

He said, "I have a coffee. Then I leave the house by seven. Breakfast is at eight—a beautiful slice of bread with prosciutto. Though sometimes no— sometimes prosciutto and mortadella." He took a breath, and rubbed his eyes. "Mortadella is good."

I agreed.

"And a half a glass of red wine. Then for lunch, *pasta asciutta* with *sugo*. A small piece of meat on the side. Half a glass of red wine. And for dinner, meat, salad—sometimes soup. Half a glass of red wine."

"Always the half glass of red wine?" I asked. "Even at breakfast?"

"Yes."

"Never more?"

"One wants to, but no—I have to work!"

We smiled.

"I've seen the weather change a great deal in my lifetime," he said.

I nodded.

He looked sad, then brightened. "During the war, I used to read postcards to a Roman guy in my army unit. He couldn't read. So I read for him. Only the postcards were in dialect, so I didn't know what they said! They were just sounds. I read, he cried, he laughed. I didn't understand a thing."

I WOULD DO a lot in Italy after Amity: I worked as a waiter; I worked as a prep cook; I went to Africa and translated for an Italian tour group; I worked in a museum. Dad endorsed it all. On the phone he told me, "Maybe you should try six months as a gondolier. How's your singing in Italian?"

"Bad."

"I'd hire you for a short trip."

I worked as a gondolier.

Dad considered it "a great accomplishment" that I'd learned Italian. It made me proud to hear him say this. The pride was mutual. He said he was so happy with the way things were going for me. He said again and again how proud he was of my progress since the—to him very sad—day he took me to the survival program in Wyoming and I took off. Now he considered me a bilingual, gondola-rowing, hardworking, nice person.

Whenever we spoke on the phone and I told him about some new job or accomplishment, he'd shout, "Good work!"

AS MOM HAD drifted further away, Dad had moved closer. This was a Dad I had never known before. And when I came back to the States, and Mom drifted closer again, I was sad to discover that this Dad didn't really exist.

I came back because I wanted to be a writer, and it was never going to happen rowing and prep-cooking and table-waiting. I needed to go back to school.

PART FOUR

·

# Resolution

*Seventeen* · BUTTER

WHEN I CAME BACK to San Francisco four years after I'd left, Dede urged me not to, saying, "Stay away from your father. It'll be better for both of you."

I almost believed her. It's hard to resist the belief that people are telling the truth. But in the end I stayed for six months. I got an internship at a newspaper and an apartment in the lower Haight.

I didn't see much of Dad. He was quick to get off the phone, saying, "Gotta go" three minutes into most conversations. He told me not to call him at home. But once a week we had a strange, clandestine lunch at a seafood restaurant near the Maritime Museum, where he wouldn't run into anyone he knew. Dad always sat in a section served by an old Italian waiter. He was proud I'd learned Italian, and liked to make me speak it. The first time we went the waiter came over and I said, in Italian, "Well, my dad here wants me to speak Italian with you. This is embarrassing to me, but if you wouldn't mind acting like I'm doing a good job, like I'm saying something interesting and complicated right now, I'd really appreciate it." He said, "Of course! You speak very well," then turned to Dad and said, "He speak very well!"

"What'd you say in Italian?" Dad asked after we'd ordered.

(The one time in these six months that I was invited to dinner with him and Dede, we went to an Italian place in the Napa Valley. Dad found another Italian waiter, and said, "Listen to how good his Italian is."

Before I could put on my show, Dede turned to me and said, "The only Italian *I* need to know is 'Bulgari.'")

At the seafood place Dad and I talked about things we'd never talked about before.

He said, "You can ask me anything you want. Any question. I'll answer it."

*Well, here's my chance,* I thought.

"O.K." I said. "Why am I never invited over to your house? You know, I'd like to come over once in a while."

He said, "You'll have to take that up with Dede. She's in charge of that."

"So it isn't your decision?" I asked.

"No," he said.

"So you *want* to have me over?"

"Yes," he said.

"Oh," I said.

"But don't tell Dede, it'll get me in trouble."

*This is impossible,* I thought.

I said, "Well, why don't you ever want to talk to me on the phone? Why do you always get off as quick as you can?"

"What is it you want to talk about?"

I couldn't think of anything. "I don't know. I just want to have a *conversation.*"

"We're having a conversation right now."

"But why don't you ever want to have a conversation on the phone?"

"I'm busy."

"When I come over to your office you talk on the phone, about *nothing*—gossip—for, like, twenty minutes, while you make me wait."

"You don't know any gossip."

I felt routed. *Fucker.*

"Why aren't there even any pictures of me in your house?"

He was silent. I continued, "It's all Todd and Trevor."

He said, "I can't do anything about that. Ask me another one."

"You had an *affair* with Dede, right?"

Dad looked down at the table, stuck his knife into the butter bowl, retrieved and ate an entire yellow square off the blade. Then he looked up and said, "I was in love."

I felt myself softening, melting to his bullshit. It was hard to resist. I couldn't quite fault Dad for *falling in love*. Plus, Dad *was* buying me lunch.

Dad said, "Your mother didn't love me the way I wanted to be loved. Dede loves me the way I want to be loved." He seemed to really mean it.

The ice in the water at the seafood restaurant came in oval chips, and it made the water, served in wineglasses, very cold.

I said, "So your marriage to Mom was a mistake."

He looked at me sideways, smiled, and said, "But it gave me you."

I was charmed.

"I haven't been easy," I said, hoping he'd say, "Oh, no, neither have I." Pay me some compliment.

"Pain in the ass," he said.

At the end of lunch Dad ordered a decaf cappuccino. I'd never seen Dad order a decaf cappuccino before. It was completely wrong to have a cappuccino in the afternoon, and a decaf cappuccino was wrong at any time of day. It made me happy. I thought, *He ordered it because of me, because I've been in Italy. Drinking this decaf cappuccino is like putting my picture on the walls inside his body.*

THE CONVERSATIONS I had with Mom were different from the ones I had with Dad. They were open and they were friendly and they were in her house, not hidden in a restaurant where nobody would see us. Mom had sold the penthouse to fund her peace work and moved to a log cabin–like place in the Haight, which she intended to have blessed by the Dalai Lama the next time he was in town. She'd named it the Enchanted Cottage. Two months after I came home she gave me two sheets of heavy paper embossed with a gold monogram and the "Montandon Crest." In her flowing, grandiose script I read the following:

March 4, 1992

This is a handwritten will—written by Pat Montandon on March 4, 1992. This will be my last will + testament as of this date. In the event of my death all my personal property goes to my only heir and Son Sean Wilsey, age 21 who resides on Page Street in San Francisco. That Property includes

1. My Home at 1591 Shrader St. San Francisco, Cal. 94117
2. all of the Personal effects within the house
3. My Mercedes Car.
4. My ownership of the Perestroika Store at Pier 39 [long story].

Sean is a helpful, Sensitive and loving Person with good judgment therefore he is to have complete say so as to any personal distribution of clothing, jewelry (mostly costume) Photographs, etc. My niece Linda Morris should assist Sean in this matter if she is willing to do so.

My love will always be with Sean and Linda, Glendora, Charles, Faye, Nina, Carlos, + Jim—my brothers and Sisters as well as the thousands of Children all over the World who have given me great joy and Love.

    Pat Montandon


Mom gave me all the furniture and cooking gear I'd ever need. I got my driver's license. Finally. I lived around the corner from Spencer Perry and his girlfriend, and we saw each other most nights.

I applied to a bunch of colleges, but the only one I got into was the New School for Social Research in New York City. Before I left San Francisco Mom said she wanted to have an exorcism, to "banish evil from our lives." She lit candles, said purgative words, and made me take some special ashes and throw them across the doorstep at Dad's Pacific Heights mansion, where Dede was sure to walk.


THEN I WENT to college in New York.

I studied for a degree, and on the side I took a welding course and got a job as a welder (almost poisoning myself by keeping a tea-colored liquid rust inducer in a Snapple bottle); I got a loft in Jersey City with an Italian roommate called Marcello, for very low rent, under the condition that we be gone between the hours of seven and midnight every Tuesday so the landlord could come over, watch T.V., and drink beer with his friends; I got a room on a century-old passenger ferry in Tribeca, where I did restoration work (chipping paint, welding); I worked for *Newsweek* as a letters correspondent (mail answerer) and *Ladies' Home Journal* as a fact-checker; I wrote and rewrote and rewrote again a novel that tells my life story but as an allegory involving a corporation that makes money from suicide and a giant casino "where all the money in the world fucks itself"; I got a job as a messenger at *The New Yorker*, thanks to my New School writing professor, Bob Dunn, to whom I owe much (particularly for letting me use his shower when the water went on the boat); I fell in love.

Dad was skeptical. Mom endorsed it all. As Dad drifted further away, Mom moved closer. Mom moving closer wasn't always easy. At one point she just about had me convinced that it would be a great idea if she moved to New York, I moved off the boat, and we shared a loft. But I came to my senses and managed to keep the whole country between us.

ON AN APRIL DAY in 1994, while I was living in Jersey, taking classes at night, and working at *Ladies' Home Journal*, Dad and Dede came to visit. Trevor Traina briefly lived in New York, too, and had a job as Seagram's youngest product manager.

I was walking on Forty-second Street, thinking about dinner (dreading conversation; anticipating food), when I realized I couldn't make out what was in front of me, only bright, indistinct spots, and large shapes. When I got to work I sat down to look at a proof. Letters looked like shiny, black stones. For words I saw glitter. I told my boss, who called her eye doctor, took me downstairs, and put me in a cab.

In the cab my vision cleared. The eye doctor had never seen or heard of what I was experiencing. He ordered an MRI and an echocardiogram, to rule out a brain tumor or a weak heart, but everything was normal. The default diagnosis was "ocular migraine," a form of migraine that disrupts vision instead of causing pain.

I met Dad and Dede at the St. Regis Hotel and told them what had happened. They were briefly interested. Then Trevor arrived and the conversation shifted to whether or not we could get a reservation at a restaurant called Lespinasse, which had just received four stars from the *New York Times* and was located, conveniently, in the hotel's lobby. Dad had tried and failed. Trevor said he'd look into it, left their suite, and went downstairs. In a few minutes he returned and said we had a table. It was obvious that Trevor possessed great skills. We went downstairs and were seated.

"How did you *do it*, Trevor?" Dad asked admiringly.

In my memory we were the only people in the restaurant. Trevor had convinced them to give us the whole place. The room was refined, classical, staid, soft-cornered, with lots of cream draperies, gold braid, high-backed armchairs. Waiters appeared and disappeared. Dad iced roll after roll with French-style butter.

Trevor had ordered the chef's tasting menu—the most desirable meal in New York City. Five courses, a bottle of champagne, and half a bottle of wine in Dad and Trevor were talking with great mutual delight. Dede, to my right, turned, held my eyes (functioning normally now), and said, "You weren't a planned child, you know. You were a mistake. Your father didn't want you. He's ashamed of you."

I was sipping a brightly flavored lobster reduction from a gold-rimmed, bone-china demitasse cup. There was just a suggestion of cream in the reduction. This was the first time I'd had lobster, and it was good.

"You are such an embarrassment to him," Dede said. "He's ashamed when his friends ask about you. Do you have any idea how bad you make him look? With your grades and ridiculous schools. Your job at *Harper's Bazaar* that someone got you as a favor to him."

Unexpectedly—surprising nobody more than myself—I put down my demitasse cup, gave Dede a bring-it-the-fuck-on look, and replied, "That is simply not true. I'm getting A's. I'm on the *honor roll*. I can take classes at Parsons School of Design, which is part of the New School, and it's a great school. Justifiably world famous! Dad had absolutely nothing to do with getting me my job, which is at *Ladies' Home Journal!* Ask him right now if you want!"

I looked over at Dad, who was still talking with Trevor. Dede severed a small morsel of lobster from a large, red-and-cream-colored hunk with tweezerlike teeth. She swallowed and said, "*Your homosexual job* at *Ladies' Home Journal.* Your father thinks you're a *faggot*. It's such a—"

I grasped the left arm of my chair—for leverage—and said, "*Dede. Shut up. Now.*" Then I held my right index finger up in the air between us.

Dad and Trevor chattered.

The encounter mixed in my brain with the taste of lobster.

Dede exhaled, surprised, then took another breath and opened her mouth to speak.

I kept my finger up and repeated, voice rising a few decibels, filling up Lespinasse, "*Now!* Dede. *Shut up now.*"

She stopped. Trevor and Dad went quiet. General silence.

Then Trevor, breezy, asked, "Sean, how's school?"

I felt like I had just fallen out of the sky and into this comfortable chair at this outstanding, ridiculous restaurant. I made a quick answer and conversation resumed. Then I stopped talking and just watched and ate and felt mighty.

*Ten more courses.*

The food was very good. Dad and Trevor talked gaily. Dede avoided my gaze for the rest of the meal. I had beaten her. I was euphoric. I felt like I had shaken something off and could see clearly. I wondered what price she might exact from Dad for this incident, and did not care.

THE FOLLOWING FALL I got a job as a messenger for *The New Yorker* magazine. I was still taking night classes at the New School. A year earlier my creative-writing professor had recommended me to his friend who ran the messenger room, I'd come in for an interview, and from October 1993 to November 1994 called every month until I was hired. I graduated from college a few months later.

The woman I fell in love with, Daphne Beal (from Milwaukee), also worked at *The New Yorker*, in the typing pool. We didn't have a conversation until one day in the park, behind the public library. It was March, my favorite month, for all its contradictions, and it was sunny; the first spring day of 1996. I'd been at *The New Yorker* for a year and a half, and felt a sense of happiness and camaraderie that I'd never experienced before. I was figuring out who I was: not my parents' child, not an Amity zealot. We came toward each other on a path, both stopped, and said, *"Hi."*

From then on we were inseparable. It was messenger/typist true love. A romance at the bottom of the editorial ladder. When she left *The New Yorker* I took a vacation and followed her to Texas, where she got a summer job working for a small newspaper. We went to Mexico and hitchhiked around the state of Chihuahua. When she came back to New York for grad school we moved in together.

THE ONLY TIME Dad came to New York without Dede to visit me, he stayed at the St. Regis again, on Fifty-fifth between Madison and Fifth, and invited me up for dinner at a restaurant around the corner, on Fifty-fourth, also between Madison and Fifth. I came up and met him in the lobby. We hugged and walked out of the hotel. I went left toward Fifth and he went right toward Madison.

I said, "Dad, this way—Fifth's got better stuff to look at."

He shook his head, and said, "We should go this way."

I said, "No, come on. Let's take Fifth."

He said, "No, Sean."

I said, "Yes, Dad."

"With me, Sean."

"With me, Dad."

"Come on, *dammit*."

"*Nuh-uh.*"

"*Now.*"

"*No,*" I said, spun, and walked off my way.

When I turned a second later to see if he was following, he was walking briskly in the other direction.

*Fucking asshole,* I thought.

We circled the block in opposite directions. As soon as I hit Fifth I sprinted to be sure I beat him. We both smiled when we saw each other.

I was a little out of breath.

"You ran," he said.

"No, I didn't," I said.

Daphne came straight from class and met us at the restaurant. Dad liked her, and she liked him. When we left, Daphne walking out first, Dad turned to me and said, "Nice little figure."

I STOPPED WORKING as a messenger at *The New Yorker*, worked in the art department, then started working as an assistant in the fiction department—the best graduate school imaginable. After Daphne and I moved in together, things got tricky with Mom. She ricocheted between manic moments and depressive moments. She told me she kept having a vivid recurring dream of medieval battle and her own fiery death. "I've just figured out what that means, Sean. I'm the reincarnation of St. Joan of Arc. A martyr burned at the stake!" Not long after that Mom asked me to take a month off my job to travel around the world with a bunch of other kids from her peace trips, "retracing our historic steps." I told her I couldn't do it. Then she asked me to take over the peace foundation ("It's time someone else did all this work!"), I didn't respond, and she disowned me. In 1996 and 1997 I received the following correspondence:

*My Darling Son, It is rewarding and fascinating to watch your progress and your admirable approach to life. It inspires me and touches my heart. Thank you for choosing me to be your mother.*

•

*Well Sean I did it! Yes today I met with Gorbachev and also saw Raisa. We had a love feast. Raisa and Mikhail told me they will be in America for quite a while this time. . . . Raisa was absolutely wonderful. She said, "We must see you again Patricia. I know we will, you are such a long time friend." . . . Carl Sagan*

*stared in lanky wonderment, Nobel prize winners and half the futurist popula-*
*tion of the planet watched as Gorbachev hugged me, kissed my cheeks, and held*
*my hands as we stood with the translator on the balcony of the Ben Swig pent-*
*house at the Fairmont.*

.

*Dear Sean Wilsey, You are indeed your fathers son. Your . . . not inviting me to*
*visit; your cool and uninterested response to my phone calls; your lack of con-*
*cern, compassion, and indifference, except when I sob, cry, beg, and have sur-*
*gery; your disinterest in having me meet the woman you are living with . . . has*
*led me to this letter in the middle of the night. . . . Although I loved you very*
*much, and have stood by you time after time . . . I no longer expect anything*
*from you and will not risk more of the same treatment I have endured for much*
*too long. You are not a son to me. Therefore I don't want to hear from you or see*
*you. All the personal photographs, your portrait, etc. are being shipped to you.*
*Your professional accomplishments mean nothing if you have no regard for oth-*
*ers except when you need or want something from them, especially when that*
*person is the woman who gave birth to you. I was a good mother to you . . . you*
*have, for the most part, been a cold, unfeeling Wilsey to me.*

.

*Dear Sean, You may Want to keep these things* [all my baby pictures] *I have*
*kept all these years, for your Own Children Someday. Patricia*

.

*Dearest Son . . . I want you to know how very much I love and respect you for all*
*your accomplishments against odds that would defeat many. Basically, regard-*
*less of things I've complained about, you are a decent, thoughtful person. You*
*would never, in my view, do anything to harm another. . . . I, again, ask you to*
*forgive my failings.*

It was confusing, but at least I was hearing from Mom. Dad called only to in-
form me of his increasingly chronic medical troubles (worsening emphysema,
more pneumonia, emergency throat surgery). When he had a quadruple bypass I
went out to San Francisco and visited him in the hospital. Dad pulled aside the
sheets and showed me the scar on his leg where they'd extracted a long, dark river
of a vein and stitched it into his heart. The scar was long and brown and Amazo-
nian in its curves. He pulled up his shirt and showed me the thick scar on his chest
where they'd slit his skin, sawed through his sternum, and prised open his rib cage.
After ten minutes Dede, who had briefly vacated Dad's hospital suite—where

she was also living, with her own bed and closet and mirrored makeup table—returned and said, "It wasn't necessary for you to come out here. You father didn't want to see you."

I felt myself about to cry, humiliatingly, so I turned toward the windows, away from them both. I wanted to ask Dad, "Is it true, you didn't want to see me?"

Dad said, "You better go. I love you, my son."

I stayed with Mom—who'd undisowned me—and returned to New York the next day.

In the spring of 1998 Dad phoned me at work and said, "Sean, I have a degenerative muscle disease, and I'm going to wind up in a wheelchair." He gave me the name of the disease—inclusion body myositis, medical abbreviation, IBM, at which I laughed, emptily—and said, "Gotta go."

The odds of contracting inclusion body myositis are about one in a million. It's an autoimmune disease that slowly, cannily, stealthily removes muscle mass from muscles' interiors, so a victim never looks any different, but feels incrementally, almost unnoticeably weaker, and weighs less and less, needle inching counterclockwise on the scale, as he fills up with holes. IBM can strike ten to fifteen years before diagnosis, which in Dad's case would've been shortly after he married Dede. Around the time he sent me away to St. Mark's. When its grip is firmly established the disease changes pattern and starts destroying muscles with brisk efficiency.

DAPHNE AND I went out to San Francisco for Christmas. We stayed with Mom at the Enchanted Cottage. For three days Daph baked and frosted cookies, with midwestern zeal. On the afternoon of the twenty-fifth we took a plate of these cookies and went over to see Dad. He looked small and couldn't get out of his chair to greet us. The disease had torn through huge pockets of muscle.

I sat down next to Dad. Daphne sat down next to me. We watched Todd and Trevor and Dede open present after present in the huge skylit room that used to be a porch. This was where Blane and I had taken a door off its hinges and broken into the house. Crumpled wrapping paper and massacred boxes from Tiffany and Co. littered the marble floor. Gratification shrapnel. The Christmas tree reached all the way to the retractable skylight. Dad watched it all dully, smiling every five minutes when Dede would discover another small box containing six figures worth of precious metal and minerals, and come over to deposit a kiss on his lips. Dad turned to me and said, "Touch my arm."

I touched it gently.

"Squeeze," he said.

Through his shirt sleeve Dad's bicep felt like a wrapped stick of room temperature butter.

As we were leaving, Dede, wearing a bathrobe to which she had pinned several just opened two hundred thousand dollar brooches, gave us a tiny, crappy, Mexican watercolor from her prebought present storage closet.

On the street Daphne said, "I can't believe I brought them cookies."

I said, "Cookies are pretty much wasted on them."

Then she told me, "I really think I might be sick." We threw away the Mexican watercolor in the first available trash can.

IN MARCH of 1999, on the beach in Brighton Beach, I asked Daphne to marry me. She said yes. We drank a bottle of Russian champagne in a Ukrainian restaurant. When we got back to Manhattan we called Mom and Dad and Daphne's parents with the news. When we told Dad and Dede it would be a September wedding they said they'd only come if it didn't conflict with the opening of the opera in San Francisco.

A couple of weeks later, Dad placed one of his chimerical telephone calls. I answered and he said, without preamble, "Did you get that FedEx I sent you?"

I said, "No."

*Some sort of engagement present?*

He said, "I need you to sign the letter inside and send it back when you get it. There's another prepaid FedEx envelope for you to do that."

I received the package the next day. It contained a short, legalistic letter, signed by Dad, saying he was "accelerating" his estate plans "with regard to Dede." He wanted all his assets to pass to her, as my favorite sentence put it, "free from trust." This meant that all Dad's money and property, which was being held in a joint trust account for tax purposes, would be shifted into her name exclusively. My signature was required to prove that I understood and approved. I had no idea what it meant. Why did I need to approve?

Dad had told me Dede was getting all his money and property when he died. It was no surprise. I called my brother Mike. He'd worked with Dad for thirty years, and now ran the family business. Dad always consulted with Mike on business matters, and had told me how much he respected his opinion. I'd always been a bit jealous of Mike as a teenager—Dad's perfect son, who was old enough to be my father. Since I'd come back from Italy (since my parents' divorce, really) we'd had few occasions to talk. He said he'd received the same letter.

"Did you sign?" he asked.

"No," I said. "Not yet."

"Me neither," he said.

"What is this?"

He told me it was a lot more complicated than I thought. In the early sixties, when Dad, my Uncle Jack, and their friend and business partner, Gerson Bakar, had first made a lot of money in real estate, they'd established a charitable foundation that still existed and was worth around five million dollars.

Mike said, "The foundation is supposed to be endowed, on Dad's death, with a third of his estate—around a hundred million dollars. It's then supposed to be run by Dad's children, by us, together with Dede. We're supposed to meet annually and decide what to do with whatever money the foundation has made that year. If the foundation were fully endowed, with a third of Dad's estate, its income would amount to several million dollars per annum. And if the majority of us agreed on a cause, we could dip into the principal to make a larger donation. This letter's the first step in making sure that doesn't happen. If all Dad's assets are moved into her name there won't be anything left for the foundation. Dede can't stand the idea of having to work with us. If you sign this letter there'll be no legal impediment to making him dissolve the foundation, and she'll get all that money, too."

I said, "*Wow.*" I was stunned to hear that Dad had this much money. And about a charitable foundation I was supposed to be a part of. Nobody had ever told me any of this.

Mike said, "They're going to put a lot of pressure on you to sign. You'll have to make your own decision about what you want to do. I'm not going to sign, but I wouldn't blame you if you did. As for Dad, Dede's calling the shots, and he'll do anything she says. Call Lad—he can give you more specifics."

Lad—Alfred Wilsey, Jr.—my younger older brother (born in June of 1945, two years after Mike) takes a distracted, fatherly role with me. A typical conversation, following my engagement to Daphne, went like this:

The phone rang.

I said, "Hello."

Lad was calling from his car.

He said, deadpan ironic, and also affectionate, "Hello, *'Dude.'*"

"Hey, Lad!"

Some static and traffic noise. "Did I? Um. Yeah—blender coming."

"What?"

"I sent you and Daphne a blender. There's no card in with it. But it's from me."

"Oh, O.K. Thanks, Lad."

"Why doesn't Daphne ever call me?"

"Uh, I don't know . . . should she be calling you?"

"I want to get to know her. And I can tell her about *you.*"

"O.K. She'd like more information."

"Give the blender to charity if you don't want it."

Then the signal went.

I called Lad and Lad confirmed what Mike had said, adding, "When I questioned Dad on all this he told me, 'Don't make my life harder than it already is. Sign the letter. Do it for me. I don't want to be out on the street.' I don't know what that means. It's ridiculous. But everything Mike told you about the foundation is true. She's trying to destroy the foundation. Don't sign the letter until you hear from us. I'm not signing for now. This is Dede trying to take control of a very physically and mentally compromised Dad. He's weak from the myositis, and she's got him where she wants him."

After hanging up I thought, *I love how no one's ever told me about any of this.* I thought about "gifting rights" on my one-sixth share of one hundred million dollars, the massive power of this, the ability to support schools that make a real difference for hopeless-seeming kids, maybe even start another Amity and do it right. Get a bigger villa. Bring John Padgett out of retirement. (He'd moved to Oregon and gotten involved with the church.) Was the foundation a last chance to turn my relationship with my father into something good? I imagined that I could do good works as a Wilsey, have a relationship with my siblings, *and even Dede,* based on generosity. I suddenly wanted this, terribly.

DAD CALLED. I told him some of what I now knew.

I said, "Will the foundation be preserved?"

He said, "This has nothing to do with the foundation."

"So you intend to keep the foundation, and have it be fully endowed when you die?"

"Yes."

"Well, great," I said. "Then I'll sign. But only if you also accelerate your plans for the foundation. Not just for Dede. Since you want to give Dede what she's going to get when you die, now, go ahead and endow the foundation with its share of your estate, *now,* too, then I'll gladly sign off on what you've just sent me."

Dad seemed taken off guard. He said, "O.K. That's an interesting idea. Maybe we should do that."

Then an odd silence. Dede had taken the phone out of his hand. "What are you saying to your father?" she demanded.

I explained what I knew. I said, "I was telling Dad he should go ahead and endow the foundation with its share of his estate, just like he wants to do with you and your share."

Dede said, "That's never going to happen."

I KEPT THINKING about the money's potential, allowing myself to formulate ever more rhapsodic plans for its charitable distribution. Dad and Dede's philanthropy had always been unimaginatively focused on museums and the Catholic church, but this would change, first with Amity Mark II—that gigantic, redemptive snot factory for America's wasted youth—then by tackling pressing global issues, like the tyranny of fossil fuel: New York and San Francisco, these great cities could lead the way in being powered by hyperefficient Wilsey Foundation windmills! The first of these would go on top of the Summit, then, for windless cities, would come other forms of clean energy generation, solar, yes, sure, but for places where it was flat and cold and sunless—*clockwork!* There would be plenty of room beneath the great plains of the Midwest to install huge *windable engines,* so the citizens of Milwaukee (Daph's home town) and Oklahoma City (I was pretty sure there was still a shuttered Wilsey butter plant there) could rise in the morning and wind up their cities like watches, employing great Wilsey Foundation levers! Clockwork and leverage—it was so beautifully obvious! Maybe *Bulgari* could make the clockwork. And—holy shit yes—*redeemed teenagers could do the winding!*

Eventually I sent Dad a letter about the foundation. I tried to state everything I now hoped and understood, as clearly as possible, with the idea that clarity and sincerity might prevail. I summoned all my sobriety. I could start talking about my ideas later, once the foundation had been secured. I was optimistic. Maybe we could work together. I even tried a little pandering to Dede in order to achieve my naive goals. (And I would be willing to pander more, *much more,* just to stay in touch with Dad.) I addressed it to both of them:

*Dear Dad and Dede,*

*I've been doing a lot of thinking about the letter I received from you. Since the issues you have raised are important issues in our family's future, I have thought hard about them and tried to get everything straight.*

*I want you both to know that I have never had any intention of questioning your decisions regarding your assets. But since you are in effect asking my opinion by sending me a letter to sign, I thought I would speak candidly about what my thoughts are.*

*I would very much like to see your holdings divided into two similarly large parts, one going to Dede, and the other going into a charitable foundation to be managed by the members of the immediate Wilsey family: Dede, Suey, Mike, Lad, Wendy and myself* [Suey and Wendy are my two half sisters]. *I imagine this to be an entity that would require us to come together a few times a year with a selfless and unifying purpose. I know from your actions over the years with the church and a multitude of other charities that you're both concerned with doing good and helping others—so this also seems like an idea in tune with your passions and concerns. And, as a son, there is nothing that would make me happier on the sorrowful occasion of losing you, Dad, than to know that the six of us would continue to come together as a whole, in your name, to share our thoughts, honor you, and do good works as a family.*

*Dad, you are the one who has brought us all together and given us your name. . . . I think we all feel strongly—and independently of our differences—the desire to bring your inspiration into the future. So in this area, and in the area of charity, we have much in common. We all want to do you proud. We all love and respect you deeply. We all look to you for guidance.*

*So, practically speaking, and to borrow your phrase, I would suggest that such a foundation also be set up in a partially accelerated manner, so that we could benefit from your guidance, and so that you would have some years to see how it all worked, and decide if it was a good idea in practice as well as in theory. Perhaps you would also like to see Todd and Trevor involved.*

*Of course I know that you both have your own ideas. You may not want to consider this option. But I would be grateful if you could explain to me your intentions for the money if the vast majority of it does not go into a charitable foundation—an idea which I know you've long been interested in yourself. And—though it's not my desire to contest your judgment—since you have asked me what I think, and I have tried to respond with my best and most serious intentions, I hope some sort of dialogue on the matter is possible.*

*Again, I think this could be a great opportunity for us to better know each other
and to do good in the world as a family.*

*Love,*

*Sean*

Dad called back a few days later. I'd just gotten out of the shower and was
standing on the concrete floor of my bathroom, dripping. He told me, "It means
that you don't love and honor me if you don't sign. How can you not love and
honor me? You're hurting me. You're bringing me pain. And if you don't sign
I'm not going to come to that wedding of yours. I won't go to the wedding of a
son who doesn't honor me." He seemed to be reading lines off a sheet of paper.

"I do love you," I said.

"The only way you can prove it to me is by signing that letter," he said. "I'm
very hurt by you. Both the girls"—my half sisters—"have signed. They're
good kids. They love me."

He seemed sincerely hurt.

"O.K. . . ." I said. "I'll sign." I was unable to resist.

"Good," he said. "Thank you."

We hung up.

Ten minutes later, dry, I called back and told him, voice shaking, "Dad, I said
what I just said to please you. To prove that I love you. But I can't sign."

"It's O.K.," he said.

"If you're not going to come to the wedding I'll be very sad. But can we
please not discuss this till after that?" At this point we'd already changed the day
to accommodate the San Francisco opera.

He agreed, and said he'd come to the wedding, schedule permitting.

THE NEXT DAY my phone rang and a voice on the other end said, "Sean, this
is your *wonderful* stepbrother Todd." Todd had become a Hollywood producer,
and he was calling to invite me to the New York premiere of a film he'd produced starring Faye Dunaway. This was surprising.

It was raining, so I took a cab to the Tribeca Film Center and ran quickly inside. I didn't notice that a large ten-by-seven-inch rectangular sticker detailing
taxi routes and prices, normally attached to the back of the partition separating
passenger from driver, was torn loose, and when I jumped out of the cab it stuck

to my pants. When I walked into the room Todd laughed and said, "What's on your pants?" I looked down and there was a map with the rates and routes for New York taxis against a bright yellow background. Perfect reunion.

I stayed for forty minutes. Todd had invited a lot of people I hadn't seen in years. He moved through the crowd, throwing down mojitos, the theme drink of the evening, laughing, grasping hands, hugging, elbowing, joking. John Traina and Danielle Steel had just announced that they were splitting up. One of Danielle's kids had died of a heroin overdose. I wanted to know if the other kids were having anything like the sort of disastrous time I'd had after my parents' divorce. When Todd and I had a moment to talk I said, "So how are your other brothers and sisters? Your dad and Danielle's kids? How are they doing?"

Todd replied, "They're all *great!* They're all *druggies!* They're throwing parties and drinking and smoking pot! They're like us!"

Before I could explain that I was wondering how his siblings were dealing with the divorce, he was pulled away by the party. I felt a rush of fondness for Todd, who, through his partiality for the Police, had gotten me into a whole genre of music I still love, and who really didn't seem to realize those years had been completely different for me.

I stood by myself for a few minutes, until a gentle, almost frail-looking man came up and said, "Hello, Sean." He held out his hand. I realized this was Dede's younger brother.

I said, "Hello!" with unexpected enthusiasm. He introduced an attractive, clear-eyed, blonde woman as his fiancée.

I said, "Congratulations."

Then there was nothing for us to say. We made some awkward small talk, and when it died out we stood in silence. Just as I was thinking of saying good-bye, he looked me in the eye and quickly said, "I'm sorry about the last twenty years."

A FEW WEEKS LATER I went to San Francisco to introduce Daphne's parents to Dad and Dede (they'd already met Mom, semidisastrously).

The day before the meeting I came by the Pacific Heights mansion for breakfast. Dede wasn't up yet, so Dad and I had the dining room to ourselves. I pulled a chair close and failed to engage him in conversation while he silently and mechanically buttered toast, ate an obscene pile of bacon, and stared at the front of the Sunday color funny section (formerly my domain) without moving an advertising insert that covered the left half of the page. He stared at the half-covered funnies without reading them, and without talking to me. This went on for forty-five minutes, till Dede arrived and said, "Why are you sitting there? Practically in your father's lap. You never used to understand that if you sat there, next to your father, the server wouldn't be able to get by."

Then she turned to Dad, who had looked up hopefully upon her arrival, like a small bird, his vacant face shifting into awareness.

"Look at you," she said to him. "Dressing like a clown." Dad looked down at himself, his expression suddenly shamed, alarmed.

He was wearing beige moleskin pants, a beige and blue plaid shirt, a blue businessman tie, and a kelly green V-neck sweater. The whole outfit looked about three sizes too big.

She turned to me, "He's always dressed that way. He's always looked like a clown." She said it as if Dad weren't even there.

I thought, *If I'd been allowed to sit here nobody would have needed to get by.* And, *Don't you dress him?*

The next day Dad and I both happened to arrive early at the restaurant where the meeting with Daphne's parents was to take place. Dad's new chauffeur dropped him off. He hobbled in slowly. We had a few minutes together at the bar. An attractive hostess walked by, and we both watched her go.

Dad turned to me and said, "Sean, we're a couple of horny bastards."

DAPHNE AND I were married on a pier in Red Hook, Brooklyn, beneath an arch of sunflowers (D.'s favorite), with the Statue of Liberty behind us. The date was September 18, 1999. Dad and Dede and Mom all came. At the rehearsal dinner, the night before, they sat directly across from each other. (Mom rearranged the place cards at the last minute, giving Dad and Dede bad seats, facing her good seat.) At the ceremony the three of them sat together in the front row. Justice Lucindo Suarez, of the New York State Supreme Court, Bronx circuit, presided. Daphne wore a red dress made of fabric she'd brought back from a trip to India, where she'd gone to report a (fucking sublime) piece of journalism. Leandro from Amity was my best man. The reception was in a loft in Queens. We got there by boat. It was a four-borough wedding!

At the reception Mom threw a tantrum, threatened to walk out, calmed down when I told her to, gave a speech that began with the line, "Perhaps some of you remember the cold war between our country and the Soviet Union," sulked, stayed in a bad mood for a month, and recovered in time to send us the most beautiful, thoughtful, and personal wedding present we received. Lad and Mike gave warm, funny, heartfelt speeches about having a brother who was young

OH THE GLORY OF IT ALL

enough to be a son. Mike said, "You turned out great in spite of us all." Dad and
Dede were silent (except when Dad said, "I'm starved! Where's the food?")
Trevor Traina, who had started an Internet comparison-shopping company
(Comparenet) and sold it to Microsoft for seventy-six million dollars, didn't
come. Todd Traina did unflattering impressions of my mom. They all left early.

Daphne and I went to Spain on a honeymoon that Dad paid for. When we got
back Dad fell out of touch again. I'd decided to ignore the letter about his estate,
and just see if he brought it up again. It seemed like the foundation had little
chance of survival, but I didn't want to sign away all my hopes for it. At this
point both my sisters and Lad had signed (Lad after adding the following adden-
dum: "This acknowledgment relies on the fact that no changes have or will be
made to the Wilsey Foundation additional funding intentions."). Mike, who had
always had a close relationship with our father, told Dad exactly what he
thought, with directness and integrity. When Mike refused to sign Dad refused
to have anything to do with him. He did his best to cut him out of his life. Mike
had been there when the foundation was set up, and he knew the intentions Dad
and Uncle Jack had once had for it. Mike had been Dad's intimate for fifty-plus
years. He ran the business. But now he spoke to Dad even less than I did.

ON THANKSGIVING I called Dad in the country and said, "Hey, Dad, happy
Thanksgiving."

He said, "Where are you?"

I said, "With Daphne's family. Who's there with you?"

He said, angrily, "Todd and Trevor and that's all."

I said, "Oh."

He said, "I want to know if you're going to sign that letter of mine."

I said, "Happy Thanksgiving?"

He said, "I want to know."

I said, "I'm not going to talk about that right now."

"I need to talk about it right now."

"I'm just not going to talk about it right now."

"Then—good-bye!"

He hung up.

So I sent Dad another letter. This time I didn't bother addressing it to Dede as
well. I figured I was maybe bringing about the end of our relationship. But
the respect of my brothers had begun to matter more to me. I said not signing
didn't mean not loving, and had nothing to do with love or respect. (My exact,

embarrassing sentence was, "When did love and respect become obedience?") I said he was obviously under a lot of stress, and didn't seem like himself, so I had decided to make my own decisions—not that they much mattered. I pointed out that on the one occasion he'd come close to being straight with me Dede had taken the phone away from him and delivered "unbelievably longwinded doubletalk." (This phrase got me in trouble.) I said, "Without a guarantee that the foundation will be preserved, and will be a viable foundation for all of us, I won't sign any letter."

TWO MONTHS LATER, late January 2000, my phone rang, I picked up, and it was Dad.

He said, "Sean, Dede's not here and I'm all by myself. I want you to know I respected your letter. And I agree with you that two people can agree about one thing and disagree on another."

I said, "Great!"

He said, "That letter showed a lot of your journalistic abilities. Did Daphne help you with it?"

"No."

"Did she read it?"

"After I sent it."

"What did she think?"

"She respected it. She thought it was the right thing."

We were quiet for a minute.

Then he said, "I fell down twenty-five stairs—backward. I cracked a rib. Myositis makes my legs give out. I don't get any warning."

"Are you O.K.?"

"I'm fine."

Quiet again.

Then he said, "Want to know who's right here next to me? Melissa. Melissa. She looks after me. She's my protector." (Melissa was his Jack Russell terrier.) "O.K.," he said. "Gotta go."

I said, "I love you."

He said, "I love you with all my heart."

"You know I feel the same, Dad."

"I love you, love you, love you, my son."

It was one of those weird, rare, agendaless, Dede's-away phone calls. It made me feel like we were close.

After that the subject of the Wilsey Foundation, and the unsigned letter, was dropped.

I  SOLD  the proposal for this book, one hundred pages about my parents' divorce and my experiences at St. Mark's and Cascade. I called Dad to tell him the news, thinking he'd be proud. It didn't seem to sink in. Then I called Mom. She told me she was also writing a memoir about the divorce and her peace work. "I think it's just incredible," she said. "A mother and her son writing about the same experiences. We can go on tour together!"

A few weeks later the phone rang, I answered, and Dad said, "What's your book about?"

I said, "Hi, Dad." Silence. "It's mostly about my experiences in schools."

He said, "You never told me your were writing a book about that."

I said, "Yes, I did. I told you I was writing a book about exactly that. It'll also deal with my youthful indiscretions."

"Oh no! You're not going to write about those. Are you going to tell them about stealing my gun?"

"Oh! I forgot about that. Maybe."

"Driving the ATV off the cliff?"

"Maybe."

A friend of mine had driven Dad's all-terrain vehicle off a cliff, and Dad always thought that I'd done it and just made the guy take the blame.

I said, "I've been writing about St. Mark's. Guess how many bottles of liquor are in the yearbook?"

"In the *yearbook?*"

"Yeah, in the yearbook."

"Twenty?"

"A hundred and fifty!"

"What?! *That can't be.* That was a good school."

"It is true. And there was a rape while I was there, too. Committed by a kid I knew. In my class."

"Who was the girl?"

"A sophomore. Pretty. Popular."

"She must have had loose morals."

Silence.

"Well, I'll be visiting. Seeing my old adviser."

"What about your friend, the Russian? You going to look him up?"

"I don't know."

"The Russian's probably making a mint in computers."

I agreed that this was possible.

"I can send you some things I have in my files, if that would be helpful."

"That would be great."

He ended up sending me all my report cards, a couple of psychiatric evaluations, and his recollections on visiting me at St. Mark's.

"What's the title for your book?"

"Don't have one yet."

"You're secretive."

"No, I'm not."

"What's your title?"

"I don't know."

"How about *The Travails of Sean?*"

ON MAY 21, 2000, my thirtieth birthday, Mom called first thing in the morning and said, "Sean, you started out as a slight swelling above my pubic bone. I had your father feel it." (This was a new variation on her usual birthday routine of calling and saying, "My water's just broken!") Then she said, "You know, I think *your* birthday should be a celebration of *me*. I was the one who did all the work. You didn't do anything!"

I was just managing not to take this personally when she told me, "I took too many anxiety pills because of those fires before you were born, and that may be why you slept for the first six months. Oh, and did you hear that Dede's house in the Napa Valley burned down? Isn't that great?"

"Yeah?" I said. It was true. Dede's country house in Oakville, where Sarabelle the dachshund disappeared, had burned to the ground: the only misfortune I've ever known to befall her. Later in the day I heard from Mike and Lad. But I didn't hear from Dad. It had gotten so that our only conversations were on important holidays, when I had an excuse to call.

A few weeks later I called to wish Dad a happy Father's Day. He said, "Hello Sean!" and started coughing.

I said, "Happy Father's Day."

It was the first time we'd spoken in two months.

"How's your mother?" he asked.

I said, "I've been hearing rumblings of discontent."

"Money troubles?"

"Of course."

"That's your mother."

At around the three minute and thirty second mark our conversation started to warm up and become natural. At which point Dede interrupted—snatching the phone away from Dad—and said, "I don't know what you think of the way your father sounds."

"He sounds fine," I lied. "A bit sleepy."

"*Exactly*," she said. "He's *very* sleepy. He's been lying in bed since we got home from a party last night at midnight."

"Two in the morning!" Dad shouted from the background.

"It *waasn't* two in the mor-*ning*," Dede said.

"It *felt* like two in the morning," Dad replied.

"Ha! Ha! Ha!"

She said, "Some of the other children—not you—are awfully paranoid when they hear his voice these days. They say, 'He's ga-ga!'"

(Mike and Lad had just told me that proving Dad was not of sound mind would be the only means of saving the Wilsey Foundation.)

"Right now he just seems sleepy," I said. She put him on again. I said, "Dad, when was the last time you flew the helicopter?"

"Back in April. I flew it to Stockton with a copilot for its regular maintenance."

"So you were eighty-one."

"Yep."

"You might be the world's oldest helicopter pilot."

This seemed to please him.

"I might be."

"That's cool."

"Gotta go."

I LEFT my job at *The New Yorker* and started working full-time on this book and editing for *McSweeney's* quarterly. Mom, meanwhile, finished her book and asked me to read it. I said I would. It arrived FedEx the next morning. After reading the scene on page nineteen, in which she yanked her Olds to the side of the road, told me she wanted to kill herself, then immediately apologized—a recast/whitewash of the deadly serious thing that happened at night on the stairs in the penthouse—I wasn't sure I could stomach her version of events. Daphne read the book for me. "It's not *so* bad," she said. "Especially the stuff about her childhood." I read it, too. Daphne was right. Everything about Mom's childhood in Texas and Oklahoma was clear and moving and full of life. The rest made me queasy.

Daphne and I applied for a shared residency with the Lannan Foundation, which owned two houses in Mom's childhood landscape, a small town in West Texas called Marfa. We were invited to stay and work in one of these houses through the summer and into the fall of 2000. Before going to Texas I went out to California for three weeks—my plan was to do research in San Francisco and write when I got to Texas. I couldn't stay with Mom. She'd sold the Enchanted Cottage and was living in a rental apartment on Nob Hill. Mike got me my own rental apartment at Northpoint, the complex across the street from the Wilsey butter offices, where Dad used to keep a place, the so-called "nooner," for his lunchtime trysts with Dede. (I may, in fact, have been staying in "the nooner.") I told Mom I would be writing about some things she would find difficult to read. "You have a right to tell your story, Sean," she said. "I'll help you in any way I can." She gave me a huge pile of press clippings on the divorce. We sorted through thousands of hours of videotape from the peace trips. She answered every question I asked her. Mike and Lad helped, too. They told me about Dad and Uncle Jack and San Francisco society. Mike's wife, Bobbie, told me, "We were worried about you after the divorce, but Dede kept the family away. And what could we do? You were your dad's son—not ours."

I went up north for five days and visited Cascade (no hard feelings), then drove over to the coast and visited Blane, who worked in a brewery in Humboldt County. When I got back to San Francisco I saw Mom and Mike almost every day for a meal or a drink. I met some old friends of Dad's. I heard a lot of stories. I spent the afternoon with a sick man and his pretty, Italian wife—Russ and Helen Reese—who'd been in the dairy business and known Dad and Uncle Jack since the forties. They told me how Uncle Jack's doctor had instructed him to cut his drinking down to a glass of wine a day, so Jack just found a glass that could hold an entire bottle of wine. This was right before he died. The more I found out the more I broadened the scope of this book. I kept seeing the parallels between my experiences and the experiences of my parents and grandparents. History repeating itself.

I saw Dad twice. The first time I visited him and Dede in Napa. They'd invited me for lunch at the dream house Dad had built for Mom. It was covered in wisteria vines, surrounded by explosions of birds and flowers. The lawn looked radioactive, like someplace where lightning had struck green and then *stayed*. Flowers were everywhere, in hectic abundance. Dede is famed for planting forty thousand tulip bulbs every year (not personally).

Mom's house had come to full fruition without her.

When I arrived there was no sign of Dede. I found Dad on the porch and sat down with him. Dad said, "Ten thousand of these tulips come from Holland every year."

I said, *"Wow."*

"It's a lot of work planting forty thousand tulips."

"Yeah?"

"Want to know how they do it?"

"Yeah."

"*Yes*. Quit the 'yeah's."

"Yes."

"We put them in three-man teams. Michael, the groundskeeper—he's a hippie—and two of the boys"—this was Dad's term for Mexican men—"they line up Indian file and walk, one poking a hole with a big stick, the next dropping in a bulb, and the last covering it up. It goes on and on for weeks like this."

Across the lawn water splashed in an eight-shaped pond with a solid slab of stone bridge, like a belt buckle at its waist. Mom had designed it.

Dad was wearing an old JC Penney shirt with a hole in the shoulder, soft moleskin pants in which his muscleless legs swam, and supersoft, fleece-lined, Velcro-closed, ankle-high suede booties.

Open blossoms swayed in the breeze; terrain gently sloped; a meadow was just visible across the creek. Two grazing horses could be glimpsed through branches.

Then Dad said, "Helen Reese tells me you speak Italian better than she does." I blinked. I hadn't told him I'd seen his old friends. *Shit, busted*, I thought.

Dede, smelling of freesia, face tight, compact, strode out of the house and said, "Who are you talking about?"

I thought, *Oh—he's warning me. He wasn't supposed to speak about this until Dede came out and she could catch me by surprise.*

I said, "This couple, the Reeses, old business associates of Dad's," and kept a straight face.

Dede said, "Why are you looking up these people? You're writing a family history! That's what you're doing, isn't it? I would be *surprised* if you weren't interested in finding out about *your family*. But if you keep snarking around you're going to find some terrible, *scandalous* things! Things that will hurt a lot of people, including *you* and your *mother* and your *siblings, very much!* Do you want to hurt your family?"

"No," I said.

Dad cleared his throat— *"hrreheh"*—looked at me, and said very slowly, "I've done some bad things that I'm not proud of."

Dede said, "He's talking about *scandalous* things that would *terrify* and *shock* you! Keep *snarking* around and *you will find them out!"*

*What? What the fuck is going on here?* I thought.

Dede said, "So what were you doing with the Reeses? I want to know."

I said, "I was finding out about the butter business." This was, in fact, what we'd spent most of our time talking about, until Mr. Reese had a beer against doctor's orders and told me about a crony of Dad's who'd taken his arm on Columbus Street, forced him down to Carol Doda's strip club, and threatened to kill him unless he faked the weight on some cream shipments. ("That's who your dad did business with.") The information jibed nicely with my idea that there was no honest way to become rich, and that the Wilsey Foundation was our family's only path to redemption.

Dede said crisply, "That's obviously not true. If you want to write about the butter business why not go see Land O'Lakes or Fleischmann's?" She squinted at me. "You're writing about your father."

Before I could answer Dad broke in, irritated, *perturbed,* and said, "Why would he go talk to the *Fleischmann's* if he's writing about *butter?* They're not in the butter business!"

Dede lost her train of thought. "Well—*margarine!"*

Dad gave a vigorous head shake no.

Recovery time for me.

I shouted, "Yeast!" They turned. "Fleischmann's makes yeast."

Dad smiled. He was enjoying himself. He looked back at Dede and told her, "They're not in butter. They make edible oils."

Dede seemed young and chastened. She looked around at the scene of expensive perfection, huffed, and started talking about her gardener. "That *stupid hippie!"* she said.

"Don't they make *yeast?"* I asked.

"Why would you do something *I* don't like?" Dede said. "I hate sunflowers. 'Where are my snapdragons you were supposed to plant in June?' I asked him.

He didn't have an answer for that. Just some mush about a misunderstanding. It's not *smart* to not do what I *want. Not smart.*"

Dad said, "He's a flower child. I call him the hippie."

I said, "I like the lawn."

Dede waved her hand at the lawn. It lapped against a stone path, just below where we were sitting.

"Because now you can *see* it," she said. "Now that there's not that stupid hedge your mother put there."

I realized Dede had ripped out a hedge. It was her one cosmetic improvement over twenty years of occupation. She hadn't even *redecorated*. She might as well have been wearing Mom's old clothes from the seventies while remarking on the hedge. The whole place screamed *"Mom!"*

I looked at the lawn and thought, *Don't be talking about my mother.*

"Sorry your house burned down," I said.

"My house never had anything as hideous as that hedge of your mother's," Dede said. "And I've rebuilt it completely since the fire. I told Todd and Trevor, 'I'm going to bring it back for you, like Brigadoon. Just like Brigadoon. It'll rise up from nothing on the horizon, every last shingle and doorknob.' You've seen *Brigadoon.*" I had no idea what she was talking about. *Brigadoon?* Sounded like a western. There was a fanatical light in her eyes.

A butler appeared and said, "Lunch is served."

We stood and slowly walked to a table that had been set on the far end of the veranda. In silence we ate a lemon infused, extremely delicate, almost effervescent soup, so light it was like a mist, and for which battery acid could have been substituted. I thought, *What's the "scandalous, terrible" thing?*

*Murder?*

*Rape?*

*Illegitimate siblings?*

*Murder . . .*

*. . . of illegitimate siblings . . .*

*. . . conceived in rape?*

Lunch featured all fresh produce, grown on the grounds.

Postsoup, conversation resumed.

Dede said, "If you want to write a family history, I can tell you about your family. Your grandfather, your father's father, had an affair with his secretary for twenty years. Until his wife died and he finally made an honest woman out of her."

Silence. I looked at Dad.

"Your father's mother hated her son," Dede continued. "I'm not going to go on for long about this because you've called me 'longwinded.' I *kept* that letter. But I want you to know that if you keep snarking around like this you're going to find terrible things you don't want to find. In fact, if you keep this up I'm going to just *tell* you. And you won't like it. Leave it alone. You don't want to know."

Ironically, Dad and Dede were changing the course of my writing, leading me to wonder about the family's history and whether it might have any relevance to my own experiences.

I said, "I have to admit, now I'm intrigued."

Dad said to Dede, "You're just fanning his curiosity."

*"Yeah!"* I said.

Then he turned and shouted at me, with surprising strength, *"Elbows!"*

At first I thought he was busting me on shouting *"Yeah!"* then I recognized the meaning of the word, and looked at my elbows.

"Get those elbows off the table!" he said.

Dede said, "Helen Reese might have done some gallivanting of her own back when she knew your father, but she probably didn't tell you about that."

"I've done some things I'm not proud of. Leave it at that," Dad said.

Dede said, "Don't you have some pictures of your wedding to show your father?"

I pulled out a stack of photos and showed them to Dad. After he'd looked I said, "These are doubles. Do you want some?"

Dad said, "No."

"You should take one," Dede said. "They're your son's wedding photos." She turned to me. "Your father had a terrible time at that wedding. All the relatives kept bothering him. They all want his money. And he just wants them to go away."

AFTER LUNCH Dede went inside to make a phone call and Dad and I returned to the wicker couch. I poured on the cheer, ran out fast, and silence prevailed. Dad looked down at his booties. I looked across the lawn at a splashing and rolling fountain. It had broken regularly and made Dad angry back in the eighties. Mike had recently told me that the house was originally going to be left to me, but now was being left to Dede, like everything else. I thought, *I could've given it to Mom.*

Dad asked, "Is your mom still mad at me?"

I said, "Yes."

He looked pained.

I thought, *Too bad.*

"Does she say nasty things about me?"

"No. She's got a sense of humor about it all now." I laughed unconvincingly.

I told Dad I'd spoken to Clifford Mooney, his old chauffeur/factotum/friend.

Dad said, "Does he ask about me?"

"Yes," I said. "Everybody does."

"I miss him."

I didn't say anything.

Dad said, "Are you going back to the city now?"

"I'm meeting a friend here." A girl I knew from Amity lived nearby.

"Are you having dinner?"

"Yes."

"Go to Piatti." A trendy local restaurant. "Use my name to get a reservation."

Looking across the property, I saw that the willow tree I used to play under had died.

Dede returned and said, "We're going to my house in Oakville now. Sean, you can come along and *see* it."

I followed their car. When they turned down the driveway to Dede's house I was amazed. It had been destroyed. But here was an absolutely perfect, scaled and detailed facsimile. For the next hour Dede took pains to show me every last closet.

She sat Dad down and gave me a guided tour. It was a 100 percent custom construction job, re-creating objects and decor that were standard when the place was built, in the 1800s, and when Dede and John Traina decorated it, in the seventies—everything specially fabricated to the specifications of her memory and old photographs. I hadn't been there since I was a teenager, and seeing the place brought on a strange form of déjà vu, a déjà vu that was not déjà vu, because I had never seen this actual place before. I was walking in Dede's memory, incarnated with Dad's money. It was all reconstructed to the last photorealistic detail, so a green sitting room with wicker furniture and a white trellis—*inside:* an indoor trellis—was expertly restored, shimmering there like a mirage: back. A long, polished, dark-wood table from some *New Yorker* cartoon about rich people filled the formal dining room. Dede told me about Victorian parlor moldings, which can still be acquired through some satanic channel. She pointed to the ceiling. "I looked at so many different moldings and showed them to Todd, and Todd didn't like any of them, so I said, 'I'm doing this for *you*. Do you think I care about this house? I don't give a damn.'" Apparently Todd had fallen in line, because there they were. There were also rosettes.

She told me, "We put up wallpaper and tore it down and replaced it because it was too buttery a yellow."

In the formal living room she pointed at a painting of a brunette in a white dress by some nineteenth-century society artist, and said, "I saw it in an auction catalogue. So I bought it and had it cleaned and installed!" This was still only the ground floor.

We continued through a sitting room, a pantry, a vast kitchen.

Then, in the front hallway, Dede opened the door to something new. An elevator. An elevator with a big painting of Dede in it! Dede faced me as I entered. Now I was trapped between two Dedes. The young, painted one leaned on a picket fence, pastel flowers in the background, a sly, conspiratorial twinkle in her eye. On the side walls were Todd and Trevor as kids. Smaller, behind them, were pets and employees: Alda, the maid, next to Snowball, the cat they'd had in the seventies, and Sarabelle, the possibly poisoned dachshund. And then I noticed Dad in his helicopter, smallest of all, far away, high in the sky, his face just a smudge. A dictator would have liked this elevator. The way it glorified and misrepresented terrible history, was full of conflation and omission and cheer. Dad had paid for this shrine, which was intended to move him upstairs—nobody else needed an elevator—but the era depicted was pre-Dad. Maybe the small helicopter Dad was a reference to the heady days when he was still married to Mom but flew over here to watch Dede wave up at him from the window of this house's ghost. Dede lured him down into her life from the sky. The fool. And here he was being mocked in his own geriatric elevator. We took it to the second floor.

On the second floor were two one bedroom apartment–sized master bedroom suites, one for Todd and one for Trevor. The twin suites were different in that one contained a fireplace and the other opened onto a massive porch with views of the valley. "I wanted to make them different, but equal," Dede said. First she showed me the one with the fireplace, Trevor's. In his bathroom she pointed out a partner-style tub and said, "Tea for Two. If you're ever looking for a big bathtub, that's the *only* brand to get. Tea for Two."

In Todd's suite she ushered me into the closet, put her hand on one of the walls, and said, "I spent so much time moving this back and forth trying to get the dimensions just right. Do you think I got it?" *What are we doing?* I wondered. *What unnatural act is this? Do I think you got the dimensions of Todd's closet right? You drove my mother insane, took away my father, and you want to know this, from me?*

I said, "Yeah. It looks good. I think you got it." And, actually, I do think she got it right.

I thought about my stepbrothers and their vast supply of rooms and closets where they stored their overflow of expensive things. Rolexes and leather jackets and Microsoft-millionaire/Hollywood-insider baseball caps. Is multiplicity what it's all about? The American dream? Multiple dwellings. Multiple vehicles. Multiple sex partners (in Dad's case). It occurred to me that T & T had at least five rooms in the various homes of their parents and stepparents and, doubtless, numerous homes of their own. They were loved. It also occurred to me that the more time I spent with Dede the more I started to think and talk like my teenage self.

We took the stairs to the third floor. Dede went first. Following behind, I thought, *Hers is not a pretty ass. It's ugly and scrunched. And what's up with the puke-green Van Halen pants with the pale rose pattern all over them?* Upstairs was a huge office with an antique partner desk. Dede told me, "I got this for Trevor and he called me the other day and said, 'Mom, guess where I am. I'm paying my bills *at the desk.*'" She showed me an adjacent screening room. *Why put a screening room in the brightest part of the house?* I wondered. A trapdoor in the ceiling led to a widow's walk on the roof. I went up and poked my head into the hot, bright day. In every direction, green vines.

We returned by stairs to the ground level. Dede pointed out and opened up several clever storage and utility closets on the way. I thought we were done; she was going to let me have a few minutes with Dad. Then she said, "Oh!" and pulled me down a flight of stairs into what used to be a dank old basement and was now deep and dry and sinister in its vast windowlessness.

It was well and efficiently lit down there, like a very nice bomb shelter. She showed me a wine cellar, an exercise room, storage, pantries.

All day I'd been afraid and hiding it. Now I was afraid and not hiding it. I was sweating. I thought, *She's going to push me into a special chamber and brick me the fuck in! She'll get me off balance, push me into some alcove, a wall'll swing closed behind me, and then a crew of bricklayers'll materialize and seal me in for eternity. No one's going to live here, anyway. She built it to entomb me against my will! My blood will make Todd and Trevor enjoy the porches and fireplaces and desk and screening room more when they visit! I'm what's missing! The final touch on this place is me!*

I took a breath. *C'mon, Dude. She thinks just showing you this place is torture enough. That's why she's doing this.*

Dede was looking at me. She said, "Sean?"

I SAID GOOD-BYE to Dad, then drove over to St. Joan of Arc, the church where we used to hold hands during the service. It's a humble church. One of the last things that still seems genuinely rural in the Napa Valley. I sat in the car and looked at it. I remembered that Mom had recently told me she believed herself to be the reincarnation of St. Joan of Arc.

I called Piatti, the restaurant Dad told me to call, and asked for a table. They said, "Will you be dining with Mr. Wilsey?"

I said, "No. It'll just be me and a friend."

They said, "But Mr. Wilsey also has a reservation for two at seven-thirty tonight."

I thought, *Wha?*

So I reserved for half an hour before him.

When Dad and Dede showed up, Dede was surprised. Dad *acted* surprised. I pretended it was a coincidence, and so did he. We got to see each other one more time.

BACK IN THE city I called Mike and told him about lunch with Dad and Dede. He said, "I don't know what they're talking about. Dad's said some strange, out of character things lately. I almost never see him, but he came into my office and cried a few months ago. Then he said, 'If I were younger and had the strength I would leave her. But I don't have it in me. I don't have the fight.' He told Lad, 'She'll throw me out if I don't do what she wants. And I don't want to live alone and shop at Safeway.'"

I called Lad and told him about lunch. I said, "She told me Dad had done 'scandalous things' that would 'terrify and shock' me. And Dad hung his head and said, 'I've done some bad things that I'm not proud of.'"

Lad seemed unsurprised. "That's the way they are," he said. "It was just Dad's medication talking. Do you want some advice on how to deal with Dad?"

"Sure."

"Be a marshmallow. He's only got one to three years left. There's no awful deed. There's no big secret. Dede's just brainwashed him into thinking and saying that there is. That's how she wants him to feel. But there's nothing. It's all just sex. Dad's a stud. He's Clinton. He can walk into a room and change the environment. Women come around him batting their eyelashes. He was that way until the myositis got him. Then he got depressed, started taking Prozac and going to a psychiatrist, who told him that he needed to look at all the bad things he'd done in his life, examine his conscience to find peace before he died. For an eighty-year-old man to be talking about everything he did wrong in his life is ridiculous! At Dad's age he should just be relaxing and enjoying his children and grandchildren and his accomplishments! But Dad started talking about his *infidelities,* which continued up until 1998. And the shrink, who's Dede's pawn, told him that he needed to try to make it right *with Dede.* So Dad started confessing his infidelities to her, and she began to use this information to extort him and get him to sign over his estate to her. He's afraid of her."

A FEW DAYS later I had lunch with Dad at Caesar's, the old Italian restaurant across from his office. I arrived first and waited on a dark vinyl bench while the middle-aged French hostess stared at me. There was opera on the sound system. After ten minutes she asked, "*Ou* are you waiting for?"

I said, "My dad, Al Wilsey."

She exclaimed, "When I saw Wilsey in the book I assumed it was your brother Michael! Oh, my! I can't believe it's *Mr.* Wilsey. And you look just like him."

Al Wilsey was going to be making one of his rare appearances.

When Dad arrived he walked carefully, robotically, through the bar, gave me a hug and a gravelly, "Hi, Sean," then executed a ninety-degree pivot and made for our booth—after a quick acknowledging veer at the maitre d'—his eyes actually gleaming at the sight of the bowl of butter that had been placed on the table. He looked like a *soft* robot. A robot very fond of warm weather and maybe a caress on his arms. A robot full of loose parts that just wiggle around. A robot that stands badly, thinks slowly, has done lots of bad things. A robot without its master, in Dede's absence. We sat down, he took up cutlery, grunted, and tried to transfer a ball of butter from its iced bowl onto the blade of his knife. The balls were too cold to cooperate.

I said, "That was a strange lunch up in the country the other day." He said nothing. He was focused, with all his strength, on trying to get the uncooperative butter onto his knife. I had already taken some, and found myself thinking, *Didn't give me any trouble. I'm more skilled at cold-butter retrieval than Dad.*

Dad had been balancing butter on the dull knives at Caesar's for half a century. But no more. Now I could do it better. It was a train of thought I'd inherited from him.

I said, "What were you and Dede talking about? What's this terrible, bad thing you've done that will terrify me?"

"Dede or I will tell you some day," he said.

One of the sweet career waiters offered us drinks.

I said, "I can't imagine anything that would shock or upset me that I don't already know."

He looked grim. His eyes were dead and preoccupied. Failing both to fend off my questions and butter his bread—which he wanted to do desperately—took everything he had.

I said, "The only thing I could imagine shocking me would be finding out that you're a Democrat." Silence. When this joke fell flat I reached out with annoyance and impatience, took his knife, flicked the butter onto the blade with my index finger, and pressed it into his bread.

He said, "Thanks."

"Sure."

He took a bite.

I said, "I know you've had a lot of extramarital affairs. It doesn't bother me. It doesn't 'shock' or 'terrify' me. I know you've had a problem with that for a long time."

I thought, *The real reason you're a philanthropist is to balance out the philandering.*

Dad nodded and ate his bread.

End of subject.

I said, "Is it hard on you having me around?"

"I miss you. I enjoy seeing you. And I'm proud of you."

When I chose to believe this the air between us changed. Dad has never been one to say nice things to spare my feelings.

"I love you and I'm proud of you, too," I said. I do not understand why I said this. *I'm proud he's my dad?* I thought. "I've heard some funny stories about you and Uncle Jack."

"Yeah?"

"I heard that Uncle Jack unloaded a tommy gun into his fireplace to break up a cocktail party."

Dad nodded.

"I also heard Jack got you to dress up like an old man and then run around feeling up all your friends' wives."

He laughed feebly. "Yeah, that's true."

I said, "Yeah, I've heard some great stories. The one about the chorus girl."
His eyes brightened.

He said, "That's true."

"Why'd you take her to church?"

He gave me just a whisper of a grin and said, "It turned out she was a Catholic."

I looked around the always empty dining room and smiled. I said, "When people tell me crazy stories about you I always tell them how I ran away from survival camp and came home a month early on the plane. That one always cracks them up. People who know you always say, 'I can't believe that happened to Al Wilsey. I would've liked to have seen his face!' Cliff told me that was the only time he ever saw you with no idea what to do."

I started chuckling.

Dad said, with unexpected strength, "That place would have been good for you. It would have taught you some good values."

We were eating our pasta course now. I said, "Remember fishing in Tahoe? How you caught that beautiful trout with a piece of cheddar cheese? We were in Secret Harbor. Everyone told you not to fish there. We were guests of that woman who had a daughter in the Moonies. Remember that?"

Dad said, "Her husband left her for a black man!"

What could I say to that?

I asked, "Do you mind me writing this book?"

He said, "No. But I don't want you writing about the family."

I said, "I understand." I understood that he didn't want me doing exactly what I was doing.

I said, "Does it bother you hearing all my misbehavior stories?"

"No." A smile. "I think they're kind of funny."

"You know, I went back to St. Mark's and visited for the book."

"They let you in?"

"Yeah. They were actually nice, and glad to see me. My old adviser, the dean, they were both really nice. And then when I was walking around looking for Mr. Engell, my old English teacher, I asked this jock with a lacrosse stick, who told me, and I found myself thinking, *What a nice young man with a lacrosse stick*. At which point I realized I was becoming *you*."

Dad laughed.

"Then I'm walking down the hall past the dining room and there's this cluster of five cute senior girls, who never would have spoken to me when I was there, and they all started smiling and paying attention. I found myself thinking, *I should come back here, finally get my high school diploma, and rule the school. I'd be cool!*"

He reached out and grabbed my hand. His eyes were alive. He was here. We were having a good time! I squeezed his hand back. We laughed. It felt good. His hand felt like him. It didn't feel old. The skin was like it always was, slightly giving—I could press in and make a dent that stayed. He squeezed and released, squeezed and released. His fingers were thick and strong and the grip was gentle but firm. Firmer than I would have thought.

I said, "Dad, you're stronger than I thought."

He said, "I'm not."

I said, "You are."

*This is all very metaphorical.*

He squeezed as hard as he could and it was much harder than I would've imagined.

We were silent.

I said, "Dad, I am suffering from hair loss. And I don't know what to do."

"You're married," he said.

"Yeah, but when this book gets done I'll need an author photo."

He said, "Hairpiece."

I laughed.

"I've seen some movies lately," he said. "In Newport."

"What have you seen?"

"*M:i-2, The Patriot.*"

"I saw *X-Men* with Mom."

"What's that?" he asked. The title seemed to strike him.

I explained. "*X-Men* are mutants with superpowers. These kids who in adolescence develop mutations that make some normal people hate them but also give them the ability to do superhuman things." I'd been into the X-Men since I was a teenager, and it was funny and typical and no surprise that Dad was clueless. But I was happy that he wanted to know now.

I noticed that he was listening carefully. And then he said, with great vulnerability and concern, "Do you think *I'm* a mutant?"

Without thinking I reached up and stroked the right side of his head, the remains of his soft hair, his right ear, and he leaned his head into my hand. *Like a little bird,* I thought. I cradled his head in my left hand and I could feel his warmth and his craving, the way he drank up my attention—loving it, like a baby. I felt I was going to cry.

*This might be the most strange and beautiful moment I've ever had with my father,*
I thought. Then my thoughts went in several different directions.

*I can't believe Dede is allowing this to happen.*

*How can he go and be this self-aware?*

*Of course he's a mutant.*

I said, "I don't think you're a mutant."

I held his head in my hand for thirty seconds. Then I took it away.

He said, grinning sheepishly and wolfishly, *"I'm pretty wild."*


I WALKED HIM to his waiting car and driver. Looking at him intently, I said,
"If you ever need anything I will be there for you. Anything at all." I was beaming him the thought: *I'd take care of you. I'd move out here if you needed me to. I'd
wipe your shit and not be embarrassed.*

He said, "I know. There's nothing I need."

I kissed him, looked at the dry skin on his face, and thought, *He's not being
taken care of.* Then I put him in his Cadillac and shut the door firmly and carefully behind him. His driver, a man around my age, whom I envied, drove him
away.


WHEN I GAVE Mom a seriously edited version of my two lunches with Dad
she said, *"You boys had better ask for an autopsy when your father dies. Dede's
poisoned his mind, so why not his body, too.* You and Mike and Lad had better see
to *that."* Now that I had a relationship with Mike and Lad, Mom was jealous.

At least, I thought, I would have Mike and Lad there when Dad died. I knew
I'd be alone when it was Mom. I was all Mom had, and this was exhausting. I
imagined the funeral oration I'd have to deliver for her, to a great cathedral full
of the world's leaders, to whom I'd have to make the case for her peace work,
speaking with such eloquence that the Norwegian Nobel Institute would be persuaded to award her the Nobel Peace Prize, posthumously. I would then have to
solve all the world's conflicts and create peace on earth in her name. I would create world peace as a memorial to her. This was the only way I could make up for
being a horrible, hated Wilsey (world peace, and maybe a few million windmills). Using the Mom-voice, I'd tell the cathedral, "This woman, my mother,
was not only the *reincarnation of St. Joan of Arc,* but all *history's great peacemak-
ers,* from *all the great religions.* She could have taught *compassion* to Mother
Teresa, the Dalai Lama, and *Mahatma Gandhi, the great soul. She* was a *great soul.*
A *soul* the likes of which we are only blessed to know once in a *millennium."* On

my knees before the open coffin now (Mom still looking great, bone structure coming through for her even in death), weeping, all the presidents and kings tearing up, too. "Thank you, thank you, *thank you, Mo*ther, for *being* my mother, for giving me *life*, for letting me *live* inside your *bod*y for nine months"—taking her folded hands—"and then for *birthing* me into the world. We must honor *you* in our deeds. Please"—I turn around now—"let us be worthy"—I spread my hands—"let *the world* be worthy."

Then I'd close the lid, pick up the coffin, and bear it alone, on my back, down the aisle and out the doors into the day.

BEFORE I LEFT FOR Texas I made an appointment with Dr. Lenore Terr, the psychiatrist I saw from age three to age five, and again for a couple years after the divorce. She had not redecorated her office, which she still shared with her husband, Abba, an allergist. When I had my weekly appointment with Dr. Terr a nun would come to get me and I'd tell my friends, "I'm going to the allergy doctor's office," which had the sort of technical purchase on truth that you'd hope a kindergartener wouldn't be able to exploit.

In her building's lobby the ceilings were high, vaulted, silver and gold, inlaid with bas-reliefs of angry gods with their tongues out, grinning heads, swastikas, abstract, pre-Columbian squiggles, snakes with big teeth and long tongues.

The offices of the Drs. Terr were at the end of a corridor on the twenty-fifth floor. A door with their names on it opened into a rectangular waiting room, dominated by an old, dark-wood, wall-mounted clock, with Roman numerals and big steel hands that ticked loudly. A high, dowel-backed bench ran the length of one wall. A wood, iron, and glass-bead chandelier, with little lampshades over its faux-flame bulbs, lit the room dimly, and shimmied from the high floor sway. Silence was broken only by the steely clock-ticking, and a high-pitched scream as wind jetted its way between old frames and windows in some distant realm of the offices.

Nothing had changed. Mom and Dad first sent me to this office because they were convinced I was going to be gay and they wanted Dr. Terr to diagnose, intervene, and cure me. A bench and the ticking clock held sway in the swaying building where Dr. Terr sought to sway me from being gay.

I waited. Then Dr. Terr, who looks like a female senator, appeared and ushered me into her office, bringing back a rush of memories.

I sat down. She said, "You came to see me for a specific diagnostic purpose. They wanted to find out if you were gay."

"I know," I said.

Then she said, "You just imitated your mother because she was larger than life. Wow. You look like your father."

I told her I was researching a book and I wanted to know what she most remembered about me and my parents. She put her hands behind her head, then down on her knees, rocked forward, and said, "Your mother was expensive. Your father was strong and compassionate. He was really concerned about you. Those eyes would mist up. He really cared."

*"Those" eyes?* I thought.

Dr. Terr said, "Your mother wouldn't leave the house without makeup on. She was a feminine extreme. Your dad was a charming, macho, man's man. Into toys and hunting and all things masculine. He would be happy today if you were a Tour de France biker. And then"—Dr. Terr tapped her hands on her knees—"Hell hath no fury! It was a Shakespearean divorce! Your mother was so infuriated that he took up with Dede, not because she'd been betrayed by her best friend, but because Dede was an *inferior specimen of womanhood*. Dede didn't have anything on her in the looks department."

It was strange to hear it all summed up this way, as if Dr. Terr had been waiting, her office unaltered for decades, to give it to me neat and simple.

I looked out the window behind her and saw something I did not remember about the unchanged office. 999 Green St., The Summit, a few clouds swabbing its sides, was erupting straight out of the top of her head. How had I not noticed during all those years of therapy?

I said, "Is there a file on me from the years I saw you? And if so, can I look at it?"

After a long pause she said, "If it exists, you have a legal right to see it."

I thanked her. She went out to her secretary. A couple minutes later she returned with a half-inch-thick Manila folder.

"Here it is," she said.

She opened it, read, grimaced at something, and said, "Don't take this too much to heart. There's some strange stuff in here."

Pause.

"Like this note." She began to read out loud, "'Bizarre child. Hears voices that tell him to do things. Terrified of the playground. Spends half time dreaming. Sister Catherine.'"

She held out the paper for me to look at. The handwriting was sloppy.

"That was written by one of the nuns that taught at your school."

Then she said, "Because of the Freedom of Information Act I'm going to let

you look at it. But I don't want you to think I agree with the things you'll find."
I followed her out of the office to a large file room in her husband's dispensary
and she left me there.

Seated at a small steel desk surrounded by the allergy records of numerous
San Franciscans, I opened the Manila folder and read Dr. Terr's initial notes,
from early 1974, written in a compact, highly legible hand.

> Tells his mother "I want to be a lady."
> Wore mother's perfume so he could, "smell like a lady."
> Wears pearls and wants to be a little girl.
> Prayed to God to make him a girl so that he could play with the girls.
> Became obsessed with breasts—wanted to grow breasts during the night.
> Wants God to make him a girl in the night.
> Wants Cinderella's glass slippers.
> Likes to wear high-heels. Lipstick. Hair in curlers.
> Has big muscles.
> Wild . . . hit a kid in the face.
> Poked a teacher in the bottom.
> Knows all about sex. Knows all the words.
> Touches his penis a lot. Holds it when anxious. Not in public.
> Told mother there was a secret Sean inside. If he let him out he would die.
> Parents went to Europe for seventeen days and when they got back he re-
> fused to believe they were his parents. Says they "put a chemical in the mir-
> ror to hide the marks" on him.
> Says life is all a dream. That none of it is real. Poked his finger in his
> mouth to prove to himself he was there.

I remembered liking Mom's hair curlers. This was because they were *machinery*. I said things in school. They were reported to my parents. My parents repeated them back to me. My parents or I told my teachers. My teachers told my
parents or me. I told Dr. Terr. Back to parents from Dr. Terr: reverberated, reiterated, reinforced.

The factuality, then the contradictoriness, then the meaninglessness sank in. I
remembered being *all these children*. Feeling all these ways. Reinventing myself
according to friends and role models and circumstances every two weeks!

*That is childhood.*

These notes did not unlock anything. I was amazed that all this stuff *existed* and had been preserved for twenty-seven years. That a file in a tall building with Meso-American lobby detailing reported on me to a microscopic degree—and yet still got everything wrong.

My passing spasms of emotion and interest accumulated until Mom and Dad decided they knew who I was. They turned me into their greatest fears. And years later, when these fears had passed, Dad was convinced I was an alcoholic just like his dead brother. Maybe the charming, macho man's man was the gay one. Maybe that was his secret? Somehow the fact that in kindergarten I'd turned a girl upside-down and pulled her underwear off went unnoticed. That memory, which fills me with shame and excitement, went unremarked in the Terr files. *What's in here is just noise*, I thought. I never mentioned what really mattered because it was too deep, too frightening, too personal.

Kids are trusting and wise and I cannot think of a less useful combination to be born with. The wisdom lets children know who they are. And then the trust lets everyone else take that knowledge away.

The notes ended and the chronology jumped ahead into the eighties, the period just after the divorce, when I went to see Dr. Terr again. There was a sequence of letters from Dad. He said he was concerned because I couldn't stand living at Mom's house, and that I insisted on calling it "The Marble Palace." He was also worried because Mom kept telling me he was "doomed to eternal damnation" and that his marriage to Dede was an "immoral act." He said he was trying to get an injunction to stop Mom from saying such things. He said I'd told him I was starting to hate her. In one letter he seemed plainly anguished about the fact that the divorce had been all over the papers, on the radio, on television, in the *National Enquirer*, in *People* magazine, and he thought it likely, some other publications of which he was unaware.

In a letter written shortly after Mom's cancer announcement he said that something mysterious was troubling me, but he didn't know what. I always needed the lights on, and I couldn't sleep at all between ten-thirty at night and two in the morning unless he let me in the bed with him.

In the next letter he was dating Dede. He wrote, "Sean has been kind and loving toward Dede."

After marrying Dede the tone changed. He pointed out my failings, and asked Dr. Terr to fix them. (My failings amounted to never being on the honor roll, not being something called a "class officer," not playing tennis or other "social sports," and always walking and running on my toes—the dreaded bouncing.) If Dr. Terr couldn't fix me, Dad felt the solution was boarding school. When I was twelve he asked for Dr. Terr's help getting me there. This letter ended with a single-word paragraph: "Help."

It's funny how easy it is to take things away from children. It only takes desire. So easy—to confuse and make kids bad, to hurt and get them lost. It is a snap for even the weakest, dullest adult. Kids have no power. Only emotions. Though everyone remembers the power of their childish emotions so well. They echo on through your whole life. Down a corridor until you arrive at a room full of them. They can push you far, far into your life before you are even aware of them, let alone reconsider them.

Which raises the question: If parents have absolute power over children, how can that not corrupt?

And yet there was something childlike about Mom and Dad—even as they destroyed my childhood.

I closed the file, left the dispensary, handed my history back to Dr. Terr's secretary, asked him to thank the doctor, and left the office. The hallway was deserted. When the elevator arrived I noticed it was also decorated with pre-Columbian designs. I found out later that Dad's second wife, who died of lung cancer, was diagnosed as terminal in this building. The doctor gave the news to Dad to give to her. I walked through the lobby and out.

IN MARFA, TEXAS, the Lannan Foundation gave Daphne and me a very comfortable house to write in (too comfortable, probably). We sat in Eames desk chairs and looked at a sweeping view of a mountain-ringed plateau formed in the Permian period and left more or less alone since. Marfa was a cranky, remote, aesthetically pleasing town of ranchers and border patrol that had been invaded by money and art. The Chinati Foundation, a museum and art institution founded in the seventies by the sculptor Donald Judd, was located there and, following Judd's death in 1994, it had begun to exert a magnetic pull on what a friend of ours termed "haute bohemia." We adopted Charlie, our wonderful dog, whose rough good looks and bursts of intransigence were commensurate with the town's. We got involved in local politics. We took singing lessons and gave a recital (Daphne was the star). We went down to Ojinaga, Mexico, with Solvi, a seraphic eight-year-old Icelandic child whose mother was one of our best friends in Marfa (on an artist's residency at the Chinati Foundation), a few other people from Chinati, and our Lannan neighbor, the novelist David Foster Wallace. Our plan was to have fish at El Bucanero—"the pirate"—a seafood restaurant located just over the border from the hottest town in the U.S., Presidio, Texas, the official border crossing, which is inhabited solely by weary border patrol and struggling onion farmers.

El Bucanero was said to have very fresh seafood, in spite of its location in the Chihuahuan desert, because it was owned by narcotics traffickers who flew the fish in as cover.

Unfortunately, it was closed, so we went to a place where they incinerated all their food in the deep-fat fryer and fleeced us with mariachis. Then we ate a lot of ice cream, ordered extremely warm club soda from a stand, and sat in the square for an hour.

On the way out of town, I was driving (we were all piled into the Chinati Foundation's Blazer) and I saw a car about one hundred yards ahead of us drive through a puddle. So I said, "Hey, Solvi, there's a *puddle* up ahead!"

"Go faster!" he shouted.

I floored it and, like an SUV ad, sent water spraying in every direction. This water turned out to be raw sewage.

When we got to the border the agent in the little window just said, "Whoa!" and we were waved through. The smell followed us all the way back to Marfa, an hour trip. Wallace taught Solvi show tunes—"Tssssssssteam heat!"—and we all sang them with the windows open.

A week later, when Wallace finished his residency, he gave me his house keys, saying, "If you ever need some space you should use my house. Nobody'll bother you. I don't think they've got anyone else coming."

My grandfather had held so many of his revivals in this part of the country. So I decided to hold a revival. I made a bunch of posters with Amity maxims on them. (I'd downloaded all the propheet music off Napster before arriving, and burned it onto a CD.) I wished Daphne good luck with her work and told her I was going to stay up for two days and have a propheet.

As I left she said, "I'm not sure what you're doing, but I'll miss you. Have a good 'propheet!'"

Then I blasted music, put myself through Amity exercises, and cried for two days.

I WROTE THESE notes:

I've attained this completely free-free state. Dancing around Wallace's.
I should do Propheet revivals for graduates.

My cheeks in strips below my eye sockets are like two inflamed little sausages. They ache.

I have put myself in that sensitive state. I have no skin. I am unfit for human company. People and their bullshit are too much for me. I must remain alone. I am wide open. Only maybe animals are O.K. company. I go out to say hello to a horse.

I have put myself through the emotional Bone Marrow Transplant. Now, stumbling around raw and deeply moved by every injustice or callousness.

I can only listen to music from musicals.

Just reading the newspaper my soul felt burned by acid.

48 pieces of snotty Kleenex. Sanctified relics.

(and counting)

Plus T-shirt.

Wept on the Eames couch onto the jute rug while looking at the NELSON BUBBLE lamps

Anything callous of tone or meaning wounds me. Anything not straightforward and full of heart. All things coarse and compromised through fakery sadden and fill me with woe. All things arrogant or boastful or rude. My feelings feel sacred. As if in them is the Amity school, protected. As if in each of my tears there is preserved the school in its entirety. I feel as all deep mourners must feel when they have grieved for a loved one and all they want to do is keep them in their heart and someone wants to talk about something fucking else.

Definitely an addictive feeling. The emotional result. I feel high.

I am sensitive to light.

My voice is in a lower register.

Starting to perceive the return of my everyday personality as horrible fakery.

Voice begins to sound nasal. Whereas before it was like John's—piped up from some deep down thermal vent.

This morning I found myself incapable of putting on anything black. It felt too dark and negative. Nor could I wear anything with a logo that seemed in any way to represent forces that were at all predatory, ironic, sarcastic, mercantile. This left me with a red plaid cowboy shirt. Usually, after a propheet, everybody who'd been in it would show up at breakfast the next morning wearing Amity T-shirts. What a coincidence! All our puffy faces and pure, childlike laughter and strong clear voices speaking from our very centers. And if someone started to waver or to go too fast you would feel a great fear, and smugness, and desire to help. You would take them aside and say, "Remember to stay slow."

My nose is still overproducing mucus. Like an assembly line that doesn't know the war's over yet.

I am getting too into this. Going too deep.

I wanted to do it like an anthropologist, but I was *moved*. And I'd turned into an unbearable, self-righteous asshole.

Then there was a knock at the door. It was Velda, the town's real estate broker. She'd sold the house to Lannan, and now she was managing it. She was wearing a denim muumuu and light-brown tinted glasses through which I could see her eyes casting around the room in confusion. *Who was I? What was this?* I had been listening to "Corner of the Sky," from the musical *Pippin,* at a very high volume. She must have knocked numerous times. Tears, hastily wiped away, had been streaming down my face; I had been leaning my head back and letting them come. The floor was littered with Kleenex, and I'd covered the walls with propheet slogans, like "NO MAN IS AN ISLAND."

She seemed completely taken aback. She said, "Oh . . . you're . . . still here!?" taking me for the just departed Wallace. (I later found out that another Marfan had observed my propheet, taken me for Wallace, and started gossiping about the novelist's eccentricity.)

I said, "No. He gave me the key. Sometimes it's nice to have another space to work in. I like to play music, and I don't want to disturb my wife."

Velda looked at the Kleenex on the floor, the strange signs on the wall. My face was still wet with tears. I picked up the Kleenex, blew my nose, and mumbled something completely unconvincing about having allergies. Marfa is probably the least allergic place in the United States.

The Lannan Foundation called the next day and asked me to give Velda the keys.

And thank God—I was becoming such an asshole. Insufferable. Completely sure of myself, my opinions, actions, goodness, righteousness. Very bad company. I was on the verge of starting another Amity out there in West Texas. It was a lucky thing Daphne didn't meet me right after I'd come back from Italy.

ON A ROLL with the research, I decided to throw myself into the mystery of my father. Texas also happened to be the right place for this investigation. Clifford Mooney—retired Marine Corps sergeant major, former chauffeur/factotum/

friend to Dad—had retired outside San Antonio. I paid him a visit. The night I arrived we stayed up talking and drinking beer from 9:30 P.M. to 2:30 A.M. For years Cliff used to pick me up after school, standing at parade rest in front of Dad's black limousine. We'd always been fond of each other.

Cliff took chilled mugs out of the deep freeze, poured our beers into them, and we talked about the principles of helicopter aerodynamics for several hours. Cliff had flown a big Huey for the *Apocalypse Now* shoot.

When I asked him about Dad he told me some anecdotes.

Dad once had Cliff spend a month walking up and down the rows of every Catholic cemetery in Marin County, because he wanted to find his mother's grave and he didn't want to call Aunt Helen and ask her where it was. Dad had Cliff obtain a set of door and dead-bolt keys for every apartment in Northpoint, home of the "nooner," where I'd just been staying a few weeks before. Hundreds of apartments—he wanted to be able to go into them all.

Hearing this story, I thought about Dad's alleged affairs. Had there really been so many of them? Was infidelity what Dad had been talking about when he said, "I've done some bad things that I'm not proud of"? I'd always assumed he'd been faithful to Dede. He'd committed what Mom called his "amoral act" with Dede, gone through a brutal divorce for Dede—why cheat again? All Lad's stuff about Dad as Clinton just seemed like hyperbole.

When it was well past midnight I asked Clifford, "So, did my dad have a lot of affairs?" I didn't really want to ask him this. And I wasn't sure he'd answer.

He said, "I had to cover up for your dad. That was part of my job."

"Often?" I asked.

He pondered the question for a minute. "A lot. I think there were eight different women in the eighties. But it wasn't about sex for your dad. All these women were talented and/or educated. He was like the old warriors that ate their enemies' livers: 'I take your power.'"

We both laughed.

I said, "Dad and Dede had me over for lunch and told me that if I kept talking to people who knew Dad I would stumble on terrible things that would hurt my mom, my siblings, and me. What do you think they were talking about?"

Cliff was silent. For a full, long minute, he stared at the floor. Then he said, "You need to put all this behind you. Stop thinking about the past. Don't you know the story of the elephant and the blind men?"

I said, "No."

"Three blind men are shown an elephant. One holds the trunk, one the middle, and one the back. The guy at the trunk says, 'This is a snake.' The one in the middle says, 'No. It's a wall.' The one in the back thinks it's something else. Each man touches a different part and thinks it's the whole thing. Your dad's the elephant. And we're all blind. No one ever saw all the parts of him."

He pushed back his chair. "I'm going to bed."

DAPHNE AND I went back to New York. I'd visited Cliff (and shortly thereafter my aunt Helen) in the hope that I would finally understand Dad. This was my fantasy: Furnished with all my father's hidden lives and actions, the elephant seen from a distance, I would complete this book, Dad would read it and (like Theoden, king of Rohan, in *The Lord of the Rings*) be restored to health and sanity through the wizardry of love and unflinching honesty. He'd realize I was the one person who truly understood him, saw him for all of who he was, and forgave him. He would then apologize to me and Mom, and divorce Dede. (Dede, who, the more I heard from Mike and Lad about her ongoing estate machinations, was like Theoden's corrupt court counselor, Wormtongue.) Dad, clear-minded, thanks to my efforts, would set right his many wrongs, endow the Wilsey Foundation with three hundred million dollars (*all his money*), and engage in the construction of numerous windmills with his faithful progeny.

Now I realized it was far more likely that he'd never live to see this book. And after talking with Cliff and Aunt Helen about Dad's talented/educated lovers, his lost mother's lost grave, his miserable childhood, his elephantine qualities, I was pretty sure the biggest secret of Dad's past was simple, and not worth hiding. He'd been unhappy. He didn't want to talk about the past because the past made him sad.

While living in the past was making me an asshole, turning me back into a teenager, taking me away from my wife and my life, a New York life that was happy, loving, full of passion and friends. I spent half my life reading and editing and engaged with the present and the other half living in my head, between ten and a hundred years before, in San Francisco, a city I loved and could never imagine returning to, because of all its history. Maybe, I thought, some nineteenth-century version of this story happened a few generations ago to my great-grandparents, Hayes Wilsey's parents, the New York City Wilseys who went back as far as New Amsterdam but ran as far away as they could, leaving an established place in society for the wilds of California.

The writing had to stop. Maybe it's possible to put things in the past by leaving them there.

·  ·  ·

IN NOVEMBER 2001, Dad had a left side–immobilizing stroke (having just survived another almost fatal bout of pneumonia). After I got the news from Mike, I called Dede to find out the details. She said he was in the hospital getting physical therapy, doing fine.

"It didn't affect his mind, obviously," she said, *Wormtongueishly,* my internal teenager thought. "I can tell you, he's calling the doctor an asshole. And the nurses names. And the ambulance driver—the ambulance driver asked him what he did for a living and he said he ran a big whorehouse. I mean, he's very funny, and he's very, very, very sharp. I mean he's *very* funny, and he's *very, very, very* sharp. I asked him, 'So what did you do today?' And he said, 'Same old shit!' So I can tell you, his mind and his humor are exactly the same."

I said, "I'd like to come see him."

She said, "He told me, 'I will not see anyone.' And you know he's like that anyway. When he's sick he refuses to talk and he refuses to see anybody. And he doesn't like to talk on the phone anyhow, as you well know."

"Well," I said, "I wanted to ask you, because I don't think I've talked to you without Dad around in a long time. You guys told me last summer that there was something Dad had done that was terrible, that I would never want to know about. Remember that conversation?"

"Uhhh. Vaguely. Yeah."

"And you said, 'I'll tell you at some point.' *What were you talking about?*"

"I *wouldn't* tell you. I wouldn't, that, ub, it's, um—"

"It's been on my mind a lot. It was a very—"

"It wasn't, that, I mean—he didn't murder anybody or anything."

"I couldn't think of anything."

"What he was upset about was that you were wandering around talking to people in his past life and it made him very *annoyed.* I think that it came off like he'd been the ax murderer or something. Which wasn't *at all* the case. He certainly did not murder anybody. But he of all people is a very private person. If you mishandle things with him you will ultimately—and I'm not talking about you now—you will ultimately pay a price where a door will close on you. And you'll say 'Whoops! I think he'll come around.' And he *won't.* He has the capacity to be one of the coldest people I've ever met, where I sometimes think, 'What *happened* to him? Where's that part of his *heart?*' I don't know. But what I know is that he's a very, very complex person, and there is a part of him I don't *understand.* I don't ever want to *go there.* I don't ever want it to happen to *me.* But he is capable of it with *anybody.* And, *he doesn't like intrusions on his privacy.* And so really what I was trying to say to you was, *'Don't go there.'* Because he could turn on *you*. Don't go there. You have a *nice* relationship with your father."

Of course she was lying, and of course I'd already decided to drop it.

THANKSGIVING 2001, I managed to call while Dede was in the shower and talk only to Dad. He sounded like he was at the end of a pipe half full of water. It was still early in the day in California.

He said, proudly, "Mike and Lad are coming for Thanksgiving."

With plain amazement I said, "How'd that happen?"

He said, "I made Dede do it." Then he said, "I wish you were here. You're my friend."

(I told Mike and Lad this later, and it turned out to be untrue. They had not been invited for Thanksgiving. It was just Dad's imagination.)

I asked, "How's the helicopter?"

He said, with enthusiasm, "Oh! It's fine!"

"Are you flying it?"

He said, "No," suddenly glum.

"I'm sorry to hear that."

He said, "Do you know I had a stroke?"

I said, "Yes. You haven't had another one since we last talked?"

"No."

"Good."

"I'm recovering great."

"Good. Taking it easy?"

"All I do is sit around the house."

"You need to rest."

"Sean, I'm gonna put the phone down and take a drink of water." He disappeared for a solid minute. I thought I'd lost him, this alternate Dad I'd happened to reach, but he slowly faded back in (I heard his shuffling footfalls approaching) and said, "I'm back. What's doing with you?"

I said, "Do you remember we have a dog?"

He said, "No. My memory is terrible."

I said, "I suppose we'll do a lot of eating today. How's your appetite?"

He said, "Don't have any."

I said, "How about drinking? Can you drink wine?"

"Yes."

"That's good."

There was a feeling of friendliness and calm between us that, though rare, felt familiar, and did not feel fragile.

"Mom's coming to New York to stay with us for Christmas."

"Oh, you poor guy."

I laughed.

He said, "How's your book?" in a voice that suggested he no longer expected to live to see it.

I was outside, by a man-made lake, at Daphne's parents' north Florida condo. To keep Dad on the phone I started talking about the ducks that were bobbing around in front of me, plane travel post–9/11, our dog's brilliance (I could shout "Escape!" and Charlie'd jump out the window onto the fire escape). Somehow, conversation was easy and leisurely and natural to the same degree that it was usually grinding and brief and impossible.

Again he said, "Sean, I'm gonna put the phone down and take a drink of water," and disappeared for another solid minute.

When he came back he said, "O.K. I'm tired."

I said, "Do you want to go now?"

"Yes."

"Is there anything I can do for you?"

"I want you to love me. I want you to be my friend."

I said, "I do love you. I am your friend. I love you more than anyone."

"Go to church and say a prayer for me," he said.

I said I would. Then he said, "Good-bye."

"Good-bye, Dad."

And it would be nice if I could say this was the last time I ever spoke to him. But it wasn't. A month later, when I called Dad to wish him a Merry Christmas, Trevor answered the phone. He said, "Hi *Sean!*" in a singsongy voice. "How are things in New York, after, *you know.*" He meant the terrorist attacks.

I said, "It's been a hard time to be here."

"Uh-huh."

"But it's also been, I don't want to say good. But interesting and inspiring to see people respond the way they have. It's been a powerful experience."

"That's *great*," he said. "I'm gonna put you on hold."

I held for several minutes, then Dad picked up. I said, "Dad! Merry Christmas! How are you?"

"I feel great," he said, and went into a paroxysm of coughing. When he recovered he said, in a commanding voice, "Brrak!"

"What?"

"Trkuk!"

"What?"

"Trlk!"

"What?"

"Talk!"

"Oh! O.K." I tried to think of something to say. "Mom's here for Christmas."

"That must be a pistol."

"It's been fun. We've had a good Christmas."

Silence.

"My friend Leandro's getting married. I'm going to be his best man. And I was the best man for my friend John this summer. He's got a big Irish family. Lots of aunts with brogues. . . . Were you ever a best man?"

"Yes!" Enthusiastically. "Lots of times!"

"For who?"

"For Mike!"

"Anyone else?"

"Can't remember."

"It's great that you were Mike's best man."

"I'll let you go."

"O.K.," I said. "But remember as you go through your day that I'm thinking of you and I love you."

"I will."

We were about to hang up, but then I remembered something I wanted to tell him.

"Oh!" I said. "We went to church for midnight mass."

"Where did you go?"

"Here nearby. The Catholic church on my block."

"Good."

"I prayed for you."

"Was God listening?"

"I think so."

"I hope so."

THIS CALL APPEARED on my phone bill a month later. It lasted eleven minutes (predominantly on hold) and cost seventy-seven cents.

*Eighteen* · SCRAPED OVER

TOO MUCH BREAD

A T HOME WITH DAPHNE, after midnight, midway through watching *Coal Miner's Daughter*, Loretta Lynn's father died. Simultaneously my phone rang.

"Listen and see who it is," Daphne said.

It was Dede. She said, her voice coiled with tension, "*E!—E!*—Uh, would you please call me. On my cell. (415) 816-————. This is—*pt*—Saturday night."

I said, "Where's the phone," and looked around the room. Daphne found it and handed it to me.

I said, "Dede, hello?"

She said, "Sean      br    j    ."

I said, "Dede, I can't hear you."

She said, "Can you hear me now?"

I said, "Yes."

She said, "     br    j    ," again.

"Dede, I can't hear you."

"Can you hear me now? I'm on a cell phone." I pictured Dede's cell phone as a Motorola. A nice one. "Can you hear me now?"

"Yes."

"I'm at UC hospital and I'm very sorry to tell you your father has just died."

I whispered, *"Dead,"* to Daphne, who was squatting in front of me. She began to cry, and hugged my knees. Even as I received the news I noticed that it did not pierce me as I'd always expected it to. It entered me almost painlessly. Dede cut out again.

I said, "Dede, I can't hear you."

She said, "Can you hear me now?"

I said, "Yes."

"    br    j    ."

"Dede, I can't hear you."

"    br    j    . I'm sorry to call you so late! What time is it there?"

"It's one o'clock. We were up."

"We were in the country—*trʒ*—nd your father wasn't looking well yest—*pt*—day. He had a cold, and today he looked worse. His color was very bad. I called his doctors and they said to bring him in. We got in the car and drove down to the city tonight, and when I got to UC they—*ikt*—eled him into the emergency room, and a few minutes later the doctor came out and told me, 'Dede, I don't know how to *tell* you this, but he's been dead for twenty minutes.'—*brʒʒkkpɪkm*—"died in the car. His doctor for twenty years said he died peacefully between two places he loved, Napa and San Francisco. And I'm here with him now, and— oh my God he's making *noise!*"

The connection went dead.

I hung up the phone and reported all of this to Daphne. "I guess he still has some air in his lungs," I said. The phone rang, I answered, heard, *"Siʒ!    dlan q!    Bp,"* and the phone went dead again.

It rang. Silence. Rang. Silence. Rang. I said, "Dede, if you can hear me, I can't hear you."

When she finally got through there was no further mention of Dad making noise. She said, "I don't think he wanted to come back to the hospital and have all those needles stuck in him. So he died in-between two places that he loved, Napa and San Francisco."

He must have died on Highway 101, passing through Marin, where he grew up.

"I guess I'll be coming out tomorrow," I said.

"Hold off! I don't know *anything* about funeral—*bd*—rrangements, except that they've been getting simpler and simpler. I just know that he wants the service to be at St. Ignatius church. But I'm going to keep him with me for a while. My mother says when her husband dies she's going to want to keep him on ice for a few weeks. I may want to put him on ice. . . . *b*    *wp*    *m*. I'm on a cell phone and there's all this machinery in here and so that's why the connection's bad. I haven't been in the bed with him in a long time. I'm just going to lie here for a while with his little arm around me."

"Well, please let me know. I can call Mike," I said. Silence at the mention of Mike.

"O.K. Thanks for calling me," I said heavily. "I'll talk to you soon."

"Good night!"

I BRUSHED my teeth. The phone rang and it was Dad's old friend and business partner Gerson Bakar.

He asked how I was. I said I was O.K.

I asked how he was. He said he was O.K.

"He's in a better place," he said.

I said, "Yes."

"O.K., buddy," Gerson said.

I liked that he said this.

We said good night.

MIKE CALLED.

I asked him how he was and he asked me how I was.

He said, softly, "My feeling is that I lost my dad a long time ago."

I said, "I definitely feel like I lost him a long time ago, too—if I ever had him."

"Well, he gave you a lot of material."

I laughed.

"Have you spoken to Dede?" he asked.

"Yeah, she called me."

"How'd she sound?"

"Pretty broken up."

"Hmm."

"Dad's been the center of her life for a long time."

"She'll go into a convent now," Mike said.

I laughed.

"I'm going to bed. See you soon. I love you," he said.

"You, too."


THE NEXT MORNING I called Mom immediately, and she immediately became weepy.

She called me back four more times that morning with various questions and thoughts.

Such as:

"Sean, it's your mom. I was talking to your cousin Linda and she said, 'Pat, do you realize that January fourth was the same day he left. The day he moved out of the penthouse.' It's true, Sean. I knew it was January, but I didn't know it was the fourth. Linda remembers everything. He chose to leave the world on the same day. January fourth, that's the day he chooses to leave. What do you suppose that means?"

"I don't know," I said.

And:

"Sean, it's your mom. Did I tell you about a dream I had a couple of weeks ago?"

"No."

"Your father was under a sort of arched portico. Everything else was black and white, but he was wearing a pink shirt. I thought it was so odd that he was wearing a pink shirt. He was sitting down and he waved. He said, 'I love you,' and waved good-bye. He said it to you, too. He said it to *both of us, Sean*. You were there, too. Then Dede came and whisked him away. She was just a shadow. A dark shadow that came and wheeled him off the stage. He was in a wheelchair at the end, too, wasn't he?"

"Yes, he was," I said.


LAD CALLED and said, "I think Dede and Todd and Trevor are having him cremated right now."

"Like, today?"

"Right now."

I felt incredibly relieved.

"Now you can publish your book!" he added.

. . .

A DAY LATER, as the winter light was fading into a luminous gray from my window, I sat at my desk, where I had just finished screaming in sudden unanticipated rage. The fact that Dad was gone, and our relationship—unredeemed— was over, had begun to sink in. I couldn't quite believe it was all ending like this. New York was cold. January's the killer month here. There are some nice days in November. December is full of holiday distractions. February is too short to worry about. March, next to April, is the red carpet to spring. But here I was at the start of January. The phone rang.

I said, "Hello," hoarsely.

Lad said, "Do you remember Al Nelder?"

"No."

"He was the police chief who got you out of juvenile hall when you were arrested. Old friend of Dad's. He got you off."

"O.K." I never knew this.

"He died the day before Dad. And his family reserved the bishop. So now the rosary's on Thursday and the service is on Friday."

"Nobody's told me any of this. What do you mean? What's a rosary?"

"It's usually in a mortuary. Everyone comes and pays their last respects, and the family sits in the front row, and the casket's right there, open—Dede's doing an open casket, which I can't believe—and so people come and they touch the face and sometimes they even *kiss* it. But there are going to be so many people that it's in a church."

"I thought he was cremated."

"They're cremating him after the service. She's got him on ice."

Now that I knew I would see him again, I imagined touching Dad on the same spot, above and behind the right ear, as I did at Caesar's.

Lad said, "On Thursday night at seven forty-five, after the rosary, I've made a reservation for a big dinner, family only. What I want to know is, should I invite your mom? Or is Patsy just going to take the whole thing over?"

I told Lad I'd check, and that I was sure she wouldn't take it over. Then I called Mom, who said she wanted to go to the party, but not the funeral. I called Lad back, and he seemed happy with this plan.

Then he said, "I've had people telling me all sorts of stuff about what a saint Dad was. And you and I know that's bullshit. He got an F in being a father to you. And you turned out wonderfully. He can't take any credit for it." Pause. "Your mom takes some. Most of it's yours."

. . .

WHEN WE ARRIVED in San Francisco Daphne and I went to Mom's (she'd moved to a bigger apartment, where there was room for us), dropped off our stuff, changed clothes, and met Mike and Lad, who took us to a funeral home with a long name—Halsted N. Gray – Carew & English. It was the most prosperous, upscale funeral home I'd ever seen. We parked in its parking lot, beside Dede's metallic-teal Mercedes convertible—the car Dad died in. Dede was seated with her back to the door as we entered the building. I stepped forward before she turned around and saw she was writing a check for two thousand dollars.

Dede was wearing a black Chanel suit and, judging from the mascara clumped in her eyelashes and collapsed in a little avalanche down her nose, she had been crying a great deal. I thought, with unwanted compassion, of reaching out and removing with a fingertip the mascara on her (retroussé, or was it aquiline?) nose. Of touching her face. The impulse surprised me.

A young blond man in black, who'd been sitting across a small, ornate desk from Dede, slid her check out of sight, stood up, and said, "I'm Graham."

Post greetings, Mike asked, "What's the accent?"

"England."

"Is this your place?"

"No. I'm the embalmer."

"We're the pallbearers," Mike said. "Is there anything we need to know?"

"Tonight you'll be bringing the casket up the stairs of the church and placing it on a rolling gurney."

"We have to carry it *up stairs?*" Mike asked. "Is it heavy?"

"It's a solid oak casket," Graham said, with a note of pride. "It weighs about three hundred pounds."

"O.K.," said Mike, somberly, and raised his eyebrows. The pallbearing muscle was Mike, Lad, Todd, Trevor, Ron, Dad's stepson from his second marriage, whom I'd never met, and me.

Graham said, "You will be wearing white gloves and boutonnieres, which we will provide. The hearse will be there already. Please arrive between six-fifteen and six-thirty, and no later than six-thirty. The service will begin promptly at seven."

"Fifty pounds each," I said to Mike. "Plus Dad."

He nodded.

Graham continued with the ceremonial aspects of the funeral. Time elapsed. I looked at Daphne's watch. It was twelve-thirty. We'd been standing there since twelve-fifteen. The coffin was being closed at one.

Mike said, "I guess we better go see Dad." We moved to go. Then Dede exclaimed, with strange desperation, "I ran into this *fellow* last night. A *homeless* man in the parking lot. I guess he sleeps back there. Not a bad place if you think about it"—a whimsical cock of her head here—"safe, quiet, maybe a little spooky, but that's not so bad!"

I imagined the Halsted N. Gray – Carew & English parking lot's homeless man befriending Dad, now also a homeless man, creeping out of his box to have a cigarette and shoot the shit in the parking lot. Dad was free to smoke now.

Lad said, "Do you lock the gates of the parking lot at night?"

"Yes, we do," Graham said.

*Glad we got that settled*, I thought.

"You'd better watch out," Dede said to Graham. "I'm thinking about kidnapping the hearse."

Dede'd have to ratchet a hearse's front seat really far forward to reach the pedals, wheel under her chin, Chanel skirt riding up, heels kicked off onto the floor. *Hearsejacker* went through my mind. I imagined the hearse blasting up the coast road, sun shining, waves crashing—an ad.

While they spoke I detached from the group and began sidling down the hall in the direction of a grooved black placard, set on an easel, that displayed names in movable plastic type. One of the white names was "Alfred S. Wilsey." Sidling on I came to a branch of three corridors, and glanced down each of them. Carpet. Yellow-white walls. Molding. Large rooms at the end of two, a turn after fifty feet on the other.

I heard the conversation break up behind me. Graham jogged over. "Let me escort you," he said. I followed him down the long hallway with the bend. We rounded it and found another long hallway, at the end of which I saw a set of double doors, right one closed, left one open. My brain was burning adrenaline. As we got closer, through the left-hand door, I saw flower arrangements on easels. Ten feet from the door the sight lines widened and the closed end of a coffin came into view. Graham, five steps ahead, at the door now, extended an arm into the room, *Here is your table*–style. I stepped past and saw, on a blazing white pillow, Dad's shrunken head. Seeing his face I inhaled sharply, then exhaled deeply, feeling everything in me fall. This was a dead person who had suffered. He looked absolutely *blasted*. That was the only word. Like he had been pounded and beaten. There was no life left in him whatsoever. This was not a sleeping man. This was not a pretty corpse. This was a man who had been kept alive as long as possible. Stretched thin. I thought of a line from *The Lord of the Rings:* "like butter that has been scraped over too much bread."

It became even clearer when I saw his deflated hands. They were the part of Dad that I knew best.

I approached the coffin. Daphne was a few steps behind me. Graham had disappeared. I stood there, then turned to Daphne and said, "I'm O.K."

She looked confused.

"I'd like to just have a minute alone," I said. I turned back to Dad.

*What had happened to him?*

His mouth was wide and drawn thin into a single curved line. Here was a face that, my whole life, I had been told I shared. Now I saw that we had the same forehead and chin, but a totally different nose. How had I never noticed this distinctive nose? It was the most unchanged thing about him. A smooth, abrupt curve.

There was gunk in his eyebrows and film over his eyelids, glue or something to keep them from opening. His eyebrows looked waxed and dyed. Every hair was distinct. His cheeks were sunken and hollow. He was ashy, except where patches of peachy red makeup had been applied to his skin. He didn't look like himself.

Dad wore a blazer, a pink shirt with a stiff, starched, white collar, and a blue tie patterned with gold circles, filled with pale pink, inside gold squares. His hands had been folded, right over left, and black rosary beads attached to a silver crucifix had been threaded through his bruised fingers. Dede was a Methodist. Dad had never owned a rosary. Where had this come from? I looked at it. His fingers against the black beads were mottled with bruises, though still hairy, like my own, as Daphne would point out later. I thought about the numerous things those hands had done, all leading to right here.

Then I reached out with my left hand, which I couldn't stop from shaking, and stroked the fringe of hair around his right ear, like I had when he asked me if I thought he was a mutant. I'd decided I would do this. I had carefully thought about it for the whole plane ride that morning. I tried to lightly rest my fingers against him. I didn't want to move his head. He felt insubstantial, weightless, like a husk. Dad looked so small. Almost like a child. They could have fit him in so many more modest places than the Solid Oak Casket. I wondered how they had dressed him. Did they have to cut the fabric and then tuck it in so it looked like it was really on? Was it all backless?

The crown of his head and his impressive nose were the only parts of him that still looked formidable, like him, as he always had looked. I touched the very point of his widow's peak and slowly stroked his thin wisps of hair. This was awful. It was not what I wanted. It felt toxic. On his forehead, where the hair began, I felt a waxy substance, probably whatever was in his eyebrows but better blended to look like skin. I stroked his hair all the way back to the little coffin pillow his head was resting on. I couldn't say anything. There were no words in my head except "Dad." I thought, *Dad kept some hair his whole life, so maybe I have a chance, too.* Then I thought, *Ha—not likely.* I heard Lad and Mike and Mike's wife, Bobbie, arrive and start talking.

I walked over to the door and said, "You can come in. It's O.K."

Everyone came in and walked to the side of the coffin. It seemed to hit Mike as it hit me. This was all Dede had left us of Dad.

"Whh," he said.

Lad said, "Hi Dad!" He stepped closer, then added, "He looks *awful*. They didn't do a good job." He waved his hand around Dad's chin. "See, they got the mouth all wrong."

I said, "Let's be quiet," and put my arm around him. We stood there quietly. Daphne stepped away. After a while Lad started looking at the various flower arrangements flanking the casket. Mike and Bobbie did the same. Bobbie inspected a three-foot-tall cross made entirely of white roses, propped on an easel. She said, "Wow! This one's from Danielle Steel!"

Lad returned to my side and, with ironic solemnity, handed me a small card with a picture of Jesus on it.

Jesus was wearing a white cassock, with a green robe draped over his arm, around his torso, and up over his shoulder. His beard and hair were very blond and very wispy, and his lips were very red. A thin gold hoop of a halo circled his head and a single red drop of fire dangled in it. A pine was behind him, and behind it were the ruins of an old fortress. He had an open, expectant, juvenile look on his face—he was God's son, and he was waiting for God to bring him something good. In gold letters it said, *"Keep Us in God's Love as We Wait for the Mercy of Jesus. (Jude, 21)"* And then in smaller, black letters, "© F ⚓ B ® MADE IN ITALY FRATELLI BONELLA COPYRIGHT"

On the flipside:

May Jesus Have Mercy on the Soul of

Alfred Spalding Wilsey
September 27, 1919–January 4, 2002

With the spirits of the righteous made perfect, give rest to the soul of Thy servant, O Savior, preserving it in the blessed life   which is with Thee, who lovest mankind.

In the place of Thy rest, O Lord, where all Thy Saints repose, give rest also to the soul of Thy servant for Thou alone art immortal.

May Christ our King Immortal and our God grant the departed soul the mercies of God, the Kingdom of Heaven, and the remission of sins. Eternal Memory. Amen.

Halsted N. Gray — Carew & English

Bobbie and Mike sat down. I sat down next to Bobbie. Daphne sat down next to me. I noticed there was a whole empty chapel behind us, lined with chairs. I began to cry. Daphne held my hand. I cried hard and loud for a minute. I looked at Dad. From this angle his deadness receded and he just looked like himself. The arch of his nose stuck up above the rim of the coffin.

I blew my nose. Daphne took the Kleenex and threw it away.

Lad said, "Danielle Steel. That's weird."

Bobbie said, "Well he had a thing for her."

"That he did," I said.

We started laughing.

Mike turned to me, pointed at Lad, and said, "Now you're just as bad as him. Anything else you want to say? Go on. Don't hold back now."

I stood up and joined Lad, looking down at Dad.

"They cut his hair!" Lad said. "He was all shaggy and scruffy and a real mess. They cleaned him up." I looked at Dad's hair. "Dad used to love this kind of stuff," he continued. "He'd go in and say hello to the corpse, rearrange the hands in the casket."

I imagined Dad doing this and thinking to himself, *They won't mind, it's me. People love me.*

Lad looked at his watch and said, "Time to go." It'd been fifteen minutes. Bobbie and Mike stood up. I stayed by the side of the coffin and said, "I'll be right there." Everyone left.

I would not have wanted to do what I did next in front of anyone.

I said, "Dad," in a whisper. "You're dead." Then I placed my right hand on top of his hands, and a jolt of electricity shot through me. Something powerful. It went straight through the top of my head and simultaneously out of my feet into Sutter between Polk and Larkin. It felt good. The hands were where I always found Dad. There was a little of him left for me there now. He'd put these hands on church pews and restaurant tables as my cue to hold them. The electricity was strong, sharp, brief like a shock—then it was gone. It was the last thing Dad ever gave me. Then I just felt cold—but not unpleasantly cold—hands beneath me. Still unmistakably his hands, the hands I'd held and been stroked and slapped and inspected by my whole life, only now there was nothing left for me in them.

I said, quietly, a little ridiculously, "Dad, I love you. Thank you. Good-bye," looked away, and did not look back.

DAPHNE AND I walked through the Tenderloin and up Nob Hill to Mom's new apartment. I looked over my shoulder a couple of times, unsettled, as if Dad's casket might be following me. I was exhausted.

Mom was surprised to see us. "You're back so fast? You've already been a pallbearer?"

"No, this was pallbearer orientation. In a few hours we'll go to the church and be pallbearers for real. But we did get to see the body." Then, without thinking, I said, "And Mom, you were right about the pink shirt. That's what he was wearing."

"Oh. You're joking," she said.

"I'm not joking. He *was* wearing a pink shirt."

Mom's eyes began to swim. *Oh, fuck,* I realized. *I'm making a big mistake.* Mom turned to Daphne and said, "*Is he telling the truth?*"

Daphne said, "It's true. He was wearing a pink shirt."

Mom's voice started to break. Crying, she said, "I can't believe it! *I can't believe it!* It's just like my dream!" She sat down, put her head in her hands, and sobbed. After a few minutes she looked up, her face red and wet, and said, "It's just like my dream. Can you believe it? *I'm blown away.*"

We crouched in front of her in our formal wear and patted her back, squeezed her knees, said, "It *is* amazing."

She looked up, her face streaked, and asked Daphne, "Did Sean tell you about my dream?"

"Yes. He mentioned it. You had it right after he died."

"No! *Before!* Several weeks before. I'm prophetic, Sean. How do I do it?"

"Don't know. It's pretty wild, Mom."

She sniffled. "So, the funeral's tonight?"

"No. Tomorrow."

"But aren't you pallbearers tonight?"

"That's just for the rosary. The pallbearers for the funeral are a bunch of his friends. Society people I don't really know."

"Oh. Who?"

I started listing names: pallbearers, ushers, and a number of other people who would be involved with funeral, and whom Mom knew. When I got to one man Mom interrupted, lifted her chin disdainfully, and declared, with horror and injury, "He *raped* me!"

"What?" I said.

"He *raped* me!" Mom repeated.

"What do you mean?" I said.

"I don't want to talk about it, Sean."

Daphne and I looked at each other, incredulous.

"I *have lots of scars*," Mom said.

ST. IGNATIUS TOWERS above Golden Gate Park and the Haight. It isn't surrounded by high-rises the way Grace Cathedral is, so you can see it from most any vantage point in the city. Dad paid to have it impressively lit up, so it particularly stands out at night. Inside I looked up at carved gothic angels and a distant ceiling covered in red paint and gold gilt. Two hundred people were there. Graham the English embalmer gave me my pair of white gloves and pinned a white carnation to my lapel. I met Ron, my stepbrother, for the first time. He was a big guy, twice my age.

Todd and Trevor and Dede were late. We stood around waiting. Nothing was happening without them. When they arrived Dede and I made blistering eye contact. We held it, held it, held it—and when Dede finally looked away her twin sister of a mother gave me her own long, curious stare. Todd and Trevor, wearing black crepe designer ties, each went for a hug. I reciprocated by wrapping my right arm around their backs, pressing, bringing my left arm around to touch my right hand and then releasing.

Dede and I held each other's gaze a second time, and said nothing. Everybody took a seat. I walked out to the street and was instructed to stand behind the hearse. A Halsted N. Gray – Carew & English employee—short, lean verging on scrawny, with swimmy eyes and kinky hair (all these mortuary men were united in their impeccable manners and the possession of a subtle, freakish physical attribute, like this guy's hair and Graham's cod-white hands)—lined us up in formation: Lad right front, me right center, Todd right rear; Mike left front, Trevor left center, Ron left rear. He told us, with great authority, "O.K., gentlemen, you on the right are going to hold with the left, and you on the left with the right. We're going to back it out and into the street, then turn around and walk up the steps into the church, where we'll sit it down on a trolley and wait for the priests to come and lead us down the aisle." The employees of Halsted N. Gray – Carew & English had a proprietary, maitre d'ey sort of attitude toward the Solid Oak Casket—possibly because it was a rental. I one-handed it for a few seconds, then realized how heavy it was and grabbed with both hands. Everyone else did the same. The white gloves were ridiculous—panty hose for hands. We got Dad on the trolley and waited for the priests. Then Lad said to Trevor, "Let's you and me switch so one of each group is in the front, and there won't be anything to say on that subject." This put me between Todd and Trevor.

After the switch a nun swished up to Trevor. I watched, standing just a foot behind him, as she whispered tenderly in his ear and slipped a rosary in his pocket. Then she walked past me to Todd and did the same thing.

This woman, I surmised, was the source of Dad's mysterious black rosary.

Five priests approached—five priests!—and sprinkled the coffin with holy water. It beaded beautifully on the varnish. We followed them up the aisle, rolling the box through the Cathedral, me behind Trevor, Todd after me, Lad across, coffin rolling between us like the drink cart in first class. We were stewards, not pallbearers. Why weren't we carrying Dad on our shoulders? He would've wanted that. I stepped on the back of Trevor's shoe.

According to Daphne, the service was beautiful. She cried. "The priests really knew your father," she said. It was an old, extremely ritualized Catholic service. A handful of priests, beyond the five that were officiating, plus the Rosary Nun, got up and said the Our Father, and there were numerous call-and-response run-throughs of the Hail Mary: one Hail Mary for each of the beads of a rosary. Thousands of white tulips filled huge urns.

Afterward, one of Mike's sons gave Daphne and me a ride back to pick up Mom. (I have a number of nieces and nephews, most of whom are around my age.) Mom wore loose-fitting silk robes, two crosses, one silver and one ceramic, a Nepalese pendant that Daphne had given her, and a choker made to look like the dove of peace. She managed to behave herself at Lad's wake/party, until encountering an old acquaintance who had testified against her in the divorce trial. This exchange ensued:

Old Acquaintance: "I'm so sorry about the divorce and everything."

Mom: "I'm sorry you lied on the stand."

Old Acquaintance: "Let's not talk about that."

Mom: "Well, *you* brought it up."

Everybody in the room was either a Wilsey or had known Dad from working in the butter business. Meanwhile, Dede, Todd, and Trevor were having a society gathering up in Pacific Heights. Mom spent a lot of time laughing and talking with Billy Breslan, an Irish-American corrugated-box salesman who used to keep Dad's butter-packing plants stocked with cardboard. It takes a particularly stout cardboard, and a resilient glue, to put up with the shipping and refrigeration of bulk-packaged butter. I loved Billy Breslan when I was a kid.

Mom shouted across the room at me and Daphne, "Billy's going to sing an Irish song!"

The room hushed. Then Billy, short and solid, stood, folded his big hands, and, at Mom's prodding, sang. Everybody cried.

*If you ever go across the sea to Ireland*
*Then maybe at the closing of your day*
*You will sit and watch the moon rise over Claddagh*
*And see the sun go down on Galway Bay*

*Just to hear again the ripple of the trout stream*
*The women in the meadows making hay*
*And to sit beside a turf fire in the cabin*
*And watch the barefoot cousins at their play*

*For the breezes blowing o'er the sea from Ireland*
*Are perfum'd by the heather as they blow*
*And the women in the uplands diggin' praties*
*Speak a language that the strangers do not know*

*For the strangers came and tried to teach us their way*
*They scorn'd us just for being what we are*
*But they might as well go chasing after moonbeams*
*Or light a penny candle from a star*

*And if there is going to be a life in the hereafter*
*And somehow I am sure there's going to be*

*I will ask my God to let me make my heaven*
*In that dear land across the Irish Sea*

THE NEXT MORNING was the funeral.

We parked Mom's car at the bottom of the hill and walked up and across a big lawn to the church, approaching it from the side. The building loomed massively, casting a cool shadow that kept the dew on the grass. I thought, *Dad's last house*. The last place he'd be able to buy his way into.

The church was already about a third full, and more people were arriving in significant numbers. We sat in the third row, behind my aunt Helen, and next to my half sister Wendy's husband, Dave, whom I've always been fond of. While we waited for things to get started he told us about a dogsled race that was being held in his and my sister's small Oregon town. They were missing it because of the funeral.

"It's called the Atta Boy 300. Atta Boy's a dog food, and they're the sponsor. A musher was going to stay at our house."

Eighty-nine-year-old Aunt Helen turned around and gave us a *What the hell?* look.

Daphne reminded me that we were supposed to process behind the casket. I went off to investigate.

A transvestite came down the aisle toward me—wrestler-sized, draped in a fur stole, and wearing a jacket with big, square, red buttons.

*What's up with that?* I thought.

There were now more than a thousand people in the church. Looking around, wondering who they all were, I recognized legions of Dad's former employees, then the mayor, two of his predecessors, and Congresswoman Nancy Pelosi, who was about to become the minority whip. Dad had been in the shrewd habit of giving money to Republicans *and* Democrats. Ranks of men in blazers stood with women in sober suits, their children, their children's children. All of San Francisco was here.

I found the man who'd directed the unloading of the hearse the night before, and asked him what we were supposed to do.

"The family is supposed to process," he said. "The sergeant-at-arms will come get you when it's time."

When I returned to our pew with this news John Traina, Danielle Steel, and their retinue were sliding into the reserved fourth row behind us.

Danielle turned to me and said, "Oh, Sean, I'm so sorry for your loss. So sorry to see you under such circumstances." She looked sincerely bereaved, though she wore a long, incongruous, leopard-print coat.

John shook my hand tanly and said, "John Traina," as if we'd never met.

Lad was the sergeant-at-arms. He took us back along the side of the church, where what looked like an entire Catholic girls' school sat in plaid skirts. Then we processed up to the front behind the casket.

For this service there were fifteen priests, one archbishop, and six thousand white roses.

The priests took turns talking, though they all said the same thing: that Dad saw the world from on high because of his helicopter. Todd Traina, sitting in front of me, cried hard until one of the priests tripped and nearly fell. Father Charles R. Gagan, Father John Lo Schiavo, Father Anthony Sauer, Father Stephen Privett, Father Mario Prietto. They all wore white robes, and looked like men at a health spa.

Then there was an unexpected silence. It lengthened to ten, fifteen, twenty seconds. The priests began to shuffle. The archbishop craned his neck around. I looked at the program. We were waiting for the general intercession, to be delivered by Sister John Martin Fixa, O.P. The Rosary Nun! I turned around and saw her taking small steps down the aisle, a beatific look on her face. She seemed to know that a good man was entering the kingdom of heaven today. Taking the microphone, she said, *"Al Wilsey walked the walk,"* and talked about Dad as a great man and a great philanthropist, equally inclined to "public giving" and "private giving."

"Al Wilsey was a man of countless unknown connections," she said.

*Amen,* I thought.

Then, turning to the coffin, she smiled and concluded, "Al, you did good. You do good."

Sister John Martin was followed by U.S. Senator Dianne Feinstein, who gave a eulogy like a campaign speech.

Then Gerson Bakar, who went back further with Dad than anyone but Aunt Helen, aggravated the archbishop by saying that Dad's devotion to the church at times got a little too extreme. All the priests shuffled around in their seats as he talked about Dad stealing the chorus girl and declaring he was taking her to mass. I felt happy until he said, "Dede, your extraordinary efforts at Al's care brought him the comfort and peace of mind that he enjoyed. In those last few years, you provided him with the major part of his enjoyment in life. On behalf of Al's friends and family, you have our most sincere thanks for that." Then I thought I might be sick. Dede, of course, had just become Gerson's business partner.

At last the archbishop, who'd spent the entirety of the service being attended to by a priest who'd place a shawl around his neck, then take it off and place a gold cap on his head, then repeat the process, stood, in magenta robes, and wrapped the whole thing up: "The helicopter was a vehicle for transcending earthly bounds," he said. A censor was lit, the "Battle Hymn of the Republic" was struck up, and we followed the coffin down the aisle, the smoke floating up and catching the light in the broad, sun-filled door before us.

ON THE STREET the coffin, covered in a woven white blanket of roses and lilies of the valley, was slotted into a shiny, late-model hearse. I peered in the side window, through the filigree of what at first glance appeared to be a silver menorah, but was in fact a metal casting of the words "Halsted N. Gray" stacked on top of the words "Carew & English."

Dede and I had another moment of eye contact. She seemed to be saying, *I've given your father the grandest funeral imaginable, and now I am done with all of you.* I replied, *I am going to tell the truth about you.* Someone fit a sprig of white edelweiss, plucked from an elaborate, flowered-cross corsage, behind her ear. It was an image from a wedding. Dede smiled and fluttered her eyelashes.

Lad patted the hearse on the roof and walked off.

I decided to stay and watch Dad pull away. Two cops on Harleys were waiting at the curb, wearing sunglasses. I assumed they would be escorting the hearse. The sidewalk was emptying. The Rosary Nun was talking with Dede. Almost no one else was left. Suddenly the Rosary Nun came at me. I thought she was going to walk by, as she had the night before, but as she drew abreast she said, "Sean."

I said, "Sister."

She said, "You've got a lot to live up to," and kept on walking.

Dede and I had another moment of physical/telepathic eye contact, the cops started their Harleys, and she and her sprig and her boys and her mother disappeared inside two limos and pulled away, cops in front of them, leaving Dad and Daphne and me behind.

"Wait. They left the hearse," I said to Daphne.

The cops were *Dede's* escorts, not Dad's. Dad didn't matter to S.F. anymore.

We walked down the hill to where we'd parked, pulled a thirty-dollar ticket off Mom's car, and drove away.

AFTER THE FUNERAL I stayed in California. I felt that I needed to stay. There was something to be done. I had a book advance. I could do my job anywhere. There was no reason not to stay. Daphne went home. We'd meet up in L.A. in a month, where Leandro, my best friend from Amity, was getting married and I was to be his best man.

I passed Halsted N. Gray — Carew & English many times on the Sutter Street bus. Once, Dede's car was in the parking lot.

I'd heard during the funeral that Dede'd brought Dad's Jack Russell terrier, Melissa (the dog Dad described as his "protector"), to the funeral home to see his body. Melissa had wagged her tail, then started shaking and whimpering. Seeing Dede's car in the funeral home parking lot I imagined that she hadn't had Dad cremated at all but had bought a permanent storage space for him at Halsted N. Gray — Carew & English, and was paying regular visits with the dogs.

Then I heard that Dede was sleeping with Dad's ashes on the pillow next to her. Dede had confided this strange, intimate detail to Aunt Helen, who repeated it to me. It amazed me that Aunt Helen, the most humble and unulterior person I've ever known, could have an ongoing relationship with Dede. It's the only piece of information that's ever made me think there was more to Dede than I know.

MOM PUT ME up in a women's club that allowed male guests on certain floors. It was down the street from Dad's funeral home. I researched the earthquake. I saw old friends. Spencer Perry and I got very drunk. I visited Sheila Krystal, Mom's Berkeley psychologist (Dad's "airy fairy"). She was sweet and unchanged.

I imagined that the Solid Oak Casket was stalking me. It wanted to get me alone, tell me things. It was sweet and friendly and earnest. But it was afraid of being caught outside the funeral home, where it didn't belong. It might get beaten up or mugged. In my mind it stood itself on one end, disguised in a Burberry trenchcoat, and snuck through the Tenderloin, toward me. When it spotted people it hid in doorways, bending a little and pulling the khaki trenchcoat around itself. *Nothing to see here. Not a Solid Oak Casket or anything.* Then it shimmied up a fire escape and started cautiously across the rooftops.

One night Mom called me and said, "Your father's been haunting me. I'm very angry about it."

"What?"

"I keep feeling his presence. The energy is very dark. I don't like it. I don't like it one bit. Sheila Krystal says he needs me to help him to the other side. Well, I don't want to. He's barking up the wrong tree. He should just leave me alone."

I thought, *It's just like Dad to go haunting a woman.* I was actually jealous that he wasn't *haunting* me. I mean, *fuck*—here I was writing a whole goddamn book about him. And he couldn't even be bothered to motherfucking *haunt* me.

MIKE AND LAD and I made an appointment to see Dede and find out where things finally stood with Dad's estate and his charitable foundation. Though Mike and I hadn't signed the letter, we hadn't taken Dad and Dede to court, as they'd feared, either. We met at Dede's mansion in Pacific Heights. Looking around at the decor I noticed a bust of Dede, done by her niece, a framed portrait of Dede holding her Maltese dog, Serena, with Todd and Trevor on either side (it had appeared in *Town & Country*), and an old picture from the eighties of Dede, Todd, Trevor, and Dad, which had sun-aged in such a way that Dad was nearly invisible, while the rest of them remained in bright color.

We sat around a vast inlaid-stone coffee table. Mike had a list of questions. Before he could ask them Dede said, "My mother's husband just died, and the funeral home told her that cremation charges range between three and twenty-eight thousand dollars! She asked why and they said, 'If you buy a twenty-five-thousand-dollar coffin and get cremated in it that's a twenty-eight-thousand-dollar cremation.' I got your father an eight-hundred-dollar rent-a-casket. It would have burned him up to *buy* the casket. No pun intended!"

I felt nauseous.

Mike asked if she could explain what had happened to Dad's estate.

Dede said, "What's to explain? He didn't consult me about it. He just did what he wanted to do and he didn't tell me about it. I don't understand what you want to know. He left it all to me."

Mike asked if we could see a copy of Dad's will. Dede said, "I don't know why you want to see it. All it says is, 'I have no possessions. I leave no estate.'"

"What about the charitable foundation?" he asked.

"He was in the process of dissolving it when he died," Dede said. "He didn't like it anymore, and he didn't want it around, being administered by relatives of his who he *didn't know*—not any of you, but the next generations. He had just ordered a large sale to fund a chair at Berkeley. He told me, 'We haven't given any money to Cal yet, and I've pledged five million. Let's give a million out of

the foundation.' And then we gave a million for something else. Nobody thought he was going to die."

So this confirmed it. He'd gotten rid of most of what was there before he died. The provision to endow the foundation had been annulled. Mike asked how much was left, and Dede said a few hundred thousand, where there was originally supposed to be a hundred million.

As Dede explained this her Maltese, Serena, kept licking its lips and staring at me with a black-eyed gaze identical to Dede's.

Lad got upset and said, "Dad wasn't of sound mind. I know what my dad wanted when he was together."

Dede said, "Oh, he was of perfectly sound mind. And there are lots of professionals who will testify to that."

There was a silence.

Dede said, "I have all the money now. Your father always told me, 'You'll have all the money when I'm gone. Look out for and give consideration to the children and grandchildren and family members that are *nice* to you. But you don't owe anything to the ones that aren't. And I mean not even a Christmas card.' And I asked him, 'If they're not nice to me you don't mind if I never give them anything or have anything to do with them?' And he said, 'No. I understand that.' That was our agreement."

Silence.

Dede said, "He never asked for my advice." She turned to Mike. "He was so upset with you and the way you talked to him that it pervaded his relationship with all his kids. That's another reason why he dissolved the will. I held the last letter he was going to send to you because I wanted to spare you that pain. I have it here, but I won't give it to you. You have to live with yourself for the rest of your life, knowing you hurt and troubled him terribly. He was very depressed and disappointed."

Mike said, "Don't worry about me. I can live with myself because I know I've behaved honorably. I don't know if others can say the same thing."

Lad asked if I had anything to say.

I'd been thinking about *niceness*. I asked, "You've said a lot about how Dad only wanted you to look out for the kids who had been nice to you. What does that mean, 'Be nice to you.'"

She smiled and said, "Well, you know what it means to be *nice* to someone, Sean. *Just be nice.* You're very nice to me. I think we have a very nice relationship. Don't you think so?"

I said, "Who isn't nice?"

"No one. You're *all* nice."

Mike said, "I thought it was *me*."

I said, "Yeah, you seemed like the most likely candidate for Not Nice."

Dede said, "What! What did Sean say?"

I said, "Mike seemed like the most likely candidate for the one who hasn't been nice."

She laughed, "You've *all* been nice."

As she said this a strange oval wrinkle wrapped around her mouth, curving up under her nose, and down to her chin, giving her jaw a muzzlelike aspect.

I said, "You've been very clear that Dad made all his own decisions and did things his way."

She nodded.

"Do you *agree* with the way he handled his estate?"

Quietly, almost piously, she said, "No, I don't."

Lad and Mike shouted, "But you're the sole beneficiary!"

I said, "What don't you agree with?"

She said, "I'm not going to say."

"But you don't agree with the way he gave it all to you?"

"No, I don't."

*Lying as an identity*, I thought to myself. *Wormtongue.*

Mike said, "Well, to make it up, you could give Sean his eight-hundred-thousand dollars." (This was what Dad was going to leave me until the will was dissolved.)

Dede said, "I wouldn't know where to find eight-hundred-thousand dollars! There *is* no eight-hundred-thousand dollars!"

Mike scoffed.

Then there was nothing left to say. The Wilsey Foundation was history. Dad had left me nothing. (Not that I'd expected him to.) Our meeting broke up. As we walked out into the entry hall, Dede with Serena in her arms, I realized this was probably the last time I would ever see her. I wanted to walk past and out the door, but she grabbed Lad, blocked me, hugged him fast, let him go, then pulled me into an embrace, too. I thought that with the dog between us I could get in one-armed and get out fast. But she moved the dog aside and brought her body close to mine. I felt the whole length of her, and before I could pull away her lips softly touched the skin above the left side of my collar bone, stuck, in a tiny, moist, lipsticky zero, and detached.

I realized Dede had gotten everything she wanted. And that was the end of the story for her. But more surprising was the realization that I did not care, that I *wasn't even angry*. Disgusted, but not angry. I'd never wanted money. I'd wanted *Dad*—and maybe truth: And as far as Dede cared, now I could have both.

THERE WERE MANY things I thought I should now do, not for my own sake, or anyone else's, but to finish this book, make it complete, make sure it's clear that all these events really happened. I should travel and telephone in Dad's wake, fifty years behind, in search of every last crumb of knowledge. I should learn to fly a helicopter. I should plumb the depths of why someone would destroy lives and stop at nothing for money and power when they seemingly already had both; talk to lawyers and comb Midwestern archives in search of the Dow Chemical Generation Skipping Trust document that had (presumably?) set Dede on her rapacious course. I should spend a month in Waurika, where Mom grew up, talking to her only remaining Oklahoma relation, a ninety-six-year-old beekeeper and professional gambler called Homer Antrim. I should look at twenty years' worth of the San Francisco *Examiner* and *Chronicle* society pages on microfilm, in search of the notorious and elusive time Dede told a reporter she had a ruby on one hand and an emerald on the other so she could play red light–green light. I should research the stage history of my grandmother Ora's eminent actress friend Helena Robertson. I should have an intimate knowledge of the butter and edible oils business in this country from the 1910s through the 1980s. I should hang out with Wilsey Bennett truckers, driving flowers from Texas to Miami. I should get to know Mike White, the guy who replaced me on Mom's peace trips, had a better meeting with the pope, and went on to write and star in a very disturbing movie called *Chuck & Buck*, and a very funny one called *School of Rock*. I should research the career of Vitaly Petrovich Ruben, originally Rubenis, and originally an agronomist before he got caught up in politics and became chairman of the Chamber of Nationalities of the Supreme Soviet of the Union of Soviet Socialist Republics. I should make it clear how much better Woodhall seems now than when I was there. I should work at Cascade and get to know the place from the other side (I came pretty close to doing this, and then it closed, in 2004.). I should find the woman who was the centerfold in that first *Playboy* Dad bought me back in 1979.

And that's when I realized I was done with this book.

At a certain point research is no different from running. I had done plenty of both. Eventually you've got to stop, make a leap, and leave the ground behind.

Dad and John Padgett and Blane Morf died while I was working on this book. I spoke at Blane's funeral. I miss him. Mrs. Morf hoped I was writing a book about him.

I wanted to be. I wanted this book to be everything to everyone. To capture all the things I've ever seen and thought and cared about. The glory of it *all!* An impossible goal.

I realized I could stop writing about Mom when I drove her down to Fresno for my aunt Faye's eighty-eighth birthday, stopped for gas at a truck stop, and found myself embarrassed and annoyed in the minimart because Mom, in a flowing white dress, her hair long, carrying sunflower seeds and a bottle of water, was talking louder than anyone, and was so luminously, radioactively conspicuous in the checkout line (anticipating this, I'd even tried and failed to make her stay in the car) that I wanted to disappear as I stood beside her. But then a thin, scrappy-looking girl in her teens came up and said, not "Shut up, lady!" as I expected, but, "What a beautiful dress! You look amazing! You are amazing!" and the whole line of truckers and folks paid her compliments and laughed at her jokes, and Mom was queen of the truck stop, and I was awed anew, for the 999,999th time, and I thought that maybe this was Mom's purpose in life, to make the whole truck stop love her; but no one more than me.

I'd made peace with Mom and Dad. I'd never make peace with Dede. But there was a peace in knowing that. And in knowing who I was.

A memoir, at its heart, is written in order to figure out who you are.

This one started as the story of Amity. I talked to Daphne so obsessively about Amity, bringing her and her parents back to see the place, unable to leave it in the past, that she told me she really thought I should write a book about it. To write about Amity I had to go back to Cascade, Woodhall, St. Mark's. In each case I was received with a kindness that did not exist when I'd been a student. Was this me changing or them changing? With this question came the realization that I wasn't really writing a book about schools. I kept saying I was, because it seemed like the simplest explanation, and I couldn't stand the word "memoir"—a word that made people look at me dubiously and say, "Aren't you a little young?" (though I wasn't)—but I wasn't. This book has been about identity. Identity is the theme. Knowing who you are. My relationship with everyone in this book has changed and evolved. And I'm grateful to everyone in this book—Rob Leggat, the St. Mark's bully included—for making me who I am. That's why I thanked Dad in his coffin. That's why I've dedicated this book to my mother. Dad and Mom and Dede all shaped and played with my identity.

Dad knew who he was in business and in the helicopter. Mom knew who she was when telling a story, giving a gift, or dazzling an audience. Dede, I have failed to understand. As a child I was tricked into loving her, and as a teenager I wanted to stick my fingers between her legs and rip her open like a fortune cookie. I don't know what I thought that fortune would have said. But it took the unlikely combination of the three of them—mother, father, stepmother—to make me who I am.

If the three of them hadn't been so consistently themselves, it might have turned out otherwise. This book might have been unwritten, and I might be living in the beautiful city where I grew up. They might have made me a society Wilsey, happily sitting on the board of the Wilsey Foundation, a philanthropist, not a memoirist in New York.

This book is the identity I've made—a better shot at salvation than trying to fix my father's mistakes. Though the decision was made for me.

I can't wait to write about something besides myself.

So now I'm putting this book to bed like Daphne and my three-and-a-half-month-old son, Owen Taylor Wilsey, named for a lake in Wisconsin where Daphne used to go every summer as a child, and for my great-grandfather Taylor, who brought Mom to California. Our son currently has the sniffles. This book probably has something worse. I fear the first reviewer who tells me I feel too sorry for myself, I'm too messy, I bounce when I walk, I've taken up too much of your time.

I hope my son has a life of his own.

To finish this book there was only one more thing for me to do.

If, on the night of January 4, 2002, a doctor at U.C.S.F. Medical Center came out of the ER and told Dede, "He died twenty minutes ago," as she said, then Dad died fifteen minutes before reaching the hospital: by my estimate it would have taken five minutes to wheel him in, examine him, and declare him dead. The night after Mike and Lad and I met with Dede, I took Mom's car, drove across town to UC, where doctors had saved Mom's life almost sixty years before, waited till fifteen minutes before the time Dede'd called me, and started driving back the way she must have come, copying her driving style—fast and assured. The traffic was similar going either direction, and on the bridge the lanes were evenly split. It was an accurate re-creation.

I went through the Richmond district first, right past Dad's childhood home, then drove through several other neighborhoods before I got on Highway 101 and crossed the Golden Gate Bridge. Now I was in Marin. Nine point nine miles from the hospital, after going through the Rainbow Tunnel—the mountains of the Marin headlands above me—and driving to the bottom of the Waldo approach, which leads down from the bridge and tunnel into the flat portion of Marin, the car's clock ticked over fifteen minutes. I was a quarter mile from the next exit. I got off and pulled up in front of a place called the Buckeye Road-house. A blue neon martini glass—Bay Area shorthand for bar—lit up the road.

It meant nothing.

I drove back to the city and went to bed.

But the next morning I remembered that it *did* mean something. Helicopters. Dad and Mom and I had driven past that spot a million afternoons on the way to Napa, and we'd always seen helicopters. Dad first started talking about buying a helicopter on one of these drives to Napa.

He'd said, "Maybe I could get one of those."

And Mom had replied, "Oh, Alfred!"

Then, before he'd married Dede, but after he'd left Mom, during his *Bandit* phase, we were alone together on the drive. He'd pointed to the side of the road and said, "Helipad." As always, I'd looked and not seen anything.

I borrowed Mom's car again, bought a twenty-seven-shot throwaway Kodak, and drove to Marin, snapping pictures through the windshield as I went—Choi's Home Video on Lombard, still in business; the towers of the Golden Gate Bridge as I drove beneath them; the bay out the side window; the Rainbow Tunnel, red, yellow, and blue outlining its curves on the San Francisco side. I got off at the same exit as I had the night before. In the daylight I saw that it was pos-sible to backtrack along a rutted dirt access road, parallel to 101, between high-way and bay, and reach the exact place where my clock had ticked over—a parking lot in front of a small, wooden building. I got out of the car. A motor-cycle on the highway flew past in high gear. Huge pylons plunged into the water where 101 leaped a finger of the bay. The building housed a seaplane rental com-pany. I walked inside.

"Hello?"

A bearded man in a sweatshirt, with a seaplane on it, came out of an office.

I said, "Is there still a helipad around here?"

"Huh?" he said.

"Is there still a helipad around here?"

He said, "Used to be. Not public anymore. Now it belongs to a guy who has a helicopter and keeps it just for his own personal use."

"I remember there used to be a lot of helicopters."

"That was a long time ago."

Then I spotted a slab of forlorn concrete out the window behind him. I pointed. "Is that it?"

The sun was shining and there was fog in the hills beyond.

"Huh?" he said, and looked confused.

"Is that it?" inclining my chin.

He gave a perfunctory glance and said, "Yep." He seemed suspicious of me.

I was wearing a couple of days' stubble and a dark, hooded sweatshirt that said, "THRASHER TWENTIETH ANNIVERSARY" across the chest. Looking for a helicopter pad near the Golden Gate Bridge was a terrorist activity.

"Thanks," I said.

I WALKED OUT of the seaplane rental office, crossed their parking lot, and stood in front of the concrete helipad. A rusty, crooked sign said, "BEWARE OF ROTOR BLAST." I looked over at the highway. This was exactly where my clock had ticked over fifteen minutes. The pad was cracked and full of weeds, but still usable. Faded red diagonals were painted across it. The concrete was thick, and a ramp led down to a gate in a low fence where I stood. It was a thoughtful gesture. Someone had once cared about this place.

*This is where Dad took his last flight*, I thought, melodramatically, Mom getting in on the act here. It was the only grave I'd ever be able to visit.

I snapped a picture, adding to my terrorist profile. Then I got in the car, took the access road back the way I'd come, got on the highway again. At the top of the Waldo approach I took a picture of the rainbow tunnel, dark and shadowy and gray here on the Marin side, with no rainbows painted around its periphery; then, entering the tunnel, I wound my camera for a shot of the bridge and the sky and the city shining in the sunlight. But the camera just kept winding. I'd shot all my film.

I put it down, came out of the tunnel, fast, and saw San Francisco for myself.

*Acknowledgments*

I WAS ONLY ABLE to write this book because of another writer who told
me she believed I could write it: Daphne Beal, whose care and laughter and
patience made it happen. Thank you, love.

Cressida Leyshon has been my dear friend, first reader, and (conscripted) editor for many years. Everything in here is truer, clearer, and mercifully shorter
because of her. Thank you Cress for treating this book with such care.

The enthusiasm of my friend and agent David McCormick kept me working,
and thanks to David this book found two editors who believed in it as much as he
did. I am grateful to Dan Menaker, who gambled that a hundred-page proposal
could be a book. Ann Godoff agreed, and stuck by me through a very long
process. Ann has been brilliant, warm, calm, and ready with wry editorial remarks—"Paging Dr. Freud!"—at just the right moments.

Dave Eggers is not just a great writer and a great editor, but a great listener
and friend who told me I could do this.

Leslie Falk's edits made many confusing sentences and thoughts come to life. Mary Norris is a sensitive and enthusiastic reader who knows Catholicism, Italians, and the English language inside out.

A NUMBER OF PEOPLE were generous with their time and recollections, and helped me to get the details right. Blane and Barbara Morf have always been like family to me, and they remembered everything I'd tried to forget. Same goes for Spencer Perry, who loves and knows S.F. better than anyone. Only Aunt Helen could have told me what life was like as a child in the post-quake city. My patient and kind brothers, Mike and Lad Wilsey, along with my sister-in-law, Bobbie Wilsey, provided a great deal of insight and support, as well as giving me the much-needed background on my dad's early adulthood and business ventures. My wonderful, generous uncle Charles and aunts Glendora and Faye talked me through the history of the Montandon family in colorful detail. Lois Harlocker shared her happy recollections of my father as a teenager. Gerson Bakar, Allan Herzog, and Pegi Brandley told me about the wild days of my father and Uncle Jack. I'm particularly grateful to Gerson for his support. Clifford Mooney and Geraldine Crumpler vividly remembered the time following my parents' divorce—their love and generosity has always been above and beyond. Diane Clayton, my lost-and-now-found cousin, was kind enough to share her memories. I'm grateful for the candor of Lenore Terr, Sheila Krystal, Russ Reese, Helen Reese, Shelly Bennett, Ralph Bennett, and Raquel Bennett.

Thanks also go to the many non-grudge-holding people from St. Mark's, Woodhall, Cascade, and Amity— particularly the teachers and friends who always tried to help: Thomas Berryman, Matthias Plum, Sally Campbell Woodhall, Jason Snyder, Michael Allgood, Ron Cavanaugh, Rosana Bartolini Cavanaugh, Michael Cruciano, John Padgett, Marci Padgett, Nicole Cimino, Ilona Rosson, and especially Leandro Tyberg.

Maya Dollarhide, Rob Whiteside, Jeff Frank, Ted Thompson, and Bill Vourvoulias were indispensable to the research for this book.

Special thanks go to the people who've become my family: Polly Beal, Bo Beal, Cecily Beal, and Jonathan Beal; and the friends who are my family in New York: Bob Dunn, Alex Smith, John J. Donohue, Sarah Schenck, Katherine Baldwin, Betsey Schmidt, Michael Meredith, Paul Greenberg, Valerie Steiker, Tracey Ryans, Cecile Barendsma, and Rob Weiner.

I'm also grateful for the help of Bruce Diones, Francoise Mouly, Alice Quinn,

Bill Buford, Deborah Treisman, David Remnick (for hard truths and a crucial vote of confidence), Willing Davidson, Rebecca Tracey, Izumi Nakamura, Liza Darnton, Darren Haggar, Sarah Larson, Sarah Hutson, Scott Seeley, and Matt Weiland.

The Lannan Foundation gave me much needed time to write. The Museum of the City of San Francisco and a number of books, particularly *The Earth Shook, the Sky Burned*, by William Bronson, gave me a solid and vivid background of facts on the '06 earthquake. Thanks as well to the San Francisco *Examiner*, the San Francisco *Chronicle*, and *The Washington Post*.

THIS BOOK wouldn't exist without the influence and insight of Leopold Caligor, the man who showed me, just in time, what it was like to have a father.

FINALLY, Mom, back to you at the end. Thank you for your unswerving support and your big, courageous heart—this is crazy, and I'm grateful to you for not just putting up with it, but, as always, embracing it.